Library of
Davidson College

CLAUDIAN'S IN RUFINUM:
AN EXEGETICAL COMMENTARY

PHILOLOGICAL MONOGRAPHS
OF THE
AMERICAN PHILOLOGICAL ASSOCIATION

NUMBER 30

Legati Hahniani ope
hic liber prodit

Accepted for publication by the Committee on the Publication of Monographs of the American Philological Association

Edited by John Arthur Hanson, Princeton University

CLAUDIAN'S IN RUFINUM:

AN EXEGETICAL COMMENTARY

By

HARRY L. LEVY

Fordham University

[With an appendix containing the author's 1935 edition of the text with Introduction and Textual Commentary]

PUBLISHED FOR
THE AMERICAN PHILOLOGICAL ASSOCIATION

BY THE PRESS OF
CASE WESTERN RESERVE UNIVERSITY

1971

© The American Philological Association 1971

Library of Congress Catalog Number: 77-145424
ISBN: 0-8295-0209-2

Composed by William Clowes and Sons Ltd
London and Beccles, England

PREFACE

This exegetical commentary is intended to complete the treatment of the *In Rufinum* which I began in 1935 with the publication of the text; of that edition, which is reproduced as part of this volume, more is said below. The present work is written for classical scholars who are not experts in the field of Claudianean studies, and for graduate students in the classics who are interested in life and letters in the Fourth Century. It may perhaps be of use to some advanced classics majors in our colleges and universities who have similar interests.

Apart from their explanatory function, the notes are intended as a bibliographical guide for the specific questions treated. For those interested in a general *aperçu*, the works listed on pages ix–xxxiii under the following headings may be useful: Demougeot (1947), (1951), Dilke (1969), Jones (1964), Levy (1958), Mazzarino (1942), Momigliano (1963), Paschoud (1967), Setton (1941), Stein-Palanque (1959), and Vogt (1965), (1967). Now that it has appeared, the most useful work of all will be Alan Cameron's *Claudian* (Clarendon Press, 1970), which, by the kindness of the author, I have been privileged to read in proof (though too late to use in the writing of this commentary).

The indulgence of those who may use the commentary as a guide to the continuous reading of the poem is asked for what may seem to be an excessive number of cross-references, and of repetitious notes calling attention to treatments of one or another aspect of the poem as a whole. They are of course intended for those who may consult the commentary at specific points only.

It remains to speak of my 1935 edition of the *In Rufinum*, which, as has been said, is reproduced for the convenience of the reader; it will be found at pages 225 ff. This contains the text, preceded by an introduction dealing with the historical background of the poem, the life and works of Claudian, and the manuscript tradition of the *In Rufinum*. Apart from the correction of a few minor errors and omissions, the work is reproduced as originally published. Such revisions of the points of view expressed in 1935 as seemed appropriate have been handled at pertinent places in the exegetical commentary, with references to the earlier treatment. The Index, while based directly only upon the exegetical commentary, will, it is hoped, serve as a guide to all essential material in the 1935 edition through the cross-references which have been provided.

I am deeply grateful to the editor, John Arthur Hanson, for the scholarly care with which he prepared my typescript for the printer and saw it through the press.

TABLE OF CONTENTS

Preface	v
Bibliography and Abbreviations	ix
Exegetical Commentary	1
Appendix: 1935 Edition of *In Rufinum*	
Introduction [7]*	225
Text, with Textual Commentary [57]	275
List of Abbreviations in Appendix [99] . . .	317
Index to the Exegetical Commentary	321

* Numerals in brackets refer to pagination of the 1935 edition, which is given conjointly with the continuous pagination of this volume.

BIBLIOGRAPHY

Ancient sources are cited, with some minor modifications, as in OLD and LSJ (see below), except for the works of Claudian, for which see the end of this Bibliography. Periodicals are cited as in *L'Année Philologique*, with some modifications.

Abel, D. H.
    1943   Genealogies of Ethical Concepts from Hesiod to Bacchylides. *TAPA* 74 (1943) 92–101.

Abel, Eugen
    1881   Orphei Lithica. Berlin.
    1885   Orphica. Leipzig.

Alföldi, Andras
    1932   Funde aus der Hunnenzeit und ihre ethnische Sonderung. Budapest.
    1934   Die Ausgestaltung des monarchischen Zeremoniells am römischen Kaiserhofe. *MDAI(R)* 49 (1934) 1–118.
    1935   Insignien und Tracht der römischen Kaiser. *MDAI(R)* 50 (1935) 1–171.

Allen, T. W., W. R. Halliday, and E. E. Sikes
    1936   The Homeric Hymns². Oxford.

Allen, W. E. D.
    1932   A History of the Georgian People. London.

Altheim, Franz
    1959   Geschichte der Hunnen. Berlin 1959–62.

Anderson, A. R.
    1928   Alexander at the Caspian Gates. *TAPA* 59 (1928) 130–63.

André, J.
    1941   Le Vocabulaire de la Couleur. *REL* 19 (1941) 132–41.

Appel, Georg
    1909   De Romanorum precationibus. Giessen.

BIBLIOGRAPHY

Assemani, G. S.
1719 — Bibliotheca Orientalis Clementino-Vaticana. Rome 1719–28.

Avery, W. T.
1940 — The *Adoratio Purpurae* and the Importance of the Imperial Purple in the Fourth Century. MAAR 17 (1940) 66–80.

Axelson, Sture
1944 — Studia Claudianea. Upsala.

Baehrens, W. A.
1913 — Vermischtes. *Eranos* 13 (1913) 18–29.

Bailey, Cyril
1928 — The Greek Atomists and Epicurus. Oxford.

Ball, A. P.
1902 — The Satire of Seneca. New York.

Ball, John
1942 — Egypt in the Classical Geographers. Cairo.

Barth, Caspar
1650 — Cl. Claudiani ... quae extant. Frankfurt.

Baylis, H. J.
1928 — Minucius Felix. London.

Baynes, N. H.
1922 — A Note on Professor Bury's "History of the Later Roman Empire." *JRS* 12 (1922) 207–29.

Bell, A. J.
1923 — The Latin Dual and Poetic Diction. London.

Benjamin, Conrad
1892 — De Iustiniani Imperatoris Aetate Quaestiones Militares. Berlin.

Béranger, J.
1939 — L'Hérédité du Principat. *REL* 17 (1939) 171–87.

Bernays, Jacob
1885 — Gesammelte Abhandlungen, ed. A. Usener. Berlin.

Berthelot, M. P. E.
1888 — Collections des Anciens Alchemistes Grecs. Paris.

Beurlier, Émile
1891 — Le Culte Impérial. Paris.

Bidez, Joseph
1913 — Philostorgius, Kirchengeschichte. Leipzig.

Bieler, Ludwig
1957 — Claudianus 104. *Lustrum* 2 (1957) 258–60.

Birt, Theodor
1892 Claudii Claudiani carmina. *MGH* 10. Berlin.
Blümner, Hugo
1892 Die Farbenbezeichnungen bei den römischen Dichtern. Berlin.
Boak, A. E. R.
1919 Imperial Coronation Ceremonies of the Fifth and Sixth Centuries. *HSCP* 30 (1919) 37–47.
Boak, A. E. R. and J. E. Dunlap
1924 Two Studies in Later Roman and Byzantine Administration. New York.
Boissier, Gaston
1913 La Fin du Paganisme[7]. Paris.
Boll, Franz
1898 Catalogus Codicum Astrologorum Graecorum. Brussels 1898–1936.
Born, L. K.
1939 Fate and Fortune in Claudian. *TAPA* 70 (1939) xxix.
Bouché-Leclercq, Auguste
1899 L'Astrologie Grecque. Paris.
Brakman, C.
1930 Observationes criticae ad Claudianum. *Mnemosyne* 58 (1930) 371–84.
1937 Review of Levy (1935). *Museum* 44 (1936–37) 121.
Brenous, Joseph
1895 Étude sur les Hellenismes dans la Syntaxe Latine. Paris.
Brown, Peter
1969 The Diffusion of Manichaeism in the Roman Empire. *JRS* 59 (1969) 92–103.
Bruère, R. T.
1964 Lucan and Claudian: The Invectives. *CP* 59 (1964) 223–56.
Brun, Jean
1966 Le Stoïcisme[4]. Paris.
Bücheler, Franz
1862 Petronii Arbitri Satirarum reliquiae. Berlin.
Buchholz, Eduard
1871 Die homerischen Realien. Leipzig 1871–84.
Burmann, Petrus
1760 Claudii Claudiani opera. Amsterdam.

Bury, J. B.
- 1923 — History of the Later Roman Empire. Vol. 1. London.
- 1928 — The Invasion of Europe by the Barbarians. London.

Byers, H. R. and R. R. Braham, Jr.
- 1948 — Thunderstorm Structure and Circulation. *Journal of Meteorology* 5 (1948) 71–86.

CAH — Cambridge Ancient History.

Cahen, Émile
- 1930 — Les Hymnes de Callimaque. Paris.

Cameron, Alan
- 1965 — St. Jerome and Claudian. *Vigiliae Christianae* 19 (1965) 111–13.
- 1968a — Notes on Claudian's Invectives. *CQ* 18 (1968) 387–411.
- 1968b — Theodosius the Great and the Regency of Stilicho. *HSCP* 73 (1968) 247–80.
- 1970 — Claudian: Poetry and Propaganda at the Court of Honorius. Oxford.

Carson, R. A. G. and H. V. Sutherland
- 1956 — Essays in Roman Coinage Presented to Harold Mattingly. Oxford.

Carter, J. B.
- 1902 — Epitheta Deorum. Leipzig.

Cary, Max
- 1949 — The Geographic Background of Greek and Roman History. Oxford.

Chatelain, E., and A.-C. Pret
- 1884 — Fragments de Scholies sur Claudien. *RPh* 8 (1884) 81–99.

Christ, Franz
- 1938 — Die römische Weltherrschaft in der antiken Dichtung. Stuttgart.

Christiansen, P. G.
- 1969 — The Use of Images by Claudius Claudianus. The Hague.
- 1970 — Claudian and the East. *Historia* 19 (1970) 113–20.

Clinton, H. F.
- 1845 — Fasti Romani. Oxford, 1845–50.

Cochrane, C. N.
- 1944 — Christianity and Classical Culture. London.

Connington, John
- 1872 — P. Vergili Maronis Opera³. London 1872–83.

Coon, C. S.
- 1939 — The Races of Europe. New York.

Courcelle, Pierre
- 1943 — Les Lettres Grecques en Occident. Paris.

Courtney, E.
- 1965 — Valeriana Tertia. *CR* 79 (1965) 151–55.

Crépin, V.
- 1933 — Claudien: Oeuvres Complètes. Paris.

CSEL — Corpus Scriptorum Ecclesiasticorum Latinorum.

Cumont, Franz
- 1929 — Les Religions Orientales dans le Paganisme Romain⁴. Paris.

D'Agostino, V.
- 1937 — Review of Levy (1935). *Mondo Classico* 7 (1937) 1–3.

Davidson, T. S.
- 1946 — A Problem of Senate Procedure in the Late Roman Empire. *AJP* 67 (1946) 168–83.

Day, John
- 1942 — An Economic History of Athens under Roman Domination. New York.

Decker, Josué de
- 1913 — Juvenalis Declamans. Ghent.

Delbrück, H.
- 1902 — Geschichte der Kriegskunst. Vol. 2. Berlin.

Delcourt, Marie
- 1955 — L'Oracle de Delphes. Paris.

Demangel, Robert
- 1945 — Contribution à la Topographie de l'Hebdomon. Paris.
- 1955 — Encore le Tribunal de l'Hebdomon. *Archaiologike Ephemeris* for 1953–54. Festschrift for Georgios Oikonomos. Athens 1955, pp. 92–98.

De Marchi, A.
- 1896 — Il Culto Privato di Roma Antica. Milan 1896–1903.

Demougeot, Émilienne
- 1947 — Les Partages de l'Illyricum à la Fin du IVᵉ Siècle. *RH* 198 (1947) 16–31.
- 1950 — Le Préfet Rufin et les Barbares. *AIPO* 10 (1950) 185–91.

1951	De l'Unité à la Division de l'Empire Romain. Paris.
Desjardins, Ernest	
1876	Géographie Historique et Administrative de la Gaule. Paris 1876–93.
Dieterich, Albrecht	
1913	Nekyia². Leipzig.
Dilke, O. A. W.	
1969	Claudian: Poet of Declining Empire and Morals. Leeds.
Doise, Jean	
1945	Le Partage de l'Arménie sous Théodose Ier. *REA* 47 (1945) 274–77.
1949	Le Commandement de l'Armée Romaine sous Théodose. *MEFR* 61 (1949) 183–94.
Dölger, Franz	
1937	Rom in der Gedankenwelt der Byzantiner. *ZKG* 56 (1937) 1–42.
Domaszewski, Alfred von	
1885	Die Fahnen im römischen Heere. Vienna.
1895	Die Religion des römischen Heeres. *Westdeutsche Zeitschrift* 14 (1895) 1–124.
Dottin, Georges	
1915	Manuel pour Servir à l'Étude de l'Antiquité Celtique². Paris.
Drexel, Friedrich	
1924	Römische Paraderüstung. Strena Buliciana (= Bulićev Zbornik). Zagreb/Split. Pp. 55–72.
DS	Daremberg, Charles and Edmond Saglio: Dictionnaire des Antiquités Grecques et Romaines.
Duckworth, G. E.	
1933	Foreshadowing and Suspense in the Epics. Princeton.
1967	Five Centuries of Latin Hexameter Poetry. *TAPA* 98 (1967) 77–150.
Eadie, John W.	
1967	The Development of Roman Mailed Cavalry. *JRS* 57 (1967) 161–73.
Egger, Rudolf	
1926	Der altchristliche Friedhof Manastirine. Forschungen in Salona, II. Vienna.
1960	Das Labarum, die Kaiserstandarte der Spätantike. Vienna.

E. H. A.
1937 Review of Levy (1935). *Hermathena* 50 (1937) 242–44.
Eitrem, Samson
1915 Opferritus und Voropfer der Griechen.... Christiania.
1933 Das Ende Didos in Vergils Aeneis. Festskrift til Halvdan Koht. Oslo.
1934 Aus "Papyrologie und Religionsgeschichte": Die magischen Papyri. *Münchener Beiträge zur Papyrusforschung und antike Rechtsgeschichte* 19 (1934) 243–63.
1941 La Magie comme Motif Littéraire chez les Grecs et les Romains. *SO* 21 (1941) 39–83.

Emonds, Hilarius
1941 Zweite Auflage im Altertum. Leipzig.
Engelhard, R.
1886 De Personificationibus. Göttingen.
Ensslin, Wilhelm
1939 Carpentum oder Carruca. *Klio* 32 (1939) 89–105.
ERE Hastings, James, and others: Encyclopaedia of Religion and Ethics.

Ernout, A.
1937 Review of Levy (1935). *RPh* 11 (1937) 290.
Ettig, G.
1891 Acheruntica. *Leipziger Studien zur Classischen Philologie* 13 (1890–91) 249–410.

Fabbri, Olindo
1916 Il Mondo degl' Inferi in Claudiano. *Athenaeum* 4 (1916) 335–38.

Fabbri, Paolo
1918 Il Genio del Male nella Poesia di Claudiano. *Athenaeum* 6 (1918) 48–61.
1938 L'Oriente nella Poesia di Claudiano. Atti del IV Congresso Nazionale di Studi Romani, Istituto di Studi Romani 1 (1938) 545–52.
1939 Del Vero Claudiano. *Athenaeum* 17 (1939) 27–40.

Fahz, Ludwig
1904 De Poetarum Romanorum Doctrina Magica. Giessen.

Faider, Paul
1937 Review of Levy (1935). *RBPh* 16 (1937) 678–80.

Fargues, Pierre
- 1933a — Claudien: Études sur sa Poésie et son Temps. Paris.
- 1933b — Claudien: Invectives contre Eutrope. Paris.
- 1936 — Review of Levy (1935). *REA* 38 (1936) 370–72.

FGrHist — Jacoby, Felix: Fragmente der griechischen Historiker.

FHG — Müller, Karl: Fragmenta Historicorum Graecorum.

Finley, M. I.
- 1967 — Utopianism Ancient and Modern. The Critical Spirit: Essays in Honor of Herbert Marcuse. Boston. Pp. 1–20.

Fischer, Wolfgang
- 1914 — Das römische Lager. Leipzig.

Fleskes, Wilhelm
- 1914 — Vermischte Beiträge zum litterarischen Porträt des Tyrannen im Anschluss an die Deklamationen. Bonn.

Fontenrose, Joseph
- 1959 — Python: A Study of the Delphic Myth and its Origins. Berkeley.

Fowler, W. W.
- 1922 — The Religious Experience of the Roman People. London.

Fraenkel, Eduard
- 1945 — Some Aspects of the Structure of Aeneid VII. *JRS* 35 (1945) 1–14.

Freese, J. H.
- 1894 — M. Tullii Ciceronis Pro L. Murena Oratio. London.

Friedländer, Ludwig
- 1910 — Darstellungen aus der Sittengeschichte Roms[8]. Leipzig.

Fürbringer, Friedrich
- 1912 — De Somniis in Romanorum Poetarum Carminibus Narratis. Jena.

Fuhrmann, Manfred
- 1968 — Die Romidee der Spätantike. *HZ* 207 (1968) 529–61.

Furneaux, Henry
- 1896 — The Annals of Tactitus[2]. Oxford.

Gennaro, Salvatore
- 1958 — Lucrezio e l'Apologetica Latina in Claudiano. Catania.

Georgacas, D. J.
- 1947 — The Names of Constantinople. *TAPA* 78 (1947) 347–67.

Gesner, J. M.
- 1759 — Cl. Claudiani Quae Extant. Leipzig.

GLM — Riese, Alexander: Geographi Latini Minores.

Glover, T. R.
- 1901 — Life and Letters in the Fourth Century. Cambridge.

Goetz, Georg
- 1888 — Corpus Glossariorum Latinarum. Leipzig. 1888–1923.

Graefe, F.
- 1922 — Kleine Studien zur Marinegeschichte des Altertums. *Hermes* 57 (1922) 430–49.

Graf, Ernst
- 1885 — Ad Aureae Aetatis Fabulam Symbolae. *Leipziger Studien zur Classischen Philologie* 8 (1885) 1–84.

Greene, W. C.
- 1944 — Moira. Cambridge, Mass.

Gregorovius, Ferdinand
- 1889 — Geschichte der Stadt Athen im Mittelalter[3]. Stuttgart.

Grillone, Antonino
- 1967 — Il Sogno nell'Epica Latina. Palermo.

Grimal, Pierre
- 1949 — L'Épisode d'Antée dans la "Pharsale." *Latomus* 8 (1949) 55–61.

Grimm, J. L. K., Andreas Heusler, and Rudolf Hübner
- 1899 — Deutsche Rechtsalterthümer[4]. Leipzig.

Grimm, J. L. K. and E. H. Meyer
- 1875 — Deutsche Mythologie[4]. Berlin.

Grosse, Robert
- 1920 — Römische Militargeschichte. Berlin.

Grumel, V.
- 1951 — L'Illyricum de la Mort de Valentinien Ier (375) à la Mort de Stilicon (408). *REByz* 9 (1951) 5–46.

Guillemin, A.
- 1924 — L'Imitation dans les Littératures Antiques. *REL* 2 (1924) 35–37.
- 1941 — L'Évolution d'un Cliché Poétique. *REL* 19 (1941) 101–12.

Gundel, Wilhelm
1907   De Stellarum Appellatione et Religione.   Giessen.

Hahn, E. A.
1930   Coordination of Non-Coordinate Elements in Vergil.   Geneva, N.Y.

Hahn, István
1962   Die Soziale Utopie der Spätantike. *Wissenschaftliche Zeitschrift der Martin-Luther-Universität, Halle-Wittenberg* 11 (1962) 1357–61.

Hammond, Mason
1933   *Concilia Deorum* from Homer through Milton. *SP* 30 (1933) 1–16.

Hampel, Erwinus
1908   De Apostrophae apud Romanorum Poetas Usu. Jena.

Harmon, A. M.
1915   Lucian.   Vol. 2.   Loeb Classical Library.   London.

Haskins, C. E.
1887   M. Annaei Lucani Pharsalia.   London.

Haverfield, E.
1888   Scholia on Claudian.   *Journal of Philology* 17 (1888) 271–73.

Haverfield, F.
1907   Three Notes.   *CR* 21 (1907) 105 f.

Heath, T. L.
1913   Aristarchus of Samos.   Oxford.

Helm, Rudolf
1936   Review of Levy (1935).   *Philologische Wochenschrift* 56 (1936) 1222 f.

Henry, James
1873   Aeneidea.   London 1873–92.

Hercher, Rudolf
1857   Erotici Scriptores Graeci.   Leipzig 1858–59.

Hermann, Peter
1968   Der römische Kaisereid.   Göttingen.

Hertel, Theodor
1848   Disputatio de Nonnullis Claudiani Carminum Locis.   Torgau.

Hicks, R. D.
1910   Stoic and Epicurean.   New York.

Hodgkin, Thomas
1875   Claudian, the Last of the Roman Poets.   Newcastle.

Hoefer, Otto
1895 De Prudentii Poetae Psychomachia. Marburg.
Hoepfner, Wolfram
1966 Herakleia Pontike—Ereğli. Vienna.
Hofmann, J. B. and A. Szantyr
1965 Lateinische Syntax und Stilistik. Munich.
Hofrichter, Werner
1935 Studien zur Entwicklungsgeschichte der Deklamation. Ohlau.
Hopfner, Theodor
1921 Griechisch-ägyptischer Opfenbarungszauber, Vol. 1. Leipzig.
1938 Ein neues Θυμοκάτοχον. ArchOrient 10 (1938) 128–48.
Hosius, Carl
1937 Review of Levy (1935). Gnomon 13 (1937) 222.
Housman, A. E.
1912 M. Manilii... Liber Secundus. London.
1927 M. Annaei Lucani Belli Civilis Libri Decem. Oxford.
Hudson-Williams, A.
1959 Imitative Echoes and Textual Criticism. CQ 53 (1959) 61–72.
Hunt, Edmund
1945 Laudatores Temporis Acti. CJ 40 (1944–45) 221–33.
Hussey, Robert
1853 Socrates Scholasticus, Ecclesiastica Historia. Oxford.
Int. Introduction to Levy (1935)=pp. 225–272 in this volume.
Janin, Raymond
1964 Constantinople Byzantine². Paris.
Johansen, K. F.
1939 Achill bei Chiron. ΔΡΑΓΜΑ Martino P. Nilsson ...Dedicatum. Lund. Pp. 181–205.
Jones, A. H. M.
1964 The Later Roman Empire, 284–602. Norman, Okla.
Jullian, C. L.
1908 Histoire de la Gaule. Paris 1908–26.

Junge, Julius
    1939   Saka-Studien. Leipzig.

Juret, A. C.
    1933   Système de la Syntaxe Latine². Paris.

Kaibel, G.
    1885   Antike Windrosen. *Hermes* 20 (1885) 579–624.

Kehding, Otto
    1899   De Panegyricis Latinis Capita Quattuor. Marburg.

Ker, Alan
    1957   Notes on Claudian. *CQ* 51 (1957) 151–58.

Kiepert, Henricus
    1892   Atlas Antiquus. Berlin.

Kiessling, Adolf and Richard Heinze
    1910   Q. Horatius Flaccus⁴. Berlin.

Koch, Julius
    1889   Claudian und die Ereignisse der Jahre 395 bis 398. *RhM* 44 (1889) 575–612.
    1893   Claudii Claudiani Carmina. Leipzig.

Koenig, G. L.
    1808   Cl. Claudiani Quae Exstant. Göttingen.

Kohl, Richard
    1915   De Scholasticarum Declamationum Argumentis. Paderborn.

Kolias, G. T.
    1939   Ämter- und Würdenkauf im früh- und mittelbyzantinischen Reich. Athens.

Kroll, Joseph
    1932   Gott und Hölle. Berlin.

Kroll, Wilhelm
    1916a   Das historische Epos. *Sokrates, Zeitschrift für das Gymnasialwesen* 4 (1916) 1–14.
    1916b   Der potentiale Konjunctiv im Lateinischen. *Glotta* 7 (1915–16) 117–52.
    1924   Studien zum Verständnis der römischen Literatur. Stuttgart.

Kromayer, Johannes and Georg Veith
    1928   Heerwesen und Kriegführung der Griechen und Römer. Munich.

Kühner, Raphael, Carl Stegmann, and Andreas Thierfelder
    1962   Ausführliche Grammatik der lateinischen Sprache: Satzlehre⁴. Munich.

Kurfess, Alfons
 1916   Invectivenspoesie des römischen Altertums. *Jahresberichte des Philologischen Vereins zu Berlin* 42 (1916) 184–202.
 1941   Zu Claudius Claudianus' Invectiven. *Hermes* 76 (1941) 93–95.

Langlois, V.
 1867   Collection des Historiens ... de l'Arménie. Paris 1867–69.

Laqueur, Richard, Herbert Koch, and Wilhelm Weber
 1930   Probleme der Spätantike. Stuttgart.

Lauer, Max
 1869   Des Moses von Chorene Geschichte Gross-Armeniens. Regensburg.

LAW   Lexikon der Alten Welt.

LeBeau, Charles
 1824   Histoire du Bas-Empire². Paris 1824–36.

Leonard, W. E. and S. B. Smith
 1942   T. Lucreti Cari ... Libri Sex. Madison.

Lévy, Isidore
 1927   La Légende de Pythagore de Grèce en Palestine. Paris.

Levy, H. L.
 1935   The Invective In Rufinum of Claudius Claudianus. Geneva, N.Y.= pp. 225 ff. in this volume.
 1941   Claudian's *In Rufinum* 1.83–84 and a Vatican Vase-Painting. *TAPA* 72 (1941) 237–44.
 1946   Claudian's *In Rufinum* and the Rhetorical Ψόγος. *TAPA* 77 (1946) 57–65.
 1947a   Two Notes on Claudian's *In Rufinum*. *AJP* 68 (1947) 64–73.
 1947b   Vergil, Ovid, and Claudian on "Licking into Shape." *CW* 40 (1946–47) 150 f.
 1948a   Claudian's *In Rufinum* and an Epistle of St. Jerome. *AJP* 69 (1948) 62–68.
 1948b   Claudian's Neglect of Magic as a Motif. *TAPA* 79 (1948) 87–91.
 1948c   Echoes of Early Eschatology in the *Iliad*. *AJP* 69 (1948) 420 f.
 1958   Themes of Encomium and Invective in Claudian. *TAPA* 89 (1958) 336–47.

1968	Hair! *CW* 62 (1968–69) 135.
Lipscomb, H. C.	
1909	Aspects of the Speech in the Later Roman Epic. Baltimore.
Lipsius, Justus	
1598	De Militia Romana. Antwerp.
Löfstedt, Einar	
1911	Philologischer Kommentar zur Peregrinatio Atheriae. Upsala.
Long, H. S.	
1948	A Study of the Doctrine of Metempsychosis in Greece. Princeton.
L'Orange, H. P.	
1947	Apotheosis in Ancient Portraiture. Oslo.
Lot, Ferdinand, Christian Pfister, and F. L. Ganshof	
1940	Les Destinées de l'Empire en Occident de 395 à 768. Paris.
LS	Lewis, C. T., and Charles Short: Harper's Latin Dictionary.
LSJ	Liddell, H. G., Robert Scott, and H. S. Jones: A Greek-English Lexicon.
LTL	Corradini, F., and J. Perrin: Lexicon Totius Latinitatis ab Aegidio Forcellini... Lucubratum.
Maenchen-Helfen, O. J.	
1945	Huns and Hsiung-Nu. The Legend of the Origin of the Huns. *Byzantion* 17 (1944–45) 222–51.
1955	The Date of Ammianus Marcellinus' Last Books. *AJP* 76 (1955) 384–99.
Marsili, Aldo	
1946a	Roma nella Poesia di Claudiano. Romanità Occidentale Contrapposta a Quella Orientale. *Antiquitas* 1.2 (April-June 1946) 3–24.
1946b	Personificazioni e Quadri Allegorici in Claudiano. *Antiquitas* 1.3–4 (July-December 1946) 49–55.
Marx, Friedrich	
1922	Molossiche und bakcheische Wortformen in der Verskunst der Griechen und Römer. *Abhandlungen der philologisch-historischen Klasse der sächsischen Akademie der Wissenschaften* 37.1. Leipzig.

Mattingly, Harold
1967   Roman Coins from the Earliest Times to the Fall of the Western Empire. London.

Mayor, J. B.
1880   M. Tulli Ciceronis De Natura Deorum. Cambridge 1880–91.
1888   Thirteen Satires of Juvenal. London 1888–89.

Mazzarino, Santo
1942   Stilicone: La Crise Imperiale dopo Teodosio. Rome.

McCartney, E. S.
1930   Greek and Roman Weather Lore of Winds. *CW* 24 (1930–31) 11–16.
1931   Classical Weather Lore of Thunder and Lightning. *CW* 25 (1931–32) 212–16.

McGovern, W. M.
1939   The Early Empire of Central Asia. Chapel Hill.

Mendelssohn, L.
1887   Zosimi... Historia Nova. Leipzig.

Merguet, H.
1912   Lexikon zu Vergilius. Leipzig.

Meurig Davies, E. L. B.
1948   Amm. Marc. 15.8.15. *Eranos* 46 (1948) 75 f.

MGH   Monumenta Germaniae Historica, Auctores Antiquissimi.

Miller, Konrad
1916   Itineraria Romana. Stuttgart.

Miniconi, Pierre-Jean
1951   Étude des Thèmes "Guerriers" de la Poésie Épique. Paris.

Minns, E. H.
1913   Scythians and Greeks. Cambridge.

Mjöberg, Josua
1944   Virgil, Aen. 1:608: *polus dum sidera pascet*. *Eranos* 42 (1944) 138–41.

Momigliano, Arnaldo
1963   The Conflict between Paganism and Christianity in the Fourth Century. Oxford.

Mommsen, Theodor
1877   Römisches Staatsrecht. Vol. 2^2. Leipzig.
1889   Das römische Militärwesen seit Diocletian. *Hermes* 24 (1889) 195–279.

1899	Römisches Strafrecht. Leipzig.
1903	Stilicho und Alarich. *Hermes* 38 (1903) 101–15.

Mommsen, Theodor and P. M. Meyer
1954	Theodosiani Libri XVI. Berlin.

Moore, C. H.
1910	Rome's Heroic Past in the Poems of Claudian. *CJ* 6 (1910–11) 108–15.

Morawski, Casimir
1917	Adnotationes Poetarum Romanorum Carminibus Adscriptae. *Eos* 22 (1917) 1–9.

Morford, M. P. O.
1967	The Poet Lucan. Oxford.

Muellner, Carolus
1893	De Imaginibus... Quae in Claudiani Carminibus Inveniuntur. *Dissertationes Philologae Vindobonenses* 4 (1893) 99–203.

Müllenhoff, Karl and Max Roediger
1890	Deutsche Altertumskunde². Berlin 1890–1920.

Müller, Carl and C. T. Fischer
1883	Claudii Ptolemaei Geographia. Paris.

Müller, K. A.
1938	Claudians Festgedicht auf das sechste Konsulat des Kaisers Honorius. Berlin.

Neue, Friedrich and Carl Wagener
1892	Formenlehre des lateinischen Sprache³. Leipzig.

Nissen, Paul
1915	Die epexigetische Copula. Keil.
NLI	Augé, Claude: Nouveau Larousse Illustré.

Nock, A. D.
1929	Greek Magical Papyri. *JEA* 15 (1929) 219–35.

Norden, Eduard
1899	Ein Panegyricus auf Augustus in Vergils Aeneis. *RhM* 54 (1899) 466–82.
1913	Agnostos Theos. Leipzig.
1916	P. Vergilius Maro, Aeneis Buch VI². Leipzig.
1959	Die germanische Urgeschichte in Tacitus Germania⁴. Leipzig.

Novák, Robert
1911	Kritische Nachlese zu Ammianus Marcellinus. *WS* 33 (1911) 293–322.

Nutting, H. C.
1925 — Studies in Latin Syntax. *University of California Studies in Classical Philology* 8 (1924–28).

Odelstierna, Ingrid
1949 — Invidia, Invidiosus, and Invidiam Facere. Upsala.

Olcott, G. N.
1904 — Thesaurus Linguae Latinae Epigraphicae, Vol. 1. Rome.

OLD — Oxford Latin Dictionary.

Opelt, Ilona
1965 — Die lateinischen Schimpfwörter. Heidelberg.

Ormsby, H. R.
1931 — France. London.

Otto, A.
1890 — Die Sprichwörter... der Römer. Leipzig.

Owen, S. G.
1936 — Latin Literature. *Year's Work in Classical Studies* 29 (1936) 11–21

Page, T. E.
1890 — Papillon and Haigh's *Aeneid*. *CR* 4 (1890) 463–66.
1900 — The Aeneid of Virgil. London.

Palanque, Jean-Rémy
1933a — Saint Ambroise et l'Empire Romain. Paris.
1933b — Essai sur la Préfecture du Prétoire du Bas-Empire. Paris.
1951 — La Préfecture du Prétoire de l'Illyricum au IVe Siècle. *Byzantion* 21 (1951) 5–14.

Parke, H. W.
1939 — A History of the Delphic Oracle. Oxford.

Parravicini, Achille
1905 — Studio di Retorica sulle Opere di Claudio Claudiano. Milan.
1914 — Le Prefazioni di Claudio Claudiano. *Athenaeum* 2 (1914) 183–94.

Paschoud, François
1967 — Roma Aeterna. Rome.

Paucker, C.
1880 — De Latinitate Claudiani... Observationes. *RhM* 35 (1880) 586–606.

Paul, T. W.
1866 — Quaestiones Claudianeae. Berlin.

Paulson, Johannes
 1911 Index Lucretianus. Göteborg.

Pearce, J. W. E.
 1936 Review of Levy (1935). *JRS* 26 (1936) 134 f.

Pearce, T. E. V.
 1968 A Pattern of Word-Order in Latin Poetry. *CQ* 18 (1968) 334–54.

Pease, A. S.
 1923 M. Tulli Ciceronis De Divinatione. Urbana.
 1935 Publi Vergili Maronis Aeneidos Liber Quartus. Cambridge, Mass.
 1958 M. Tulli Ciceronis De Natura Deorum Libri Secundus et Tertius. Cambridge, Mass.

Petersen, Leiva
 1939 Zur Geschichte der Personifikation in griechischer Dichtung und bildender Kunst. Wurzburg.

Petersen, Eugen, Alfred von Domaszewski, and Guglielmo Calderini
 1896 Die Marcus-Saüle. Munich.

Pfister, Friedrich
 1930 Die Religion der Griechen und Römer. Leipzig.

PGM Preisendanz, Karl: Papyri Graecae Magicae. Leipzig 1928–33. Citation is by papyrus-number and line: e.g. 34.1 = Papyrus 34, line 1; cf. Vol. 2, p. 159.

Pipping, Hugo
 1944 Zur Erklärung des Stellungsgesetzes von Marx. Societas Scientiarum Fennica (Finska vetenskapssocieteten), Commentationes Humanarum Litterarum 13 (1944) 2.1–8.

Platnauer, Maurice
 1922 Claudian. Loeb Classical Library. London.

Platt, Arthur
 1891 Virgil, *Aeneid* vi.567. *CR* 5 (1891) 337.

Postgate, J. P.
 1895 Review of Birt (1892) and of Koch (1893). *CR* 9 (1895) 162–69.
 1917 Lucani ... Liber VIII. Cambridge.

Poteat, H. M.
 1912 Repetition in Latin Poetry. New York.

Pr. Preface. Page-numbers of prefaces thus cited are given in Arabic numerals.

Préchac, François
1921 · Sénèque, De la Clémence. Paris.
Preller, L. and C. Robert
1894 · Griechische Mythologie⁴. Berlin 1894–1926.
Premerstein, Anton von
1937 · Vom Werden und Wesen des Principats. Munich.

Rackham, Harris
1938 · Pliny: Natural History. Loeb Classical Library. Cambridge, Mass.
Ranstrand, Gunnar
1951 · Querolusstudien. Stockholm.
Rattenbury, R. M.
1942 · An Ancient Armoured Force. *CR* 56 (1942) 113–16.
Rauschen, Gerhard
1897 · Jahrbücher der christlichen Kirche. Freiburg.
RE · Wissowa, G. and Wilhelm Kroll: Paulys Real-Encyclopädie der classischen Altertumswissenschaft.

Reid, J. S.
1925 · M. Tulli Ciceronis De Finibus. Cambridge.
Reinach, Salomon
1909 · Répertoire de Reliefs Grecs et Romains. Paris 1909–12.
Riess, Ernst
1935 · Religious Gleanings from the Magical Papyri. *CW* 28 (1934–35) 105–11.
Robert, Paul
1960 · Dictionnaire ... de la Langue Française. Paris 1960–64.
Rohde, Erwin
1921 · Psyche: Seelencult und Unsterblichkeitsglaube der Griechen⁷⁻⁸. Tübingen.
Rolfe, J. C.
1919 · Claudian. *TAPA* 50 (1919) 135–49.
Roscher, W. H.
1890 · Über Selene und Verwandtes. Leipzig.
1895 · Nachträge zu ... Selene und Verwandtes. Leipzig.
1937 · Ausführliches Lexikon der griechischen und römischen Mythologie. Leipzig 1884–1937.

Rossbach, August
1853   Untersuchungen über die römische Ehe. Stuttgart.

Rostovtzeff, M. I.
1926   The Social and Economic History of the Roman Empire. Oxford.

Rowland, R. J.
1968   Foreshadowing in Vergil, *Aeneid*, VIII, 714–28. *Latomus* 27 (1968) 832–42.

Ruhl, Ludwig
1903   De Mortuorum Iudicio. *Religionsgeschichtliche Versuche und Vorarbeiten* 2 (1903) 33–105.

Rushforth, G. McN.
1891   Virgil *Aen*. vi.567–9. *CR* 5 (1891) 232.

Saint-Denis, E. de
1941   Les Romains et le Phénomène des Marées. *RPh* 15 (1941) 134–62.

Sandalgian, Joseph
1917   Histoire Documentaire de l'Arménie. Rome.

Sandbach, F. H.
1952   Guilty Men? *CR* 66 (1952) 6 f.

Sander, Erich
1939   Die Germanisierung des römischen Heeres. *HZ* 160 (1939) 1–34.

Sauter, Franz
1934   Der römische Kaiserzeit bei Martial und Statius. Stuttgart.

Schamberger, Maximilianus
1917   De Declamationum Romanarum Argumentis. Halle.

Scheffer, Johannes
1671   De Re Vehiculari. Frankfurt.

Schissel von Fleschenberg, Otmar
1941   Spätantike Anleitung zum Bogenschiessen. *WS* 59 (1941) 110–24, 60 (1942) 43–70.

Schlicher, J. J.
1915   The Historical Infinitive. *CP* 10 (1915) 54–74.

Schmidt, Ludwig
1910   Geschichte der deutschen Stämme. Berlin 1910–18.
1934   Geschichte der deutschen Stämme...: Die Ostgermanen^2. Munich.

Schoener, Chr.
 1881   Über die Titulaturen der römischen Kaiser. *Acta Seminarii Philologici Erlangensis* 2 (1881) 449–99.
Schol. A   = Chatelain-Pret (1884)
Schol. B   = Haverfield (1888)
Schrader, Otto and Alfons Nehring
 1917   Reallexikon der indogermanischen Altertumskunde². Berlin 1917–29.
Schredelseker, Paul
 1913   De Superstitionibus Graecorum Quae ad Crines Pertinent. Heidelberg.
Schroff, Helmut
 1927   Claudians Gedicht vom Gotenkrieg. Berlin.
Schuster, Mauriz
 1940   Die Hunnenbeschreibungen bei Ammianus, Sidonius, und Iordanis. *WS* 58 (1940) 119–30.
Schwenn, Friedrich
 1927   Gebet und Opfer. Heidelberg.
Scott, Kenneth
 1941   The *Sidus Iulium* and the Apotheosis of Caesar. *CP* 36 (1941) 257–72.
Seeck, Otto
 1876   Notitia Dignitatum. Berlin.
 1896   Das deutsche Gefolgwesen auf römischem Boden. *ZRG* 17 (1896) Ger. Abt. 97–119.
 1913   Geschichte des Untergangs der antiken Welt. Vol. 5, with Anhang. Berlin.
 1919   Regesten der Kaiser und Päpste. Stuttgart.
 1920   Geschichte des Untergangs der antiken Welt. Vol. 6, with Anhang. Stuttgart 1920–21.
Semple, E. C.
 1931   The Geography of the Mediterranean Region. New York.
Semple, W. H.
 1936   Rev. of Levy (1935). *CR* 50 (1936) 228 f.
 1937i   Observations on...Lucan...: A Reply. *CQ* 31 (1937) 16–21.
 1937a   Notes on Some Astronomical Passages of Claudian. *CQ* 31 (1937) 161–69.
 1937b   Claudian, *In Rufinum* II. 156–61. *CR* 51 (1937) 167.

1939	Notes on Some Astronomical Passages of Claudian (continued). *CQ* 33 (1939) 1–8.
Setton, K. M.	
1941	Christian Attitudes toward the Emperor in the Fourth Century. New York.
Seure, Georges	
1925	Chars Thraces. *BCH* 49 (1925) 347–437.
SHA	Scriptores Historiae Augustae.
Sidgwick, Arthur	
1891	Letter to the Editor. *CR* 5 (1891) 64 f.
Sittl, Carl	
1890	Die Gebärden der Griechen und Römer. Leipzig.
Sommer, Ludwig	
1912	Das Haar in Religion und Aberglauben der Griechen. Münster.
Stangl, Thomas	
1912	Ciceronis Orationum Scholiastae. Vienna.
Steele, R. B.	
1911	The Endings *-ere* and *-erunt* in Dactylic Hexameter. *AJP* 32 (1911) 328–32.
Stein, Ernst and Jean-Rémy Palanque	
1959	Histoire du Bas-Empire. Bruges.
Steinbeiss, Heinz	
1936	Das Geschichtsbild Claudians. Halle (Saale).
Steinmetz, Helmuth	
1907	De Ventorum Descriptionibus. Göttingen.
Stengel, Paul	
1910	Opferbraüche der Griechen. Leipzig.
1920	Die griechischen Kultusaltertümer[3]. Munich.
Stoecker, Ernst	
1889	De Claudiani Poetae Veterum Rerum Romanarum Scientia. Marburg.
Straub, Hans (Johannes)	
1938	Kaiser und Heer in spätrömischer Zeit. *Geistige Arbeit* 5 (1938), No. 10, pp. 7 f.
1939	Vom Herrscherideal in der Spätantike. Stuttgart.
1952	Parens Principum. *NClio* 4 (1952) 94–115.
SVF	Arnim, J. von: Stoicorum Veterum Fragmenta.
Text. Comm.	Textual Commentary, in Levy (1935) 57–98 = pp. 275–316 in this volume.

Thomson, J. O.
   1948   History of Ancient Geography. Cambridge.

Thörnell, G.
   1918   Studia Tertullianea. Upsala.

Tidner, Erik
   1922   De Particulis Copulativis apud Scriptores Historiae Augustae. Upsala.

TLL   Thesaurus Linguae Latinae.

Tobler, Titus and Augustus Molinier
   1879   Itinera Hierosolymitana, Vol. 1. Geneva.

Todd, O. J.
   1945   Charon the *Portitor*. CP 40 (1945) 243–47.

Tomsin, A.
   1940   La Légende des Amours d'Aréthuse et d'Alphée. AC 9 (1940) 53–56.

Tozer, H. F.
   1935   History of Ancient Geography^2. Cambridge.

Trump, Fridericus
   1887   Observationes ad Genus Dicendi Claudiani ... Spectantes. Breslau.

Vahlen, Johannes
   1905   Beiträge zur Berichtigung der römischen Elegiker. SDAW (1905) 759–81.
   1907   Opuscula Academica. Leipzig.

Van der Horst, P. C.
   1943   Fatum, Tria Fata; Parca, Tres Parcae. *Mnemosyne* 11 (1942–43) 217–27.

Van Millingen, Alexander
   1899   Byzantine Constantinople. London.

Várady, L.
   1968   Stilicho Proditor Arcani Imperii. AAntHung 16 (1968) 413–22.

Vidal de la Blache, P. and L. Gallois
   1927   Géographie Universelle. Paris 1927–48.

Villeneuve, François
   1918   Essai sur Perse. Paris.

Vischer, Rüdiger
   1965   Das einfache Leben; Wort- und motivgeschichtliche Untersuchungen zu einem Wertbegriff der antiken Literatur. Göttingen.

Vogt, Joseph
1965 Der Niedergang Roms: Metamorphose der antiken Kultur. Zürich. Available in Eng. trsl. by Janet Sondheimer, "The Decline of Rome," New York 1968.
1967 Kulturwelt und Barbaren. Wiesbaden.

Vollrath, Otto
1910 De Metonymiae in Cl. Claudiani Carminibus Usu. Weide.

Wachsmuth, Curt
1874 Die Stadt Athen im Altertum. Leipzig 1874–90.

Wagner, Norbert
1967 Getica. Berlin.

Walbank, F. W.
1945 Phalaris' Bull in Timaeus. CR 59 (1945) 39–42.

Waser, Otto
1894 Skylla und Charybdis. Zürich.

Wellesley, Kenneth
1968 Virgil's Araxes. CP 63 (1968) 139–41.

Werner, P. O.
1906 De Incendiis Urbis Romae. Leipzig.

Wesseley, K.
1888 Griechische Zauberpapyrus von Paris und London. Vienna (= Denkschriften der Kaiserlichen Akademie der Wissenschaften, Wien, Phil.-Hist. Classe, 36.2. Pp. 27–208).

Wetmore, M. N.
1911 Index Verborum Vergilianus. New Haven.

Weyman, Carl
1926 Beiträge zur Geschichte der christlich-lateinischen Poesie. Munich.

Whittle, E. W.
1959 A Note on *Perikeiromene* 87–88. CQ 53 (1959) 57–60.

Will, E.
1943 Sur la Nature du Pneuma Delphique. BCH 66–67 (1942–43) 161–75.

Wissowa, Georg
1912 Religion und Kultus der Römer². Munich.

Witstrand, Erik
1946 Invidia. *Eranos* 44 (1946) 355–69.

Wölfflin, Eduard
 1879   Lateinische und romanische Comparation. Erlangen.
 1882   Über die Aufgaben der lateinischen Lexicographie. *RhM* 37 (1882) 83–123.

Zeller, E.
 1923   Die Philosophie der Griechen[5]. Dritter Teil, Erste Abteilung. Leipzig.

Ziegler, Konrat
 1905   De Precationum apud Graecos Formis. Breslau.

ABBREVIATIONS USED IN CITING CLAUDIAN'S POEMS

		Gesner's Numbers
BG:	De bello Gildonico	15
BP:	De bello Pollentino sive Gothico	25,26
CM:	Carmina minora (cited as in Birt and in Koch)	
CS:	De consulatu Stilichonis	21–24
EH:	Epithalamium de nuptiis Honorii Augusti	9,10
FH:	Fescennina de nuptiis Honorii Augusti	11–14
3H:	Panegyricus de tertio consulatu Honorii Augusti	6,7
4H:	,, ,, quarto ,, ,, ,,	8
6H:	,, ,, sexto ,, ,, ,,	27,28
IE:	In Eutropium	18–20
IR:	In Rufinum	2–5
MT:	Panegyricus dictus Manlio Theodoro consuli	16,17
PO:	,, ,, Probino et Olybrio consulibus	1
RP:	De raptu Proserpinae	32–36

Prefaces are cited thus: CS 3 Pr.21 = the twenty-first verse of the *Praefatio* to the third book of De consulatu Stilichonis.

BOOK 1. PREFACE

1 Pr.1–18: *When Apollo killed Python, the world was rid of an oppressive monster. Now Stilicho, a new Apollo, has rid us of Rufinus, a new Python.* Of the eleven works of Claudian which Birt (1892) 15 classifies as "Carmina Maiora et Publica," IR, BG, IE, FH, EH, 3H, 4H, MT, CS, 6H, and BP, all but three, BG, FH, and 4H, are provided with prefaces in the elegiac distich. Among the poems mentioned, only IR has a separate preface for each book: cf. Int. 39 f. For an analysis of Claudian's prefaces, and a comparison with those of Prudentius, Ausonius, and others, cf. Parravicini (1914). He traces (189–94) the writing of prefaces back to Martial and Catullus, and to the prologues of the comic poets. For an exhaustive study of the influence on this Preface of Lucan and of Lucan's models and imitators, cf. Bruère (1964) 223–25. For the rest of IR, Bruère confines his attention to the influence on Claudian of Lucan alone.

1 Pr.1 Phoebeo domitus Python cum decidit arcu: for Apollo's victory over Python, cf. 4H 537 f. *Caeruleus tali prostratus Apolline Python / implicuit fractis moritura volumina silvis;* PO 188 f. *Phoebus adhuc nigris rorantia tela venenis / extincto Pythone gerens;* Stat. *Theb.* 1.562–69 *Postquam caerulei sinuosa volumina monstri / terrigenam Pythona deus septem orbibus atris / amplexum Delphos squamisque annosa terentem / robora, Castaliis dum fontibus ore trisulco / fusus hiat, nigro sitiens alimenta veneno, / perculit, absumptis numerosa in vulnera telis, / Cirrhaeique dedit centum per iugera campi / vix tandem explicitum;* 5.531–33. Cf. also Ov. *Met.* 1.438–47; Luc. 6.407–9; Roscher (1937) s.v. *Python* 3400–6; Fontenrose (1959), esp. 13–27, 61, 62 f., 365–77, 465–74.

The victorious battle of Phoebus Apollo against the dragon Python, the dread of mankind (Ov. *Met.* 1.439 f. *populis . . . / terror*) is chosen by Claudian to symbolize the victory of Stilicho over Rufinus (cf. Int. 7–26, esp. 7–11 and 18 f.; cf. also 39–41). The contrast (cf. Bury

[1923] 113) between the radiant god of the sun and the dark earth-monster (4H 537 caeruleus ... Python; cf. also Stat. *Theb.* 1.562 f., quoted above) is in accord with Claudian's symbolic use of darkness and light (cf. n. 1.25–73) elsewhere in the poem: cf. 1.29 f. pestes ... quascumque ... / Nox gemuit, 49 facibus ... atris, 62 f. Stygiis invadere nubibus astra / ... flatu violare diem, 129 f. (Megaera) Phoebi ... egressa serenos / infecit radios, 275 (Stilicho) sidus ceu dulce, 378 (to Megaera) expellere die, 2.454 f. (the universe rejoices at Rufinus' death) Senserunt convexa necem ... / ... iam respirantibus astris. The concept of a conflict between light and darkness may have adhered to the Apollo-Python story from its origin (if Türk's theory is valid) as a lunar myth; cf. Roscher (1937) s.v. *Python* 3401 f., with the ftn. expressing Roscher's dissent. On the Apollo-Python struggle viewed as a conflict between heavenly and chthonic powers, cf. Fontenrose (1959) 433. On a possible effect of Claudian's concept of Stilicho as a latter-day Apollo upon the poet's use of a Thyestes myth, cf. Levy (1941) 239 f.

The extensive use of mythological themes is one of Claudian's major characteristics; Fargues (1933a) 153 f. calls him "l'auteur latin du IVe siècle qui accorde la plus large place à la mythologie dans son oeuvre." Cf. n. 1.25–73, para. 3; n. 1.45–65, sect. 7.

1 Pr.2 *a* **Cirrhaeo:** = *Delphico*; cf. Stat. *Theb.* 1.562–69 (quoted in n. 1 Pr.1); TLL *Onomasticon* s.v. *Cirrha* 456 f.

1 Pr.2 *b* **anhela:** cf. Hom. *h. Ap.* 359 (of the she-dragon) ἀσθμαίνουσα. For the change from the nameless female dragon of the Homeric Hymn to the masculine Πύθων, cf. Allen-Halliday-Sikes (1936) 246 f.; Fontenrose (1959) 365–74.

1 Pr.3 f. *a*: the three characteristics mentioned in these two lines are found, among others, in Menander Rhetor (441 Spengel): Πύθων ... καταλαμβάνει ... Παρνασσόν, ὄρος τῶν ὑπὸ τὸν οὐρανὸν τὸ μέγιστον. ... τοῦτο τοίνυν ἐκάλυπτε μὲν ταῖς σπείραις καὶ τοῖς ἑλιγμοῖς, καὶ ἦν τοῦ ὄρους γυμνὸν οὐδέν, τὴν κεφαλὴν ὑπὲρ αὐτὴν τὴν ἄκραν ἔχων, ... ἄνω μετεωρίζων πρὸς αὐτὸν τὸν αἰθέρα. καὶ ἡνίκα μὲν πίνειν ἔδει, ποταμοὺς ὅλους ἐδέχετο; cf. Fontenrose (1959) 80. Cf. also Menander's mention of Themis a few lines later on; for the text, cf. n. 1 Pr.14 *a*.

1 Pr.3 f. *b* **qui ... tegeret ... hauriret ... tangeret:** contrast the mood in 2.442 manus, quae sceptra sibi gestanda parabat; IE 2 Pr.1, Qui modo sublimes rerum flectebat habenas. The clause first cited refers to Rufinus before his fall, the second to Eutropius in similar case; they are thus exactly parallel to the present clause. The subjunctive here is apparently used *metri gratia*, perhaps principally to avoid the inadmissible *hauriebat*. Cf. Kroll (1916b) 144; Hofmann-Szantyr (1965) 560 f. Birt (1892) Pr.223 f., sect. 7. cites several instances in Claudian of mood-variation in parallel verbs (e.g. RP 1.27–31 flexit...possedit... erraverit...cesserit); cf. also 2.11–13 tuebor...queam, and n. 2.405 f., n. 2.480 f. On similar variations in tense, cf. Text. Comm. on 1.131.

1 **Pr.3 spiris tegeret montes:** cf. Call. *Del.* 93 Παρνησὸν... περιστρέφει ἐννέα κύκλοις; Stat. *Theb.* 5.531 f. sacri spiris intorta movebat / cornua Parnassi. On Python's coils as a reflection of his origin as a river, cf. Fontenrose (1959) 143 f., 545–49.

1 **Pr.3 f. *c* hauriret hiatu flumina:** cf. *AP* 9.128.1 f. Εἷρπε δράκων καὶ ἔπινεν ὕδωρ· σβέννυντο δὲ πηγαὶ / καὶ ποταμὸς κεκόνιστο; 129.2 f. ὁ διψήσας ποταμῷ ὑπέθηκε γένειον· / πᾶς δ' ἄρα Κηφισὸς εἴσω ῥέεν; Stat. *Theb.* 7.349 f. Cephisi glaciale caput, quo suetus anhelam / ferre sitim Python amnemque avertere ponto; Fontenrose (1959) 84, 126, 203, 263, 501.

1 **Pr.4 *a* sanguineis...iubis:** cf. Verg. *A.* 2.206 f. (the serpents from Tenedos) iubae... / sanguineae superant undas.

1 **Pr.4 *b* tangeret astra:** cf. Sil. 6.185–87 (a serpent) tantus...sub astra coruscum / extulit assurgens caput atque in nubila primam / dispersit saniem et caelum foedavit hiatu. Claudian, though possibly influenced here by Menander Rhetor (cf. n. 1 Pr.3 f. *a*) may have in mind also his later representation of Rufinus as a plague to heaven and earth: cf. 1.370 f. terras...ipsumque fatigat / aethera, 2.454 f. senserunt convexa necem tellusque nefandum / amolitur onus iam respirantibus astris. Cf. also the quotation from Weston, Int. 39.

1 **Pr.7 *a* concussae...diu...orni:** cf. Stat. *Theb.* 1.563–65 Pythona.../ ...squamis...annosa terentem / robora, 5.515 (a serpent) vastas tenuat complexibus ornos.

1 **Pr.7 *b* tractibus:** for this word of a snake's movements, cf. BP 22 f. insopitisque refusam / tractibus aurati custodem velleris anguem, 3H 141; Verg. *G.* 2.154 squameus in spiram tractu se colligit anguis; Stat. *Theb.* 5.506.

1 Pr.8 **explicuere:** Steele (1911) 331 reports that in 322 occurrences of the 3rd pl. perf. ind. act., Claudian uses the -*ere* form 281 times, the -*erunt* form only 41 times. This ratio of over 6:1 is substantially higher than the average of the dactylic poets whom Steele studied: 2183 occurrences of -*ere* as against 557 of -*erunt*, a ratio of less than 4:1.

1 Pr.9 **spumavit ... veneno:** cf. Stat. *Theb.* 1.360 spumavit Lerna veneno; Sil. 6.677 f. spumabat Bagrada ... / vipereo sanguine; Fontenrose (1959) 144.

1 Pr.10 **Cephisos:** cf. Plin. *Nat.* 4.3.8 amnis Cephisos praefluens Delphos. Schol. B cites Stat. *Theb.* 7.349 f. (quoted in n. 1 Pr.3 f. *c*).

1 Pr.11 f. **Omnis "Io Paean" regio sonat; omnia Phoebum rura canunt:** cf. Call. *Ap.* 102 f. ἐπηΰτησε δὲ λαός / ‛Ἰὴ ἰὴ παιῆον. On the origin and meaning of the cry celebrating Apollo's victory, cf. Cahen (1930) 81–83; Fontenrose (1959) 383 f.

1 Pr.12 **tripodas plenior aura rotat:** the word *aura* refers to the vapor which in Alexandrian and later times was believed to issue from a cleft or chasm in the rock at Delphi (cf. the passage from Lucan quoted in n. 1 Pr.14 *a*). Over this cleft a tripod was placed, on which sat the Pythia, the oracular priestess of Apollo; intoxicated by the vapor, she uttered prophecies. For an analysis of this account, and references to ancient sources, cf. Parke (1939) 19–25; Will (1943); Delcourt (1955) 31 f., 73 f., 140–43.

I have been unable to find elsewhere any trace of Claudian's notion that the vapor caused the tripod to rotate. Claudian may have been influenced by Lucan's expressions *immotos tripodas* and *tripodas cessare* (5.121, 157; cf. 5.166 *plenior* with the same word in our passage), though Lucan seems to have meant simply that the tripod had stood unused, had not been disturbed. Koenig (1808) *ad loc.* suggests that Claudian refers to an illusion of circular motion produced in the priestess by the vertigo resulting from her inhalations; he cites Verg. *A.* 3.91 f. totusque moveri / mons circum.

1 Pr.13 **Musarum:** cf. Strabo 10.10 (468) αἱ Μοῦσαι θεαὶ καὶ Ἀπόλλων μουσηγέτης ... αἱ μὲν τῶν χορῶν προεστᾶσιν, ὁ δὲ καὶ τούτων καὶ τῶν κατὰ μαντικήν; *RE* s.v. *Musai* 701.61–702.5. Here the Muses sing in glorification of Apollo's victory, as Claudian sings of Stilicho's.

1 Pr.14 a **Themidis ... antra:** cf. Lucan 5.80–85 Paean Pythona sagittis / explicuit, cum regina Themis tripodasque teneret. / Ut vidit Paean vastos telluris hiatus / divinam spirare fidem ventosque loquaces / exhalare solum, sacris se condidit antris, / incubuitque adyto, vates ibi factus Apollo. On the form of the myth in which Apollo and Themis share the oracle amicably, which Claudian here follows, cf. Roscher (1937) s.v. *Themis* 586 f. Menander Rhetor, in the passage following that quoted in n. 1 Pr.3 f. *a*, mentions Python's baleful effect on Themis' oracle before Apollo slew him (441 Spengel): οὗτος ἀβάτους μὲν ἐποίει Δελφοὺς τοῖς ἅπασιν, ᾤκει δὲ τὸν τόπον οὐδείς, ἦν δὲ τὸ Θέμιδος μαντεῖον ἔρημον.

1 Pr.14 b **severa:** as belonging to the goddess of Law; cf. MT 154 leges ... severae; EH 201.

1 Pr.14 c **dei:** a graceful compliment to Claudian's auditors (cf. n. 1 Pr.16).

1 Pr.15–18: in two other prefaces (3H Pr.15–18, exactly corresponding in numerical order to our present verses, and CS 3 Pr. 21–24) Claudian repeats the pattern of reserving the last four verses for a specific introduction to the poem which follows. Cf. also IR 2 Pr. 13–20, MT Pr.17–20.

1 Pr.15 a **alio ... Pythone:** the reference is of course to Rufinus. Cf. CS 3 Pr.21 f. alter / Hannibal, said of Gildo, the African rebel (cf. Stein-Palanque [1959] 231–33).

1 Pr.15 b **domini:** Stilicho; cf. CS 3.174 Stilicho praeclare, 191 f. Mavortia plebes / te dominum ... fatetur, and Birt (1892) Pr.38, ftn. 1. The word *domini*, with no immediate modifier or apposite, is curiously unemphatic; contrast CS 3 Pr.21 Noster Scipiades Stilicho; cf. Text. Comm. on 1 Pr.17–18. On Stilicho's career, cf. Mazzarino (1942), esp. 99–113.

1 Pr.15 c **domini telis:** cf. 2.402 f. (to Rufinus) Hac Stilicho ... dextra / te ferit; hoc absens invadit viscera ferro; also 2.305–7.

1 Pr.16 **sacra caterva:** a group of members of the Imperial court, called *sacra* because of their connection with the "sacred" person of the Emperor; cf. FH 1.14 sacris vulneribus, referring to wounds inflicted by Honorius; EH 32, 131; cf. also Int. 12 and ftn. 49; CAH 12.361 f. The term *caterva* is applied to a similar group of auditors in MT Pr.1; cf. MT Pr.7 f.

Despite the objections of Fargues (1936) 371, I still hold the view (Int. 39 and ftn. 248; cf. Birt [1892] Pr.38) that neither Honorius nor Stilicho was present at the first reading of the poem, for which reading this Preface was composed. Though Fargues is right in pointing out that Stilicho is not apostrophized in CS 3 Pr., which was certainly read in his presence, there is one factor which seems to me decisive in our present passage: the extreme unlikelihood that Honorius and Stilicho, or either of them, would have been included in such a group designation as *caterva*.

1 Pr.17 *a* **stabilem servans Augustis fratribus orbem:** the assertion that the dying Theodosius had left both young Emperors (and not merely Honorius) in Stilicho's charge was first enunciated by Claudian in a poem written shortly before the present work: 3H 153 (Theodosius, on the point of death, addresses Stilicho) geminos dextra tu protege fratres. On the dating of the two poems, cf. Int. 39; Koch (1889) 576, 581–83; Birt (1892) Pr.24, 36 f.; Fargues (1933a) 13–15. Thenceforth, this assertion was one of the poet's most oft-repeated themes: in addition to our present passage, cf. 2.5 f. tibi credita fratrum / utraque maiestas; 4H 432 f. (Theodosius is addressed) Stilichone . . . quem fratribus ipse / discedens clipeum defensoremque dedisti; EH 307 f.; CS 1.140 f., 2.54 f., 59–62; 6H 583.

That Theodosius, in some manner or other, actually commended both his sons to Stilicho must, despite the doubts of Fargues (1933a) 61, be considered established by the express testimony of Ambrose (*De obitu Theodosii* 5 nihil habebat novum . . . nisi ut eos praesenti commendaret parenti; cf. Int. 19; Palanque [1933a] 304, ftns. 57, 58; Mazzarino [1942] 106, ftn. 3). The Bishop of Milan was friendly to Rufinus (cf. Int. 9), and none too well disposed toward Stilicho (cf. Palanque [1933a] 304 f.); he would have no motive for magnifying the pretensions of the latter at the expense of the former. It is the exact nature of the *commendatio* which is a matter of doubt. It may well have been a matter of doubt even to contemporaries, for Theodosius' act corresponded to no clearly defined legal concept (cf. Int. 19). Whether or not Theodosius' deathbed adjuration was intended to supplant his action of 394 in placing Arcadius under Rufinus' guidance (cf. Zos. 4.57.4, Stein-Palanque [1959] 216) must apparently remain an open question. Olympiodorus represents the affirmative point of view; cf. fr. 2 (= FHG 4.58; reference is to Stilicho) καταστὰς ἐπίτροπος τῶν παίδων Ἀρκαδίου καὶ Ὀνωρίου ὑπ' αὐτοῦ τοῦ πατρὸς αὐτῶν Θεοδοσίου τοῦ μεγάλου; Eunapius the negative: fr. 63 (= FHG 4.42) Ῥουφῖνος.... ἦσαν δὲ οὗτός τε καὶ Στελίχων ἐπίτροποι τῶν Θεοδοσίου παίδων; cf. Jo. Antioch. fr. 188 (= FHG 4.610). Zosimus varies as he follows the one or the other (cf. n. 1.178-249, para. 4): when he is following Olympidorus, he writes (5.34.6) Στελίχων ... ἀμφοῖν αὐτοῦ τοῖν παίδοιν τὰς βασιλείας ἐπιτραπείς; in a passage in which he follows Eunapius, he sets the idea forth merely as a claim of Stilicho's: 5.4.3 ὁ Στελίχων ... ἔλεγε ... ἐπιτετράφθαι παρὰ Θεοδοσίου τελευτᾶν μέλλοντος τὰ κατ' ἄμφω τοὺς βασιλέας ἔχειν ἐν πάσῃ φροντίδι. The position taken by Claudian must be regarded as that officially espoused by Stilicho; cf. Fargues (1933a) 57 f.; Mazzarino (1942) 61. Whether Stilicho enunciated that position soon after Theodosius' death, as Fargues holds, (1933a) 61 and ftn. 3, or only after the murder of Rufinus, as is maintained by Birt (1892) Pr.28, can scarcely be determined. I incline to the former theory, in view of the longstanding animosity between Stilicho and Rufinus; cf. Int. 10. On the entire question, cf. Baynes (1922) 211-14; Mazzarino (1942) 106 f.

1 Pr.17 *b* stabilem servans ... orbem: an allusion to Atlas is perhaps intended; cf. n. 1.273 f.; Christ (1938) 134; also 9, 16. For *orbis* used to denote the Roman Empire, cf. CS 1.149 f. (after Theodosius' death) tanto ... remoto / principe mutatas orbis non sensit habenas; Ov. *Fast.* 1.616 (of Tiberius) omine suscipiat, quo pater, orbis onus; Christ (1938) 4-18. On a similar use of *mundus* and *terrae*, cf. n. 1.143 *b*; n. 1.51 *b*.

1 Pr.17 f. servans ... regit: cf. Text. Comm. *ad loc.* For the separation of the relative from its antecedent, cf. 1.151-53, where *herbarum* is separated from *quas* by *gramine, Caucasus, crimina,* and *rupes.* For Stilicho as *rector,* cf. 2.265.

1 Pr.18 *a* iustitia pacem, viribus arma regit: for this dual praise of Stilicho, cf. CS 1.16 f. Narrem iustitiam? plus splendet gloria Martis. / Armati referam vires? plus egit inermis; 3H 144 Stilicho, cuius ... robor in armis, / pace probata fides. Cf. also MT 162 f., CS 1.301 f., 2.1 f., 15 f.

1 Pr.18 *b* iustitia pacem ... regit: on Stilicho's control of Imperial legislation in the West, cf. Stein-Palanque (1959) 226 f. The present passage is in line with Claudian's effort to make Stilicho's regime acceptable to the Senatorial party: cf. CS 1.325–32, 2.297; Glover (1901) 157, ftn. 2; Steinbeiss (1936) 2, 58 f.; Mazzarino (1942) 231–49; Stein-Palanque (1959) 226 f.; Levy (1958) 338–46. Claudian himself was apparently in high favor among the senatorial aristocrats; his close attachment to prominent families of this group is shown by his composition of PO in 395 and of MT in 399. It was at the request of the Senate that the honorific statue to Claudian was erected: cf. CIL 6.1710 (Dessau 2949) Claudiano . . . imperatores, senatu petente, statuam . . . erigi . . . iusserunt; BP Pr.9 adnuit . . . princeps titulum petente senatu; Fargues (1933a) 26 f.; Steinbeiss (1936) 66.

BOOK 1

1.1–24 Exordium: *The death of Rufinus has resolved the dilemma as to whether chance or divine providence rules the world, and has justified the ways of gods to men. Rufinus was raised high only to fall more grievously. Tell me, o Muse, whence sprang this dread plague.* Claudian's dilemma (1.2 f. curarent superi terras an nullus inesset / rector et incerto fluerent mortalia casu) reflects the conflict between the Stoic doctrine of divine providence (1.7 consilio ... dei) and the tenets of Epicurean philosophy (1.15 f. causae ... viam ... / alterius) which maintained the basic fortuitousness of the world and its works. Cf. Plu. *Moralia* 2.1051E (of Chrysippus) πρὸς τὸν Ἐπίκουρον μάλιστα μάχεται καὶ πρὸς τοὺς ἀναιροῦντας τὴν πρόνοιαν; Cic. N.D. 1.8.18–10.24, 2.7.18 f.; Lucr. 2.1090–1104, 5.156–99, 1194–1240; Sen. *Dial.* 1.1; Hicks (1910) 39 f., 304; Zeller (1923) 485–87; Leonard-Smith (1942) 33 f.; Greene (1944) 356–61. Claudian himself summarizes the controversy in two verses: MT 82 f. Hi vaga collidunt caecis primordia plagis, / numina constituunt alii casusque relegant.

Cameron (1968a) 388 regards the whole introductory paragraph of IR 1 as based on Juvenal 13.86–88 sunt in fortunae qui casibus omnia ponant / et nullo credant mundum rectore moveri / natura volvente vices et lucis et anni. Cameron rightly points out that Claudian's viewpoint here is very similar to that of Juvenal. Juvenal presents Epicureanism as encouraging perjury by removing the fear of divine retribution; Claudian holds that Rufinus' punishment confounds the Epicurean, who does not fear such retribution for his misdeeds. This anti-Epicurean stance on Claudian's part renders it highly unlikely, as Cameron (1968a) 388, ftn. 1, shows, that Claudian was here imitating Lucretius directly, despite the arguments of Gennaro (1958).

For the passage (1.4–11) dealing with providence, Hammond (1933) 2, and ftn. 1, compares Cic. *Tusc.* 1.28.68, regarding Claudian's verses as a borrowing of "almost the very words." The correspondence of ideas is fairly close (save that Claudian does *not* mention the stars, while Hammond quotes *stellas... eosdem cursus servantes*), but hardly convincing as an indication of direct borrowing.

Bruère (1964) 225 compares Luc. 2.4–5 cur hanc tibi, rector Olympi, / sollicitis visum mortalibus addere curam?; I should add verses 7–13 sive parens rerum ... // fixit in aeternum causas, qua cuncta coercet / se quoque lege tenens ... // sive nihil positum est, sed fors incerta vagatur / fertque refertque vices et habet mortalia casus; Bruère also cites Luc. 7.454 f.; 487.

Birt (1892) Pr.65 points to the similarity between our passage and Minuc. Fel. 17.3 as one indication of Claudian's familiarity with the *Octavius* (on Minucius as an exponent of Stoic doctrine, cf. Baylis [1928] 108–44, esp. 127). In the Minucian passage there are numerous correspondences, more or less exact, which I indicate by parenthetical references to IR: Minuc. Fel. 17.3–9 mihi videntur qui hunc mundi totius ornatum non divina ratione perfectum volunt, sed frustis quibusdam temere cohaerentibus (1.16–18) conglobatum, mentem, sensum, oculos denique ipsos non habere.... Caelum ipsum vide ... iam scies, quam sit in eo summi moderatoris mira et divina libratio (1.11). Vide et annum, ut solis ambitus faciat (1.5).... Quid tenebrarum et luminis dicam recursantes vices (1.6) ... ? ... Quae singula ... ut ... disponerentur (1.4) ... rationis eguerunt.... Ordo temporum ac frugum stabili varietate distinguitur (1.8).... Mari intende: lege litoris stringitur (1.5). Cf. also Minuc. Fel. 5.12, where the opposing view is expressed: Quod si mundus divina providentia et alicuius numinis auctoritate regeretur, numquam mereretur Phalaris... regnum ... Socrates venenum (1.13). These correspondences with our passage are more numerous than those which I have been able to find in any one other ancient source, or even in any two or three combined. This fact lends weight to Birt's contention (rejected by Fargues [1933a] 158 f.) that Claudian was familiar with the *Octavia*, unless of course both authors drew from a common source now lost. On Minucius and Claudian, cf. Gennaro (1958) 43 f., 58; cf. also n. 2.8 *c*.

On Claudian's rather confused views regarding divine providence, cf. Fargues (1933a) 179–81. Cf. also n. 1.5 *b*, on the poet's neglect of the Stoic συμπάθεια.

On the relation of this Exordium to the ψόγος-pattern, cf. Levy (1946) 60.

1.1–3: cf. Juv. 13.86–88, quoted in n. 1.1–24; also Tac. *Ann*. 6.22 Sed mihi ... in incerto iudicium est fatone res mortalium et necessitate immutabili an forte volvantur. Quippe ... reperies ... multis insitam opinionem non initia nostri, non finem, non denique homines dis curae.

1.1 *a* Saepe: the idea of frequent fluctuation is reinforced by the use of the imperfect in 1.6 rebar, 1.14 cadebat, and 1.15 sequebar. Cf. 1.20 tandem.

1.1 *b* dubiam traxit sententia mentem: for the resultative-predicate ("propleptic") use of the adjective, cf. 1.344 Festinas urgete manus, RP 1.184 f. pingunt maculosa ... / terga notae; Ov. *Met*. 1.184 inicere ... captivo bracchia caelo; Hofmann-Szantyr (1965) 413 f.

1.1 *c* dubiam ... sententia mentem: cf. Verg. *A*. 11.314 quae sit dubiae sententia menti; Ov. *Met*. 9.517 haec dubiam vicit sententia mentem. Claudian's echo is purely verbal.

1.2 curarent superi terras: cf. Cic. *N.D*. 1.44.123 Quae enim potest esse sanctitas, si di humana non curant?; Sen. *Nat*. 1.1.4 Videbimus an rerum omnium certus ordo ducatur et alia aliis ita implexa sint ut quod antecedit aut causa sit sequentium aut signum. Videbimus an diis humana curae sint.

1.3 *a* incerto fluerent mortalia casu: cf. Luc. 7.446 f. cum caeco rapiantur saecula casu, / mentimur regnare Iovem.

1.3 *b* fluerent: cf. Sen. *Nat*. 3 Pr.7 (of Fortune) nihil stabile ab illa datum fuisse, eius omnia aura fluere mobilius.

1.4 *a* dispositi ... mundi: cf. 2.25 f. (Rufinus deliberately planned world-wide ruin) cladem divisit in orbem / disposuitque nefas; Ov. *Met*. 1.32 Sic ubi dispositam, quisquis fuit ille deorum / congeriem secuit, sectamque in membra coegit; Minuc. Fel. 17.6 Quae ... ut disponerentur ... perfectae rationis eguerunt.

1.4 *b* foedera mundi: cf. Luc. 1.79 f. tota ... discors / machina divolsi turbabit foedera mundi; Verg. *G*. 1.60 f.; Sil. 14.346 f. Cf. also 1.65 rerum ... fidem, BP 55 f. Some influence of the Stoic doctrine of συμπάθεια, generally lacking in this passage, may perhaps be seen here: cf. n. 1.5 *b*.

1.5 a praescriptos ... mari fines: cf. Minuc. Fel. 17.9 mari intende: lege litoris stringitur.

1.5 b praescriptos ... annis ... meatus: for the thought, cf. Minuc. Fel. 17.5 vide et annum, ut solis ambitus faciat; Juv. 13.88 vices ... anni (for context see n. 1.1–24). Cf. also Cic. N.D. 2.7.19 Possetne uno tempore florere, dein vicissim horrere terra? aut, tot rebus ipsis se immutantibus, solis accessus discessusque solstitiis brumisque cognosci? ... Haec ita fieri, omnibus inter se concinentibus mundi partibus, profecto non possent, nisi ea uno divino et continuato spiritu continerentur. The passage from Cicero is cited at some length to exemplify an aspect of the traditional Stoic cosmological proof of divine providence to which Claudian makes no explicit (cf. n. 1.4 b) reference: the notion of συμπάθεια, the harmony between celestial and terrestrial phenomena. Cf. the phrases *tot rebus ipsis se immutantibus* and *omnibus inter se concinentibus mundi partibus* in the Ciceronian passage just quoted; cf. also Minuc. Fel. 17.4 cum oculos in caelum sustuleris et quae sunt infra circaque lustraveris; Arr. *Epict.* 1.14.2 συμπαθεῖν τὰ ἐπίγεια τοῖς οὐρανίοις; Zeller (1923) 172 f.; Greene (1944) 340; Brun (1966) 59–61.

The word *meatus* seems otherwise unexampled as applied to *annus*, but cf. Verg. A. 6.796 extra anni solisque vias; 849 caeli ... meatus; Lucr. 1.128 solis lunaeque meatus.

1.5 c mari ... annis: cf. Text. Comm. *ad loc.*; cf. also Cameron (1968a) 387 f.; he prefers the reading *anni*, citing Juv. 13.86–88 (cf. n. 1.1–24) and Verg. A. 6.796. He thus has Claudian mention "three distinct groups: boundaries of the sea, path of the sun, and alternation of day and night."

1.6 a lucis noctisque vices: cf. Stat. *Theb.* 4.282 lucis ... vices noctisque; Juv. 13.88 vices ... lucis; Minuc. Fel. 17.5 tenebrarum et luminis ... recursantes vices.

1.6 b rebar: on the tense, cf. n. 1.1 *a*.

1.7 consilio ... dei: the πρόνοια of the Stoics: cf. Cic. N.D. 1.8.18 Stoicorum πρόνοιαν, quam Latine licet providentiam dicere. Cf. also τὴν πρόνοιαν in Lucian. *JTr* 20, quoted in n. 1.12–19; Zeller (1923) 161 and ftns. 2, 3; 163; 318; 347 and ftn. 2; 366 f.; Brun (1966) 69–71.

1.7 f. lege moveri sidera: cf. Sen. *Dial.* 1.1.2 non sine aliquo custode tantum opus stare nec hunc siderum coetum discursumque fortuiti impetus esse... hanc inoffensam velocitatem procedere aeternae legis imperio.

1.8 fruges diverso tempore nasci: cf. Minuc. Fel. 17.7 ordo temporum ac frugum stabili varietate distinguitur; Arr. *Epict.* 1.14.3 Πόθεν γὰρ οὕτως τεταγμένως καθάπερ ἐκ προστάγματος τοῦ θεοῦ, ὅταν ἐκεῖνος εἴπῃ (cf. iusserit, 1.9) τοῖς φυτοῖς ἀνθεῖν, ἀνθεῖ, ὅταν εἴπῃ βλαστάνειν, βλαστάνει, ὅταν ἐκφέρειν τὸν καρπόν, ἐκφέρει;

1.9 *a* variam Phoeben: cf. *Hymni Magici* 5.9 (= Abel [1885] 293) πολύμορφε; Lyd. *Mens.* 3.7 πολυφάσματος; cf. also Wessely (1888) 32.25 δαιδάλη. That one must go so far afield to find parallels for Claudian's characterization of the moon as *varia* is symptomatic of the almost complete lack of interest which the ancients seem to have manifested in the variability of the moon's appearance as it goes through its different phases. No other occurrence of the adjective *varius* or any semantic equivalent in connection with *Phoebe* (*Luna, Diana*) is reported for Latin verse either in the special lexica or in Carter (1902) 28–31, 152. As for the Greek authors, the three citations appearing above are the only pertinent items (and δαιδάλη is of doubtful pertinence: cf. LSJ s.v. δαίδαλος for other meanings) which can be gleaned from among the 300-odd epithets listed by Roscher (1895) 46–50. Among these epithets, on the other hand, words meaning "bright," "beautiful," "torch-bearing," "golden," and "horned" occur repeatedly: cf. Roscher (1890) 18–36. For the name *Phoebe*, cf. Roscher (1890) 17 f.

1.9 *b* alieno... igni: cf. MT 130 f. quae linea Phoeben / damnet et excluso pallentem fratre relinquat (cf. Semple [1937a] 169). Cf. also Cat. 34.15 f. notho... lumine Luna; Verg. G. 1.396 fratris radiis obnoxia... luna; Sen. *Med.* 97 Phoebe... lumine non suo. For the origin of the ancients' knowledge that the moon shines by borrowed light, cf. Pl. *Cra.* 409A (of Anaxagoras) νεωστὶ ἔλεγεν ὅτι ἡ σελήνη ἀπὸ τοῦ ἡλίου ἔχει τὸ φῶς; Heath (1913) 78 f.; Pease (1923) on Cic. *Div.* 2.10 lunaque suo lumine.

1.9 *c* iusserit: cf. Ov. *Met.* 1.36 f. freta diffundi... iussit [quisquis fuit ille deorum]; cf. also εἴπῃ, n. 1.8.

1.9 *d* igni: on the variation between this form of the ablative and *igne* (e.g. 2.468) cf. Birt (1892) 521 s.v.

1.10 compleri: cf. Verg. A. 3.645 lunae se cornua lumine complent.

1.10 f. porrexerit undis litora: cf. 1.5 praescriptos ... mari fines; Ov. Met. 1.13 nec bracchia longo / margine terrarum porrexerat Amphitrite (note the contiguous citation from Ovid in n. 1.11).

1.11 tellurem medio libraverit axe: cf. Man. 1.279 aera per gelidum tenuis deducitur axis, / libratumque regit diverso cardine mundum; Ov. Met. 1.12 f. tellus / ponderibus librata suis; Minuc. Fel. 17.5 summi moderatoris ... divina libratio. Cf. also Achilles, Isagoge 4 (= SVF 2.175) ἐν δὲ τῷ μεσαιτάτῳ τὴν γῆν εἶναι, κέντρου τάξιν καὶ μέγεθος ἐπέχουσαν, ὡς ἐν σφαίρᾳ ... πανταχόθεν ὑπὸ τοῦ ἀέρος ὠθουμένην ἰσορρόπως; Cic. Tusc. 1.17.40 terram in medio mundo sitam, 5.24.69 terra ... quibus librata ponderibus; Hyg. Astr. 1.8 Terra mundi media regione collocata, omnibus partibus aequali dissidens intervallo centron obtinet sphaerae; hanc mediam dividit axis in dimensione totius terrae (Schol. B refers to a quotation from this passage in Isid. Nat. rer. 48). Bruère (1964) 225 compares Luc. 1.57 f. (if the deified Nero chooses a part of the heavens not directly above Rome) sentiet axis onus. Librati pondera caeli / orbe tenet medio; 5.94.

1.12–19: with this whole passage cf. Lucian. *JTr* 19 f. (Momus explains Epicureanism as arising from the gods' failure properly to order the world) οὔτε τῷ Ἐπικούρῳ ἄξιον ὀργίζεσθαι οὔτε τοῖς ὁμιληταῖς αὐτοῦ καὶ διαδόχοις τῶν λόγων, εἰ τοιαῦτα περὶ ἡμῶν ὑπειλήφασιν. ἢ τί γὰρ ἂν αὐτοὺς ἀξιώσειέ τις ἂν φρονεῖν, ὁπόταν ὁρῶσι τοσαύτην ἐν τῷ βίῳ τὴν ταραχήν, καὶ τοὺς μὲν χρηστοὺς αὐτῶν ἀμελουμένους, ἐν πενίᾳ καὶ νόσοις καὶ δουλείᾳ καταφθειρομένους, παμπονήρους δὲ καὶ μιαροὺς ἀνθρώπους προτιμωμένους καὶ ὑπερπλουτοῦντας καὶ ἐπιτάττοντας τοῖς κρείττοσι. ... Εἰκότως τοίνυν ταῦτα ὁρῶντες οὕτω διανοοῦνται περὶ ἡμῶν ὡς οὐδὲν ὅλως ὄντων ... ἡμεῖς δὲ ἀγανακτοῦμεν, εἴ τινες ἄνθρωποι ὄντες οὐ πάνυ ἀνόητοι διελέγχουσι ταῦτα καὶ τὴν πρόνοιαν ἡμῶν παρωθοῦνται; cf. also Sen. *Dial.* 1 passim (the so-called *De providentia*).

1.12 a caligine volvi: for the expression cf. Verg. A. 9.36 (an unknown enemy approaches) Quis globus ... caligine volvitur atra?; Sil. 4.306 f. (the beginnings of a forest-fire) nigranti piceus sensim caligine vertex / volvitur; on the thought, cf. n. 1.12 *b*.

1.12 b caligine: Koenig (1808) *ad loc.* interprets *caligine volvi* as meaning *in occulto esse, nec posse ulla ratione indagari*. In the meaning given to *caligo* he is followed by TLL s.v. 2 *caligo* 161.3 and by Platnauer (1922), who translates it "impenetrable mist." This interpretation seems to involve a contradiction. If human affairs are shrouded in impenetrable mist, how can the poet discern that the wicked triumph and the good are sore afflicted? I suggest that *caligo* here is the darkness, not of visual obscurity, but of evil: cf. IE 1.490–93 (Roma begs Stilicho to protect her from Eutropius) neu tradita libris / omina vestitusque meos, quibus omne quod ambit / Oceanus domui, tanta caligine mergi / calcarique sinas; Cic. *Red. sen.* 3.5 ex superioris anni caligine et tenebris; Amm. 29.2.18 Quanta in illa caligine temporum correxisses; n. 1 Pr.1 *a*, para. 2. Cf. also the words τοσαύτην ... ταραχήν in the passage from Lucian quoted in 1.12–19.

1.13 -que: the conjunction is explicative; the words *laetos ... diu florere nocentes vexarique pios* amplify and explain, but do not add essentially new matter, to *res hominum caligine volvi*. For explicative (epexegetical) conjunctions in Claudian, cf. 1.109 f. fateor vinci rapidoque magistram / praevenit ingenio; 1.363 Linque homines sortemque meam; 2.464 rimosam patriam dilectaque pumicis antra; 2.471 f. findit / aequora triste gemens et fletu concita plangit; Axelson (1944) 40 f. Cf. also Nissen (1915) 26–35; Thörnell (1918) 1; Tidner (1922) 123–29; Ranstrand (1951) 121 f.

1.14 cadebat: on the tense, cf. n. 1.1 *a*.

1.14 f. cadebat relligio: cf. Cic. *N.D.* 1.43.121 Epicurus vero ex animis hominum extraxit radicitus religionem, cum dis immortalibus et opem et gratiam sustulit.

1.15 *a* viam: cf. Lucr. 6.27 (of Epicurus) viam monstravit; Cic. *Fin.* 1.18.57 (Epicureanism is praised) o praeclaram beate vivendi ... viam!

1.15 b non sponte: this expression of personal repugnance toward Epicureanism is in line with Claudian's general sympathy for Stoic ideas: cf. Fargues (1933a) 179 f.

1.15 c sequebar: on the tense, cf. n. 1.1 *a*.

1.16 a vacuo ... motu: cf. Text. Comm. *ad loc.* As regards the extended use of adjectives, cf. also 1.77 cognata caede, 4H 329 murali ... pulsu; Stat. *Ach.* 1.45 f. profunda / tempestate, "a tempest on the deep." On the Epicurean theory of the motion of atoms, cf. Bailey (1928) 310-38.

1.16 b currere: Lucretius does not use this word for the motion of atoms through the void; cf. Paulson (1911) 34. His favorite word for this action appears to be *fero* in the passive; there are nine occurrences of it in Lucr. 2.80-250.

1.16 c semina: for this word used to denote the primordial components of matter, cf. RP 1.249-51 (Proserpina embroiders a scene representing the cosmogony) *veterem qua lege tumultum / discrevit Natura parens et semina iustis / discessere locis*; Lucr. 1.58-62 *quae nos materiem et genitalia corpora rebus / reddunda in ratione vocare et semina rerum / appellare suëmus*; cf. also Verg. *Ecl.* 6.32. On Lucretius' use of the term, cf. Bailey (1928) 343 f.

1.17 a magnum ... per inane: cf. MT 80 (Epicurus) *immensum per inane volat*, RP 2.281; Lucr. 1.1018 *copia ferretur magnum per inane*; Verg. *Ecl.* 6.31 f. *magnum per inane coacta / semina*.

1.17 b novas ... figuras: both Birt (1892) 510 and TLL s.v. *figura* 729.74-81 take *figuras* here in the sense of "atoms": cf. Lucr. 2.384 f. *ignem / suptilem magis e parvis constare figuris*. The difficulty with this interpretation lies in the adjective *novas*. Birt classifies the use of *novus* here (he calls special attention to its inclusion, Birt [1892] 546) with the occurrences of the adjective in 1.47 *Quae nova corrupit nostros clementia mores?*; IE 1.471 *Ite, novi proceres*, 2.41 f. *nasci ... / infantum ... novi vultus*. But the epithet "strange," "new-fangled," "freakish" seems inappropriate to describe the atoms, the basic feature of a philosophical theory which Claudian introduces here and in MT 82 as well-known enough to justify his use of its technical terms in their philosophical sense (1.16 *semina*, MT 81 *primordia*). That Birt himself was dissatisfied with his interpretation is shown by the fact that he suggests (though he does not print) the emendation *vagas* for *novas*: Birt (1892) 18. The sense "newly-created" would likewise be inappropriate for *immortali primordia corpore*, which are *servata per aevum* (Lucr. 1.545, 549). The remedy is to be found in an interpretation for *figuras* in a sense other than that of "atoms." The collocation of *novas* and *magnum ... per inane* suggests that by *novas ... figuras* Claudian is here referring to new worlds of varied shape (Epicur. *Ep.* 1.74 τοὺς κόσμους οὔτε ἐξ ἀνάγκης δεῖ νομίζειν ἕνα σχηματισμὸν ἔχοντας) which the Epicureans believed were constantly being created in the void by the fortuitous concourse of atoms: cf. MT 79–81 (of Epicurus) Ille ferox unoque tegi non passus Olympo / inmensum per inane volat finemque perosus / parturit innumeros angusto pectore mundos. Cf. also Cic. *Fin.* 1.6.21 innumerabiles mundi ... qui ... oriantur ... cotidie; Lucr. 2.1048–76; Bailey (1928) 360–62.

1.18 f. *a*: Bruère (1964) 225 compares Luc. 745 f. (Fortune is to blame for the slaughter at Pharsalus) sunt nobis nulla profecto / numina, cum caeco rapiantur saecula casu.

1.18 *a*: **fortuna ... regi**: cf. Lucr. 5.107 fortuna gubernans.

1.18 *b*: **non arte regi**: for the expression, cf. Ov. *Trist.* 1.4.12 nec regit arte ratem; for the thought, cf. MT 82 caecis ... plagis; Lucr. 1.1021 f. Nam certe neque consilio primordia rerum / ordine se suo quaeque sagaci mente locarunt.

1.18 f. *b* **sensu ambiguo**: cf. Cic. *N.D.* 1.31.86 (of Epicurus) Dubium est enim, utrum dicat aliquid ... esse ... immortale, an si quid. Non animadvertunt hic eum ambigue locutum esse.

1.19 *a* **vel nulla ... vel nescia nostri**: cf. Minuc. Fel. 19.8 Epicurus ille, qui deos aut otiosos fingit aut nullos; Cic. *N.D.* 1.44.123 Verius est igitur nimirum illud ... nullos esse deos Epicuro videri, quaeque is de dis immortalibus dixerit, invidiae detestandae gratia dixisse. Neque enim tam desipiens fuisset, ut ... deum fingeret ... nihil cuiquam tribuentem .... Quae natura primum nulla esse potest, idque videns Epicurus re tollit, oratione relinquit deos; Bailey (1928) 438; Greene (1944) 334.

Platnauer (1922), unless his "or ... or" means "either ... or," apparently goes back to Gesner's interpretation of a variant reading not cited by Birt (1892), *censet / ambigua* (Gesner [1759] *ad loc.*). He translates "that philosophy which believes in God in an ambiguous sense, or holds that there be no gods, or that they are careless of our doings." But the ambiguity itself is represented by the alternatives introduced by *vel ... vel.*

1.19 *b* **nescia nostri**: cf. Lucr. 2.646–48 omnis enim per se divom natura necessest / inmortali aevo summa cum pace fruatur / semota ab nostris rebus seiunctaque longe.

1.20–23 Abstulit — ruant: on the use of the prooemium to forecast the action of the poem, cf. Duckworth (1933) 6 f. Here the forecast is of a most general nature, merely hinting at Rufinus' rise to guilty heights, and the ruin involved in his punishment (cf. n. 1.20 c).

1.20 a hunc... tumultum: for *tumultus* of mental disturbance, cf. 4H 255 f. (the Roman ruler must calm the turbulence of his passions) Hos igitur potuit si quis sedare tumultus / inconcussa dabit purae sacraria menti; Luc. 7.183 mentis... tumultum. For the thought, cf. 1.1 dubiam... mentem.

1.20 b tandem: on the relationship of this word to 1.1 saepe, and to the verbs in the imperfect tense which intervene, cf. n. 1.1 a.

1.20 c Rufini poena: for Rufinus' murder (cf. Int. 25 f.) viewed as *poena*, cf. 1.369 poenas tuus iste dabit, 2.406 fessi poenam... orbis; cf. also Symmachus *Ep.* 6.14.1 Dubitare vos video, an Rufini poenam secuta sit etiam publicatio facultatum; Int. 16, ftn. 95. In *Cod. Theod.* 9.42.14 (cf. Int. 26) the neutral term *obitus* is used.

1.21 a absolvit... deos: for the concept of the gods on trial before the bar of human opinion, cf. Sen. *Dial.* 1.1.1 causam deorum agam. On Claudian's later implicit repudiation of the thesis that Rufinus' punishment had justified the ways of the supernatural powers, cf. n. 2.421–23.

1.21 b culmina rerum: cf. EH 316 f. (Stilicho deserves an exalted place) quem sic Romana decerent / culmina?; IE 2 Pr.5 (Eutropius demoted) Culmine deiectum; Luc. 8.8 (Pompey fallen) summo de culmine lapsus.

1.22 f. tolluntur in altum, ut lapsu graviore ruant: cf. [Sen.] *Oct.* 379 alte extulisti, gravius ut ruerem; Lucian. *Cont.* 14 ἐπαιρέσθων ὡς ἂν ἀφ' ὑψηλοτέρου ἀλγεινότερον καταπεσούμενοι; Minuc. Fel. 37.7 in hoc altius tolluntur, ut decidant altius; cf. also Juv. 10.106 f. excelsae turris tabulata, unde altior esset / casus.

1.23 Vos pandite vati: only here and at PO 71 f. does Claudian utter the customary invocation to the Muses. But cf. CS 2.5 mitior incipiat fidibus iam Musa remissis; cf. also RP 1.20–31.

1.25–73: *The Furies, convoked by Allecto, rage at the triumph of Justice under Theodosius.* Fabbri (1918) 50 f. discusses Claudian's development to its logical conclusion of the concept, already adumbrated in the *Aeneid* (7.324–26, 337 f.), of the Furies as prime movers of evil; cf.

Roscher (1937) s.v. *Furiae* 1564. In this development Fabbri (53 f.) sees evidence that Claudian was influenced by the dualistic doctrine of a principle of evil in the universe actively inimical to a principle of good. Fabbri thinks that Claudian may have become familiar with the idea through contact with Christians (or Christian writings) involved in the Manichaean controversy (cf. Cochrane [1944] 342, 382, 447; Brown [1969] 97–100). On Claudian's familiarity with Christian writers, cf. Birt (1892) Pr.64 f. Fargues (1933a) 158 f. goes too far in his rejection of Birt's position; cf. e.g. the parallels between Claudian and Minucius cited in n.1.1–24. On dualism as a force in Roman religious thought, cf. Cumont (1929) 141 f., 184.

On Claudian's avoidance of Tisiphone ("Avenger of Murder") as inappropriate to embody the principle of evil in a dualistic scheme, cf. Levy (1947a) 68–73. In the absence of Tisiphone, the role of leader of the Furies (cf. Verg. *A.* 6.571 f., RP 1.38–41, RE s.v. *Teisiphone* 150 f.) devolves upon Allecto. A part similar to that played by the Vergilian Allecto (*A.* 7.323–571) is assigned by Claudian to Megaera (1.74–172, 354–79).

Following the general practice of Augustan and later poets (save Lucan) Claudian disregards any incongruity which might be felt to exist between the contemporaneity or recency of the events described and the mythological character of the treatment. Cf. Kroll (1916a). Cf. also Lipscomb (1919) 19 f.: "One of the most striking features of the poems of Claudian ... is the prominence of the rôle given to mythological figures, who deliver 40 ... of the 102 speeches." Cf. n. 1 Pr.1 *fin.*; n. 1.45–65, sect. 7. Note that the narrative portion of IR begins (1.25) with a verse quite similar to that found at a corresponding place in a purely mythological poem, RP 1.32 Dux Erebi quondam tumidas exarsit in iras; cf. also CM 53.1. On the temporal incongruity, cf. n. 1.25 a.

On Claudian's place in the tradition of the *concilium deorum* as an epic theme, cf. Hammond (1933).

1.25 a quondam: on the actual date of Rufinus' entry into public life, cf. Int. 8 f.; the lapse of two decades, at most, between that event and the composition of the IR makes the use of this adverb, from a logical point of view, quite incongruous.

1.25 b stimulis incanduit: cf. MT 225 f. cum viscera felle /

canduerint, ardet stimulis; 4H 252 stimulis... flagrant; IE 2.46 stimulis ignescere; Stat. *Theb.* 5.489 sontibus accensae stimulis.

1.26 *a* Allecto: "The Restless" (ἄλληκτος, cf. λήγω); cf. Verg. *A.* 7.324–26 Allecto . . . / . . . cui tristia bella / iraeque insidiaeque et crimina noxia cordi.   On her role in IR, cf. n. 1.25–73.

1.26 *b* placidas late cum cerneret urbes: cf. Verg. *A.* 7.45 f. Rex arva Latinus et urbes / iam senior longa placidas in pace regebat. Reference here is apparently to the treaties with the Goths (cf. 1.308) concluded by Theodosius early in his reign: cf. Stein-Palanque (1959) 193 f.

1.27 infernas ... sorores: cf. Verg. *A.* 6.571 f. Tisiphone ... / ... vocat agmina saeva sororum; Roscher (1937) s.v. *Furiae* 1564.   Birt (1892) 426 s.v. *Allecto* points out that the term *sorores* includes the allegorical figures of 1.28–38, even though *Morbus, Livor, Timor,* and *Luxus* are masculine.   On the inclusion of the four last-named among the feminines (cf. also 1.116 cunctae) cf. Hoefer (1895) 13 f.

1.28 Glomerantur in unum: cf. Stat. *Theb.* 2.585 f. densi glomerantur in unum / Ogygidae.

1.29–38: with this enumeration cf. Verg. *A.* 6.273–80 vestibulum ante ipsum primisque in faucibus Orci / Luctus et ultrices posuere cubilia Curae, / pallentesque habitant Morbi tristisque Senectus / et Metus et malesuada Fames ac turpis Egestas, / terribiles visu formae, Letumque Labosque; / tum consanguineus Leti Sopor et mala Mentis / Gaudia mortiferumque adverso in limine Bellum, / ferreique Eumenidum thalami et Discordia demens; Ov. *Met.* 4.481–85; Sil. 13.581–86; these conglomerations of personified abstractions are also located in the Lower World.   For similar enumerations in Claudian (but only that in CS 2.113 f. connected with Tartarus) cf. CS 2.103–15; 6H 322 f. (with the note of Müller [1938] *ad loc.*); EH 78–85; MT 166–71. On the personification of abstractions, cf. Roscher (1937) s.v. *Personifikationen abstrakter Begriffe* 2068–2169, with an index at 2164–69; s.v. *Unterwelt* 76–78, where Audacia, Avaritia, and Timor, all figuring in our present passage, are omitted; RE s.v. *Personifikationen* 1042–58, esp. 1048; Petersen (1939); Abel (1943); Marsili (1946b), the last with special reference to Claudian.

This is the first passage of IR which Christiansen (1969) treats from the standpoint of the use of images by Claudian, at p. 122.   I shall mention each of his remarks *suo loco*, without comment save where I find his interpretation faulty.

1.29 f. *a* **pestes Erebi, quascumque ... Nox genuit:** cf. Cic. *N.D.* 3.17.44 fratres et sorores qui a genealogis antiquis sic nominantur, Amor, Dolus, Metus, Labor, Invidentia, Fatum, Senectus, Mors, Tenebrae, Miseria, Querella, Gratia, Fraus, Pertinacia, Parcae, Hesperides, Somnia, quos omnes Erebo et Nocte natos ferunt. For comparative genealogies of demonic personifications in Hesiod, Cicero, Vergil, Hyginus, Seneca, Silius, and Claudian, cf. Engelhard (1886), Plates I and II (facing p. 24). Cf. also Abel (1943).

1.29 f. *b* **quascumque sinistro Nox genuit fetu:** cf. Luc. 6.670 (vile substances used by Erichtho in necromancy) quidquid fetu genuit natura sinistro.

On the word-pattern here (and in 1.167 f.), consisting of noun (*fetu*) separated from its modifier (*sinistro*) by an unmodified noun (*Nox*) and a verb (*genuit*), as a trait of Latin verse, cf. Pearce (1968) 334–54, esp. 351 and 346. Cf. also Duckworth (1967) 143–50.

1.30 *a* **Nox:** on the symbolic use of darkness in IR, cf. n. 1 Pr.1.

1.30 *b* **nutrix Discordia belli:** cf. Verg. *A.* 8.702 scissa gaudens ... Discordia palla (cf. n. 1.33); Sil. 13.586 f. Discordia gaudens / permiscere fretum caelo; Stat. *Theb.* 7.50. The placing of Discordia at the head of the list may be intended to heighten the contrast with 1.26 placidas urbes. Strife engendered by Rufinus is a prominent theme of IR: cf. 1.105 doctus ... unanimos odiis turbare sodales; 1.181 f. commoti pectoris ignem / nutrit; 1.300 accendit proelia; 1.308 Getas ... movet; 1.361 f. quas ... Rufinus strages ... / ... praebeat; 2.9 f. terras accendere bellis / inchoat; 2.24 laxavit ... viam bellis; 2.138 torquetur pace futura; 2.235 f. Getis discordia nostra / proderit; 2.501 stimulator perfidi Martis. On a possible Vergilian identification of Discordia with Allecto, cf. Fraenkel (1945) 14.

1.31 *a* **imperiosa Fames:** cf. Verg. *A.* 6.276 malesuada Fames; Stat. *Theb.* 10.44 nil non ausa Fames. Schol. B cites both passages.

1.31 *b* **leto vicina Senectus:** cf. Verg. *A.* 6.275 tristis ... Senectus; Sil. 13.583 queribunda Senectus; Sen. *Oed.* 594, *Herc. F.* 695 f.

1.32 impatiens ... sui: cf. Sen. *Ep.* 56.8 nos male habet inertia sui impatiens.

1.32 f. Livor ... secundis anxius: cf. Sil. 13.584 angens utraque manu sua guttura Livor.

1.33 scisso maerens velamine Luctus: cf. Stat. *Theb.* 3.125 f. sanguineo discissus amictu / Luctus atrox. For rent garments as a sign of grief, cf. BG 136 rescissae vestes; RP 3.149 f. (Ceres) amictus / conscindit; Sittl (1890) 22, 25, 68.

1.34 caeco praeceps Audacia vultu: cf. Ov. *Hal.* 75 audacia praeceps; Sen. *Ag.* 145. The word *audacia* is of rare occurrence among dactylic poets; cf. TLL s.v.; it is used five times by Claudian, according to Birt (1892) 475.

1.35 f. Luxus ... quem semper ... comitatur Egestas: cf. Pl. *Trin.* Prol. 8 f.: Primum mihi Plautus nomen Luxuriae indidit: / tum hanc mihi gnatam esse voluit Inopiam; Mart. 3.10.3 Luxuriam premeret cum crastina semper Egestas. For a more extensive sketch of personified *Luxuries*, cf. CS 2.131–37.

1.37 a Avaritiae ... matris: cf. CS 2.111–13 (Stilicho rejects the forces of evil) scelerum matrem, quae semper habendo / plus sitiens patulis rimatur faucibus aurum, / trudis Avaritiam. That Avaritia is presented here as the mother of a vast number of unspecified anxieties is perhaps an allusion to Rufinus' greed: cf. Int. 15, ftns. 82, 83.

1.37 b complexae: the participle seems to refer, not to the present scene, but rather to an action often repeated in the past: *complexae pectora*, if taken to refer to the situation as here described, would be ludicrously inconsistent with *longo ... examine* in the next verse. The translation of Platnauer (1922), "the long company of sleepless Cares, hanging round the foul neck of their mother," presents an impossible picture; read rather "which have often hung round"; so with the *se pressant* of Crépin (1933). On the *konstatierendes Perfekt*, cf. Hofmann-Szantyr (1965) 318.

1.38 a insomnes ... Curae: cf. Luc. 2.239 insomni ... cura.

1.38 b longo ... examine: cf. Stat. *Theb.* 3.196 longo examine matres.

1.39 ferrata sedilia: for the adjective, cf. Verg. *A.* 6.280 ferrei ... Eumenidum thalami. By the use of the word *sedilia* here, *curia* in the next verse, and *decernite* in 1.61, together with the expressions *surgit ... de sede*, 1.74, *si vestrae res est accommoda turbae*, 1.112, and *cunctae ... /*

porrexere manus, 1.116 f., Claudian creates the atmosphere of a parliamentary debate.

1.42 *a* obstantes in tergum reppulit angues: cf. Ov. *Met.* 4.474 f. Tisiphone . . . / . . . obstantes reiecit ab ore colubras.

1.42 *b* reppulit angues: these two words (each, however, in a different clause) occur in Verg. *A.* 7.450 (Allecto interrupts Turnus) reppulit et geminos erexit crinibus angues; cf. n. 1.44, n. 1.66 *c*.

1.42 *c* angues: cf. 1.66 totos serpentum erexit hiatus; 1.134, 1.362, 1.378 f.; RP 1.39; Roscher (1937) s.v. *Erinys* 1313, s.v. *Furiae* 1563. For the same trait reflected in the magical papyri, cf. PGM 4.2800 f. (the three-headed goddess Persephone-Megaera-Allecto) ἡ φοβερῶν ὀφίων χαίτην σείουσα μετώποις.

1.43 *a* per . . . umeros: cf. Ov. *Met.* 4.492 (Tisiphone blocks the exit of Athamas and his wife) caesariem excussit; motae sonuere colubrae / parsque iacent umeris.

1.43 *b* errare dedit: for a similar use of the infinitive with *do*, cf. BP 541 (Romans have been given as slaves to Alaric) servire dati; Verg. *A.* 1.79 tu das epulis accumbere divum; Hofmann-Szantyr (1965) 345.

1.43 f. corde sub imo inclusam . . . iram: cf. 4H 239–43 quippe opifex veritus confundere sacra profanis / distribuit partes animae sedesque removit. / Iram sanguinei regio sub pectore cordis / protegit imbutam flammis avidamque nocendi / praecipitemque sui; Laqueur-Koch-Weber (1930) 37 f.

1.44 rabidis patefecit vocibus: cf. Verg. *A.* 7.451 (Allecto speaks to Turnus) rabido . . . haec addidit ore (note contiguity of the lemma with that quoted in n. 1.42 *b*).

1.45–65 Sicine — fidem: the following statistics concerning direct quotation in IR (exclusive of the cry "*Io Paean*" at 1 Pr.11) are presented for comparison with those assembled by Lipscomb (1909) 7–47 for Vergil's *Aeneid*, Lucan, Valerius Flaccus, Statius' *Thebaid* and *Achilleid*, and Silius Italicus, as well as for Claudian's major works taken as a whole.

1. IR contains 20 instances of direct quotation: 1.45–65, 86–115, 140–61, 170 f., 334–39, 342–48, 357–67, 368–87; 2.11–21, 88–99, 144–68, 206–19, 228–47, 247–51, 261–77, 297–316, 330–33, 385–90, 402 f., 498–527. The frequency of occurrence with reference to the 952 verses of the poem is thus

one for each 48 verses; this compares with the average in the *Aeneid* of 1:30 verses; in Claudian's major works of 1:79 verses: Lipscomb (1909) 15.

2. Direct quotation is represented by approximately 281 out of 952 verses, or 29%; in the *Aeneid*, 38%; in Claudian's major works, 30%: Lipscomb (1909) 15.

3. The average length of a speech is ca. 14 verses; in the *Aeneid*, 11 +; in Claudian's major works, ca. 24: Lipscomb (1909) 15.

4. The longest speeches are 1.86–115 and 2.498–527, each of 30 verses (longest in the *Aeneid*, 103; in Claudian's major works, 139); the shortest, the two half-lines of 1.170 f. (shortest in the *Aeneid*, 4 words; in Claudian's major works, 2 words): Lipscomb (1909) 15.

5. In at least three situations in which the spoken word is represented as of great importance, the exact words used are left to the reader's imagination: 1.172, the Fury's admonition to Rufinus to go East; 2.169 f., 195 f., the imperial command issued to Stilicho in Thessaly; 2.382 f., Rufinus' demand that Arcadius declare him co-Emperor; cf. also 2.340–42, and Lipscomb (1909) 23–30.

6. Of the four dialogue-sequences (1.45–65, 86–115; 1.140–61, 170 f.; 1.357–67, 368–87; 2.206–19, 228–47, 247–51) only the last is extended to a third speech, in which the first speaker replies to the response of the second: cf. Lipscomb (1909) 27; he gives only three other instances of such a triple sequence in Claudian: BG 230–324, 4H 214–416, PO 126–73.

7. Assigned to mythological characters are eight speeches: 1.45–65, 86–115, 140–61, 342–48, 357–67, 368–87; 2.330–33(?), 498–527; or 40% of the total number; in the *Aeneid*, 19% in Claudian's major works, 39%: Lipscomb (1919) 19; cf. n. 1.25–73, para. 3.

8. Beginning within the verse are eight direct quotations: 1.170, 368; 2.11, 88, 247, 330, 385, 402; ending within the verse are four: 1.65, 171; 2.247, 251. Thus of the 40 beginnings and endings of the 20 speeches, 12, or 30%, involve a shift from narrative to direct quotation within the verse. The corresponding figure for the *Aeneid* is 24.5%: Lipscomb (1909) 37 (columns 3 and 5 averaged).

The foregoing figures bear out for IR the following among the general conclusions reached by Lipscomb (1909) 46 f. concerning the speech in the later Roman epic (I have inserted parenthetical numbers referring to the sections above):

In the later Roman epic, in general, one finds a restriction of the conversational side of speech with a nearer approach to declamation, for, compared with the standard of Vergil, the later epics show a decrease in the amount of speech employed (2) as well as in the number of speeches (1) . . . . Moreover, the average length of the speech tends to increase (3) .... Again, the tendency which Vergil shows to restrict the length of dialogue and to confine the speech-scene within narrow limits is even more noticeable in the later epic (6) .... Through the conventional use of the supernatural as a motivating force the gods are given an important place in all the Roman epics with the exception of the Pharsalia. Especially notable in this respect is the usage of Claudian (7) .... [A striking departure] from the custom of the Greek epic ... [is] found in the habit of beginning and ending the speech within the verse (extended in the later epic) ... (8).

The only marked deviation of IR from the general pattern is the complete lack of speeches over 40 verses long (4): cf. Lipscomb (1909) 46, "Lucan, Silius Italicus, and Claudian employ a larger number of speeches exceeding 40 verses ... in length than does Vergil." Cf. also n. 1.65 *b*.

1.45 tranquillo ... cursu: on the *pax Theodosiana*, cf. n. 1.26 *b*.

1.47 Quae nova ... clementia?: cf. IE 2.391 (the military leader Leo calls for action) Quis novus hic torpor?; Verg. *A*. 5.670 (Ascanius attempts to restrain the Trojan women's fury) Quis furor iste novus?

1.47 f. corrupit ... perit: cf. Text. Comm. *ad loc*.; Brakman (1937) 121.

1.48 Quo rabies ... perit?: cf. Luc. 7.75 (Cicero pleads with Pompey to prosecute the war against Caesar) Quo tibi fervor abit aut quo fiducia fati? I have been unable to find a parallel for the use of *pereo* with a word denoting end of motion.

1.49 *a* verbera ... facibus: cf. Verg. *A*. 7.335–37 (Juno to Allecto) tu potes ... / ... verbera tectis / funereasque inferre faces; Roscher (1937) s.v. *Erinys* 1313, s.v. *Furiae* 1563. Cf. also PGM 4.2799 f. (the three-headed goddess Persephone-Megaera-Allecto) ἡ χέρας ὁπλίζουσα κελαιναῖς λαμπάσι δειναῖς.

1.49 *b* facibus ... atris: cf. Verg. *A*. 7.456 f. (Allecto shoots a brand at Turnus) facem iuveni coniecit et atro / lumine fumantes finxit sub pectore taedas (cf. also 9.74–76); Sen. *Med*. 13–15. On the symbolic use of darkness, cf. n. 1 Pr.1, and Pease (1935) on Verg. *A*. 4.384.

1.49 *c* nequiquam cingimur: cf. Verg. *A*. 11.536 (Camilla) nostris nequiquam cingitur armis.

1.50 f. Iuppiter — terris: on the ruler of Rome as the earthly analog of Jupiter, cf. Ov. *Met.* 15.858–60 Iuppiter arces / temperat aetherias ... / terra sub Augusto est. Cf. also Verg. ap. ps.-Suet. *Vita Vergilii* (= 66 Reifferscheid) divisum imperium cum Iove Caesar habet; Christ (1938) 21 f., 126–29.

1.51 *a* Theodosius: cf. Text. Comm. *ad loc.*

1.51 *b* terris: for the plural *terrae* used to denote the Roman Empire, cf. BG 47 (Rome speaks) domui terras; Verg. *A.* 6.781 f. Roma / imperium terris ... aequabit; Christ (1938) 21 f. On a similar use of *orbis* and *mundus*, cf. n. 1 Pr.17 *b*, n. 1.143 *b*.

1.51 f. En — redit: for the concept of a primordial Age of Gold, cf. RP 2.285 f. pretiosior aetas, / aurea progenies, MT 123 prisci ... tempora ... auri; Hes. *Op.* 109 f. χρύσεον μὲν πρώτιστα γένος μερόπων ἀνθρώπων / ἀθάνατοι ποίησαν, 111–20; Arat. *Phaen.* 114 γαῖα γένος χρύσειον ἔφερβεν, 108–13; Ov. *Met.* 1.89 Aurea prima sata est, 89–112, 15.96; Verg. *G.* 1.125–54, 2.536–40; Preller-Robert (1894) 1.87 f.; Graf (1885).

For the concept of an actual or prospective return of the Golden Age under the beneficent guidance of a contemporary ruler, cf. 1.372–87 (Honorius), CS 2.454–66 (Stilicho); Verg. *Ecl.* 4.6, 8 f., 18–45 (*puer nascens*), *A.* 6.792–94, 8.174–28 (Augustus). On these passages, as well as on those referring to other rulers from Caligula to Constantine, cf. Christ (1938) 97–115; Sauter (1934) 19–24; Finley (1967) 9 f.; Rowland (1968); cf. also Norden (1899) 476. On the Golden Age in Claudian and other late authors, with special reference to the community of real property (cf. IR 1.380–87) cf. Hahn (1962), where our present passage is wrongly cited as 1.45 f.

1.52–57 Concordia — leges: cf. Symmachus, *Ep.* 10.8.2 credimus ... ad regnum suum redire virtutes. On the use of imagery here, cf. Christiansen (1969) 119 f.

1.52 f. Concordia, Virtus cumque Fide Pietas: cf. Hor. *Saec.* 57–59 Iam Fides et Pax et Honor Pudorque / priscus et neglecta redire Virtus / audet; Christ (1938) 154 f. On the personification, cf. n. 1.29–38.

1.53 alta cervice: cf. EH 84 f. petulans alta cervice Iuventa / excludit Senium; BP 627 f. (Alaric's wife dreams of having Roman matrons as slaves) Demens ... / Romanas ... alta famulas cervice petebat; IR 2.294 magna cervice triumphat, 2.446 f. Aspiciat quisquis nimium sublata secundis / colla gerit; cf. also Verg. G. 3.552 f. Tisiphone ... / in ... dies avidum surgens caput altius effert.

1.54 canunt ... triumphum: cf. CS 1.3 f. regia ... / ... cecinit fuso Gildone triumphos; Ov. *Met.* 1.560 f. laeta triumphum / vox canet; *Trist.* 4.2.53; *Am.* 1.2.34.

1.55 f. ipsa — Iustitia: for Iustitia as a heavenly body, the constellation Virgo of the zodiac, translated to the heavens after a sojourn on earth during the early ages of mankind, cf. MT 116 f. (Iustitia, seeing Manlius on earth, descends and appears to him) liquida cessantem vidit ab aethra / Iustitia, 119 f. deserit Autumni portas, qua vergit in Austrum / Signifer et noctis reparant dispendia Chelae (cf. IR 1.364–66), 122 f. laetatur terra reverso / numine, quod prisci post tempora perdidit auri, 132 aspexit fulgentia Virginis ora; Arat. *Phaen.* 96 f., 101–5, 112–14, 129–36; Eratosth. *Cat.* 9 (= 82–84 Robert); Hyg. *Astr.* 2.25 VIRGO. Hanc Hesiodus Iovis et Themidis filiam dicit; Aratus autem Astraei et Aurorae filiam existimari, quae eodem tempore fuerit cum aurea saecula hominum, et eorum principem fuisse demonstrat; quam propter diligentiam et aequitatem Iustitiam appellatam.... Denique causam pervenisse usque eo, dum diceretur aeneum genus hominum natum, itaque iam non potuisse pati amplius et ad sidera evolasse. Cf. also Verg. G. 2.473 f., *Ecl.* 4.6 iam redit et Virgo; Ov. *Fast.* 1.249 f., *Met.* 1.149 f.; Preller-Robert (1894) 1.90 and ftn. 2; 150, 479; Roscher (1937) s.vv. *Astraia, Iustitia, Parthenos* 1655 f., *Sternbilder usw. bei Griechen u. Römern* (Vol. 6) 959–61; RE s.v. *Iustitia*; Semple (1939) 3 f. For Iustitia's role later in the poem, cf. 1.354–87. On Claudian's interest in astrology, cf. Rolfe (1919) 147 f.; Brakman (1930) 383 f.; Fargues (1933a) 174–79; Semple (1937a), (1939). On the use of imagery here, cf. Christiansen (1969) 117.

1.55 liquidas delapsa per auras: cf. MT 116 f. liquida ... vidit ab aethra / Iustitia. Cf. also Verg. *A.* 6.202 (doves seen by Aeneas) liquidum ... per aëra lapsae, 11.595; Ov. *Pont.* 3.2.61 f.; Stat. *Silv.* 5.1.103.

1.56 a stirpe recisis: cf. Verg. *A.* 12.208 (Latinus swears by his scepter) imo de stirpe recisum.

1.57 elicit oppressas tenebroso carcere leges: for laws held prisoner by an oppressor, cf. 2.85 maerent captivae ... leges; for their release, cf. BP 37 f. claustris ... solutae / tristibus exangues audent procedere leges; 4H 512. On the importance of *leges* for the concept of the *pax Romana*, cf. Christ (1938) 113 f. For the corresponding imprisonment of the forces of evil, cf. 1.377–79 (Iustitia to Megaera) tu ... gravibus ferri religata catenis // ... imo barathri claudere recessu, n. 1.379. Bruère (1964) 225 compares Lucan's account of the exiled Marius, 2.79 viderat immensam tenebroso in carcere lucem.

1.59 omnibus eiectae regnis: cf. 1.50 f. (the Furies) quas Iuppiter arcet Olympo, / Theodosius terris, 1.359 (Megaera to Iustitia, ironically) nec locus est usquam Furiis?

1.61 nefas ... decernite: cf. Luc. 5.203 f. (Why did not the oracle disclose Pompey's fate?) An nondum numina tantum / decrevere nefas?

1.62 f. Stygiis invadere nubibus astra ... flatu violare diem: cf. RP 1.1 f. (Pluto darkens the stars by approaching them in his chariot) adflata ... curru / sidera Taenario. On the Furies as storm-goddesses, cf. Roscher (1937) s.v. *Erinys* 1310–12. On Claudian's treatment of the theme of a threatened revolt of the powers of darkness against those of light, cf. Kroll (1932), esp. 520; cf. also n. 1 Pr.1; n. 1.68 f.

1.63 f. laxare — ripis: for the destruction of the world by inundation, cf. 2.209 f. (Stilicho prefers that the world be destroyed by flood rather than by Rufinus' machinations) prorumpat in arva / libertas effrena maris; BG 139–41; n. 2.209–11.

1.63 violare diem: cf. Luc. 9.461 f. (a smoky fire pollutes the air) quantum ... licet consurgere fumo / et violare diem.

1.64 frena: for bodies of water thought of as steeds controlled by the bridle, cf. RP 2 Pr.17 frenantur ... undae; Ov. *Met.* 1.280–82 (Neptune orders the rivers to flood the lands) "fluminibus vestris totas immittite habenas." / Iusserat; hi redeunt ac fontibus ora relaxant / et defrenato volvuntur in aequora cursu; Verg. *G.* 4.136. For a similar idea applied to the winds, cf. 2.22 f. ventis veluti si frena resolvat / Aeolus, n. 2.22 *b*.

1.65 *a* rerum ... fidem: cf. ps.-Verg. *Aetna* 226 nosse fidem rerum dubiasque exquirere causas. Schol. A *ad loc.*, with a glance backward at 1.4, remarks: quod superius vocavit foedera mundi, hic vocat fidem: ubi enim est fides, ibi est foedus. On a speech ending within the verse, cf. n. 1.45–65, sect. 8.

1.65 *b* Sic fata: on the use of similar phrases to indicate the resumption of the narrative after a direct quotation, cf. Pease (1935) on Verg. *A*. 4.30 sic effata. In IR we find: 1.116 Orantem sequitur clamor, 162 Dixerat, 171 ait, 340 audiit illa, 349 Sic fatus: 2.22 Haec fatus, 169 Haec ubi, 220 His dictis, 251 nec plura locutus, 317 talibus acclamat dictis, 334 Has canit ambages, 404 Sic fatur. The foregoing citations show resumptive phrases or their equivalents following 13 out of the 20 direct quotations in IR (cf. n. 1.45–65). The remaining 7 fall into three groups: (a) 1.367 is followed by *Diva refert*, 2.247 interrupted by *Dux inde vetat*, each phrase marking a change of speaker; 2.99 by *Talibus ... procellis*, which may with some latitude be taken as a resumptive phrase; (b) 1.387 and 2.527 close their respective books, the latter the entire poem; (c) thus 2.277 and 2.390 are the only clear-cut instances (2 out of 20) of the resumption of narrative after direct quotation without a phrase to mark the change.

1.65 f. cruentum mugiit: for *cruentus = crudelis* cf. IE 1.192 f. cruentam / ... avaritiam; TLL s.v. *cruentus* 1240.37–80. The adverbial use of the neut. acc. sing. adjective is a favorite locution of Claudian's: cf. 2.344 regale tumens, 355 saevum nutant, 472 triste gemens; cf. also IE 2 Pr.26; EH 61; 4H 37; MT 237; CS 2.458 f.; RP 2.8, 3.340. Cf. Verg. *Ecl*. 3.63 suave rubens, *G*. 4.270; Stat. *Theb*. 4.10; Hofmann-Szantyr (1965) 40.

1.66 *a* mugiit: on cattle-like bellowing as an attribute of the Furies, cf. Roscher (1937) s.v. *Erinys* 1315; PGM 4.2802 f. (the three-headed goddess Persephone-Megaera-Allecto) ἡ ταύρων μύκημα κατὰ στομάτων ἀνιεῖσα.

1.66 *b* totos ... hiatus: for *totus = omnis* cf. Stat. *Theb*. 1.81 totos in poenam ordire nepotes (Serv. on Verg. *A*. 1.185 remarks: id est, omnes); Birt (1892) 593 s.v. *totus, fin.*; Wölfflin (1882) 107 f.; Hofmann-Szantyr (1965) 203.

1.66 *c* totos serpentum erexit hiatus: cf. Verg. *A*. 7.450 (Allecto) geminos erexit crinibus angues (cf. n. 1.42 *b*); Stat. *Theb*. 2.27 Cerberus ... omnes capitum subrexit hiatus; n. 1.42 *c*.

1.67 noxia ... effudit concusso crine venena: cf. Ov. *Met*. 4.492–94 (Tisiphone) caesariem excussit; motae ... colubrae ...

saniem ... vomunt; Luc. 9.635 (Medusa's locks) vipereum ... fluit depexo crine venenum. For *concusso crine* cf. BP 487 (an aged Goth) concutiens ... comam; Stat. *Theb.* 7.3 (Jupiter) concussit ... caput.

1.68 vulgi. Pars maxima: for a similar collocation of words, cf. Luc. 7.47 f. miseri pars maxima vulgi / non totum visura diem.

1.68 f. bellum indicit superis: Fabbri (1939) 29 remarks upon Claudian's fondness for themes involving a revolt against the supernal gods; cf. CM 53 and RP 1.32–47; n. 1.62 f.

1.69 *a* indicit: for the conative present, cf. RP 1.135 (suitors make their offers) Mars donat Rhodopen, Phoebus largitur Amyclas; Text. Comm. on 1.142 f.; Juret (1933) 30.

1.69 *b* Ditis iura: cf. RP 1.63–65 ne pete firmatas pacis dissolvere leges / quas dedimus nevitque colus, neu foedera fratrum / civili converte tuba; Hom. *Il.* 15.189–93; Schol. Dan. on Verg. *A.* 1.139 Iuppiter et Neptunus et Dis pater ... cum de mundi possessione certamen inissent, placuit ut imperium sorte dividerent: ita effectum est, ut caelum Iuppiter, maria Neptunus, Dis pater inferos sortirentur; Roscher (1937) s.v. *Poseidon* 2801.

1.70–73: cf. Ov. *Fast.* 2.775 ut solet a magno fluctus languescere flatu / sed tamen a vento, qui fuit, unda tumet (Rolfe [1919] 144); Luc. 5.217 f. ut tumidus Boreae post flamina pontus / rauca gemit (Bruère [1964] 225 f.); Sen. *Her. F.* 1089–92, *Her. O.* 710 f.; Stat. *Theb.* 1.479–81, 7.86–89. Bruère (1964) 226 on 1.72 dubium ... per aestum, compares Luc. 5.492, 602 dubium aequor. On the use of imagery here, cf. Christiansen (1969) 111 f.

1.71 *a* impacata quies pelagi: Bruère (1964) 226 compares Luc. 5.442 saeva quies pelagi.

1.71 *b* flamine fracto: for *frango* thus used of a wind which dies down by itself (as here, since the image is that of a storm on the open sea) rather than of one which is stopped by a barrier (the more common usage, cf. BG 521 f., Luc. 9.450), cf. Stat. *Silv.* 4.5.8 in Zephyros Aquilone fracto; Sen. *Nat.* 1.1.13 frangi tempestatem et desinere ventos.

1.74–117: *Megaera offers to bring Rufinus, once her nurseling, to the Court, where he will re-establish the reign of Evil. The plan meets with approval.*

1.74 a surgit: for rising to address a gathering (cf. n. 1.39) cf. Cic. *Att.* 1.14.3 Crassus...surrexit ornatissimeque...locutus est; RE Supp. 6 (1935) s.v. *Senatus (Regierung)* 706.47–49.

1.74 b Megaera: "The Envious" (μεγαίρω); on her role in IR, cf. n. 1.25–73.

1.75 f.: on the connection of the Furies with insanity, cf. Roscher (1937) s.v. *Erinys* 1315.

1.77 cognata caede: for the extended use of the adjective, cf. Sen. *Med.* 522 f. Non ut in socerum manus / armes nec ut te caede cognata inquines. Cf. also RP 3.200 f. cognata vulnera cernis / invidiae; Text. Comm. on 1.16; n. 1.16 *a*.

1.77 f. cruorem...bibit: for the Furies' thirst for blood, cf. A. *Eu.* 254 ὀσμὴ βροτείων αἱμάτων με προσγελᾷ, 264 f. ἀντιδοῦναι δεῖ σ' ἀπὸ ζῶντος ῥοφεῖν / ἐρυθρὸν ἐκ μελέων πέλανον; Petr. 120.96 f. (Dis Pater speaks) iam pridem nullo perfundimus ora cruore / nec mea Tisiphone sitientis perluit artus; cf. also Amm. 14.1.2 (the wife of the Caesar Gallus) Megaera quaedam mortalis...humani cruoris avida; Rohde (1921) 1.270, Dieterich (1913) 55.

1.78 patrius quem fuderit ensis: the slaughter of their offspring in fury-inspired madness is attributed to Hercules (1.79 f.; cf. Sen. *Her. F.* 100–22, 982–1038) and to Athamas (1.81; cf. Ov. *Met.* 4.464–519).

1.79 *a* quem dederint fratres: on a possible reference here to the murder by Thyestes and Atreus of their half-brother Chrysippus, cf. Levy (1941) 240 f.

1.79 *b* haec terruit Herculis ora: Schol. B cites Luc. 1.576 f. iussu Iunonis iniquae / horruit Alcides viso iam Dite Megaeram; cf. also Sen. *Her. F.* 100–2 Incipite, famulae Ditis.../...agmen horridum anguibus / Megaera ducat; *Her. O.* 1005 f., 1014.

1.80 defensores terrarum...arcus: cf. Sen. *Her. O.* 282 f. licet / totus...pacem debeat mundus tibi; 1990 orbis...pacator; Var. *L.* 7.82 Herculem...cognominatum ἀλεξίκακον ab eo quod defensor esset hominum. As an example of the word *defensor* used of inanimate objects, Henry (1873) 2.257 cites Caes. *Gal.* 4.17 (piles were erected above the bridge) ut, si arborum trunci sive naves... essent a barbaris immissae, his defensoribus earum rerum vis minueretur.

1.81 *a* Athamantheae: cf. Serv. on Verg. *A.* 5.241 Athamas post furorem a Iunone immissum cum, occiso Learcho filio, dum eum feram credit, Melicertam alterum filium cum ... uxore sua persequeretur; cf. also Ov. *Met.* 4.464–519; Stat. *Silv.* 2.1.143, *Theb.* 1.12 f.

1.81 *b* direxit spicula dextrae: cf. Ov. *Met.* 12.606 letifera direxit spicula dextra; Verg. *A.* 7.497 f., 11.654, 12.403.

1.82 *a* Agamemnonios inter ... Penates: cf. Sen. *Thy.* 249–52 (Atreus speaks) Excede, Pietas, si modo in nostro domo / unquam fuisti. Dira furiarum cohors / discorsque Erinys veniat et geminas faces / Megaera quatiens.

1.82 *b* bacchata: cf. 1.368 (Iustitia to Megaera) Non ulterius bacchabere demens; Verg. *A.* 10.41 Allecto medias Italum bacchata per urbes; Stat. *Theb.* 7.466 f.

1.83 *a* alternis ... iugulis: Schol. A *ad loc.* cites Ov. *Ep.* 8.51 f. (Hermione to Orestes) iugulo ... Aegisthus aperto / tecta cruentavit quae pater ante tuus.

1.83 f. *a* hac auspice taedae Oedipoden matri ... iunxere: cf. Sen. *Oed.* 644 (Laius speaks) mecum Erinyn pronubam thalami traham. Schol. A *ad loc.* cites Stat. *Theb.* 1.68 f. (Oedipus speaks) Si dulces furias et lamentabile matris / conubium gavisus inii.

1.83 f. *b* hac auspice taedae ... natae iunxere Thyesten: on the possibility that a vase-painting in the Vatican Library represents a Fury as instigator of Thyestes' incest (Claudian's version of the myth is unparalleled in classical literature) cf. Levy (1941).

1.83 *b* auspice: cf. Cic. *Div.* 1.16.28 nuptiarum auspices ... re omissa nomen tantum tenent, and Pease (1923) *ad loc.*; Luc. 2.371 (Cato and Marcia remarry) iunguntur taciti ... auspice Bruto; Juv. 10.336; Serv. on Verg. *A.* 4.45.

1.83 *c* taedae: for the marriage-torch, cf. EH 229 f. (Maria has no thought of wedlock) taedas ... parari nescia; Verg. *A.* 4.338 f. nec coniugis umquam / praetendi taedas, and Pease (1935) *ad loc.* An ironic reference may also be intended to the *Eumenidum taedae;* cf. IE 2.484, also Ov. *Met.* 6.428–30 (at the wedding of Tereus to Procne) non pronuba Iuno, / non Hymenaeus adest ... : / Eumenides tenuere faces de funere raptas.

1.84: cf. IE 1.289 f. Oedipodes matrem, natam duxisse Thyestes / cantatur. On a similar repetition of a formula within Claudian's own poems, cf. n. 1.102 f.

1.86–115: on direct quotation in IR, cf. n. 1.45–65, esp. sections 4 and 7.

1.86 o sociae: cf. Text. Comm. *ad loc.*; Fargues (1936) 371; Faider (1937) 679.

1.87 *a* nec fas est: Claudian seems to have forgotten that he has just attributed to Allecto the point of view that *nefas* (1.61) is the proper concern of this council.

1.87 *b* nec posse reor: for *posse=fieri posse*, cf. Ov. *Am.* 1.12.2 Infelix hodie littera posse negat; Hofmann-Szantyr (1965) 422.

1.87 f. laedere mundum si libet: for *mundus* = ἡ οἰκουμένη, (cf. 1.88 populis) cf. Stat. *Silv.* 3.3.87 f. partae . . . per omnis / divitiae populos magnique impendia mundi; Luc. 5.469 miseri . . . spes inrita mundi, 1.160. On the inhabited world as a battle-ground between the forces of good and evil, cf. Cumont (1929) 184.

1.88 commune . . . letum: cf. 2.19 f. Everso iuvat orbe mori: solacia leto / exitium commune dabit.

1.89–93: contrast with these verses the boast of the goddess Roma about Probinus and Olybrius, PO 142–44 Sunt mihi pubentes alto de semine fratres, / pignora cara Probi, festa quos luce creatos / ipsa meo fovi gremio.

1.89–91: on the relation of these verses to the ψόγος-pattern, cf. Levy (1946) 64, ftn. 28; on the use of imagery here, cf. Christiansen (1969) 85.

1.89 cunctis immanius hydris: cf. Ov. *Met.* 13.804 calcato immitior hydro; for a long series of such comparisons, each with its ablative, cf. *ibid.* 789–807.

1.90 tigride mobilius feta: Bruère (1964) 226 compares Luc. 5.405 (of Caesar) ocior . . . tigride feta; cf. also Sil. 12.458–62; Plin. *Nat.* 8.25.66 Tigrim Hyrcani et Indi ferunt, animal velocitatis tremendae, et maxime cognitae dum capitur totus . . . fetus; n. 1.227 *a*. For Rufinus' swiftness, cf. 1.239 f. Cetera segnis, / ad facinus velox, and Int. 21.

1.90 f. violentius Austris acribus: cf. Luc. 9.448 Syrtis violentius excipit Austrum.

1.91 *a* Euripi refluis incertius undis: in addition to the citations in the Text. Comm. *ad loc.*, cf. Sen. *Her. O.* 779 f.; Mela 2.7.108 Euripon vocant, rapidum mare, et alterno cursu septiens die ac septiens nocte fluctibus in vicem ... versis ... fluens; Saint-Denis (1941) 136. On Claudian's fondness for geographical allusions, cf. Fargues (1933a) 52–54.

1.91 b refluis: cf. Text. Comm. *ad loc.*; Semple (1936) 229; Brakman (1937) 121; Faider (1937) 679; Bieler (1957) 259; Bruère (1964) 254, ftn. 5.

1.91 c incertius: for Rufinus' alleged inconstancy, cf. 1.223 sociat perituro foedere dextras.

1.92–111: on the relation of these verses to the ψόγος-pattern, cf. Levy (1946) 61, 65.

1.92 f. quem — gremio: cf. Stat. *Theb.* 1.59–61 (Oedipus prays) Tisiphone ... / ... si me de matre cadentem / fovisti gremio, *Silv.* 1.2.109 f.; V. Fl. 1.355 f. (Cometes takes care of his infant son) Asterion, quem matre cadentem / ... gemino fovit pater amne. On the possible influence upon Claudian here of the passages just quoted, cf. Hudson-Williams (1959) 65.

1.92 prima: on this adjective in agreement with the subject in lieu of the adverb *primum*, cf. Birt (1892) 561 s.v. *primus*; he cites RP 1.54 prima ... Lachesis clamabat, 3.220 f. Prima Venus ... / ingerit. In general, cf. Hofmann-Szantyr (1965) 161, sect. 95b.

1.93 isto: for *iste* = *meus*, cf. Luc. 1.342 miles ... iste, 2.539 f. ista ... / proelia, 6.242 gladio ... isto, 3.126, 5.287, 351; Stat. *Theb.* 7.523 f. ista ... / ubera; Hofmann-Szantyr (1965) 184 on Cat. 17.21 Iste meus stupor.

1.95 f. quaesivit ... finxerunt: on the change of subject, cf. Text. Comm. on 2.124, last sentence.

1.95 linguis ... trisulcis: cf. Verg. *A.* 2.475 (a snake) linguis micat ore trisulcis (= G. 3.439); Stat. *Theb.* 5.571.

1.96 mollia lambentes finxerunt membra cerastae: for the she-wolf licking Romulus and Remus, cf. Verg. *A.* 8.634 mulcere alternos et corpora fingere lingua; Ov. *Fast.* 2.418 fingit lingua corpora bina sua. The notion of "licking into shape" springs from the idea, common in ancient folklore, of the mother-bear's formative functions with regard to her cubs: cf. Ov. *Met.* 15.379–81, Plin. *Nat.* 8.54.126, Gel. 17.10.2–4; Levy (1947b).

1.97 artes ... nocendi: cf. Verg. *A.* 7.337 f. (to Allecto) tibi ... / mille nocendi artes.

IN RUFINUM 35

1.98 f. simulare — risu: for elaboration of these alleged traits of Rufinus, cf. 1.104 f., 179 f., 222 f., 228 f., 238 f.; 2.367 f. Cf. also the *Suda* s.v. Ῥουφῖνος (4.300 Adler) βαθυγνώμων ἄνθρωπος καὶ κρυψίνους; Zos. 5.2.3 οὐδενὶ τὴν γνώμην ἣν εἶχεν ἐκφήνας, 5.2.4 διδοὺς ἅπασιν ὑπονοεῖν ὡς [Λουκιανὸς] οὐ τεθνηκὼς εἴη, τεύξεται δὲ πάντως φιλανθρωπίας (cf. n. 1.240 f.). Contrast with these traits the qualities which Claudian attributes to Stilicho: CS 2.34 f. invisos odisse palam, non virus in alto / condere, non laetam speciem praemittere fraudi.

1.100 plenus saevitiae: for elaboration, cf. 1.225–28, 230–37, 243–47, 261 f., 265, 291–96, 298–300, 305; 2.7 f., 61–72, 141 f.

1.100–4 lucri — siti: on Rufinus' avarice, cf. Int. 15, ftn. 82 (add 1.296, 305), ftn. 83; Int. 16, ftn. 95.

1.101–11: on the relation of these verses to the ψόγος-pattern, cf. Levy (1946) 61, 65.

1.101 f. Non ... non: on *non* at the beginning of a verse as a cliché in rhetorical amplifications, cf. Guillemin (1941) 101–12, esp. 111 f. On the metrical treatment of repeated monosyllables, cf. Poteat (1912) 48–55 (also 40 f.), and Duckworth (1967) 143–50.

1.101 Tartesiacis ... harenis: the adjective, literally applying to the city of Tartessus (cf. RE s.v. *Tartessos*) in Spain, is loosely used in the sense "Far-Western"; cf. (in an *adynaton*) CM 40.13 f. Lucem iam condet Hydaspes, / et Tartesiaco, Sol, oriere vado; cf. also Ov. *Met.* 14.416 Sparserat occiduus Tartessia litora Phoebus; Sil. 6.1 f. (and 3.399).

1.102 tempestas: I have been unable to find a parallel to the use of this word to denote the (presumably violent) current of a river, as we use the word "flood." Claudian himself uses it of billowing clouds of incense (CM 27.98 f.); other metaphorical uses, not really parallel to our present passage, are those of Verg. *A.* 12.284 tempestas telorum ac ferreus ingruit imber, and, probably in imitation of the foregoing, Sil. 15.627 f. (of an attacking army) ferrea ... / tempestas.

1.102 f. Tagi ... Pactoli ... Hermum: cf. PO 50–54 aurum, / quantum stagna Tagi rudibus stillantia venis / effluxere decus, quanto pretiosa metalli / Hermi ripa micat, quantas per Lydia culta / despumat rutilas dives Pactolus harenas (on a similar repetition of a formula, cf. n. 1.84). Cf. Serv. on Verg. *A.* 10.142 Pactolus et Hermus Lydiae flumina sunt, aurum sicut Tagus trahentia; Plin. *Nat.* 33.4.66; Otto (1890) 340.

1.103 f. exhauserit ... ardebit: for this type of quasi-conditional expression, cf. Hor. *S.* 1.1.45 f. Milia frumenti tua triverit area centum, / non tuus hoc capiet venter plus ac meus; V. Fl. 1.642–46; Kühner-Stegmann-Thierfelder (1962) 2.166. On the use of imagery here, cf. Christiansen (1969) 84 f.

1.104 a ardebit ... siti: cf. 1.186 f. fluctibus auri / expleri calor ille nequit, 220 Crescebat scelerata sitis. Cf. also Ov. *Rem.* 533 sitis ista ... qua perditus ardes.

1.104 b fallere: cf. 1.238 Causis fallacibus instat; 2.367 fallere cuncta solebat; n. 1.98 f.

1.105 unanimos odiis turbare sodales: cf. Verg. *A.* 7.355 f. (among Allecto's qualities) unanimos armare in proelia fratres / atque odiis versare domos. Cf. also IE 2.539–41 Rufinus origo / prima mali: geminas inter discordia partes / hoc auctore fuit.

1.107 f.: for these fabled pairs of inseparables, cf. Mart. 7.24.3–6 Te fingente nefas Pyladen odisset Orestes, / Thesea Pirithoi destituisset amor // et Ledae poteras dissociare genus (i.e. Castor and Pollux); Stat. *Theb.* 1.475–78 fidem, quanta partitum extrema protervo / Thesea Pirithoo, vel inanem mentis Oresten / opposito rabidam Pylade vitasse Megaeram. On the friendship of Theseus and Perithoos, cf. Roscher (1937) s.v. *Peirithoos* 1766 f., Otto (1890) 347.

1.109 a fateor vinci: cf. Stat. *Ach.* 1.483 cedit turba ducum vincique haud maesta fatetur; on the syntax, cf. Hofmann-Szantyr (1965) 364.

1.109 b -que: on the explicative conjunction, cf. n. 1.13.

1.109 f. magistram praevenit: cf. Luc. 1.326 (Pompey) docilis Sullam scelerum vicisse magistrum.

1.111 scelerum: cf. 1.297 f. Certamen ... / virtutum scelerumque.

1.112 a si vestrae res est accommoda turbae: on the use of language suitable to a parliamentary debate, cf. n. 1.39.

1.112 b vestrae ... turbae: cf. 6H Pr.24 (of the Emperor's entourage) turba verenda, and Müller (1938) *ad loc.*; Luc. 8.79 pia turba senatus; 3.104, 5.20.

1.113 a regalem: for the use of *rex* and its derivatives with reference to the Roman Emperor, cf. 2.144 (of Honorius) per fratris regale iubar, 195 f. (Arcadius' commands) mandata ... / regia; EH 198,

253; CS 3.113-15 Fallitur egregio quisquis sub principe credit / servitium: numquam libertas gratior extat / quam sub rege pio, 2.355, 361. Cf. also Amm. 14.1.1 regiae stirpis; Pacatus, *Panegyricus dictus Theodosio Augusto* 12 adfinitas regia; Spartianus *Hadr.* 23.8 (SHA 1.24.21) servis regiis; Schoener (1881) 481–84, 488 f.; Bernays (1885) 2.122 f.

1.113 *b* summi...principis: Theodosius the Great; cf. Int. 8.

1.114 f.: cf. Stein-Palanque (1959) 191, "Pour être un souverain vraiment grand, Théodose aurait dû surveiller de plus près ses favoris du moment"; 192 (a comparison of Theodosius with Constantine) "C'est à cet empereur que Théodose fait penser par l'amabilité du caractère, exploitée chez tous les deux par des favoris." On Rufinus as a favorite of Theodosius, cf. Int. 9, 15. Here and elsewhere, Claudian attempts to excuse Theodosius' failure to withstand Rufinus' evil influence: cf. 1.177 subrepsit, 180 ambitos a principe...honores, 1.320 eluso principe; cf. also 1.244 f. neu perderet ullum / Augusto miserante nefas.

1.114 *a* ipse: for this word used of the Emperor, cf. 3H 173 (Theodosius) quas partes velit ipse sequi; MT 259 (Honorius) quam quater ipse gerit; TLL s.v. *ipse* 343.32–344.12.

1.114 *b* Numa: cf. 4H 491–93 fruimir...quietis /...bonis.../ ceu placido moderante Numa. Cf. also n. 1.252–55, *fin*.

1.114 *c* Minos: for Minos' actual rôle at the end of the poem, cf. 2.476–527.

1.116 f. *a*: Bruère (1964) 226 compares two passages from Lucan, the first a reversed reminiscence: 2.596 (Pompey's troops are unfavorable to his address) verba ducis nullo partes clamore secuntur; 8.551 f. (Ptolemy's murder of Pompey) profanas / inseruisse manus.

1.116 f. *b* sequitur...porrexere...laudant: on the variation in tense, cf. Axelson (1944) 75 f.; he cites also 1.131–33 sentit...quatit ...substitit...torpuit, on which see Text Comm. on 1.131.

1.117 porrexere manus: for this gesture of approval, borrowed from Greece, cf. Cic. *Flac.* 6.15–7.17 sic sunt expressa ista praeclara quae recitantur psephismata, non sententiis neque auctoritatibus declarata, non iure iurando constricta, sed porrigenda manu profundendoque clamore multitudinis concitatae.... Porrexerunt manus; psephisma natum est. Cf. also RE s.v. χειροτονεῖν, χειροτονία.

1.118–75: *Megaera ascends to the world above. She appears to Rufinus in the guise of an old man, and bids him to travel to Constantinople. He obeys.*

1.118 *a* caeruleo ... angue: cf. Verg. G. 4.482 f. caeruleos ... implexae crinibus angues / Eumenides, A. 7.346 f. (Allecto infects Amata) huic dea caeruleis unum de crinibus anguem / conicit.

1.118 *b* vestes conexuit angue: cf. Ov. Met. 4.483 (Tisiphone) induitur pallam tortoque incingitur angue.

1.119 *a* nodavit ... adamante comas: cf. Verg. A. 4.138 (Dido's coiffure) crines nodantur in aurum. Either a hair-pin (cf. Sil. 15.26 fronte decor quaesitus acu) or a *fibula* is meant (cf. Verg. A. 7.815 f. [Camilla] ut fibula crinem / auro internectat); cf. Pease (1935) on Verg. A. 4.138.

1.119 *b* Phlegethonta: cf. 2.467 f. Plegethon ... inamoenus ... / alveus ... igne redundat; n. 2.466 f.; Verg. A. 6.550 f. rapidus flammis ambit torrentibus amnis, / Tartareus Phlegethon.

1.119 *c* sonorum: cf. Verg. A. 6.551 Phlegethon torquet ... sonantia saxa.

1.120 ab aggere ripae: cf. Luc. 6.778 (a shade summoned to earth for necromancy) tacitae revocatus ab aggere ripae.

1.121 succendit ... pinum: cf. RP 3.390 f. (Megaera) Phlegethontis ad undam / constitit et plenos excepit lampade fluctus; Sil. 2.609–11 Erinnys / lampada flammiferis tinctam Phlegethontis in undis / quassat, 12.714.

1.122 *a* pigra ... veloces: for the contrasting adjectives, cf. Verg. A. 11.62 f. solacia luctus / exigua ingentis.

1.122 *b* concutit alas: cf. Verg. A. 7.476 Allecto ... Stygiis se concitat alis; cf. also Roscher (1937) s.v. *Erinys* 1311.

1.123–33: post-Homeric speculation located the scene of the Nekyia in various western lands: cf. Roscher (1937) s.v. *Odysseus* 632–38. On Homer's own localization of the episode in the West παρὰ ῥόον Ὠκεανοῖο (Od. 11.13–37), cf. Roscher (1937) s.v. *Kimmerier*. Claudian's concept that the summoning of the ghosts took place in Gaul (1.123) seems to be without parallel; the poet was obviously motivated by the desire to have the Fury emerge in the province of Rufinus' birth and early residence (cf. 1.137; Int. 8). It has been suggested that there is some connection between Claudian's placing the Nekyia episode in Gaul and the tale told by Procop. Goth. 4.20.48–58 (cf. Tz. ad Lyc.

1204) about fishermen of the Gallic coast who ferried the spirits of the dead to the isle of Brittia at night: cf. Grimm-Meyer (1875) 2.696; Ettig (1891) 386, ftn. 2.

J. Schmidt in Roscher (1937) s.v. *Odysseus* 637 assumes that Claudian thought of the Nekyia as having occurred in the immediate vicinity of Elusa, Rufinus' birthplace (cf. Int. 8). Apparently on the basis of our passage alone, he suggests the existence of a tradition connecting the name of the town with Elysium. Elusa, however, was not on or near the coast (cf. 1.123 f. locus... pandit qua Gallia litus / Oceani praetentus aquis; on the location of Eauze, cf. Desjardins [1876] 2.364, 367, and map facing 368). Moreover, Schmidt has neglected the geographical data given by Claudian in 1.131–33: the Fury's howl reaches Britain, the *arva Senonum*, and the Rhine (the naming of Tethys adds nothing to 1.123 f.). If Schmidt's assumption were correct, we should have to believe that Claudian represented the Fury's voice as traveling northward only. Now in a parallel passage in IE (2.160–65, quoted in n. 1.131–33) the sound of Mars' shield, emanating from a peak of the Haemus range, reaches the Danube to the North and Mt. Athos to the South; in Luc. 7.478–83 (quoted in n. 1.131–33) the trumpet-blast at Pharsalus reaches the Haemus range to the North, Mt. Pelion to the East, Mt. Oeta to the South, and the Pindus range to the West. Hence, had Claudian imagined the Fury's cry as coming from somewhere in Aquitania, he would almost certainly have mentioned the Pyrenees, Spain, or perhaps even Africa as the southern limit of its range. Norden (1959) 186 f. is therefore justified in regarding the data given in 1.131–33 as delimiting the area in which Claudian's *locus* is to be sought: somewhere along the Gallic coast, opposite Britain, between the Rhine on the North and an extension of the *ager Senonicus* on the South. Cf. also Grimm-Meyer (1875) 2.696. This area has the additional merit of being better suited than the Aquitanian coast to the designation *extremum... litus* (1.123) and also of corresponding to the area described by Procopius. To go further, and to fix upon an actual town (Norden names the sea-port of Bononia or Gesoriacum, now Boulogne-sur-Mer), is, I believe, going too far. There is nothing in Claudian or in Procopius to suggest a town; an almost deserted stretch of coastline would be more appropriate to the supernatural activities in question.

Claudian disregards the Fury's journey from the coast to Elusa (1.129 Hinc... egressa, 134–37 Tunc... invadit), a poetic treatment quite as appropriate to the 450-odd miles which separate Eauze from the Channel coast as to the 70-odd miles which lie between that town and the nearest coastal point.

1.123 Est locus: for the cliché consisting of these words at the beginning of a hexameter and followed by a description (as also in 2.466), cf. Verg. *A.* 1.530 f. (=3.163 f.) est locus, Hesperiam Graii cognomine dicunt, / terra antiqua, 7.563; Ov. *Met.* 8.788 f. Est locus, extremis Scythiae glacialis in oris, / triste solum, 2.195 f.; *Fast.* 2.491 f., 4.337 f.; *Pont.* 3.2.45. It does not occur in Lucan, but appears in Statius (*Theb.* 2.32, *Silv.* 5.1.222) and Silius (11.505). Cf. also Guillemin (1941).

1.124 ubi fertur: on the use of this phrase despite the apparent lack of basis in tradition for Claudian's localization, cf. Norden (1959) 187.

1.124 f.: cf. Hom. *Od.* 11.35–37 τὰ δὲ μῆλα λαβὼν ἀποδειροτόμησα / ἐς βόθρον, ῥέε δ' αἷμα κελαινεφές· αἱ δ' ἀγέροντο / ψυχαὶ ὑπὲξ Ἐρέβευς νεκύων κατατεθνηώτων; RE s.v. *Nekromantie* 2220 f. On blood-offerings to the dead, cf. Rohde (1921) 1.56–58; Stengel (1910) 24; Eitrem (1915) 416–21; ERE s.v. *Blood* 718, sect. 7; Pfister (1930) 140 f., sect. 99.3; Roscher (1937) s.v. *Unterwelt* 81.

1.125–28: on various echoes of Lucan here, cf. Bruère (1964) 226.

1.125 populum... silentem: cf. RP 2.237 f. (Diana bids farewell to Proserpina) populo... silenti / traderis, heu! Luc. 6.513 (of the witch Erichtho) coetus audire silentum; Stat. *Theb.* 4.528 f.; Roscher (1937) s.v. *Unterwelt* 82.

1.126–28: cf. Stat. *Theb.* 2.48–51 (the entrance to the Lower World thought to exist at Taenarus in Laconia) hoc, ut fama, loco pallentes devius umbras / trames agit nigrique Iovis vacua atria ditat / mortibus. Arcadii perhibent si vera coloni, / stridor ibi et gemitus poenarum.

1.126 f. umbrarum... volantum...; simulacra: cf. Ov. *Am.* 1.6.9 quondam... simulacra... vana timebam, 13 f. venit amor. Non umbras nocte volantis / ... timeo.

1.128 *a* pallida: cf. Pease (1935) on Verg, *A.* 4.26 pallentis.

1.128 *b* migrare figuras: cf. Verg. *A.* 10.641 morte obita quales fama est volitare figuras.

1.128 c figuras: cf. Text. Comm. *ad loc.*; also Fargues (1936) 371. E. Vetter, in TLL s.v. *figura* 729, errs in attributing the reading *catervas* here to Birt instead of to Koch.

1.129 dea: for this word applied to a Fury, cf. Verg. *A.* 7.324 luctificam Allecto dirarum ab sede dearum; cf. 7.346.

1.129 f. Phoebi... egressa serenos infecit radios: cf. Stat. *Theb.* 1.124 (Tisiphone comes to the Theban palace) adsueta... infecit nube penates, 7.40-46, esp. 45 f. laeditur adversum Phoebi iubar, ipsaque sedem / lux timet, et dirus contristat sidera fulgor. On the struggle between light and darkness, cf. n. 1.62 f.

1.130 ululatu... aethera rupit: cf. Verg. *A.* 7.394 (frenzied companions of Amata) ululatibus aethera complent.

1.131–33 sensit — urna: for similar recitals of geographical boundaries (cf. n. 1.123-33, para. 2) limiting the range of a mighty sound, cf. IE 2.160-65 (Mars strikes his shield) clipeo... // intonuit. Responsat Athos Haemusque remugit; / ingeminat raucum Rhodope concussa fragorem, / cornua cana gelu mirantibus extulit undis / Hebrus et exanguem glacie timor adligat Histrum, 171-73; Luc. 7.478-83 (the trumpet is blown at Pharsalus) Extremi... fragor convexa inrumpit Olympi, // excepit resonis clamorem vallibus Haemus, / Peliacisque dedit rursus geminare cavernis; / Pindus agit fremitus, Pangaeaque saxa resultant, / Oetaeaeque gemunt rupes; Stat. *Theb.* 1.114-20. On Claudian's fondness for geographical enumerations as an outgrowth of his rhetorical training, and also as showing imitation of Lucan, cf. Fargues (1933a) 52-54. On the use of imagery here, cf. Christiansen (1969) 63.

1.131 sensit: cf. Text. Comm. *ad loc.*; Fargues (1936) 371; Brakman (1937) 121; Axelson (1944) 76.

1.132 f. a revoluta — urna: for bodies of water represented as affected by violent noises, cf. Verg. *A.* 8.239 f. intonat aether, / dissultant ripae refluitque exterritus amnis, 9.124 f. cunctatur et amnis / rauca sonans revocatque pedem Tiberinus ab alto; 3.672-74; Henry (1873) 3.679 f.

1.132 f. b revoluta... Tethys substitit: for *revolvo* of a violent disturbance of the sea (cf. 1.132 *quatit arva*) cf. Verg. *A.* 10.660 avulsam... rapit revoluta per aequora navem; Sen. *Ag.* 487-90. For *subsisto* of subsidence (cf. 1.133 *torpuit*) cf. Verg. *A.* 8.87-89 (the Tiber) ita substitit... / mitis ut in morem stagni... / sterneret aequor. Platnauer (1922) seems mistaken in taking *revoluta* as a reference to the tide, unless he means the word in the general sense of "waves."

1.133 Rhenus proiecta torpuit urna: cf. RP 2.69 f. (at the festival of Bacchus) laetatur in antro / amnis et undantem declinat prodigus urnam; Verg. *A.* 7.792 amnem fundens pater Inachus urna; Roscher (1937) s.v. *Flussgötter* 1492.

1.134–36: for a similar transformation, cf. Verg. *A.* 7.415–18 Allecto torvam faciem et furialia membra / exuit, in vultus sese transformat aniles; / et frontem obscenam rugis arat, induit albos / cum vitta crines, 7.328 (Allecto can assume many guises) tot sese vertit in ora. On the Furies' faculty of changing their shapes as a reflection of their original character as cloud-divinities, cf. Roscher (1937) s.v. *Erinys* 1310 f. Cf. also Ov. *Met.* 3.275 for a similar disguise adopted by Juno.

1.134 in canitiem mutatis...colubris: cf. IE 2.186 (Bellona assumes the shape of a Gothic woman) virides flavescere iusserat angues; on the snaky locks, cf. n. 1.42 c.

1.135 mentita senem: for the accusative, cf. Mart. 3.43.1 Mentiris iuvenem tinctis... capillis; cf. also BP 320, CS 1.253, 2.249; Axelson (1944) 36.

1.136 ficto...passu: cf. IE 2.182 (Bellona in disguise) mentito... gressu.

1.137 *a* Elusae: on Rufinus' birthplace, cf. Int. 8.

1.137 *b* notissima dudum: cf. 1.92–96. Cf. also Stat. *Theb.* 1.100 f. (Tisiphone, Oedipus' nurse [1.60 f.] returns to his birthplace) arripit... / notum iter ad Thebas.

1.138 f. haesit peiorem mirata virum: with this conceit, contrast EH 241 f. (Venus sees Maria and her mother) Cunctatur stupefacta Venus: nunc ora puellae / nunc... miratur... matrem.

1.140–61: on direct quotation in IR, cf. n. 1.45–65, esp. sect. 7.

1.140 *a* Otia: of Rufinus' early career nothing is known: cf. Int. 8.

1.140 *b* iuventae: on Rufinus' age, cf. Int. 8.

1.141 patriis inglorius arvis: perhaps a conflation of Verg. *A.* 11.793 (Arruns offers to give up fame in return for Camilla's death) patrias remeabo inglorius urbes, and 10.52 (Venus proposes as a last resort a refuge for Ascanius where he may live) positis inglorius armis.

1.142–44: Heu — velis: Bruère (1964) 226 compares Luc. 8.557 f. (denunciation of young Ptolemy's part in Pompey's murder) Nescis, puer improbe, nescis / quo tua sit fortuna loco; also 8.553 (had Pompey not been so mighty) non domitor mundi.

1.142 f. *a* **fata . . . fortuna:** cf. RP 3.300 f. (Ceres turns from indignation to entreaties) quamcumque dedistis / fortunam, sit nota: feram fatumque putabo; on Fate and Fortune in Claudian, cf. Born (1939).

1.142 quid sidera donent: cf. PO 146 (the stars ordained the birth of Probinus and Olybrius) magnos proferrent sidera partus. On Claudian's interest in astrology, cf. the references cited in n. 1.55 f. *fin.*

1.142 f. *b* **donent . . . paret:** cf. Text Comm. *ad loc.*

1.143 *a* **toto dominabere mundo:** cf. Verg. *A.* 3.97 domus Aeneae cunctis dominabitur oris.

1.143 *b* **toto . . . mundo:** here apparently of the Roman Empire, as distinguished from the οἰκουμένη (cf. n. 1.87 f.): cf. 2.212 f. procumbere mundum / hoc auctore pudet, 3H 64 quatit discordia mundum; Luc. 1.160 mundo . . . subacto; Christ (1938) 18–21, though the distinction is often blurred or non-existent. On the use of *orbis* and *terrae* of the Roman Empire, cf. n. 1 Pr.17 *b*, n. 1.51 *b*.

1.143 *c* **dominabere:** cf. Text. Comm. *ad loc.*

1.144 Artus ne sperne seniles: cf. Verg. *A.* 7.452 f. (Allecto, casting aside her old woman's disguise, speaks ironically to Turnus) En ego victa situ, quam veri effeta senectus / arma inter regum falsa formidine ludit!

1.145–60: as will be seen from the following notes, the elements of magic here referred to by Claudian are all otherwise attested in literary sources, while all except those mentioned in 1.158 (Ire vagas quercus et fulmen stare coegi) also appear in the magical papyri edited by Preisendanz (cf. abbreviation PGM). On the correspondence between the literary treatment of magic and the practices reflected in the papyri, cf. Nock (1929) 225–27; Eitrem (1933), (1934), (1941); Riess (1935); cf. also Fahz (1904) 110–21, 144–70.

For similar enumerations of thaumaturgic feats, cf. Ov. *Met.* 7.199–209, Tib. 1.2.43–52; Luc. 6.461–84; Sen. *Med.* 754–79; Pease 1935) on Verg. *A.* 4.489 sistere; DS s.v. *Magia* 1495.

This extended passage devoted to magic is not characteristic of Claudian's work as a whole, where, in a corpus of nearly 10,000 verses, we find less than 30 concerned with the magical arts. For a possible explanation of Claudian's relative neglect of magic as a motif, cf. Levy (1948b).

1.145 f. aevi ... futuri praescius: cf. Verg. *A.* 8.627 (Vulcan, the forger of Aeneas' shield) haud ... venturi inscius aevi, 6.66 (the Sibyl) praescia venturi.

1.146 f. quo — iubar: for Thessalian witches represented as able to draw the moon down from the sky, cf. BP 237 f. Thessalidas patriis lunare venenis / incestare iubar; Hor. *Ep.* 5.45 f. quae sidera excantata voce Thessala / lunamque caelo deripit, 17.77 f.; Luc. 6.499–505 (of Thessalian women) primum / ... Phoebe ... serena / ... diris verborum obsessa venenis / palluit ... / et patitur tantos cantu depressa labores; Sen. *Phaed.* 420 f.; Plin. *Nat.* 30.1.7 ut Menander quoque ... Thessalam cognominaret fabulam complexam ambages feminarum detrahentium lunam, 25.2.10; Eitrem (1941) 50. For Thessaly as the home of magic in general, cf. Apul. *Met.* 2.1 reputans ... me media loca tenere, quo artis magicae nativa cantamina totius orbis consono ore celebrentur; Eitrem (1941) 46, 70, 72 f., 77, ftn. 3.

For the drawing down of the moon by witches (without reference to Thessaly) cf. Verg. *Ecl.* 8.69, Ov. *Met.* 7.207; PGM 34.1 f. κἂν σελήνη κελεύσω, καταβήσεται; 4.1326, 4.2245.

1.146 Thessala cantu: cf. Stat. *Theb.* 4.504 rabido iubeat si Thessala cantu. With *cantu* cf. the frequent use of such words as ᾠδή in the magical papyri: e.g. PGM 1.317, 2.83, 4.2789, 4.3151, 7.889. Cf. also IR 1.156 canendo, n. 1.156; Eitrem (1941) 59, 70.

1.147 *a* lunare iubar: for *iubar* used of the luminosity of heavenly bodies, cf. BP 237 f. lunare ... / iubar; RP 1.45 caeleste iubar; 3H 45 aestivum ... iubar; Ov. *Met.* 1.767–69 (Clymene to Phaethon) spectans ... ad lumina solis, / "per iubar hoc," inquit, "radiis insigne coruscis, / nate, tibi iuro." Cf. Pease (1935) on Verg. *A.* 4.130 iubare exorto.

1.147 *b* signa: the word apparently refers to χαρακτῆρες such as occur in the magical papyri, e.g. PGM 1.268, 3.293, 298, 7.196, 392, 421, 464, 588, 860, 923, 930–40, 11.3, 13.1054; cf. Hopfner (1938) 132 f., 137 f. For a discussion of these figures, cf. Hopfner (1921)

1.145 f., 222 f.; RE Suppl. 4.1183–88. Some of them are apparently derived from hieroglyphic symbols (cf. Hopfner [1921] 1.222 f.) and some from astrological (cf. Hopfner [1921] 1.145 f., PGM 7.923 and parenthetical note in translation); 7.810–21; thus the interpretations of Gesner (1759), *characteres magici ex hieroglyphicis illis forte orti*, and of Birt (1892) 580, s.v. *signum*, where he lists our present occurrence under the rubric *astrologica*, seem each to be partially justified. For *signum*= χαρακτήρ cf. the gloss in Codex Sangallensis 912, Goetz (1888) 4.215.40 caracter: signum vel nota. Cf. also Damigeron Latinus, *De Lapidibus* 7, Abel (1881) 169 insculptum nomen noctilucae, hoc est Hecates signum; Hopfner (1921) 1.222 f.; Amm. 17.4.10 f. ita prisci ... scriptitarunt Aegyptii ... his signis ostendentes (the reading *signis* is, however, doubtful: cf. Novák [1911] 308; he reads *insignibus*).

1.147 f. sagacis Aegypti: for the adjective, cf. Gel. 11.18.16 apud veteres Aegyptios, quod genus hominum constat ... extitisse ... in cognitione rerum indaganda sagaces. On Egyptian culture as a source of Graeco-Roman magic, cf. Nock (1929) 228.

1.148 gens Chaldaea: cf. 6H 348 f. Chaldaea mago seu carmina ritu / armavere deos; CS 1.60 f.; Hsch. s.v. Χαλδαῖοι: γένος μάγων πάντα γιγνωσκόντων; Cod. Theod. 9.16.4 (A.D. 357) Chaldaei ac magi et ceteri, quos maleficos ob facinorum magnitudinem vulgus appellat.

1.149 imperet ... deis: Schol. A *ad loc.* refers to Luc. 6.497–99 an habent haec carmina certum / imperiosa deum, qui mundum cogere, quidquid / cogitur ipse, potest? Cf. also Luc. 6.440 f. plurima surgunt / vim factura deis; 445 f., 492–97, 527 f., 598 f.; ps.-Quint. *Decl.* 10.7 magum ... cuius horrido murmure imperiosisque verbis dii superi manesque torquentur.

Cf. also PGM 12.316 f. ὁσάκις ἂν βούλει ἐπιτάσσειν τῷ θεῷ, τὸν μέγιστον Οὔφωρα εἰπὼν ἐπιτάσσει, καὶ τελεῖ; 4.2252–54 τὸ δεῖνα ποιήσεις, κἂν θέλῃς κἂν μὴ θέλῃς, ὅτι οἶδά σου τὰ φῶτα πρὸς στιγμῆς μέτρον; 4.1036–38, 2255–58, 3106–12; 14.21 f.

1.149 f. fluentes arboribus suci: cf. BG 171–73 Mors nulla refugit / artificem: varios sucos spumasque requirit / serpentum virides. Cf. also Sen. *Med.* 712 f. aut quos ... sucos legunt / lucis Suebae nobiles Hyrcaniis; Stat. *Theb.* 6.101 f. metuenda ... suco / taxus; PGM 8.72 ὀπὸς συκαμίνου (cf. 7.223, 12.429); Eitrem (1941) 46, 56, ftn. 2. Claudian or his models may possibly have had in mind such exudates as styrax and myrrh; cf. PGM 4.1308-12, 2460, 2642-49, 2872; 7.434; 13.16-20.

1.150 f. funestarum ... herbarum: cf. Verg. G. 3.283 miscuerunt ... herbas et non innoxia verba; Luc. 6.438 Thessala ... tellus herbas ... nocentes / ... ingenuit. Cf. n. 1.151 f. *b*, n. 1.152 *a*. Cf. also Plin. *Nat.* 25.2.15 plerosque ita video existimare, nihil non herbarum vi effici posse, 24.17.156-67, 26.4.18-20. For thyme and aloes used in a death-charm, cf. PGM 7.430, 434. Cf. also Hopfner (1921) 1.114-41, and Pease (1935) on Verg. *A.* 4.514 herbae.

1.151 f. *a* quidquid ... vernant: for the accusative cf. CS 2.262-64 Oenotria ... // vina fluens; on the development of intransitives into transitives, cf. Hofmann-Szantyr (1965) 31 f.

1.151 f. *b* letali gramine pollens Caucasus: cf. Sen. *Med.* 706-9 congerit in unum frugis infaustae mala // quae fert opertis hieme perpetua iugis / sparsus cruore Caucasus Promethei; V. Fl. 7.356 f. Prometheae florem de sanguine fibrae / Caucaseum; Eitrem (1941) 56, ftn. 2.

1.151 gramine: cf. Text. Comm. *ad loc.*; Fargues (1936) 371; Bieler (1957) 260.

1.152 *a* Scythicae ... rupes: cf. Ov. *Met.* 7.406 f. huius in exitium miscet Medea, quod olim / attulerat secum Scythicis aconiton ab oris (note the mention of Medea in our next verse); Stat. *Theb.* 4.505 f. Scythicis ... medicata venenis / Colchis aget.

1.152 *b* vernant in crimina: cf. Text. Comm. *ad loc.*; Semple (1936); Faider (1937); Ernout (1937). Cameron (1968a) 388 f. prefers Heinsius' conjecture *carmina* on the ground that Megaera, as the aged wizard, was not boasting of her power for evil, but only of her command of "run-of-the-mill magic and spells." He supports his view by instancing, among other things, the innocuous turning of Rufinus' doorpost into gold. But Cameron, though he is right in his remarks on the importance of *carmina* in witchcraft (cf. n. 1.146), apparently overlooks one boast that is scarcely innocuous: 1.156 f. multos ... canendo / ... peremi (cf. n. 1.156 f.). As for the turning of the doorpost into gold, that may have contained a special, and to Claudian not at all an innocuous, implication: cf. n. 1.160-69.

1.153 *a* quas legit Medea: cf. Luc. 6.441 f. Colchis / legit in Haemoniis quas non advexerat herbas.

1.153 *b* **Medea ferox:** cf. Hor. *Ars* 123 (advice to writers) sit Medea ferox.

1.153 *c* **Medea ... et ... Circe:** cf. Theocr. 2.15 f. φάρμακα ταῦτ᾽ ἔρδοισα χερείονα μήτε τι Κίρκας / μήτε τι Μηδείας; Stat. *Theb.* 4.551 Colchis et Aeaeo simulatrix litore Circe. Cf. also Plin. *Nat.* 25.2.10 Certe quid non repleverunt fabulis Colchis Medea aliaeque, in primis Itala Circe; Hopfner (1921) 1.115 f.

1.154 f. *a* **Manes ... Hecaten:** on ψυχαγωγία and the summoning of Hecate, cf. Rohde (1921) 2.87 and ftn. 2.

1.154 *a* **horrendos Manes ... citavi:** cf. Sen. *Oed.* 568 manes voce ... citat; Verg. *A.* 4.490 nocturnas ... movet manis, and Pease (1935) *ad loc.*; cf. also Hor. *S.* 1.8.29; Tib.1.2.47 f.; Sil. 1.97 f.; Stat. *Theb.* 4.413 f.; also Cod. Theod. 9.16.5 (A.D. 357) Multi magicis artibus ... manibus accitis audent ventilare, ut quisque suos conficiat malis artibus inimicos. Cf. also PGM 4.1418–20 πέμψον δὲ Ἐρίνυν ... ψυχὰς καμόντων ἐξεγείρουσαν πυρί; 12.303 f. ψυχὰς μετατρέπειν, πνεύματα κινεῖν; 4.222–49, 1454–95, 1949, 2039–54, 2140–56; 13.1077; 51.5; 58.8. Cf. Pease (1923) on Cic. *Div.* 1.58.132 psychomantia, RE s.v. *Nekromantie*.

1.154 *b* **citavi:** cf. Text. Comm. *ad loc.*; Semple (1936); Faider (1937); Bieler (1957). Cameron (1968a) 389 f. would retain the vulgate *litavi*, on the interesting ground that Servius' teaching with regard to the propriety of the formula *deos litamus* might well have been Claudian's basis for the use of the word here. But, in regard to another part of his presentation, Hecate was not as exempt from summons as Cameron suggests: cf. PGM 4.2751–53 δεῦρ᾽ Ἑκάτη, ... καλῶ σε, 4.2714; Rohde (1921) 2.87 and ftn. 2. Crépin (1933), who prints *litavi*, none the less translates "J'ai ... fait apparaître à mon appel."

1.154 f. *b* **sacris ... citavi nocturnis Hecaten:** cf. Verg. *A.* 4.609 nocturnis ... Hecate triviis ululata, 4.510 f. ter centum tonat ore deos, Erebumque Chaosque / tergeminamque Hecaten, 6.247; Luc. 6.700 f. nostraeque Hecates pars ultima per quam / manibus et mihi sunt tacitae commercia linguae, 6.736–38; Stat. *Theb.* 4.515 turbare Hecaten. Cf. also PGM 4.2751–53 (quoted in n. 1.154 *b*); 3.45–47; 4.1432–65, 2119, 2714–30; 36.185–90; Roscher (1937) s.v. *Hecate* 1894 f.

1.154 f. *c* **sacris ... nocturnis:** cf. Cod. Theod. 9.16.7 (A.D. 364)

Ne quis deinceps nocturnis temporibus aut nefarias preces aut magicos apparatus aut sacrificia funesta celebrare conetur; RE s.v. *Nekromantie* 2227.

1.155 f. condita funera traxi carminibus victura meis: cf. Luc. 6.639 f. miserum trahitur ... cadaver / victurum (where, however, *traho* refers to dragging by physical means; for the same verb used of magical attraction, as in our present passage, cf. Luc. 6.652 f.). Bruère (1964) 227 compares Luc. 6.527–32 superi ... / ... carmen ... timent audire.... / Viventes animas ... / infodit busto, fatis debentibus annos / mors invita subit; perversa funera pompa / rettulit a tumulis. Cf. also Hor. *Ep.* 17.79 possim crematos excitare mortuos; Stat. *Theb.* 2.21 f. te furiata sacerdos / Thessalis arcano iubet emigrare sepulcro, 3.140 f.; Apul. *Met.* 2.28 corpus ... istud postliminio mortis animare, 3.18 illa corpora ... spiritum mutuantur humanum et sentiunt et audiunt et ambulant; PGM 13.277–82 ἔγερσις σώματος νεκροῦ· "ὁρκίζω σε, πνεῦμα ἐν ἀέρι φοιτώμενον, εἴσελθε, ἐνπνευμάτωσον, δυνάμωσον, διαέγειρον τῇ δυνάμει τοῦ αἰωνίου θεοῦ τόδε τὸ σῶμα, καὶ περιπατείτω ἐπὶ τόνδε τὸν τόπον, ὅτι ἐγώ εἰμι ὁ ποιῶν τῇ δυνάμει τοῦ Θαῦθ ἁγίου θεοῦ." λέγε τὸ ὄνομα; 19.14 f.

1.156 f. multos ... canendo, quamvis Parcarum restarent fila, peremi: cf. Luc. 6.530 f. (quoted in n. 1.155 f.), 6.609 f. quamvis fecerit omnis / stella senem, medios herbis praerupimus annos. Cf. also Cod. Theod. 9.16.5 (A.D. 357) Multi magicis artibus ... vitas insontium labefactare non dubitant. For death-charms cf. PGM 12.378–80 (a drug causing insomnia) ἐν ἀποκρούσει δὲ αὐτὸ ἀποτέλει τριταίας οὔσης τῆς θεοῦ, καὶ ἄυπνος τελευτήσει ⟨ἡ δεῖνα⟩ μὴ διαμηκύνασα ἡμέρας ζ΄. λύσιν οὐκ ἔχει τοῦτο οὐδεπώποτε; 36.245–50 κύριοι ἄγγελοι, ὥσπερ ὁ βάθρακος [= βάτραχος] οὗτος καταρρεῖ καὶ ξηρένεται [= ξεραίνεται], οὕτως καὶ τὸ σῶμα τοῦ δεῖνα; cf. also 3.74–76, 121–24, 4.2446–52, 2455–2500; 12.6–11.

The words *multos ... canendo ... peremi* may, as T. Hopfner in RE s.v. *Nekromantie* 2227 suggests, refer to the procurement of βιοθάνατοι for necromantic purposes (cf. Luc. 6.559 f. et quotiens saevis opus est ac fortibus umbris / ipsa facit manes). The inclusion of magical murder here results in, and may have been motivated by a desire for, a contrasting doublet (1.155–57 funera traxi / ... victura ..., multos ... canendo / ... peremi) of the type found in other thaumaturgic enumerations: e.g. Ov. *Met.* 7.200–2 concussa ... sisto, / stantia concutio ...; nubila pello / nubilaque induco, ventos abigoque vocoque; Sen. *Her. O.* 462; Luc. 6.529–32; Berthelot (1888) 262 τοῦτο τὸ ὕδωρ τὰ νεκρὰ ἀνιστᾷ καὶ τὰ ζῶντα νεκροῖ, τὰ σκοτεινὰ φωτίζει καὶ τὰ φωτεινὰ σκοτίζει.

For the intervention of witchcraft against the decrees of fate, cf. Luc. 6.651 f. quamvis Thessala vates / vim faciat fatis; also 6.605–15 for limitations on such intervention.

1.156 canendo: for the use of this word for magical incantations, cf. Stat. *Theb.* 3.141 hominem renovare canendo; Ov. *Met.* 12.263 f. deduxisse canendo / ... cornua lunae; n. 1.146.

1.157 Parcarum restarent fila: cf. Juv. 3.27 dum superest Lachesi quod torqueat; contrast Stat. *Silv.* 3.1.171 f. Parcarum fila tenebo / extendamque colus: duram scio vincere mortem.

1.158 *a* Ire vagas quercus: cf. Verg. *A.* 4.491 (Dido speaks of magic) descendere montibus ornos, and Pease (1935) *ad loc.*; Ov. *Met.* 7.205 (Medea speaks) silvas moveo. I have been unable to find even an approximate parallel in PGM; we are thus apparently dealing with what in Claudian's time was a purely literary tradition, ultimately going back to Orphic antecedents.

1.158 *b* fulmen stare: cf. Sen. *Her. O.* 454 f. iussi ... fulmen stare; 469 f. cantu fugax / stat deprehensum fulmen. Bruère (1964) 227 compares Luc. 6.519 f. Thessala ... / ... nocturna ... fulmina captat. The nearest parallel in PGM is apparently the stopping of the sun in its course: 13.871–73 ἐπικαλοῦμαί σου τὸ ὄνομα, τὸ μέγιστον ἐν θεοῖς· ὃ ἐὰν εἴπω τέλειον ... ὁ ἥλιος στήσεται.

1.159 *a* versa ... curvavi flumina: cf. Ov. *Am.* 1.8.6 (Dipsas has magic powers) in ... caput liquidas arte recurvat aquas; Tib. 1.2.46 (a witch's powers) fluminis haec rapidi carmine vertit iter; cf. n. 1.159 *c*, n. 1.160. Cf. also PGM 4.3052–54 ὁρκίζω σε μέγαν θεὸν Σαβαώθ, δι' ὃν ὁ Ἰορδάνης ποταμὸς ἀνεχώρησεν εἰς τὰ ὀπίσω (though this does not necessarily mean that the user of the formula wished to repeat the miracle); Pease (1935) on Verg. *A.* 4.489 sistere.

1.159 *b* versa ... curvavi: on the resultative-predicate use of the adjective, cf. n. 1.1 *b*.

1.159 *c* non prono ... lapsu: Bruère (1964) 227 compares Luc. 6.473 f. amnis ... cucurrit / non qua pronus erat.

1.160 in fontes reditura suos: cf. Ov. *Met.* 7.199 f. (through Medea's witchcraft) amnes / in fontes rediere suos; Sen. *Med.* 762.

1.160–69: in contrast with Vergil's Allecto, who convinces the incredulous Turnus by resuming her shape as a Fury (*A.* 7.445–59), Megaera offers a Midas-like miracle as a proof of the authenticity of her words. Thus Claudian, though losing the dramatic force of Vergil's device, gains an additional opportunity to tax Rufinus with his besetting sin of greed (1.164 f.); cf. n. 1.100–4. He is also enabled to introduce a note of ill omen through the analogy of the Midas legend; cf. 2.134–36. (In the Text. Comm. on 2.393, the citation of 1.164–69 should now be deleted).

The notion of a miraculous power (apart from the pseudo-science of alchemy) of changing baser substances to gold occurs in classical literature apparently only, as here, in connection with the Midas story: cf. TLL s.v. *aurum* 1530.22 f. There is a mention of magic gold in PGM 1.108 εὐθὺς περιθήσει [ὁ πάρεδρος] χρυσόροφα δώματα, but the practitioner is warned that it may not be entirely genuine: 109 f. καὶ ταῦτα ἡγεῖ τὰ μὲν ἀληθῆ, τὰ δὲ βλέπεσθαι μόνον; cf. also 100 χρυσόν.

1.162 Dixerat: on the use of phrases marking the end of direct quotations, cf. n. 1.65 b.

1.163 ditari: cf. CS 3.230 ditabat rutilo quidquid Mida tangeret auro, 4H 38 Hesperidum ... quos ditat fabula ramos. The use of *dito* in the sense "make golden" is apparently original with Claudian: cf. TLL s.v. 1556.33–36. Cf. also CM 27.22 (of blue feathers dappled with gold) color sparso ... ditescit in auro.

1.164 f. avaro ... aspectu: for the extended use of the adjective, cf. 1.243 avidae ... curae, CS 3.229 voti ... famem ... avari. Cf. also Text. Comm. on 1.16, and 1.166 pulchro ... tactu, 2.130 exanguis ... horror.

1.165–69: for the Midas myth, cf. Ov. *Met.* 11.85–145; Roscher (1937) s.v. *Midas*.

1.165 *a* pascitur aspectu: cf. Verg. G. 2.285 (of mere visual pleasure) animum ... uti pascat prospectus inanem.

1.165 f. rex ... Maeonius: cf. Ov. *Met.* 11.91 f. Phryges ... / ad regem duxere Midan, and IE 2.242–46 Gens una fuere // appellata Phryges; sed ... / ... dicti post Maeona regem / Maeones. For Maeonia = Lydia cf. Sil. 1.157 f., RE s.v. *Maionia* 583.

1.165 b ad prima: cf. Tertullian, *De oratione* 22 (= Reifferscheid-Wissowa 1.196.14 f.) *ex ea die... qua ad primum... expaverint.* Birt (1892) Pr. 9 considers *ad prima* here a Grecism, but I have not been able to find any occurrence of the supposed Greek idiom ὡς τὰ πρῶτα which he cites, following Gesner (1759) and Koenig (1808) *ad loc.* Vergil's *ad prima* (G. 2.134) has a different meaning, "especially;" cf. Thuc. 3.39.2, 3.56.6 ἐς τὰ πρῶτα.

1.165 c tumebat: cf. 2.344 *regale tumens.* Cf. also Ov. *Met.* 11.118 (of Midas) *vix spes ipse suus animo capit.*

1.166 pulchro... tactu: on the use of the adjective, cf. n. 1.164 f.

1.167 a riguisse: cf. Ov. *Met.* 11.122 (bread touched by Midas) *Cerealia dona rigebant.*

1.167 f. fulvam... revinctos in glaciem vidit latices: contrast Ovid's notion that liquids changed to gold by Midas remained fluid: *Met.* 11.126 *fusile per rictus aurum fluitare videres,* 11.117 *unda fluens... Danaen eludere posset.* On the word-order, cf. Pearce (1968) 351, and n. 1.29 f. *b.*

1.167 b revinctos: cf. Ov. *Tr.* 3.10.25 *vincti concrescant frigore rivi.* On Claudian's fondness for *re-* compounds, particularly at the end of a verse, cf. Birt (1892) Pr. 222, sect. v 2.

1.168 munus acerbum: cf. Ov. *Met.* 11.104 (Bacchus confers a baneful gift on Midas) *nocitura... munera.*

1.169 inviso votum damnavit in auro: for the thought, cf. Ov. *Met.* 11.128 (Midas is driven by suffering to repentance) *quae modo voverat, odit,* 130 *inviso meritus torquetur ab auro.* The use of *in* here seems to be modeled on its use with *laetor, gaudeo,* and the like: cf. Hofmann-Szantyr (1965) 120; on the later extension of this usage, 126.

1.170 a animi victus: for the use of *animi,* cf. Verg. G. 4.491 *immemor heu victusque animi*; Hofmann-Szantyr (1965) 75, where the long-held view that *animi* in such expressions is an old locative is rejected in favor of its interpretation as a true genitive.

1.170 f. Sequimur — numen: on direct quotation in IR, cf. n. 1.45–65, esp. sects. 4, 8.

1.170 b Sequimur quocumque vocabis: cf. Verg. *Ecl.* 3.49 *veniam quocumque vocaris,* A. 4.576 f. *sequimur te, sancte deorum, / quisquis es;* Stat. *Theb.* 10.680.

1.171 a seu tu vir seu numen: cf. Verg. A. 1.327 f. o—quam te memorem, virgo? Namque haud tibi vultus / mortalis, nec vox hominem sonat: o dea certe.

1.171 b ait: on the use of phrases marking the end of direct quotation, cf. n. 1.65 b.

1.171–77 patria — aulam: on the date of Rufinus' arrival at Constantinople (ca. A.D. 385) cf. Int. 8, 30. Cf. also Lyd. *De mag.* 3.23 ὁ 'Ρουφῖνος ... δι' ἑαυτοῦ ἐπὶ τὴν ἕω ἦλθε.

1.172 a Furiae iussu: on the omission of the exact words used in situations of great importance, cf. n. 1.45–65, sect. 5.

1.172 b tendebat ad arces: Bruère (1964) 227 compares Luc. 6.14 (Caesar hastens to seize Dyrrhacium) rapiendas tendit ad arces.

1.173 instabiles ... olim Symplegadas: cf. IE 2.30 (an earthquake shakes the Symplegades loose again) instabilem rursus Symplegada. Schol. A cites Luc. 2.718 f. (the Argo escapes the Clashing Rocks) vana ... percussit pontum Symplegas inanem / et statura redit. Gesner (1759) *ad loc.* points out that Rufinus, on his journey from the West, would have no need to pass the Symplegades, thought of as being at the Black Sea end of the Bosphorus (cf. RE s.v. *Symplegades* 1170); the allusion to the celebrated rocks is intended as a mythological ornament (cf. Koenig [1808] *ad loc.*).

1.174 a Thessalicis: for this adjective applied to the Argo, a reference to Jason's provenience, the Thessalian city of Iolcos, cf. V. Fl. 1.380 f. te quoque Thessalicae, Nestor, rapit in freta puppis / fama.

1.174 b celsa ... urbe: on the hills of Constantinople, cf. RE s.v. *Byzantion* 1117; cf. also 2.55 despectat.

1.175 a Odrysiis: = *Thraciis*; cf. 3H 147 Odrysium Hebrum; V. Fl. 1.470 Odrysius ... Orpheus; Plin. *Nat.* 4.11.40 Thracia sequitur. ... Populorum eius quos nominare non pigeat. ... Odrysarum gens fundit Hebrum; RE s.v. *Odrysai* 1900 f.

1.175 b discriminat: cf. Text. Comm. *ad loc.*

1.176–300: *The greed, cruelty, and violence of Rufinus crush and terrify the East. Only Stilicho can prevail against him.*

1.176–258: on the relation of these verses to the ψόγος-pattern, cf. Levy (1946) 61 f., 65.

1.176–78 ut ... subrepsit ... ilicet ... nasci: the use of *ilicet*

IN RUFINUM 53

(= *ilico*) in correlation with a temporal conjunction is apparently original with Claudian; cf. TLL s.v. *ilicet* 329.54 f.

1.176 f. maligno stamine fatorum: cf. 6H 267 nimium diversi stamine fati; BG 202 f. voces adamante notabat / Atropos et Lachesis iungebat stamina dictis; Van der Horst (1943) 218. Only here does Claudian attribute the rise of Rufinus to Fate rather than to the interposition of the Furies (cf. 1.172). On Claudian's concept of Fate, cf. Born (1939).

1.177 subrepsit: the translation of Platnauer (1922) "won his way" does not convey the right shade of meaning; "wormed his way" would be more appropriate. On Claudian's attempts to avoid implicating Theodosius in Rufinus' misdeeds, cf. n. 1.114 f.

1.178-249: several of the accusations of evil-doing which Claudian brings against Rufinus in these verses may be linked with historical events otherwise attested. I have listed the pertinent historical events below in what I regard as the descending order of the probability of their connection with the indicated portions of the text. As will be seen from the corresponding notes, I follow Seeck (in RE s.v. *Rufinus* 1190 f.) in regard to the first four items (cf. also Koch [1889] 595 f., Fargues [1933a] 69–71). I believe that my suggestions concerning the last two have not previously been made.

1. Punishment of Proculus and Tatianus: n. 1.243–49.
2. Trial of Tatianus: n. 1.238 f.
3. Civil disqualification of the Lycians: n. 1.232 f.
4. Punishment of Lucianus: n. 1.240 f.
5. Massacre at Thessalonica: n. 1.181 f. *a*.
6. Institution of 30-day stay in execution of all death sentences: n. 1.234–36.

Only the passage covered by n. 1.234–49 is sufficiently detailed to justify us in regarding the connection noted above as established with virtual certainty. However, in view of the importance which contemporaries seem to have attached to Rufinus' proceedings against Tatianus and Proculus (cf. Stein-Palanque [1959] 211 f., and Int. 17, ftns. 101–5), the connections indicated for the next two items may be considered as fairly well established. The objection of Koenig [1808], in his note on 1.232 excindere cives, to seeing in 1.232 f. a reference to the disqualification of the Lycians is not convincing, being based solely on the order in which Claudian presents the material. As regards items 4 and 5, if we cannot be sure that Claudian refers specifically in 1.240 to Rufinus' swiftness in taking action against Lucianus, or in 1.181 f. to his alleged part in the Thessalonica episode, we may at least regard the incidents as illustrative of the type of activity which Claudian has in mind; the parallels drawn in n. 1.179 f. *a*, para. 1, n. 1.179 f. *b*, and n. 1.222 f. are to be taken in the latter sense. The linking of the sixth item with 1.234–36 is a purely conjectural interpretation, for which no more than possibility is urged.

In assessing the degree of probability to be attributed to the various lines of connection drawn between Claudian's accusations and specific historical events, it should be kept in mind, on the one hand, that Claudian's auditors (cf. n. 1 Pr.16) were doubtless well-versed in court intrigues, and would presumably find in Claudian's verses the reflection of actual or rumored occurrences; on the other hand, that there was a well-established rhetorical tradition concerning the stereotype of a tyrant (cf. Fargues [1933a] 70, 221–23), which may have led Claudian to introduce purely imaginative elements into his portrait of Rufinus.

Apart from specific charges, many of the generalized accusations of misdeeds and of vicious character traits which Claudian makes against Rufinus in this passage (and elsewhere) are otherwise attested in the sources (cf. Int. 15, ftns. 82, 83; n. 1.98 f., n. 1.178, n. 1.179 f. *a*, para. 2, n. 1.187 *a*, n. 1.187–89 *a*, n. 1.188–92, n. 1.192 *a*, n. 1.193 f., n. 1.194 f., n. 1.238 f.), especially in the accounts of Eunapius (in the *Suda* s.v. ‛Ρουφῖνος) and Zosimus. Eunapius, it should be noted, is as unfavorable to Stilicho as he is to Rufinus (cf. RE s.v. *Eunapios* 1122.65 f.); in some of his strictures the two rivals are assailed jointly. Where Zosimus follows Eunapius, he likewise presents both men in a most unfavorable light; beginning with Zos. 5.26, where the source is Olympiodorus, there is a complete change of tone with regard to Stilicho: cf. Mendelssohn (1887) Pr. 14, 35; RE s.v. *Olympiodoros* 203; n. 1 Pr.17 *a*. Cf. also the *Suda* s.v. Στελίχων (4.428 Adler), and Bury (1923) 107 f., ftn. 3.

1.178 ambitio nasci: cf. Zos. 4.51.2 ὁ ‛Ρουφῖνος ... ἦν ἅπασιν ἔγκοτος διὰ φιλοπρωτείας ὑπερβολήν.

1.178 f. nasci, discedere ... dari: on Claudian's use of the historical infinitive, cf. Schlicher (1915) 65 f., 73.

1.179 f. *a* **venum cuncta dari; ... ambitos a principe vendit**

IN RUFINUM 55

honores: cf. Zos. 5.1.1 ἀπῄει κεκρατηκὼς ὁ χρημάτων τὴν ψῆφον ὠνούμενος, 5.1.2 τῶν μὲν δωρεαῖς θεραπευόντων ... ἑτέρων δὲ τὰ οἰκεῖα προιεμένων ὑπὲρ τοῦ τυχεῖν ἀρχῆς ἢ ἄλλον τινὰ πρίασθαι τῶν πόλεων ὄλεθρον, 5.2.1 Λουκιανὸς ... ἐχρῆτο προστάτῃ Ῥουφίνῳ, τὰ τιμιώτατα τῶν ὄντων αὐτῷ κτημάτων εἰς ἐκεῖνον μετενεγκών· ἐφ' οἷς ὁμολογῶν χάριτας ὁ Ῥουφῖνος τῷ νεανίσκῳ διετέλεσεν, ἐπαίνους αὐτοῦ παρὰ τῷ βασιλεῖ Θεοδοσίῳ διεξιών (cf. Int. 21, and n. 1.178–249, para. 2).

Cod. Theod. 2.29.2 (= Cod. Iust. 4.3.1, A.D. 394), addressed to Rufinus, and hence presumably dictated by him (cf. RE s.v. *Rufinus* 1191), recognizes and regulates on a contractual basis the payment of fees for the use of influence (*suffragium*) on behalf of those who sought governmental office or special privileges: cf. RE s.v. *suffragium* 656–58, and Kolias (1939), esp. 31–34.

1.179 profert arcana: for the same charge, cf. 1.229 nusquam reverentia mensae, 2.488 f. arcana ... / prodere.

1.179 f. *b* clientes fallit: reference is perhaps to Rufinus' treatment of Lucianus: cf. Zos. 5.2–4 Λουκιανὸς ... ἐχρῆτο προστάτῃ Ῥουφίνῳ. ... ὁ Ῥουφῖνος ... τὸν Λουκιανὸν συναρπάσας εἰς εὐθύνας ἄγει. ... σφαίραις ... μολυβδίναις αὐτὸν ... ἐνεκελεύετο παίεσθαι (cf. Int. 21, and n. 1.178–249, para. 2). Cf. also n. 1.98 f.

1.180 *a* ambitos: Crépin (1933) translates *que l'on sollicite*; read rather *qu'il a sollicité*; Platnauer (1922) well renders "that had been wheedled."

1.180 *b* a principe: on Claudian's attempt to avoid implicating Theodosius in Rufinus' misdeeds, cf. n. 1.114 f.

1.181 f. *a* reference is possibly to Rufinus' alleged part in encouraging Theodosius' outrageous punishment of the Thessalonicans (cf. Int. 9, and n. 1.178–249). The *crimen* would then be the actual guilt of the mob, which Rufinus exaggerated (*ingeminat*) by inflaming Theodosius' mind (*ignem nutrit*) and exacerbating (*acerbat*) his sense of grievance (for a different interpretation, cf. Fargues [1933a] 69). For *ingemino* = *augeo*, cf. RP 3.69 f. noctes ... timorem / ingeminant; Verg. A. 7.578 terrorem ingeminat. Platnauer (1922) wrongly translates "He followed up one crime with another."

Contrast Claudian's praise of Stilicho, CS 2.16 f. ut non infensus alendis / materiem praestes odiis.

1.181 f. *b* **ignem nutrit:** cf. Ov. *Met.* 6.492 f. (Tereus inflames his passions by recalling Philomela's beauty) ignes / ipse suos nutrit.

1.182 acerbat: cf. Verg. *A.* 11.407 (Drances uses his pretended fear of Turnus to add bitterness to his charges) formidine crimen acerbat.

1.183–95: on the relation of these verses to the ψόγος-pattern, cf. Levy (1946) 62, 65.

1.183–87 Ac velut — nequit: cf. Ov. *Met.* 8.835 f. (Erysichthon, worked upon by the goddess Hunger, is insatiable) Utque fretum recipit de tota flumina terra / nec satiatur aquis peregrinosque ebibit amnes; 840 f. Sic epulas omnes Erysichthonis ora profani / accipiunt, poscuntque simul; Sen. *Dial.* 1.1.2 maria ... nec ullum incrementum fluminum sentiant; Lucr. 6.608–15.

Cf. also Aristid. *Or.* 26.62 (= 2.108.20–24 Keil) (of the sea) οὔτε γὰρ ἐκείνη μείζων ὑπὸ τῆς ἐμβολῆς τῶν ποταμῶν γίγνεται ... ἐξιόντων καὶ εἰσιόντων ἴση οὖσα καὶ φαινομένη; on Claudian's apparent imitations of the panegyrists, cf. Kehding (1899) 28–44; n. 1.220 f.; n. 2.440–53. On the use of imagery here, cf. Christiansen (1969) 85. His suggestion that Nereus is used as an image of Rufinus' hypocrisy seems too far-fetched even for "a reminder."

1.185 *a* **bibat:** wrongly cited by TLL s.v. 1964.60 under the rubric *poetarum in sermone ... quo commoratio alicuius vel origo significetur*; contrast 1.312, which is correctly cited, *ibid.* 1964.61.

1.185 *b* **aestivum ... Nilum:** cf. CM 28.27–31 cum tristis hiems alias produxerit undas, / tunc Nilum retinent ripae; cum languida cessant / flumina, tunc Nilus mutato iure tumescit. / Quippe quod ex omni fluvio spoliaverit aestas / hoc Nilo natura refert; 41 f. saepius, aestivo iaceat cum forte sopore, / cernit cum stabulis armenta natantia pastor. Cf. also Luc. 10.210–39 (and n. 1.269 *a*). On the ancient geographers' knowledge of the Nile, cf. Ball (1942) 9, 12, 24, 43–45, 69, 100 f., 117, 120.

1.185 *c* **septeno gurgite:** cf. EH 51 septem despectat cornua Nili, CM 27.99 f. aura / ostia nigrantis Nili septena vaporat; Luc. 8.445 gurgite septeno rapidus mare summovet amnis, 10.253; Ball (1942) 124.

186–95 sic fluctibus — regno: on Rufinus' avarice, cf. Int. 15 f., ftn. 82 (add 1.296, 305), ftns. 83, 95.

1.186 manet: cf. Text. Comm. *ad loc.*

1.187 a **expleri ... nequit**: for the expression, cf. 4H 251 (of *cupido*) expleri pascique nequit; Verg. *A.* 1.713 (Dido) expleri mentem nequit. For the thought, cf. Zos. 5.7.6 (=Philostorgius 11.3) τῷ ἀπλήστῳ; Lyd. *Mag.* 2.10 'Ρουφῖνον τὸν ἐπίκλην ἀκόρεστον.

1.187 b **calor**: cf. 1.220 f. praedae ... / ... flagrabat amor. For the use of the word with a similarly extended meaning, cf. 2.287 f. mentis ... calorem / non sermone viae, non inter pocula rumpi; TLL s.v. *calor* 181.40–182.24.

1.187–89 a **Cuicumque monile — Rufino populandus erat**: cf. Cod. Theod. 2.29.2 si quid ... in auro vel argento vel in ceteris mobilibus datum fuerit, traditio sola sufficiet, et contractus habebit perpetem firmitatem; on the significance of this constitution, addressed to Rufinus, cf. n. 1.179 f. *a*, para. 2, and n. 1.188–92. Cf. also the *Suda* s.v. 'Ρουφῖνος (4.301.1 f. Adler=Eunapius frag. 63 = FHG 4.42) (on Rufinus and Stilicho; cf. n. 1.178–249, para. 3) ἄμφω τὰ πάντα συνήρπαζον ... καὶ οὐδεὶς εἶχεν ... οὐδέν, εἰ μὴ τούτοις ἔδοξε.

1.187–89 b **Cuicumque ... fuissent ... erat**: on the syntax, cf. n. 1.224 f.; the relative clause here parallels the conditional clause there discussed.

1.188–92 **praedia — finibus**: cf. Cod. Theod. 2.29.2 si praedia rustica vel urbana placitum continebit, scriptura, quae ea in alium transferat, emittatur; cf. n. 1.179 f. *a*, para. 2. The purpose of this section of the constitution was apparently to give Rufinus ground for demanding written transfer of real property offered for his *suffragium*, so that there could be no dispute later as to the petitioner's intent. Cf. also the *Suda* s.v. 'Ρουφῖνος (=4.301.3–6 Adler=Eunapius frag. 63 = FHG 4.42) πολὺς ἦν ὄχλος τῶν περιθεόντων εἴ που τινὶ χωρίον ὑπάρχοι παντομιγές τε καὶ εὔκαρπον· καὶ ὁ δεσπότης εὐθὺς συνήρπαστο.

1.192 a **aut aufert vivis aut occupat heres**: cf. BG 165 (the tyrant Gildo) instat terribilis vivis, morientibus heres. Cf. also Cod. Theod. 9.42.14 ea quae Rufinus ... quoquo pacto possedit (cf. Int. 21).

1.192 b **occupat heres**: on *captatio testamentorum* cf. Friedländer (1910) 1.419–26. For the persistence of the practice, cf. Auson. *Ecl.* 7.2 (=362).45 (89 Peiper) captatoris praeda est heredis egenus, and

Novella Maiorani 6.11 (A.D. 458; Mommsen-Meyer [1954] 2.166) captatorum etiam aviditas conprimenda est.

1.193 orbis ... ruinas: Bruère (1964) 227 compares Luc. 10.150 (Caesar's greed) opes mundi quaesisse ruina, 7.752 f., 1.351. On *orbis* of the Roman Empire, cf. n. 1 Pr.17 b.

1.193 f. orbis ... ruinas accipit una domus: cf. Symmach. *Ep.* 6.14 Dubitare vos video, an Rufini poenam secuta sit ... publicatio facultatum. ... non fuit ambigendum, quod spolia orbis desideraret aerarium; Zos. 5.1.3 ὁ ... ἀπανταχόθεν πλοῦτος εἰς τὴν Ῥουφίνου καὶ Στελίχωνος οἰκίαν εἰσέρρει (cf. n. 1.178–249 *fin.*).

1.194 f. populi ... plenaque ... oppida: cf. Cod. Theod. 9.42.14 Hoc ... per omnes provincias praecipimus divulgari, quo cuncti sciant iacturam se perpessuros graviorem ... nisi ... manus ab his, quae Rufinus vivus possederat, voluerint abstinere.

1.195 regno: on the almost regal position and style of the Praetorian Prefect, cf. Int. 11–14.

1.196–219: these verses may be considered an illustration of Rufinus' lack of φρόνησις (cf. Levy [1946] 62, 65) in that they represent him as insanely (1.196 vesane) lacking in comprehension of the ends which the material possessions of man should serve (cf. 1.215–17). If this is so, this passage is the only place in which Claudian impugns Rufinus' intelligence (2.53 *iners* refers to military ineptitude), which seems to have been considerable: cf. Philostorgius 11.3 εὐμήκης ... ὁ Ῥουφῖνος ἦν ... καὶ τὴν σύνεσιν αἵ τε ὀφθαλμῶν κινήσεις ἐδήλουν καὶ τῶν λόγων ἡ ἑτοιμότης. The passage may also be regarded as a treatment of the rhetorical *loci communes de saeculo* and *de divitiis*; cf. Sen. *Con.* 1 Pr.23 translaticias ... sententias ... quae ... de saeculo, de divitiis dicuntur; Decker (1913) 19–38, 44–50; Fargues (1933a) 241–44. For a conjecture as to the history of the passage, cf. Text. Comm. on 1.205 f. para. 2. Cf. also Bieler (1957) 260; Emonds (1941).

1.196 Quo, vesane, ruis?: cf. Verg. *A.* 10.811 (Aeneas to Lausus) Quo moriture ruis?

1.196–99 Teneas — quaestu: cf. 4H 257–60 (Theodosius to Honorius) Tu licet extremos late dominere per Indos, / te Medus, te mollis Arabs, te Seres adorent: / si metuis, si prava cupis, si duceris ira, / servitii patiere iugum.

1.196 f. utrumque ... Oceanum: cf. Verg. *A.* 7.100 f. (Latinus hears a prophecy of Roman greatness) omnia sub pedibus, qua Sol utrumque recurrens / aspicit Oceanum, verti regique videbunt. Cf. also BG 48; Ov. *Met.* 1.338.

1.197 f. laxet — tiara: cf. IE 1.213 f. (Eutropius controls the wealth which Persia conquered from Lydia) Pollentem solio Croesum victoria Cyri / fregit ut eunucho flueret Pactolus et Hermus? On Croesus, cf. Otto (1890) 98 f.

1.197 rutilos... Lydia fontes: on Lydia, cf. n. 1.102 f.

1.199 *a* numquam dives eris: cf. Sen. *Ep.* 16.7 Istuc... ab Epicuro dictum est: si ad naturam vives, numquam eris pauper; si ad opiniones, numquam eris dives.

1.199 *b* numquam satiabere: cf. the adjectives ἄπληστος and ἀκόρεστος quoted in n. 1.187 *a*.

1.200–16: on the relation of these verses to the ψόγος-pattern, cf. Levy (1946) 64.

1.200 Semper inops quicumque cupit: cf. Sen. *Ep.* 2.6 non qui parum habet, sed qui plus cupit, pauper est; Otto (1890) 123.

1.200–3 Contentus — tegebat: cf. 4H 413–15 (Theodosius to Honorius) Pauper erat Curius, reges cum vinceret armis; / pauper Fabricius, Pyrrhi cum sperneret aurum, / sordida dictator flexit Serranus aratra, BP 131 f.; Verg. *A.* 6.843 f. (Anchises to Aeneas) parvo... potentem / Fabricium vel te sulco, Serrane, serentem. Bruère (1964) 227 compares Lucan's contrast between Caesar's greed and the parsimony of the great Romans of old: 10.151–53 Pone duces priscos et nomina pauperis aevi, / Fabricios Curiosque graves, hic ille recumbat / sordidus Etruscis abductus consul aratris. Cf. also Pacatus, *Panegyricus Theodosio Augusto dictus* 9.5 Sic agrestes Curii... sic nomina reverenda Fabricii... inter aratra vivebant; Moore (1910) 114; Laqueur-Koch-Weber (1930) 19; Fargues (1933a) 248–53; Steinbeiss (1936) 24–36; Christ (1938) 199 f.; Hunt (1945); Vischer (1965), esp. 155–57.

1.200 f. *a* Contentus... parvo: cf. Verg. *A.* 6.843 f. parvo... potentem / Fabricium; Otto (1890) 129.

1.200 f. *b* honesto... parvo: for *honestum* as a substantive qualified by an adjective, cf. Luc. 2.389 (Cato) rigidi servator honesti.

1.201 *a*: cf. 4H 414 (quoted in n. 1.200–3), BP 131 pectora Fabricii donis invicta, IE 1.452 f.; Sen. *Con.* 5.2 (cf. 2.1.29) Fabricius aurum a

Pyrrho accipere noluit; beatior fuit animo quam ille regno. Cf. also RE s.v. *Fabricius* 1934 f.

1.201 *b* **regum:** = 4H 414 Pyrrhi (cf. n. 1.200–3); on the plural, cf. Bell (1923) 77.

1.202 *a*: cf. 4H 415 (quoted in n. 1.200–3); IE 1.453 f.; Verg. *A.* 6.844 te sulco, Serrane, serentem; Cic. *Sest.* 33.72 ille Serranus ab aratro; RE s.v. *Atilius* 2094 f.

1.202 *b* **consul:** Serranus is called *dictator* in 4H 415 (cf. n. 1.200–3). On the confused tradition attached to the name Atilius Serranus, cf. RE s.v. *Atilius* 2095; Stoecker (1889) 49.

1.203 *a*: cf. 4H 413 (quoted in n. 1.200–3); BP 124 f. sublimi certe Curium canit ore vetustas, / Aeaciden Italo pepulit qui litore Pyrrhum; RE s.v. *Curius* 1844 f.

1.203 *b* **casa...angusta:** cf. Sen. *Con.* 1.6.4 (Rome's humble beginnings) nudi hi stetere colles, interque tam effusa moenia nihil est humili Romuli casa nobilius. Bruère (1964) 227 sees here a reflection of Luc. 5.523, 527 f. (the poor fisherman who piloted Caesar).

1.203 *c* **pugnaces:** Enn. *ap.* Cic. *Rep.* 3.3.6 (= frag. 373 Vahlen^2) (of Manius Curius) quem nemo ferro potuit superare nec auro.

1.203 *d* **Curios:** for the plural, cf. IE 1.457 Curii veteres, CS 2.379; Luc. 1.169 Curiorum; on this use of the plural to denote the entire class of men resembling a famous bearer of the name, cf. Bell (1923) 76 f.; Fargues (1933a) 252.

1.204–19: cf. CM 20; Verg. *G.* 2.458–74, 493–540; Sen. *Phaed.* 483–552; Vischer (1965). With the idealized portrayal of rural life painted here and in CM 20, contrast the realistic picture of the farmers' wretchedness given by Claudian's contemporary St. John Chrysostom: *In Matt. Hom.* 61.3 (= Migne Gr. 58.591 f.); Stein-Palanque (1959) 196.

1.204 *a* **mihi:** I cannot agree with Fargues (1936) 372 in his coupling of this word with *tuis* in the next verse to form a contrastive pair. *Mihi* is, as Platnauer (1922) and Crépin (1933) take it ("To my mind," "J'estime"), a *dativus iudicantis* (cf. Hofmann-Szantyr [1965] 96) qualifying the rest of the sentence; the element contrasting with *culminibus... tuis* is *haec tecta*, where *haec* = not *mea*, but *Curiorum*.

1.204 *b* **opulentior:** cf. *Laus Pis.* 108 ipsa... possesso mens est opulentior auro.

1.205 f. *a* **Ibi quaerit ... hic donat:** cf. Text. Comm. *ad loc.*; Fargues (1936) 372, Bieler (1957) 260. Cf. also Emonds (1941) on variant readings traceable to the author.

1.205 f. *b* **inanes ... cibos:** cf. Ov. *Met.* 8.826 exercet ... cibo ... guttur inani (cf. 824 petit ille dapes sub imagine somni). Bruère (1964) 227 sees here the influence of Lucan's description (10.155–57) of Cleopatra's banquet: infudere epulas ... / ... quod luxus inani / ambitione furens ... quaesivit.

1.206 f. **inemptas ... dapes:** cf. Verg. *G.* 4.133 (the old pirate turned rustic) dapibus mensas onerabat inemptis.

1.207 f. **Rapiunt — vestes:** cf. 1.384 f. nec murice tinctis / velleribus quaeretur honos; Pease (1935) on Verg. *A.* 4.134 ostro. Bruère (1964) 227 sees in 1.207–11 an echo of Luc. 10.122–24; cf. esp. his ftn. 7, p. 254.

1.207 **Rapiunt:** for *rapio* of the absorption or drinking of liquids, cf. Luc. 4.629 f. rapit arida tellus / sudorem, 3.345, 9.924; Stat. *Theb.* 4.834 f. raptas ... refundit / Arcus aquas (cf. Verg. *G.* 1.380 f.), *Silv.* 1.4.27 f. Cf. also Verg. *G.* 3.137 rapiat sitiens. All these parallels lend added weight to Postgate's rejection, (1895) 163, of the suggestion of Birt (1892) Pr. 8 f., ftn. 4, that Claudian, in using *rapio* in the sense of *sorbeo* here and in 2.121, was influenced by the similarity in sound between *rapio* and the Greek ῥοφέω.

1.208 *a* **picturatae saturantur:** on the resultative-predicate use of the participle, cf. n. 1.1 *b*.

1.208 *b* **picturatae ... vestes:** cf. CM 9.12–14 (the porcupine's quills) picturata seges ... / alba subit radix, alternantesque colorum / tincta vices, spatiis internigrantibus, 31.3 picturatae ... volucres; Verg. *A.* 9.614 picta croco et fulgenti murice vestis.

1.208 *c* **saturantur:** cf. Text. Comm. *ad loc.*

1.209 *a* **radiant:** the use of this verb to refer to the colors of flowers is not otherwise exemplified either in Claudian, or, apparently, in the rest of Latin verse. In CM 30.3–5 Claudian mentions the radiance of gems in contradistinction to that of mere flowers: solitam consurgere gemmis / et Rubro radiare mari si floribus ornes / reginae ... comam. He elsewhere uses *radio* of purple garments (4H 552 f. vestis radiato murice solem / combibit; cf. Sil. 16.354 Cinyphio rector cocco radiabat Hiberus, 17.395); here the verb is transferred to the flowers, which, in the rural scene, correspond to the purple garments in the contrasting picture.

1.209 *b* **viva voluptas:** this striking phrase, enhanced by the alliteration, is apparently all Claudian's own!

1.210 ingenio ... suo: cf. Ov. *Met.* 3.157–59 est antrum ... / arte laboratum nulla: simulaverat artem / ingenio natura suo; Col. 3.1.2 (of trees) Sed quae non ope humana gignuntur silvestres ac ferae, sui cuiusque ingenii poma vel semina gerunt.

1.210 f. Fulgentibus — toris: Bruère (1964) 227 compares Luc. 10.122 f. (Cleopatra's banquet) Fulget gemma toris et ... supellex / stat mensas onerans, variaque triclinia veste / strata micant, Tyrio ... fuco / cocta diu.

1.211 *a* **surgunt:** cf. CM 29.29 f. roseis ... cubilia surgunt / floribus, EH 226 f.

1.211 *b* **mollis ... herba:** Bruère (1964) 227 traces this expression to Lucan's description (5.520 f.) of the seaweed bed of Caesar's humble guide.

1.212: cf. Verg. *G.* 3.530 (the ploughman's simple life) nec somnos abrumpit cura salubres. Note that in the Vergilian parallel *salubres* is unaffected by *nec*, while here the negative force of *non* is felt both with *sollicitum curis* and with *abruptura*; cf. Vahlen (1905) 766.

1.213: cf. Verg. *G.* 2.461 f. (happy the farmer's lot) Si non ingentem foribus domus alta superbis / mane salutantum totis vomit aedibus undam, 467 at secura quies.

1.215 Vivitur exiguo melius: cf. Hor. *Carm.* 2.16.12 Vivitur parvo bene; Verg. *G.* 2.472 exiguo ... assueta iuventus; Otto (1890) 376.

1.215 f. beatis omnibus esse dedit: for the predicate dative, cf. Hor. *S.* 1.1.19 licet esse beatis; Ov. *Met.* 8.690 f. vobis immunibus ... / esse ... dabitur; Hofmann-Szantyr (1965) 349 f.

1.216 *a* **si quis cognoverit:** on Claudian's free use of the subjunctive, cf. n. 1 Pr.3 f. *b*.

1.216 *b* **uti:** for this verb used absolutely, cf. Hor. *Ep.* 1.7.57 quaerere et uti, 2.2.190; Hofmann-Szantyr (1965) 35.

1.217 simplice cultu: for a lament on the complexity of Roman civilization in the generation preceding Claudian's, cf. Amm. 28.4.6–34.

Bruère (1964) 227 compares Luc. 5.527–29 (of Caesar's humble guide) o vitae tuta facultas / pauperis ... o munera nondum / intellecta deum.

1.218 f. non (*quater*): cf. Text. Comm. on 1.219; cf. also 1.230–32, CS 3.320 f., 339–41, and n. 1.101 f.

1.218 a classica: for *classica* as a symbol of warfare, cf. CM 20.7 (the old man of Verona) non classica miles [tremuit]; Verg. G. 2.539 (the happy age of Saturn) necdum audierant inflari classica.

1.218 b gemerent: cf. Text. Comm. *ad loc.*

1.219 a non ventus quateret puppes: for navigation as a symbol of man's fall from primeval innocence, cf. Verg. *Ecl.* 4.31–33 vestigia fraudis / quae temptare Thetim ratibus... / ... iubeant (cf. 39 f.); Hor. *Carm.* 1.3.21–24 nequiquam deus abscidit / prudens Oceano dissociabili / terris, si tamen impiae / non tangenda rates transiliunt vada; Tib. 1.3.37.

1.219 b machina muros: cf. 4H 328 f. (Theodosius' advice to Honorius) Fidit si moenibus hostis, / tum tibi murali libretur machina pulsu. There is probably a verbal echo of Verg. *A.* 2.46 (Laocoon's warning) haec in nostros fabricata est machina muros, where, of course, the *machina* is not an ordinary siege-engine.

1.220–29: on the relation of these verses to the ψόγος-pattern, cf. Levy (1946) 62, 65.

1.220 f. Crescebat — amor: cf. Pacatus, *Panegyricus Theodosio Augusto dictus* 25.6 f. (the greed of the tyrant Maximus) Crescebat in dies habendi fames et parandi rabiem parta irritabant. Ut aegrorum sitim potus accendit... ita... divitiae aviditatem ieiunae mentis acuebant; n. 1.183–87, para. 2. Cf. also the reflections on Maximus' fate quoted in n. 2.440–53.

1.220 a Crescebat: the imperfect here, the pluperfect in 1.256, and the temporal adverb *iam* (1.305, 308) give the effect of a narrative moving forward in time rather than that of an exposition proceeding from topic to topic. Yet if verses 1.240 f. are correctly linked with the punishment of Lucianus (cf. n. 1.240 f. and n. 1.178–249), they refer to a happening of later date (393 or 395, cf. Int. 21, ftn. 133) than do verses 1.306–53, which are concerned with events of the years 391 and 392 (cf. n. 1.306–53). On the relative chronology of IR 1 and IR 2, cf. n. 1.240 f. *fin.*

1.220–22 scelerata — pudor: on Rufinus' avarice, cf. Int. 15 f. ftn. 82 (add 1.296, 305), ftns. 83, 95.

1.220 b praedae . . . recentis: cf. Verg. A. 7.748 f. (the warlike Aequi delight in plunder) semper . . . recentes / . . . praedas, 9.612 f.

1.221 flagrabat: for strong emotion expressed in terms of heat, cf. 1.187 calor; also 2.287 calorem.

1.221 f. petendi cogendive pudor: for *pudor* with the genitive of the gerund, cf. Ov. Met. 14.571 deponendi . . . pudore; Luc. 7.525 pudore timendi.

1.222 f. crebris periuria nectit blanditiis: cf. Zos. 4.52.3 (Rufinus deceives Tatianus and Proclus) ὁ Ῥουφῖνος . . . μετελθὼν ἀπάτῃ τὸν πατέρα καὶ ὅρκοις, καὶ τὸν βασιλέα πείσας ὑποφῆναι καὶ αὐτῷ καὶ τῷ παιδὶ μεγίστας ἐλπίδας (cf. Int. 17 and n. 1.178–249, para. 2). Cf. also n. 1.98 f.

1.222 periuria nectit: for the verb, cf. 1.315 innectit . . . moras (and n. 1.315); Ov. Am. 2.2.35 (= 2.9.45) iurgia nectat; Stat. Theb. 11.289 Tiresias . . . oracula nectit.

1.223 a sociat perituro foedere dextras: cf. n. 1.179 f. b.

1.223 b perituro foedere: cf. Luc. 7.211 (the poet will arouse by his narrative prayers that are destined to come to naught) peritura . . . vota; Stat. Theb. 5.194 (Venus inspires a short-lived love) miseros perituro adflaverat igni. Contrast the following said in praise of Stilicho: CS 2.38 f. amicitias . . . / mansuro . . . adamante ligat. The translation which Crépin (1933) gives for *perituro foedere* is unfortunately ambiguous: *cette amitié sera mortelle*. The French reader might well suppose that Claudian means that the alliance will be deadly in its effects, instead of what he does mean, namely that it will be of short duration.

1.224 f. Si . . . negasset . . . quatiebat: for the moods and tenses cf. BG 56 f. (Rome's former diverse sources of grain) Memphis si forte negasset, / pensabam Pharium Gaetulis messibus annum; Hofmann-Szantyr (1965) 663 f., and n. 1.187–89 b.

1.224 a semel: for this word adding the idea of immediacy, cf. Verg. A. 10.569 f. Aeneas desaevit . . . / ut semel intepuit mucro; Hofmann-Szantyr (1965) 663 f., 636 f. Platnauer (1922) seems to join *semel* with *e tantis*; he translates "Should any dare to refuse his demand for one thing out of so many." I have, however, found no parallel for a numeral adverb with *ex* and the ablative. Joining *e tantis* (cf. n. 1.224 *b*) with the indefinite *quisque* (cf. n. 1.224 *c*) seems to avoid this difficulty and to yield satisfactory sense: *e tantis . . . quisque* = *e tot hominibus quivis*: cf. TLL s.v. *ex* 1117.19–40; Hertel (1884) 4.

1.224 *b* tantis: = *tot*; cf. 2.52 tantis . . . annis, 106 f. tantae . . . / . . . manus nec tot discrimina vocum, 150 f. Tantis . . . armis? / Tot signis . . . ?; IE 1.60 f.; Luc. 9.34 ratibus tantis (cf. 32 mille carinis), 10.190; Stat. *Theb.* 2.495 tantis . . . armis (cf. 494 quinquaginta), 4.627; Hofmann–Szantyr (1965) 206.

1.224 *c* quisque: = *quivis*; cf. Apul. *Met.* 7.3 crimen, non modo latrocinium, verum etiam parricidium quisque rectius nominarit, 2.5 Nam simul quemque conspexerit speciosae formae iuvenem, venustate eius sumitur; Hofmann–Szantyr (1965) 202, 562.

1.225 *a* praetumido: cf. CS 3.81 praetumidi . . . Orientis. In addition to this adjective and to the familiar *praeclarus* (cf. Hofmann–Szantyr [1965] 167), Claudian uses the following adjectives compounded with the intensive *prae*-: *praedives*, *praedurus*, and *praelargus*; cf. Birt (1892) 560 f., Hofmann–Szantyr (1965) 164.

1.225 *b* quatiebat: Koenig (1808) *ad loc.* is apparently right in regarding the subject of *negasset*, 1.224, as the subject of this verb as well. Birt (1892) 566 s.v. *quatere* supplies *Rufinus* as the subject of *quatiebat*. Though the change of subject offers no obstacle (cf. Text. Comm. on 2.124, para. 2, and IE 2.191–93), the apparent absence of any parallel to the use of *quatio* of a person acting upon his own emotions militates against this view. Birt's interpretation might perhaps be defended on the ground that Claudian is thinking of the comparison in 1.226: cf. Luc. 1.208 (the lion lashes himself into a fury) ubi se saevae stimulavit verbere caudae; Hom. *Il.* 20.170 f.

1.226–28: on the relation of these verses to the ψόγος-pattern, cf. Levy (1946) 64, ftn. 28. On the use of imagery here, cf. Christiansen (1969) 85.

1.226: cf. Stat. *Theb.* 6.787 f. (Capaneus is wounded, and rages) non leo, non iaculo tantum indignata recepto / tigris; Verg. *A.* 12.4–6 (with the Latins defeated, Turnus becomes even more violent) Poenorum qualis in arvis / saucius ille gravi venantum vulnere pectus / . . . leo; Hom. *Il.* 20.167 f.

1.227 *a*: cf. quotation from Pliny in n. 1.90; also Sil. 12.461 f. (the tigress) fulmineo partus vestigia cursu / colligat et rabiem prenso consumat in hoste; Stat. *Theb.* 4.315 f.; Mart. 3.44.6-8. Cf. also Verg. *A.* 4.367 Hyrcanae ... tigres, and Pease (1935) *ad loc.*

1.227 *b* partus: cf. Text. Comm. *ad loc.*

1.228 *a* serpens calcata: cf. Ov. *Met.* 13.804 (from a description of Galatea) calcata immitior hydro. Cf. also Verg. *A.* 2.379-81 (Androgeos, who realizes that he has fallen among enemies, is compared with one who has accidentally trodden on a snake) improvisum ... qui ... anguem / pressit humi nitens, trepidusque repente refugit / atollentem iras.

1.228 f. Iurata deorum maiestas teritur: on allegations of Rufinus' perjury, cf. n. 1.222 f.

1.228 *b* Iurata: for *iuro* used transitively, cf. Stat. *Theb.* 7.160 Styge iurata, 8.100 iurandus Apollo; cf. also BP 81 numen iuraverat; Verg. *A.* 6.324 iurare ... numen, 351; 12.197; Brenous (1895) 215. Cf. also 1.328 occisos ... iurare parentes.

1.229 *a* maiestas: cf. Apul. *Met.* 6.15 quod ... vos deieratis per numina deorum, deos per Stygis maiestatem solere.

1.299 *b* nusquam reverentia mensae: for the misuse of secrets divulged at banquets, cf. Sen. *Cl.* 1.26.2 Omnia maesta, trepida, confusa; ... non convivia securi ineunt, in quibus lingua sollicite etiam ebriis custodienda est; cf. also n. 1.179.

1.229 *c* mensae: for *mensa* as a symbol of hospitality, cf. Verg. *A.* 10.460 per patris hospitium et mensas; Sil. 17.68.

1.230-58: on the relation of these verses to the ψόγος-pattern, cf. Levy (1946) 62, 65.

1.230-56: as Fargues (1933a) 222 f. points out, this passage and 2.61-70 seem to echo the rhetorical *locus communis de crudelitate*: cf. Sen. *Con.* 1 Pr.23 translaticias ... sententias ... quae ... de crudelitate ... dicuntur; Decker (1913) 19-21, 50-54. This *locus*, especially appropriate to declamations dealing with tyrants (cf. Sen. *Con.* 2.5.4, 6; 5.8; Decker [1913] 53) presumably received great attention in the rhetorical schools, where speeches against tyrants or in behalf of tyrannicides constituted an important part of the curriculum. Cf. Juv. 7.150 f. Declamare doces? O ferrea pectora Vetti, / cum perimit saevos classis numerosa tyrannos; Lucian. *Bis. acc.* 32 τυράννων κατηγορίας; D. H. *Rh.* 10.15 ἐν ... ταῖς δικανικαῖς τὸ δεῖν τὸν ἠριστεύκότα, τὸν ἀνῃρηκότα τύραννον δωρεὰν λαμβάνειν; Fleskes (1914); Kohl (1915) 45-48; Schamberger (1917) 24 f., 31, 33 f., 37 f., 41-43, 45, 47, 53-55, 64-66; Villeneuve (1918) 266 f.; RE s.v. *Melete*; Fargues (1933a) 221; Hofrichte (1935) 26-28.

1.230-33: cf. Sen. *Cl.* 1.26.4 (the tyrant's aim) a singulorum deinde caedibus in exitia gentium serpere.

1.230 ipse: on this word used absolutely to denote the husband in relation to his wife, cf. TLL s.v. 344.47-52.

1.230-32: Non (*quinquies*): cf. n. 1.101 f. and n. 1.218 f.

1.232 a egisse: perhaps *in exilium* is to be supplied, as TLL s.v. *ago* 1368.41 hesitantly suggests; cf. 1369.33-39 (so Platnauer [1922] and Crépin [1933]); possibly, however, the verb is to be interpreted in the more general sense of "persecute," "hound," "harass": cf. 2.91 f. quos barbarus illinc, / hinc Rufinus agit; n. 2.92 a.

1.232 f. exscindere — laborat: reference is probably to the civil disqualification of the inhabitants of the province of Lycia, upon all of whom Rufinus is said to have vented his animosity toward the Lycian Tatianus: cf. Int. 18; RE s.v. *Rufinus* 1191; Stein-Palanque (1959) 212; cf. also n. 1.178-249.

Apparently following Koenig (1808) (cf. n. 1.178-249), Platnauer (1922) interprets this passage in general terms as referring to the *gens Romana* as a whole ("every citizen of Rome," "our race"); not so Crépin (1933): "leurs concitoyens, leur pays."

1.232 b exscindere: cf. Verg. *A.* 4.425 f. (Dido speaks) Non ego ... Troianam exscindere gentem / ... iuravi.

1.234 f. crudelibus ... suppliciis fruitur: for other allegations of Rufinus' joy at the sufferings of mankind, cf. 2.61 f. Obsessa ... ille ferus laetatur in urbe / exsultatque malis; 68-70 Inmensa voluptas / et risus plerumque subit; dolor afficit unus, / quod feriat non ipse manu; 138 Torquetur pace futura. For condemnation of joy derived from the infliction of punishment, cf. MT 224 f. (a contrast between Theodorus and an imagined martinet) Qui fruitur poena, ferus est legumque videtur / vindictam praestare sibi; CS 2.14 f. (Stilicho has absorbed the teachings of Clementia) docet ut poenis hominum vel sanguine pasci / turpe ferumque putes; Sen. *Cl.* 1.25.1 f. ferina ista rabies est sanguine gaudere ac vulneribus. ... Hoc est, quare vel maxime abominanda sit saevitia, quod ... nova supplicia conquirit, ingenium advocat, ut instrumenta excogitet, per quae varietur atque extendatur dolor; delectatur malis hominum; tunc illi dirus animi morbus ad insaniam pervenit ultimam, cum crudelitas versa est in voluptatem et iam occidere hominem iuvat; 1.26.3; 1.11.4. On possible echoes of Sen. *Cl.* in Claudian, cf. Préchac (1921) Pr. 50–53. Cf. also Sen. *Ben.* 7.19.8 Si vero sanguine humano non tantum gaudet, sed pascitur, sed et suppliciis omnium aetatum crudelitatem insatiabilem exercet, nec ira, sed aviditate quadam saeviendi furit, si in ore parentum liberos iugulat [cf. IR 1.246 f.], si non contentus simplici morte [cf. IR 1.238] distorquet....

Note however that the words *suppliciis fruitur* are said approvingly, 6H 112, of Theodosius' satisfaction at the punishment meted out to Alaric and to Gildo.

1.234–36 Nec celeri — parat: reference here may possibly (cf. n. 1.178–249) be to the policy expressed in Cod. Theod. 9.40.13 Si vindicari in aliquos severius... iusserimus, nolumus statim eos... subire poenam, ... sed per dies xxx super statu eorum sors et fortuna suspensa sit. Reos sane accipiat vinciatque custodia, et excubiis sollertibus vigilanter observet. This enactment is believed to have been promulgated by Theodosius after the massacre at Thessalonica: cf. Seeck (1919) 278, Stein-Palanque (1959) 208 f.; for Rufinus' connection with that incident and its sequel, cf. Stein-Palanque (1959) 209 and ftn. 111; also Int. 9.

1.236 mucrone... ense: for the sword as an instrument of punishment, cf. MT 227–30 dis proximus ille / ... qui ... / consilio punire potest. Mucrone cruento / se iactent alii; BG 465 solito... mucrone; CS 2.15 f. ut ferrum, Marte cruentum, / siccum pace feras. Cf. also Ulpian *ap.* Iust. *Dig.* 48.19.8.1 Vita adimitur, ut puta si damnatur aliquis, ut gladio in eum animadvertatur. Sed animadverti gladio oportet, non securi vel telo vel fusti vel laqueo vel quo alio modo; Mommsen (1899) 924. Contrast 1.247 stricta cecidere securi.

1.236 f. Pro — dolori: Bruère (1964) 228 cites as the source of these words Luc. 2.179 f. (the torture of M. Marius Gratidianus) nihil animae letale datum, moremque nefandae / dirum saevitiae, pereunti parcere morti. If both the theory propounded in n. 1.234–36 and Bruère's suggestion are correct, Claudian is here adapting to his concept of the tortures inherent in the judicial delay of execution

Lucan's description of the sadistic savagery of those unwilling to give a dying victim the *coup-de-grace*.

1.237 parcendi rabies: cf. Verg. *A.* 9.63 f. (the hunger of a wolf) edendi / ... rabies. With the oxymoron here, cf. MT 90 f. dixit ... tacendo / Pythagoras.

1.238 *a* Mors adeone parum est?: for the language, cf. Stat. *Theb.* 4.673 Usque adeone parum cineri data mater iniquo? For the thought, cf. Sen. *Ben.* 7.19.8 non contentus simplici morte distorquet; n. 1.234 f.; Ov. *Her.* 10.82 mors ... minus poenae quam mora mortis habet.

1.238 *b* parum est: cf. Text. Comm. *ad loc.* In defense of Birt's view may be cited Stat. *Theb.* 4.673 (cf. n. 1.238 *a*). On the omission of *est* cf. also Cameron (1968a) 400.

1.238 f. Causis — iudice: cf. Zos. 4.52.2 Τατιανὸς ... ἤγετο εἰς κρίσιν .... καὶ τῷ μὲν φαινομένῳ κοινωνεῖν ἐτάχθησαν ἕτεροι 'Ρουφίνῳ τῆς κρίσεως, ἐκεῖνος δὲ μόνος εἶχε τῆς ψήφου τὸ κῦρος; Cod. Theod. 9.38.9 Tatiani ... temporalis offensio teterrimi iudicis inimici; Int. 17; RE s.v. *Rufinus* 1190; n. 1.178–249. Cf. also the *Suda* s.v. 'Ρουφῖνος (=4.301.5–7 Adler=Eunapius frag. 63=FHG 4.42) κατηγορίας πεπλασμένης εὐλόγου ... ὁ ἀδικούμενος ἠδικεῖτο τοῦ ἀδικοῦντος κρίνοντος (cf. n. 1.178–249, para. 2).

1.239 *a* Cetera segnis: perhaps a reversed reminiscence of Sil. 1.244 f. (Hannibal) nec cetera segnis, / quaecumque ad laudem stimulant. For the adverbial use of *cetera*, cf. BG 438 f. (the Moorish horseman) Dextra movet iaculum, praetentat pallia laeva; / cetera nudus eques; Verg. *A.* 3.594; TLL s.v. *ceterus* 973.64–974.25.

1.239 *b* segnis: reference is to Rufinus' lack of military prowess: cf. 2.53 iners, 1.268 fuga ... inerti.

1.240 f. ad facinus — vias: cf. Zos. 5.2.3 ἐπὶ τὴν Ἀντιόχειαν ἵεται, νυκτός τε βαθείας ἐπιδημήσας τῇ πόλει τὸν Λουκιανὸν συναρπάσας εἰς εὐθύνας ἄγει; Int. 21; RE s.v. *Rufinus* 1190; Birt (1892) Pr. 29; Koch (1889) 595 f.; n. 1.178–249. Fargues attempts to support an early dating of the Lucianus incident (cf. Fargues [1933a] 70 f.; Int. 21, ftn. 133) by an argument based on the inclusion at this point in the poem of a reference to the event. Fargues' argument is far from convincing. Though the action of IR 1 is evidently intended to be taken (cf. n. 1.220 *a*) as belonging to the period before Theodosius' death (cf. 2.1-3, and n. 2.1-4), it may be argued that Claudian included a reference to the Lucianus incident at this point both because of the appropriateness of the action to a *locus de crudelitate* (cf. Fargues [1933a] 223) and because he wished to dispose within the compass of IR 1 of all less important incidents, so as to reserve IR 2 for the uninterrupted narrative of the crucial events summarized in Int. 22 (last para.)–26. Moreover, even if the incident were correctly to be dated to 393, its mention before verses 1.306-53 would still involve a departure from chronological order: cf. n. 1.220 a. Demougeot (1951) 127 agrees with the position taken in Int. 21 and ftn. 133 in dating the event to 395; cf. Stein-Palanque (1959) 541, ftn. 58 *infra*.

1.240 a penitus ... remotas: cf. CM 30.84 f. (Stilicho grew up far from Spain) penitus ... remoto / orbe; Verg. *A.* 1.512 (the tempest had driven the Trojans far off course) penitus ... alias avexerat oras; *Ecl.* 1.67.

1.240 b regione remotas: cf. Ov. *Tr.* 3.4.73 f. (Ovid in exile) quamvis longe regione remotus / absim.

1.242 a bruma ... stridens Aquilone: cf. Verg. *A.* 1.102 stridens Aquilone procella, and Henry (1873) 1.345-47 *ad loc*.

1.242 b Riphaeo ... Aquilone: reference is to the Riphaean mountains in Scythia: cf. 6H 27 (Apollo's sojourn in the far North) lustrat Hyperboreas ... aras; 30 f. (his return to Delphi) at si ... grypha iugalem / Riphaeo, tripodas repetens, retorsit ab axe (and Müller [1938] 32 on 6H 25 f.); Verg. *G.* 1.240 (the northern limit of the world's sphere) Scythiam Riphaeasque ... arces; RE s.v. Ῥίπαια ὄρη.

1.243 a torquebant: for allegations of Rufinus' anguish at the absence of suffering, cf. 2.138 torquetur pace futura; n. 2.138.

1.243 b avidae ... curae: on the extended use of the adjective, cf. n. 1.164 f.

1.243-49: reference is undoubtedly to the execution of Proculus and the banishment of Tatianus; cf. Int. 17 f.; RE s.v. *Rufinus* 1190 f.; n. 1.178-249. Note the parallels:

neu perderet ullum Augusto miserante nefas . . . . colla ante patrum vultus . . . cecidere . . . ; ibat grandaevus . . . post trabeas exul.

Zos. 4.52.4 ὁ βασιλεὺς ἔστελλε μὲν δῆθεν τὸν ἀνακαλεσόμενον ... τὸ ξίφος· ὁ δὲ συνθήματι Ῥουφίνου πειθόμενος σχολαίτερον ἀπιὼν ἔφθασεν ἤδη πεσοῦσαν τὴν κεφαλήν. Asterius, Hom. 4 (= Migne Gr. 40.224C–25A) ἐπεῖδε τὸν ἑαυτοῦ παῖδα ἀποτμηθέντα τῆς κεφαλῆς. τὸν δὲ ἐξ ὑπάρχων ἐκεῖνον ... οἷα τοῦ βίου καταστροφὴ διεδέξατο. ... ζήσας δὲ ὀλίγον ὀδύναις ... ὁ πρεσβύτης, ... ἐν ἀτιμίᾳ ἀπῆλθεν τοῦ βίου, τοῦτο τῆς μεγάλης ὑπατείας τὸ τέλος εὑράμενος. Zos. 4.52.4 Τατιανοῦ ... τῇ τῆς πατρίδος οἰκήσει παραδοθέντος (i.e. Tatiano in patriam relegato).

1.244 f. neu — nefas: Bruère (1964) 228 compares Luc. 10.370 f. (Pothinus to Achillas, as they discuss Pompey's murder) per te quod fecimus una / perdidimusque nefas.

1.245–50: Bruère (1964) 228 cites a number of passages from Lucan as underlying our present passage:

Claudian	Lucan
non flectitur annis, / non aetate labat	2.104–7 (Marius' proscription) nulli sua profuit aetas: / non senis extremum piguit vergentibus annis / praecepisse diem, nec ... / infantis miseri nascentia rumpere fata.
rorantia colla	2.122–24 (the triumvir's grandfather beheaded) Antoni, cuius laceris pendentia canis / ora ferens miles festae rorantia mensae / imposuit (cf. n. 1.246).
quis prodere tanta ... / funera, quis caedes possit deflere nefandas?	2.118 (in the midst of so many deaths of nobles) cui funera vulgi / flere vacet? (cf. n. 1.249 f.)
post trabeas exul	2.69 f. (Marius) post ... triumphos / exul.

1.245 Augusto miserante: on Claudian's effort to avoid implicating Theodosius in Rufinus' misdeeds, cf. n. 1.114 f.

1.245–49 Non flectitur — exul: cf. Pacatus, *Panegyricus Theodosio Augusto dictus* 25.2 (under the tyranny of Maximus) Vidimus ... exutos trabeis consulares et senes fortunarum superstites et infantum sub ipso sectore ludentium flendam securitatem; n. 1.183–87, *fin.*

1.245–48: Claudian uses both *anni* and *aetas* either in the sense of *iuventus* (cf. 4H 365–67, 517) or of *senectus* (cf. BP 480–84, 521). Platnauer (1922) translates *annis* as "age" and *aetate* as "youth," maintaining a chiastic order: *iuvenum ... patrum ... grandaevus nato.*

1.246 rorantia: cf. Verg. *A.* 12.511 f. (Turnus carries the heads of Amycus and Diores) abscissa duorum / suspendit capita et rorantia sanguine portat. The occurrence of *rorantia* in Luc. 2.122–24, cited in n. 1.245–50 as having influenced Claudian, may itself go back to the Vergilian passage, and indeed Claudian may have been thinking of both.

1.247 *a* ante patrum vultus: cf. Verg. *A.* 6.308 (untimely deaths of the young) impositi... rogis iuvenes ante ora parentum; Sen. *Ben.* 7.19.8 in ore parentum liberos iugulet (cf. n. 1.234 f.).

1.247 *b* securi: cf. n. 1.236. The implements of execution forbidden by the rule of Ulpian there cited, whether in actual use or not, continued to be referred to, perhaps in a figurative sense, as we use the term "hanging judge" even in jurisdictions in which the noose is no longer employed. Cf. also Asterius, *Hom.* 4 (= Migne Gr. 40.224D–25A) τῆς σχοίνου ἤδη προσαχθείσης τῷ στόματι.

1.248 ibat grandaevus: the spondees may possibly be intended to correspond to the aged man's slow tread. Cf. Duckworth (1967) 143–50.

1.249 f. Quis — nefandas: cf. Verg. *A.* 2.361 f. (the fall of Troy) quis funera fando / explicet aut possit lacrimis aequare labores? Cf. also Bruère (1964) 228, and n. 1.245–50. On Claudian's treatment of the Vergilian reminiscence, whereby he recalls the thought but avoids the exact language, cf. Rolfe (1919) 144; cf. also Guillemin (1924).

1.249 Quis ... tanta relatu: cf. Stat. *Theb.* 8.515 f. (Hercules speaks of how much he owes Pallas) quis tanta relatu / aequet?

1.251–56: on the relation of these verses to the ψόγος-pattern, cf. Levy (1946) 64, ftn. 28.

1.252–55: of the eight malefactors to whom Claudian refers here, five (all except those connected with Roman history) are mentioned in a single passage by Lucian: *VH* 2.23.10 (cf. also *Bis. acc.* 8). He makes them the ringleaders in a revolt of the damned. Lucan refers to the cruelty of Sulla and Cinna in one passage (4.821 f.) and to Spartacus in another (2.554). It is typical of Claudian's interest in Rome's heroic past (cf. Moore [1910], esp. 114) that he adds historical figures drawn from it to the traditional Hellenistic catalogue of torturers (cf. Fargues [1933a] 223). Cf. also 1.114 Sit licet ipse Numa gravior, sit denique Minos.

1.252 Sinis Isthmiaca pinu: cf. Ov. *Met.* 7.440–42 Occidit ille

Sinis magnis male viribus usus / qui poterat curvare trabes et agebat ab alto / ad terram late sparsuras corpora pinus; Roscher (1937) s.v. *Sinis* 923.

1.252 f. rupe profunda Sciron: cf. BP 188 Scironia rupes; Stat. *Theb.* 1.333 infames Scirone petras; D.S. 4.59.4 (Theseus' benefactions) ἐκόλασε δὲ καὶ Σκείρωνα τὸν οἰκοῦντα τῆς Μεγαρίδος τὰς ὀνομαζομένας ἀπ' ἐκείνου Σκειρωνίδας πέτρας· οὗτος γὰρ εἰώθει τοὺς παριόντας ἀναγκάζειν ἀπονίπτειν ἑαυτὸν ἐπί τινος ἀποκρήμνου τόπου, λακτίσματι δ' ἄφνω περιεκύλιε κατὰ τῶν κρημνῶν εἰς θάλατταν; Roscher (1937) s.v. *Skiron* 1005 f.

1.253 a Phalaris tauro: cf. IE 1.163–66 Sic opifex tauri tormentorumque repertor, / qui funesta novo fabricaverat aera dolore / primus inexpertum Siculo cogente tyranno / sensit opus docuitque suum mugire iuvencum; Cic. *Ver.* 4.33.73 ille nobilis taurus, quem crudelissimus omnium tyrannorum Phalaris habuisse dicitur, quo vivos supplici causa demittere homines et subicere flammam solebat; ... monumentum ... crudelitatis; RE s.v. *Phalaris* 1650 f.; Walbank (1945).

1.253 b carcere: I have been unable to find clear historical grounds for mentioning a *carcer* in connection with Sulla as an analog to Phalaris' *taurus* or Sciron's *rupes*. Claudian apparently uses *carcer* here to symbolize political punishment in general: cf. IE 1.177 f. Procerum squalore repletus / carcer.

It is possible that by *carcer* Claudian refers to Sulla's notorious slaughter of the *dediticii* in the Villa Publica, as related in the Periocha of Livy 88: Sylla ... pulcherrimam victoriam crudelitate, quanta in nullo hominum fuit, inquinavit. Octo milia dediticiorum in villa publica trucidavit (cf. Flor. *Epit.* 2.9.24 f.; Dio frag. 109.5). The victims were hemmed into a small space: cf. Sen. *Ben.* 5.16.3 L. Sulla ... legiones duas ... in angulo congestas contrucidavit; Luc. 7.306 clausi proelia Campi (cf. 2.196–206); RE s.v. *Cornelius* 1548 f. The massacre is variously reported as having occurred in the Villa Publica (cf. DS s.v. 891 f.) or in the nearby *saepta* or *ovilia* (cf. DS s.v. *saeptum* 997).

For *carcer* used of a place beset by hostile soldiery, cf. Cic. *Phil.* 5.7.18 in cella Concordiae conlocari armatos, latrones, sicarios; de templo carcerem fieri.

For another connection of Sulla with a prison, cf. Ap. BC 1.94 Λουκρήτιος δ' ἐπεὶ Πραινεστὸν εἷλε, τῶν ἀπὸ τῆς βουλῆς ... τοὺς μὲν αὐτίκα ἀνῄρει, τοὺς δ' ἐς φυλακὴν ἐσέβαλλεν· οὓς ὁ Σκύλλας ἐπελθὼν ἀνεῖλε.

1.253 c Sylla: cf. Text. Comm. *ad loc.*

1.253 d Sylla: for Sulla as a typical tyrant, cf. Luc. 4.821 f. ius licet in iugulos nostros sibi fecerit ensis / Sulla potens (cf. n. 1.255 a); 1.326, 2.171, 7.307; Stat. *Silv.* 4.6.107 saevi ... vox horrida Syllae; Sen. *Cl.* 1.12.1 f. L. Sullam tyrannum appellari quid prohibet, cui occidendi finem fecit inopia hostium; RE s.v. *Cornelius* 1548–50, 1566.

1.254 a Diomedis equi: cf. RP 2 Pr.11 f. (Hercules tamed the man-eating mares) Dira ... sanguinei vertit praesaepia regis / et Diomedeos gramine pavit equos; Ov. *Met.* 9.194 f. (Hercules speaks) Thracis equos humano sanguine pingues / plenaque corporibus laceris praesaepia vidi; Roscher (1937) s.v. *Diomedes.* Bruère (1964) 228 compares Luc. 2.162 f. (Sulla's butcheries outdid Diomedes').

1.254 b Busiridis arae: cf. IE 1.159–62 (evil counsellors reap the fruits of their wickedness) vates ... / hospite qui caeso monuit placare Tonantem / inventas primus Busiridis imbuit aras / et cecidit saevi; quod dixerat, hostia sacri; RP 2 Pr.43; Apollod. 2.5.11 ἐβασίλευε Βούσιρις Ποσειδῶνος παῖς. ... οὗτος τοὺς ξένους ἔθυεν ἐπὶ βωμῷ Διός. ... ἐννέα γὰρ ἔτη ἀφορία τὴν Αἴγυπτον κατέλαβε, Φράγιος δὲ ἐλθὼν ἐκ Κύπρου μάντις ... ἔφη τὴν ἀφορίαν παύσεσθαι ἐὰν ξένον ἄνδρα τῷ Διὶ σφάξωσι κατ' ἔτος. Βούσιρις δὲ ἐκεῖνον πρῶτον σφάξας τὸν μάντιν τοὺς κατιόντας ξένους ἔσφαζε; RE s.v. *Busiris* 1076.

1.255 a Cinna: for Cinna as a typical tyrant, cf. Luc. 4.812 f. ius licet in iugulos nostros sibi fecerit ensis / ... Cinna cruentus (cf. n. 1.253 d); Cic. *Phil.* 11.1.1 L. Cinna crudelis; [Victor] *De viris illustr.* 69.1 Cinna flagitiosissimus rem publicam summa crudelitate vastavit; Vell. 2.22–24; RD s.v. *Cornelius* 1285–87.

1.255 b Spartace: for Spartacus as a type of savage cruelty, cf. BP 155–59 vilis cum Spartacus omne / per latus Italiae ferro bacchatus et igni // ... strage pudenda / fuderit imbelles aquilas servilibus armis; Luc. 2.554 (Caesar is as guilty as Spartacus); Cic. *Phil.* 4.6.15 Est ... populo Romano ... omne certamen cum percussore, cum latrone, cum Spartaco (cf. 3.8.21); RE s.v. *Spartacus* 1536.

On the use of the vocative to lighten the monotony of enumeration, and also to avoid metrically inadmissible or undesirable forms, cf. Hampel (1908) 23, 36–42, 49 f.; Kroll (1924) 257; Parravicini (1905) 26: Fargues (1933b) on IE 2.98. Cf. also 1.287 f., 2.280.

1.256 Deiecerat: on the tense, cf. n. 1.220 *a*.

1.257 *a* terror: for the fright alleged to have been caused by Rufinus, cf. 2.93 f. *maior oberrat / intra tecta timor*; cf. also Int. 11, ftn. 40.

1.257 f.: cf. 2.86–88 *Quae murmura furtim! / (nam miseris nec flere quidem aut lenire dolorem / colloquiis impune licet)*; Pacatus, *Panegyricus Theodosio Augusto dictus* 25.2–5 *miseri vetabamur agere miseros, immo etiam cogebamur mentiri beatos.... Ita fleri non licebat amissa, metu reliquorum.... Nulla maior est poena quam esse miserum nec videri*; n. 1.183–87, *fin*. Bruère (1964) 228 compares Luc. 1.247 (the people of Ariminium silently resent Caesar's entry) *tacito mutos volvunt in pectore questus*, 257 f. *gemitu sic quisque latenti / non ausus timuisse palam*.

1.257 *b* sepultos: for this word used of stifling one's sorrow, cf. Cic. *Tusc.* 2.13.32 *Amittenda igitur fortitudo est aut sepeliendus dolor*.

1.259–300: this is the first appearance in the body of the poem of a *laus Stilichonis* (cf. Kurfess [1941] 94; Int. 39; Birt [1892] Pr. 37), which forms a sharp contrast to the *vituperatio Rufini*; for other passages lauding Stilicho, cf. 1.332–53; 2.1–6, 100–29, 171–292. On the relation of these verses to the ψόγος-pattern, cf. Levy (1946) 59, 65.

1.259 f. At non — metu: Bruère (1964) 228 compares Luc. 2.234 f. *At non magnanimi percussit pectora Bruti / terror*.

1.259 At ... Stilichonis: for *at* marking a sharp change of subject, cf. 2.102 *At Stilicho*, 130 *At ... Rufinum*; cf. also Pease (1935) on Verg. *A.* 4.1 *At*.

1.260 *a* solus medio sed turbine: cf. Text. Comm. *ad loc*. Bruère (1964) 228 compares Luc. 2.243 f. (on Cato) *virtutis iam sola fides, quam turbine nullo / excutiet fortuna tibi*. On the use of imagery here, cf. Christiansen (1969) 57.

1.260 *b* solus: cf. 1.264 *sola*, BP 267 f. *Solus erat Stilicho, qui desperantibus augur / sponderet meliora manu*; IE 2.501 f. *Iam sola renidet / in Stilichone salus*.

1.260 *c* turbine rerum: cf. 2.90 *funesto turbine rerum*; Ov.

Met. 7.614 (Aeacus overcome by the woes of a pestilence) attonitus tanto miserarum turbine rerum; Stat. *Theb.* 3.251, *Silv.* 2.2.127.

1.261–63: cf. Apollod. 2.3.1 f. (Bellerophon slays the Chimaera) Ἰοβάτης δὲ ... ἐπέταξεν αὐτῷ Χίμαιραν κτεῖναι ... εἶχε δὲ προτομὴν μὲν λέοντος, οὐρὰν δὲ δράκοντος, τρίτην δὲ κεφαλὴν μέσην αἰγός, δι' ἧς πῦρ ἀνίει. καὶ τὴν χώραν διέφθειρε, καὶ τὰ βοσκήματα ἐλυμαίνετο. ... ἀναβιβάσας οὖν ἑαυτὸν ... ἐπὶ τὸν Πήγασον, ὃν εἶχεν ἵππον ... πτηνόν ... εἰς ὕψος ἀπὸ τούτου κατετόξευσε τὴν Χίμαιραν; 4H 558–60; Roscher (1937) s.v. *Bellerophon* 763–67. On the use of imagery here, cf. Christiansen (1969) 86.

1.261 f. rapacem ... feram: for the tyrant as a wild beast, cf. Cic. *Rep.* 2.26.48 tyrannus, quo neque taetrius neque foedius ... animal ullum cogitari potest; qui quamquam figura est hominis, morum tamen immanitate vastissimas vincit beluas (cf. Fleskes [1914] 15, ftn. 1); Sen. *Cl.* 1.25.1 ferina ista rabies est sanguine gaudere ac vulneribus et abiecto homine in silvestre animal transire, 1.26.3. On possible echoes of Sen. *Cl.* in Claudian, cf. Préchac (1921) Pr. 50–53; cf. also n. 1.234 f.

On *fera* as a term of abuse, cf. Opelt (1965) 143 f., 179, 197. On a possible echo of *feram* here in a letter of St. Jerome's, cf. Levy (1948a) 67.

1.262 f. volucris — habenis: for a similar comparison between Stilicho and the heroes of mythology, to the disadvantage of the latter, and with the repeated use of *non* to disparage the second term of the comparison, cf. 1.280 f. te non penna vehit; ... / tu non viperco defensus crine Medusae; 1.288–91; cf. also CM 30.177 f. On a use of *sed* similar to that of *non* here, cf. n. 1.279 *c*. On the disparagement of the second term of a comparison, cf. also n. 1.283, n. 1.289 *b*.

1.263 Pegaseis ... habenis: cf. 4H 560 (Pegasus) Bellerophonteas indignaretur habenas; Pausanias 2.4.1 (explaining Athena's epithet Χαλινῖτις) Ἀθηνᾶν γὰρ ... συγκατεργάσασθαι τά τε ἄλλα Βελλεροφόντῃ φασὶ καὶ ὡς τὸν Πήγασον οἱ παραδοίη χειρωσαμένη τε καὶ ἐνθεῖσα αὐτὴ τῷ ἵππῳ χαλινόν.

1.264 *a* Hic ... hic: cf. Text. Comm. *ad loc.*

1.264 *b* quies: cf. Stat. *Theb.* 3.295 (Mars to Venus) O mihi bellorum requies!

1.264 f. *a* hic sola pericli turris erat: Bruère (1964) 228 compares Luc. 2.243 (cf. n. 1.260). On the imagery here, cf. Christiansen (1969) 22.

1.264 f. *b* pericli turris: for the figure of a "tower of strength" cf. Cic. *Parad.* 1.12 duo propugnacula belli Punici, Cn. et P. Scipiones; Hom. *Od.* 11.556 (Odysseus to Telamonian Ajax) τοῖος γάρ σφιν πύργος ἀπώλεο.

1.265 clipeus: for the figure of a defender as a shield, cf. 4H 432 f. (to Theodosius) Stilichone ... quem fratribus ipse / discedens clipeum defensoremque dedisti, CS 2.62, IE 2.601; *A. A.* 1438 (Clytemnestra speaks of Aegisthus) οὗτος γὰρ ἡμῖν ἀσπὶς οὐ σμικρὰ θράσους.

1.265–68 erat .... minatus haerebat: on the abrupt change of subject (from Stilicho to Rufinus), cf. Text. Comm. on 2.124; also n. 2.124, para. 2.

1.266 profugis sedes: cf. Ov. *Met.* 3.539 (refugees from Tyre have established themselves at Thebes) hac profugos posuistis sede penates.

1.267 *a* castra: cf. Liv. 44.39.3 Castra sunt victori receptaculum, victo perfugium.

1.267 *b* bonis: for this word of Stilicho's political allies, cf. IE 2.557 f. (Eutropius has rejected the *boni*) pulsisque bonis et faece retenta / peiores legit socios.

1.267 f. Hucusque — inerti: for *hucusque* marking the high point of an enemy's success, cf. BP 60 f. Fatales hucusque manus crebrisque notatae / prodigiis abiere minae. Bruère (1964) 228 compares the phrase *huc usque licet* as applied by the goddess Roma to the Rubicon, Luc. 1.192.

1.267 *c* Hucusque: local rather than temporal as Paucker (1880) 599 thought: cf. BP 548 Huc iter usque datur. Cf. also BP 60 Fatales hucusque manus, which Platnauer (1922) correctly translates "Thus far came the fatal hordes" (his marking a new paragraph at BP 61 resolves the difficulties of interpretation mentioned by Schroff [1927] *ad loc.*). Here of course the locus is figurative, corresponding to *haerebat* and *cedebat* in the next verse.

1.268 inerti: on Claudian's stress upon Rufinus' unwarlike nature, cf. n. 1.239 *b*.

1.269–72: cf. Stat. *Theb.* 3.671–76 Ut rapidus torrens, animos cui verna ministrant / flamina et exuti concreto frigore montes, / cum vagus in campos frustra prohibentibus exit / obicibus, resonant permixto turbine tecta, / arma, armenta, viri, donec stetit improbus alto / colle minor magnoque invenit in aggere ripas; Verg. A. 7.586–90, 10.693–96. On the use of imagery here, cf. Christiansen (1969) 87.

1.269 a hiberno tumidus ... vertice torrens: the Graeco-Roman literary tradition which represents floods as a characteristic of winter is apparently based on the south Mediterranean climate, which has maximum rainfall in the winter months: cf. Vidal de la Blache-Gallois (1927) 7.241. According to Cary (1949) 4 the entire Mediterranean area receives more than two-thirds of its rainfall in the winter months; cf. also Semple (1931) 85–94, 110. Cf. RP 2.198 f. (Pluto's horses gallop more rapidly than a winter torrent) torrentius amne / hiberno; CM 28.27 f. (the Nile is not like other rivers) cum tristis hiems alias produxerit undas, / tunc Nilum retinent ripae (cf. Luc. 10.228 f., and n. 1.185 b); Hom. Il. 5.87 f. θῦνε γὰρ ἂμ πεδίον ποταμῷ πληθόντι ἐοικὼς / χειμάρρῳ.

1.269 b hiberno ... vertice: on the extended use of the adjective, cf. Text. Comm. on 1.16, and n. 1.16 a.

1.269 f. vertice torrens saxa rotat: cf. Verg. A. 7.567 dat sonitum saxis et torto vertice torrens, 10.362 f. saxa rotantia late / impulerat torrens.

1.270 a volvit ... nemus: cf. MT 237 f. Torrentes ... / ... volvant spumoso vertice silvas; Verg. A. 2.305–7 torrens // praecipites ... trahit silvas.

1.270 b pontes ... revellit: cf. MT 237 f. Torrentes ... lassis ... minentur / pontibus; Luc. 4.14 Sicoris ... / saxeus ingenti quem pons amplectitur arcu / hibernas passurus aquas.

1.271 frangitur obiectu scopuli: cf. Luc. 6.265 f. mare ... / frangentem fluctus scopulum ferit.

1.272 a: cf. Verg. A. 7.589 f. (Latinus stands firm as a rock) scopuli nequiquam et spumea circum / saxa fremunt laterique illisa refunditur alga.

1.272 b illisa: cf. Text. Comm. ad loc.

1.273–84: the apostrophe to Stilicho commenced in these verses is resumed in 1.299 f., 316, 333.

1.273 Qua — feram: for a similar formula, cf. BP 13 f. Quae tibi ... / sufficient laudes, Stilicho?

1.273 f. qui — orbi: a comparison with the feat of Hercules in assuming the burden of Atlas (cf. Preller-Robert [1894] 2.494 f.) is apparently intended (cf. n. 1 Pr.17 *b*, n. 1.278–96): cf. CS 1.142–47 (addressed to Stilicho) Ancipites rerum ruituro culmine lapsus / aequali cervice subis: sic Hercule quondam / sustentante polum melius librata pependit / machina ... / perpetuaque senex subductus mole parumper / obstupuit proprii spectator ponderis Atlas; Christ (1938) 134 f.; to the citations there given add 4H 59–61. As regards the soundness of Claudian's estimate of Stilicho's achievement, cf. Stein-Palanque (1959) 227: "Si ... il fut encore possible, durant peu de temps, de maintenir en apparence l'ancienne puissance de l'Empire, un jugement non prévenu devra l'attribuer à l'énergie infatigable, à la souplesse politique et aux remarquables talents stratégiques de Stilicon."

Bruère (1964) 229 compares this passage with Cato's words in Luc. 9.385: durum iter ad leges patriaeque ruentis amorem. On the use of imagery here, cf. Christiansen (1969) 22.

1.275 trepidae ... carinae: cf. Luc. 5.568 (Caesar's boatman warns of a storm) Tunc rector trepidae fatur ratis.

1.275–77: cf. IE 2.507 f. (the people of the East long for Stilicho as for a star amidst the stormy seas of trouble) hoc tantis ... sidus in undis / sperant. A reference to the stars Castor and Pollux may be intended; cf. BG 219–22 (the elder and younger Theodosii come to bring peace to the world like the Dioscuri in a storm) Sic cum praecipites artem vicere procellae / adsiduoque gemens undarum verbere nutat / descensura ratis, caeca sub nocte vocati / naufraga Ledaei sustentant vela Lacones; Stat. *Silv.* 3.2.8–10; Sil. 15.82 f.; V. Fl. 1.570–73; Sen. *Nat.* 1.1.13 in magna tempestate apparere quasi stellae solent velo insidentes; adiuvari se tunc periclitantes aestimant Pollucis et Castoris numine; Plin. *Nat.* 2.37.101. It is possible, however, that reference is not specifically to the star or stars of the Dioscuri, but simply to any guiding star: cf. IE 2.424 and Stat. *Theb.* 6.452 (both quoted in n. 1.277 *a*). On the imagery here, cf. n. 1 Pr.1, para. 2; also Christiansen (1969) 20.

1.276 *a* geminis ... procellis: cf. CM 30.203–6 incumbat si turbidus Auster et unda / pulset utrumque latus ... nautae / ... sese ...

pavere / confessi; Sil. 17.268 f. diversis flatibus acta / in geminum ruit unda latus; Stat. Theb. 5.704 f.; Luc. 5.569 f.; V. Fl. 1.639 f.

1.276 b lassa: cf. Ov. Met. 11.531 fessam ... carinam; also MT 237 f. lassis ... / pontibus.

1.277 a victo — magistro: cf. IE 2.423 Sic orba magistro / fertur in abruptum casu, non sidere puppis; Stat. Theb. 6.451–53 lassa veluti ratione magister / in fluctus, in saxa ruit nec iam amplius astra / respicit et victam proiecit casibus artem; Luc. 7.125–27; Ov. Tr. 1.4.12.

1.277 b caeca: for this word applied to things, cf. IE 2.545 f. caeca futuri / gaudia; Plin. Ep. 4.22.5 tela ... caeca et improvida. The present passage should be listed in TLL s.v. *caecus* in the same section as the two lemmata last cited, 44.29–69, sect. IB2, under the rubric *active ... de eo qui non videt ... translate ... de rebus*, instead of IIB2 (46.66 f.) under *passive ... translate ... de eis rebus quae cognosci male possunt*. The *carina* is *caeca* in the same sense that it is *trepida* (1.275) and *lassa* (1.276). Cf. also Verg. A. 2.335 caeco Marte resistunt, 9.518.

1.278–96: for a similar comparison of Stilicho's achievements with the feats of legendary heroes, cf. BP 13–35; cf. also CS 3.232; n. 1.273 f. On the relation of these verses to the ψόγος-pattern, cf. Levy (1946) 64.

1.278–82: for the exploit of Perseus, cf. Lucian. DMar. 14.3 ἐπεὶ δὲ κατὰ τὴν παράλιον ταύτην Αἰθιοπίαν ἐγένετο, ἤδη πρόσγειος πετόμενος, ὁρᾷ τὴν Ἀνδρομέδαν προκειμένην ἐπί τινος πέτρας προβλῆτος προσπεπατταλευμένην.... κατὰ μικρὸν δὲ ἁλοὺς ἔρωτι ... βοηθεῖν διέγνω· καὶ ἐπειδὴ τὸ κῆτος ἐπῄει μάλα φοβερὸν ὡς καταπιόμενον τὴν Ἀνδρομέδαν, ὑπεραιωρηθεὶς ὁ νεανίσκος, πρόκωπον ἔχων τὴν ἅρπην, τῇ μὲν καθικνεῖται, τῇ δὲ προδεικνὺς τὴν Γόργονα λίθον ἐποίει αὐτό, τὸ δὲ τέθνηκεν ὁμοῦ καὶ πέπηγεν αὐτοῦ τὰ πολλά, ὅσα εἶδε τὴν Μέδουσαν· ὁ δὲ λύσας τὰ δεσμὰ τῆς παρθένου ... ὑπεδέξατο ... κατιοῦσαν ἐκ τῆς πέτρας; Roscher (1937) s.v. *Perseus* 2010, 2012, 2014, 2020–22. Claudian's version agrees with Lucian's in connecting the Gorgon's head (1.280) with the slaying of the sea-monster; contrast Ov. Met. 4.720, 727, 734; Man. 5.594, 600 f., 609; Roscher (1937) s.v. *Perseus* 2014.16–20.

1.278 a Inachius ... Perseus: for Perseus as a descendant of Inachus, cf. Ov. Met. 4.720 Inachides; Apollod. 2.1.1 Ἐπειδὴ δὲ τὸ

τοῦ Δευκαλίωνος διεξεληλύθαμεν γένος, ἐχομένως λέγωμεν τὸ
'Ινάχειον, 2.4.3 Περσέα; Roscher (1937) s.v. Inachos.

1.278 b rubro ... in aequore: cf. Lucian. DMar. 14.3 (quoted
in n. 1.278-82) Αἰθιοπίαν; Plin. Nat. 6.35.196 Aethiopum terram
universam cum mari rubro patere in longitudinem |XXI| LXX p. ...
Agrippa existimavit. For the name *rubrum mare* applied to the *sinus
Arabicus* (the present "Red Sea"), cf. Plin. Nat. 6.28.107 f.; Mela
3.8.73; RE s.v. *Arabicus sinus* 362; cf. also BG 454 f. (the Roman
Empire once extended to the Nile and the Red Sea) ius Latium quod
tunc Meroe rubroque solebat / oceano cingi. On the use of the term
to denote the Indian Ocean, cf. n. 2.242 f.

The interpretation given by Koenig (1808) of *ruber* here as meaning
tinctus cruore beluae runs counter to the form of the myth which Claudian
uses, stressing the Gorgon's head (1.280 f.), and omitting any mention
of the scimitar referred to by Lucian (cf. n. 1.278-82); Koenig is followed by Crépin (1933).

1.279 a Neptuni: for this god in the Andromeda legend, cf.
Apollod. 2.4.3 Ποσειδῶν ... ἔπεμψε ... κῆτος.

1.279 b pecus: cf. IE 2.427 (the whale) *immensum pecus*. The
plural "monsters" used by Platnauer (1922) is wrong, despite Hor.
Carm. 1.2.7 *omne cum Proteus pecus egit*; cf. Apollod. 2.4.3 κῆτος;
Ov. Met. 4.689 belua, Man. 5.545 belua, Lucian. DMar. 14.3 τὸ κῆτος.

1.279 c sed: cf. 4H 455 f. (Stilicho's feats surpass those of the
Drusi) Nobilitant veteres Germanica foedera Drusos, / Marte sed anci-
piti, sed multis cladibus empta; on a similar use of *non*, cf. n. 1.262 f.

1.279 d alis: for Perseus' wings, cf. Ov. Met. 4.724 *avidos morsus
velocibus effugit alis*; Man. 5.593; Lucian. DMar. 14.2 ὑπόπτερον ...
αὐτὸν ἡ 'Αθηνᾶ ἔθηκεν.

1.280 f. a te non penna vehit ... tu non — Medusae: on the
repeated use of *non* to disparage the second term of a comparison, cf.
n. 1.262 f.; on a similar use of *sed*, cf. n. 1.279 c.

1.280 f. b rigida — Medusae: on the form of the legend followed
by Claudian, cf. n. 1.278-82, *fin*.

1.280 rigida: for the causative use of the adjective, cf. Lucr. 1.355
rigidum permanat frigus ad ossa.

1.283 Taceat superata vetustas: for this formula used in claiming
superiority for the poet's own heroes and heroines over those of the

past, cf. PO 202 f. (Proba surpasses Thetis) Taceat Nereida nuptam / Pelion, CM 30.42 (Serena surpasses Cornelia) Claram Scipiadum taceat Cornelia gentem. Cf. also Nazarius, *Panegyricus dictus Constantino Augusto* 15.1 Cedat tibi ... totius memoriae vetustas; n. 1.183–87, *fin*. Cf. also Axelson (1944) 49. Bruère (1964) 229 compares Luc. 4.590 (Curio marches to the site of Antaeus' struggle with Hercules) Antaei ... regna vocat non vana vetustas; 4.654.

1.284–96 Herculeos — hydrae: cf. Verg. *A.* 6.801–3 (Augustus' realm will cover a vaster area than Hercules' travels) Nec vero Alcides tantum telluris obivit, / fixerit aeripedem cervam licet aut Erymanthi / pacarit nemora et Lernam tremefecerit arcu; Lucr. 5.22–54. Muellner (1893) 122 points out that the Nemean (or Cleonaean) lion, the Arcadian boar, the Cretan bull, the Lernaean hydra, and Geryon are mentioned by Claudian in the same order as they appear in Lucretius, though the latter makes no mention of Antaeus.

1.284 actus: for the word *actus* in the sense of *factum*, *opus*, cf. 2.481, BG 291, CS 1.14; Luc. 2.390 f. nullos ... Catonis in actus / subrepsit ... voluptas; TLL s.v. *actus* 453.

1.285 *a*: for the Cleonaean lion, cf. Apollod. 2.5.1 ὁ Ἡρακλῆς ... τὰ προσταττόμενα ὑπὸ Εὐρυσθέως ἐτέλει. Πρῶτον μὲν οὖν ἐπέταξεν αὐτῷ τοῦ Νεμέου λέοντος τὴν δορὰν κομίζειν.... πορευόμενος οὖν ἐπὶ τὸν λέοντα ἦλθεν εἰς Κλεωνάς; D.S. 4.11.3 f.; Preller-Robert (1894) 2.440–43. Cf. also RP 2 Pr.33–35.

1.285 *b* Cleonaeum ... leonem: cf. Sil. 3.32–34 in foribus labor Alcidae ... / ... nexu ... elisa leonis / ora Cleonaei patulo caelantur hiatu; Stat. *Theb*. 1.487. Bruère (1964) 229 compares Luc. 2.612 (Hercules' lion-skin) Cleonaei ... terga leonis.

1.285 *c* silva: cf. Stat. *Theb*. 4.825–28 silvarum, Nemea, longe regina virentum, / ... quam tu non Herculis actis / dura magis, rabidi cum colla comantia monstri / angeret; 5.44 f.

1.286 f. *a* Arcadiae — aper: for the Arcadian boar, cf. D.S. 4.12.1 Τρίτον δὲ πρόσταγμα ἔλαβεν ἐνεγκεῖν τὸν Ἐρυμάνθιον κάπρον ζῶντα, ὃς διέτριβεν ἐν τῇ Λαμπείᾳ τῆς Ἀρκαδίας; Apollod. 2.5.4; Preller-Robert (1894) 2.447 f. Cf. also RP 2 Pr.36.

1.286 f. *b* Arcadiae saltum vastabat ... aper: cf. Ov. *Met*. 9.192 Arcadiae vastator aper.

1.287 f. *a*: for the Antaeus legend, cf. Apollod. 2.5.11 (Heracles' travels) Λιβύην διεξῄει. ταύτης ἐβασίλευε παῖς Ποσειδῶνος Ἀνταῖος, ὃς τοὺς ξένους ἀναγκάζων παλαίειν ἀνῄρει. τούτῳ παλαίειν ἀναγκαζόμενος Ἡρακλῆς ἀράμενος μετέωρον ἅμμασι κλάσας ἀπέκτεινε· ψαύοντα γὰρ γῆς ἰσχυρότερον συνέβαινε γίνεσθαι· διὸ καὶ Γῆς τινες ἔφασαν τοῦτον εἶναι παῖδα; Text. Comm. on 1.287 (also Ov. Met. 9.184 f.); Preller-Robert (1894) 2.514–17. On Lucan's use of the Antaeus episode to heighten the dramatic effect of Cato's suicide, cf. Grimal (1949).

1.287 f. *b* **tu ... o ... Antaee:** on the use of apostrophe in enumeration, cf. n. 1.255 *b*, para. 2.

1.287 *a* **tuque o:** for this formula, cf. 3H 7, RP 2.367; Verg. A. 6.196.

1.287 *b* **compressa matre rebellis:** cf. Text. Comm. *ad loc.*; Fargues (1936) 371. Additional examples of the ablative absolute in close connection with an adjective are: IE 1.392 f. domito ... Saxone ... / mitior; 6H 529 f. insignior auctis / collibus; CM 27.54 mutata melior ... figura; Verg. A. 6.837 caesis insignis Achivis; Luc. 9.1015 genero secure perempto. The translation of Platnauer (1922), "rebel Antaeus, holding thy mother earth in thine embrace," does not adequately reflect the causal relationship between Antaeus' contact with the earth and his ability to keep fighting back.

Bruère (1964) 229 compares Luc. 4.615 parum fidens pedibus contingere matrem.

1.289 *a*: for the Cretan bull, cf. Apollod. 2.5.7 (among Heracles' labors) ἕβδομον ἐπέταξεν ἆθλον ... τὸν Κρῆτα ἀγαγεῖν ταῦρον; Paus. 1.27.9 Κρησὶ τήν τε ἄλλην γῆν καὶ τὴν ἐπὶ ποταμῷ Τεθρίνι ταῦρος ἐλυμαίνετο; Preller-Robert (1894) 2.456–58. Cf. also RP 2 Pr.33 f.

1.289 *b* **sola ... Creta:** for the purposes of this passage Claudian has adopted the Vergilian form of the myth (A. 8.294 tu Cresia mactas / prodigia; cf. Preller-Robert [1894] 2.458, ftn. 3) which has Hercules kill the bull on the island of Crete, rather than the common version in which the bull is brought alive to Greece, where it commits further depredations: Apollod. 2.5.7; Paus. 1.27.9 f.; Schol. Dan. on Verg. A. 8.294; cf. D.S. 4.13.4, Sen. Ag. 833 f. The restriction of the bull's area of damage is perhaps another technique for disparaging the second term of a comparison: cf. n. 1.262 f., n. 1.279 *c*, n. 1.283.

1.289 c fulmineo ... iuvenco: cf. V. Fl. 7.582 (the bull attacks Jason) Bis fulmineis se flatibus infert.

1.290 a: for the Lernaean hydra, cf. Apollod. 2.5.2 (among Heracles' labors) δεύτερον δὲ ἆθλον ἐπέταξεν αὐτῷ τὴν Λερναίαν ὕδραν κτεῖναι· αὕτη δὲ ἐν τῷ τῆς Λέρνης ἕλει ἐκτραφεῖσα ἐξέβαινεν εἰς τὸ πεδίον καὶ τά τε βοσκήματα καὶ τὴν χώραν διέφθειρεν; D.S. 4.11.5; Ov. *Met.* 9.69–74, 192 f.; Stat. *Theb.* 2.376 f.; Preller-Robert (1894) 2.444–47. Cf. also RP 2 Pr.41.

1.290 b Lernaeam: the emphatic position of this word partially compensates for the lack of a restrictive expression to correspond with 1.285 una, 1.286 unum, 1.288 non ultra, 1.289 sola. Cf. also 1.291 non una palus.

1.291–96: on the relation of these verses to the ψόγος-pattern, cf. Levy (1946) 64, ftn. 28.

1.291 Hoc monstrum: for this term applied to Rufinus, cf. 2.99 avidi ... monstri.

1.292 Latia — subactum: on Claudian's feeling for the ancient center of the Empire, cf. Laqueur-Koch-Weber (1930) 19, "besteht für ihn ... der tatsächlich längst verschwundene Unterschied zwischen dem siegreichen Rom, welches die Herrschaft auf alle erstreckt hatte ... und dem von ihm unterworfenen Gebiet ... noch fort. Rom erscheint dem Dichter ... als das notwendige Zentrum ...;" Levy (1958) 340 f.

1.293 a a primis Ganges horrebat Hiberis: Claudian has fused the two forms of expression seen in Ov. *Pont.* 1.4.29 f. (Caesar) quem solis ab ortu / solis ad occasus utraque terra tremit, and in *Fast.* 1.717 horreat Aeneadas et primus et ultimus orbis.

1.293 b primis ... Hiberis: for *primus* of one extreme of a tract being measured, cf. Luc. 9.413 f. Nec enim plus litora Nili / quam Scythicus Tanais primis a Gadibus absunt. Cf. also Ov. *Fast.* 1.717, quoted in n. 1.293 a.

1.293 c Ganges horrebat: for the name of a river used metaphorically for the people who dwell on its banks, cf. 1.308 (Rufinus stirs up the Danubian peoples) Histrum ... movet; 6H 414 f. (the awe felt by the Mesopotamians) timebant / Tigris et Euphrates; Vollrath (1910) 23 f.

1.294 a Geryon triplex: cf. Apollod. 2.5.10 (among Heracles' labors) δέκατον ἐπετάγη ἆθλον τὰς Γηρυόνου βόας ἐξ Ἐρυθείας κομίζειν. . . . ταύτην κατῴκει Γηρυόνης . . . τριῶν ἔχων ἀνδρῶν συμφυὲς σῶμα, συνηγμένον εἰς ἓν κατὰ τὴν γαστέρα, ἐσχισμένον δὲ εἰς τρεῖς ἀπὸ λαγόνων τε καὶ μηρῶν; Sil. 1.278 f.; Preller-Robert (1894) 2.465–83.

1.294 b Geryon: cf. Var. L. 9.51.90 Reprehendunt, cum ab eadem voce plura sunt vocabula declinata, quas συνωνυμίας appellant, ut . . . Geryon . . . Geryones; Birt (1892) Pr. 211; Neue-Wagener (1892) 1.857 f.

1.294 c triplex: cf. Ov. Ep. 9.91 f. prodigium . . . triplex . . . / Geryones, Met. 9.184 f. Cf. also CM 4.2 tergemino . . . Geryoni, RP 2 Pr.39; Verg. A. 8.202 tergemini . . . Geryonae.

1.294 f. a turbidus Orci ianitor: cf. Apollod. 2.5.12 (among the labors of Heracles) δωδέκατον ἆθλον ἐπετάγη Κέρβερον ἐξ Ἅιδου κομίζειν; D.S. 4.25.1, 4.26.1; Ov. Met. 7.410–14 Tirynthius heros // . . . nexis adamante catenis / Cerberon adtraxit, rabida qui concitus ira / implevit . . . ternis latratibus auras; Sil. 3.35–37; Preller-Robert (1894) 2.483–88. Cf. also RP 2 Pr.34.

1.294 f. b Orci ianitor: cf. Verg. A. 8.296 (in a hymn to Hercules) te Stygii tremuere lacus, te ianitor Orci. Cf. also RP 1.85 f. latratum triplicem compescuit ingens / ianitor; Sil. 3.35, 2.551 f.

1.296 a vis hydrae: cf. n. 1.290 a.

1.296 b Scyllae . . . fames: cf. Hom. Od. 12.245 f. (Odysseus speaks) τόφρα δέ μοι Σκύλλη κοίλης ἐκ νηὸς ἑταίρους / ἓξ ἕλεθ', 256 αὐτοῦ δ' εἰνὶ θύρῃσι κατήσθιε κεκληγόντας; Ov. Ep. 12.123 nos Scylla rapax canibus misisset edendos, Ib. 383; Roscher (1937) s.v. Skylla 1024–35.

For a tradition connecting Scylla with the labors of Hercules, cf. Tz. ad Lyc. Alex. 45 Ἡρακλῆς τὰς Γηρυονείους βοῦς ἐλαύνων ἐξ Ἐρυθείας ὡς ἐγένετο κατὰ τὸν πορθμὸν τὸν μεταξὺ Ἰταλίας καὶ Σικελίας, ἁρπάσασά τινας τῶν ταύρων ἡ ῥηθεῖσα Σκύλλα καὶ ἀνελοῦσα, καὶ αὐτὴ ὑφ' Ἡρακλέος ἀναρεῖται; Roscher (1937) s.v. Skylla 1032.

A reference to Rufinus' avarice is probably intended here; cf. Int. 15 f., ftns. 82, 83, 95.

1.296 c flamma Chimaerae: cf. Verg. A. 6.288 (among the monsters in the Lower World) flammis . . . armata Chimaera. Cf. also 1.261 letiferos rictus, and n. 1.261–63.

The inclusion of a monster slain by Bellerophon (cf. Roscher [1937] s.v. *Bellerophon* 763) in an enumeration otherwise devoted to the exploits of Hercules (cf. n. 1.296 *b*, para. 2) may be explained on the ground that the Chimaera is frequently associated with Scylla: cf. Verg. *A*. 6.286–88, Tib. 3.4.86–89; Waser (1894) 29, ftn. 40.

1.297 sublime: i.e. carried out by the highest dignitaries of the Roman state, short of the Emperors themselves: cf. IE Pr.1 f. (of Eutropius before his fall) Qui modo sublimes rerum flectebat habenas / patricius; Sil. 16.600 consul sublimis. For the use of *sublimis* as part of the official title of the Praefectus Praetorio, cf. Int. 26, ftn. 166. Bruère (1964) 229 sees in *sublimis* a figurative echo of the struggle between Hercules and Antaeus, in which the hero held the giant high above the ground (Luc. 4.649).

1.299 f. tu prohibes ... tu reddis. ... instauras ... vincis: on the apostrophe to Stilicho, cf. n. 1.273–84.

1.299 *a* ditem spoliat: on Rufinus' exactions, cf. n. 1.187–89 *a*, n. 188–92.

1.299 *b* tu reddis egenti: for praise of Stilicho's generosity, cf. CS 3.223–36.

1.300: on the possibility that verses numbered in even hundreds seemed to Claudian especially appropriate to mark pauses in the sense, cf. Birt (1892) Pr. 218 f.; cf. also 2.100.

1.301–31: *Rufinus incites the barbarians to invade the Empire.* On the relation of these verses to the ψόγος-pattern, cf. Levy (1946) 63, 65.

1.301–4: for descriptions of plagues, cf. Hom. *Il.* 1.50–52; Lucr. 6.1090–1286; Ov. *Met.* 7.523–613; Luc. 6.89–105; Sil. 14.582–617. Cf. also Verg. *G*. 3.478–566. Lemmata from these passages are quoted below to parallel the description of the plague in its various stages as Claudian conceives it. On the use of imagery here cf. Christiansen (1969) 86.

1.301 *a* infecto — caelo: cf. Lucr. 6.1096–1100 (the behavior of disease-causing atoms) ea cum casu sunt forte coorta / et perturbarunt caelum, fit morbidus aer / atque ea vis omnis morborum pestilitasque / ... extrinsecus ut nubes nebulaeque superne / per caelum veniunt; Ov. *Met.* 7.529 f. (a pestilence) principio caelum spissa caligine terras / pressit; Luc. 6.89 f. (failure of fresh fodder causes the death of horses, and then a plague) traxit iners caelum fluvidae contagia pestis / obscuram in nubem; Sil. 14.582–84.

1.301 b morbus crudescere: cf. Verg. G. 3.504 (a stage in an autumnal plague) coepit crudescere morbus.

1.302 a primos — artus: cf. Hom. Il. 1.50 οὐρῆας μὲν πρῶτον ἐπῴχετο καὶ κύνας ἀργούς; Ov. Met. 7.536 strage canum primo volucrumque oviumque bovumque; Sil. 14.594–96.

1.302 b depascitur artus: cf. Verg. G. 3.458 artus depascitur arida febris; Sil. 14.613.

1.303 a mox — rapit: cf. Ov. Met. 7.551 f. pervenit ad miseros damno graviore colonos / pestis et in magnae dominatur moenibus urbis.

1.303 b mox populos . . . rapit: cf. Hom. Il. 1.10 ὀλέκοντο . . . λαοί, 51 f.; Luc. 6.93 inde labant populi.

1.303 c urbes . . . rapit: cf. Gal. Pis. (= 14.281 Kühn) ὥσπερ γάρ τι θηρίον καὶ αὐτὸς ὁ λοιμὸς οὐκ ὀλίγους τινάς, ἀλλὰ καὶ πόλεις ὅλας ἐπινεμόμενος διαφθείρει.

1.303 f. ventis — amnes: cf. Ov. Met. 7.532 f. letiferis calidi spirarunt aestibus austri. / Constat et in fontes vitium venisse lacusque; Sil. 14.585–87.

1.304 a amnes: cf. Luc. 6.93 f. caelo . . . paratior unda / omne pati virus.

1.304 b corruptos: on the resultative-predicate use of the participle, cf. n. 1.1 b.

1.305 a avidus praedo: on Rufinus' avarice, cf. Int. 15 f., ftns. 82, 83, 95 (where note Symmachus' use of the word praedo).

1.305 b iam non per singula: for iam non, cf. 2.56 iam non finitimo . . . terrore movetur; Ov. Pont. 1.1.1 iam non novus incola, Met. 14.165.

1.305 c iam: on the implication of a chronological order here, cf. n. 1.220 a.

1.306–53: the conflicts with the Goths and other barbarians to which reference is made in these verses (and in CS 1.94–115) occurred in 391 and 392: cf. Rauschen (1897) 336, 370 f.; Stein-Palanque (1959) 194 f.; Schmidt (1934) 424; Mazzarino (1942) 256 f. Cf. also n. 1.308 b, n. 1.308 c.

Claudian accuses Rufinus of causing and prolonging these conflicts by treacherous dealings with and on behalf of the barbarians (cf. 1.308 f., 1.314 f., 1.319 f.). A like charge concerning the invasions of 395 is made in IR 2 (cf. 2.9 f., 23–26). The latter accusation apparently echoes, or at any rate parallels, a contemporary belief that was widespread, at least among Rufinus' enemies: cf. n. 2.22–60; Int. 23. The present charge, however, has no parallel in other sources, save perhaps in the statement of Zos. 4.51.3 that Rufinus suborned the barbarians to ambush Promotus (cf. Int. 10). Fargues (1933a) 75 f. seems entirely justified in maintaining that this earlier accusation is a mere invention of Claudian's. I suggest that Claudian may be attempting here, as well as in 2.22–85 (cf. esp. n. 2.78–85) to direct against Rufinus, and thus perhaps to deflect from Stilicho, some of the strong anti-Germanic and generally anti-barbarian sentiment which was currently prevalent in military and court circles, and which ultimately caused Stilicho's downfall: cf. Seeck (1913) 315–17, Grosse (1920) 260–65; Stein-Palanque (1959) 226 f., 235 f., 237 f., 247, 253 f.; Levy (1958) 344 f.

As has been observed (cf. Schmidt [1934] 424, ftn. 6; the reference to "Bessell" is explained at p. 261, ftn. 3), the narrative of events given in this passage differs in some points from that set forth in CS 1.94–115. With considerable recourse to conjecture, the two accounts may perhaps be reconciled somewhat as follows:

(a) Stilicho engages a force composed of Goths and Bastarnae (and others? cf. n. 1.308 c). In revenge for Promotus' death, he annihilates the Bastarnae; he drives the Goths (and others?) into their wagon-enclosure: CS 1.94–96 Quis—ruina, CS 1.102–4 turmas—datur; IR 1.316 f. Nam—letum. The expressions *pars una* ... / *debilior* (IR 1.317) and *tot barbara* ... / *milia* (CS 1.106 f.), despite their disparity, seem to refer to the same troops: cf. CS 1.108 conclusa, IR 1.318 facilis ... capi. The difference in expression corresponds to a difference in emphasis: in our present passage, the point is the ease with which Stilicho could have rounded out his victory, had it not been for Rufinus' interference; in the other, stress is laid upon the vast numbers of potential expiatory victims, which are contrasted with the meager offerings of Aeneas and of Achilles.

(b) Orders from Imperial headquarters forbid Stilicho to press the fight against the beleaguered barbarians, pending negotiations in line with Theodosius' pro-Gothic policy (cf. n. 1.314–20): IR 1.314 f. vetat—differt, 318–20 tunc—pugnas, CS 1.113 f.

(c) Reinforcements for the barbarians arrive during this period of delay: IR 1.321 f., CS 1.109–11. Stilicho engages in skirmishes with the augmented force; possibly these occur when troops sally forth from the barbarian encampment to meet their oncoming allies: IR 1.332–53. This ends the account in IR; no explicit indication is given of the outcome of these engagements, but *maestam*, IR 1.355, does not imply any marked success on Stilicho's part.

(d) As a result of the negotiations referred to in (b) above, the campaign ends in a lifting of the siege and a treaty with the barbarians: CS 1.115. This phase is not mentioned by Claudian here, possibly so as not to conflict with his representation of the Goths later in IR as the persistent enemies of the Romans: e.g. 2.36–38, 70–85, 186–94, 215 f., 235 f.

1.306 sceptris: = *imperio Romano*: cf. 1.307 Romanas ... prosternere vires, 319 proditor imperii. Cf. also Sil. 10.645 f. (the defence of the Roman Republic in the Second Punic War) pro ... arce et sceptris et libertatis honore / vel famulas armare manus, 17.627 (Scipio Africanus) securus sceptri, 6.103, 10.628, 11.606. Birt (1892) 576 s.v. *sceptrum* takes *sceptris* as = *Augusto*. The contrast with *per singula* (1.305) seems to favor the wider interpretation; cf. also 1.303 populos urbesque. The translation "kings" of Platnauer (1922) is quite inappropriate, that offered by Crépin (1933), "jusqu'au trône," somewhat less so.

1.308–14 iamque Getas — manus: Bruère (1964) 229 sees in these verses the marked influence of several passages from Lucan: 2.296 f. (Rome's fall would stir barbarians) motura Dahas ut clade Getasque, 3.94 (quoted in n. 1.310 a), 3.282 f.

On the enumeration of multi-ethnic troops as an epic theme, cf. Miniconi (1951) 158; also 53, 55, 61, 124–26. This is the first reference to IR in Miniconi's useful book on warlike themes in the ancient epic. He comments on some two dozen passages from IR, each of which will be noted *suo loco*.

1.308 a iam: on the implication of a chronological order here, cf. n. 1.220 a.

1.308 b Getas: by this name (cf. 1.316, 319; 2 Pr.12; 2.36, 83, 235) Claudian denotes the Goths (cf. Müllenhoff-Roediger [1890] 3.162; Wagner [1967] 150 f.) and almost always, as here, the Visigoths (cf. Birt [1892] 440 s.v. *Getae*); in a parallel passage he uses the name Visi in what is apparently a reference to the same people (CS 1.94;

cf. CS 1.111, and Schmidt [1934] 203). For other references to these barbarians, cf. CM 25.89 saevis ... Getis, BP 33-35 Getarum / ... quos tantis aluit Bellona tropaeis / totaque sub galeis Mavortia canuit aetas, 134, 645; Schmidt (1934) 195-249, 400-29; Bury (1923) 1.97 f., 105, 109 f.; McGovern (1939) 370-72; Stein-Palanque (1959) 192-95.

1.308 *c* **Histrum ... Scythiam:** to the peoples enumerated in 1.308-21 (Getae, Sarmatae, Daci, Massagetae, Alani, Geloni, Huni), Claudian in a parallel passage, CS 1.94-115, adds the Bastarnae: CS 1.96. Birt (1892) Pr. 26 and Schmidt (1934) 424, ftn. 1, seem right in regarding the list as amplified for the purpose of poetic ornamentation.

Apparently the Massagetae (1.312) no longer existed as a people distinct from the Alani (1.312: cf. Amm. 23.5.16 Massagetas, quos Halanos nunc appellamus, 31.2.12; RE s.v. *Massagetai* 2124 f.; cf. also Amm. 22.8.38 and RE s.v. *Hunni* 2589.9-11; McGovern [1939] 463); they are, however, mentioned by Jerome *Ep.* 77.8.1 in a passage concerned with the Hunnish invasions of 395 (cf. n. 2.20-36).

Reference to the Daci (1.310) is apparently nothing more than a reminiscence of Vergil and Lucan (cf. n. 1.310 *a*), for that people had long since ceased to be active as a separate tribe: cf. RE s.v. *Dacia* 1975.

Aside from their mention by Claudian, the Bastarnae do not appear in any source dealing with the history of the Fourth Century: cf. Schmidt (1934) 95. However, since the defeat of this people is one of the earliest military victories with which Claudian credits Stilicho (cf. Seeck [1913] 270 f.) we may be reasonably certain that their mention in CS 1.96 corresponds to an actual fact. Moreover, if we except a mere listing of their name by Ov. *Tr.* 2.198, there is nothing in the poetic tradition which might have suggested the inclusion of the Bastarnae. Perhaps Claudian assimilated to the Ovidian name the actual appellation of some barbarian tribe which sounded similar.

The importance given to the Goths in Claudian's account (they are listed in first place both in 1.308 and in CS 1.94; cf. also 1.316 and 1.319), and the mention of *foedera* (CS. 1.115: cf. Stein-Palanque [1959] 195) seem to obviate any doubt that this people was actually involved in the events in question.

This leaves the Sarmatae, the Alani, the Geloni, and the Huni. Unlike the Massagetae and the Daci, these cannot be dismissed with confidence as mere poetic ornaments, for all are mentioned elsewhere as active in the closing years of the Fourth Century; cf. Amm. 31.16.3, 31.2.14; Zos. 4.16 f., 25 f., 35; McGovern (1939) 370, 373–75 (on the Alani and the Huni). On the other hand, Claudian may be following Vergil, Lucan, Statius, and Silius in naming the first three peoples (cf. n. 1.310 *a*, n. 1.312 f., n. 1.312 *c*, n. 1.313 *a*), and may have included the Huns merely so as to open the way for the striking ethnography which he gives (1.323–31). The question of the actual participation of these four peoples in the events under discussion seems to be insoluble, and both Stein and Schmidt leave the matter open: Schmidt (1934) 424, "Goten, Bastarnen und andere Völker von der Donau," and ftn. 1; Stein-Palanque (1959) 194, "des Goths et d'autres Barbares." On the Alani, Huni, Massagetae, and Sarmatae, cf. Junge (1939) s.vv., 113–15; Minns (1913).

1.308 *d* Histrum: on the metaphorical use of river-names for peoples, cf. n. 1.293 *c*.

1.308 *e* receptat: for this word in a pejorative sense, cf. Tac. *Ann.* 3.60 complebantur templa pessimis servitiorum; eodem subsidio ... suspecti ... capitalium criminum receptabantur; Flor. *Epit.* 1.45.9 (= 3.10.9) Nec Rhenus ergo immunis; nec enim fas erat ut liber esset receptator hostium atque defensor.

1.309 f. suas ... relliquias: i.e. the survivors of his oppressive policies as already represented, 1.220–58; cf. Verg. *A.* 1.30 Troas, reliquias Danaum atque immitis Achilli, 3.87.

1.310 *a* Mixtis descendit Sarmata Dacis: cf. Verg. *G.* 2.497 coniurato descendens Dacus ab Istro; Luc. 3.94 f. iuncto Sarmata velox / Pannonio Dacisque Getes admixtus (and n. 1.308 *c*).

1.310 *b* Mixtis ... Dacis: for *mixtus* in agreement with an ablative element in the expression of a mixture, probably to be construed as an ablative absolute, cf. Verg. *Ecl.* 10.55 mixtis lustrabo Maenala Nymphis; Luc. 3.518 senes mixtis armavit ephebis.

1.310 *c* Sarmata: cf. IE 2.338 feriat si Sarmata portas; FH 4.14 f.; Amm. 17.12.1–3, 31.4.12; RE s.v. *Sarmatae* 2547–50; McGovern (1939) 462 f. Cf. also n. 1.308 *c*.

1.311 f. qui — Massagetes: cf. Sen. *Oed.* 470 lactea Massagetes qui pocula sanguine miscet; Stat. *Ach.* 1.307 f. lactea Massagetae ... pocula fuscant / sanguine; Sil. 3.360 f.; cf. also Verg. *G.* 3.461–63; Luc. 3.282 f., and n. 1.308 *c*.

1.312 f. Massagetes ... Gelonus: for the coupling of these two peoples, cf. Luc. 3.283 Massagetes ... volucresque Geloni.

1.312 *a* caesam ... bibens Maeotin Alanus: cf. Text. Comm. *ad loc.*; n. 1.375.

1.312 *b* bibens Maeotin: for expressions of this type denoting a people's geographical location, cf. PO 37 f. si quis ... / nascentem, te, Nile, bibit; Verg. *A.* 7.715 qui Tiberim ... bibunt: Luc. 8.213 f.; Stat. *Theb.* 1.686; TLL s.v. *bibo* 1964.39–66 (cf. n. 1.185 *a*). For a variation, cf. 2.111–14.

1.312 *c* Alanus: cf. CS 1.109 terrisonus stridor venientis Alani; n. 1.308 *d*. Cf. also 2.271 impacatis ... Alanis; Luc. 8.223 duros aeterni Martis Alanos; Amm. 31.2.12–25; RE s.v. *Alani* 1282 f.; McGovern (1939) 40, 362–64, 370–77, 463.

1.313 *a*: cf. Verg. *G.* 2.115 pictos ... Gelonos (Serv. *ad loc.* stigmata habentes). On the tattooing of the Geloni, cf. RE s.v. *Geloni* 1018.

1.313 *b* Gelonus: cf. CS 1.110 (in a list of those who could not subdue Stilicho) non falce Gelonus; n. 1.308 *c*. Cf. also Amm. 31.2.14; RE s.v. *Geloni* 1017 f.

1.314–20 Vetat — pugnas: on Theodosius' lenient policy toward the Goths, which Claudian attributes in this instance to Rufinus' influence, cf. Fargues (1933a) 75, Stein-Palanque (1959) 193–95. Schmidt (1934) 424 accepts Claudian's claim that Rufinus influenced Theodosius to restrain Stilicho from further action against the barbarians, and suggests that Rufinus may have been prompted by a desire to block Stilicho's aggrandizement. Cf. Mazzarino (1942) 256, ftn. 1; 254 f., ftn. 3. Cf. also n. 1.306–53, sects. b and d. For an apparent later reference to Rufinus' alleged interference here, cf. 2.235 f. Semperne Getis discordia nostra / proderit?

1.314 Vetat ille domari: cf. Text. Comm. *ad loc.*; also Stat. *Theb.* 6.529 (Neptune keeps Arion from defeat) vetat aequoreus vinci pater.

1.315 innectit ... moras: for the verb, cf. Verg. *A.* 4.51 (Anna urges Dido to delay Aeneas' departure) causas ... innecte morandi (and Pease [1935] *ad loc.*); Stat. *Theb.* 5.743 (a prayer for a further delay in hostilities) plures innectere pergas, / Phoebe, moras. For a kindred verb in official language, cf. Cod. Theod. 2.29.2 (cf. n. 1.179 f. *a*, para. 2) si ... moras nectent.

1.316 *a*: for these victories of Stilicho's in 391 and 392, cf. CS 1.102 f. *turmas equitum peditumque catervas / hostilesque globos . . . prosternis*; n. 1.306–53.

1.316 *b* **tua:** on the apostrophe, cf. n. 1.273–84.

1.317 ulta — letum: for Stilicho's action to avenge the slaughter of Promotus by barbarians, cf. CS 1.95 f. *saeva Promoti caede tumentes / Bastarnas una . . . delere ruina*; cf. n. 1.308 *d*. Cf. also Int. 10, where I did not represent Claudian's statement quite accurately; I should have written ". . . he was prevented by Rufinus from completing his vengeance."

1.317 f. pars — capi: for this phase of Stilicho's campaign, cf. CS 1.107 f. *milia . . . / finibus exiguae vallis conclusa tenebas*; n. 1.306–53, sect. a.

318–20 impius — pugnas: for Rufinus' alleged intervention, cf. CS 1.112–14 *Extincti . . . forent penitus, ni more maligno / falleret Augustas occultus proditor aures / . . . strictumque retunderet ensem*; n. 1.314–20.

1.318 facilis . . . capi: cf. IE 2.275 f. *urbes / . . . faciles . . . capi*; Luc. 2.656 *Roma capi facilis*.

1.319 *a* **proditor imperii:** for this and kindred words applied to Rufinus, cf. 2.50–53 *Imperium . . . proditor . . . vertit*, CS 1.113 *occultus proditor*, BP 517 *proditio*.

1.319 *b* **coniuratus . . . Getarum:** the use of the substantive *coniuratus* in the singular is cited as exceptional in TLL s.v. *coniuro* 341.37 f., but cf. Cic. *Sul.* 31.88 *coniurati et consceleratI et proditoris filius*. More exceptional is the use of the genitive denoting those with whom the *coniuratus* is allied. I have been unable to find a single parallel among the citations in TLL s.v. *coniuro* or elsewhere. Despite this fact, I believe that Birt (1892) 440 s.v. *Getae*, TLL s.v. *coniuro* 341.37 f., Platnauer (1922) *ad loc.*, and Axelson (1944) 24 are right in construing *Getarum* wih *coniuratus* (against Koenig [1808], followed by Crépin [1933], who took it with *pugnas*): cf. CM 30.233–35 *Rufino meditante nefas, cum quaereret artes / in ducis exitium coniuratosque foveret / contra pila Getas*; cf. also 2.72–85.

1.321–31: on the Huns, cf. Amm. 31.2.1–12; Zos. 4.20.3; RE s.v. *Hunni* 2583–2615 (esp. 2583 f., 2601, 2614); Bury (1923) 101–4; Bury (1928) 51; Schmidt (1934) 249–52; Schuster (1940); Stein-Palanque

(1959) 188. The long-favored identification of the Huns with the Hiung-nu (Hsiung-nu) of Chinese history was challenged by Maenchen-Helfen (1945), and is rejected by Altheim (1959) 1.369, at least "wie sie bisher meist vertreten wurde." Maenchen-Helfen (1945) 234 holds that Claudian's description is largely based upon Ammianus' discourse, which in turn, he says, was apparently based upon Trogus Pompeius' description of the Scythians. Cf. also Maenchen-Helfen (1955) 393–95. On the Huns as equestrian bowmen, cf. n. 2.80.

1.321 Hunorum ... opem: on the Huns as Stilicho's opponents, cf. CS 1.110 vaga Chunorum feritas; n. 1.306–53, sect. c; n. 1.308 d. For an earlier mention of Huns as associated with Goths, cf. Amm. 31.16.3 Gothi Hunis Alanisque permixti, nimium bellicosis et fortibus. Axelson (1944) 24 strangely takes *Hunorum* as equivalent to a dative: i.e. Rufinus desired to render assistance *to* the Huns; quite the reverse; he is alleged to have favored delay until he could put the help of the Huns at the Goths' disposal. Cf. Axelson's citations of Birt's index, which he seems not to have understood.

1.322 a invisis ... castris: for this encampment, cf. CS 1.94 f. Visos in plaustra ... / reppulit (cf. n. 2.126–29), 106–8 tot barbara ... / milia iam pridem miseram vastantia Thracen / finibus exiguae vallis conclusa tenebas.

1.322 b coniungere: for the present infinitive of a future action, cf. 2.450 qui Sidonio velari credidit ostro, IE 2.319 (the barbarian will not submit to Eutropius) se ... servire negat, BP 81 f., and Schroff (1927) *ad loc.*; Hofmann-Szantyr (1965) 357 f.

1.323 a Est genus: as a beginning of an ethnic description, this resembles *est locus* for a topographical: cf. n. 1.123; for the rhythm and sound of the entire verse, cf. Ov. *Met.* 8.788, there quoted.

1.323 b ortus: i.e. *solis ortus*; cf. 2.104 (Stilicho moves East) castra movens Phoebi properabat ad ortus.

1.324 a gelidum Tanain: cf. RP 2.65 f. (the Amazons range widely) rigentem / ... Tanaim fregere; Verg. G. 4.517 hyperboreas glacies Tanaimque nivalem. Cf. Amm. 31.2.13 amnem Tanaim ... qui Asiam terminat ab Europa; RE s.v. *Tanais* 2165 f., s.v. *Phasis* 1888 f. The Tanais is the modern Don: cf. RE s.v. *Tanais* 2164.50–68.

1.324 b quo non famosius ullum: cf. Verg. A. 4.174 Fama, malum qua non aliud velocius ullum.

1.324 c famosius: cf. Text. Comm. *ad loc.*; Fargues (1936) 371. Cameron (1968a) 390 f. argues persuasively for *animosius*, but I cannot quite share his complete confidence that this is what Claudian wrote. He bases his argument on two grounds: (1) that the adjective in question need not have been unfavorable, since Claudian was not writing an invective against the Huns; (2) that to reject *animosius* would leave the Huns without an epithet for their ferocity, a prime point in Ammianus' account. (1) Though the Huns are not Claudian's main target, they are allies of the arch-traitor Rufinus and of his predatory Goths, cheek by jowl with them (1.322 invisis mox se coniungere castris); this surely entitles them to a bit of vituperation *en passant*; (2) in a passage in which, in Cameron's view, (1968a) 391, Claudian never makes the same point twice, he *does* refer to the ferocity of the Huns' attacks in 1.330 f. acerrima . . . / mobilitas; not merely the tactics, *mobilitas* and *recursus* (1.330 f.), but the nature of the *mobilitas*, namely *acerrima* (cf. Amm. 31.2.8 cum caede vasta). For *acer* denoting ferocity, cf. TLL s.v. 357.74–358.5. Cf. also the quotation which Cameron gives from Sen. *Dial.* 3, with the doublet *animosius . . . acrius*, and the same doublet in V. Max. 2.7.1 acrem . . . et animosam Numantiam. If any single stroke is missing, and needed to complete the picture, it is a general word of contempt for the Huns.

1.325 Turpes habitus: cf. Amm. 31.2.5 f. Indumentis operiuntur linteis vel ex pellibus silvestrium murum consarcinatis; nec alia illis domestica vestis est, alia forensis. Sed semel obsoleti coloris tunica collo inserta, non ante deponitur aut mutatur, quam diuturna carie in pannulos diffluxerit defrustata. Galeris incurvis capita tegunt, hirsuta crura coriis munientes haedinis, eorumque calcei formulis nullis aptati vetant incedere gressibus liberis; 10 taetra . . . vestimenta.

1.325 f. obscaena . . . visu corpora: cf. Amm. 31.2.2 f. prodigiose deformes et pandi, ut bipedes existimes bestias, vel quales in commarginandis pontibus effigiati stipites dolantur incompte. In hominum autem figura, licet insuavi. . . .

1.326 mens — labori: cf. Amm. 31.2.4 pruinas famem sitimque perferre ab incunabulis adsuescunt; 7 perrumpunt quicquid inciderit.

1.327 a praeda — Ceres: cf. Amm. 31.2.3 ita victu sunt asperi, ut neque igni neque saporatis indigeant cibis, sed radicibus herbarum agrestium, et semicruda cuiusvis pecoris carne vescantur, quam inter femora sua equorumque terga subsertam, fotu calefaciant (cf. Maenchen-Helfen [1945] 233); 10 Nemo apud eos arat nec stivam aliquando contigit.

1.327 *b* frontem ... secari: cf. Amm. 31.2.2 quoniam ab ipsis nascendi primitiis infantum ferro sulcantur altius genae, ut pilorum vigor tempestivus emergens, corrugatis cicatricibus hebetetur, senescunt imberbes; Maenchen-Helfen (1945) 235.

1.327 *c* frontem: =*faciem*: for the fact, cf. Amm. 31.2.2 sulcantur ... genae; Jordanes, *Get.* 24.128 facies ... sulcata. For the use of the word *frons* in this sense, cf. FH 4.8 f. (the gatherer of honey must not fear for his face) nec spoliat favos / si fronti caveat; Min. Fel. 22.5 Ianus ... frontes duas gestat; TLL s.v. *frons* 1359.4–14.

1.327 f. secari ... et ... iurare: for the shift in voice, cf. 2.431 f. iuvat ire ... / pressaque ... vestigia ... tingui; Verg. *A.* 3.61 linqui ... hospitium et dare ... Austros; Luc. 9.687 f. iussit non laedere terras / et parci populis.

1.328 *a* ludus: cf. CS 3.156 f. (the *pax Romana* makes distant voyages mere sport) cernere Thylen / lusus et horrendos ... penetrare recessus; Verg. *A.* 9.606 flectere ludus equos et spicula tendere cornu; Stat. *Ach.* 2.155 f. (=441 f. Queck).

1.328 *b* occisos ... parentes: the practice of geronticide is imputed to the Massagetae by Herodotus (1.216) and to other Eastern barbarians by various authors: to the Iazyges by Valerius Flaccus (6.122–28, 282 f., 289–91, 308–10); to the Scythians by Sextus Empiricus (*P.* 3.24.210). Claudian seems simply to have transferred the stock accusation to the Huns: cf. Maenchen-Helfen (1945) 237 f.; Cameron (1968a) 391.

1.328 *c* pulchrum: cf. BP 91 f. ignoscere pulchrum / iam misero; Verg. *A.* 2.317 pulchrum ... mori ... in armis.

1.328 *d* iurare parentes: on the transitive use of *iuro*, cf. n. 1.228 *b*. For the idea, cf. V. Fl. 6.287–91, where one of the Iazyges invokes the shade of the father whom, according to their custom, he has slain (cf. n. 1.328 *b*).

1.329 f. Nec — equis: cf. Amm. 31.2.6. ad pedestres parum accommodati sunt pugnas, verum equis prope affixi ... et muliebriter eisdem non numquam insidentes, funguntur muneribus consuetis. Ex ipsis quivis in hac natione pernox et perdius emit et vendit, cibumque sumit et potum, et inclinatus cervici angustae iumenti, in altum soporem... effunditur. Bruère (1964) 229 sees here an echo of Luc. 3.198, quoted in n. 1.329 c.

1.329 a nubigenas: for this term applied to the Centaurs, cf. Verg. A. 7.674 f. duo nubigenae ... / ... Centauri; Ov. Met. 12.211, 541; Luc. 6.386 f.; Schol. in Hom. Il. 1.268 (= 1.40 f. Dindorf) Ἰξίων ... Ἥρας ... ἠράσθη. Ζεὺς δὲ βουλόμενος αὐτὸν δοκιμάσαι εἰ τῷ ὄντι τολμᾷ ποιῆσαι τοῦτο, νεφέλην ἀπεικάσας Ἥρᾳ παρέκλινεν αὐτῷ. ὁ δὲ μιγεὶς τῇ νεφέλῃ, ὡσανεὶ τῇ Ἥρᾳ, ἔσχε παῖδα Κένταυρον, ἀφ' οὗ τὸ τῶν Κενταύρων γένος; D.S. 4.69 f.; Roscher (1937) s.v. *Kentauren* 1033 f., 1063.

1.329 b duplex natura: cf. Lucr. 5.878 f. Sed neque Centauri fuerunt, nec... / esse queunt duplici natura; Ov. Met. 12.502 (a Centaur speaks) fortissima rerum / in nobis duplex natura animalia iunxit.

1.329 c biformes: cf. Ov. Met. 9.121 (to a Centaur) Nesse biformis, Am. 2.12.19 f.; Luc. 3.198 (the legendary Centaurs) populum Pholoe mentita biformem. Cf. also 4H 542 f. (Honorius excels in horsemanship) Non te... /... ipsi poterunt aequare bimembres.

1.330 cognatis ... equis: cf. 2.359 (of the *cataphractarii*, armored men riding armored horses) credas simulacra moveri / ferrea cognatoque viros spirare metallo.

1.330 f. acerrima — recursus: cf. Amm. 31.2.8 Ut... ad pernicitatem sunt leves et repentini, ita subito de industria dispersi incessunt, et incomposita acie cum caede vasta discurrunt, nec invadentes vallum, nec castra inimica pilantes, prae nimia rapiditate cernuntur.

1.331 a mobilitas: = *velocitas*; cf. n. 1.90.

1.331 b insperati ... recursus: for this tactic in Roman equestrian exercise, cf. 4H 539–41 (to Honorius) Cum vectaris equo simulacraque Martia ludis, / quis mollis sinuare fugas ... / acrior aut subitos melior flexisse recursus?

1.332–53: *Stilicho girds himself to stem the barbarian tide; he prays to Mars, who comes to fight at his side.* On these verses as part of a *laus Stilichonis*, cf. n. 1.259–300, para. 1.

1.332 f. Quos ... contra ... tendis: for *tendo* of hostile movement, cf. Verg. A. 9.794–96 (a baffled lion) neque terga / ira dare aut virtus patitur, nec tendere contra / ille ... potis est; 768 (Lynceus attacks) Lyncea tendentem contra (and Henry [1873] 3.878 f.); Sil. 7.496 praeceps tendebat in hostem, 6.335, 8.37, 17.571.

1.332 *a* Quos: not merely the Huns, but the other barbarians: cf. 1.322 invisis ... se coniungere castris, and CS 1.109-11, 3H 147 f.; n. 1.306-53, sect. c.

1.332 *b* spumantis ... Hebri: cf. Stat. *Theb.* 9.438 spumifer ... Hebrus.

1.333 *a* tendis: on the apostrophe, cf. n. 1.273-84.

1.333-39 sic — quercu: for a *votum* to Mars on the eve of battle, cf. Ov. *Fast.* 5.571-77 ille manus tendens, hinc stante milite iusto / hinc coniuratis, talia dicta dedit: /// Mars ades, et satia scelerato sanguine ferrum / stetque favor causa pro meliore tuus! / Templa feres, et, me victore, vocaberis Ultor. Cf. also Sil. 10.553; Appel (1909) 8, 56; Wissowa (1912) 383, ftn. 2.

On the emphasis placed by Claudian upon Mars as a guardian of Rome, cf. Steinbeiss (1936) 16; on the actual worship of Mars in the army of the Empire, cf. Domaszewski (1895) 33-36; RE s.v. *Mars* 1929.

The location of the battle, in Thrace at the river Hebrus (1.332, 338; cf. Stein-Palanque [1959] 194) and the fact that it was fought against the Goths, whom Claudian calls *Getae* (cf. n. 1.308 *b*), make the present prayer to Mars (contrast 3H 33-38 to Jupiter) and his participation in the battle (1.340-53) especially appropriate:

(1) Thrace: IE 2.103 f. Gradivus ... / arva ... repetebat Thracia; *Hom. Il.* 13.301 (Ares and Phobos) τὼ μὲν ἄρ' ἐκ Θρῄκης ... θωρήσσεσθον; Verg. *A.* 3.13 f. Terra ... Mavortia ... / (Thraces arant), 12.335; Man. 4.691; Roscher (1937) s.v. *Ares* 482; RE s.v. *Ares* 642-44.

(2) Hebrus: cf. PO 122 f. (Gradivus') cornus ... / ... ferit splendoribus Hebrum; Verg. *A.* 12.331 f. Qualis apud gelidi cum flumina concita Hebri / sanguineus Mavors clipeo increpat; Stat. *Theb.* 9.438 f.

(3) Getae: cf. CM 53.75-77 Mavors ... / ... impellit equos, quibus ille ... / ... Getas turbare solet; Verg. *A.* 3.35 Gradivum ... patrem, Geticis qui praesidet arvis; Stat. *Theb.* 3.220 f.; Sil. 17.488 f.

That Claudian represents Stilicho, who was at least a nominal Christian (cf. Seeck [1913] 297-99, 560; Mommsen [1903] 115, ftn. 2; Fargues [1933a] 155-57; Mazzarino [1942] 231, ftn. 1) as praying to a pagan god, is in accord with Claudian's custom, throughout his major poems, of ignoring the existence of Christianity. Cf. 3H 33–38, where Theodosius prays to Jupiter; Int. 22; n. 2.2 f., para. 2; Fargues (1933a) 154.

1.333 *b* **ante tubas aciemque:** cf. Stat. *Theb.* 6.147 (Eurydice mourns her sons before the battle commences) ante tubas ferrumque; cf. also CS 1.192 (Stilicho subdues the Germans by the mere terror of his name) Ante tubam nobis audax Germania servit; Verg. *A.* 11.424 (Turnus spurns Drances' cowardice) Cur ante tubam tremor occupat artus? Cf. also 2.195. On the sounding of the trumpet as an epic theme, cf. Miniconi (1951) 166.

1.333 *c* **aciem:** = *proelium*; cf. CS 1.238 f. Acie nec iam pulsare rebelles, / sed vinclis punire licet; Verg. *A.* 6.829 quantas acies stragemque ciebunt; TLL s.v. *acies* 409.41–81.

1.334–39: on direct quotation in IR, cf. n. 1.45–65.

1.334–36: seu (*quater*): cf. CS 3.208–11, EH 300 f.; Stat. *Theb.* 1.696–701, *Silv.* 3.1.23–25. The mention of various localities in connection with a god seems related to the similar practice in regard to appellations, as seen in Hor. *Saec.* 14–16 Ilithyia... / sive tu Lucina probas vocari / seu Genitalis (cf. Norden [1913] 144–47); cf. also Stat. *Theb.* 1.696–719, where several localities (1.696–701) as well as several appellations (1.715–19) are given; Schwenn (1927) 60. Bruère (1964) 229 f. sees in this prayer an echo of several passages in Lucan: beside 3.198, already cited (n. 1.329 *c*), he lists Luc. 1.679 f. video Pangaea nivosis / cana iugis latosque Haemi sub rupe Philippos; 7.449 f. petet Pholoen... / inmeritaeque nemus Rhodopes.

1.334 *a* **procumbis:** for Mars depicted as reclining, cf. PO 120 procubat... Getico Gradivus in arvo; 2 Pr.17 f. Fertur et indomitus tandem post proelia Mavors / lassa per Odrysias fundere membra nives; Stat. *Silv.* 4.2.46 f. Rhodopes in valle recumbit / dimissis Gradivus equis.

1.334 *b* **Haemo:** cf. 1.340 scopulis... nivalibus Haemi, IE 2.106 (Mars) vertice constitit Haemi; Stat. *Theb.* 12.733 Haemi de vertice Mavors / impulerit currus; 7.42; Sil. 11.464 Mavortius Haemus.

1.335 Rhodope: cf. 4H 526 flumina laverunt puerum Rhodopeia Martem; Stat. *Silv.* 4.2.46 f., quoted in n. 1.334 *b*.

1.335 f. remige — Athos: for Xerxes' piercing of Mt. Athos, cf. 2.122 f. Bruère (1964) 229 compares Luc. 2.676 f. cum vela ratisque /

in medium deferret Athon. Cf. also Hdt. 7.22–24; Cic. *Fin.* 2.33.112 Xerxes, cum tantis classibus ... Athone perfosso ... terram navigasset; RE s.v. *Athos* 2067; CAH 4.269. On the popularity of this and related themes with the rhetoricians, cf. n. 2.121–23.

1.336 Athos: on a possible connection of Mt. Athos with the worship of Ares, cf. RE s.v. *Ares* 642.53–64.

1.336 f. nigris ilicibus: for the word *niger* applied to this tree, cf. Verg. *A.* 9.381 ilice nigra, *Ecl.* 6.54; André (1941) 132, 140.

1.337 Pangaea: for this Thracian mountain, cf. IE 2.103–5 Gradivus ... / arva ... repetebat Thracia curru; / subsidunt Pangaea rotis; Stat. *Theb.* 6.665 f. clipeus Mavortis ... / luce mala Pangaea ferit; Luc. 1.679 f., quoted in n. 1.334–36.

1.338 Thracas ... tuos: cf. n. 1.333–39, para. 2.

1.339 vestita — quercu: for Mars' trophies in the form of decorated oak-trees, cf. 1.345 f.; CS 2.371 f. cruentum / ditibus exuviis ... quercum; Verg. *A.* 11.5–11, esp. 5–8 Ingentem quercum decisis undique ramis / constituit tumulo fulgentiaque induit arma, / Mezenti ducis exuvias, tibi, magne, tropaeum, / Bellipotens, 10.541 f.; Stat. *Theb.* 2.704–12. Cf. also Var. *Bimarcus* (ap. Non. 55 s.v. *tropaei*) spolia capta, fixa in stipitibus, appellantur tropaea; RE s.v. τρόπαιον 663 f.

1.340–53: on the intervention of warrior-gods as an epic theme, cf. Miniconi (1951) 169.

1.340 a Audiit illa: cf. Verg. *G.* 4.7 audit ... vocatus Apollo; Ziegler (1905) 65–67. Cf. also n. 1.65 *b*, on the use of phrases to indicate the resumption of the narrative after a direct quotation.

1.340 b pater: cf. IE 2.108 pater; Verg. *A.* 3.35 Gradivum ... patrem; Carter (1902) 65 f.; Steinbeiss (1936) 16.

1.341 surgit: on reclining Mars, cf. n. 1.334 *b*.

1.341–44 hortatur — manus: for descriptions of Mars (Ares) and his retinue, cf. CS 2.367–76; IE 2.103–11; PO 119–23; Hom. *Il.* 13.298–300, 15.119 f.; Verg. *A.* 8.700–3, 12.331–36; Stat. *Theb.* 3.420–31, 7.64–74, 105–16; Sil. 4.430–39; V. Fl. 3.89 f.

1.342–48: on direct quotation in IR, cf. n. 1.45–65, esp. sect. 7.

1.342 a galeam: cf. Sil. 4.432 f. (the helmet of Mars) galeam ... deorum / haud ulli facilem. On the helmet as an epic theme, cf. Miniconi (1951) 164.

1.342 b Bellona: for Bellona as a member of Mars' retinue, cf.

CS 2.371–73 currum ... patris Bellona ... // praecedit; IE 2.109–11; Stat. *Theb.* 7.72–74 regit atra iugales / sanguinea Bellona manu longaque fatigat / cuspide; Sil. 4.439; RE s.v. *Bellona* 256 f. (at 256.60 read "Amm. 31.1.1"); Roscher (1937) s.v. *Bellona* 775 f.

1.342 f. nexus ... rotarum tende: Barth (1650) *ad loc.* suggests that the word *nexus* here may refer to one or the other of two items which Poll. *Onomast.* 1.145 f. glosses in his enumeration of parts of the chariot:

(1) The παραξόνιον, "linch-pin," τὸ ... κωλῦον ἐκπίπτειν τὸν τρόχον, ἐμπηγνύμενον τῷ ἄξονι, παραξόνιον· ἢ ὡς Γοργίας, ἐπίβολος, ἢ ὡς Ἐρατοσθένης, ἔμβολος (cf. Phryn. *PS* s.v. παραξόνια [= 100.5–7 de Borries]). The linch-pin which figures in the tale of Pelops' victory over Oenomaus is called ἔμβολος in Pherecyd. fr. 37a (=FGrHist 1.72.27), *obex* in Sid. Apoll. *Carm.* 2.492, and *clavus* in Hyg. *Fab.* 84. As Burmann (1760) *ad loc.* points out, this first suggestion of Barth's is valueless, since the verb *tendo* is not appropriate to a pin or peg.

(2) The ἐμβολοδέτης "linch-pin-binder," ὁ ... τοῦ παραξονίου δεσμός. Though this second suggestion is not further developed by Barth, it may perhaps point to the correct interpretation.

There is apparently no evidence, either archaeological or literary, bearing upon the structure or material of the ἐμβολοδέτης. A παραξόνιον similar to a modern cotter-pin may be seen in one of the reliefs on the column of Marcus Aurelius: cf. Petersen-Domaszewski-Calderini (1896) 85 and Plate 102 (forward wheel of wagon in left-hand photograph). A παραξόνιον of this type required no δεσμός, since its end was bifurcated, and was spread to keep the pin from dropping out. In a different section of the same monument we see another παραξόνιον, apparently in the form of a solid wedge or spike: *ibid.* 58, and Plate 22 (wheel of *carroballista* in left-hand photograph). It was presumably for a παραξόνιον of this general type that the δεσμός, the ἐμβολοδέτης, might be used (though none appears in this instance), especially if the chariot was intended for rough usage. E. Saglio, in DS s.v. *currus* 1635 (cf. Scheffer [1671] 39, 41), suggests that the ἐμβολοδέτης was a second and smaller pin, thrust through the end of the παραξόνιον. No such part can be discerned in the elaborate device which Saglio pictures in Fig. 2202. Nor does anything in Pollux indicate that the ἐμβολοδέτης is a pin or peg. Etymologically, both δεσμός and -δέτης seem to suggest tying (δέω) rather than pegging (ἐμβάλλω, ἐμπήγνυμι).

On the slender basis of (1) Phrynichus' use of the word δεσμός and of the termination -δέτης, and of (2) Claudian's use of *tendo* here (cf. Verg. G. 4.399 f. vincula capto / tende), I venture to suggest that Claudian's *nexus* were straps or thongs used to secure the παραξόνιον against the possibility of working loose. The fastening of such δεσμοί would be one of the final steps in assembling the chariot for combat: cf. PO 81 hic ligat axe rotas; cf. also Hom. *Il.* 5.722, and Buchholz (1871) 2.224. A pin from a Thracian chariot, pictured in Seure (1925) 407, Fig. 1, though apparently used for another purpose, is provided with rings which Seure believes were used to hold retaining-straps such as I have in mind: "L'ensemble était sans doute ... maintenu par deux lanières, ou mieux par deux queues de rats, insérées à bloc dans les deux premiers anneaux latéraux."

1.343 *a* Pavor ... Formido: for comparable allegorical figures in Mars' retinue, cf. CS 2.373 licior ... Metus cum fratre Pavore, 375 f. propius ... iugales / Formido ... vibrat ... securim; Hom. *Il.* 15.119 f. ἵππους κέλετο Δεῖμόν τε Φόβον τε / ζευγνύμεν, 13.298 f. Ἄρης πολεμόνδε μέτεισι, / τῷ δὲ Φόβος φίλος υἱὸς ἅμα ... / ἕσπετο; Verg. *A.* 12.335 f. circum ... atrae Formidinis ora / Iraeque Insidiaeque, dei comitatus, aguntur; Stat. *Theb.* 3.425, 7.108 f.; Roscher (1937) s.v. *Deimos*; s.v. *Mars* 2423.

1.343 *b* rapidos: cf. Text. Comm. *ad loc.*; Fargues (1936) 371; Bieler (1957) 259; also Ov. *Fast.* 1.858 Mars ... citos ... urget equos.

1.344 Festinas urgete manus: on the resultative-predicate use of the adjective, cf. n. 1.1 *b*.

1.345 f. qui — cristas: cf. n. 1.339. Note esp. Verg. *A.* 11.8 cristas.

1.347 f. Communes — canunt: for the blaring of the *lituus* as a signal for battle, cf. CM 30.213 f. saeva vocantibus arma / ... lituis; Ov. *Fast.* 3.216 lituus pugnae signa daturus erat; Kromayer-Veith (1928) 323 f., 517 f.; RE s.v. *lituus* 804 f.

1.348 iuncto ... curru: for *currum iungo* of yoking a chariot, cf. PO 77 (Roma's chariot is made ready) Famuli currum iunxere, 81 f. Hic ligat axe rotas: hic sub iuga ferrea nectit / cornipedes rigidisque docet servire lupatis; Ov. *Fast.* 2.858 Mars ... citos iunctis curribus urget equos.

1.349–53: on the use of imagery here, cf. Christiansen (1969) 17.

1.349 *a* **Sic fatus:** on the use of phrases indicating the end of direct quotation, cf. n. 1.65 *b*.

1.349 *b* **insiluit:** on another *salio* compound connected with Mars, cf. Serv. on Verg. *A.* 3.35 Gradivum ... θοῦρον Ἄρηα, id est exsilientem in proelia.

1.350 f. Stilicho ... Gradivus ... pares: cf. Sil. 11.580 f. (Hannibal is the equal of Mars) germanus in armis / ille tuus par Gradivo. Cf. also n. 2 Pr.17–20.

1.350 *a* **Gradivus:** on this epithet for Mars, cf. RE s.v. *Gradivus* 1688 f.; Carter (1902) 64 f.

1.350 *b* **turmas:** for this term referring to troops in general, cf. 2.105 Gallica discretis Eoaque robora turmis, 343 salutatum reduces ... turmas; Luc. 9.400 equitem peditum praecedere turmas.

1.351 *a* **mole:** for this term applied to a mighty man, cf. Verg. *A.* 12.161 ingenti mole Latinus; Sil. 15.337 (Marcellus) moles illa viri.

1.351 *b* **stat:** cf. Verg. *A.* 6.779 stant vertice cristae; Ov. *Met.* 6.672.

1.351 f. cassis ... hirsuta iubis: for horse-hair crests, cf. Verg. *A.* 10.869 aere caput fulgens cristaque hirsutus equina.

1.352 sidereis ... iubis: for Mars' gleaming crest, cf. CM 53.78 f. nitentes / ... iubae, IE 2.108 f. cristis ... micantem / ... galeam. For *sidereus = nitens* cf. Verg. *A.* 12.167 sidereo flagrans clipeo; V. Fl. 8.122 f. (the Golden Fleece) villis ... comantem / sidereis ... pellem, 2.104. Particular reference is probably intended here to the gleam of a comet: cf. Verg. *A.* 10.270–73 cristis ... a vertice flamma / funditur ... / non secus ac ... si quando ... cometae / ... rubent; Sil. 1.460 f., 463 f. For *sidus = cometes*, cf. also Luc. 1.528 f. crinem ... timendi / sideris ... cometen; Plin. *Nat.* 2.23.92 cometes ... terrificum sidus. Platnauer (1922), apparently following the far-fetched interpretation of Gesner (1759), *sidereus = versus sidera erectus*, translates "bristling."

1.353 *a* **aestuat:** *= calet*; cf. CM 28.35 (of the sun's rays) radiis potentibus aestuat axis; Verg. *G.* 1.107 exustus ager ... aestuat; Luc. 1.16 dies medius flagrantibus aestuat horis, 9.400; Stat. *Silv.* 2.3.46 f. igne superno / aestuet; for Claudian's use of *aestus = calor* cf. Birt

(1892) 466 s.v. *aestus*. Cf. also Stat. *Theb.* 9.700 pugna / cassis anhela calet. Neither in TLL s.v. *aestus* nor elsewhere have I been able to find a parallel to support the *sudore perfunditur* of Koenig (1808), or the "flash" of Platnauer (1922) as interpretations of *aestuat* here; Crépin (1933) does better with "en est brûlant."

1.353 *b* largo — cornus: cf. Ov. *Fast.* 5.575 Mars . . . satia scelerato sanguine ferrum; Luc. 7.317 quanto satiavit sanguine ferrum; Sil. 4.435, 7.534 f. For *saturo* = *satio*, cf. Verg. *Ecl.* 10.30 nec cytiso saturantur apes nec fronde capellae, *A.* 5.608; V. Fl. 6.647.

1.354–87: *Megaera encounters Justice, and glories in the disorder which her pupil Rufinus has caused. Justice prophesies Rufinus' evil end, and the return of the Golden Age under Honorius.* On the relation of these verses to the ψόγος-pattern, cf. Levy (1946) 63, 65.

1.354 *a* voto: for *votum* denoting the accomplishment of something prayed for, cf. BG 7 f. (the poet can scarcely grasp the reality of Gildo's defeat) manifesta . . . gaudia differt, / dum . . . tanto cunctatur credere voto. Approaching this usage are two occurrences of the word in Ovid: *Ars* 1.671 quantum defuerat pleno . . . voto?, 737 ut voto potiare tuo; cf. also Petr. 11.1 (success in love) fruor votis usque ad invidiam felicibus.

1.354 f. multis . . . luxuriata malis: cf. Ov. *Tr.* 5.1.44 (let Ovid's verse put behind it its reveling in evil) sit semel illa meo luxuriata malo. Cf. also n. 1.25–73, para. 1.

1.354 *b* Megaera: for her previous part in the action, cf. 1.74–172; also n. 1.25–73, para. 2.

1.355 *a* maestam: for this word as giving some slight indication of the outcome of Stilicho's campaign, cf. n. 1.306–53, sect. c.

1.355 *b* arce: as Birt (1892) 474 s.v. *arx* (2) points out, this word denotes a place somewhere on earth, not in the heavens: cf. 1.363 linque homines sortemque meam, pete sidera. For *arx* of a lofty mountain, cf. Ov. *Am.* 3.3.35 Iuppiter igne suos lucos iaculatur et arces; Sen. *Ag.* 562, 566; TLL s.v. *arx* 741.52–742.31. The conversation is evidently thought of as taking place on a height overlooking ravaged Thrace: cf. 1.359 Huc lumina flecte.

1.356 Iustitiam: already spoken of as an adversary of the Furies: 1.55–57; cf. n. 1.55 f.

1.357–67: on direct quotation in this poem, cf. n. 45–65, esp. sect. 7.

1.357–59 En ... ? En ... ?: for this word introducing an emotional interrogation, cf. Verg. *A.* 6.346 En haec promissa fides est?; Ov. *Met.* 15.776 en acui sceleratos cernitis enses?; Stat. *Theb.* 9.514–17; TLL s.v. *en* 545.74–79.

1.357 *a* prisca — saecula: an ironic echo of Allecto's words, 1.51 f. En aurea nascitur aetas, / en proles antiqua redit; cf. n. 1.51 f.

1.357 *b* renovata ... rursus: for *rursus* reinforcing the idea of repetition expressed by the prefix of a verb compounded with *re-*, cf. EH 260 f. rursus / ... redi; FH 3.5 f.; MT 73, 140; CM 30.150; RP 2.195 f.; Verg. *A.* 4.531 rursus resurgens (and Pease [1935] *ad loc.*), 6.750 f., 9.391, *G.* 2.231 f., 480; Ov. *Met.* 3.684 redeunt ... rursus, 7.788, 10.288, *Pont.* 3.5.55, *Tr.* 2.16; Luc. 1.391 rursus redeuntis, 3.262, 5.36 f., 635, 7.719; Stat. *Silv.* 2.5.4 rursus ... reverti; Sil. 7.508 rursus ... referri, 8.96, 14.336 f. For this usage in prose, cf. Caes. *Civ.* 3.93.1 rursus renovato cursu; Apul. *Met.* 3.12 rursum reverterim, 4.18; Hofmann-Szantyr (1965) 798.

1.358 ut rebare: for the expression, cf. Verg. *A.* 10.608 ut rebare. For the thought, cf. 1.55 f. (Allecto speaks) ipsa mihi ... / Iustitia insultat.

1.358 f. nostra — Furiis: an ironic echo of 1.48–51, 58 f.

1.359 f. Huc lumina flecte. Aspice: cf. Verg. *A.* 6.788 Huc geminas nunc flecte acies, hanc aspice gentem. Cf. also Verg. *A.* 4.369 Num lumina flexit? (and Pease [1935] *ad loc.*); Ov. *Met.* 8.864 f. in nullam lumina partem / ... flexi; Luc. 3.4; Stat. *Ach.* 1.795, *Silv.* 5.1.217; Sil. 3.188, 8.139.

1.360 f.: Bruère (1964) 230 compares Luc. 1.24–26 (the devastation caused by the Civil War) quod moenia ... / urbibus Italiae ... / ... iacent, and 3.627 f. (a Roman ship off Massilia is a scene of carnage) strage virum cumulata ratis multoque cruore / plena.

1.362 quantis — hydri: cf. IE 2.110 f. (Bellona combs her snaky locks) pingues pectebat stragibus hydros.

1.363–66: Bruère (1964) 230 compares Luc. 1.53–59 (parts of the heavens to be avoided or to be chosen by the deified Nero).

1.363 *a* Linque — meam: the Fury speaks either (1) as if she were, or identified herself with, one of the three major deities (cf. n. 1.69 *b*) who had partitioned the world among themselves by lot: cf.

RP 2.220 (Minerva to Pluto) Fratris linque domos, alienam desere sortem, CM 30.123 f. (Diana and Minerva) revisunt / aequorei sortem patrui; Sen. Phaed. 1211 f., Her. F. 609; or else (2) as if she herself were an heiress who had received mankind as a bequest (cf. 6H 84 sortem; Liv. 1.34.3 sortem bonorum). The parallelism with RP 2.220 weighs in favor of the interpretation given first.

1.363 b homines sortemque meam: on the explicative -*que*, cf. n. 1.13.

1.363 c pete sidera: Claudian probably has in mind Iustitia's former withdrawal: cf. n. 1.55 f., esp. Arat. Phaen. 133 f. μισήσασα Δίκη κείνων γένος ἀνδρῶν / ἔπταθ' ὑπουρανίη; Hyg. Astr. 2.25 Iustitiam ... iam non potuisse pati amplius et ad sidera evolasse; Ov. Fast. 1.249. Bruère (1964) 230 compares Luc. 1.46 (Nero's deification) astra petes.

1.363 f. notis Autumni ... plagis: for the autumnal tract of the heavens as the abode of Astraea-Iustitia-Virgo, cf. MT 119 (Iustitia) deserit Autumni portas, CS 2.465 autumni maturet germina Virgo (cf. n. 1.55 f.); Man. 2.176 f. nam desinit aestas, / incipit autumnus media sub Virgine utrimque, 266 autumnus Virgine surgit; Housman (1912) Pr. 10 on Man. 2.265-69; Semple (1939) 3 f. On Claudian's interest in the stars, cf. n. 1.55 f., *fin*.

1.364-66 Autumni — Signifer ... gelidae — Librae: for a similar concatenation, cf. MT 119 f. Autumni portas, qua vergit in Austrum / Signifer, et noctis reparant dispendia Chelae (on *Chelae*=*Libra*, cf. cf. RE s.v. *Libra* 118.6-21).

1.364 f. qua vergit in Austrum Signifer: in the direction of the sun's apparent course from the summer to the winter solstice, the boundary between the section of Virgo and that of Libra (Χηλαί, Ζυγός: cf. RE s.v. *Libra* 117.3-65) marks the beginning of the southern hemicycle of the Zodiac (cf. n. 1.365 a): cf. Gem. Elem. Astr. 6.40 f. (=82.19-26 Manitius) ἐν ἓξ ζῳδίοις, Κριῷ Ταύρῳ Διδύμοις Καρκίνῳ Λέοντι Παρθένῳ, ὅπερ ἐστὶν ἡμικύκλιον τοῦ ζῳδιακοῦ κύκλου ἀπὸ Κριοῦ πρώτης μοίρας μέχρι Παρθένου μοίρας τριακοστῆς· βόρειόν ἐστιν.... ἐν τοῖς ἀπολειπομένοις ζῳδίοις, Ζυγῷ Σκορπίῳ Τοξότῃ Αἰγοκέρῳ Ὑδροχόῳ Ἰχθύσιν, ὅπερ ἐστὶ πάλιν ἡμικύκλιον τοῦ ζῳδιακοῦ κύκλου ἀπὸ Ζυγοῦ πρώτης μοίρας μέχρις Ἰχθύων μοίρας τριακοστῆς· νότιόν ἐστι (cf. Manitius' apparatus criticus *ad loc.*); Boll (1898) 7.128.20 f.; Semple (1939) 3 f. The line dividing the Zodiac into northern and southern hemicycles is of course the celestial equator: Gem. *Elem. Astr.* 5.6 (= 44.21 Manitius) ἰσημερινὸς ... κύκλος, Hyg. *Astr.* 1.6 (= 24.20 Bunte) circulus aequinoctialis; RE s.v. *Kykloi* 2322.10–13; cf. also Gem. *Elem. Astr.* 5.51 f. (= 60.25–62.8 Manitius). For the shift of the celestial equator from Hipparchus' time to the present, cf. Bouché-LeClercq (1899) 140 f.

The constellation Virgo extended past its own 30-degree section into the section belonging to Libra, and hence into the southern hemicycle of the Zodiac: cf. Hipparch. 2.1.8 (= 126.13 f. Manitius) ἡ ... Παρθένος ... τῶν Χηλῶν ἐπιλαμβάνει; RE s.v. *Libra* 120.12–15; Bouché-LeClercq (1899) 140 f.

The phrase *qua vergit in Austrum* also appears in 2.348 of terrestrial topography.

1.365 *a* Signifer: for this term for the Zodiac, cf. Cic. *Arat.* 317–19 Zodiacum hunc Graeci vocitant nostrique Latini / orbem signiferum perhibebunt nomine vero, / nam gerit hic volvens bis sex ardentia signa; Censorin. 8.4 Circulus est, ut ferunt, signifer, quem Graeci vocant ζωδιακόν. Cf. also PO 241, MT 120, CS 1.145, CM 51.9; Mayor (1880) on Cic. *N.D.* 2.20.53 signiferum orbem.

1.365 *b* aestivo — Leoni: = CS 3.209.

1.365 *c* aestivo ... Leoni: cf. PO 25 f. fulva Leonis / ira; Arat. *Phaen.* 148 f. Λέων ... / ἔνθα ... ἠελίοιο θερείταταί εἰσι κέλευθοι; Cic. *N.D.* 2.43.110 (= Arat. frag. 23) magnu' Leo tremulam quatiens e corpore flammam; RE s.v. *Leo* 1981 f.

1.365 f. sedes vicina Leoni ... confinia Librae: cf. Hipparch. 2.1.8 (= 126.13 f. Manitius) ἡ ... Παρθένος καὶ τοῦ Λέοντος καὶ τῶν Χηλῶν ἐπιλαμβάνει; RE s.v. *Leo* 1975.43–46, s.v. *Libra* 120.12–15; Bouché-LeClercq (1889) 138–41; Semple (1939) 3 f.; note Semple's dissent from the translation of Crépin (1933).

1.366 *a* iam pridem ... vacant: presumably since early in Theodosius' reign, when Iustitia descended to Earth: cf. 1.50 f. (the Furies) quas ... arcet ... / Theodosius terris, 55 f. delapsa per auras / Iustitia.

1.366 *b* gelidae ... Librae: cf. Boll (1898) 7.104.11–19 φθινόπωρον Ζυγὸς Σκορπίος Τοξότης ... τὸ δὲ φθινόπωρον ψυχρόν ἐστι καὶ ξηρόν· ἔοικε δὲ τῷ βορρᾷ; RE s.v. *Libra* 126.48–51.

1.367 *a*: for the Furies' frustrated desire to invade the heavens, cf. 1.62 cupio Stygiis invadere nubibus astra, 69 pars Ditis iura veretur (cf. n. 1.69 b), 86 f. Signa ... divos attollere contra / nec fas est nec posse reor.

1.367 b convexa: for this term of the vault of heaven, cf. Verg. A. 4.451 (Dido has grown weary of the sky) taedet caeli convexa tueri, and Pease (1935) ad loc. Bruère (1964) 230 compares Luc. 9.4 (the ascension of Pompey's ghost) sequitur convexa Tonantis.

1.368–87: this prophetic passage is evidently modeled in large part on Verg. A. 1.261–96. Note the correspondence in language between A. 1.279 f. Iuno, / quae mare nunc terrasque metu caelumque fatigat, and IR 1.370 f. terras qui nunc ipsumque fatigat / aethera, and in thought between (1) the advent of Julius Caesar in A. 1.286–90, and that of Honorius in IR 1.372–76; (2) the incarceration of Furor in A. 1.294–96, and that of Megaera in IR 1.377–79; (3) the age of peace in A. 1.291–93, and that in IR 1.380–87 (on other Vergilian echoes in our passage, cf. n. 1.376 c, n. 1.374–76, n. 1.380–87).

On the use as a forecasting device of a prophecy made by one immortal to another, cf. Duckworth (1933) 16. The opening verses of each passage (A. 1.261–64 Hic — contundet, and IR 1.369–71) forecast events which are to take place within the scope of the poem: cf. Duckworth (1933) 41–43; cf. also n. 1.20–23, n. 2.281–83, n. 2.330–34. The remainder of the Vergilian prophecy is largely devoted to events which are to occur during the many centuries which separate the dramatic from the actual date of the *Aeneid*: cf. Duckworth (1933) 35 f. With a corresponding span of less than five years (cf. n. 1.372 a, Int. 39), Claudian is of course precluded from an analogous development. On the other hand, the Vergilian prophecy (like those of A. 6.756–859, 868–883, and 8.626–731) is not concerned with the actual future, save for the implications of continuing glory and felicity contained in A. 1.278 nec tempora pono, 291 positis mitescent saecula bellis. It is the theme of the future which is dealt with by Claudian (1.372–87), who borrows from the *Aeneid*, and transfers to the new time-sphere, the touches already noted, and in addition draws upon the fourth Eclogue, in which Vergil does of course present a prophecy concerning events actually yet to come: cf. n. 1.380–87.

On the use of direct quotation in IR, cf. n. 1.45–65, esp. sects. 6, 7.

1.368 a Diva refert: on the transition from quotation to narrative, cf. n. 1.65 b.

1.368 *b* bacchabere: cf. n. 1.82 *b*. Bruère (1964) 230 compares Luc. 5.169 (the Bacchic priestess) *bacchatur demens ... per antrum.*

1.369 *a* poenas: on Rufinus' murder viewed as *poena,* cf. n. 1.20 *c.*

1.369 *b* tuus iste: cf. 1.89 (Megaera claims Rufinus as her own).

1.369 *c* debitus: for this word of what is foreordained, cf. 2.276 f. *debita ... / victima;* also Verg. *A.* 7.120 *Salve, fatis mihi debita tellus,* 6.713 f. *animae, quibus altera fato / corpora debentur;* without *fato* or *fatis,* Stat. *Ach.* 2.32 (=318) *vastator debite Troiae;* V. Fl. 5.277 *debitus ... dux.* The collocation *debitus ... promissus* (1.372) is repeated in 2.276 f. *debita ... promissis.*

1.369–76 ultor — Araxes: for a similar coupling of Stilicho (cf. n. 1.369 *d*) and Honorius, cf. MT 265 f. *Nil licet invidiae, Stilicho dum prospicit orbi / sidereusque gener;* IE 1.377–79 *Tum forte decorus / cum Stilichone gener pacem implorantibus ultro / Germanis responsa dabat.*

1.369 *d* ultor: cf. 2.402 f. (to Rufinus, at the moment of his assassination) *Hac Stilicho ... dextra / te ferit.* Stilicho is called *ultor* also in 2 Pr.6, CS 2.322, BP 434.

1.370 f. terras ... ipsumque fatigat aethera: for Rufinus as an oppressor of the universe, cf. 2.406 *fessi ... orbis,* 454 f. *tellus ... nefandum / amolitur onus iam respirantibus astris;* n. 1 Pr.4 *b.* Cf. also Verg. *A.* 1.279 f., quoted in n. 1.368–87.

1.371 *a* nec — harena: for the unburied state of Rufinus' corpse, cf. 2.450–53; Int. 26. For the horror with which that state was viewed, cf. BG 398 *tenuem caesis invidit harenam;* Hor. *Carm.* 1.28.23–25 *Vagae ne parce ... harenae / ossibus et capiti inhumato / particulam dare;* Verg. *A* 4.620 (and Pease [1935] *ad loc.*), 6.325 f.

1.371 *b* nec vili: cf. Text. Comm. *ad loc.*

1.372–87: on the Roman ruler as the founder of a golden age, cf. n. 1.51 f., para. 2.

1.372 *a* Iam ... aderit ... Honorius: at the dramatic date of this conversation (392: cf. n. 1.306–53) Honorius was in his eighth year (cf. Seeck [1913] 267, 545). Cf. 4H 371 f. (Theodosius speaks to Honorius after raising him to the rank of Augustus in 393) *Veniet robustior aetas, / ne propera. Necdum decimas emensus aristas;* 385–87 *Sed proelia differ / in iuvenem patiensque meum cum fratre tuere / me bellante locum;* 387–95.

1.372 b laeto . . . aevo: cf. 1.380–87, 3H 184 (Arcadius and Honorius) saecula qui rursus formant meliore metallo (cf. Verg. A. 6.792 f. Augustus Caesar, Divi genus, aurea condet / saecula qui rursus). On the resultative-predicate use of the adjective, cf. n. 1.1 b.

1.372 c promissus: for this word of that which is foreordained, cf. CS 2.336 promissam subolem (cf. 335 Lachesis); V. Fl. 2.486 (a chained maiden to her fated deliverer) auguriis promisse et sorte deorum. Cf. also Verg. A. 6.791 f. Hic vir, hic est tibi quem promitti saepius audis, / Augustus Caesar.

1.373 a: cf. Verg. A. 10.129 nec Clytio genitore minor nec fratre Menestheo.

1.373 b nec . . . genitore minor nec fratre: cf. 4H 354 f. (Honorius to Theodosius) nec me fratri tibique / dissimilem populi . . . videbunt.

1.373 c fratre: Claudian's tone with regard to Arcadius varies from eulogy (expressed only when Arcadius is linked with Honorius, as here, and in 3H 182–84, 4H 652 f.) to more or less thinly veiled disparagement (cf. IE 2 Pr.49 f., 2.68 f., EH 23–25 [cf. Int. 21], BG 236–319, 6H 85 f.): cf. Birt (1892) Pr. 41; n. 2.145; n. 2.170. Mazzarino (1942) 94 regards EH 23–25 as Claudian's last personal attack on Arcadius; however, the tone of BG 236–319 and 6H 85 f. is certainly hostile.

1.373 d corusco: F. X. Burger, in TLL s.v. *coruscus* 1077.20 f (following Birt [1892] 490) takes this word in the sense of *purpuratus*. Though there is a single instance in Claudian (apparently none elsewhere) of the use of *coruscus* with reference to purple (PO 264 Tecta . . . ostro . . . infecta corusco), it seems better to take the word here as referring to the supposed Imperial effulgence or *nimbus* (cf. n. 2.144 c): cf. 6H 359 (of the goddess Roma) vultus . . . confessa coruscos. On the comparison of Emperors, while still alive, to stars, cf. Sauter (1934) 138–45. Platnauer (1922) appropriately translates "brilliant."

1.374–76: for prayers that the *imperium Romanum* may still expand, cf. PO 160–63 sic nobis Scythicus famuletur Araxes, / sic Rhenus per utrumque latus, Medisque subactis, / nostra Semiramiae timeant insignia turres; / sic fluat attonitus Romana per oppida Ganges; cf. also IE 2.102, 4H 257 f., 387–89; cf. also Verg. A. 6.794–805. On the rhetorical τόπος of the expansion of empire as an element of the βασιλικὸς λόγος, and particularly of the ἐγκώμιον Ἀλεξάνδρου, cf.

Norden (1899) 467-73; Christ (1938) 29. Bruère (1964) 230 compares Luc. 1.19, a vision of what Rome might have achieved had civil war been avoided.

1.374 *a* **subiget ... proteret:** cf. Text. Comm. *ad loc.*

1.374 *b* **subiget Medos:** cf. PO 161 (an element in a prayer) Medis ... subactis (cf. n. 1.374-76), IE 2.102 (Eutropius and his sister return from a pleasure-trip with triumphal pomp) ceu vinctos traherent Medos. Actually, the establishment of peaceful relationships between the Roman and the Persian empires was one of Theodosius' notable accomplishments: cf. Stein-Palanque (1959) 205 f., and EH 224 f. Misit Achaemenio quidquid de Tigride Medus, / cum supplex emeret Romanam Parthia pacem.

1.374 *c* **Indos:** for the idea of Rome's conquering India, cf. PO 163 (an element in a prayer) fluat ... Romana per oppida Ganges; BG 20 (Roma as conqueror) trepidos summittit fascibus Indos; IE 2.102; cf. also Verg. *A.* 6.794 f. (Augustus) super ... Indos / proferet imperium; Luc. 7.427 f. Vergil's mention of India as a land to be conquered is perhaps due to the influence of the ἐγκώμιον Ἀλεξάνδρου: cf. n. 1.374-76, n. 1.376 *b.*

1.375 asper: for this term applied to ice, cf. CM 53.24 glacies asperrima durat; Verg. *Ecl.* 10.49 ne teneras glacies secet aspera plantas; TLL s.v. *asper* 808.27 f., where our present passage is confused with CM 53.24, just quoted. For the Phasis as a frigid stream, cf. IE 2.575 gelidus Phasis; Luc. 2.585 f. gelidas ad Phasidos undas / Arctos; RE s.v. *Phasis* 1888.33-38. Cf. also Text. Comm. on 1.312, *fin.*

1.376 *a* **Phasis ... Araxes:** on the enumeration of rivers in descriptions of the actual or hoped-for greatness of the Roman Empire, cf. Christ (1938) 47-51 (add to the citations Verg. *A.* 8.726-28; cf. Christ [1938] 32).

1.376 *b* **Phasis:** for the Phasis as a boundary between the Roman Empire and the barbarians to the East, cf. IE 1.245 f. Trans Phasin aguntur / Cappadocum matres, 2.574 f. (Aurora speaks) nec iam mihi Caucasus hostes / nec mittit gelidus Phasis; Procop. *Goth.* 4.2.27-29; RE s.v. *Phasis* 1888 f.

1.376 *c* **pontem — Araxes:** cf. Verg. *A.* 8.728 pontem indignatus Araxes; Stat. *Silv.* 1.4.79. The bridging of the Araxes is perhaps another (cf. n. 1.374 *c*) element borrowed from the ἐγκώμιον

Ἀλεξάνδρου: cf. Curt. 5.5.3 f. ad Araxen ... pervenit. ... pontem ... strenue induxit; 4.5.4; D.S. 17.69.2; Arr. 3.18.6, 10; Serv. and Schol. Dan. on Verg. A. 8.728 Araxes: hic fluvius Armeniae ... cui Alexander Magnus pontem fecit, quem fluminis incrementa ruperunt. Postea Augustus firmiore ponte eum ligavit. The scholiasts' story of a bridge built by Augustus over the Araxes seems not to be otherwise attested; for Augustus' own statement about his exploits in Armenia, cf. *Anc.* 27. On the Araxes, cf. Wellesley (1968) 140 f.

1.377–79: for the imprisonment of evil force in a prophesied happy age, cf. Verg. *A.* 1.294–96 (Jupiter to Venus) Furor impius intus / saeva sedens super arma et centum vinctus aënis / post tergum nodis fremet horridus ore cruento.

1.377 religata catenis: cf. Ov. *Fast.* 1.701 f. (under Augustus and his line) religata catenis / iam pridem vestro sub pede Bella iacent.

1.378 expellere die: for the antithesis between the bright daylight and the dark Furies, cf. 1.62 f. Iam cupio ... / ... flatu violare diem, 129 f. Phoebi ... egressa serenos / infecti radios; n. 1 Pr.1 a.

1.378 f. *a* debellatas ... tonsa comas: cf. IE 1.383 militet ut nostris detonsa Sygambria signis; cf. TLL s.v. *detondeo* 818.72, and 4H 446 f. Ante ducem nostrum flavam sparsere Sygambri / caesariem; Levy (1968). Shearing the hair in token of the loss of freedom was a custom of the Greeks as well as of the Germans: cf. Schrader-Nehring (1917) 1.425; Sommer (1912) 58–61; Schredelseker (1913) 14 f.; RE s.v. *Haartracht und Haarschmuck* 2119.29–35; DS s.v. *coma* 1362, ftns. 141–43; Grimm-Heusler-Hübner (1899) 1.202. Cf. also Epaminondas *ap.* Paus. 9.15.6 ἡμετέραις βουλαῖς Σπάρτη ... ἐκείρατο δόξαν (cf. Cic. *Tusc.* 5.17.49 consiliis nostris laus est attonsa Laconum).

1.378 f. *b* draconum ... comas: on the Furies' snaky locks, cf. n. 1.42 *c*.

1.379 imo — recessu: in the actual working out of the prophecy (2.523–25), it is not upon Megaera, but upon her nurseling Rufinus that this punishment is inflicted. With this verse cf. Stat. *Silv.* 5.1.168 (if Caesar but had power over Death) caeco gemeret Mors clausa barathro.

1.380–87: for the general picture of a golden age, cf. Verg. *Ecl.* 4.18–45; cf. also n. 1. 51 f., and esp. the reference there to Hahn (1962).

For specific resemblances between the two passages, cf. n. 1.381 f., n. 1.382, n. 1.383, n. 1.384–86, n. 1.384, n. 1.387.

1.380 tellus communis: cf. [Sen.] *Oct.* 401-3 cingere assuerant suas / muris nec urbes; pervium cunctis iter, / communis usus omnium rerum fuit. Cf. also Verg. *G.* 1.127 in medium quaerebant.

1.380 f. limite — ager: cf. Verg. *G.* 1.125–27 Ante Iovem ... / ne signare quidem aut partiri limite campum / fas erat; Tib. 1.3.43 f.; Sen. *Phaed.* 528 f.

1.381 f. nec — findetur: cf. RP 1.198 f. (Ceres promises Sicily immunity from the plough in return for the safeguarding of Proserpina) nullo rigidi versabere vomeris ictu; Verg. *Ecl.* 4.40 non rastros patietur humus (cf. 31–33 priscae vestigia fraudis // ... quae iubeant telluri infindere sulcos), *G.* 1.125; Ov. *Met.* 1.101 f. (in the Golden Age) immunis rastroque intacta nec ullis / saucia vomeribus ... tellus, 109 tellus inarata.

1.381 obunco: cf. Text. Comm. *ad loc.*; Faider (1937) 679; D'Agostino (1937) 1.

1.382 subitis — aristis: cf. RP 1.199 f. (Ceres promises Sicily freedom from the plough) sponte tuus florebit ager; cessante iuvenco / ditior oblatas mirabitur incola messes; Hes. *Op.* 117 f. (in the Golden Age) καρπὸν ... ἔφερεν ζείδωρος ἄρουρα / αὐτομάτη πολλόν τε καὶ ἄφθονον; Verg. *Ecl.* 4.39 omnis feret omnia tellus, *G.* 1.127 f.; Ov. *Met.* 1.102-9; [Sen.] *Oct.* 404 f.

1.383 Rorabunt querceta favis: cf. PO 250 (the god Tiber orders all Nature to celebrate) Mella ferant silvae; Verg. *Ecl.* 4.30 durae quercus sudabunt roscida mella, *G.* 1.131; Ov. *Met.* 1.112; Tib. 1.3.45.

1.383 f. stagnantia — fluent: cf. PO 250 f. (the god Tiber orders all nature to celebrate) iam profluat ebrius amnis / mutatis in vina vadis; Verg. *G.* 1.132 (Jupiter terminated the Golden Age) passim rivis currentia vina repressit; Ov. *Met.* 1.111.

1.384–86 nec murice — greges: cf. CM 30.72 f. (at Serena's birth wondrous changes occurred) Duria ... / vellere purpureo passim mutavit ovile; Verg. *Ecl.* 4.42–45 nec varios discet mentiri lana colores, / ipse sed in pratis aries iam suave rubenti / murice, iam croceo mutabit vellere luto; / sponte sua sandyx pascentes vestiet agnos.

1.384 olei ... lacus: Claudian here substitutes oil for the milk of

Vergil (*Ecl.* 4.21), Ovid (*Met* 1.111), and Tibullus (1.3.46), none of whom mentions oil in connection with a golden age. Elsewhere Claudian follows the more usual pattern: cf. CS 1.85 f. (the Earth rejoiced at the marriage of Stilicho and Serena) mellis... lacus et flumina lactis / erupisse solo.

1.384 f. *a* **murice tinctis velleribus:** cf. 1.207 f. Rapiunt... Tyrios... vellera sucos / et picturatae saturantur murice vestes; n. 1.207 f.

1.384 f. *b* **tinctis... quaeretur honos:** on the resultative-predicate use of the participle, cf. n. 1.1 *b*.

1.385 honos: cf. CM 35.5 (the beauty of a crystal is enhanced) Auctus honor; Ov. *Ars* 2.277 f. plurimus auro / venit honos; TLL s.v. *honor* 2930.49–72.

1.386 attonito pastore: cf. IE 1.3 (among prodigies surpassed by Eutropius' becoming consul) attonito pecudes pastore locutas.

1.386 f. pontum — algae: reference is apparently to the "pearls" supposedly found growing on coral, which was thought of as a green sea-plant: cf. Plin. *Nat.* 32.2.22 (on coral) forma est ei fruticis, colos viridis. Bacae eius candidae sub aqua ac molles, exemptae confestim durantur et rubescunt qua corna sativa specie et magnitudine (cf. EH 169–71 Mergit se subito vellitque corallia Doto: / vimen erat dum stagna subit; processerat undis: / gemma fuit; RE s.v. *Koralle* 1373 f.). Ordinary sea-weed *pontum... per omnem*, now a type of worthlessness (cf. Verg. *Ecl.* 7.42 proiecta vilior alga; Otto [1890] 13) is to become *dives* like that of the *rubrum mare*: cf. 4H 597 f., CM 29.14 f.

1.387 ridebunt: for this verb applied to places and things which present a joyous appearance, cf. CM 30.71 f. Callaecia risit / floribus, MT 273 riserunt floribus amnes; Verg. *Ecl.* 4.20 mixta... ridenti colocasia fundet acantho.

BOOK 2. PREFACE

2 Pr.1–20: *Helicon is free from barbarian inroads. Rejoice, ye Muses. Stilicho, pause from your labors to hear my song.* On the Gothic invasion of Greece under Alaric in 396 and 397 (and thus outside the chronological framework of IR), and the campaign of Stilicho in the latter year whereby the barbarians were driven from Arcadia (cf. n. 2 Pr.9) to a tightly surrounded area in the Pholoe range of eastern Elis, cf. Stein-Palanque (1959) 230 f.; also Koch (1889) 582 f.; Birt (1892) Pr. 30, 38; Seeck (1913) 280, 553. It was upon Stilicho's return to Italy after this expedition that the entire poem, accompanied by this Preface, was read in Stilicho's presence: cf. Int. 39 f., Kurfess (1941) 94 f. On Claudian's use of prefaces, cf. n. 1 Pr.1–18.

2 Pr.1 Pandite ... Helicona: cf. Verg. *A.* 7.641 (=10.163) Pandite nunc Helicona, deae, cantusque movete. To the general sense of the Vergilian *Pandite ... Helicona* is here apparently added the specific idea of a reopening of a place thitherto closed by siege: cf. CS 2.191–93 obsidione solutus / ... clausa tot annis / oppida laxatis ausus iam pandere portis. For the drawing of a similar connection between the fabled abode of the Muses (cf. Roscher [1937] s.v. *Musen* 3240) and military events occurring nearby (on Alaric's siege of Thebes, cf. Stein-Palanque [1959] 231), cf. Stat. *Theb.* 7.628–31 Nunc age, Pieriae, non vos longinqua, sorores, / consulimus, vestras acies vestramque referte / Aoniam; vidistis enim, dum Marte propinquo / horrent Tyrrhenos Heliconia plectra tumultus.

2 Pr.2 Permissis: cf. Text. Comm. *ad loc.*; Brakman (1937) 121. Cf. also Luc. 6.271 permissa licentia. Apart from any question of pleonasm, *permissis* may be regarded as an instance of the resultative-predicate use of a participle: cf. n. 1.1 *b*.

2 Pr.3 Aonios: =*Boeotios*; cf. MT 270–72 (the news of Manlius' consulship reaches the abode of the Muses) fama ... moverat Aonios audito consule lucos, / concinuit felix Helicon fluxitque Aganippe;

Verg. G. 3.11 Aonio...deducam vertice Musas; RE s.v. *Aones* 2657.42–46. The "Italy" of Platnauer (1922) is undoubtedly a mere slip.

2 Pr.4 *a* mugitu: for *mugio* used of trumpets, cf. Verg. A. 8.526 Tyrrhenus...tubae mugire per aethera clangor; Stat. *Theb.* 6.120 f. cornu grave mugit adunco / tibia.

2 Pr.4 *b* deteriore: cf. Non. 432 (=696 Lindsay) PEIVS et DETERIVS his sensibus discernuntur, quod sit peius a malo;... deterius vero a bono, ut minoris sit meriti quam id quod placet. Vergilius, Georg. lib. IV ⟨89 f.⟩ deterior qui visus, eum, ne prodigus obsit, / dede neci; idem, ⟨A.⟩ lib. VIII ⟨324–26 Aurea...fuere / saecula. Sic placida populos in pace regebat /⟩ deterior donec paulatim et decolor aetas.

2 Pr.5 *a* securis — Delphis: on his march from Thermopylae to Thebes (cf. Stein-Palanque [1959] 231) Alaric presumably used the road running through Elatea and Chaeronea (cf. Miller [1916] 566, 573 f., 577 f.); when midway between the two last-named cities, he would be less than 20 miles (as the crow flies) from Delphi.

2 Pr.5 *b* securis pulsa formidine: on Claudian's use of an adjective in close relation with an ablative absolute, cf. Text. Comm. on 1.287.

2 Pr.6 *a* floribus...cinge: for the omission of some such word as *caput, frontem,* or *comas,* cf. Sen. *Ag.* 779 victrice lauru cinctus Agamemnon; Sil. 15.100 cinctus...lauro Triumphus.

2 Pr.6 *b* ultorem, Delie,...tuum: for the mention of Stilicho in connection with Apollo, cf. 1 Pr., CS 3.60.

2 Pr.7 f. Castalios — flumina: for the Castalian waters as connected with prophecy, cf. CM 3.1 Quidquid Castalio de gurgite Phoebus anhelat, 6H 25–33; Stat. *Theb.* 8.175 f. Hoc antra lacusque / Castalii tripodumque fides? Sic gratus Apollo?; Amm. 22.12.8 venas fatidicas Castalii fontis...praecinentibus aquis; RE s.v. *Kastalia* 2338.

2 Pr.7 Castalios latices: cf. Luc. 5.125 (Apollo's priestess is wandering) Castalios circum latices.

2 Pr.8 *a* flumina: on the little stream flowing from the *fons Castalius,* cf. RE s.v. *Kastalia* 2337. Claudian elsewhere speaks of Castalia's waves: 6H 27 f. (in Apollo's absence) Nil...Castaliae rivis communibus undae / dissimiles.

2 Pr.8 *b* polluto...ore: for the expression, cf. Ov. *Met.* 15.98

(the Golden Age was vegetarian) nec polluit ora cruore; Bruère (1964) 230 compares Luc. 6.706 f. (the witch Erichtho, speaking of her own mouth) ore . . . / polluto. For the concept of pollution through blood, cf. 4H 362 polluta potestas (cf. 363 cruoris); Luc. 1.331 f. (Pompey, like Sulla, is stained with blood) nullus semel ore receptus / pollutas patitur sanguis mansuescere fauces (cf. n. 2.8 *a*); cf. also Livy 45.5.4 (Atilius addresses the Samothracians about the sacredness of their island) cur . . . polluit eam homicida, sanguine regis Eumenis violavit, et, cum omnis praefatio sacrorum eos, quibus non sunt purae manus, sacris arceat, vos penetralia vestra contaminari cruento latronis corpore sinetis?; Paul. *Fest*. 117 (= 104.23 f. Lindsay) Laureati milites sequebantur currum triumphantis, ut quasi purgati a caede humana intrarent Urbem; Wissowa (1912) 416, ftn. 3; Fowler (1922) 33. The concept is much more prominent in Greek than in Roman culture: cf. Stengel (1920) 156.

2 Pr.9-12: for the fabled water-course connecting the Alpheus in Arcadia with Arethusa in Sicily, cf. CS 1.186 f. (Stilicho's victories over the Goths in Arcadia) Alpheus Geticis angustus acervis / tardior ad Siculos etiam nunc pergit amores, RP 2.60 f.; Verg. *A*. 3.694-96 Alpheum fama est huc Elidis amnem / occultas egisse vias subter mare, qui nunc / ore, Arethusa, tuo Siculis confunditur undis; Sil. 14.53 f.; cf. also Str. 6.2.4; Plin. *Nat*. 2.106.225, 31.5.55; Sen. *Nat*. 3.26.5; RE s.v. *Alpheios* 1633-36; Roscher (1937) s.v. *Alpheios* 257 f.; Tomsin (1940). Bruère (1964) 230 compares with 2 Pr.9-11 the following passages from Lucan: 6.421 f. (Sextus Pompey) Scyllaeis exul grassatus in undis / polluit aequoreos Siculus pirata triumphos; 7.871 (naval victory of Agrippa) flebilis unda Pachyni. On rivers bearing the signs of carnage as an epic theme, cf. Miniconi (1951) 174.

2 Pr.9 Alpheus: the coupling of the Arcadian river Ladon with the Alpheus in CS 1.185 f. shows that reference here is to the headwaters of the Alpheus in Arcadia: cf. Seeck (1913) 280, 553.

2 Pr.12 Geticam: on Claudian's use of *Geta* and *Geticus*, cf. n. 1.308 *b*.

2 Pr.16 tenuem . . . moram: Birt (1892) Pr. 38, followed by Mazzarino (1942) 262, ftn. 3, holds that these words refer to the interval between the end of the campaign against Alaric and the beginning of the expedition against Gildo. Though this interval was indeed slight (cf. Stein-Palanque [1959] 231 f.), I do not believe that it is referred to in its entirety here. For one thing, the festive tone of 2 Pr.1–12 would be marred by a reference, however covert, to a struggle yet to come; for another, Birt's interpretation makes Claudian suggest that Stilicho devote the entire period between campaigns to his verses (2 Pr.14 nostrae lyrae), which seems presumptuous. I suggest, on the contrary, that *tenuem* is deprecatory (cf. Hor. *Carm.* 1.6.9 tenues grandia); it is but a slight pause that Claudian can hope for; so Platnauer (1922) "a few moments," Crépin (1933) "un moment."

2 Pr.17–20: for another comparison of Stilicho with Mars resting after victory, cf. CS 2.367–76; cf. also n. 1.350 f. Bruère (1964) 230 compares Luc. 8.363 f. On comparisons with Mars as an epic theme, cf. Miniconi (1951) 197, where these verses are wrongly assigned to the body of IR 2 instead of to the Preface.

The notion of ἀκίθαρις Ἄρης (A. *Supp.* 681 f.) finding relaxation in the strains of the Muses is apparently an *ad hoc* invention of Claudian's; cf. Muellner (1893) 116; n. 2 Pr.17. The obviously appropriate example of Apollo (cf. Hor. *Carm.* 2.10.19 f. suscitat musam neque semper arcum / tendit Apollo) could not be used here because of the role assigned to that god in 2 Pr.6.

2 Pr.17 Fertur: on the use of this word to introduce one of the poet's own inventions (cf. n. 2 Pr.17–20, para. 2), cf. n. 1.124.

2 Pr.17 f. Mavors . . . per Odrysias . . . nives: on the location of this scene, cf. n. 1.333–39, para. 2.

2 Pr.18 Odrysias: = *Thracias*; cf. n. 1.175 a.

2 Pr.19 a oblitus . . . sui: cf. IE 1.229 (Eutropius is so dazzled by opulence as to forget that he is a eunuch) oblita sui . . . mens, RP 2.343 f.; Verg. *A.* 3.628 f. nec . . . Ulixes / oblitus . . . sui est. The poet apologizes for Mars' unaccustomed role (cf. n. 2 Pr.17–20, para. 2).

2 Pr.19 b posita clementior hasta: cf. CS 2.368 f. Gradivus . . . / deposito mitis clipeo; on the ablative absolute in close relation with an adjective, cf. Text. Comm. on 1.287.

2 Pr.20 aures: Birt (1892) Pr. 38, ftn. 2, cites this word to sustain his view that the poem was actually recited in Stilicho's presence.

BOOK 2

2.1–6: *The dying Theodosius has left the two-fold Empire in Stilicho's charge.* On the basis for this assertion, cf. n. 1 Pr.17 *a*. On these verses as part of a *laus Stilichonis*, cf. n. 1.259–300, para. 1.

2.1–4 iam ... iam: the temporal adverb marks the transition to the period following Theodosius' death; cf. n. 1.240 f.

2.1 f. post — Hesperiae: reference is to Theodosius' defeat in 394 of the usurper Eugenius, whom the *magister militum* Arbogastes had set up as Augustus in the Western provinces: cf. Zos. 4.54, 58; Int. 18; Stein-Palanque (1959) 210 f., 216 f.

2.1 edomitas Alpes: for Theodosius' expeditions across the Alps to subdue the usurpers Maximus and Eugenius, cf. 2.389 rupimus Alpes; PO 74 Belliger Augustus trepidas laxaverat Alpes, 105–8 Alpes / claustra ... durissima ... tendunt / ... pervia tantum / Augusto, geminisque fidem mentita tyrannis; Zos. 4.58.1 τῆς διὰ τῶν Ἄλπεων παρόδου κρατήσας [ὁ Θεοδόσιος]; Stein-Palanque (1959) 207, 216 f.; Cameron (1968a) 391 f., correcting Platnauer (1922).

2.2 parentem: = *Theodosium*, as the adoptive father of Stilicho's wife Serena; cf. Stein-Palanque (1959) 226.

2.2 f. merita — mundus: on the metamorphosis into a star of a deified ruler, cf. 3H 109 (Theodosius delayed his departure to heaven) Distulit Augustus cupido se credere caelo, 163–84, esp. 172–74 (constellations vie for the honor of Theodosius' proximity) Invitant ... novum sidus, pendentque vicissim / ... quibus esse sodalis / dignetur stellis, 4H 428 f.; Verg. *Ecl.* 9.47 Ecce Dionaei processit Caesaris astrum (and Serv. *ad loc.*); Ov. *Met.* 15.840 f.; Luc. 1.45 f.; Stat. *Theb.* 1.25–31; Sil. 3.626–28. Cf. also Plin. *Nat.* 2.23.94 Ipsis ludorum meorum diebus sidus crinitum per septem dies ... est conspectum. ... Eo sidere significari vulgus credidit Caesaris animam inter deorum immortalium numina receptam; Gundel (1907) 223–26, Sauter (1934) 148–53; Scott (1941); Courcelle (1943) 121.

On the application to Christian emperors of the pagan concept of deification, cf. Beurlier (1891) 287–89, 330; Boissier (1913) 2.221; RE Supp. 4 s.v. *Kaiserkult* 852.38–57; Setton (1941); L'Orange (1947) 119. Cf. also n. 1.333–39, para. 3, *fin*.

2.3 auctior adiecto ... sidere: on Claudian's use of an ablative absolute in close relation with an adjective, cf. Text. Comm. on 1.287.

2.5 *a* apex: for this word used to designate supreme power, cf. 6H Pr.23 En princeps, en orbis apex aequatus Olympo; IE 2.350 (ironically, of Eutropius and Hosius) Considunt apices gemini dicionis Eoae; Pacatus, *Panegyricus Theodosio Augusto dictus* 6.2 principem qui princeps esse debuerit, qui hunc Romani fastigii apicem ... potuerit aequare; Amm. 30.8.10 (the Emperors) sunt dignitatum apices maximi; TLL s.v. *apex* 228.11–41 (our passage belongs in sect. 2, rather than in sect. 1, where it is listed).

2.5 *b* fratrum: = *Arcadii et Honorii*; cf. 1 Pr.17 Augustis fratribus, n. 1 Pr.17 *a*.

2.6 geminae ... exercitus aulae: for Stilicho's two-fold army, cf. 2.104–6 utraque castra movens ... / Gallica discretis Eoaque robora turmis / complexus, 106–19; CS 1.151 geminas acies. The army led by Stilicho comprised not only a large part (cf. n. 2.105 *b*) of the Eastern forces which Theodosius had led against the usurper Eugenius, but also the Western troops (cf. n. 2.105 *a*) which the Emperor had acquired through his victory; cf. 2.156–58, 161–63; CS 1.160 f. Ductor Stilicho tot gentibus unus / quot vel progrediens vel conspicit occiduus sol; Zos. 5.4.2 ἅπαν σχεδὸν τὸ ʽΡωμαίων στρατόπεδον ὑπήκοον εἶχε. ... στρατηγὸς ὢν τοῦ παντὸς στρατεύματος ὁ Στελίχων; Int. 18, 22, 24; Stein-Palanque (1959) 216 f., 228; Mazzarino (1942) 105.

Cameron (1968b) 277 f. holds that Stilicho had no legal right to regard himself as commander of the Eastern troops. He supports this point of view with arguments based upon his interpretation of IR 2. Whatever may be thought of his arguments here (and I find them less cogent than most which he presents), he surely goes too far when he says "It is equally *clear* [italics mine] both from Claudian and John of Antioch" that in marching East Stilicho was definitely exceeding his authority. I pass over the fact that, as Cameron admits (ftn. 56), John may not even be referring to the events narrated in IR 2. I call attention merely to Cameron's own phrases "reveals by implication" (277.30) and "The explanation of Stilicho's conduct implicit in *In Rufinum*" (278.14). That which is deduced by interpreting implications may indeed be correct, but it should not be called "clear." It is perhaps a mistake to attempt to define the *de iure* situation so precisely, when the *de facto* state of affairs was, as Cameron (in his turn) implies in his concluding sentences, that Stilicho had the power, had he not lacked the will "to march on Constantinople and establish his 'regency' by force."

2.7-21: *Rufinus, feeling himself doomed, decides to involve the world in his own ruin.*

2.7-99: on the relation of these verses to the ψόγος-pattern, cf. Levy (1946) 63, 65.

2.7 quietem: reference is to the interval of peace in the Eastern provinces which followed the suppression of the barbarian disturbances of 391-92: cf. n. 1.306-53, para. 1.

2.8 *a* pollutae — fauces: Bruère (1964) 230 compares Luc. 1.331 f. (quoted in n. 2 Pr.8 *b*); cf. also Luc. 4.239-41. On the concept of blood-pollution, cf. n. 2 Pr.8 *b*. On the use of imagery here, cf. Christiansen (1969) 86.

TLL s.v. *aresco* 509.63 f. suggests hesitatingly that our passage may be proverbial in origin: it compares [Lact.] *De mort. persecut.* 21.9 (of the sufferings of martyrs) *arescentibus siccitate faucibus*. Not cited is the passage from Lucan on which our present passage is apparently based, and which does not contain the word *aresco*. Commentators on Lucan have not discovered any pertinent proverb. Moreover, it is unlikely that the words of a derogatory proverb would have been applied to the venerable martyrs. On the other hand, Claudian's use of the verb *aresco* in a non-classical sense (cf. n. 2.8 *b*) may point to the currency in the Fourth Century of some locution containing the words *aresco* and *fauces*, which might have influenced both Claudian and Ps.-Lactantius.

2.8 *b* arescere: cf. 2.509 f. (of a possible punishment for Rufinus like that of Tantalus) *te refugi fallant latices atque ore natanti / arescat decepta sitis*. Claudian's use of *aresco* in connection with thirst is apparently paralleled only in the Vulgate and in Christian writers: cf.

TLL s.v. *aresco* 509.60–510.2 (in Plin. *Nat.* 22.24.108 and Cels. 7.12.1 *aresco* is used of dryness due to disease, not to thirst). This usage may possibly indicate Claudian's acquaintance with Christian writings (cf. n. 1.1–24, para. 5; n. 1.19 *a*; n. 1.22 f.), but it seems more likely that it simply reflects one of the infrequent triumphs of contemporary Latinity over Claudian's classical models.

2.9 f. iterum ... solito ... tumultu: reference is to the earlier disturbances alleged to have been caused by Rufinus: cf. n. 1.306–53, para. 2. On the use of imagery here, cf. Christiansen (1969) 87 f.

2.9 *a* infandis ... terras accendere bellis: cf. Verg. *A.* 12.804 *infandum accendere bellum*, 7.644.

2.9 *b* terras: on *terrae* of the Roman Empire, cf. n. 1.51 *b*.

2.10: Bruère (1964) 230 compares Luc. 4.210 (Petreius breaking up fraternization at Ilerda) *et multo disturbat sanguine pacem* (despite, as he says, the small verbal similarity between the passages).

2.11–21: on Claudian's rather infrequent use of the monologue, cf. Lipscomb (1909) 43; 38–42. Cf. also n. 1.45–65, esp. sect. 8. On the despairing monologue, cf. Pease (1935) on Verg. *A.* 4.534 *quid ago*; para. 2. Bruère (1964) 231 gives extensive parallels from Lucan.

2.11–13 tuebor ... queam: on the variation in mood, cf. n. 1 Pr.3 f. *b*.

2.12 fragilem: the adjective seems to foreshadow the nautical metaphor in 2.12 f. *Qua—queam?*; cf. Hor. *Carm.* 1.3.10 f. *fragilem ... / ... ratem*, 3.2.28 f.; Ov. *Pont.* 1.4.35 *fragili ligno vastum sulcavimus aequor*; Sen. *Med.* 302.

2.12 f.: on the use of imagery here, cf. Christiansen (1969) 87.

2.13 *a* Premor — cingor: cf. Pacatus, *Panegyricus Theodosio Augusto dictus* 38.3 (the tyrant Maximus deliberates) *Quid ergo faciam inter arma et odia medius? A tergo premor hostibus, a fronte criminibus*; on Claudian and the panegyrists, cf. n. 1.183–87, para 2.

2.13–15 Premor hinc odiis ... non ... auxiliatur amor: cf. IE 2 Pr.34 (to Eutropius) *cingeris hinc odiis, inde recessit amor*. Contrast the love for Stilicho which is one of Claudian's chief themes: cf. n. 2.225.

2.13 *b* hinc ... hinc: cf. Luc. 10.366 f. (Pothinus to Achillas) *nil undique restat / auxilii: rex hinc coniunx, hinc Caesar adulter*.

2.13 c odiis: on the hatred aroused by Rufinus, cf. Int. 26 and ftn. 164.

2.13 d milite cingor: reference here can scarcely be to the bulk of the Eastern armies, which was with Stilicho in Italy (cf. 2.101–4, n. 2.6; cf. also 2.301–6). Claudian apparently means that Rufinus felt surrounded by the hostility of such military contingents as had remained in Constantinople: cf. Int. 19, ftn. 121.

2.14 a Heu quid agam?: cf. Verg. *A.* 12.486 (Aeneas tries in vain to confront Turnus) Heu quid agat?

2.14 b Non arma mihi: reference is to the absence of the bulk of the Eastern forces: cf. n. 2.6.

2.14 f. non principis — amor: apparently a covert reference to Rufinus' unsuccessful attempt (cf. Int. 20–22) to marry his daughter to Arcadius: cf. Birt (1892) 34, *app. crit. ad loc.*, Pr.28; Koch (1889) 597, ftn. 1.

2.15 Matura pericula: for *maturus* of an evil which is ripe to bursting, cf. IE 2.14 maturam...luem; Luc. 1.644 f. generi... paratur / humano matura lues, 7.668. Cf. also Cic. *Catil.* 1.31 scelerum ac...furoris et audaciae maturitas in nostri consulatus tempus erupit.

2.16 a impositi — enses: cf. Cic. *Tusc.* 5.21.61 f., esp. 62 (Dionysius hangs a sword over Damocles) mensae conquisitissimis epulis exstruebantur. Fortunatus sibi Damocles videbatur. In hoc medio apparatu fulgentem gladium e lacunari saeta equina aptum demitti iussit, ut impenderet illius beati cervicibus; Hor. *Carm.* 3.1.17 f. (and Porphyrio *ad loc.*); RE s.v. *Damokles* (6). Cf. also BG 175–81, esp. 179 (Gildo's victim fears for his life) intentos capiti circumspicit enses. On the use of imagery here, cf. Christiansen (1969) 87.

2.16 b impositi: for this word in the sense "suspend over," cf. Ov. *Ars* 2.469 (first there was Chaos) mox caelum impositum terris.

2.16 c radiant: cf. Cic. (quoted in n. 2.16 a) fulgentem gladium.

2.17–21: Stoecker (1889) 80, followed by Kurfess (1916) 197 and Fargues (1933a) 74, ftn. 4, 227, ftn. 4, cites as a parallel to our passage a remark attributed to Catiline by Cicero and Sallust: Cic. *Mur.* 51 si quod esset in suas fortunas incendium excitatum, id se non aqua, sed ruina restincturum; Sal. *Cat.* 31.9 quoniam quidem circumventus... ab inimicis praeceps agor, incendium meum ruina restinguam. An important difference, however, must be noted. Catiline, it is true, threatens to demolish the fabric of the Roman constitution, but his announced purpose is the extinction of a hostile conflagration; he compares himself to a fireman who tears down a building to arrest the spread of the blaze; cf. Freese (1894) 95 on Cic. *Mur.* 51 ruina; cf. also Petr. 78 vigiles ... rati ardere Trimalchionis domum ... cum aqua securibusque tumultuari ... coeperunt; Werner (1906) 67. Thus, for all Catiline's fury (cf. Sall. *Cat.* 31.9 furibundus), his destructiveness is attributed to efforts at self-preservation, and not to mere wantonness. Rufinus, however, is described as realizing himself doomed, and determined wantonly to involve the innocent peoples of the world in his downfall. A truer parallel is to be found in a passage of Lucan, where an attitude like that here attributed to Rufinus is clearly delineated by contrast with that actually manifested by Pompey: 7.654–61 Nec, sicut mos est miseris, trahere omnia secum / mersa iuvat gentesque suae miscere ruinae: / ut Latiae post se vivat pars maxima turbae, / sustinuit dignos etiamnum credere votis / caelicolas volvitque sui solacia casus. / "Parcite," ait, "superi, cunctas prosternere gentes; / stante potest mundo Romaque superstite Magnus / esse miser." On the parallels between Claudian and Lucan here, cf. Bruère (1964) 231; note also the contrast between IR 2.19 everso ... orbe, and Luc. 7.660 stante ... mundo.

2.17 *a* **novo:** in contrast with earlier disturbances; cf. n. 2.9 f.

2.17 *b* **luctu:** Birt (1892) 487 s.v. *confundere* wrongly construes this as a dative. Where the formula *rem rei confundo* is used (cf. TLL s.v. *confundo* 265.25–29) the two nouns denote elements of similar nature which are mingled together: cf. EH 199 f. sociam plebem non indignata potestas / confundat turbae proceres; Ov. *Med.* 61 (in a prescription for mixing face-powder) ubi [omnia] pulvereae fuerint confusa farinae; Verg. *A.* 3.696 (the river Alpheus) Siculis confunditur undis; Hor. *Ep.* 2.1.195 confusa ... panthera camelo (and Kiessling-Heinze [1910] *ad loc.*). Here it is not a question of commingling *cuncta* with *luctus*, but rather of throwing *cuncta* into confusion by means of *luctus*: cf. 4H 551 f. confusa ... motu / caesaries; Stat. *Theb.* 1.136 vario confundunt limite sulcos, *Ach.* 1.881 f. (= 2.207 f.); Sil. 11.101, 12.619 f., 15.759 f.; TLL s.v. *confundo* 265.29 f. On Claudian's wide use of the ablative, cf. Birt (1892) Pr. 222.

2.19 Everso — mori: for the thought, cf. Sen. *Her. F.* 1284–94, esp. 1290 urbe versa condar, 1293 f. onus omne media parte quod mundi sedet / ... in meum vertam caput; *Her. O.* 1147–50 regnum omne, genitor, aetheris dubium tibi / mors nostra faciet ... / ... conde me tota, pater, / mundi ruina.

2.19 f. solacia — dabit: the likelihood of a similar thought is attributed to the tyrant Gildo in CS 1.339 f. (Stilicho forbore to use his full strength against Gildo, lest) missurus ... sibi certae solacia mortis, / oppida dirueret flammis.

2.20 f. nec territus — potestas: by attributing to Rufinus the resolution to yield his power only with his life, Claudian both foreshadows and justifies his actual end (cf. n. 1.368–87).

2.22–60: *Rufinus summons barbarian hordes to invade the Empire.* The charge that Rufinus instigated the barbarian inroads of 395 (cf. Int. 22 f.; also Stein-Palanque [1959] 228 f., Schmidt [1934] 427 f.), unlike the similar accusation with regard to the disturbances of 391 and 392 (cf. n. 1.306–53), is paralleled in a number of places by our other sources. Cf. Zos. 5.5.3 f. Ῥουφῖνος [τὸν Ἀντίοχον] ... ἀνθύπατον καθίστησι τῆς Ἑλλάδος, ἕτοιμον ἐθέλων τοῖς ἐπιοῦσι βαρβάροις ποιῆσαι τὴν αὐτῆς ἀπώλειαν.... ταῦτα Ῥουφῖνος πονηρευσάμενος, ἐπειδὴ στασιάζοντα καὶ ἀλλοτριώσαντα τῶν νόμων ἑαυτὸν ἐθεώρησεν Ἀλάριχον ... τότε τοίνυν ἐσήμαινε δι᾽ ἀπορρήτων αὐτῷ προσωτέρω τοὺς σὺν αὐτῷ βαρβάρους ... ἐξαγαγεῖν, ὡς ἑτοίμων ἁπάντων εἰς ἅλωσιν ἐσομένων; 5.7.1 Ῥουφῖνος ... ἀγγελθέντος αὐτῷ τοῦ περὶ τὴν Ἑλλάδα πάθους, ἐπίδοσιν ἐλάμβανεν ἧς εἶχε περὶ τὴν βασιλείαν ἐπιθυμίας· συνταραττομένου γὰρ τοῦ πολιτεύματος οὐδὲν ἐμποδὼν ᾤετο αὐτῷ φανήσεσθαι πρὸς τὴν τοιαύτην ἐπιχείρησιν; Jo. Antioch. frag. 190 (= FHG 4.610), on the uncertain chronology of which cf. n. 2.6, para. 2; Oros. 7.37.1 sibi ... adfectans regale fastigium, ut rebus repente turbatis necessitas reipublicae scelus ambitus tegeret, barbaras gentes ille inmisit; Marcellinus Comes 8.4 (= MGH 11.64.18–21) Rufinus patricius Arcadio principi insidias tendens Alaricum Gothorum regem missis clam pecuniis infestum rei publicae fecit et in Graeciam misit; Socr. 6.1.6 ὑπωπτεύετο ... εἰς τυραννίδα ὁ Ῥουφῖνος· καὶ δόξαν εἶχεν, ὡς αὐτὸς εἴη τοὺς Οὔννους τὸ βάρβαρον ἔθνος ἐπικαλεσάμενος εἰς τὴν Ῥωμαίων χώραν;

Sozomen. 8.1.2 Οὖννοι βάρβαροι Ἀρμενίας καὶ τῆς πρὸς ἕω ἀρχομένης μέρη τινὰ κατέδραμον. ἐλέγετο δὲ ὡς λάθρα τούτους ἐπηγάγετο ἐπὶ ταραχῇ τῆς βασιλείας Ῥουφῖνος, ὁ τῆς ἀνατολῆς ὕπαρχος, ὕποπτος ὢν καὶ ἄλλως ὡς τυραννεῖν βούλεται; cf. also Assemani (1719) 1.262 f., where a passage from a late fifth-century Syrian annalist is translated as follows: quum Hunni Orientem sub Honorio et Arcadio invasissent totamque Syriam ... proditione Rufini patricii ... occupassent. These citations seem to reflect a widespread belief (however unjustified, cf. Demougeot [1950]) that Rufinus was responsible for the invasions of 395. Koch (1889) 598 f. suggests that both the contemporary belief and its echo in later writers may be traced back to our present passage and other portions of IR (cf. Rauschen [1897] 435 and ftn. 6). This seems rather unlikely: cf. Fargues (1933a) 72, Mazzarino (1942) 252, ftn. 1. Orosius, Marcellinus Comes, Socrates, Sozomen, John of Antioch (if he is talking about 395), and, to a lesser extent, Zosimus, all connect Rufinus' alleged part in the barbarian invasions with his plot to force his nomination as Arcadius' colleague. This is not the point of view presented by Claudian. To him, the instigation of the inroads is seen as an act of desperate wantonness (cf. 2.17-21, 61-70), not of ambitious calculation. Rufinus' imperial ambitions are represented by Claudian as really coming into play only after the removal of Stilicho from the Eastern provinces: 2.297 Vicimus, expulimus, facilis iam copia regni, 309-16. Moreover, some indication of an independent tradition may perhaps be seen in the mention by the other sources (cf. n. 2.26-30) of the Huns, who, as Koch himself points out (Koch [1889] 598, ftn. 1), play no part in the invasions of 395 as Claudian depicts them. Both Koch and Fargues cite the so-called *Pithoei Chronicon* for the year 395 (= MGH 9.650, sect. 34), but this citation (Rufinus ... interficitur Chunorum, quo fulciebatur, praesidio superato) is hardly pertinent except as reflecting the charge that Rufinus was friendly with the barbarians (cf. Int. 25, ftn. 163; Text. Comm. on 2.76).

For a similar accusation, i.e. of inciting the barbarians to invade the Empire, lodged by the anti-Stilichonian party against Stilicho, cf. Rutil. 2.41-60; Seeck (1913) 273 f.; Mazzarino (1942) 251-53. Cf. also n. 2.53 a, n. 2.78-85, para. 3.

2.22-26 Haec fatus — nefas: on the imagery here, cf. Christiansen

(1969) 88; he fails to make clear that his "wall" is itself metaphorical, not an actual fortification which Rufinus breached or allowed Alaric to breach.

2.22 *a* Haec fatus: on the use of phrases marking the end of direct quotation, cf. n. 1.65 *b*.

2.22 f. ventis — fudit: for advancing armies compared with winds released, cf. Sil. 12.185–88 (the Romans burst forth from Nola) effusae ... ruunt ... turmae /// ut rupto terras invadunt carcere venti. For the reverse image, winds compared with armies, cf. 3H 96 f. fundit ab antris / Aeolus armatas hiemes; Verg. *A.* 1.81–83 (Aeolus releases the winds) cavum conversa cuspide montem / impulit in latus, ac venti, velut agmine facto, / qua data porta, ruunt. Bruère (1964) 231 compares Luc. 7.124–26 (the effect of Pompey's speech) frenos ... / laxat et ut victus violento navita Coro / dat regimen ventis.

2.22 *b* frena: for the winds thought of as reined horses, cf. RP 2 Pr.17 venti frenantur; Verg. *A.* 1.53 ventos ... / ... vinclis et carcere frenat. For a similar metaphor applied to bodies of water, cf. 1.63 f. laxare profundo / frena mari; n. 1.64.

2.23 abrupto ... obice: on the varying gender of *obex*, cf. Serv. on Verg. *A.* 10.377 magna ... obice: Modo usus habet, ut "hic obex" dicamus. ... antiqui etiam "haec obex" dicebant. ... Caper tamen in libris dubii generis probat dici et "hic obex" et "haec obex," quod, ut diximus, hodie de usu recessit; LTL s.v. *obex*, 424, col. 3.

2.24–26 ne — regio ... disposuit ... nefas: Bruère (1964) 231 compares Lucan's apostrophe to Fortune, 8.603 f. Disponis gladios, ne quo non fiat in orbe, / heu, facinus civile tibi.

2.25 cladem — orbem: for *divido* with *in* and the accusative, cf. Sen. *Thy.* 101 furorem divide in totam domum; TLL s.v. *divido* 1605.10–17 (cf. 1596.47–49, 60–64). On *orbis* of the Roman Empire, cf. n. 1 Pr.17 *b*.

2.26–30 Alii per terga ... Danuvii ... ruunt ... alii per Caspia claustra ... invadunt: for the two-fold invasion, cf. Philostorg. 11.8 τῶν Οὔννων ... οἱ μὲν ... τῆς ἐντὸς Ἴστρου Σκυθίας τὴν πολλὴν χειρωσάμενοι ... ἔπειτα παγέντα τὸν ποταμὸν διαβάντες, ἀθρόως εἰς τὴν Ῥώμην [read τὰ Ῥωμαίων; cf. Bidez (1913) *ad loc.*, and Caesarius *Dial.* 1.68 = Migne Gr. 38.936] εἰσήλασαν, καὶ κατὰ πᾶσαν ἀναχθέντες τὴν Θράκην, ὅλην τὴν Εὐρώπην ἐληΐσαντο· οἱ δὲ πρὸς ἥλιον ἀνίσχοντα τὸν Τάναϊν ποταμὸν διαβάντες καὶ τῇ Ἑῴᾳ ἐπεισρυέντες, δι' Ἀρμενίας τῆς μεγάλης εἰς τὴν καλουμένην Μελετινὴν κατερράγησαν. ἐκ ταύτης δὲ Εὐφρατησίαν τε ἐπέθησαν καὶ μέχρι τῆς κοίλης Συρίας ἤλασαν, καὶ τὴν Κιλικίαν καταδραμόντες φόνον ἀνθρώπων εἰργάσαντο ἀνιστόρητον; Sozomen. 8.25.1, 8.1.2; Socr. 6.1.6 f.; cf. Jerome *Ep.* 77.8.1 f. ecce subito discurrentibus nuntiis oriens totus intremuit, ab ultima Maeotide inter glacialem Tanain et Massagetarum immanes populos, ubi Caucasi rupibus feras gentes Alexandri claustra cohibent, erupisse Hunorum examina, quae ... caedis pariter ac terroris cuncta complerent. Aberat tunc Romanus exercitus et bellis civilibus in Italia tenebatur; 60.16.4 f. Immunis ab his malis videbatur oriens et tantum nuntiis consternatus: ecce tibi anno praeterito ex ultimi Caucasi rupibus immissi in nos ... septentrionis lupi tantas brevi provincias percucurrerunt. ... Obsessa Antiochia et urbes reliquae, quas Halys, Cnydus, Orontes, Euphratesque praeterfluunt (cf. n. 2.32–35); Assemani (1719) 262 f.; Int. 22; Rauschen (1897) 435 f., 438 f.; Seeck (1913) 274, 549; Schmidt (1934) 425–28; Stein-Palanque (1959) 228 f.

Apart from the question of the identity of the invaders, Claudian is thus supported by the other sources in his account of a two-fold invasion, with one horde crossing the Danube (2.26–28 Alii—rotis), the other penetrating the Caucasus mountains (2.28 f. alii—ducti; cf. n. 2.28 *b*). It should be noted that, after mentioning the two separate hordes, Claudian narrates their several campaigns of depredation in chiastic order. The spoliation of the *Orientis opes* by the second horde is narrated first, 2.30–36 Iam—Asiae, so that the second account, 2.36–44 Geticis—aristas, must refer to the first-mentioned horde. Thus Claudian identifies the crossers of the frozen Danube as Goths (cf. n. 1.308 *c*), while he gives no name to the other group.

Now Philostorgius and Sozomen, who speak of both hordes, identify both as Huns; Caesarius, who refers only to the former group, uses no ethnic designation. Socrates and Jerome speak only of the latter group, and identify them as Huns. The identification as Huns of the latter horde, those who broke through the Caucasus to invade Armenia and Syria, is undisputed: cf. Koch (1889) 598; Rauschen (1897) 438 f.; Birt (1892) Pr. 28 f.; Seeck (1913) 274, 549; Schmidt (1934) 427; Stein-Palanque (1959) 228. In regard to the first-named horde, those who crossed the frozen Danube, there seems to be no criterion for deciding between the identification of Claudian, who calls them Goths, and that of Philostorgius and Sozomen, who call them Huns. Their identification as Huns is accepted by Seeck (1913) 274 and Stein-Palanque (1959) 228; they are called Goths by Koch (1889) 598, Birt (1892) Pr. 29, ftn. 13, and Schmidt (1934) 425.

2.26 f. terga ... Danuvii solidata: cf. Philostorg. 11.8 παγέντα τὸν ποταμὸν διαβάντες; Caesarius, *Dial.* 1.68 (= Migne Gr. 38.936) ὅρα ... τὸν ... Ἴστρον. ... χειμῶνος πηγνυμένου, καὶ εἰς λιθώδη ἀντιτυπίαν μεθισταμένης τῆς μαλακῆς τοῦ ῥείθρου φύσεως, ὡς οἷαν τε φέρειν ἐπιπορευομένων πολεμίων ... πλῆθος. οὕτω τοι καὶ τὸ αὐτὸ ἐκ τοῦ ὕδατος παγὲν στερέωμα ... ὑπερστέγει ... ἵππον καὶ ἀναβάτην, ἐν χιλιάσι δέκα πολλάκις ὁρώμενον; Text. Comm. on 1.312, *fin.*

2.27 f. experta — rotis: cf. BP 338 f. (the Rhine and the Danube) Ambo habiles remis, ambo glacialia secti / terga rotis, 3H 150, 4H 347 f.; Verg. G. 3.361 f. (in the frozen North) unda ... iam tergo ferratos sustinet orbes, / puppibus illa prius, patulis iam hospita plaustris; Luc. 5.439–41 (the frozen seas of the North) nec pervia velis / aequora frangit eques, fluctuque latente sonantem / orbita migrantis scindit Maeotida Bessi.

2.28 a frangunt: cf. Text. Comm. *ad loc.*; cf. also Luc. 5.440 (quoted in n. 2.27 f.).

2.28 b Caspia claustra: cf. Jerome *Ep.* 77.8.1 ubi Caucasi rupibus feras gentes Alexandri claustra perhibent, erupisse Hunorum examina (cf. n. 2.26–30). Reference is most probably to the pass located at about the mid-point of the Caucasus range, the modern Pass of Dariel (Darial, Daryal, Persian *Dar-i-Alan*, "The Gate of the Alani": cf. Allen [1932] 10, 31; CAH 12, Map 8 [facing p. 109], grid CD 1). Though Pliny objects to the designation "Caspian" for this pass, he indicates that the alleged misnomer was in wide use: Plin. *Nat.* 6.12.30 Portae Caucasiae magno errore multis Caspiae dictae, 6.15.40; cf. RE s.v. *Kaukasiai Pylai*; Müller-Fischer (1883) 911 on Ptol. 5.8.5 αἱ Σαρματικαὶ Πύλαι; Furneaux (1896) on Tac. *Ann.* 6.33.4 Caspia via (cf. *Hist.* 1.6 claustra Caspiarum).

Koch (1899) 598 (cf. Rauschen [1897] 438) identifies our *Caspia claustra* with the coastal pass near Derbend (cf. CAH 12, Map 8 [facing

p. 109], grid D 1). There are three objections to this identification: (1) The passage from Jerome cited above, with its reference to *Alexandri claustra*, points to the Pass of Dariel, the fortification of which was credited to Alexander by the legend: cf. Procop. *Pers.* 1.10.3–9; Müller-Fischer (1883) 911. (2) Though modern scholars assert that the coastal pass was also called *Caspiae portae* (cf. Postgate [1917] 61 on Luc. 8.222 Caspia claustra; RE s.v. *Kaspioi* 2272.41–43, s.v. *Kaukasiai Pylai* 58.55; Rackham [1938] 2.358, ftn. *a*), they do not cite, nor have I been able to find, any ancient source which bears out this assertion, however reasonable it may seem in view of the location of the pass on the Caspian Sea. (3) In IE 2.152 per Caucasias accito turbine valles, the expression *Caucasias ... valles* is in better accord with an inland pass than with a passageway between the mountains and the sea.

Anderson (1928) discusses the question of the Caspian Gates at some length; he cites our passage, which he wrongly assigns (136) to *Carm. Min.*, as referring *either* to Dariel *or* to Derbend, but later (149 f., ftn. 36) he identifies the pass mentioned by Jerome *Ep.* 77.8.1 as Dariel.

2.29 *a* **Armenias ... nives:** cf. IE 1.16 f. ruptone Niphate / rursum barbaricis Oriens vastabitur armis? On the supposed connection between the name Niphates and νιφάς, "snowflake," cf. RE s.v. *Niphates* 706.65–67. Armenia is specifically mentioned by Philostorgius, Sozomen, and Socrates: cf. n. 2.26–30.

2.29 *b* **inopino:** the translation of Platnauer (1922), "newly-discovered," seems unduly to extend the meaning of this word. There is no reason to depart from the interpretation of Koenig (1808) *ad loc.*: *inopino tramite*, "per quem nemo exercitum ductum iri expectaverat"; Crépin (1933) "où on ne les attendait pas." Cf. RP 3.165–67 attonitus stabulo ceu pastor inani / cui pecus aut rabies Poenorum inopina leonum / aut populatrices infestavere catervae, 4H 102 f., 6H 216 f. On the unexpectedness of the Huns' attack, cf. the quotations from Jerome in n. 2.26–30.

2.30 Orientis opes: cf. Jerome *Ep.* 60.16.4 Immunis ... videbatur oriens ...; ecce ... lupi tantas brevi provincias percucurrerunt; n. 2.26–30.

2.30–48: for similar descriptions of devastation, cf. IE 1.243–50, 2.114 f., 550–53, 565–75.

2.30–36 Iam — Asiae: on the identity of the invaders referred to here, cf. n. 2.26–30, para. 2 f.

2.30 f. pascua ... Cappadocum — equorum: for Cappadocia as a breeder of horses, cf. CM 47.4 f. (in a poem on a gift to a horse, he discusses its birthplace) seu te Cappadocum gelida sub valle natantem / Argaeae lavere nives, CM 30.190–92; Solinus 45.1–5 (= 173 f. Mommsen) Cappadocia ... ante alias altrix equorum (cf. 45.4 [= 174 Mommsen] Argaeus nivalibus iugis arduus); Opp. C. 1.169–71; Veget. Ars vet. 4.6 (= 249 f. Lommatzsch); RE s.v. *Kappadokia* 1913.21–34. In the *Itinera Hierosolymitana* 577.5 f. (= CSEL 39.16.16 f.) there is mention of a *Villa Pampati* at Andabilis (cf. RE s.v.) *unde veniunt equi curules*; Andabilis is approximately fifty miles from Mt. Argaeus.

2.32–35 rubet ... Halys ... proterit — Orontem: cf. Jerome Ep. 60.16.4 f. quantae fluviorum aquae humano cruore mutatae sunt! Obsessa Antiochia et urbes reliquae, quas Halys, Cnydus, Orontes Eufratesque praeterfluunt (cf. n. 2.26–30). On the likelihood that Jerome was influenced by our present passage in writing the sentences just cited, cf. Levy (1948a); Maenchen-Helfen (1955) 387, ftn. 21, 393; Cameron (1965) 112. Cf. also n. 2.37, n. 2.187–91.

2.32 *a* rubet ... Halys: for *rubeo* used to describe bloodstained objects without the actual occurrence of some such word as *sanguis* or *caedes*, cf. RP 2 Pr.43 rubuit Busiride Nilus; Stat. Theb. 3.211 io quanti crudele rubebitis amnes; Sil. 1.267.

2.32 *b* Halys: this river, together with Mt. Taurus, cf. n. 2.32 f., was regarded as forming the boundary between Asia proper and Asia Minor: cf. RE s.v. *Halys*.

2.32 f. nec — Cilix: cf. BP 184 f. non obice Pindi / servati Dryopes. For Mt. Taurus as a barrier protecting Cilicia, cf. IE 2.468 per Cilicas rupto descendere Tauro; Curt. 3.4.6 perpetuo iugo montis asperi ac praerupti Cilicia includitur; RE s.v. *Tauros* 46.44–48. For the invasion of Cilicia, cf. Philostorgius 11.8, quoted in n. 2.26–30.

2.33–35 Syriae — Orontem: cf. IE 2.569–71 Nuper ab extremo veniens equitatus Araxe / terruit Antiochi muros, ipsumque decorae / paene caput Syriae flammis hostilibus arsit; Philostorg. 11.8 μέχρι τῆς κοίλης Συρίας ἤλασαν; Jerome Ep. 60.16.5 Obsessa Antiochia; n. 2.26–30.

2.34 f. assuetum ... choris et laeta plebe canorum ... imbel-

lem ... Orontem: cf. Juv. 3.62–65 iam pridem Syrus in Tiberim / defluxit Orontes / et linguam et mores et cum tibicine chordas / obliquas nec non gentilia tympana secum / vexit; Lucian. *Salt.* 76 οἱ ... Ἀντιοχεῖς, εὐφυεστάτη πόλις καὶ ὄρχησιν μάλιστα πρεσβεύουσα; RE s.v. *Antiocheia* 2442 f. Cf. also IE 1.434 famae contemptor Orontes.

2.36–48 Geticis — usus: on the attribution to the Goths of the devastation described here, cf. n. 2.26–30, para. 2 f. Cf. also n. 2.45–48.

2.36–44: on the use of imagery here, cf. Christiansen (1969) 68.

2.36 Europa: cf. Philostorg. 11.8 ὅλην τὴν Εὐρώπην ἐληΐσαντο; n. 2.26–30.

2.37 ludibrio: for the ironic use of this word, cf. 6H 139 (a ship) ludibrium pelagi; IE 2.535; Verg. *A.* 6.75 (the Sibyl's leaves) ne ... volent rapidis ludibria ventis; Luc. 7.380 (Pompey) ludibrium soceri, 8.710, 10.26. Cf. also Jerome *Ep.* 60.16.3 (during the barbarian invasions) Quot matronae ... his beluis fuere ludibrio; n. 2.32–35.

2.37 f. *a* frondentis ... Dalmatiae: for the productiveness of Dalmatia, cf. CS 3.302 Dalmatiae lucos; Str. 7.5.10 (the coasts of Dalmatia and of Italy) ἐλαιόφυτοι ... καὶ εὐάμπελοι; *Expositio totius mundi et gentium* 53 (= GLM 119) Dalmatia ... tigna tectis utilia ... emittit; Rostovtzeff (1926) 222, 545 ftn. 11, 553 ftn. 59.

2.37 f. *b* ad usque Dalmatiae fines: for epigraphic evidence that the city of Salona in Dalmatia was spared at least until July 395, cf. Egger (1926) 43, 84.

2.38 f. omnis — undas: cf. Jerome *Ep.* 123.16.1 (on the devastation of Roman territory by barbarians) Olim a mari Pontico usque ad Alpes Iulias non erant nostra, quae nostra sunt. Jerome attributes the disasters to the treachery, not of Rufinus, but of Stilicho (cf. CSEL 56.93, ftn. 11).

2.39 aequor et ... interiacet undas: for *interiaceo* governing two accusatives, cf. CS 1.215 Oceanum fontesque interiacet Histri; Stat. *Theb.* 3.337 et Asopon veteresque interiacet Argos; *Ach.* 1.710 (= 2.36) portum celsamque interiacet urbem; Liv. 7.29.6 planitiem quae Capuam Tifataque interiacet.

2.40–42: for Libya as a type of wasteland, cf. 4H 436 Libyae squalentis harenas, IR 2.241. Bruère (1964) 231 compares Luc.

5.39 (Curio met his death) Libyae squalentibus arvis, and 9.690 f. (Perseus, avoiding the cultivated lands of Europe, flies with the death-dealing Gorgon's head over Libya) quae nullo consita cultu / sideribus Phoeboque vacat. Bruère, referring to the "badlands of the northern Balkans," and to "this sterile region," does not make it sufficiently clear that, while Libya was a perpetual and typical wasteland, Claudian's whole point here is that the other regions mentioned and bemoaned had, in the memory of man, been fertile; it is only because of the repeated raids of the barbarians that the inhabitants had become benumbed (2.48 sensum ... malis detraxerat usus), and it was only because of this numbness that "the loss of this [now] sterile region was mourned by none," 2.46 iam nulli flebile damnum. With the lemma just quoted, Bruère (1964) 231 compares Luc. 7.691 (among the losses in the Civil War) flebilis Africa damnis. As so often, Claudian has given his own twist to a borrowing from Lucan. On the imagery here, cf. Christiansen (1969) 68.

2.42 a nescit mansuescere: cf. Verg. G. 4.470 (the inexorable hearts of Tartarus' rulers) nescia ... humanis precibus mansuescere corda.

2.42 b mansuescere: for this word of land subdued to cultivation, cf. Verg. G. 2.238 f. Salsa autem tellus et quae perhibetur amara; / frugibus infelix ea, nec mansuescit arando.

2.43 f.: both Zos. 5.5.5 and Socr. 7.10 mention the devastation of Thessaly by the Goths under Alaric. However, because Zosimus' chronology of the years 395–97, and Socrates' for the entire period 395–410 are confused (cf. Clinton [1845] 1.536; Stein-Palanque [1959] 540, ftn. 51; for a somewhat different position Cameron [1968b], esp. 247 f.; Hussey [1853] 3.507; Bury [1923] 111, ftn. 3), it cannot be held with any degree of certainty (despite Schmidt [1934] 428, ftn. 2) that the passages cited refer to events preceding the first expedition of Stilicho to Greece in 395, and not rather to those which followed his withdrawal later in that year: cf. n. 2.187–91, Stein-Palanque (1959) 230 f.

2.45–48: Schmidt (1934) 428 holds that the invaders of Pannonia in 395 were not Visigoths, but Marcomanni, Quadi, and other trans-Danubian peoples. His views are more fully set forth in his first edition, Schmidt (1910) 1.117, and are followed by Stein-Palanque

(1959) 228 and Cameron (1968b) 270. Note that Claudian does not state explicitly that it was the Goths who invaded Pannonia. Rather, the present passage constitutes a sort of *praeteritio* (cf. 2.45 Nam) intended to set off, by contrast with the long-standing woes of Pannonia, Thrace, and Moesia (cf. Stein-Palanque [1959] 182 f., 186, 192 f., 194 f., 204 f., covering the years 374–87), the horrors now caused by the Gothic invasions of Thessaly and Macedonia (2.43 f.), which regions Claudian would apparently have us believe had been hitherto unscathed. Actually, however, the two last-named regions had been ravaged just a few years before: cf. Stein-Palanque (1959) 194 f.

2.46 a Mysorum: cf. Text. Comm. *ad loc.*

2.46 b nulli flebile damnum: cf. Jerome *Ep.* 123.16.1 (A.D. 409) per annos triginta fracto Danubii limite in mediis Romani imperii regionibus pugnabatur. Aruerunt vetustate lacrimae; Stein-Palanque (1959) 182–95, esp. 189; 204 f.

2.47 cursus: for this word of barbarian raids, cf. IE 2.567 f. quas urbes et quanto tempore Martis / ignaras uno rapuerunt proelia cursu; Luc. 1.254–56 (the inhabitants of Ariminum bewail their fall) Nos primi Senonum motus Cimbrumque ruentem / vidimus et Martem Libyae cursumque furoris / Teutonici (note the word *furori* at the end of the present verse, and cf. Bruère [1964] 231).

2.47 f. campus ... furori expositus: reference is apparently to the collapse of the Danuvian *limes*: cf. n. 2.46 b.

2.48 sensum ... detraxerat usus: cf. the last three words in the quotation from Jerome, n. 2.46 b.

2.49 brevibus ... causis: cf. Text. Comm. *ad loc.*; cf. also CM 9.40 (the porcupine) brevis ... bestia.

2.50–53: on the relation of these verses to the ψόγος-pattern, cf. Levy (1946) 63, 65.

2.50 Imperium — sanguine: cf. BG 75 f. (Roma speaks) arva / vulneribus quaesita meis; Christ (1938) 146 f.

2.52 tantis: on *tantis = tot* cf. n. 1.224 b.

2.53 a proditor: the same term is applied to Stilicho by Jerome *Ep.* 123.16.2 (cf. CSEL 56.93, ftn. 11) and by Rutilius (2.51 Geticis grassatus proditor armis); cf. n. 2.22–60, para. 2; Várady (1968).

2.53 b iners: for this adjective used of the unwarlike, cf. IE 2.54–56 (in the face of dreadful portents) Haud equidem contra tot signa Camillo / detulerim fasces, nedum... inerti / mancipio; Verg. A. 9.55–57 Teucrum mirantur inertia corda, /... non obvia ferre / arma viros; Tib. 1.1.53, 57 f.; Luc. 6.419 f. Turbae sed mixtus inerti / Sextus erat, Magno proles indigna parente; Stat. Theb. 11.484 f.; Sil. 11.237–40. Cf. also Liv. 44.38.10. For a similar epithet applied to Rufinus, cf. 2.198 ignavo... nocenti; on the unpopularity of the civilian Rufinus with the military, cf. Int. 10, 25.

2.54–99: this is the sole direct reference in our sources to the march of a Gothic army upon Constantinople (cf. Seeck [1913] 549 on 275.12–25). Corroboration may perhaps be found in the bare mention in another source of Alaric's withdrawal from the city: Socr. 7.10 Ἀλάριχος... ἀναχωρήσας... τῆς Κωνσταντινουπόλεως ἐπὶ τὰ ἑσπέρια μέρη διέβαινε; cf. Rauschen (1897) 435, ftn. 7, followed by Schmidt (1934) 427, ftn. 6; on the uncertainty of Socrates' chronology, cf. n. 2.43 f. Hence the authenticity of the details given in our passage rests almost (cf. n. 2.76 f.) entirely upon Claudian's word alone.

2.54 a: for Constantinople as a new Rome, cf. BG 60 f. (Roma speaks) cum subiit par Roma mihi, divisaque sumpsit / aequales Aurora togas; Socr. 1.16.1; Jul. Or. 1.8B–C; Notitia Urbis Constantinopolitanae 1.1 f. (= Seeck [1876] 229) VRBS CONSTANTINOPOLITANA NOVA ROMA; the Suda s.vv. Κωνσταντῖνος ὁ μέγας, Κωνσταντινούπολις, Γρατιανός (= 3.176.9, 3.177.2–12, 1.539.10 Adler); RE s.v. Constantinopolis 964; Dölger (1937); Christ (1938) 89; Georgacas (1947) 354. On the rivalry between Constantinople and Rome as seen by Claudian, cf. Marsili (1946a); Fuhrmann (1968).

2.54 b magnae: on this and similar epithets for Rome, cf. Christ (1938) 83 f.

2.55 a Calchedonias: on the spelling, cf. TLL, Onomast. s.v. Calchedon 73.2; RE s.v. Kalchedon 1555.

2.55 b despectat: on Constantinople as a lofty city, cf. n. 1.174 b.

2.56 iam non finitimo: on iam non, cf. n. 1.305 b.

2.57–59 lucere — aspicit: the verb aspicio here is extended to include auditory (rauca sonare / cornua) as well as strictly visual (lucere faces, peti fastigia) perception, a shade of meaning of which TLL s.v. aspicio apparently takes no notice. Cf. Ov. Met. 12.527–29 (Mopsus perceives Caenaeus in the form of a bird) lustrantem leni sua castra volatu / Mopsus et ingenti circum clangore sonantem / aspexit. The words *rauca* and *clangore* in the two passages seem to require that *aspicit* and *aspexit* be taken to denote actual sense-perception, not mere mental cognition (contrast, e.g. V. Fl. 7.431 f. illa tremens, ut supplicis aspicit ora / conticuisse viri, iamque et sua verba reposci).

2.60 iunctis ... portus munire carinis: for a chain of boats used to blockade a port defensively, cf. Liv. 30.10.4-6 Scipio ... onerariarum quadruplicem ordinem pro muro adversus hostem opposuit, easque ipsas ... malis antennisque de nave in navem traiectis ac validis funibus inligatis velut uno inter se vinculo comprehendit; Graefe (1922) 445-49. For a chain of logs similarly used, cf. Luc. 2.669-78. Apparently none of the other poets mentions a similar stratagem.

2.61-85: *Rufinus rejoices in the suffering caused by the barbarians, with whom he openly consorts.*

2.61-70 Obsessa — manu: on Rufinus' alleged joy at the sufferings of others, cf. n. 1.234 f. On this passage as a reflection of the rhetorical *locus de crudelitate*, cf. n. 1.230-56. On echoes of Lucan here, cf. Bruère (1964) 232.

2.62 *a* summae ... ex culmine turris: cf. Ov. *Met.* 5.291 (Pyreneus leaps) e summae culmine turris.

2.62 f., 70 ex culmine turris ... cernit spectacula. ... Videt omnia late: on τειχοσκοπία as an epic theme, cf. Miniconi (1951) 168; also 35, 58, 77, 89, 91, 107, 138.

2.62 *b* turris: the attribution of an *arx* to the *tyrannus* was a stock feature of the rhetorical treatment of tyrants and tyrannicides (cf. n. 1.230-56). Cf. Sen. *Con.* 3.6 Pr. tyrannum ex arce fugientem, 2.5.6 ex arce, 9.4 Pr. tyrannus patrem in arcem ... accersiit; Quint. *Inst.* 7.4.22 multum interest tyrannum iuvenis occiderit an senex ... in arce an domi; [Quint.] *Decl.* 274 (= 121.27-29 Ritter), 267 (= 88.18-20 Ritter), 288 (= 155.22-25 Ritter); Lucian. *Tyr.* 7, 9, 16, 19; cf. also Juv. 10.307 saeva ... in arce tyrannus; Mayor (1888) 2.159-61; Decker (1913) 53.

2.63 spectacula: for *spectaculum* of a sight yielding grim gratification, cf. 6H 271 (Alaric's defeat gives the Alps their revenge) desolatus et exspes / debita pulsato reddit spectacula monti; Luc. 7.797 (Caesar refuses cremation to the corpses of the Pompeians slain at Pharsalus) ne laeta furens scelerum spectacula perdat; Sil. 10.453, 12.239, 16.531.

2.67 f. nec canos — sinus: for the tyrant's cruelty exercised equally upon young and old, cf. 1.245-49; n. 1.245-50, n. 1.245-49, n. 1.247 a.

2.69 risus: cf. Ov. Met. 2.778 (in a description of Invidia) Risus abest, nisi quem visi movere dolores.

2.71 exceptis ... suis: in over-strict conformity with my announced procedure (Int. 50 f.) of discussing only those readings in which Jeep, Birt, and Koch differed from one another or I from all of them, I regrettably failed to call attention at this point in the Text. Comm. to the fact that the reading *exceptis* is based upon reports of two non-extant manuscripts given in the Florentine and Gyraldine excerpts (cf. Int. 44 f.). As I stated in Int. 23, ftn. 147, Fargues rejects *exceptis* in favor of *praeceptis*, the unanimous reading of the extant manuscripts. Cameron (1968a) 392 also prefers *praeceptis*, but on different grounds, for which he argues most persuasively. He may be right in holding that Claudian wrote *praeceptis*. If he is, we shall have to conclude that a scribe at some point in the tradition was capable of inventing a reading which was not only *difficilior* but considerably *acutior*. The charge that Rufinus had summoned the barbarians to perform their acts of devastation has already been made, and made forcefully, in 2.22-26; to state at this point that these wolves required *praecepta* in the carrying out of their depredations would be otiose, to say the least. The one additional charge that could render Rufinus' guilt more hideous would be that the beloved estates of the ἄπληστος, the ἀκόρεστος, the *praedo annosus* (Int. 15, ftn. 83), were left untouched amidst the general ruin by the *carus hostis* (2.72), the *fidi hostes* (2.133). This is not to argue, as Seeck (1913) 273 f. does, that Rufinus' possessions were in fact the only ones spared; in details like this we are dealing with Claudian's imaginative rhetoric, not with the sober report of a historian.

In a recent private communication, Cameron, while still rejecting *exceptis*, has generously provided a parallel passage in support of it: Theophanes *Chronologia* (288.2-4 de Boor; the Emperor Maurice speaks to a suspected usurper) ὦ Γερμανέ, δύο εἰσὶ τεκμήρια τῆς ὑπονοίας μου· τά τε ἐκ τοῦ λαοῦ πρός σε γράμματα, καὶ τοῦ φείδεσθαι τὸν λαὸν τῆς ἀγελαίας ἵππου τῆς νεμομένης σοι εἰς τὰ προάστεια. πάντα γὰρ διήρπασαν, καὶ τῶν σῶν ἐφείσαντο.

2.72 carum — hostem: the idea is repeated in 2.133 fidos... hostes.

2.73–85: for Rufinus' negotiations with Alaric, cf. Zos. 5.5.4, quoted in n. 2.22–60; Stein-Palanque (1959) 229; Int. 24 f. Zosimus' words δι' ἀπορρήτων do not accord with Claudian's story of open negotiations. Fargues (1933a) 99, ftn. 3, suggests that Claudian purposely refrains from mentioning Alaric by name in IR so as not to jeopardize Stilicho's possible friendly relations with him in the future.

2.73 f. iactabat ... quod ... paterent ... foret ... permissa: for *iacto* with a subjunctive *quod*-clause, cf. Tac. *Ann.* 6.25 (Tiberius on Agrippina's death) iactavit... quod non... strangulata neque... proiecta foret. On Claudian's use of the *quod*-clause as a substitute for the infinitive with subject accusative, cf. Paucker (1880) 605 f.; Trump (1887) 36; on the general development of the usage, cf. Hofmann-Szantyr (1965) 576–79.

2.74 a sermonum ... vicibus: cf. Verg. *A.* 6.535 (conversation between Aeneas and Deiphobus) Hac vice sermonum; Ov. *Tr.* 4.4.79, *Ep.* 21.18, *Pont.* 2.10.35.

2.74 b foret ... permissa: Birt (1892) 556 s.v. *permittere* takes *permissa* as an attributive participle; he cites it along with 4H 618 permissi... voti, and FH 4.31 permissis iocis. In neither of these, however, is *permissus* pleonastic, as it would be here. It seems better, therefore, to take the view that *foret permissa* is a compound verb: cf. CM 29.51 (to Cupid) Quae tibi, saeve puer, non est permissa potestas? This interpretation also avoids the necessity of taking *vicibus* directly with *facultas*; the dative with this noun is otherwise apparently unexampled in verse, and is rare in prose: cf. TLL s.v. *facultas*, e.g. 148.3 f.

2.75 a egregii: for this word used ironically, cf. BG 239 (of Gildo) scilicet egregius morum; CM 22.54; Verg. *A.* 6.523 (Deiphobus, of his treacherous wife) Egregia... coniunx, 7.556; Stat. *Theb.* 9.98; TLL s.v. *egregius* 289.24–42.

2.75 b quotiens exisset: on the subjunctive here, cf. n. 1.187–89 b, n. 1.224 f.

2.75 c foederis: on Rufinus' alleged negotiations with Alaric, cf. n. 2.73–85.

2.76 f.: cf. Text. Comm. on 2.76; in the last sentence of that note, for "verses 78–80," read "verses 78–83." Seeck (following Mommsen [1889] 235, ftn. 3) originally identified Rufinus' *socii* as Goths: cf. Seeck (1896) 109, ftn. 1 (cf. also RE s.v. *bucellarii* 936.31–39; Seeck [1913] 275, 549); in this he was followed by Grosse (1920) 86, ftn. 3 (where our passage is wrongly assigned to IR 1), 286, ftn. 4. Later, on the basis of *Pithoei Chronicon* (for 395 = MGH 9.650, sect. 34) Rufinus ... interficitur Chunorum, quo fulciebatur, praesidio superato (cf. Int. 25, ftn. 163), Seeck altered his position, and identified Rufinus' *armata clientum agmina* as Huns: Seeck (1920) 100 f., 412. In this latter position he is followed by Stein-Palanque (1959) 239.

Barbarian bodyguards for Roman officials from the time of Honorius to that of Justinian seem to have been drawn in greatest numbers from among the Goths, with the Huns holding second place: cf. Olymp. frag. 7 (= FHG 4.59) τὸ βουκελλάριος ὄνομα ἐν ταῖς ἡμέραις Ὀνωρίου ἐφέρετο κατὰ στρατιωτῶν οὐ μόνον Ῥωμαίων, ἀλλὰ καὶ Γότθων τινῶν; Zos. 5.34.1 οἳ Στελίχωνι προσεδρεύοντες ἔτυχον Οὖννοι; Benjamin (1892) 33 f.; Grosse (1920) 289. Whatever may have been the actual nationality of Rufinus' barbarian retainers, it is evident from 2.78–83 (esp. 2.83 ritus vestemque Getarum) that Claudian intended to represent them as Goths. Strangely enough, he seems to have included among the *ritus vestemque Getarum* a trait of Hunnish, not of Gothic, culture: cf. n. 2.80. Mazzarino (1942) 254 f., ftn. 3, mistakenly cites 2.71 in support of the statement that Rufinus' bodyguards were Huns.

2.77 privatis ... signis: as a civilian magistrate, Rufinus had no right to official military *signa*. What sort of standard, if any, Rufinus is supposed to have used for his *bucellarii* is not clear; Claudian is probably speaking metaphorically.

2.78–85: the Emperor Gratian is also said to have assumed the garb of his barbarian bodyguards, to the indignation of the regular Roman troops: cf. [Victor.] *Epit. de Caes.* 47.6 Nam dum exercitum negligeret et paucos ex Alanis, quos ingenti auro ad se transtulerat, anteferret veteri ac Romano militi, adeoque barbarorum comitatu et prope amicitia capi∗, ut nonnumquam eodem habitu iter faceret, odia contra se militum excitavit; RE s.v. *Exercitus* 1628.44–50.

The costume of skins (cf. n. 2.79 *b*) served as a convenient symbol of barbarism in expressions of anti-barbarian sentiment (cf. n. 1.306-53, para. 2): cf. Synes. *De regno* 15 (= Migne Gr. 66.1093A) τὴν βουλαίαν Θέμιν αὐτήν, καὶ Θεὸν οἶμαι τὸν στράτιον ἐγκαλύπτεσθαι, ὅταν ὁ σισυροφόρος ἄνθρωπος ἐξηγῆται χλαμύδας ἐχόντων (cf. Stein-Palanque [1959] 235 f.); Prudent. *Contr. Symm.* 2.695 f. (= Migne Lat. 60.234A) Tentavit Geticus nuper delere tyrannus / Italiam, 698 mastrucis proceres vestire togatos. For attempts to curb the wearing of barbarian dress in Rome, cf. Cod. Theod. 14.10.2, 3, 4; Cochrane (1944) 307; Sander (1939) 17 f.

Rutilius reproaches Stilicho with betraying Rome to his *satellites pelliti*: cf. Rutil. 2.49-51 Ipsa satellitibus pellitis Roma patebat, / et captiva prius, quam caperetur, erat. / Nec tantum Geticis grassatus proditor armis; n. 2.22-60, para. 2; n. 2.53 *a*.

2.79 *a* revocat... in pectora: for *revoco* of drawing to the front of the body a portion of a garment draped over the back, cf. Serv. on Verg. *A.* 7.612 Gabinius cinctus est toga sic in tergum reiecta, ut una eius lacinia a tergo revocata hominem cingat. Cf. also Juv. 1.27 umero revocante lacernas, and Mayor (1888) *ad loc.*

2.79 *b* pelles: for a garment of skins as a national costume of the Goths, cf. BP 481 f. pellita Getarum / curia, 4H 466; Prudentius as quoted in n. 2.78-85; Sidon. *Ep.* 1.2.4 (in a description of the court of Theodoric, King of the Goths) pellitorum turba satellitum; Sander (1939) 15 f.

2.80: the mention of *frena* along with *pharetrae* and *arcus* shows that Claudian has in mind the accoutrements of the mounted archer. These he wrongly represents as part of the *ritus vestisque Getarum* (2.83), for equestrian bowmen were apparently not found among them, nor (despite Luc. 8.221 arcus Geticis intendite nervis, on which cf. Postgate [1917] 60 f.; Schmidt [1934] 518, ftn. 4) was the bow in high esteem among them: cf. Procop. *Goth.* 1.27.27 Ῥωμαῖοι μὲν σχεδόν τι ἅπαντες καὶ οἱ σύμμαχοι Οὖννοι ἱπποτοξόται εἰσὶν ἀγαθοί, Γότθων δὲ τὸ ἔργον τοῦτο οὐδενὶ ἤσκηται, ἀλλ' οἱ μὲν ἱππεῖς αὐτοῖς μόνοις δορατίοις τε καὶ ξίφεσιν εἰώθασι χρῆσθαι, οἱ δὲ τοξόται, πεζοί τε ὄντες καὶ πρὸς τῶν ὁπλιτῶν καλυπτόμενοι, ἐς μάχην καθίστανται; Sidon. *Ep.* 1.2.5 (of Theodoric) arcum lateri innectere citra gravitatem regiam iudicat; Schmidt (1934) 246, 518. On the other hand, the Huns were famous for equestrian bowmanship, and esteemed archery highly: cf. Zos. 4.20.4 (the Huns) ἐκ τῶν ἵππων κατατοξεύοντες; Olymp. frag. 18 (= FHG 4.61) διαλαμβάνει ... περὶ τῶν Οὔννων, καὶ περὶ τῶν ῥηγῶν αὐτῶν τῆς εὐφυεστάτης τοξείας; Jordanes, *Get.* 24.128 (the Huns) ad equitandum promptissimi ... et ad arcus sagittasque parati; Grosse (1920) 293; Alföldi (1932) 18–24, esp. 24. Thus it is presumably a trait of Hunnish warfare which Claudian here attributes to the Goths. On the possibility that Rufinus' bodyguards were actually Huns, cf. n. 2.76 f.

2.82–85: with Claudian's indignation at Rufinus' adoption of barbarian dress, Bruère (1964) 232 compares Lucan's at the ex-centurion Septimus, the murderer of Pompey, who used Egyptian arms instead of Roman: Luc. 8.597 f.

2.82 *a* Ausonios — regentem: as Cameron (1968a) 393 points out, the translation of Platnauer (1922), "One who drives a consul's chariot and enjoys a consul's powers," is incorrect; that of Crépin (1933), "qu'on a vu en Italie sur un char de triomphe," is no better. Reference is rather to Rufinus' pomp and authority as Praetorian Prefect: cf. n. 2.82 *b*, n. 2.82 *c*.

2.82 *b* Ausonios currus: reference is to the chariot which was a well-known official appurtenance of the Praetorian Prefect: cf. Lyd. *Mag.* 2.14 ὄχημα ... ὁποῖον ἴσμεν; Cassiod. *Inst.* 1.32.5 (= 81.13 f. Mynors) si praefectum vox praeconis enuntiet, si carpentum ipsius strepentibus rotis transire noscamus, *Var.* 6.3.2; Int. 14; Birt (1892) 493 s.v. *currus*, where the present passage is erroneously cited as 2.8; Alföldi (1934) 109 f., 115, Plate 10; Ensslin (1939) 92, 98, 100. For the word *Ausonius* used of the traditional trappings of Roman officialdom, cf. 4H 566 (Honorius borne aloft in a procession) Ausonio ... succinctus amictu.

2.82 *c* iura: on the Praetorian Prefect's juridical functions, cf. Int. 12 f.; cf. also 1.239, 2.85 iudice.

2.84 f. the preeminent position of the Praetorian Prefect in the Roman judiciary (cf. 2.82 iura regentem; Int. 12 f.) is at the basis of Claudian's conceit that the laws themselves were forced to change their costume when Rufinus changed his. The laying aside of Roman dress is then equated with foreign captivity, with which it would ordinarily be associated: cf. Hor. *Carm.* 3.5.9–11 sub rege Medo Marsus et Apulus / ... togae / oblitus. Bruère (1964) 232 compares Lucan's personification of the laws in 3.139 f. (Caesar speaks) si voce Metelli / servantur leges, malint a Caesare tolli. On the use of imagery here, cf. Christiansen (1969) 88.

2.84 Latii: the word is chosen to emphasize Rufinus' deviation from ancient Roman tradition: contrast CS 1.294 f. (of Stilicho) nihil in tanto circum terrore locutus / indignum Latio; cf. Steinbeiss (1936) 11; Laqueur-Koch-Weber (1930) 19.

2.85 pellito: cf. 2.79 revocat in pectora pelles; n. 2.79 b.

2.86–99: *The oppressed people long for Stilicho.* Claudian here represents the inhabitants of Constantinople much more sympathetically than he does in IE 2.133–37 (esp. 136 Graios ... Quirites), 326–45. Though the latter poem (A.D. 399) still expresses Stilicho's hopes of eventual domination in the East (cf. IE 2.574–602), such hopes must have diminished somewhat in the intervening years; hence Claudian seems to have felt free in 399 to express the antipathy of the Romans of the West (with whom the poet identifies himself; cf. Levy [1948b]) for their titular fellow-citizens at the other end of the Mediterranean: cf. Stein-Palanque (1959) 228; Fargues (1933a) 137–39; Steinbeiss (1936) 50 f., 55; Fabbri (1938); Mazzarino (1942) 95; Courcelle (1943) 119 f.; Marsili (1946a).

2.86 murmura furtim: for an adverb qualifying a substantive, cf. IE 1.476 retro ducibus; Birt (1892) Pr. 221, sect. II; Hofmann-Szantyr (1965) 171.

2.87 f. nam — licet: for the suppression of the right to complain, cf. 1.257 f. taciti ... sepultos / suspirant gemitus indignarique verentur; n. 1.257 f.

2.87 nec ... quidem: cf. Text. Comm. *ad loc.*

2.88–99: there are two other occurrences in IR (2.228–47, 261–77) of the collective speech, representing as a single utterance the words of several speakers. On speeches of this type in the later Roman epic, cf. Lipscomb (1909) 44–46. Cf. also n. 1.45–65, esp. sect. 8.

2.90 turbine rerum: on this expression, cf. n. 1.260 c.

2.91 f. illinc, hinc: explained by 2.93 f. per rura ... / intra tecta.

2.92 *a* agit: for *ago* in the sense "harass," cf. BG 148 f. (the goddess Africa prefers to be harassed by heat rather than oppressed by Gildo) medius flagrantis Olympi / me quoque limes agat; Verg. *A.* 4.465 f.

(Aeneas troubles Dido's dreams) Agit ipse furentem / in somnis ferus Aeneas; TLL s.v. *ago* 1368.12–44. Cf. also n. 1.232 *a*.

2.92 *b* **fretum ... negatur:** for the interruption of navigation, cf. 2.60 iunctis—carinis.

2.93 f.: on the use of imagery here, cf. Christiansen (1969) 86.

2.94 timor: cf. 1.256 f. Deiecerat omnes / ... terror; Int. 11, ftn. 40.

2.94 f. *a* **Tandem — Stilicho:** cf. IE 2.592 f. (Aurora speaks) Stilicho, ... succurre ruenti, / eripe me tandem, servilibus eripe regnis. Cf. also Hor. *Carm.* 1.2.25 f. Quem vocet divum populus ruentis / imperi rebus?, 30 Tandem venias precamur.

2.94 f. *b* **ruenti ... patriae:** cf. Jerome *Ep.* 60.16.3 Romanus orbis ruit. On the likelihood of a connection between the two passages, cf. n. 2.32–35.

On the recital by Claudian and the panegyrists of Rome's very real dangers for the purpose of magnifying the glory of her rescuers, cf. Christ (1938) 72.

2.95 Dilecta hic pignora: Stilicho's wife Serena presumably left their children in Constantinople when, earlier in the year, she accompanied her cousin Honorius to Italy: cf. 6H 92–100, Stein-Palanque (1959) 218, 229, and ftn. 57.

2.96 f.: Stilicho's marriage to Serena, niece of Theodosius, took place in Constantinople in A.D. 384: cf. CS 1.76–88 (esp. 88 Bosphorus); RE s.v. *Serena* (2); Rauschen (1897) 175, sect. 10.

2.96 *a* **hic domus:** cf. CS 1.295–98 (Stilicho always behaved with proper loftiness towards the officials of the East, even though he might thus have endangered his holdings there) responsa quod ardua semper / Eois dederis ... / securus, quamvis et opes et rura tenerent / insignesque domos; Stein-Palanque (1959) 231.

2.96 *b* **thalamis ... genialibus:** cf. Paul. *Fest.* 94 (83.23 f. Lindsay) genialis lectus, qui nuptiis sternitur in honore genii, unde et appellatus; Rossbach (1853) 367–69; Wissowa (1912) 176 and ftn. 9. The comment of Schol. A *ad loc.*, thalami geniales sunt in quibus filii generantur, follows the etymology given by Serv. on Verg. *A.* 6.603 a generandis liberis, and copied by Isid. *Etym.* 20.11.5.

2.96 *c* **primum ... omen:** cf. Verg. *A.* 1.345 f. (Dido and Sychaeus) pater intactam dederat primisque iugarat / ominibus; Serv. *ad* *loc.* Ominibus: auguriis. Et secundum Romanos locutus est, qui nihil nisi captatis faciebant auguriis, et praecipue nuptias; Cic. *Div.* 1.16.28 nihil fere quondam maioris rei nisi auspicato . . . gerebatur, quod etiam nunc nuptiarum auspices declarant, qui omissa re nomen tamen tenent; Rossbach (1853) 293–307; DeMarchi (1896) 1.152–55; Wissowa (1912) 386.

2.97: cf. 3H 154–56 (Theodosius adjures Stilicho) per consanguineos thalamos . . . / per taedas, quas ipsa tuo regina levavit / coniugio socrusque nurum produxit ab aula.

2.98 f. *a* **solus — languescent:** cf. Pacatus, *Panegyricus Theodosio Augusto dictus* 30.5 Et te quidem, imperator Auguste, ad adserendam rem publicam usurpandamque victoriam suffecisset in bella vel solum venire. . . . nonne tu . . . legionibus otiosis rem totam visus egisses?; n. 1.183–87, para. 2.

2.98 f. *b* **Te . . . viso . . . cadet dementia:** for a similar compliment paid to the consul Manlius, cf. MT 248 f. Quae non seditio, quae non insania vulgi / te viso lenita cadat?

2.99 *a* **avidi:** on Rufinus' avarice, cf. Int. 15 f., ftns. 82, 83, 95.

2.99 *b* **monstri:** for this epithet applied to Rufinus, cf. 1.291 Hoc monstrum.

2.100–29: *Stilicho marches East at the head of a mighty host, the combined armies of the East and the West. His very approach checks the barbarian raids.* On Stilicho's march from Italy to Thessaly, for which Claudian is our only source, cf. Int. 24; Seeck (1913) 275, 549 (on Seeck's bias against Stilicho, cf. Int. 23, ftn. 145); Stein-Palanque (1959) 229. On the shortcomings of Zosimus and Socrates for this period, cf. n. 2.43 f. On the legitimacy of Stilicho's claim to command both armies, cf. n. 2.6. On this passage as part of a *laus Stilichonis*, cf. n. 1.259–300.

2.100 *a*: on a possible significance of the verse-number here, cf. n. 1.300. On the use of imagery here, cf. Christiansen (1969) 68 f.

2.100 *b* **Talibus . . . procellis:** on these words as marking the transition from direct quotation to narrative, cf. n. 1.65 *b*.

2.101 *a* **At Stilicho:** on *at* marking sharp changes of subject, cf. n. 1.259.

2.101 f. Zephyris — pruinis: on the basis of these words, Seeck (1913) 549 dates Stilicho's departure from Italy to April or May 395.

2.101 b bruma remitti: Bruère (1964) 232 compares Luc. 1.17 (the Scythian winter) bruma ... nescia vere remitti.

2.103 pace: cf. 2.159 (Rufinus speaks of Stilicho) ille quidem tranquilla pace fruetur ...? From the defeat of Eugenius in September 394 to the uprising of Gildo in 397, the peace of the Western part of the Empire was undisturbed: cf. Stein-Palanque (1959) 216 f. For the expression *tuta sub pace*, Bruère (1964) 232 compares Luc. 2.348 (Marcia complains) cur tuta in pace relinquar?

2.104–6 utrasque castra movens ... Gallica — complexus: on the bipartite nature of Stilicho's forces, cf. n. 2.6.

2.104 properabat: on the lack of information concerning the actual speed of Stilicho's movement, cf. Int. 24; Fargues (1933a) 100.

2.105 a Gallica ... robora: the troops which Theodosius took over after the defeat of Arbogastes and Eugenius, and which subsequently became Stilicho's (cf. n. 2.6), apparently included both Gallic and Germanic components: cf. Oros. 7.35.12 Arbogastes ... adversus ... Theodosium collectis Gallorum Francorumque viribus exundavit; Seeck (1913) 256, 541 on 250; Stein-Palanque (1959) 211. Claudian both here and at 2.110, 147 f., 174, and BG 431 Gallos causa, non robore vinci, mentions only the Gauls.

2.105 b Eoa ... robora: cf. 2.161 f. Eoa ... / agmina, 217 miles Eous. In these passages, reference is to the troops which Theodosius had assembled in the East for his campaign against Arbogastes and Eugenius in 394: cf. 2.156 f. Quascumque paravit / hic Augustus opes, 3H 68 f. Iam princeps molitur iter gentesque remotas / colligit Aurorae, 69–72, CS 1.154 f. totam pater undique secum / moverat Auroram, 155–61; Int. 18, 22; Seeck (1913) 250 f., 541 f.; Stein-Palanque (1959) 216. Not included, of course, are the Gothic troops under Alaric, which had returned East earlier: cf. Int. 22 f.; Seeck (1913) 273, 548 f. on 273; Stein-Palanque (1959) 216, 228 f.

2.105 c turmis: on this term, cf. n.1.350 b.

2.106 a complexus: cf. Text. Comm. *ad loc.*

2.106 f. Numquam — vocum: for the polyglot character of Stilicho's troops, cf. CS 1.152–54 Certe nec tantis dissona linguis / turba nec armorum cultu diversior umquam / confluxit populus. Bruère (1964) 233 compares two Lucanian catalogs: 3.288–90 (foreign troops in the Civil War) coiere nec umquam / tam variae cultu gentes, tam dissona volgi / ora, 7.360-62; cf. also Sil. 16.19-21 (Hannibal's troops) tot dissona lingua / agmina, barbarico tot discordantia ritu / corda virum mansere gradu. For a favorable attitude toward the mixture of many ethnic groups, in addition to the present passage and to that first cited above, cf. CS 2.122 f. (to Stilicho) Lectos ex omnibus oris / evehis, et meritum, non quae cunabula, quaeris; Mart. *Sp.* 3.11 f.; Laqueur-Koch-Weber (1930) 20. On the enumeration of multi-ethnic troops as an epic theme, cf. Miniconi (1951) 158; also 53, 55, 61, 124-26.

2.106 *b* tantae: on *tanti=tot*, cf. n. 1.224 *b*.

2.107 discrimina: there is apparently no exact parallel to this use of *discrimina* in the sense of "differences," "variations," "varieties." Cf., however, 2.474 nulla discrimina fati; Sil. 5.393 clamor vario discrimine vocum. Despite the difference in sense (cf. TLL s.v. *discrimen* 1357.5-11), Claudian may have been influenced here by Verg. *A.* 6.646 (of seven musical notes) septem discrimina vocum.

2.108-10 *a* illinc ... inde: the use of these two adverbs as a contrasting pair is apparently otherwise unexampled: cf. TLL s.v. *illinc* 381.32.

2.108-10 *b* Armeniae vibratis crinibus alae ... truces flavo ... vertice Galli: Claudian parallels in his antithesis of East and West the contrast drawn by Pliny between the inhabitants of the North and the South: cf. *Nat.* 2.78.189 Aethiopas vicini sideris vapore ... gigni barba et capillo vibrato ... et adversa plaga mundi ... esse gentes flavis promissas crinibus, truces vero ex caeli rigore.... For similar contrasts, cf. Luc. 10.129-32, Mart. *Sp.* 3.9 f.

For the Armenian (cf. n. 2.108 *a*) and the Gallic (cf. n. 2.105 *a*) troops as representatives respectively of the Eastern and the Western armies, cf. 2.174 f. Armeniis frons laeva datur; per cornua Gallos / dexteriora locat.

2.108 *a* Armeniae ... alae: for the Armenian component in Theodosius' army (cf. n. 2.105 *b*), cf. 3H 68 f. princeps ... gentes ... remotas / colligit Aurorae, 72 Armenii Phasin ... liquere, BG 243-45, CS 1.155-57; Seeck (1913) 250. On Theodosius' relations with Armenia, cf. Stein-Palanque (1959) 205 f.; Doise (1945).

For Armenian cavalry, cf. Str. 11.14.9 ἱπποβότος σφόδρα ἡ χώρα.... Ἀρταουάσδης δὲ Ἀντωνίῳ χωρὶς τῆς ἄλλης ἱππείας

αὐτὴν τὴν κατάφρακτον ἑξακισχιλίαν ἵππον ἑκτάξας ἐπέδειξεν. ...
ταύτης δὲ τῆς ἱππείας. ... Ἀρμένιοι ζηλωταὶ γεγόνασιν, 11.14.12;
Sandalgian (1917) 2.549.

2.108 b vibratae crinibus: cf. CS 1.156 f. crine decorus / Armenius; Coon (1939) 628: "The hair form of the Armenians is mostly low waves; ... hairiness is an outstanding Armenian feature." Though Coon refers to the modern Armenians, he holds (625) that the type has changed little from pre-Turkish times. Cf. also the description of Haik, the mythical founder of the Armenian people, attributed to Mar Apas Catina by the Armenian historian Moses of Chorene (A.D. ca. 407–ca. 492), 1.10 f. This is translated by Langlois (1867) 1.16, col. 2.1 f. "Haïg ... célèbre par ... sa chevelure bouclée;" cf. also 1.18, col. 1.22 f.; 1.35, ftn. 2; also Lauer (1869) 19.

2.109 a herbida: for this word in the sense "green," cf. Plin. *Nat.* 12.14.56 folio ... herbidi coloris, 16.24.88. For green garments, cf. Mar. 5.23.1 Herbarum fueras indutus ... colores; Stat. *Silv.* 2.1.132–34. The wearing of green by the Armenians is not otherwise attested. The orientalist Saint-Martin *ap.* LeBeau (1824) 5.110, ftn. 2, translates *herbida* here by the words "fait d'herbes tissues," which may be correct.

2.109 b collectae ... velamina nodo: cf. Verg. *A.* 1.320 (Venus disguised as a huntress) nodo ... sinus collecta fluentes.

2.110 a truces ... Galli: for the epithet Bruère (1964) 233 compares Luc. 7.231 inde, truces Galli; cf. also CS 2.241 Gallia ... ferox; RE s.v. *Gallia* 637.51–60.

2.110 b flavo ... vertice: cf. CS 2.240 f. flava repexo / Gallia crine; Pease (1935) on Verg. *A.* 4.590 flaventis ... comas.

2.111–13 quos Rhodanus ... Araris ... ambit, et quos ... explorat ... Rhenus quosque rigat ... unda Garumnae: stylistic variations from the formula *qui hoc vel illud flumen bibit*: cf. n. 312 *b*. On geographical enumerations, cf. n. 1.131–33.

2.111 a Rhodanus velox, Araris ... tardior: the contrast was a stock theme of the poets: cf. MT 53 Lentus Arar Rhodanusque ferox; IE 2.269; Luc. 6.475 f. (in a magical reversal of nature) Rhodanum ... morantem / praecipitavit Arar (cited by Schol. A *ad loc.*); Bruère (1964) 233 also cites Luc. 1.433 f. Cf. also Sen. *Apoc.* 7 and Ball (1902) 185 *ad loc.*; Sil. 15.500 f., 3.448–54; Plin. *Nat.* 3.4.33 Rhodanus amnis ex Alpibus se rapiens ... segnemque deferens Ararem.

2.111 b **Araris:** this form of the nominative also occurs in IE 1.405; cf. Prisc. 5.13 (=2.149 f. Keil) Arar, quod etiam Araris dicitur ... "hic Araris"; TLL s.v. *Arar* 397.2–6. Fargues (1933b) on IE 1.405 mistakenly cites as nominative a form occurring in CIL 13.1674 (=Orelli 4018) ad confluentes Araris et Rhodani (a common formula: cf. Olcott [1904] 425, col. 1.6–23).

2.112 **nascentes — Rhenus:** for the notion that the Gauls plunged their newborn infants into the Rhine as a test of legitimate paternity, cf. Jul. Or. 2.81D ὑπάρχειν δέ φασι ... Κελτοῖς ποταμὸν ἀδέκαστον κριτὴν τῶν ἐκγόνων, Ep. 16.383D οὐδὲ ὁ ʽΡῆνος ἀδικεῖ τοὺς Κελτούς, ὃς τὰ μὲν νόθα τῶν βρεφῶν ὑποβρύχια ταῖς δίναις [cf. *gurgite*] ποιεῖ ... ὅσα δ᾽ ἂν ἐπιγνῷ καθαροῦ σπέρματος, ὑπεράνω τοῦ ὕδατος αἰωρεῖ; AP 9.125.1 f. Κελτοὶ ποταμῷ ζηλήμονι ʽΡήνῳ / τέκνα ταλαντεύουσι; Eust. 8.7.1–3 (=Hercher [1858] 2.241.18–25); Dottin (1915) 185 f. The custom of using the waters of a river as a test of paternity is not attested before Julian. The trait of plunging newborn infants into a river is attributed to πολλοί ... τῶν βαρβάρων by Arist. *Pol.* 7.17.3 1336A (where the mention of Κελτοί in another connection may be at the root of our present story), to an Italic people by Verg. *A.* 9.603 f., and to the Germans by Galen (6.51 Kühn). The very tentative suggestion of Dottin (1915) 186 that Julian uses the term Κελτοί in the passages cited above to refer to the Germans (cf. RE s.v. *Galli* 611.5–13) is without merit; Julian carefully distinguishes between Κελτοί and Γερμανοί; cf. *Ad Ath.* 278D–279B πολλῶν πάνυ Γερμανῶν περὶ τὰς πεπορθημένας ἐν Κελτοῖς πόλεις ἀδεῶς κατοικούντων ... οὐδὲ νέμειν ἐξῆν τοῖς Κελτοῖς τὰ βοσκήματα, *Mis.* 359B, *Caes.* 320D, *Gal.* 116A; cf. also *Mis.* 340D τὴν φίλην Λουκετίαν· ὀνομάζουσι δ᾽ οὕτως οἱ Κελτοὶ τῶν Παρισίων τὴν πολίχνην. Crépin (1933) completely misunderstands the passage, translating "dont les yeux se sont ouverts sur les flots profonds du Rhin." Cameron (1968a) 393 f., who corrects the inadequate "laved" of Platnauer (1922), and who gives an informative summary of passages dealing with the river-testing of babies, unfortunately refers our present passage to the Germans instead of to the Gauls. Bruère (1964) 233 compares Luc. 4.696 f. and 1.432 f.

2.113 f. **retro — aestu:** for the Garonne as a tidal river, cf. Mela 3.2.21 [fluvius] ... diu vadosus et vix navigabilis fertur. At ubi obvius oceani exaestuantis accessibus adauctus est, isdemque retro remeantibus suas illiusque aquas agit, aliquantum plenior, et quanto magis procedit eo latior fit, ad postremum magni freti similis; nec maiora tantum navigia tolerat, verum more etiam pelagi saevientis exurgens iactat navigantes atrociter; *Itinerarium a Burdigala Hierusalem Usque* (= Tobler-Molinier [1879] 3.5–8); Sidon. *Carm.* 7.393–97, 22.101–13, *Ep.* 8.12.5; RE s.v. *Garumna* 850.15–33; NLI s.v. *Garonne* 777; Ormsby (1931) 237.

2.114 aestu: for a careful study of the semantics of this word, cf. Saint-Denis (1941) 158–62. Bruère (1964) 233 compares Luc. 4.102 f.

2.115–19: for the general spirit of amnesty and reconciliation which followed Theodosius' victory over Eugenius, cf. 4H 111–17, esp. 115 post acies odiis idem qui terminus armis; Zos. 4.58.6 οἱ μετὰ τὴν νίκην ὑπολειφθέντες ἐπὶ τὸν βασιλέα δραμόντες τοῦτόν τε Αὔγουστον ἀνεβόησαν καὶ ἐπὶ τοῖς ἡμαρτημένοις ἠξίουν ἔχειν συγγνώμην, καὶ ὁ βασιλεὺς ῥᾷον ἐπένευεν; Stein-Palanque (1959) 217. That Stilicho continued Theodosius' policy is shown by Cod. Theod. 15.14.11 Fas est sequi nos paternae dispositionis arbitrium atque adeo universos cuiuslibet ordinis viros ... ad veniam volumus pertinere et beneficia inopinantibus ultro deferimus, sancientes hac lege, ne is, qui tyranni tempore militavit ... notam infamiae [sustineat]; cf. 15.14.12. Both these constitutions were promulgated in Milan on 18 May 395, four months after Theodosius' death: cf. Seeck (1919) 100 f.

At the start of Stilicho's expedition, less than ten months had passed since the defeat of Eugenius: cf. Stein-Palanque (1959) 217, 229.

2.115 f.: Steinbeiss (1936) 62.1–17 wrongly interprets these verses as if they referred in general to the Roman history of the period, instead of specifically to the events of 394–95; cf. n. 2.115–19.

2.115 Mens eadem cunctis: Bruère (1964) 233 compares Luc. 3.324 (the Massilians beg for peace) sit mens ista quidem cunctis.

2.118 bellatrix ... ira: cf. Cic. *Tusc.* 4.54 bellatrix iracundia.

2.119 eximium: on this reading cf. Faider (1937) 679; Fargues (1936) 371; Bieler (1957) 260. Cameron (1968a) 394 advances strong reasons for preferring *eximii*.

2.120 f. Xerxen — secutus ... exercitus: cf. Hdt. 7.61–99 for a catalog of Xerxes' expeditionary forces; on the actual number and provenience of the forces, cf. CAH 4.271–73.

2.120 toto ... orbe: Claudian here extends to Xerxes' realm a term often used of the Roman Empire: cf. n. 1 Pr.17 *b*.

2.121–23 rapuisse — aequor: Claudian here includes all four of the rhetorically celebrated elements of Xerxes' expedition: (a) the drinking up of rivers by his army; (b) the darkening of the sun by his bowmen's arrows; (c) the canal cut through Mt. Athos (cf. n. 1.335 f.); and (d) the bridge of boats built over the Hellespont. There is apparently no other passage in which all four appear. The combination of (a), (c), and (d) is found in Juv. 10.174–78 as providing a rhetorical topic (Schol. A on our present passage cites 10.177). Three others, (b), (c), and (d), are combined in Lucian. *Rh. pr.* 18 ἀεὶ ὁ Ἄθως πλείσθω καὶ ὁ Ἑλλήσποντος πεζευέσθω καὶ ὁ ἥλιος ὑπὸ τῶν Μηδικῶν βελῶν σκεπέσθω (cf. *Anth. Lat.* 239.3–6, 442.3 f. [= 1.1.197, 333 Bücheler-Riese]). For (a) and (b) combined, cf. Aristid. 23.43 (= 1.782 Dindorf, 2.43.14 f. Keil; the combination of (c) and (d) is found with perhaps the greatest frequency: cf. n. 2.122 f. *a*. On the recital of Xerxes' feats as a rhetorical commonplace, cf. Reid (1925) 217 f. on Cic. *Fin.* 2.34.112 maria—navigasset; Reid strangely omits the words ὃ πάντες θρυλοῦσιν from his citation of Isoc. *Paneg.* 89. On Xerxes' exploits as an epic theme, cf. Miniconi (1951) 210.

2.121 *a* rapuisse vagos ... amnes: cf. Hdt. 7.21 κοῖον δὲ πιόμενόν μιν ὕδωρ οὐκ ἐπέλιπε, πλὴν τῶν μεγάλων ποταμῶν; D.S. 11.5.3. For a similar feat credited to Stilicho's army, cf. CS 1.171 arebant tantis epoti militibus amnes; to Alaric's, cf. BP 527 arescere vidimus amnes.

2.121 *b* rapuisse: on the use of *rapio* to denote drinking, cf. n. 1.207.

2.122 telis umbrasse diem: cf. Hdt. 7.226 ἐπεὰν οἱ βάρβαροι ἀπιέωσι τὰ τοξεύματα, τὸν ἥλιον ὑπὸ τοῦ πλήθεος τῶν ὀϊστῶν ἀποκρύπτουσι· τοσοῦτό τι πλῆθος αὐτῶν εἶναι; V. Max. 3.7, ext. 8 sagittis Persarum solem obscurari solere. For a similar feat credited to Stilicho's army, cf. CS 1.258. On a dense shower of arrows as an epic theme, cf. Miniconi (1951) 165.

2.122 f. *a* classibus — aequor: Xerxes' two antithetical feats of piercing Mt. Athos with a canal and bridging the Hellespont with boats captured the imagination of the ancient world to a high degree: cf. Isoc. *Paneg.* 88 f. περὶ οὗ τίς οὐχ ὑπερβολὰς προθυμηθεὶς εἰπεῖν ἐλάττω τῶν ὑπαρχόντων εἴρηκεν; ὃς ... βουληθεὶς ... τοιοῦτον μνημεῖον καταλιπεῖν, ὃ μὴ τῆς ἀνθρωπίνης φύσεώς ἐστιν, οὐ πρότερον ἐπαύσατο, πρὶν ἐξεῦρε καὶ συνηνάγκασεν, ὃ πάντες θρυλοῦσιν, ὥστε τῷ στρατοπέδῳ πλεῦσαι μὲν διὰ τῆς ἠπείρου, πεζεῦσαι δὲ διὰ τῆς θαλάττης; D. Chr. 3.30 f.; CAH 4.269; Reid (1925) 217 f. Cf. also Cic. Fin. 2.34.112 si Xerxes, cum tantis classibus tantisque equestribus et pedestribus copiis Hellesponto iuncto, Athone perfosso maria ambulavisset, terram navigasset; [Verg.] Cul. 31–34; Luc. 2.672–77; Stat. Silv. 4.3.56–58.

2.122 f. b classibus — scopulos: for the canal cut through Mt. Athos, cf. 1.335 f. remige Medo / sollicitatus Athos; n. 1.335 f.

2.123 a tectum — aequor: for Xerxes' bridge of boats over the Hellespont, cf. Hdt. 7.33–36; CAH 4.269. Cf. also Lucr. 3.1029–32 ille quoque ipse, viam qui quondam per mare magnum / stravit iterque dedit legionibus ire per altum / ac pedibus salsas docuit super ire lacunas / et contempsit equis insultans murmura ponti.

2.123 b pedes: for this word as a singular collective noun in apposition (here with *exercitus*) cf. Verg. A. 7.624 pars pedes ire parat campis.

2.124 a Vix — erat: cf. Text. Comm. *ad loc.*; Fargues (1936) 371; Faider (1937) 679; Brakman (1937). On Stilicho as the subject of *transgressus erat*, cf. Birt (1892) 426 s.v. *Alpis*; Seeck (1913) 549; Fargues (1933a) 101, ftn. 1 (with Fargues, however, I differ in the interpretation of *Alpes*: cf. n. 2.124 b).

For an additional example of an abrupt change of subject, cf. IE 2.191–93 (Tarbigilus recounts his lack of success; Bellona, disguised as his wife, mourns) Ille iter ingratum, vanos deflere labores, / quos super eunuchi fastus, quae probra tulisset. / Continuo secat ungue genas.

With this passage Bruère (1964) 233 compares Luc. 1.183 iam gelidas Caesar cursu superaverat Alpes. If Bruère is right in connecting the two passages, Lucan's *superaverat* provides support for the reading *transgressus erat* rather than for *egressus*, which Bruère cites.

2.124 b Alpes: Birt (1892) 426 s.v. *Alpis* is undoubtedly right in taking this word to refer to the Julian Alps. Fargues (1933a) 101, ftn. 1, would interpret the word as designating "les hauteurs séparant l'Epire de la Thessalie." But Stilicho is represented as marching swiftly (2.104 properabat) eastward; Claudian is evidently trying to create the impression that the terror of the general's name outran even his swift approach (cf. 2.125 adventum ... timens). To maintain that the barbarians were struck with fear when Stilicho had scarce left Italy is quite in harmony with Claudian's hyperbolic manner (cf. CS 1.188 f. Miramur rapidis hostem succumbere bellis, / cum solo terrore ruant?). There is no need to weaken the rhetorical effect of the passage by a metonymic interpretation of *Alpes* which might bring the recital into closer accord with sober historic truth. Fargues himself (1933a) 100 f., mentions the Julian Alps as having been crossed just before the supposed crossing of the second mountain-chain.

2.125 f. unam planitiem: Claudian later makes it clear that he places this plain in Thessaly: cf. 2.171 Stilicho iam laetior hoste propinquo / nec multo spatii distantibus aequore vallis, 179 implet Thessaliam ferri nitor, 278 Haemoniis miles digressus ab oris. Fargues (1933a), 101 and ftn. 7, suggests that Stilicho probably met the Goths in the valley of the Peneus. However, the passage (Socr. 7.10) on which this suggestion is based is questionable as regards its chronology (cf. n. 2.43 f.).

2.126–29 tuto — iuvencis: for the Gothic circular wagon-barricade, or *carrago*, cf. CS 1.94 f. Quis enim Visos in plaustra feroces / reppulit ... ?; Amm. 31.7.5 vulgus inaestimabile barbarorum, ad orbis rotundi figuram multitudine digesta plaustrorum, tamquam intramuranis cohibitum spatiis, otio fruebatur, 31.7.7 manus ... ad carraginem (quam ita ipsi appellant) ... regressae, 31.8.1; Veget. *Epit. rei milit.* 3.10 omnes barbari carris suis in orbem conexis ad similitudinem castrorum securas a superventibus exigunt noctes; RE s.v. *carrago*; Suppl. 3 s.v. *Germani* 573.33–39; Delbrück (1902) 2.289; Müllenhof-Roediger (1890) 4.203.

2.126 pascua: Claudian represents the *carrago* as large enough to encompass pasture-land for the Goths' cattle: cf. RE Suppl. 3 s.v. *Germani* 565.45–61; Delbrück (1902) 2.289. Cf. also 2.129 caesis ... iuvencis, and n. 2.127–29.

2.127–29: the recital of the extraordinary defensive measures, (1) the double trench (cf. n. 2.127); (2) the double palisade (cf. n. 2.128 *b*); and (3) the slaughtering of cattle to provide protective screens of bull-hide for the wagons (cf. n. 2.129 *a*), is apparently intended to heighten the picture of the Goths' terror at Stilicho's approach (2.125

adventum ... timens). None of these measures seems to be otherwise attested in connection with the Gothic wagon-barricade.

2.127 duplici fossa ... vallum: for a rampart protected by a double trench, cf. Hirt. *Gal.* 8.9.3 haec imperat vallo ... muniri ... fossam duplicem ... deprimi; Fischer (1914) 26.

2.128 *a* asperat: cf. CM 9.24 (of a porcupine) consanguineis hastilibus asperat armos; Stat. *Theb.* 4.304 (of a warrior wearing a bear's jaws as a headdress) rictu caput asperat ursae; cf. also Var. *R.* 1.52.1 (a threshing-sledge) fit e tabula lapidibus aut ferro asperata.

2.128 *b* alternis sudibus: for *alternus* in the sense of "double," "two-fold," cf. Stat. *Theb.* 12.431 f. (flames leap from two corpses) exundant diviso vertice flammae / alternosque apices abrupta luce coruscant; MT Pr.16 (Parnassus is the meeting-place for a double flight of birds) contulit alternas Pythius axis aves; n. 2.226.

Platnauer (1922) translates "planted stakes two deep at intervals along its summit." The expression "at intervals" seems unwarranted, for if *alternus* has the sense of "double," "two-deep," it can scarcely at the same time convey the alternation of stakes with unprotected spaces; the latter concept, moreover, weakens the idea of extremely strong fortifications (cf. n. 2.127–29). Despite the agreement of F. Vollmer (TLL s.v. *alternus* 1757.40), Birt (1892) 468 s.v. *alternus* is wrong in connecting the *alternae sudes* with the *duplex fossa*. The stakes belong atop the wall, not down in the trenches: cf. BP 216 (the Goths') vallum densaeque sudes; Veget. *Epit. rei milit.* 3.8 aggerem faciunt, supra quem valli, hoc est sudes vel tribuli lignei, per ordinem digeruntur; Kromayer-Vieth (1928) 341 f.

2.129 *a* caesis ... iuvencis: cf. Luc. 4.131 f. (a boat is constructed of willow-withes and bull-hide) salix ... / ... caeso ... inducta iuvenco; cf. also IE 2.387 (Leo shakes his vast belly instead of a huge shield) non septem vasto quatiens umbone iuvencos; Stat. *Theb.* 3.591; Verg. *A.* 10.784 f. On the slaughtering of the cattle, cf. n. 2.127–29.

2.129 *b* plaustra iuvencis: possibly an echo (if so, a purely verbal one) of Verg. *G.* 2.205 f. (a land rich in cattle) non ullo ex aequore cernes / plura domum tardis decedere plaustra iuvencis.

2.130–70: *Rufinus, alarmed for his own safety, persuades Arcadius to bid Stilicho dispatch the Eastern troops to Constantinople, and return to Italy* *with the Western forces*. The entire account of Rufinus' persuasion, Arcadius' acquiescence, and the compliance of Stilicho rests on Claudian's word alone, though both John of Antioch and Zosimus mention the restoration of the Eastern troops to Constantinople, the latter in a fashion quite at variance with Claudian's: Jo. Antioch. frag. 10 (= FHG 4.610, col. 2.24–26) ὁ τοῦ Ἀρκαδίου στρατὸς ἔκ τε τῆς Εὐγενίου καθαιρέσιως καὶ τῆς τῶν βαρβάρων τῶν κατὰ τὴν Ἰλλυρίδα διώξεως ἐπὶ τὴν Κωνσταντίνου πόλιν ἐχώρει (on the uncertainty of John's chronology, cf. Cameron [1968b] 277, ftn. 56); Zos. 5.7.3 ὁ Στελίχων ... πρὸς τὸν βασιλέα ποιεῖται λόγους Ὀνώριον ὡς προήκει τέλη τινὰ στρατιωτικὰ στεῖλαι πρὸς Ἀρκάδιον τὸν ἀδελφόν.

On the relation of these verses to the ψόγος-pattern, cf. Levy (1946) 63, 65. On Claudian's lack of concern with the possibilities of dramatic irony inherent in this passage, cf. n. 2.152–63.

2.130 a At ... Rufinum: on *at* marking a sharp change of subject, cf. n. 1.259.

2.130 b procul: the scene now shifts back (cf. n. 2.54 a, n. 2.125 f.) to Constantinople: cf. 2.142 fores praedivitis aulae.

2.131 stetit ore gelato: cf. Stat. *Theb.* 4.497 gelat ora pavor, 404 f. Bruère (1964) 233 compares Luc. 7.339 (Pompey before the battle of Pharsalus) stat corde gelato; also 3.589.

2.132 fugam: since Claudian represents Stilicho's sphere of activity as extending over the entire Roman world (cf. 1 Pr.17 stabilem servans ... orbem, 2.4–6; n. 1 Pr.17 a), and since defection to the enemy is separately mentioned in 2.133, Claudian may here be suggesting that Rufinus contemplated taking refuge in a place of asylum, as his wife and daughter actually did after his death: cf. Zos. 5.8.2, and RE s.v. *Asylon* 1885.39–43.

2.132 f. veniam ... subactus posceret: there may be an implication that pardon humbly begged might have been granted even to a Rufinus; for Claudian's representation of Stilicho's clemency, cf. CS 2.6–29; cf. also n. 2.115–19.

2.133 fidos ... hostes: the Goths; cf. 2.72 carum ... sibi non abnuit hostem.

2.134 f. divitiae ... fulvi — congeries: on Rufinus' avarice, cf. Int. 15 f., ftns. 82, 83, 95.

2.135 f. purpureis — moles: on Rufinus' magnificent estate, cf. Int. 15 f.; Janin (1964) 151 f., and Map 13.

2.135 purpureis: cf. Luc. 10.115 f. (of Cleopatra's palace) stabat ... / purpureus ... lapis. According to Blümner (1892) 192, reference is probably to porphyry or red granite. The choice of color may perhaps be intended as a subtle accusation of long-held aspirations on Rufinus' part toward the imperial crown: cf. n. 2.346 *b*.

2.137 f. numerat — vitam: contrast CS 3.2–4 (of Rome's longing for Stilicho) Iam tempora desine longae / dinumerare viae visoque adsurgere semper / pulvere.

2.138 Torquetur pace futura: on allegations of Rufinus' joy at the sufferings of others, cf. n. 1.234 f.; also n. 1.230–56. Here the thought of the war's end (cf. 2.98 f. [to Stilicho] Te proelia viso / languescent) and of the consequent termination of his savage pleasures (cf. 2.61–70) brings him anguish: cf. 1.243 f.

2.139 nec recipit somnos: for *recipio* in this sense, cf. Ov. *Met.* 1.686 sopor est oculorum parte receptus; cf. also Verg. *A.* 4.529–31 (Dido) neque umquam / solvitur in somnos oculisve aut pectore noctem / accipit.

2.140 poenam — poenae: for the rhetorical paradox, cf. Sen. *Ep.* 70.8 timore mortis mori; Morawski (1917) 5; Rolfe (1919) 146.

2.141 faciem: cf. Text. Comm. *ad loc.*; Bieler (1957) 259; Cameron (1968a) 394 f. The second sentence of the note in the Text. Comm. should be disregarded; it was written under the misapprehension that the word *terrore* in 2.143 referred to terror felt by Rufinus, when in fact it refers to terror inspired by him.

2.141 f. scelerum ... immane ... ingenium: cf. 1.109–11 (Megaera's praise of Rufinus) magistram / praevenit ingenio; ... / solus habet scelerum quidquid possedimus omnes.

2.142 *a* sacras ... fores: on the adjective *sacer* used of the Emperor, and of persons and things closely connected with him, cf. n. 1 Pr.16.

2.142 *b* praedivitis: on Claudian's use of adjectives compounded with *prae-*, cf. n. 1.225 *a*.

2.143 *a* Arcadium: on the domination of the Emperor Arcadius by Rufinus, cf. Int. 18. As evidence of Arcadius' docility, cf. Zos. 5.12.1, where Eutropius, Rufinus' successor in power, is described as κυριεύων ᾿Αρκαδίου καθάπερ βοσκήματος; cf. Seeck (1913) 277. On Claudian's attitude toward Arcadius, cf. n. 1.373 c; cf. also n. 2.145, n. 2.170.

2.143 b terrore: for this word in a causative sense, cf. CS 2.25 f. (Stilicho emulates Jupiter in his willingness to rely on the fear he inspires, rather than to use actual force) contentus solo terrore ... / aetherii patris exemplo; Ov. Met. 2.483 f. (a terrifying voice) vox iracunda minaxque / plenaque terroris; Stat. Theb. 9.107 f., 1.535 f. For Rufinus' fear-inspiring words, cf. 2.164–68, and n. 2.168; for their effect, cf. BG 304 (Theodosius' shade addresses Arcadius) Rufinum ... quem tu tremuisse fateris.

2.144–68: on direct quotation in IR, cf. n. 1.45–65.

2.144 a fratris: to represent even the treacherous Rufinus as paying homage to Honorius as well as to Arcadius is in line with Claudian's policy of upholding the essential unity of the Empire: cf. Int. 33.

2.144 b regale: on the use of this and similar terms in connection with the Roman Emperors, cf. n. 1.113 a.

2.144 c iubar: for the celestial effulgence, or nimbus, supposed to emanate from the persons of the Emperors, cf. 6H 539 principis et solis radiis; Mart. 8.65.4 (of Domitian) purpureum fundens Caesar iubar; Stat. Silv. 1.1.76–78; Mamertinus, *Panegyricus Maximiniano Augusto dictus* 3.2 (= 246 Mynors) illa lux divinum verticem claro orbe complectens; RE s.v. Nimbus 614.10–616.24, 622.41–623.6; cf. also 1.373 (of Arcadius) fratre corusco; n. 1.373 d.

2.144 f. parentis aetherii: for *aetherius* of a deified Emperor, cf. 3H 175 (to Theodosius) O decus aetherium! The usage is apparently not otherwise attested (cf. TLL s.v. aetherius 1153.5–14, 1154.7–11). The term *aetherius pater* in CS 2.26 and Stat. Silv. 3.1.108 refers to Jupiter; *aetherii parentes* in Stat. Theb. 1.704 are Jupiter and Latona. On the application of the term to the Christian Theodosius, cf. n. 2.2 f., para. 2.

2.145 florem ... tui ... aevi: it is characteristic of Claudian's attitude toward Arcadius (cf. n. 1.373 c) that he represents Rufinus as finding no aspect of Arcadius worthy to serve as a basis for adjuration but his flourishing youthfulness (he was about 18 years of age in 395; cf. Seeck [1913] 545 on 265.18).

IN RUFINUM 157

2.147 *a* nostram: Arcadius is not included; cf. 2.151 unum petitur caput.

2.147 f. Gallia ... coniurata: cf. Hor. *Carm.* 1.15.6 f. Graecia ... / coniurata.

2.147 *b* Gallia: for the Gauls as representative of Stilicho's Western troops, cf. 2.105 Gallica ... robora, 110 Galli; n. 2.105 *a*.

2.148 f. Quidquid — Britannos: in having Rufinus mention Britons, Claudian endows him with a gift for hyperbole like the poet's own; the Britons are not mentioned in 2.105–14.

For the Britons, dwelling by their northern Ocean, as the remotest inhabitants of the Western world, cf. BP 202–4 a Gadibus usque Britannum / terruit Oceanum et nostro procul axe remotam / ... tremefecit ... Thylen, CS 3.148 f.; Verg. *Ecl.* 1.67 penitus toto divisos orbe Britannos; Sen. *Apoc.* 12; *Anth. Lat.* 424.3 f. (= 1.325 Bücheler-Reise).

2.149 volitat: for *volito* of warriors swarming over a territory, cf. Verg. *A.* 11.546 circumfuso volitabant milite Volsci.

2.150 f. Tantis — caput: cf. Stat. *Theb.* 2.490 f. (of an ambush set for Tydeus) exit in unum / plebs ferro iurata caput, 495 Macte animi, tantis dignus qui crederis armis.

2.150 *a* Tantis: on *tanti* = *tot*, cf. n. 1.224 *b*.

2.150 *b* capiendi credimur: the gerundive in the predicate (cf. Hofmann-Szantyr [1965] 371 f.) with the passive of *credo* is not otherwise attested (cf. TLL s.v. *credo* 1141.38–1142.4) save for a late fifth-century example, in which, however, the gerundive with *esse* is merely the equivalent of a future passive infinitive: cf. Hofmann-Szantyr (1965) 312: Faustus Reienzis *De gratia* 1.16 (= CSEL 21.49.6 f.) etiam impii ... resuscitandi esse creduntur. The nearest parallels in the works of Claudian's predecessors are apparently (as regards the passive of *credo*) Luc. 3.99 f. creditur, ut captae, rapturus moenia Romae, / sparsurusque deos, and (as regards the gerundive) Ov. *Ars* 1.613 Sibi quaeque videtur amanda; cf. *Met.* 14.474, *Tr.* 3.11.37, 5.14.7.

2.151 f. cruoris ... sitis: for the desire to kill represented as a thirst for blood, cf. BP 604 miles sitiens haurire cruorem; Ov. *Met.* 13.768 caedis amor, feritasque, sitisque immensa cruoris, *Tr.* 3.11.57; Luc. 1.330 f. sic et Sullanum solito tibi lambere ferrum / durat, Magne, sitis; Stat. *Theb.* 11.173 f.; Sil. 16.616 f. Cf. also n. 1.77 f., n. 2.232 *b*.

2.152–63: Geminum — heres: Rufinus bolsters his plea for personal protection by representing as a necessary measure of Arcadius' imperial policy the issuance of orders (1) that Stilicho return to Italy (2.161 Deserat Illyricos fines), and (2) that he dispatch the Eastern troops to Constantinople (2.161 f. Eoa remittat agmina). The groundwork for the first demand is laid in 2.153–56 Succumbere—capit, for the second in 2.156–58 Quascumque—curat (cf. n. 2.157). When Rufinus' purpose is achieved, he is represented as again stressing these two aspects of his program: cf. 2.299 (speaking of himself) tanto ... munitum milite; 301 f. remotus / ... Stilicho; 2.309 f. Detrusimus orbe / te medio tantisque simul spoliavimus armis.

By pressing the demand regarding the Eastern troops, Rufinus, as Claudian represents the events, unwittingly becomes the instrument of his own destruction, for it is these troops, upon their arrival at the capital, who encompass his death (cf. 2.275–417; Int. 25 f.). Claudian, ignoring the irony inherent in this situation, makes no use of such explicit indications of ill-fated persistence as the Vergilian *frustra*, *demens*, *ignarus*, *fatis debitus*, or the like (cf., in a different situation, 2.322 frustra, and Duckworth [1933] 75 f.). It may be possible to assign a cause, apart from mere inadvertence, for the absence of this touch. If the dispatch of Stilicho to Italy, and of the Eastern troops to Constantinople, had been pointed up as the destined mechanism of Rufinus' destruction, then the Imperial orders effecting these movements could not have been represented as wholly bad. It may have been a desire to let nothing interfere with the representation of these orders as an unmitigated evil (2.169 facinus, 198 ignavo tantum licuisse nocenti, 2.186–94) that kept Claudian from exploiting the possibilities of dramatic irony here.

2.152 Geminum caeli ... axem: for *geminus axis* of the Eastern and Western parts of the Roman world, cf. 4H 129–31 (Honorius belongs to both parts) Hesperio de limite surgit origo, / sed nutrix Aurora tibi ... / ... geminus civem te vindicat axis, CS 2.59 f., 3.139; Luc. 7.422–24 (Rome covered almost the whole world) Te geminum Titan procedere vidit in axem; / haud multum terrae spatium restabat eoae, / ut tibi nox, tibi tota dies, tibi curreret aether; RE s.v. *Axis* 2633.32–40; TLL s.v. *axis* 1639.50–53; Christ (1938) 53–57. Cf. also 2.264 f. axis / ... Hesperius; n. 2.264 f.

2.154 regit ... coercet: for these two verbs used as synonyms, cf. Ov. *Pont.* 3.3.61 f. sic regat imperium terrasque coerceat omnes / Caesar. In view of this parallel, it seems scarcely likely that *coercet* here is intended to refer to the strained relations between the *Comes Africae* Gildo and the regime of Theodosius and Honorius (cf. Seeck [1913] 282 f.; Stein-Palanque [1959] 205, 207, 231 f.).

2.154 f. Italiam Libyamque ... Hispanis Gallisque: the first pair represents the *Praefectura Praetorio Illyrici Italiae et Africae*, the second the *Praefectura Praetorio Galliarum*; these two prefectures constituted the Western part of the Empire: cf. Stein-Palanque (1959), Map, "Imperium Romanum Anno 390 P. Chr.," sections colored yellow and green; maps follow p. 672.

Note that of the first-named prefecture's three titular divisions, Claudian has Rufinus concede to Stilicho only the last two, thus avoiding mention of Illyricum, part of which was then the subject of dispute: cf. n. 2.161.

2.155 *a* Hispanis Gallisque iubet: though the dative with *iubeo* is otherwise attested both in Claudian and elsewhere (see below), apparently no other author uses *iubeo* (with either accusative or dative) in the sense exemplified here of "control," "rule," "give orders to." The only other example is CS 3.85 f. (Rome is in command) Ipsa iubet signis, bellaturoque togatus / imperat ... senatus, where the parallelism with *impero* in the sense just mentioned (cf. IR 1.148 f. gens Chaldaea ... / imperet ... deis, TLL s.v. *impero* 588.2–18, 45–53) points to the genesis of our present construction.

Claudian also uses *iubeo* with a dative and dependent infinitive: CM 26.86 (the divine author of the universe has given Aponus healing qualities) telluri medicas fundere iussit aquas. This usage is otherwise clearly attested only in Cat. 64.139 f. non haec quondam blanda promissa dedisti / voce mihi, non haec miserae sperare iubebas, where the parallelism with *dedisti / ... mihi* seems to account for the dative in *miserae ... iubebas*. In CM 26.86, as in CS 3.85, Claudian apparently follows the pattern of *impero*: cf. Verg. *A.* 7.35 f. Flectere iter sociis ... / imperat; Ov. *Met.* 2.118 iungere equos Titan velocibus imperat Horis; TLL s.v. *impero* 585.35–49. Though these two developments (*iubeo* meaning "control," "give orders to," with the dative, and *iubeo* meaning "command," with dative and infinitive) are, with the Catullan exception noted, peculiar to Claudian, the general trend of assimilating *iubeo* to *impero* is evident elsewhere. The instances fall into two categories: (1) *iubeo* meaning "command," with dative and dependent subjunctive: Tac. *Ann.* 13.15.3 Britannico iussit exsurgeret, 13.40.3 quibus iusserat ut ... resisterent; Capitolin. *Maximin.* 3.1 (= SHA 2.318 Loeb) iussit ... tribuno ut eum coerceret (parallel with TLL s.v. *impero* 584.76–585.16, 585.26–34); (2) *iubeo* meaning "impose," "enjoin," with dative and accusative: Tac. *Ann.* 4.72.1 tributum iis Drusus iusserat (cf. Furneaux [1896] *ad loc.*); Stat. *Theb.* 7.32 f. pacem ... iubebo / omnibus, 373 tuus armatis iubet ecce silentia frater (parallel with TLL s.v. *impero* 583.6–45); Löfstedt (1911) 151 f.; Bährens (1913) 21, Hofmann-Szantyr (1965) 31, 646.

2.155 f. non orbita — capit: the gibe apparently echoes the traditional rhetorical castigation of Alexander's boundless ambition: cf. Sen. *Suas.* 1.1 Satis sit hactenus Alexandro vicisse, qua mundo lucere soli satis est; 2 Tempus est Alexandrum cum orbe et cum sole desinere; 5 ipsa suasoria insolentiam eius coarguit: orbis illum suus non capit; Curt. 9.4.18 (Alexander's soldiers refuse to proceed further) Trahi extra sidera et solem cogique adire quae mortalium oculis natura subduxerit; on Curtius as reflecting the rhetorical treatment of Alexander, cf. RE s.v. *Suasoria* 471.1–6; s.v. *Curtius* 1889–91; on Alexander and the οἰκουμένη, cf. RE s.v. *Oikumene* 2139–41. For a similar thrust at Romans in general, cf. Petr. 119.1–3 orbem iam totum victor Romanus habebat, / qua mare, qua terrae, qua sidus currit utrumque, / nec satiatus erat; Christ (1938) 58.

Platnauer (1922) translates so as to differentiate between *orbita solis* and *natura*: "The sun's path circumscribes him not, no, nor the whole universe." Despite the appropriateness of the crescendo to the rhetorical tone of the passage, it seems better to take *natura* jointly with *orbita solis* (cf. n. 155 b) as designating the οἰκουμένη, that part of the world lit by the sun and intended by nature for man's use: note the four-fold use of the word *natura* in the contexts of the passages cited above from Seneca (not quoted) and Curtius; cf. also Sen. *Herc. O.* 46 (of Hercules' travels) natura cessit, terra defecit gradum; 631 (after a list including various far-off places) avidis natura parum est; Pacatus, *Panegyricus Theodosio Augusto dictus* 23.1 dum ultra terminos rerum metasque naturae regna orientis extendis.

IN RUFINUM 161

2.155 *b* orbita solis: for this expression denoting the apparent diurnal path of the sun (on a different meaning cf. para. 2, below) cf. Sil. 16.295 *septima cum solis renovabitur orbita caelo*, 303 *Iamque dies praedicta aderat*. For the οἰκουμένη defined in terms of the sun's illumination, in addition to the passages from Seneca and Curtius cited in n. 2.155 f., where note especially the phrases *qua mundo lucere soli satis est, qua lucet, cum orbe et cum sole*, and *extra . . . solem*, cf. CS 3.138–40 (Rome) *exiguis quae finibus orta tetendit / in geminos axes, parvaque a sede profecta / dispersit cum sole manus*; BG 47 f., FH 2.39 f.; Verg. *A.* 7.99–101 *nepotes / omnia sub pedibus, qua Sol utrumque recurrens / aspicit Oceanum, verti regique videbunt*; Ov. *Fast.* 2.136; Luc. 2.583 f. *tota . . . / terra . . . quocumque iacet sub sole*; Stat. *Silv.* 3.3.47; Christ (1938) 53–57.

The expression *orbita solis* is also used to denote the ecliptic, the apparent annual path of the sun through the Zodiac, a meaning which cannot be intended here, since the lands lying directly beneath the ecliptic and the Zodiac were in the middle or torrid zone, and regarded as uninhabitable: cf. Plin. *Nat.* 2.68.172 *media . . . terrarum, qua solis orbita est, exusta flammis et cremata comminus vapore torrentur*; Luc. 9.691 f. *premit orbita solis / exuritque solum*; cf. also Verg. *G.* 1.238 f. (and Macr. *Somn. Scip.* 2.8 *ad loc.*); RP 1.259–61, BG 148–50; Tozer (1935) 180; RE s.v. *Oikumene* 2159.18–28, Suppl. 4 s.v. *Geographie* 578–80; Semple (1939) 5–7.

2.156 natura: on the interpretation of this word, cf. n. 2.155 f., para. 2.

2.156–58 Quascumque — habet: on the two-fold division of the troops (cf. n. 2.157) left under Stilicho's command, cf. n. 2.6, n. 2.105 *a*, n. 2.105 *b*.

2.157 opes: for this word used to denote troops, cf. BP 400–2 (Stilicho persuades the Goths to resume their allegiance) *Hoc monitu pariter nascentia bella repressit / et bello quaesivit opes, legitque precantes, / auxilio mensus numerum qui congruus esset*; cf. Serv. Dan. on Verg. *A.* 8.171 "*opes*" *antiqui vocabant milites*; Nep. *Con.* 4.3 *ducem fortem, prudentem regiis opibus praefuturum*, *Thr.* 2.4; Mommsen (1903) 103, ftn. 6. Platnauer (1922) translates *opes* as "wealth," Crépin (1933) "richesses, trésors." This interpretation is not impossible (cf. CS 2.88–94; Fargues [1933a] 100, "bijoux") but it would leave this part of the speech without any reference to the troops which are represented as forming an important item in Rufinus' program (cf. n. 2.152-63).

2.158 possessa — curat: cf. Luc. 1.317 (Caesar on Pompey) *ille semel aptos numquam dimittit honores?*

2.159 tranquilla pace: cf. 2.103 *partibus Italiae tuta sub pace relictis;* n. 2.103.

2.159 f. fruetur ... premet: cf. Text. Comm. *ad loc.*; Semple (1936) 229; Faider (1937) 697.

2.160 a obsidio: reference is apparently to the possibility of a future siege in the absence of sufficient military forces, not to the actual siege mentioned in 2.54-99. This had presumably been lifted by the withdrawal of Alaric to Greece: cf. 2.124 f. *nec iam amplius errat / barbarus;* Socr. 7.10 Ἀλάριχος ... ἀναχωρήσας ... τῆς Κωνσταντινουπόλεως (and n. 2.54-99); Int. 24; Stein-Palanque (1959) 229.

2.160 b Pontum [read **partem**] **invadere:** cf. Text. Comm. *ad loc.*; Fargues (1936) 372; Helm (1936) 1223; Owen (1936) 20; Semple (1936) 229, (1937b); E. H. A. (1937) 243; Faider (1937) 679; Hosius (1937); Axelson (1944) 11-13; Bieler (1957) 259 f.; Cameron (1968a) 395.

The excellent suggestion of Semple (1937b)—cf. Cameron (1968a) 395—obviated the need for emendation, and I now believe that *partem,* the reading of the codices, should be retained. Semple interprets *invadere* not in a military but in a juridical sense: "to make away with," "embezzle," "usurp." "The sense is then ... that Stilicho is a fraudulent trustee who means to misappropriate the share of Theodosius' estate which really belongs to Arcadius," as Semple explains. He cites, among other passages, Cic. *Phil.* 2.16.41 ... *vi eiectis veris heredibus, tamquam heres esset, invasit.* A striking confirmation of Semple's interpretation may be added: Ulpian *ap.* Just. *Dig.* 5.3.25.3 (cf. 5.3.20.6) *Quod autem ait senatus "eos qui bona invasissent," loquitur de praedonibus, id est de his qui, cum scirent ad se non pertinere hereditatem, invaserunt bona, scilicet cum nullam causam haberent possidendi.*

For *pars* in the sense of a hereditary share of the Empire, cf. 6H 82-85 (addressed to Honorius) *quotiens optare tibi quae moenia malles / alludens genitor regni pro parte dedisset, / divitis Aurorae* solium sortemque paratam / sponte remittebas fratri; cf. also Stat. *Theb.* 2.386 f. (of the usurper Eteocles) Iura ferus populo trans legem ac tempora regni / iam fratris de parte dabat.

2.161–63: on the two parts of the demand, cf. n. 2.152–63.

2.161 Deserat Illyricos fines: cf. 2.201 (of Stilicho's eagerness to fight with Alaric) Illyricis ardet succurrere damnis. Thessaly, where Stilicho now had his armies (cf. n. 2.125 f.) was in the diocese of Macedonia, in the eastern part of Illyricum: cf. Stein-Palanque (1959), Map, "Imperium Romanum Anno 390 P. Chr."; maps follow p. 672.

On the vexed question of the partition of Illyricum, the dividing line of which became the boundary in Europe between the Eastern and Western parts of the Empire (cf. 2.309 f. Detrusimus orbe / te medio), cf. Int. 23 f., 32–34; Mazzarino (1942) 1–49; Demougeot (1947); Stein-Palanque (1959) 228–31, 249. The conclusions of Demougeot (1947) 30 f. are in substantial accord with Stein's, upon which those in the Int. are based. In the *Actes de VIᵉ Congrès International d'Études Byzantines* (Paris 1950) 1.87–92, Demougeot took account of the numismatic data, thus satisfying the desideratum of Pearce (1936) 135: "The coins should at least be allowed a hearing." The most recent discussions of the problem, which seems as far as ever from a final solution, will be found in Grumel (1951), Palanque (1951), and Cameron (1968b) 271 f.

2.162 *a* fraternas: for the use of this word of the joint concerns of Arcadius and Honorius, cf. IE 2.546 f. Fraterno coniungi coeperat orbis / imperio.

2.162 *b* hastas: the use of this word to denote troops is apparently otherwise unexampled (cf. TLL s.v. *hasta* 2552.34–48, where Honorius is wrongly substituted for Stilicho as the subject of *dividat*). For a similar use of *gladii*, cf. Luc. 3.323 ut gladiis egeant civilia bella coactis. The common term is of course *arma*: cf. 6H 461–63 (Stilicho had only a small force) paucis comitatus erat, nam plurima retro / ... liquerat arma / extera vel nostras acies; TLL s.v. *arma* 600.44–601.44.

2.163 *a* sceptri ... heres: this term is applied here, as in 6H 76, in a popular (cf. TLL s.v. *heres* 2654.14–42), not in a juridical sense; both Arcadius and Honorius, who had been Augusti for some time when Theodosius died (cf. Seeck [1913] 265, 268, 545 f.), from the standpoint of the law simply continued in that position: cf. Mommsen

(1877) 1110. Cf. the loose application of the term ἐπίτροπος ... Ἀρκαδίου καὶ Ὀνωρίου in Olymp. frag. 2 (= FHG 4.58); Int. 19.

On the quasi-hereditary transmission of imperial power, cf. Premerstein (1937) 267–72; Béranger (1939) 171–87; CAH 12.370 f.

2.163 *b* **fueris tantum:** on this reading, cf. Fargues (1936) 371; Faider (1937) 679.

2.164–68: this is the threat foreshadowed by 2.143 mixto terrore; cf. n. 2.143 *b*. For another instance in which Rufinus is represented as using forceful language in dealing with Arcadius, cf. 2.381 f. graviter ... morantem / increpat Augustum.

2.164 *a* **dissimulas ... succurrere:** for *dissimulo* with the infinitive in the sense of "refuse," "neglect," "fail," cf. *Anth. Lat.* 218.7 f. (= 1.185 Bücheler-Riese) si dissimulas ... venire, / oscula ... mitte; Amm. 20.4.8 (Julian warns Florentius) si procurare dissimulasset, ipse propria sponte proiceret insignia principatus.

2.164 *b* **nostrae succurrere morti:** for the dative with *succurrere* denoting, not the person helped, but the evil against which the help is given, cf. 2.201 Illyricis succurrere damnis; Cic. *Ver.*, *Act. Pr.* 1.2 ut infamiae communi succurrerem, *Phil.* 11.11.26; Liv. 3.58.4 cum eo ... cuius adversae fortunae velit succursum; Petr. 110 huic tristitiae ... succurrit ancilla. The usage seems to have been common in medical language: cf. Cels. 2.11 (= 56.12 f. Daremberg) nec posse vehementi malo nisi aeque vehemens auxilium succurrere, 2.8, 3.19 (= 46.37–47.2, 103.22 Daremberg).

2.165 Manes — testor: for the adjuration, cf. Stat. *Theb.* 3.63 f. Noctis vaga lumina testor / et socium manes; Henry (1873) 3.326 on Verg. *A.* 6.458 f.

2.167 *a* **nec ... incomitatus:** for a vengeful slaying viewed ironically as providing an escort to Hades for the soul of one in whose behalf the vengeance is inflicted, cf. Hom. *Il.* 13.414–16 οὐ μὰν αὖτ' ἄτιτος κεῖτ' Ἄσιος, ἀλλὰ ἕ φημι / εἰς Ἀϊδός περ ἰόντα πυλάρταο κρατεροῖο / γηθήσειν κατὰ θυμόν, ἐπεί ῥά οἱ ὤπασα πομπόν. The idea is apparently unparalleled in the Latin epic, for in Verg. *A.* 12.362 huic comitem Asbyten coniecta cuspide mittit, and in similar passages (*A.* 9.765, 12.881; Sil. 1.400, 5.467, 8.66; Stat. *Theb.* 2.607; V. Fl. 6.213), the *comes* is not slain to revenge the man first killed, but is on the contrary simply another victim of the same slayer. The Homeric idea, which is perhaps distantly paralleled in our passage, may itself spring ultimately from a reminiscence of primitive sacrifices intended to provide the soul of the departed with companions, servants, and animals for use in the next world: cf. RE s.v. *Menschenopfer* 950 f.; ERE s.v. *Human Sacrifice* 847, 860; Stengel (1920) 129; Levy (1948c).

2.167 *b* **umbras:** cf. Text. Comm. *ad loc.*; Fargues (1936) 371.

2.168: cf. Text. Comm. *ad loc.*; E. H. A. (1937) 243. Like the reviewer just cited, Cameron (1968a) 396 finds the interpretation given in the Text. Comm. unacceptable, and prefers Birt's emendation *ridebis*. In a private communication, Cameron has kindly referred me to Verg. *A*. 10.739 f. (Orodes' dying speech) non me, quicumque es, inulto / victor, nec longum laetabere, and to Courtney (1965) 152 *ad loc.* I am convinced by this parallel that Rufinus indeed meant Arcadius, and not Stilicho, as the person who will not be able to laugh at Rufinus' death, and gratefully retract the admittedly tortuous interpretation given in the Text. Comm. However, I am not completely convinced that it is necessary, in making this interpretation, to change *ridebit* to *ridebis*. Even meaning Arcadius, and speaking directly to him, Rufinus can still use the third person to refer to him, as the Greek ironically uses τὶς: cf. S. *Aj*. 1138 τοῦτ' εἰς ἀνίαν τοὔπος ἔρχεταί τινι; cf. also Creon's misinterpretation, in S. *Ant*. 751, of Haemon's τινα as a threat against Creon himself, to whom Haemon is talking.

2.169 *a* **Haec ubi:** on the use of phrases marking the end of direct quotation, cf. n. 1.65 *b*.

2.169 *b* **dictatur facinus:** the actual terms of the imperial orders (2.195 f. mandata ... / regia) are nowhere specifically set forth, but are implied in 2.161 f., 213–19, 264 f.; cf. n. 2.152–63. On the lack of direct quotation here and in 2.195 f., cf. n. 1.45–65, sect. 5.

2.170 extortas — voces: about four years later (cf. Birt [1892] 189), in writing his panegyric on Stilicho's consulship, Claudian is still concerned with absolving Arcadius from responsibility for the acts of Rufinus: cf. CS 1.112 f. (the barbarians) extincti ... forent penitus, ni more maligno / falleret Augustas occultus proditor aures; 2.79–81 (to Stilicho) nec, si quid iners atque impia turba / praetendens proprio nomen regale furori / audeat, adscribis iuveni. This concern is no longer discernible in a passage written in 402 (cf. Birt [1892] 259):

BP 516 f. (to Alaric) extinctus ... fores, ni te sub nomine legum / proditio regnique favor texisset Eoi. The change of attitude here and in 6H 85–87 (cf. n. 1.373 c) apparently reflects the cooling of Stilicho's hopes that he might eventually acquire a controlling influence at the court of Arcadius: cf. Stein-Palanque (1959) 229 f., 231, 235, 236 f.

On Claudian's attitude toward the Eastern part of the Empire, cf. now Christiansen (1970).

2.171–96: *Stilicho has reached the encampment of the barbarians, and is ready to do battle, when the Emperor's command arrives.* Claudian represents Stilicho as preparing to attack the Goths upon his arrival in their vicinity (2.171–73 laetior hoste propinquo // ... accendit voce cohortes); on the actual chronology, cf. Int. 24.

2.171–292: on this passage as a part of a *laus Stilichonis*, cf. n. 1.259–300.

2.171 laetior hoste propinquo: for Stilicho's alleged eagerness to come to grips with the enemy, cf. 2.104 properabat; n. 2.124 b.

2.172 a multo spatii: for the ablative of a neuter adjective of quantity used substantively with a partitive genitive, cf. PO 52 f. quanto ... metalli / Hermi ripa micat. The construction is apparently otherwise unexampled; Kühner-Stegmann-Thierfelder (1962) 1.429, Anm. 7 b cites examples with the adjective in the nominative and the accusative only.

2.172 b aequore: for the Thessalian plain on which Stilicho met Alaric, cf. 2.126 planitiem; n. 2.125 f.

2.172 c vallis: Platnauer (1922) seems justified in taking this word as referring to the Gothic fortifications alone. Gesner (1759) *ad loc.*, Birt (1892) 596 s.v. *vallum*, and Crépin (1933) make it apply to the several encampments of the two opposing forces. For *vallis* (ablative) referring to a single encampment, cf. Verg. A. 10.120 At legio Aeneadum vallis obsessa tenetur, whether *vallis* there is from *vallus*, as Page (1900) *ad loc.*, following Connington (1872), holds, or from *vallum*, as Merguet (1912) 732 and Wetmore (1911) 529 more plausibly take it. After the stress which Claudian had laid on the circumvallation of the Goths as an indication of their fear (cf. n. 2.127–29), it seems less likely that he would call attention to any defensive measures taken by Stilicho.

2.173: for Stilicho exhorting the troops before battle, cf. BP

559–80; on the actual use of such exhortations in the army of the Fourth Century, cf. Grosse (1920) 249.

2.174 a Armeniis ... Gallos: on the contrast, cf. n. 2.108–10 b.

2.174 b frons laeva: for the wing of an army thus designated, cf. Tac. *Hist.* 2.24 dextera fronte; Luc. 7.220 dextri frons...Martis; TLL s.v. *frons* 1361.33–37.

2.175–81 Spumis — radiat: for other descriptions of troops in splendid array, cf. 2.351–65, 3H 132–41, 6H 566–77. On the mustering of troops as an epic theme, cf. Miniconi (1951) 159.

2.175 Spumis ignescere: for *ignesco* meaning to become fiery red with blood, cf. Stat. *Theb.* 3.78 ignescunt sanguine vultus; cf. also CM 9.7 Oculis rubet igneus ardor; Luc. 9.791 f. rubor igneus ora / succendit. For the foam of horses' mouths blood-stained from their champing at the bit, cf. CS 2.350–52 spumis fucantem ... frena / sanguineis ... / ... equum; Sil. 12.254 f. equum spumantia saevo / frena cruentatum morsu. The interpretation of Platnauer (1922) "covered with warm foam," seems incorrect, despite RP 2.202 sanguine frena calent. If taken in his sense, *ignescere* would presumably refer to the heating of the *frena*, which would not be caught by the eye of the spectator, as the blood-red color would (cf. 2.176 videres). The translation of Crépin (1933), "se couvrent d'écume fumante," is not quite as open to this objection.

2.176 pulveris extolli nimbos: on the dust-cloud accompanying military action as an epic theme, cf. Miniconi (1951) 167.

2.177 f.: for the dragon-banners, which were regularly used in the Roman army of the Fourth Century as the standard of a legionary detachment (the eagle remaining the standard of the full legion), cf. 2.364 f. spiris ... remissis / mansuescunt varii vento cessante dracones, 3H 138–41 Hi volucres tollunt aquilas, hi picta draconum / colla levant, multusque tumet per nubila serpens / iratus stimulante Noto, vivitque receptis / flatibus, et vario mentitur sibila tractu, EH 193, 4H 545, 6H 566–68; Amm. 16.10.7 (Constantius' triumphal entry into Rome) circumdedere dracones, hastarum aureis gemmatisque summitatibus illigati, hiatu vasto perflabiles, et ideo velut ira perciti sibilantes, caudarumque volumina relinquentes in ventum; Veget. 2.13 Primum signum totius legionis est aquila, quam aquilifer portat. Dracones etiam per singulas cohortes a draconiariis feruntur ad proelium; Zos. 3.19.1;

RE s.v. *Draco* (2); Grosse (1920) 231–33; Kromayer-Veith (1928) 585; cf. also Reinach (1909) 1.256, Plate 2; Straub (1939) 258, ftn. 48.

Blümner (1892) 194 misunderstands this passage entirely. Miniconi (1951) 196 has mechanically included this passage among comparisons drawn from mythology or legend, apparently not realizing that these were actual, not metaphorical, dragon-banners. On the absence of any mention of the Christian *labarum*, cf. n. 2.366.

2.177 *a* purpureis: for the color, cf. Amm. 15.5.16 (Silvanus assumes the purple at Cologne) cultu purpureo a draconum et vexillorum insignibus ad tempus abstracto, ad culmen imperiale surrexit; Stein-Palanque (1959) 142. These two passages contradict the theory set forth by Fiebiger, RE s.v. *Draco* (2) 1634.21–27, Grosse (1920) 232, and Kromayer-Veith (1928) 585 (it goes back to Lipsius [1598] 172 = 4.5) that the color was at least one of the distinctive characteristics of the *draco* by which Julian was recognized on the battlefield: cf. Amm. 16.12.39 quo agnito per purpureum signum draconis, summitati hastae longioris aptatum, velut senectutis pandentis exuvias. Since Silvanus was neither Caesar nor (as yet) Augustus, and yet had at hand *dracones* and *vexilla* adorned with purple, it is clear that the color could not have been the distinguishing feature in Julian's case. It may be, as Lipsius himself suggests, that the taller *hasta* (*hastae longioris*; cf. n. 2.177 *b*) was the significant item; perhaps it was a correspondingly larger size, or some peculiarity of design denoted by the words *velut — exuvias*, that served to distinguish the *draco* of the Caesar or Augustus from that of the legionary detachment (cf. n. 2.177 f.)

2.177 *b* hastas: for the *hasta* as a flagstaff, cf. Amm. 16.10.7 dracones, hastarum... summitatibus illigati, 16.12.39; Veget. 1.20 draconarii atque signiferi, qui sinistra manu hastas gubernant; Domaszewski (1885) 50, ftn. 1.

2.179–82: on geographical enumerations, cf. n. 1.131–33; note especially the quotation from Lucan given there. Here Mt. Olympus roughly marks the northern, Mt. Oeta the southern boundary of Thessaly.

2.179 Thessaliam: on the location of this episode, cf. n. 2.125 f.

2.179–81 implet — radiat: on the gleam of arms as an epic theme, cf. Miniconi (1951) 164 f. Bruère (1964) 233 suggests as Claudian's prototype here Luc. 7.477–83 (the battle of Pharsalus commences); he also cites Luc. 1.151-53 (the comparison of Caesar to a thunderbolt).

2.179 f. antra — Achilli: for Achilles as the pupil of the Centaur Chiron in his cave near the river Sperchius in Thessaly, cf. Stat. *Ach.* 1.232 f. (Thetis takes the young Achilles from Chiron) celeres ... recursus / ... Chiron rogat, 237-40 Illum non alias rediturum ad Thessala Tempe / ... iam ... ingemuit ... / ... tenuis Sperchius aquis speluncaque docti / muta senis; Roscher (1937) s.v. *Achilleus* 25 f., s.v. *Cheiron* 889 f. Cf. also 3H 60 f.; on the popularity of the theme with the rhetoricians, cf. Levy (1946) 61 and ftn. 17.

2.180 a tenero — Achilli: for Achilles' tender age when he was given over to Chiron, cf. Stat. *Ach.* 2.382 f. (Achilles speaks) in teneris et adhuc reptantibus annis / Thessalus ut ... senior ... me ... recepit; A.R. 4.812 f.; Roscher (1937) s.v. *Achilleus* 25.24-30; Johansen (1939) 182, ftn. 2.

2.180 b amnis reptatus: for the mention of a body of water when reference to its banks is intended, cf. 2.290 Percurritur Hebrus (and Text. Comm. *ad loc.*; n. 2.290 b); CS 2.199 f. opacum vitibus Histrum conserit; Verg. *A.* 7.682-84 qui ... arva Gabinae / Iunonis gelidumque Anienem ... / ... colunt, 714 Casperiam ... colunt Forulosque et flumen Himellae; V. Fl. 1.43 f.; Sil. 3.322.

2.180 c amnis: Schol. A *ad loc.* correctly identifies the river as the Sperchius; cf. Stat. *Ach.* 1.628 f. (Achilles speaks) Quaerisne meos, Sperchie, natatus?; Roscher (1937) s.v. *Spercheios* 1294.

2.180 d reptatus: for the passive of *repto*, cf. 4H 134 Creta ... tenero reptata Tonanti; Stat. *Theb.* 5.581.

2.181 f. Clamore ... fragor: Platnauer (1922) does not differentiate between these two words; he translates, "Ossa re-echoes to the sound and Olympus smitten therewith sends it back two-fold." Crépin (1933) follows much the same interpretation. H. Hoppe, in TLL s.v. *clamor* 1257.29, cites Clamore ... / Ossa tonat under the rubric rerum ... sonitus, fragor. However, it seems more likely that *clamor* here is the war-cry, *fragor* the sound of the shield struck in a display of martial spirit: on both these traits, cf. Grosse (1920) 249 f., 327. For *clamor* of the war-cry, cf. Luc. 1.388 It ... ad aethera clamor (cf. also Verg. *A.* 9.504, 566, 664, 11.622); DS s.v. *clamor* 1220 f. For the *barritus*, the fourth-century Roman war-cry of Germanic origin, cf.

Veget. 3.18 clamor autem, quem barritum vocant, prius non debet adtolli, quam acies utraque se iunxerit; RE s.v. *Barditus* 11.7–26; Grosse (1920) 38.24–28, 250.1–4. For *fragor* of the sound made by striking the shield, cf. IE 2.160–64 (Mars) clipeo ... // intonuit ...; / ingeminat raucum Rhodope concussa fragorem (cf. also CM 9.22–26); Amm. 15.8.15 militares omnes horrendo fragore scuta genibus inlidentes, 21.5.9, 27.6.10. Cf. also Serv. on Verg. *A.* 8.527 fragor est proprie armorum sonus. For the striking of shields as troops advance to battle, cf. Amm. 29.5.38 f. conglobatis suis scutaque in formidabilem moventibus gestum, [Theodosius] controversas eisdem [*sc.* barbaris] opposuit manus. Quamquam ... manipuli furentium [*sc.* barbarorum] imminebant, ipsi quoque parmas genibus inlidentes, where the word *quoque* identifies the gesture as made by the Roman soldiers. On the Ammianus passage, cf. Meurig Davies (1948) 76.

2.182 tonat ... geminatur: for these verbs used to denote the reverberation of sound, cf. (1) Verg. *A.* 12.756 f. Tum vero exoritur clamor ... / ... et caelum tonat omne tumultu, 9.541; Sen. *Tro.* 174 f. nemus / fragore vasto tonuit; (2) Luc. 7.480 f. (cf. n. 1.131–33) excepit resonis clamorem vallibus Haemus / Peliacisque dedit rursus geminare cavernis. Cf. also IE 2.163 ingeminat raucum Rhodope concussa fragorem; Verg. *G.* 3.45; Ov. *Met.* 3.369.

2.183–94: on martial fury as an epic theme, cf. Miniconi (1951) 169 f.

2.183 Intumuit virtus: for the expression, cf. Stat. *Theb.* 3.333 Tunc quoque lassa tumet virtus.

2.183 f. lucis prodigus ... impetus: for the thought, cf. Stat. *Theb.* 8.406 vitae prodiga virtus, 3.69 f.; Ov. *Am.* 3.9.64 sanguinis atque animae prodige Galle tuae; Sil. 1.225.

2.184 f. vetarent ... stravissent: Claudian uses the imperfect as well as the pluperfect subjunctive in unreal expressions referring to the past (cf. CS 1.112–15, 176–80, 2.317, 3.20 f., 354 f., 6H 223); on this use of the two tenses, cf. Hofmann-Szantyr (1965) 662. Elsewhere the choice of the imperfect might be accounted for on metrical grounds; the use of *vetarent* here instead of the metrically equivalent *vetassent*, as a parallel to the pluperfect *stravissent*, seems to indicate that Claudian regarded the two tenses as freely interchangeable in this construction.

2.186–94: the validity of Claudian's claim that Stilicho could have defeated the forces of Alaric at this time had he been permitted to do so is of course a matter of conjecture. Bury (1928) 69 holds that "there is no doubt that he could easily have crushed the Goths and rendered Alaric harmless"; cf. Bury (1923) 112. For a contrary view, cf. Fargues (1933a) 101.

2.186 acies collata fuisset: for *aciem confero* used of committing an army to battle, cf. BG 386 f. collata ... nescit / maiestatem acies. The expression in this sense is apparently otherwise unexampled: cf. TLL s.v. *confero* 180.6–18. The usage in Pl. *Epid.* 547, orationis aciem contra conferam, is figurative, and in Stat. *Theb.* 6.297 f. neque enim generosior umquam / alipedum conlata acies, the *acies* is the entire group of contestants. The expression used here is evidently modeled on *manum confero, signa confero,* and the like: cf. TLL s.v. *confero* 180.40–65.

2.187–91: for a similar list of places under barbarian domination at the time this poem was written, cf. Jerome *Ep.* 60.16.4 (A.D. 396) Quid putas nunc animi habere Corinthios, Athenienses, Lacedaemonios, Arcadas, cunctamque Graeciam, quibus imperant barbari? On the likelihood of a connection between the two passages, cf. n. 2.32–35.

On the devastation wreaked upon Greece by Alaric after Stilicho's withdrawal, cf. Zos. 5.5.5–5.6.5 (on the uncertainty of his chronology, cf. n. 2.43 f.); Stein-Palanque (1959) 230 f.

2.188 Pelopeia: for this adjective used to denote locations in the Peloponnese, cf. Verg. *A.* 2.193 f. ultro Asiam ... Pelopea ad moenia ... / venturam; RE s.v. *Peloponnesus* 382.28–49.

2.189: for both thought and expression, cf. Verg. *A.* 2.56 Troiaque nunc staret, Priamique arx alta maneres. Cf. also Luc. 6.306–11, and Bruère (1964) 233.

2.190 *a*: cf. BP 612 (in an enumeration of Gothic spoils) rapta ... flagranti spirantia signa Corintho; 4H 471 (after Stilicho's expedition of 397; *Ephyre = Corinthus*) Excutiat cineres Ephyre. Claudian is our only authority for the burning of Corinth: Zos. 5.6.4 says simply ἡ Κόρινθος πρώτη κατὰ κράτος ἡλίσκετο; cf. Stein-Palanque (1959) 231; 542, ftn. 68 *bis*.

2.190 *b* mare ... geminum: for the expression, cf. IE 1.90 f. (a woman of Corinth) Lais / e gemino ditata mari; Ov. *Ep.* 12.104 maris gemini distinet Isthmos aquas, *Tr.* 1.10.32; Stat. *Theb.* 7.106 f.

2.191 *a*: cf. Philostorgius 12.2 Ἀλλάριχος Γότθος ... τὰς Ἀθήνας εἷλεν. On the story of Zos. 5.5.8–5.6.2 that Athens was saved from a hostile incursion by the miraculous interposition of Athena Promachos, cf. Wachsmuth (1874) 1.715 f.; Gregorovius (1889) 1.37, 41; Day (1942) 269, ftn. 31.

2.191 *b* **Cecropiae:** =*Athenienses*: cf. Plin. *Nat*. 7.56.194 oppidum primum Cecrops a se appellavit Cecropiam quae nunc est arx Athenis; TLL *Onomast*. s.v. *Cecrops* 292.3–45.

2.192 f.: for the thought, cf. Luc. 6.312 ultimus dies potuit tibi, Roma, malorum; and Bruère (1964) 233.

2.194 Invida ... Fortuna: for a similar thought, cf. 1.176 f. maligno / stamine fatorum; n. 1.176 f.

2.195 tubas: on the use of the word *tubae* to denote the start of a battle, cf. n. 1.333 *b*.

2.195 f. mandata: for the substance of the orders, cf. 2.161 f. Deserat Illyricos fines; Eoa remittat / agmina; n. 2.152–63; n. 2.169 *b*.

2.196 regia: on the use of this and similar terms in connection with the Roman Emperor, cf. n. 1.113.

2.197–219: *Stilicho deliberates briefly, then decides to obey*. For Stilicho's dilemma and its resolution, cf. CS 2.95–97 Mittitur et miles, quamvis certamine partes / iam tumeant. Hostem munire robore mavis / quam peccare fidem; Int. 24; Stein-Palanque (1959) 229. Certain scholars have been at pains to find motivation of Stilicho's obedience to Arcadius' demands beyond the former's fidelity to the senior Augustus (cf. Int. 24, n. 2.202) and his hopes of establishing himself as protector of the Eastern court, once Rufinus was put out of the way: cf. Int. 24 f.; n. 2.170; Stein-Palanque (1959) 229. Bury (1923) 112 and Lot-Pfister-Ganshof (1940) 26, as well as Mazzarino (1942) 258, suggest that Stilicho was influenced by the presence in Constantinople of members of his family, who might be regarded as hostages (cf. n. 2.95). Stein-Palanque (1959) 229 rightly rejects this suggestion on the ground that the military power at Stilicho's disposal (especially, it may be added, if he did *not* restore the Eastern troops to Arcadius) obviated any real threat to his family. Fargues (1933a) 102, ftn. 2, suggests that Stilicho avoided entering into armed conflict with Arcadius' court for fear that the officers of the Eastern troops would not stand by him in such a conflict. This suggestion seems hardly tenable in view of the action of Gainas and the troops in slaying the chief minister of the Eastern court in the Emperor's presence (cf. Int. 25). The question is reviewed by Cameron (1968b) 277 f.

2.198 ignavo: for a similar epithet ridiculing Rufinus' non-military status, cf. 2.53 proditor... iners; n. 2.53 *a*.

2.201 *a* Illyricis... damnis: for the invasion of the Illyrian Prefecture (cf. n. 2.161), cf. 2.36-44 Geticis—aristas; Caesarius *Dial.* 1.68 (= Migne Gr. 38.936) πρὸς τὰ Ῥωμαίων, Ἰλλύριά τε καὶ Θρᾴκεια μέρη; cf. also the citations from Zosimus and Socrates in n. 2.43 f., with the caution there noted; Stein-Palanque (1959) 228 f.

2.201 *b* succurrere damnis: on this use of *succurro* with the dative cf. n. 2.164 *b*.

2.202-4 timet... metus: only here, and in the paradox CS 1.341 ne timeare times, does Claudian ascribe to Stilicho the emotion of fear. The words *timet* and *metus* here probably denote a feeling of awe with regard to the Emperor's commands and his possible displeasure (cf. however n. 2.204). For *timeo* and *metus* of the affectionate awe in which Stilicho himself was allegedly held, cf. EH 330-32 Non odium terrore moves... / ... ; diligimus pariter pariterque timemus. / Ipse metus te noster amat.

2.202 Reverentia: for Stilicho's deep sense of loyalty to both Arcadius and Honorius as Theodosius' sons, cf. CS 2.50-53 Nec vivis adnexus amor meminisse sepultos / desinit; in prolem transcurrit gratia patrum. / Hac tu Theodosium, tenuit dum sceptra, colebas, / hac etiam post fata colis; 86 f. cuius fulta fide mediis dissensibus aulae / intemeratorum stabat reverentia fratrum; BG 288-308; Baynes (1922) 213 f.; Fargues (1933a) 122 f.; Stein-Palanque (1959) 225 f.

2.203 virtutis stimulos: for the expression, cf. Luc. 8.328-30 quos Lentulus omnis / virtutis stimulis et nobilitate dolendi / praecessit.

2.204 invidiae: Platnauer (1922) is apparently correct in interpreting this word as referring to the Emperor's displeasure. For *invidia* denoting resentment, with no derogatory connotation as regards the person who feels the emotion, cf. 2.249, n. 2.248 f.; Stat. *Silv.* 3.5.41 f. (the gods spared the poet for fear of his wife's displeasure) superi... potentes / invidiam timuere tuam, 5.5.78; Sil. 10.224 f. (Servilius' death augments the Romans' anger) magnam... cadens leto addidit uno / invidiam Cannis. Cf. also Ov. *Met.* 4.548; Witstrand (1946); Odelstierna (1949) 28.

It is also possible (so Crépin [1933]) that Claudian has in mind the *invidia* of the general's enemies at Arcadius' court, and the danger that they might find in Stilicho's disobedience a source of ammunition in their campaign completely to discredit him with the young Emperor (cf. n. 2.170). Stilicho is represented as having been in some danger even at Theodosius' court from the *invidia* of rivals: cf. CM 30.228–30 (Serena guards Stilicho's interests) vigili tu prospicis omnia sensu / ne quid in absentem virtutibus obvia semper / audeat invidiae rabies neu fervor iniquus.

2.204 f. ad astra extollit palmas: for the gesture, cf. Verg. *A.* 2.153 (Sinon prays) sustulit ... ad sidera palmas, 3.176 f., 9.16 f.; Sittl (1890) 174; Appel (1909) 194–96.

2.206–19: on the use of direct quotation in IR, cf. n. 1.45–65, esp. sect. 6.

2.206–13: Numina — pudet: for the thought, cf. Luc. 2.56–58 (Romans pray the gods to avert civil war) perdere nomen / si placet Hesperium, superi, conlatus in ignes / plurimus ad terram per fulmina decidat aether.

2.206 *a* Romanis ... ruinis: for a similar reference to current disasters, cf. 2.94 f. ruenti / ... patriae; n. 2.94 f. *b*.

2.206 *b* necdum: here used in the sense of simple *nondum*, without any of the conjunctional force of *nec*. Birt (1892) 544 s.v. holds that this is the only meaning of *necdum* in Claudian: he apparently overlooks IE 2.554–56 erat invidiosa potestas, / sed tamen eunuchi, necdum sibi publica iura / sumere nec totas audebat vertere leges (cf. also CM 30.46). For *necdum* used as in the present passage, cf. 4H 383–85 sic pascua parvus / vindicat et necdum formatis cornibus audax / iam regit armentum vitulus, CM 53.6 erumpunt crebri necdumque creati (note the addition of *et* in the first lemma and *-que* in the second); Col. 10.55 Atque ubi iam tuto necdum confisus Olympo; V. Fl. 4.208 f.; Hofmann-Szantyr (1965) 449.

2.206 *c* satiata ruinis: cf. Petr. 121.119 f. ingenti satiare ruina, / pallida Tisiphone.

2.208 saecula: for this word to denote the human race (cf. n. 2.209), cf. 2.473 f. (in a description of the Lower World) Huc post emeritam mortalia saecula vitam / deveniunt, 4H 99 f., 6H 151; Lucr. 5.805 tum tibi terra dedit primum mortalia saecla, 1169, 1238; Verg. G. 1.468; Luc. 10.110.

2.209 humani generis: for this expression to denote the inhabitants of the Roman Empire, cf. CS 3.151 (Rome protects mankind) humanum ... genus communi nomine fovit; Ov. Met. 15.758 f. (the gods favor Rome under Augustus) Quo praeside rerum / humano generi, superi, favistis abunde; Christ (1938) 28.

2.209-11 prorumpat — habenas: on the concept of the destruction of the world by fire and water, cf. Roscher (1937) s.v. Phaëthon 2189-95. Cf. also n. 1.63 f.

2.210 *a* effrena: for the sea in flood thought of as an unbridled steed, cf. 1.63 f. laxare profundo / frena mari; n. 1.64.

2.210 f. *a* limite — habenas: for the Phaëthon legend, cf. 4H 62-69, 6H 186-90; Ov. Met. 1.750-2.400; on Claudian's use of the legend, cf. Roscher (1937) s.v. Phaëthon 2193.50-63.

2.210 f. *b* limite ... devius: the use of *devius* with an ablative of separation is perhaps paralleled in Sil. 15.583 f. ubi arma / avertisse suo cognovit devia vallo; TLL s.v. *devius* 867.15-17. Cf. also Ov. Pont. 3.1.27 procul haec regio est et ab omni devia cursu.

2.210 *b* limite: for *limes* denoting the sun's path, cf. 4H 286 f. limite Phoebus / contentus medio (cf. 6H 411 f.), BG 149, RP 1.261; Ov. Met. 2.130 (of the Zodiac) sectus in obliquum est lato curvamine limes.

2.212-16 mundum ... orbem: on the use of these words to denote the Roman Empire, cf. n. 1.143 *b*, n. 1 Pr.17 *b*.

2.212 f. procumbere — pudet: Bruère (1964) 234 compares Luc. 7.672 (Pompey fears his death might lead to general disaster) supra ... ducem procumberet orbis.

2.215: in a passage in Lucan similar to 2.206-19, Pompey calls Rome to witness that he joins battle against his better judgment: Luc. 7.91 f. Testor, Roma, tamen Magnum quo cuncta perirent / accepisse diem. With IR 2.214-26 Bruère (1964) 234 compares Luc. 7.333, 411-14.

2.216 f.: these two verses correspond respectively to the two parts of the demand voiced by Rufinus in 2.161 f.: Deserat Illyricos fines; Eoa remittat / agmina; cf. n. 2.152-63.

2.216 cedo equidem: for the expression, cf. Verg. *A.* 2.704 cedo equidem, nec, nate, tibi comes ire recuso; 12.818.

2.217–19: for the rapid succession of brief sentences, evidently intended to reproduce the laconic style of military command, cf. Luc. 1.226 f. (Caesar at the Rubicon) Te, Fortuna, sequor. Procul hinc iam foedera sunto. / Credidimus fatis. Utendum est iudice bello. Cf. also the commands of Minos to his minions at the end of IR: 2.520–23.

2.217 a Flectite signa, duces: for a command similar in form, opposite in meaning, cf. Luc. 5.41 (Lentulus encourages the Pompeians) Tollite signa, duces.

2.217 b Flectite: for *flecto* in the sense "turn back," cf. 2.252 f. flexit iter ... qualis ... / impatiens remeare leo, 4H 541, BP 594; TLL s.v. *flecto* 894.29.

2.217 c duces: for this term denoting subordinate military commanders, cf. IE 2.342 Pars humili de plebe duces, 345 f. sed prima potestas / Eutropium praefert Hosio subnixa secundo; TLL s.v. *dux* 2322.39–62. On the official use of the term, cf. RE s.v. *Dux* 1869–72.

2.217 d miles Eous: on this expression cf. n. 2.105 b.

2.218 a Taceant litui: on the *lituus* as an instrument used for sounding the attack, cf. n. 1.347 f.

2.218 b sagittas: for the mention of this weapon, cf. 2.229 solvi curvatos imperat arcus; cf. also Grosse (1920) 335 f., Schissel von Fleschenberg (1941).

2.219 Rufinus praecipit: for an exclamatory parenthesis similarly placed, cf. Stat. *Theb.* 6.918 f. Ne precor, ante aciem, ius tantum casibus esse, / fraternisque sinas—abigant hoc numina—votis; on the use of parentheses, cf. Hofmann-Szantyr (1965) 472 f.

2.220–56: *The soldiers implore Stilicho not to separate the two forces, but he stands firm.*

2.220 His dictis: on the use of phrases marking the end of direct quotation, cf. n. 1.65 b.

2.220–23 omnes — poscunt, 225–27 sibi — queruntur: with these passages Bruère (1964) 234 compares Luc. 7.45–49 (Pompey's soldiers are eager for battle) mixto murmure turba / castrorum fremuit fatisque trahentibus orbem / signa petit pugnae ... pars maxima volgi / ... queritur ... tumultu.

2.220-22 fremuere — Coris: for a similar comparison, cf. Stat. *Theb.* 3.593-96 bella ore fremunt; it clamor ad auras, / quantus Tyrrheni gemitus salis, aut ubi temptat / Enceladus mutare latus; procul igneus antris / mons tonat; cf. also Luc. 6.692 f. On the use of imagery here, cf. Christiansen (1969) 59.

2.221 f. quantum non (*bis*): for this expression used in a comparison *a maiore ad minus*, cf. RP 2.199 f. (the speed of Pluto's horses) torta ... ruunt pernicius hasta, / quantum non iaculum Parthi, non impetus Austri (cf. also EH 215 f.); Luc. 6.165 f. Movit tantum vox illa furorem / quantum non primo succendunt classica cantu; Stat. *Theb.* 6.806 f. Vergil uses the expression in a different sense, "save in so far as"; cf. *A.* 6.731 quantum non corpora noxia tardant.

2.221 *a*: on comparisons with the violence of the waves as an epic theme, cf. Miniconi (1951) 192 f.; he should have included verse 222 under the rubric *Tonnerre*, not under *Mer et vagues*.

2.221 *b* Italo ... fluctu: this designation for the Adriatic is apparently otherwise unexampled. For the Adriatic as a type of the raging sea, cf. Hor. *Carm.* 2.14.13 f. Frustra ... carebimus / fractis ... rauci fluctibus Hadriae, 1.3.15 f., 1.33.15, 3.3.5, 3.9.22 f.; Sen. *Thy.* 361 f.; RE s.v. *Adria* 418.60-69, s.v. *Notos* 1117.19-35.

2.221 *c* Ceraunia: the headland jutting out into the Adriatic is more specifically called Acroceraunia: cf. Hor. *Carm.* 1.3.19 f. mare turgidum et / infames scopulos, Acroceraunia; TLL s.v. *Acroceraunia* 429.20-46; RE s.vv. *Akrokeraunia, Keraunia* (1).

2.222 *a* madidis ... Coris: for Corus or Caurus (Greek Ἀργέστης: cf. RE s.v. *Caurus*; Steinmetz [1907] 43, ftn. 2) associated with rain, cf. CM 28.3 graviter flantes pluviali frigore Coros; Stat. *Theb.* 4.833-35 (in praise of an ever-flowing river) neque enim tibi cana repostas / bruma nives raptasque alio de fonte refundit / arcus aquas, gravidive indulgent nubila Cori (for *gravidus* in connection with rain, cf. 5.362 f. gravidam ... imbri / ... nubem); Plin. *Nat.* 18.35.354 cum ab Austro vel Coro aut Favonio nocte serena fulgurabit (cf. *tonitrua* in our passage), ventum et imbrem ex iisdem regionibus demonstrabit; Kaibel (1885) 604; McCartney (1930) 13.

2.222 *b* elisa tonitrua Coris: for the concept that thunder and lightning are produced by the action of winds upon clouds, cf. Lucr. 6.96-99 tonitru quatiuntur caerula caeli / propterea quia concurrunt sublime volantes / aetheriae nubes, contra pugnantibu' ventis, 124–203; Luc. 1.151–53 Qualiter expressam ventis per nubila fulmen / aetheris impulsi sonitu mundique fragore / emicuit (this citation is used by Lactantius on Stat. *Theb.* 1.258 to illustrate his words: fulmen esse sine aere non potest.... Etenim si non fuerint nubes aere collisae, fulmen nullum est); McCartney (1931) 216. For a report on modern scientific research on thunderstorms, with a statement that such storms "'breathe,' ... 'inhaling' air from the surroundings at heights between 2000 and 25,000 feet, and 'exhaling' at both top and bottom," cf. *New York Times* 97 (29 January 1948) 25, col. 7; Byers-Braham (1948).

2.223 secerni ... negant: for *nego* in the sense "refuse," "be reluctant," with a passive infinitive denoting that which the person refuses to have done to him, cf. Sen. *Herc. F.* 493 (a refusal of marriage) copulari pertinax taedis negat, *Tr.* 903 f.; V. Fl. 5.28 f.

2.224 a populus: for this word used of a multitude of soldiers (cf. the Homeric λαός, e.g. *Il.* 16.129 λαὸν ἀγείρω), cf. 2.290; cf. also Luc. 7.841 (the dead at Pharsalus) non omnis populus pervenit ad ossa, 6.633–36; Stat. *Theb.* 12.22 f. (the Theban dead) Itur in exsanguem populum bellique iacentis / relliquias. Note, however, that Lucan and Statius use the word of troops that have been slain.

2.224 b defendit: for *defendo* in the sense of "claim," "assert one's right to," cf. Stat. *Silv.* 1.3.4 (two villas vie for their master's affection) certantes ... sibi dominum defendere villas; TLL s.v. *defendo* 295.80–84.

2.225 amore: the army's love for Stilicho was a favorite theme of Claudian's (cf. 2.261), and, as Schroff (1927) on BP Pr. 18 remarks, was a theme which Stilicho himself was apparently delighted to have stressed: cf. EH 332, CS 2.173, 397 f., 412, 3.52, 222.

2.226 alternam ... fidem: on *alternus* in the sense "two-fold," cf. n. 2.128 b. The idea of reciprocity conveyed by 4H 283 alterna fides (the mutual good faith of ruler and subject) is of course absent here.

2.226 f. non inlaudata ... seditio: for the oxymoron, cf. Stat. *Theb.* 10.240 f. (Adrastus rejoices that his soldiers protest against his excluding them from a war-party) pulchra meorum / seditione fruor.

2.228–47: on the use of direct quotation in IR, cf. n. 1.45–65, esp. sect. 6.

2.228 mihi: according to Lipscomb (1909) 45, the singular is found only occasionally in collective speeches (cf. n. 2.88–99). Note also

2.232 mihi, 235 patiar, 241 comitabor, 245 relinquam, 269, 275 mihi. On the plurals (2.239) *sumus* and *sequemur*, cf. n. 2.239.

2.229 arcus: on the mention of this weapon, cf. n. 2.218 *b*.

2.230 stricto — ferro: cf. Text. Comm. *ad loc.* Bieler (1957) 260 sees in the variants (1) *leges vibrato imponere ferro* of *Em^bVC* and (2) *stricto leges imponere ferro* of the other codices, another instance of the kind which I posited in Text. Comm. on 1.205 f., para. 2.: cf. n. 1.205 f. *a.* Cameron (1968a) 397 argues strongly against the point of view that Claudian could not have written *leges vibrato*.

2.231: Bruère (1964) 234 regards this *sententia* as a reversed adaptation of Luc. 1.330–32, especially of 331 f. (Pompey, accustomed to licking Sulla's bloody sword, cannot put aside violence) *Nullus semel ore receptus / pollutas patitur sanguis mansuescere fauces.* The words *sitientia pila cruores* in the next verse of our passage lend weight to Bruère's suggestion.

2.232 *a* mihi: on the singular in a collective speech, cf. n. 2.228.

2.232–34: for the attribution of a hostile *animus* to weapons, cf. Hom. *Od.* 16.294 αὐτὸς ... ἐφέλκεται ἄνδρα σίδηρος; V. Fl. 5.540 *virum trahit ipse chalybs*; RE s.v. *Personifikationen* 1043.

2.232 *b* sitientia pila cruores: for weapons personified as blood-thirsty beings, cf. Sil. 12.264 *non hunc sitiens gravis hasta cruorem*; cf. also MT 297 *caedis sitientem ... arcum*; Verg. *A.* 11.804 (a spear) *virgineum ... alte bibit acta cruorem*; Petr. 120.98; Stat. *Theb.* 12.750. On the concept of blood-thirstiness, cf. n. 2.151 f. Cf. also Hom. *Il.* 11.574, 15.317, 21.70.

2.235 patiar: on the singular in a collective speech, cf. n. 2.228.

2.235 f. Semper — proderit: reference is apparently to Rufinus' alleged interference on behalf of the Goths in 391–92; cf. n. 1.314–20.

2.236–38 En iterum — aquilas: here Claudian's desire for rhetorical effect has led him into an absurdity which is patent from the standpoint not only of objective history but of what the poet himself wants us to believe. The end of the *bellum civile* (Theodosius' suppression of Eugenius' revolt) had occurred scarcely a year before: cf. 2.115 f. *animi ... recentia ponunt / vulnera*, 117 f. *civilia nuper / classica*; n. 2.115–19. Note also the impatient tone of *En iterum* here, suggestive of but a short interval. Claudian himself, in a neighboring passage, emphasizes that the two contingents of troops were of diverse origin (cf. 2.105–14; n. 2.105 *a*, *b*) and had fought on opposite sides (cf. 2.115 f., esp. 116 *victus victorve*; n. 2.115–19). Yet the combined troops are now represented as calling each other *consanguineae* and *olim concordes*. The adverb *olim*, despite the hesitation of Birt (1892) 549 s.v., if it is to have any meaning in the context, must be taken to refer to a considerable lapse of time. Claudian is rarely so clumsy.

2.239–47 Te qua — patria est: for a similar profession of willingness to follow a military leader to any lengths, cf. Luc. 1.367–86, and Bruère (1964) 234; cf. also n. 2.244 f., and CS 1.176–80. The influence of the *laudatio Alexandri* is perhaps to be seen in this passage; cf. n. 1.374–76; contrast the *vituperatio Alexandri*, n. 2.155 f. On the actual contemporary policy of not employing troops too far from their places of origin, cf. Straub (1952) 110.

2.239 sumus ... sequemur: these plurals may possibly be intended to emphasize momentarily the actual existence of two separate contingents of the army (cf. 2.217 *miles Eous*) which elsewhere in 2.228–47 is perhaps played down by the use of the singular (cf. n. 2.228). *Per contra* note the apparently purposeless intrusion of the singular *mihi* (2.269, 275) among the plurals of 2.261–77.

2.240–44 Thylen — Nili: for a similar catalog of widely separated geographical limits, cf. RP 3.319–25 (Ceres will traverse the entire world, if necessary, to find Proserpina); Luc. 1.10–20.

2.240 *a* Hyperboreo ... sidere: the constellation Ursa Major in the extreme northern sky: cf. Luc. 5.23–25 (the Senate's domination extends from the frozen North to the torrid South), esp. 23 *Hyperboreae plaustrum glaciale sub Ursae*; Sen. *Herc. O.* 1523 f.; Ov. *Pont.* 4.10.39 f.; RE s.v. *Arktos* (2) 1173.49–62.

2.240 *b* Thylen: to Claudian, Thyle is evidently the Shetland Islands, off the Orkney group: cf. 4H 31 f. (the elder Theodosius' northern conquests) *Maduerunt Saxone fuso / Orcades, incaluit Pictorum sanguine Thyle*. Cf. Tac. *Ag.* 10.5 f. (Agricola) *insulas, quas Orcadas vocant, invenit.... Dispecta est et Thule*; RE s.v. *Thule* (*Thyle*) 629.48–65.

2.241 *a* incensas Libyae ... harenas: cf. n. 2.40–42.

2.241 *b*: on the use of the singular, cf. n. 2.228.

2.242 f. rubri ... litoris: on the term "red" (ἐρυθρός, *ruber*) applied to the Indian Ocean as well as to what we now call the Red Sea (*sinus Arabicus*: cf. n. 1.278 *b*), cf. Thomson (1948) 81, 299.

2.243 *a* auriferum . . . Hydaspen: the epithet is intended as a general designation of opulence: cf. 3H 4 Hydaspeis . . . gemmis, MT 29 ditavit Hydaspes; Sen. *Med*. 725, *Herc. O*. 628.

2.243 *b* poturus Hydaspen: for the commonplace of soldiers' drawing their drinking-water from the rivers of the lands in which they serve, cf. IE 2.248-51 Gallorum exercitus . . . pro Rheno poturus Halyn; also BP 532 galeis . . . Padum victricibus hausi, with the note of Schroff (1927) *ad loc*.

2.244 calcare Notum: Claudian's choice of verb shows how stereotyped had become the metonymic use of the name of a wind for the name of its country of origin: cf. Birt (1892) 448 s.v. *Notus* (2).

2.244 f. secreta . . . Nili nascentis: for the mystery of the Nile's source, cf. Luc. 1.20 gens siqua iacet nascenti conscia Nilo; perhaps Claudian had this passage in mind as well as that cited by Bruère (1964) 234, i.e. Luc. 1.367-86. Cf. also Ov. *Met*. 2.254 f. Nilus . . . / occuluit . . . caput, quod adhuc latet; RE s.v. *Nil* 556.61-561.35.

2.245 *a* mundum post terga relinquam: Bruère (1964) 234 compares Luc. 1.369 ut victum post terga reliquerit orbem. Cf. also Luc. 4.353 securum . . . orbis patimur post terga relicti.

2.245 *b* relinquam: on the use of the singular, cf. n. 2.228.

2.246 f. *a* quocumque loco — patria est: Bruère (1964) 234 sees here a reminiscence of Luc. 1.396 tentoria fixa.

2.246 f. *b* figet . . . est: cf. Text. Comm. *ad loc*.

2.247 inde: on words indicating the resumption of the narrative, cf. n. 1.65 *b*.

2.247-51 Desistite . . . differte . . . ite: Stilicho addresses only the Eastern contingent; the Westerners returned to Italy with him (Int. 25). On the direct quotation, cf. n. 1.45-65, esp. sects. 6, 8.

2.248 f. Cadat . . . invidiae cumulus: cf. Luc. 4.279, where *cadat* is used in a similar passage, 4.273-84 (Caesar forbids his soldiers to fight). Platnauer (1922) wrongly translates *invidiae cumulus* "mountain of hatred that towers over me"; *invidia* here is the understandable (cf. n. 2.204, para. 1) resentment of the frustrated soldiery.

2.249 f. Non est victoria — mihi: on this *sententia* "in Lucan's manner" cf. Bruère (1964) 234; he cites Luc. 3.51 f. nec vincere tanti, /

ut bellum differret, erat, and the paradoxes in 4.356, 362. Cf. also Luc. 2.323 ne sibi se vicisse putet, 4.274. For a similar *sententia*, cf. 4H 295 (Theodosius to Honorius) Non tibi, nec tua te moveant, sed publica vota.

2.251 *a* **ite, mei quondam socii:** cf. Verg. *Ecl.* 1.75 ite meae, felix quondam pecus, ite capellae. For the term *socii* addressed by a commander to his troops, cf. Luc. 1.299 bellorum o socii.

2.251 *b* **Nec plura locutus:** on formulae for closing quotations, cf. n. 1.65 *b*.

2.252–56 vacuo — silvas: for similar images drawn from the animal world, cf. Sil. 7.718–22 averso pastore lupus ... /// ... spirantem dentibus imis / reiactat praedam, et vacuo fugit aeger hiatu; V. Fl. 3.589, 738; Stat. *Silv.* 2.5.14 f. Tunc cunctis cecidere iubae, puduitque relatum / adspicere, et totas duxere lumina frontes; Christiansen (1969) 23 f., Miniconi (1951) 199–202. Cf. also Verg. *A.* 9.792–96. All these images can perhaps ultimately be traced to Hom. *Il.* 17.61–67, 108–12, 133–36, 657–64, a remarkable series. One may wonder whether Claudian's *demissa lumina velat* came through the Statian passage just cited, or another Latin work, or directly (as Skutsch *ap.* Koch [1893] Pr. 22 suggests) from *Il.* 17.136 ἐπισκύνιον κάτω ἕλκεται ὄσσε καλύπτων.

2.252 flexit iter: cf. Luc. 8.471 flexit iter; n. 2.217 *b*.

2.253 impatiens remeare: for *impatiens* in the sense "reluctant," cf. RP 1.35 (Pluto rejects his unwed state) impatiens nescire torum; Sil. 6.231 f. (a horse balks at the rein) freno ... teneri / impatiens, 254 (a serpent disdains retreat) impatiens dare terga.

2.255: Schol. A *ad loc.* remarks: per jubas intelligit vexilla et signa Stiliconis, quae quasi demissa et inclinata fuerant ... per jubas leonis prius erectas ostenditur ira Stiliconis quae prius erat ad bellum....

2.257–77: *The Eastern soldiers vow loyalty to Stilicho and vengeance upon his enemies.*

2.257 legio: Platnauer (1922) translates in the plural, "armies." However, it is only the Eastern army that might be said to have been deserted: cf. n. 2.247–51. For *legio* of an entire army, cf. IE 1.256, Verg. *A.* 9.174, Haverfield (1907) 105.

2.258–60: for a grief-stricken army, cf. Stat. *Theb.* 8.162–68, esp.

163 fletus galeis cecidere solutis. Both passages contrast the stern implements of war with the pitiful tears and sighs of the soldiers.

2.259 pressam ... morantia vocem: these words anticipate 2.262 exclamant. The army, in its tight cuirasses (cf. Stat. *Theb.* 4.723 f. arctos / thoracum nexus) was too strangled by sobs to shout out at once.

2.261–77: on direct quotation in IR, cf. n. 1.45–65.

2.261 amorem: on the theme of the army's love for Stilicho, cf. n. 2.225.

2.263 a quas — probavit: on Stilicho's military commands under Theodosius, cf. Doise (1949) 185–91.

2.263 b Bellona: cf. n. 1.342 b.

2.264 Nos adeo viles?: cf. Luc. 5.682–84 (his friends chide Caesar for having left them to take a sea-voyage) quo te, dure, tulit virtus temeraria, Caesar, / aut quae nos viles animas in fata relinquens / ... dabas tua membra procellis?

2.264 f. Adeo felicior axis Hesperius: cf. IE 2.536 f. (Aurora chides Stilicho for having abandoned her, first to Rufinus, then to Eutropius) solam ... tueris / Hesperiam?

2.265 rectore: cf. Text. Comm. on 1 Pr.17 f. servans ... regit; n. 1 Pr.18 b.

2.266–68 Quid — nihil: on these "improbable declarations," as he calls them, cf. Bruère (1964) 234. He points out that they are a treatment in reverse of the *locus* in Luc. 9.230 f. patrios permitte penates / desertamque domum dulcesque revisere natos. Cf. also Sinon's speech in Verg. *A.* 2.137 f.

2.268 Te sine dulce nihil: cf. Verg. *A.* 12.882 f. (Juturna to Turnus) quicquam mihi dulce meorum / te sine, frater, erit?

2.270 iam: cf. Text. Comm. *ad loc.*

2.270 f. Hunis ... Alanis: cf. n. 1.308 c.

2.271 impacatis ... Alanis: cf. Luc. 8.223 duros aeterni Martis Alanos. Though Claudian could scarcely have known this, the Alans seem in fact to have been conquered by the Huns ca. A.D. 375: cf. McGovern (1939) 366.

2.272 quamquam non ... defecerit: for the subjunctive with *quamquam*, cf. 6H 13 f., Hofmann-Szantyr (1965) 602 f.

2.273: cf. Text. Comm. *ad loc.*; cf. also IE 2.121 (how destructive has been a time of peace) quantum nocuerunt otia ferri, where the connection between the last two words is scarcely more strained than that between *penuria* and *ferri* in the present passage. With the idea of *penuria ferri*, contrast 2.183 lucis prodigus. Cf. also Luc. 1.147 parcere ferro, 7.225 largus habenae; Stat. *Theb.* 7.533 ferri ... ardor, 6.914 ingens copia leti. These passages, paralleling or nearly paralleling various aspects of our present passage, have made me somewhat less dubious about the reading. Cameron (1968a) 397 f., *per contra*, defends the emendation of Paul (1866) 12, who proposed to read *tantave gestati fuerint periuria ferri*. Cameron translates *periuria* "forswearing," and takes it to refer to the soldiers' military oath. But the *sacramentum* in the late Empire was taken *in verba Augusti*, in other words, to an Emperor, never to a military leader who bore the title neither of Augustus nor of Caesar: D.S. s.v. *sacramentum* 952. Given Claudian's firm and constant representation of Stilicho's loyalty to the house of Theodosius (cf. n. 2.202), it is hard to see how the poet could have conceived of any defection from Stilicho as *periuria*, though *infidelitas* it would certainly have been. Cf. also E. H. A. (1937) 243.

2.274 a licet ... maneas: the "libre à toi de demeurer" of Crépin (1933) does not clearly convey the concessive force of the expression.

2.274 b cardine solis: cf. Text. Comm. *ad loc.*; Faider (1937) 680.

2.275-77 absens ... longe: these words emphasize the function of the Eastern army as a long-range weapon in Stilicho's hands, and are to be contrasted with Rufinus' confidence in his own safety because of the distance which would separate him from Stilicho once the latter was back in the West: cf. 2.305-7. Ker (1957) 157 is therefore right in translating *longe* "at a distance," and Platnauer (1922) wrong in rendering it "of old," Crépin (1933) "anciennement" (he prints *longum*).

2.276 a fĭdem ... prīdem: Gesner (1759) *ad loc.* calls attention to the (of course unintentional) leonine rhyme, disregarding in the mediaeval fashion the vowel-quantities in the penultimate syllables.

2.276 f. Dabitur — sacris: on the use of imagery here, cf. Christiansen (1969) 89.

2.276 b debita: on *debitus* of what is foreordained, cf. n. 1.369 *c*.

2.277 f.: on the unusual absence here of a phrase marking the transition from direct quotation to narrative, cf. n. 1.65 *b*.

2.278–92: *The Eastern army's plan is kept secret as they march toward Constantinople.*

2.278 Haemoniis ... oris: on the location of the episode in Thessaly, cf. n. 2.125 f.

2.279 Macetum: the form Μακέτης for Μακεδών is not attested in any Greek author, according to LSJ s.v. Cf. Gel. 9.3 *Macetae*; the femine Μακέτις is found in Str. 10.4.10. For the use of the word in Roman poets, cf. Sil. 14.5; Luc. 10.28 Macetum fines (as in our passage), 5.2.

2.279 f. muros ..., Thessalonica, tuos: on the use of the vocative, cf. n. 1.255, para. 2.

2.280 Thessalonica: Koenig (1808) *ad loc.* remarks that Claudian makes no mention of the blood-bath which occurred in Thessalonica in 390, and in the sequel to which, at least, Rufinus was involved. Koenig attributes Claudian's silence to his desire not to mention an episode disgraceful to Theodosius. At any rate, the incident deeply involved Theodosius' relations with the Church, a topic which Claudian studiously avoids: cf. Int. 22; n. 2.366. For a possible covert reference to the Thessalonica blood-bath, cf. n. 1.181 f.

2.281–83 Tacitas — tempora: on foreshadowing in IR, cf. n. 1.368–87. Claudian chooses the idea of *tacitas* for amplification in 2.283–90. In fact, the success of the anti-Rufinian faction in keeping the plotted assassination a secret was complete: cf. Int. 25 f. It must be noted, however, that Rufinus' intelligence services were highly inept: cf. the Eudoxia episode, Int. 21 f. Of course, despite *vulgi* (2.286) and *populo* (2.290), we have no way of determining how long before the date of the assassination any but Gainas (cf. Int. 24) and his immediate entourage actually became privy to the plot.

2.282 odiis: on the hatred which Rufinus—all Stilichonian propaganda aside—seems actually to have inspired, cf. Int. 25 f.; Stein-Palanque (1959) 230.

2.285: on the use of an appeal to the expected wonderment of posterity as a device to emphasize the near-incredibility of a statement, cf. Schroff (1927) on BP 423. Claudian foreshadows the paradox of 2.290 fuit arcanum populo: cf. n. 2.290 *a*.

2.287 *a* **facinus:** apparently used here only by Claudian of an act which he deems laudable: cf. Birt (1892) 506 s.v. Cf. Serv. on Verg.

A. 1.51 "bonum facinus" et "malum facinus" dicimus; Gel. 12.9.1 vocabula quae nunc in sermonibus vulgi unam certamque rem demonstrent ita fuisse media et communia ... ut "tempestas," "valetudo," "facinus."

2.287 *b* **calorem:** on the use of this word here, cf. n. 1.187 *b*.

2.288 rumpi: on *rumpo* of "the release of feelings long pent up," cf. Pease (1935) on Verg. *A.* 4.553.

2.290 *a* **populo:** cf. Text. Comm. *ad loc.* Like Jeep, Platnauer (1922) fails, by his translation "the people's secret was kept," to do justice to the epigrammatic nature of *fuit arcanum populo* (cf. n. 2.285). Some such translation as "There existed such a thing as a secret kept by an entire host!" (cf. n. 2.224) might be appropriate.

2.290 *b* **Hebrus:** by an oversight, Platnauer (1922) prints *Haemus*, translates "Hebrus"; cf. Text. Comm. *ad loc.* Cameron (1968a) 404, discussing the army's route (2.290-92), objects to *Hebrus* (preferring *Haemus*) on the basis of a strict interpretation of the verb *percurro*; he rejects my parallel, RP 2.68 f. In the case of a poet who could write CS 2.199 f. opacum vitibus Histrum ... conserit (cf. n. 2.180 *b*) and 2.244 calcare Notum (cf. n. 2.244), such strictness of interpretation might be misplaced. Probably the matter of the army's route must be left *sub iudice*.

2.291 deseritur: this looks like a slightly distorted reminiscence of Luc. 3.199 deseritur Strymon, 225 f. deseritur Taurique nemus Perseaque Tarsus / Coryciumque ... antrum, where the point is that the places named were stripped of their youth, who rushed to join Pompey. A mention of Thrace immediately precedes the first *deseritur* in Lucan's long enumeration.

2.292 Herculei ... nominis urbem: on Heracle-Perinthus, cf. RE s.v. *Perinthos* (1); Hoepfner (1966). The city, now Ereğli (Marmaraereğlisi), is on the Thracian coast of the Propontis, some fifty miles from Constantinople.

2.293–323: *Rufinus rejoices with his friends at Stilicho's withdrawal. He prepares to ascend the throne as Arcadius' colleague.*

2.293–383: on the relation of these verses to the ψόγος-pattern, cf. Levy (1946) 63, 65.

2.293 f. cessisse ducem ... venisse cohortes cognita: I have been unable to find a parallel for the neuter plural *cognita* agreeing collectively with two items in *oratio obliqua*; for the usual construction with *cognitum* (*est*), cf. the lemmata in TLL s.v. *cognosco* 1518.2–19. Cf. however Verg. A. 1.667–69.

2.294 magna cervice: on this expression, cf. n. 1.53.

2.295 a omnia tuta ratus: a reversed reminiscence (cf. Bruère [1964] 234 on 2.266–68) of Verg. A. 4.298 *omnia tuta timens*. On a later contradiction of this idea, cf. n. 2.326.

2.295 b sceptrum . . . capessere: for the charge that Rufinus aspired to the throne, cf. the following passages (some of them, of course, traceable to identical sources): Zos. 5.1.4 τὴν βασιλείαν ἑαυτῷ μνᾶσθαι ʽΡουφῖνος ὠνειροπόλει; Socr. 6.1.6 ὑπωπτεύετο γὰρ εἰς τυραννίδα ὁ ʽΡουφῖνος; Sozom. 8.1.2 ʽΡουφῖνος . . . ὕποπτος ὢν . . . ὡς τυραννεῖν βούλεται, 4 ʽΡουφῖνον ἐπίβουλον ὄντα τῆς αὐτῶν [= ʼΑρκαδίου καὶ ʽΟνωρίου] ἀρχῆς; Lyd. Mag. 2.10 ʽΡουφῖνον . . . τυραννίδα μελετήσαντα, 3.7, 23; Philostorg. 11.3 ὁ . . . ʽΡουφῖνος . . . τὸ τῆς βασιλείας ὄνομα εἰς ἑαυτὸν μεθέλκειν ἐτέχναζεν. . . . ὁ . . . ʽΡουφίνου τῆς βασιλείας ἔρως; Int. 19 f., 25.

2.296 hortatur . . . clientes: the unwarlike Rufinus (cf. n. 2.53) addresses his civilian followers in what looks like a parody of a general's *contio* before his troops on the eve of battle: cf. Miniconi (1951) 170; 119 f.; 129–32. Miniconi, however, does not call attention to the mock-military nature of this harangue. Cf. particularly 2.297 *Vicimus*, 2.309 *has . . . manus*, 2.310 *spoliavimus*; n. 2.313.

2.297–316: on direct quotations in IR, cf. n. 1.45–65.

2.297 Vicimus: on the warlike tone, cf. n. 2.296.

2.298 a poscere: for this verb in the sense "challenge," cf. Verg. A. 8.614 *in proelia poscere Turnum*; Sil. 1.420 *ductorem avido clamore in proelia poscit*. However, nowhere else either in Claudian or in any other author have I found *posco* in this sense without *in proelia* or the like.

2.298 b solum: Claudian represents Rufinus as completely disregarding Arcadius.

2.299 tanto munitum milite: cf. n. 2.152–63.

2.299 f. vincat . . . ferat: on the subjunctive in rhetorical questions equivalent to declarative sentences (*quis vincat* = *nemo vincit, vincet*), cf. Kuhner-Stegmann-Thierfelder (1962) 1.178.

2.301 *a* I nunc: on the ironic rhetorical figure of *permissio*, cf. Pease (1935) on Verg. *A*. 4.381 I, sequere Italiam.

2.301 *b* remotus: cf. 2.403 absens; n. 2.152–63.

2.303 *a* mediis ... undis: for *medius* describing an object which separates two others dissimilar to itself, cf. Ov. *Tr*. 2.192 Danuvii mediis vix prohibentur aquis, 3.10.7 medio defendimur Histro; TLL s.v. 583.34–62.

2.303 *b* interstrepat: cf. Text. Comm. *ad loc*.

2.304 Alpinas ... rupes: for the (Julian) Alps as the boundary between East and West, cf. IE 1.431–33 Peregrina piacula forti / pellantur longe Latio, nec transeat Alpes / dedecus. Thus the effective beginning of Stilicho's expedition to the East in 395 (cf. Int. 24) is marked by the words *Vix Alpes transgressus erat* (cf. Text. Comm. on 2.124). Cf. also IE 2.504 f. (the possibility of Stilicho's marching East again) quem si procedere tantum / Alpibus audissent.

2.305 illinc: = *ab Italia*, 2.307.

2.306 *a* ensem: for the sword whereby Stilicho had Rufinus cut down, cf. 2.400.

2.306 *b* ad moenia tendi: cf. Verg. *A*. 1.410 gressum ... ad moenia tendit; Stat. *Theb*. 12.255 dextram ... ad moenia tendens.

2.308 Quisnam: cf. Text. Comm. *ad loc*. The comment of Koenig (1808), which has since become accessible to me, adds nothing of value.

2.309 has ... manus: on the warlike tone, cf. n. 2.296.

2.309 f. orbe ... medio: these words repeat the ideas expressed above by 2.302 f. dum nos longissima tellus / dividat et mediis Nereus interstrepat undis; cf. n. 2.303 *a*. Cf. also n. 2.161, n. 2.152–63. Platnauer (1922) correctly translates "from the centre of the ... world," Crépin (1933) erroneously "d'une moitié du monde."

2.310 *a* tantis ... armis: Platnauer (1922) wrongly, "of thy great army," which would imply that Stilicho had yielded up all, not merely the Eastern troops (cf. Int. 24 f.); rather "such a mighty army."

2.310 *b* spoliavimus: on the warlike tone, cf. n. 2.296.

2.311 Nunc epulis tempus: the modern Latinist will think of Hor. *Carm*. 1.37 Nunc est bibendum, and Alc. frag. 20; one may query whether it is likely that Claudian had either or both of these passages in mind.

2.311 f. epulis ... aurum: foreshadowing 2.341 f.

2.312 *a* novis: Birt (1892) was troubled by this reading, found in all the codices (cf. his *appar. crit.*, and Pr. 105), presumably because the veteran Eastern troops could not appropriately be called "new"; he suggests, but does not print, *bonis*. Koch (1893) Pr. 22, who had proposed *meis*, later withdrew the suggestion. However, Koch's citation of 4H 35, in which *novis = usque adhuc non visis*, is completely beside the point; Rufinus must have had ample occasion to view some of these very troops when he was in Theodosius' entourage in the East in 391–94 (cf. Int. 10, 18). *Novis* may simply mean "which have just arrived" (which Koch may perhaps mean by his *pro 'advenis'*); cf. FH 2.39 *novo* (of the sun which has just appeared on the horizon). However, the word may refer to the new allegiance which the soldiers would assume *iurantes in verba Rufini*: cf. DS s.v. *sacramentum* 952; Hermann (1968); also 2.341 f. quod post vota daretur / ... aurum.

2.312 *b* aurum: on donatives to the troops at an emperor's accession, cf. Mattingly (1967) 152–55, 183–85. Cf. also Kent in Carson-Sutherland (1956) 193–202, who takes 2.341 f., quod post vota daretur / ... aurum, as evidence of a "mint in the eastern parts" (202). This is surely too uncritical an acceptance of an otherwise unsupported detail which may well be a propagandistic invention on Claudian's part. It is otherwise with Claudian's main contention, that Rufinus expected to be named Emperor: cf. n. 2.295 *b*, and Int. 25, ftn. 159.

2.313 lux crastina: cf. Verg. A. 10.244 f. (Cymodocea prophesies to Aeneas his victory over the Rutulians) Crastina lux ... / ingentis Rutulae spectabit caedis acervos. The reminiscence may be intended as a slight reinforcement of the mock-military tone (cf. n. 2.296).

2.314 *a* nolit: on the subjunctive by attraction here, cf. Birt (1892) Pr. 224.

2.314 *b* coactus: Rufinus' verbal threats (cf. n. 2.143 *b*) are now, in his opinion, given absolute cogency by the presence of the troops which he expects to control.

2.315 *a* in partem mihi regna dari: cf. 2.383 participem sceptri, socium declaret honoris; Zos. 5.3.3 ʿΡουφίνου οἰουμένου ... κοινωνήσειν ... αὐτῷ ... τῆς τῶν ὅλων ἀρχῆς. On the limited aim (i.e. collegiality with, not displacement of, Arcadius) with which Claudian charges Rufinus here, cf. Int. 20.

2.315 b in partem: adverbial: cf. Verg. *A.* 7.709 in partem data Roma Sabinis. Neither the "portion" of Platnauer (1922) nor "ma part" (Crépin [1933]) is quite right; "to share with him" would express the idea better: cf. 2.383 participem sceptri. Perhaps Claudian would have us believe that what Rufinus was aiming at was something like the relationship which the Augustus Theodosius had with his sons after he had named them Augusti.

2.316 privati ... modum: TLL s.v. *modus* 1263.50–53 (*i.q. vitae condicio modestior*) cites the following parallels to our present passage: V. Max. 6.9.7 altiora modo suo sperare ausos; Curt. 6.1.17 maiores res erant, quam quas praefecti modus caperet; Tac. *Ann.* 13.2.4. For Claudian to represent Rufinus as regarding *modus* as something to be avoided, rather than, *more Romano*, to be sought after, is in line with his usual depiction of Rufinus' avarice: cf. Int. 15, ftn. 82, to which add IR 1.296, 305.

2.317 a Talibus: on *talibus* and similar words summarizing a direct quotation, cf. Pease (1935) on Verg. *A.* 4.219; cf. also n. 1.65 b.

2.317 b acclamat: for the *acclamatio* following an imperial *contio*, cf. Ael. Lamprid. *Diad. Antonin.* (= SHA 16) 1.4–8. W. Bannier in TLL s.v. *acclamo* 326.44 f. has misunderstood our passage completely, unless *Rufinus* is a misprint for *Rufini*.

2.317–21: for an account of Rufinus' supporters, cf. the *Suda* s.v. Ῥουφῖνος (= 4.301.9–13 Adler = Eunap. frag. 63 = FHG 4.42) καὶ ὁ τῶν κολάκων περὶ αὐτὸν ὄχλος ἦν πολύς. οἱ δὲ κόλακες χθὲς μὲν καὶ πρώην δεδρακότες τοῦ καπηλείου καὶ τοῦ τὰ βάθρα καλλύνειν καὶ τοὔδαφος κορεῖν, ἄρτι δὲ χλαμύδας τάς τε εὐπαρύφους ἐνδεδυκότες καὶ περόναις χρυσαῖς διαπεπερονημένοι καὶ σφραγῖσι χρυσοδέτοις διεσφιγμένοι.

2.320 funesta tacere: cf. Text. Comm. *ad loc.*; Fargues (1936) 371 f.

2.321 f. conubia ... aliena: i.e. marriages with the women of the dignitaries whom they will displace. So, in CM 53.38–40, the earth-born monsters plan for victory over the supernal gods, and for goddesses as wives, the spoils of victory: hic sternere Martem cogitat, hic Phoebi laceros divellere crines; / hic sibi promittit Venerem speratque Dianae / coniugium. Neither Platnauer (1922) with "foreign wives" nor Crépin (1933) with "les joies de l'adultère" hits the mark.

2.322 frustra: for the foreshadowing, cf. 2.334 f., and n. 1.368–87.
2.323 quas ... quas: cf. Text. Comm. *ad loc.*

2.324–35: *In sleep, Rufinus beholds a vision which seems to promise him success.* On the similarity between this dream sequence and Pompey's dream in Lucan 7, cf. Bruère (1964) 235; Morford (1967) 75–84. Cf. also Verg. *A.* 2.268–97, Fürbringer (1912), Grillone (1967) 151–60, esp. 156 f. For Claudian's own treatment of the dream as a reflection of the dreamer's workaday concerns, cf. 6H Pr., and Müller (1938) on 6H Pr.1 f. On the use of imagery here, cf. Christiansen (1969) 114.

2.325 nox: on night-scenes, cf. Pease (1935) on Verg. *A.* 4.522.

2.326: this representation of Rufinus' mental agitation, and its repetition at 2.330 f. Quid plurima volvis / anxius, are at sharp variance with 2.295 omnia tuta ratus, and with the euphoric speech and scene which follow; we are brought back to the situation as Rufinus saw it before Stilicho's withdrawal (2.130–70). Perhaps Claudian is influenced here by the account of Dido's anxieties which Vergil contrasts with his peaceful night-scene (*A.* 4.522–32).

2.327 *a* labitur in somnos: cf. the same expression in Stat. *Theb.* 5.504.

2.327 *b* Toto vix: Helm (1936) 1223 agrees with the choice of reading in preference to Jeep's *vix toto*, and refers to a law formulated by Marx (1922) 198, "Folgt auf die Semiquinaria ein Monosyllabon oder pyrrhichisches Wort verbunden mit einem spondeischen Wort ... so steht das spondeische Wort an erster Stelle." Cf. also Pipping (1944); Axelson (1944) 54; Duckworth (1967) 143–50.

2.328 alludere protinus: neither Platnauer (1922), "flit before his eyes," nor Crépin (1933) "il croit voir aller et venir," does justice to the idea of sportiveness (here *in malam partem*, mockery; cf. n. 2.239 *b*) contained in *alludo*. The word is rarely used of physical movement: cf. TLL s.v. 1697.73, with the gloss *ludendo, iocando appetere*, and the citations which follow. For a similar meaning, but *in bonam partem*, cf. Ov. *Met.* 2.864 (Jupiter in the guise of a bull frolics near Europa) nunc adludit, viridique exsultat in herba; Stat. *Silv.* 2.6.101 f.

2.328 f. umbras quas dedit ipse neci: these (*animae quas ille fero sub iure peremit*) reappear at 2.458–65, as Rufinus enters the Lower

World, and, like a swarm of angry bees, impel him toward the tribunal. For other references to Rufinus as a murderer, cf. 1.231, 246–50; 2.61–70, 423, 429 f., 502 f.; n. 1.243–49.

2.329 *a* dedit ... neci: cf. Verg. G. 3.480 (a destructive plague) *genus omne neci pecudum dedit*.

2.329 *b* clarior una: by contrast, this implies that the other shades were gibbering confusedly.

2.330–34: on irony and ambiguity in epic prophecies, cf. Duckworth (1933) 77–79; cf. also n. 1. 368–87. On possible parallels to this passage, cf. Whittle (1959) 57. Bruère (1964) 235 sees here an echo of the ambiguities in Lucan 5.224 f. and 1.637 f.

For a similar fallacious prophecy, cf. BP 546–55 (Alaric mistakes the name of the river Urbs for *Urbs Roma*: cf. Birt [1892] Pr. 51, and ftn. 3).

2.330–33 Pro — vulgi: on the use of direct quotation in IR, cf. n. 1.45–65, esp. sect. 8.

2.330 f. Quid — anxius: on Rufinus' anxiety, cf. n. 2.326.

2.332 f. plebe ... altior: *plebe* cannot be meant in the sense *quam plebs*, for Rufinus already held a position in the East second only to the Emperor (cf. Int. 11–15); *plebe redibis altior* is therefore simply a theme of which *manibus portabere vulgi* (2.333) is a variation.

For the custom of carrying a conquering hero aloft, cf. Ael. Lamprid. *Alex. Sev.* (= SHA 18) 57.5 *levabatur manibus hominum Alexander, vixque illi per horas quattuor ambulare permissum est*.

For the actuality foreshadowed by this ambiguous prophecy, cf. 2.335 *capitis ... fixi*, and 2.434 f.

2.334 Has canit ambages: on phrases used to indicate the resumption of the narrative after a direct quotation, cf. n. 1.65 *b*. For *canit ambages*, cf. Verg. A. 6.98 f. *Sibylla / horrendas canit ambages*.

2.335 capitis ... fixi: for the language, cf. Verg. A. 9.465 f. (the Rutulians display the heads of Nisus and Euryalus) *arrectis ... in hastis / praefigunt capita*; for the event, cf. 2.434 f.

2.336–47: *On the morrow, Rufinus makes preparations for his coronation.* The day is 27 November 395: cf. Int. 25.

2.336–38: Bruère (1964) 235 sees here a reversed reminiscence of the sun's reluctant rise on the day of Pharsalus, Luc. 7.1–3 *segnior ... /*

luctificus Titan... / ...cursum...retorsit (on which verses cf. Semple [1937i] 17). Cf. also Luc. 1.233 f. dies primos belli visura tumultus / exoritur.

2.336: the sunrise is seen from the viewpoint of one looking westward from Constantinople at the reflection of the rising sun on the mountain peaks. On descriptions of morning, cf. Pease (1935) on Verg. *A.* 4.6 and 4.118 f.

2.337 solito properantior: for comparatives with *solito*, cf. 4H 567 solito conspectior, 6H 537; Luc. 9.463.

2.337–39 urget... Titan: desiluit [Rufinus]: on abrupt changes of subject, cf. Text. Comm. on 2.124, para. 2.

2.339 f. densae... capacia turbae atria: on Rufinus' magnificent mansion, cf. Int. 15 f., Janin (1964) 151 f.

2.341 f. *a* dapes... aurum: cf. 2.311 f. epulis... / ...aurum.

2.341 f. *b* quod post vota daretur... aurum: cf. n. 2.312 *b*. *Vota* refers to the *sacramentum*: cf. n. 2.312 *a*.

2.342 aurum fatale: cf. Stat. *Theb.* 4.212 f. (a golden necklace used as a disastrous bribe) aurum fatale penates / inrupit.

2.343 turmas: on the use of this word, cf. n. 1.350 *b*.

2.344–47: Christiansen (1969) 132 f. (cf. 89) contrasts this regal image of Rufinus with that of a trapped beast given in 2.394–99.

2.344 *a* regale tumens: on the adverbial use of the neuter adjective, cf. n. 1.65 f. For *tumeo* of regal pride, cf. 1.165 f. (Midas rejoices in the golden touch) Sic rex ad prima tumebat / Maeonius.

2.344 *b* principe celsior: Platnauer (1922) makes *principe* general, and translates metaphorically: "in... arrogance above a prince's." It seems better to take the expression both specifically and literally, "taller than the Prince," i.e. Arcadius. Cf. Philostorgius 11.3, quoted in ftn. 113 to Int. 18. Crépin (1933) correctly translates "plus élevé que l'empereur."

2.345 *a* colla... mollia: on the resultative-predicate use of the adjective, cf. n. 1.1 *b*.

2.345 *b* solvebat: cf. Text. Comm. *ad loc.*, where I neglected to call attention to another objection to the reading *gestabat*: it would give us the collocation *gestabat... gestu*.

2.346 *a* imperii certus: for the genitive with *certus*, cf. MT 114 (Manlius had found his *métier*) telluris iam certus eras; Verg. *A.* 4.554

(Aeneas sleeps before his departure for Italy) *iam certus eundi*; Luc. 8.119 f.; Sil. 6.27; Hofmann-Szantyr (1965) 78.

2.346 *b* purpura: for the purple as a symbol of imperial majesty, cf. 6H 614 *veneratur purpura vulgus*; Avery (1940).

2.347 gemmae: for this word referring to a jewel-ornamented headband, cf. 6H 527 (a bride is bedecked by her mother) *substringit ... comam gemmis*; Ov. *Am.* 3.13.25 *virginei crines auro gemmaque premuntur*. Here apparently uniquely in verse of the imperial diadem; cf. Amm. 21.1.4 (Julian at his *quinquennalia*) *ambitioso diademate utebatur, lapidum fulgore distincto*. On the diadem, cf. Alföldi (1935) 145–50.

2.348–370: *The army is drawn up in splendid array at the Hebdomon. Rufinus and Arcadius review the troops.*

2.348–50: on the Hebdomon, the plain at the seventh milestone from Constantinople on the Via Egnatia, cf. Text. Comm. on 2.350; Int. 25; Demangel (1945) 6 f.; Janin (1964) 446–49, and Map 9. Claudian's *trames* (the "causeway" of Text. Comm. on 2.350) would seem best identified with the stretch of road (between the two present-day bridges over *Tchaouch bachi déré* and *Tchirpédji déré*) which passes the promontory called by Demangel (cf. his fig. 1) *Cap de la Magnaure Jetée*.

2.348 *a* ab: for *a, ab* in the sense "on the side of," "adjacent to," cf. TLL s.v. 21.5–22.40.

2.348 *b* angusto tractu: the "narrow stretch" of Constantinople is apparently the extreme southwest part of the city, where the Wall of Constantine met the Propontis: cf. Janin (1964), Map 1, grid 8CD. The shore road from this region leads westward toward the Hebdomon, a distance of some five kilometers. The rendition of Platnauer (1922), "crowded quarter," does not receive support from any entry in TLL s.v. *angustus*. That of Crépin (1933), "Dans le voisinage de la ville, un peu vers le midi," ignores or misinterprets *ab angusto tractu*.

2.348 *c* qua vergit in Austrum: on Claudian's fondness for this formula, cf. n. 1.364 f., *fin*.

2.351 ornatu lucida Martis: i.e. in parade armor: cf. Drexel (1924).

2.352 cuneos: for this word used of military formations of various

IN RUFINUM 195

types, cf. TLL s.v. 1404.37-1405.80, esp. 1404.37-41; Kromayer-Veith (1928) 598. The disposition of the troops is referred to resumptively in 2.363.

2.353 illinc: cf. *hinc*, 2.355; different sectors of the *pars dextra* (cf. 2.352 *sinistra*).

2.355-62: cf. 6H 569-78 (a girl views a parade of armored cavalry, *cataphracti* or *cataphractarii*) ut chalybe indutos equites et in aere latentes / vidit cornipedes, "Quanam de gente," rogabat, / "ferrati venere viri? Quae terra metallo / nascentes informat equos? Num Lemnius auctor / indidit hinnitum ferro simulacraque belli / viva dedit?" Gaudet metuens et pollice monstrat / quod picturatas galeae Iunonia cristas / ornet avis vel quod rigidos vibrata per armos / rubra sub aurato crispentur serica dorso (and Müller [1938] 113 f.); Amm. 16.10.8 (Constantius conducts a dress-parade including *cataphractarii*) et incedebat hinc ordo geminus armatorum, clipeatus atque cristatus, corusco lumine radians, nitidis loricis indutus, sparsique cataphracti equites, quos clibanarios dictitant, personati, thoracum muniti tegminibus, et limbis ferreis cincti, ut Praxitelis manu polita crederes simulacra, non viros; quos lamminarum circuli tenues apti corporis flexibus ambiebant, per omnia membra diducti, ut quocumque artus necessitas commovisset, vestitus congrueret, iunctura cohaerenter aptata. Müller rightly takes the passage just quoted from Ammianus as the model for the verses from 6H quoted above; for other evidence of Claudian's imitation of Ammianus, cf. Maenchen-Helfen (1945) 234, (1955) 393-95. On the *cataphractarii* cf. Rattenbury (1942), Eadie (1967); Stein-Palanque (1959) 137, 488, ftn. 35 *supra*.

2.355 *a* saevum ... vertice nutant: on the adverbial use of the neuter adjective, cf. n. 1.65 f. Cf. Hom. *Il.* 3.337 δεινὸν δὲ λόφος καθύπερθεν ἔνευεν, which Birt (1892) Pr. 72, ftn. 3, regards as the direct ancestor of our present passage. Verbally, though not as regards context, Claudian may have been thinking of Verg. *A.* 2.629 (a mighty ash is felled) comam concusso vertice nutat.

2.355 *b* cristato vertice: the *cristae* were probably peacock plumes: cf. 6H 575 f. (in a dress-parade) Iunonia cristas / ornat avis; Drexel (1924) 56 f.

2.356 f. tremulos umeris gaudent vibrare colores, quos operit formatque chalybs: in taking *colores* as the antecedent of *quos*, I reject the interpretations both of Birt (1892) 47 *ad loc.*, who writes: "Quos] mihi ex alii [355] pendere visum est," and of Buecheler, whom Birt cites as making it depend on *umeris*. (1) For *quos* to leap-frog the immediately adjacent *colores* and go back three words to *umeris* or eleven to *alii* would be strained (despite my remarks in Text. Comm. on 1 Pr.17–18); (2) to say that the metal "forms" the bodies or the shoulders of the cavalrymen would be quite contrary to the words which follow, which emphasize (as in the passages from 6H and from Ammianus quoted in n. 2.355–62) the flexibility of the armor in following the movements of the men; besides, it would imply that the men are flabby and need some sort of stay. My interpretation is not without its own difficulties, since it makes Claudian say that the metal both "covers" and "forms" the shimmering colors. As I take the words, the colors are below and constricted by the metal; they are not colors which are painted or enameled on it (as "the flashing colours of their shoulder armour," Platnauer [1922], suggests). I owe my interpretation to Gesner (1759) *ad loc.*; he holds that the *colores* are those of the silken garment worn just below the armor: cf. 6H 576 f. rigidos vibrata per armos / rubra sub aurato crispentur serica dorso, which Müller (1938) *ad loc.* translates "über den festen Bug herabwallend, die rote Seidendecke unter dem vergoldeten Rücken kräuselt," Platnauer (1922) "beneath the golden armour ... the red silk waves and ripples over the strong shoulders." Thus the light silk, covered and constricted by the metal above it, none the less emerges through the interstices between the plates of armor, and flaps in the breeze. That Claudian conceived of the present scene as beginning in the midst of a stiff breeze is shown by 2.364 f. spiris ... remissis / mansuescunt varii vento cessante dracones.

2.359 Horribles: cf. Text. Comm. *ad loc.*

2.360 cognato ... metallo: cf. Claudian's description of a lobster, where *cognatus* is of course literally appropriate: CM 24.2 cognatus dorso durescit amictus; n. 1.330.

2.362 securi vulneris: Bruère (1964) 235 cites Luc. 1.212 (a lion wriggles free from a spear) per ferrum tanti securus volneris exit.

2.363 f. Metuenda voluptas ... pulcherque timor: for the oxymora, cf. 6H 574 Gaudet metuens, RP 2.155 perterrita gaudet; cf. also Stat. *Theb.* 6.72 miseranda voluptas.

IN RUFINUM 197

2.365 dracones: on the dragon-banners, cf. n. 2.177 f.

2.366: as is to be expected (cf. Int. 22) Claudian makes no specific reference to the Christian *labarum* (on which cf. Egger [1960] 20), though it must have been the subject of Arcadius' *veneratio*.

2.367 f. quo — affatu: cf. Text. Comm. *ad loc.*

2.368 a affatu: on Rufinus' skill in speech, cf. Philostorg. 11.3 τῶν λόγων ἡ ἑτοιμότης. Perhaps the placing of a stone in his mouth after he was slain (ibid. τῷ στόματι λίθον ἐνέθησαν) was in mockery of his eloquence.

2.368 b devota: on *devotus* as an official military term of approval, cf. TLL s.v. *devoveo* 884.18–20; cf. also Luc. 3.311, 4.533.

2.369 a nomine quemque vocat: here presented as the reverse of what Claudian represents, in his praise of Stilicho, as a most laudable trait; but note that the personal address is joined by Stilicho with laudatory reminders of military service: CS 2.153–55 nomine quemque / compellas clari, sub te quod gesserat olim, / admonitum facti; Rufinus can report only on the home front, 2.269 f. natos—incolumes. For the language, cf. Verg. A. 11.731 (Tarchon encourages his troops) nomine quemque vocans (= 12.759).

2.369 b natos patresque: cf. Text. Comm. *ad loc.*; on the thought, cf. n. 2.369 a.

2.370–83: *Rufinus is quietly surrounded. Not observing this, he urges Arcadius to declare him his colleague.*

2.371 intendere: cf. Text. Comm. *ad loc.*

2.372 suprema: the *cornua* of 2.375; for *supremus* in the sense of "furthermost," cf. BP 640 f. Oceani stagnis excita supremis / Cimbrica tempestas, 554.

2.373 circuitu: for the encircling pincers movement, cf. Zos. 5.7.5 ἀπολαβόντες ἐν μέσῳ. Cf. also Int, 25. ftn. 163.

2.373 f. decrescere campus incipit: cf. Stat. Theb. 8.397 (two hostile forces close the gap between them) medium ... vident decrescere campum.

2.375 sinuantur: for *sinuo* of a skilfully executed evasive movement, cf. 4H 540 (Honorius is skilled in equestrian manoeuvres) mollis sinuare fugas.

2.376–79 sic ligat — oras: Bruère (1964) 235 f. calls attention to echoes here of three passages in Lucan: 6.41 f. (Caesar's salt works near Dyrrhachium) saltus... / et silvas vastaque feras indagine claudit, 9.441–47, and 1.605–7 (a propitiatory procession) dum... illi effusam longis anfractibus urbem / circumeunt, Arruns dispersos fulminis ignes / colligit.

Cf. also (hunting scenes) Verg. *A.* 4.121 saltus... indagine cingunt; Sil. 10.80 lustrat inaccessos venantum indagine saltus. On the use of imagery here, cf. Christiansen (1969) 59; on comparisons drawn from the chase as an epic theme, cf. Miniconi (1951) 203 *bis*. Parravicini (1905) 9 notes that, except for IE 1.113–18 (Eutropius is like dry, barren corn, or a moulting, moribund sparrow), Claudian always draws both elements of a double simile from the same type of imagery: myths, animals, plants, or (as here) human activities.

2.378 f. raros ... plagarum ... anfractus: on *rarus* in the sense "wide-meshed," cf. Pease (1935) on Verg. *A.* 4.131. For *anfractus* in the sense "coil," "spiral," (cf. OLD s.v.), cf. V. Fl. 7.523 immensis recubantem anfractibus anguem, and the final quotation from Lucan in n. 2.376–79. On comparisons drawn from fishing as an epic theme, cf. Miniconi (1951) 204, s.v. *Pêcheur*; the passage should not also be listed s.v. *Pilote*.

2.379 oras: for this word in the sense "outer edge," cf. Verg. *A.* 10.243 (Aeneas' shield) ignipotens ... oras ambit auro.

2.380 alios: Platnauer (1922) correctly, "all others," i.e. those not in the plot; Crépin (1933) wrongly, "Le cortège impérial." We see from the next verse (*adprensa veste*) that Arcadius is still next to Rufinus; the Emperor cannot have been thought of as being without some additional escort.

2.381 f. graviter ... morantem increpat Augustum: on Rufinus' treatment of Arcadius, cf. n. 2.164–68.

2.382 f. scandat — honoris: on the use of *oratio obliqua*, cf. n. 1.45–65, sect. 5. On the ceremony accompanying the creation of a new Augustus, cf. Straub (1938). He distinguishes three steps: (1) the *commendatio*, in which the candidate is presented to the troops; (2) the *acclamatio*, in which they receive him with shouts of approval; and (3) the *nuncupatio*, or formula accompanying the new Emperor's actual investiture with purple and diadem. Cf. also Boak (1919) 45 f.

2.382 a scandat sublime tribunal: almost repeated in IE 1.311 scandit sublime tribunal.

2.382 b sublime tribunal: on the identification of an extant ruin with this edifice, cf. Demangel (1945) 7–16; Demangel (1955); Janin (1964), Map. 9. Cf. also Philostorg. 11.3 τὸν Ῥουφῖνον ὁ... στρατὸς ... ἐν τῷ λεγομένῳ τριβουναλίῳ πρὸς αὐτοῖς τοῦ βασιλέως ποσὶ ταῖς μαχαίραις κατεκόψατο.

2.383 participem sceptri, socium... honoris: on the limited nature of Claudian's charge here, cf. n. 2.315 a.

2.384–427: *A mighty voice denounces Rufinus. The soldiers draw their swords, and hack him to pieces.*

2.384 a cum: for *cum inversum*, cf. MT 116 f. (Manlius had already committed himself to a life of studious ease) cum subito liquida cessantem vidit ab aethra / Iustitia et tanto viduatas iudice leges; Sil. 10.102; Hofmann-Szantyr (1965) 623, sect. (d).

2.384 b vox... ingens: presumably that of the Goth Gainas, whom Zos. 5.7.4–6 mentions as having given the signal for Rufinus' slaughter (cf. Int. 25). Thus the translation of Crépin (1933), "un tonnerre de cris," is presumably wrong, that of Platnauer (1922), "a mighty voice," right. On Claudian's failure to mention Gainas—or anyone else who might detract from Stilicho's glory—cf. Fargues (1933a) 43, 64, (1933b) 86 f. on IE 2 Pr.19.

2.384 c desuper: perhaps Gainas is to be thought of as mounted. However, the manoeuvre described in 2.370–80, said to have been accomplished by the same men as were engaged in conversation with Rufinus (Illi dum... sermone petunt, intendere... flexus... parant) seems to belong to infantry soldiers (2.352 f.); cf. 2.374 clipeis... iunctis. The same is true of the scene described in 2.391–93. Perhaps Gainas was a man of very tall stature, and was thought of as on foot.

2.385–90 Nobis — tyranno: on the use of direct quotation in IR, cf. n. 1.45–65, esp. sect. 8. If the attribution of this speech to Gainas is correct, the tentative classification of this passage in Lipscomb (1909) 45 as collective speech should be discarded.

2.385 Nobis... nobis: for the shift of ictūs, cf. Luc. 8.556 f. Quid viscera nostra / scrutaris gladio? Nescis, puer improbe, nescis; Ov. *Met.* 1.514.

2.386 famulas ... catenas: for the relatively few examples of the adjective *famulus* in the sense of *servilis*, cf. TLL s.v. 270.6–11; the list is meant to be exhaustive: cf. 269.36.

2.387–90: the two civil wars mentioned in these verses, both of which forced Theodosius to march his Eastern forces westward across the Julian Alps, were (1) that of Maximus in 388; cf. Stein-Palanque (1959) 207; and (2) that of Eugenius in 394; cf. Stein-Palanque (1959) 217. This pair of victories was one of Claudian's favorite themes: cf. 4H 69–73, PO 107 f., BG 376 f., BP 284, 6H 91.

2.387 audire satelles: for *audio* in the sense "hear oneself called," "have the name or title of," cf. PO 61 f. (Probinus and Olybrius have outdone their father Probus) Sed nati vicere patrem solique merentur / victores audire Probi. The construction is not found elsewhere in Latin epic (cf. however Hor. S. 2.7.101, Ep. 1.7.38), and its use by Claudian may betray his Greek origin: cf. LSJ s.v. ἀκούω 54, col. 1, sect. III.

2.388 libertatem: Claudian, deeply conscious of the old Republican tradition (cf. Moore [1910]), seems to have been somewhat sensitive about the use of this word in his contemporary context: cf. his defensive verses CS 3.113–15 Fallitur egregio quisquis sub principe credit / servitium. Numquam libertas gratior extat / quam sub rege pio. Contrast IR 2.390 servire tyranno.

2.389 civile nefas: the same expression occurs in Stat. *Silv*. 1.1.80.

2.390 f.: on the unusual absence here of a phrase marking the transition from direct quotation to narrative, cf. n. 1.65*b*.

2.391 *a* Deriguit: cf. Verg. *A*. 3.259 f. (the Harpy Celaeno terrifies the Trojans) sociis ... sanguis / deriguit; Stat. *Theb*. 9.36 (Polynices hears of Tydeus' death) Deriguit iuvenis.

2.391 *b* Spes nulla fugae: cf. IE 2.276 f. (the Goths attack Phrygia) spes nulla salutis, / nulla fugae; Verg. *A*. 10.121 (the Trojans are trapped) Nec spes ulla fugae (=9.131). That the passage from *A*. 10 was in Claudian's mind here is made likely by his use of *corona* in a neighboring verse: cf. n. 2.393 *b*.

2.391–93 Seges — coronae: Bruère (1964) 236 calls this passage a remodeling of Luc. 1.319–21 (Milo's court is ringed by armed men) Quis castra timenti / nescit mixta foro, gladii cum triste micantes / iudicium insolita trepidum cinxere corona. On Vergilian reminiscence here, cf. n. 2.391 *b*, n. 2.393 *b*; on the use of imagery, cf. Christiansen (1969) 59.

2.391 c Seges ... ferri: cf. 3H 135 (a dress-parade) nudi ... seges Mavortia ferri; Verg. *A.* 7.525 f., 12.663 f. (battle-scenes) atra ... late / horrescit strictis seges ensibus; strictis ... seges mucronibus horret / ferrea, 3.45 f.

2.393 a mucrone: cf. Text. Comm. *ad loc.*, where the reference to 1.164–69 should now be deleted; cf. n. 1.160–69; cf. also Brakman (1937) 121.

2.393 b coronae: cf. Gel. 6.4.4 circumstatio militum "corona" appellata; Verg. *A.* 10.121 f. (the Trojans are trapped) nec spes ulla fugae. Miseri stant turribus altis / nequiquam et rara muros cinxere corona, 12.744. Note 2.391 *b* calls attention to the juxtaposition of *spes ... fugae* and a form of the word *corona* in both 2.391–93 and in the Vergilian passage just quoted; note also that the reflection of Verg. *A.* 9.551 (ut fera, quae densa venantum saepta corona) in the image of the trapped beast which follows our passage (2.394–99) carries along the chain of Vergilian reminiscence: *spes fugae, corona, ut fera saepta corona.*

2.394–99: on this imagery, cf. n. 2.344–47. On Vergilian reminiscence here, cf. n. 2.393 *b.* Bruère (1964) 236 sees here a companion-piece to Luc. 1.327–29 (following closely on 1.319–21, quoted in n. 2.391–93), dealing with tigers which have never lost their fierceness; he also cites Luc. 4.708 f. harenae / muneribus (cf. n. 2.395 f.). Miniconi (1951) 201 lists this passage among those in which a comparison with lions is an epic theme, but the wild beast here is unidentified. He also lists the passage at page 203, under *Chasseur*, without making it clear that the *vir* is a huntsman only in the limited sense of the *venator* in a Roman spectacle.

2.395 f. harenae muneribus: on the so-called *venationes*, the beast-fights in the Circus, cf. RE and DS s.v. *Bestiarii*; LAW s.v. *Amphitheatralische Spiele.*

2.396 f. vir murmure contra hortatur: Platnauer (1922), in a rare slip, takes the deponent *hortatur* as passive: "the gladiator, heartened by the crowd's applause." What is meant by *murmure* instead is the gladiator's cry used to impel the beast to run onto his spear. Gesner (1759) *ad loc.* gives the cry used by eighteenth-century German boar-hunters; *Hui Sau!* Cf. TLL s.v. *hortor* 3009.16–18; Petr. 74.9 (a slave-boy "sicks" a dog onto his master) catellam hortatus ... est ut ad rixam properaret.

2.398 theatri: seems to be used in the sense of *amphitheatri*, as the translation of Platnauer (1922) takes it; cf. Aug. *Anc.* 22 venationes bestiarum ... aut in foro aut in amphitheatris populo dedi; LAW s.v. *Amphitheatralische Spiele*. I have not found a clear parallel; cf. Ov. *Met.* 11.25 f. (a deer falls prey to dogs in the arena) structo ... utrimque theatro / ... cervus periturus harena, where *utrimque* takes the place of *amphi-*.

2.400 audendi pronior: on this rare, if not otherwise unexampled use of the genitive with *pronus*, cf. Housman (1927) 20 on Luc. 1.460 f. inde ruendi / in ferrum mens prona viris. Housman joins *ruendi* with *mens*, not with *prona*. Regardless of the correctness of Housman's interpretation as to Lucan's intention, one may suppose that Claudian imitated what he thought was Lucan's phrase, *ruendi ... prona*. Cf. Text. Comm. on 2.303.

2.401 dictis ... et vulnere torvus: Platnauer (1922) renders "with fierce words and flashing eye"; he seems to be translating *lumine*, a variant of *vulnere*, though he prints the latter (cf. the *appar. crit.* of Birt [1892] *ad loc.*). The joining of words and deed, *dicta et vulnus*, is recapitulated in 2.404 sic fatur meritoque latus transverberat ictu. One might perhaps translate "fierce both in speech and in swordsmanship."

2.402 f. Hac — ferro: for the same viewpoint, cf. Philostorg. 11.3 τὸν ... Ῥουφῖνον ὁ ... στρατὸς ... κατακόψατο ... ἔχοντες ἐντολὰς παρὰ Στελίχωνος ἐξεργάσασθαι. Cf. also Verg. *A.* 12.948 f. On the use of direct discourse in IR, cf. n. 1.45–65, esp. sect. 8.

2.402 iactas pellere: cf. 2.297 (Rufinus gloats over Stilicho) Vicimus, expulimus.

2.403 a hoc absens invadit viscera ferro: cf. 2.306 f. Quaere ferox ensem, qui nostra ad moenia tendi / possit ab Italia; n. 1 Pr.15 c.

2.403 b invadit ... ferro: Bruère (1964) 236 calls attention to the similarity of these words to those in Luc. 2.315 (Cato offers himself as a victim) me solum invadite ferro; cf. also Stat. *Theb.* 2.487 f. (Eteocles prepares to attack Tydeus) invadere ferro / ... cupit.

2.404 a Sic fatur: on the use of formulae of transition from direct discourse to narrative in IR, cf. n. 1.65 b.

2.404 b transverberat ictu: cf. Verg. *A.* 10.484 (Turnus slays Pallas) [clipeum] cuspis medium transverberat ictu.

2.405 f.: for the formula, cf. 6H 101 f. (Theodosius rejoices at Honorius' succession) Felix ille parens, qui te securus Olympum / succedente petit! The use of the indicative *petit* (metrically = *petat*) where the present passage has the subjunctives *hauserit* and *libaverit* virtually proves that the latter verbs are in the subjunctive *metri gratia*, or in other words that Claudian did not feel a sufficiently clear distinction between the two moods in subordinate clauses to prevent such a variation; cf. n. 1 Pr.3 f. *b*.

2.406 a poenam: on Rufinus' murder as *poena*, cf. n. 1.20 *c*.

2.406 b libaverit: for a similar use of this verb, cf. Stat. *Theb.* 5.586 f. (the wind coming from Jove's thunderbolt stirs the crest of Capaneus' helmet as a first taste of punishment to come) aura ... / ... summas libavit vertice cristas (note the proximity of a dismemberment scene, 596–604, as in our next passage); 8.527 f.

2.406 c orbis: on this term for the Roman Empire, cf. n. 1. Pr.17 *b*.

2.407–39: on dismemberment as an epic theme, cf. Miniconi (1951) 126–29, 172 *bis*. On echoes of Lucan here, cf. Bruère (1964) 236 f.; to be added perhaps is the gruesome passage Luc. 6.540–67. Fargues (1933a) 228 sees resemblances to Christian martyrologies.

2.407 omnes: Philostorg. 11.3 also attributes the slaying to the entire army: ʽΡουφῖνον ὁ ... στρατὸς ... κατεκόψατο ... διότι μυκτηρίζων αὐτοὺς ἐπεφώρατο; so also Zos. 5.7.5 δόντος Γαΐνου τὸ σύνθημα πάντες ὁμοῦ τὸν ʽΡουφῖνον ... τοῖς ξίφεσι παίουσι.

2.408 tepescunt: cf. Verg. *A.* 10.569 f. sic toto Aeneas desaevit in aequore victor / ut semel intepuit mucro (cf. *mucrone* in our next verse); Stat. *Theb.* 1.611 (a monster tears apart two infants) ferrati ... ungues tenero sub corde tepescunt (note also the further resemblances between Stat. *Theb.* 1.611–23, the slaughter and dismemberment of the monster, and IR 2.407–53).

2.409: Bruère (1964) 236 compares Luc. 2.113 (victors in the Sullan revolution gather severed heads) dum vacua pudet ire manu.

2.410 avidos: on Rufinus' avarice, cf. Int. 15 f., ftns. 82, 83, 95.

2.410 f. spirantia ... lumina: for the admittedly strained use of the participle here as applied to *lumina*, Weyman (1926) 87 f. cites Quint. 1.8.11 aures ... respirant, and Stat. *Theb.* 4.466 f. semineces fibras et adhuc spirantia ... viscera. Cf. also Stat. *Theb.* 2.712 membris spirantibus, and Luc. 8.670 (Septimus seizes the head of Pompey, just slain) spirantia ... occupat ora, with the comment of Bruère (1964) 237; he also cites Luc. 2.183 f. spiramina naris aduncae / amputat (cf. *Amputat* in our next verse).

2.411 truncatos ... rapuere lacertos: on the resultative-predicate use of the participle here, cf. n. 1.1 *b*.

2.412 f. solutis nexibus: apparently a transfer to the field of physical violence of a reminiscence of Verg. *A.* 4.695 (Iris is sent to release Dido's soul) quae luctantem animam nexosque resolveret artus; cf. Pease (1935) *ad loc.*

2.414 f. hic — latebras: though the context is entirely different, Claudian seems to have in mind Arruns' inspection of the *exta* in Luc. 1.621–25: 621 cernit ... iecur, 622 f. pulmonis anheli / fibra latet, 625 produnt ... suas omenta latebras; cf. Bruère (1964) 237.

2.415 f. Spatium — odiis: cf. Stat. *Theb.* 1.623 (the crowd dismembers a monster; cf. n. 2.408) nequit iram explere potestas (cited by Schol. A on our passage); Amm. 14.9.6 (Eusebius is tortured) qui ita evisceratus ut cruciatibus membra deessent; Ov. *Met.* 3.237.

2.416 f. Consumpto — cadaver: Bruère (1964) 237 compares Luc. 2.119–21 (Baebius is dismembered during the Marian massacres) vix te sparsum per viscera, Baebi, / innumeras inter carpentis membra coronae / discessisse manus. On the treatment of corpses as an epic theme, cf. Miniconi (1951) 173; also 55, 57, 59, 61, 74, 114, 126–29.

2.416 *a* Consumpto funere: on *funus* = *cadaver*, cf. Birt (1892) 515 s.v. *funus* (3); TLL s.v. *funus* 1605.36–67.

2.416 *b* vix tum: cf. Text. Comm. *ad loc.*; Helm (1936) 1223.

2.417 sparsum ... perit per tela cadaver: cf. Juv. 3.260 (men are crushed under a load of stone blocks) obtritum ... perit omne cadaver.

2.418–20: in *Met.* 3.701–33, Ovid joins two myths, that of Pentheus dismembered by the Maenads for opposing the worship of Dionysus, and that of Actaeon changed to a stag and torn to pieces by his own hounds for having seen the naked Artemis; he deals with the Actaeon myth alone in *Met.* 3.174–252. Cf. Roscher (1937) s.v. *Aktaion* 214 f., *Pentheus* 1927–29. In constructing a double simile here, Claudian follows the rule discovered by Parravicini; cf. n. 2.376–79, para. 2.

Claudian returns to the Pentheus theme in another poem in referring to Rufinus' slaughter, CS 2.212 f. (the gods turn Stilicho's enemies against themselves) Aut in se vertunt furiis aut militis ense / bacchati laniant Pentheo corpora ritu. It appears that, though confining himself to the Pentheus myth in CS 2.212-15, Claudian specifically recalled to mind the whole of our present passage with its double simile: he mentions Molossian hounds in CS 2.215 (the gods are keen as Molossians in tracking down Stilicho's enemies), though the *Molossi* belong to the Actaeon (IR 2.419 f.) and not to the Pentheus myth.

2.418 *a* mons Aonius: Cithaeron or Parnassus; cf. Roscher (1937) s.vv. *Aktaion, Pentheus*; on *Aonius*=*Boeotius*, cf. TLL s.v. *Aon* 204.59-68.

2.418 *b* ferrent: the word itself is neutral, and derives its violent meaning here solely from the context: cf. TLL s.v. 531.80-532.24.

2.419 subito mutatum ... cornu: for Actaeon's transformation into a stag, cf. Ov. *Met.* 3.194-97, and n. 2.418-20.

2.421-23 Criminibus — suppliciis: as Gesner (1759) *ad loc.* points out, Claudian here repudiates his lofty thesis of 1.20-23, that the punishment of Rufinus has justified the ways of the supernatural powers.

2.423 Una tot milia morte rependis: cf. BP 633 f. (the Romans recoup their losses at Pollentia) uno ... die Romana rependit / quidquid ter denis acies amisimus annis.

2.424-27 Eversis — populis: a quasi-parallel to the distribution of Rufinus' members among the countries which he had destroyed is to be found in Petr. 120.65 f. (Fortune has scattered the remains of the Triumvirs among three lands) et quasi non posset tot tellus ferre sepulchra / divisit cineres; cf. also *Anth. Lat.* 402.

2.424 divide: for the ironic *permissio*, cf. 2.301 I nunc; n. 2.301 *a*.

2.425 Odrysiis: = *Thraciis*; cf. n. 1.175 *a*.

2.426 f. Quid — populis?: for a similar question intended to convey the enormity of Rufinus' crimes, cf. 2.518 f.

2.426 Nec: =*ne ... quidem*: cf. PO 147 f. (Rome holds Probinus and Olybrius in higher esteem than even her ancient worthies) His ego nec Decios pulchros fortesve Metellos / praetulerim, 6H 429; Hofmann-Szantyr (1965) 449 f. Birt (1892) 544 s.v. was not justified in questioning this interpretation here.

2.427–39: *The citizenry stream forth to trample Rufinus' body in the dust, and to make sport of his head and right hand.*

2.427 f. Vacuo plebs undique muro iam secura fluit: the people are apparently thought of as having maintained a sort of τειχοσκοπία in anticipation of the army's arrival; cf. BP 455 f. (a crowd on the walls of Rome await Stilicho's return, as yet unconfirmed) Pulveris ambiguam nubem speculamur ab altis / turribus, incerti socios adportet an hostes. The Romans' reaction to the sight of Stilicho closely parallels, in the reverse sense, the language of our own passage: BP 461 f. Portas secura per omnes / turba ... effunditur obvia. On τειχοσκοπία in the epic, cf. n. 2.62 f., 70.

2.427 a Vacuo: on the resultative-predicate use of the adjective here, cf. n. 1.1 b.

2.427 b: on the people's hatred of Rufinus, cf. Zos. 5.1.5 τὸ κατ' αὐτοῦ ηὐξάνετο μῖσος; Philostorg. 11.3 (money is collected in Rufinus' severed hand) ἐν τοῖς ἐργαστηρίοις τῆς πόλεως; Int. 23, 26, ftn. 164.

2.427 c undique: cf. Text. Comm. *ad loc.* Cameron (1968a) 398 argues for the reading *obvia*, which, as the Text. Comm. notes, would convey a tone of bitter irony. The reading *obvia* may receive some support from BP 462: cf. n. 2.427 f., *fin.*

2.427 d muro: if Claudian reflects the contemporary topography of Constantinople, this must be the Wall of Constantine, since the Wall of Theodosius (II) was of course not built as yet: cf. Janin (1964) 263–65. The poet may be only generalizing, however.

2.430 gaudia: cf. the same word used of the delight taken by those who viewed the remains of a destructive monster: Stat. *Theb.* 1.620 magna ... post lacrimas etiamnum gaudia pallent, and cf. n. 2.408.

2.431 a Laceros ... artus: Bruère (1964) 236 compares Luc. 2.177 (Marius' body mistreated) Laceros artus, 2.165. The same expression occurs in Ov. *Met.* 9.169 (Hercules' flesh is rent by the poisoned robe).

2.431 b iuvat ire: cf. Verg. *A.* 2.27 f. (the Trojans delight in visiting the Greek camp) iuvat ire et Dorica castra / ... videre; Stat. *Theb.* 1.616 f. Claudian uses the same metrical scheme embracing the words *iuvat ire* elsewhere: CS 3.277 steriles iuvat ire per aestus.

2.432 calcato ... sanguine: cf. Verg. *A.* 12.340 (Turnus' horses trample down his enemies) mixta ... cruor calcatur harena. Cf. also IR 2.447 calcandus spargitur. Claudian seems to refer again to this trampling of Rufinus in CS 3.109 (Stilicho reinvigorates the Roman people) excitat ut magnos calcet metuendus honores.

2.433-39: The parading of Rufinus' head mounted on a pike, and the carrying of his hand around the city, with its fingers manipulated by the tendons to imitate begging gestures, seem to have made a deep and lasting impression. Cf. Jerome, *Ep.* 60.16.1, and Philostorg. 11.3, quoted in Int. 26, ftn. 165; also Zos. 5.7.6 ὁ δὲ τὴν κεφαλὴν τοῦ τραχήλου χωρίσας ἀπῄει, παιᾶνας ᾄδων ἐπινικίους, ἐς τοσοῦτον δὲ ἐπετώθασαν ὥστε τὴν χεῖρα πανταχῇ τῆς πόλεως περιάγειν, αἰτεῖν τε ἀργύριον δοῦναι τῷ ἀπλήστῳ τοὺς προστυγχάνοντας; Marcell. Com. 8.5 (=MHG 11.64.22-26) Rufinus... merito trucidatus est. Caput eius manusque dextra per totam Constantinopolim demonstrata.

2.434 de cuspide summa: cf. n. 2.335 for a Vergilian parallel; cf. also Luc. 2.160 (the Sullan massacres) colla ducum pilo trepidam gestata per urbem, 9.137.

2.435 digna rediens... pompa: cf. Aster. *Hom.* 4 (= Migne Gr. 40.224, with ftn. 30) ἐπομπεύθη... μετὰ θάνατον μᾶλλον ἢ ὅτε φερόμενος ἐπὶ τοῦ δίφρου ἐγαυρία τοῦ ἀξιώματος (cf. Int. 14, ftn. 71).

2.436-39 ludo... vivosque — nervis: cf. Schol. A *ad loc.*: Ludum tangit puerorum qui pedem gruis vel aliae [*sic*] avis tenentes, nervos solent attrahere, et vel detractione nervorum digitos claudere vel laxatione eosdem solent dissolvere et aperire. Bruère (1964) 237 sees the influence of Luc. 3.612 f. (a severed hand holds firm to the side of a ship) illa tamen nisu, quo prenderat, haesit / deriguitque tenens strictis inmortua nervis.

2.437 *a* aera petens: Bruère (1964) 237 seems to have misread *aera* (acc. plu. of *aes*; cf. *quaestum* and χρυσίον in n. 2.438 *a*, ἀργύριον in n. 2.433-39) as *aëra* (acc. sing. of *aër*), for he remarks, "Rufinus' severed hand, which the Byzantine populace first tossed sportively into the air."

2.437 *b* fraudes: cf. Text. Comm. *ad loc.*; Faider (1937) 680.

2.437 *c* animi... avari: on Rufinus' avarice, cf. Int. 15 f., ftns. 82, 83, 95.

2.438 *a* terribili lucro: cf. 2.445 feralem quaestum; Philostorg. 11.3 πολὺ χρυσίον ἡ αἴτησις ἠρανίσατο· οἷα γὰρ ἐπὶ καταθυμίῳ θεάματι προθύμως τὸ χρυσίον οἱ ὁρῶντες ἀντεδίδοσαν.

2.438 *c* **retentus:** apparently first used by Claudian; cf. Paucker (1880) 588.

2.440–53: *The fate of Rufinus teaches that pride goes before a fall.* On this passage as a treatment of the rhetorical *locus de fortuna* (cf. 2.421–27), cf. Fargues (1933a) 235 f., Decker (1913) 19–22, 38–44. Cf. also Jerome *Ep.* 60.16.2 (following an account of Rufinus' fall) Non calamitates miserorum, sed fragilem humanae condicionis narro statum, and n. 2.32–35. Cf. also Bruère (1964) 237; he compares Luc. 8.694–700; 9.1012, 1083; 8.867 f.

With the whole passage cf. Pacatus, *Panegyricus Theodosio Augusto dictus* 45 Quisquis purpura quandoque regali vestire humeros cogitabit, Maximi ei exutus occurrat. Quisquis aurum gemmasque privatis pedibus optabit, Maximus ei plantis nudis appareat. Quisquis imponere capiti diadema meditabitur, avulsum humeris Maximi caput et sine nomine corpus aspiciat; n. 1.183–87, para. 2; n. 1.220 f.

2.443 f. cuius se totiens summisit ad oscula supplex nobilitas: on bending the knee and kissing the emperor's hand as a part of late Roman court ceremonies, and on the spread of these ceremonies from the Emperor as recipient down to less exalted dignitaries, cf. Alföldi (1934) 46 f., 65; Cochrane (1944) 308, citing Cod. Theod. 6.22.7, which insists upon scrupulous observance of differences in rank. Eutropius, an official of lower rank than Rufinus (cf. Boak-Dunlap [1924] 184, 194 f., 279), received the kisses of *senatus, duces,* and *omnis potestas* (IE 2.64–66).

2.444 inhumata: cf. 1.371 nec vili moriens condetur harena, 2.452 f.; n. 1.371 *a*.

2.444 f. misero ... revulsa corpore: cf. Verg. *A.* 2.558 (Priam's mutilated corpse) avulsum ... umeris caput, et sine nomine corpus (cf. last sentence in quotation from Pacatus, n. 2.440–53).

2.445 post fata: = *post mortem*: cf. BG 292 (the shade of Theodosius) quae vidi post fata, loquar; CS 2.53; Birt (1892) 508 s.v. *fatum* (2); TLL s.v. *fatum* 359.21–360.77.

2.446 f. nimium sublata secundis colla gerit: cf. 2.345 f. colla ... femineo solvebat mollia gestu / imperii certus.

2.448 f. *a*: on Rufinus' mausoleum as part of his magnificent estate, cf. Int. 15 f. Bruère (1964) 237 f. compares Lucan's contrast between the unburied wretchedness of Pompey and the regal splendor of the Ptolemies' burial, 8.694–700; cf. esp. 695–98 [cum] regum cineres exstructo monte quiescant, / cum Ptolemaeorum manes ... / pyramides claudant indignaque Mausolea, / litora Pompeium feriunt; cf. also 9.155–57.

2.448 f. *b* non cedentia templis ... culmina: cf. Luc. 10.111 f. (Cleopatra's palace) templi ... instar erat; Juv. 14.88–90.

2.450 *a* velari: on the present infinitive for a future action, cf. n. 1.322 *b*.

2.450 *b* credidit: cf. Text. Comm. *ad loc.*

2.450 *c*. ostro: on the imperial purple, cf. n. 2.346 *b*.

2.451–53: on Rufinus' unburied state, cf. n. 1.371 *a*.

2.451 *a* nudus pascit aves: Bruère (1964) 238 compares Luc. 4.810 (Curio is unburied) pascit aves nullo contextus Curio busto. Cf. also Verg. *A*. 9.485 f. praeda ... / alitibus, and of course Hom. *Il*. 1.5 οἰωνοῖσι ... δαῖτα, if, indeed, δαῖτα is the correct reading. For *nudus* = *insepultus*, cf. Verg. *A*. 5.871 nudus in ignota, Palinure, iacebis harena; Luc. 9.157.

2.451 *b* possidet orbem: on Rufinus' wide-spread holdings, cf. Int. 26, and esp. these words of Cod. Theod. quoted: per omnes provincias ... quae Rufinus vivus possederat. On *orbis* of the Roman Empire, cf. 1 Pr.17 *b*.

2.451 *c* possidet: the present tense ironically stresses the suddenness as well as the awfulness of Rufinus' fate: "Lo, he who until this moment possesses the world, lies. ..."

2.452 inops: for this word of the unburied, cf. Verg. *A*. 6.325 haec omnis, quam cernis, inops inhumataque turba est.

2.454–527: for the conclusion of IR, Claudian turns once more to the supernatural surroundings of the Lower World, in which he set the Assembly of the Furies, the first scene of the poem (1.25–122). Thus, save for a brief interlude of divine intervention at the end of IR 1 (340–87), we have terrestrial action bounded at beginning and end by infernal.

The final scenes in Hades naturally invite comparison with the literary tradition of the *catabasis* from the *Nekyia* of *Od*. 11 down. As usual, Claudian is widely eclectic. Among literary influences, the most clearly discernible are those of *Aeneid* 6, Seneca's *Apocolocyntosis*, and Lucian's *Cataplus, Necyomantia*, and *De luctu* (unless, instead of being influenced by Seneca and Lucian, Claudian was inspired here, as Lévy [1927] 121 f. suggests, by a source common to all three).

This portion of IR has been discussed in detail by Lévy (1927) 120–22 (cf. also 116–18); Fargues (1933a) 185–88, 229–31; Levy (1947a); and Bruère (1964) 238 (cf. also Ruhl [1903] 66 f., 90 f.; cf. also 56–64). On the declamatory tradition of penalties awaiting tyrants in the Lower World, cf. Fleskes (1914) 44 f. On the relation between this passage and the ψόγος-pattern, cf. Levy (1946) 64 f.

2.454–65: *The spirit of Rufinus comes to the Lower World, where it is surrounded by the enraged shades of its victims, who drive him to the judgment-seat of Minos.*

2.454 f.: cf. Petr. 124.264 f. (the balance of the universe is upset as gods join men in strife) Sentit terra deos mutataque sidera pondus / quaesivere suum. Cf. also Weston's remark on cosmic forces quoted at Int. 39. Bruère (1964) 238 compares Luc. 1.57 (if the deified Nero choose a part of the heavens not directly above Rome) sentiet axis onus. For *convexa* and *axis* Bruère compares Luc. 5.632.

2.454 convexa: = *caelum*: cf. n. 1.367 *b*.

2.455 *a* amolitur onus: cf. Luc. 5.354 f. (Caesar rejoices at being relieved of cowardly soldiers) Heu, quantum Fortuna umeris iam pondere fessis / amolitur onus!

2.455 *b* astris: on the heavenly bodies as symbols of light in the scheme light:darkness::Stilicho:Rufinus, cf. n. 1 Pr.1.

2.456 Infernos gravat umbra lacus: in order to bring the shade of Rufinus to judgment, Claudian must disregard the tenet that the unburied dead may not cross the Styx (cf. Verg. *A*. 6.374 f.). The poet exploits this necessity by the use of *gravat*, thus reinforcing the idea of oppressive weight already presented in 2.454 f. nefandum / ... onus. This is of course quite different from the concept of the skiff weighted down by the still-living Aeneas in Verg. *A*. 6.413.

2.456 f. Aeacus ... Cerberus: in presenting Aeacus as the border-guard of Hades, side by side with Cerberus, Claudian follows Lucian (or a common source: cf. Lévy [1927] 121 f.): cf. Lucian. *Luct.* 4

Αἰακὸς ἕστηκε τὴν φρουρὰν ἐπιτετραμμένος, καὶ παρ' αὐτοῦ κύων τρικέφαλος, Nec. 8 τὴν τοῦ Αἰακοῦ φρουράν.

2.457 intrantem ... etiam latratu Cerberus urget: for the point of *etiam*, cf. Lucian. *Luct.* 4 κύων τρικέφαλος ... τοὺς μὲν ἀφικνουμένους φίλιόν τι καὶ εἰρηνικὸν προσβλέπων, τοὺς δὲ πειρῶντας ἀποδιδράσκειν ὑλακτῶν. Schol. A *ad loc.* remarks: qui omnibus intrantibus solet esse mitis et benignus. Platnauer (1922) uses italics effectively: "bays to stop, in this case, the *entry* of a ghost." For *latratu*, cf. Verg. *A.* 6.417. The passage from Lucian seems to render unnecessary the suggestion of Cameron (1968a) 399 that *arcet* be read for *urget* (*urguet*); according to Lucian, all that Cerberus would have done to "any ordinary deceased mortal" was to look at him benignly, not usher him in with barking.

2.458–60 Tunc animae — fremitu: cf. Lucian. *Cat.* 26 (Megapenthes' victims surround him in the Lower World) ἀκρίτους ... ἀπέκτεινε πλείονας ἢ μυρίους ... ἄκλητοι ... πάρεισι καὶ περιστάντες ἄγχουσιν αὐτόν.

2.458 *a*: cf. 2.328 f. umbras / quas dedit ipse neci; n. 2.328 f. The equivocal prophets can now enjoy the fulfilment of their predictions in their hidden sense.

2.458 *b* fero sub iure: on Rufinus' juridical functions, cf. n. 2.82 *c*, n. 2.84 f.

2.459 *a* nigri ... ad iudicis urnam: on Minos as the examining judge, cf. n. 2.476–78.

2.459 *b* trahunt: metaphorically "drive," not physically "drag": cf. *infesto fremitu* in the next verse, and the bee-simile which follows; cf. also 2.459 f. circumstant ... trahunt ... / ... fremitu, and Verg. *G.* 4.216 (the bees surround their king protectively) circumstant fremitu.

2.460–65 veluti — velant: for the bee-simile, cf. Verg. *A.* 12.587–92; Stat. *Theb.* 10.574–79. Claudian has blended and reworked his models, omitting the smoke element from the Vergilian model, and the stress on the pathetic element of the bees' losses from the Statian. Christiansen (1969) 62 seems to have misinterpreted the passage. The bees here are meant to typify formidable adversaries; the shades who are compared with them are capable of compelling Rufinus to proceed at once to the throne of justice.

2.461 glomerantur apes: with the *catabasis* of *Aeneid* 6 in mind,

Claudian here echoes Verg. *A.* 6.311 (the shades cluster about the bank of Styx like birds flying South) quam multae glomerantur aves.

2.461 f. raptu . . . vehit: for *raptu* with a verb of conveying, cf. RP 1.27 (Proserpina abducted) ducta ferox Proserpina raptu.

2.462 pennas . . . cient et spicula tendunt: cf. Verg. *G.* 4.73 f. (bees at war) pennis . . . coruscant / spiculaque exacuunt rostris.

2.463 cinctae: cf. Text. Comm. *ad loc.*

2.464 rimosam patriam dilectaque pumicis antra: cf. Verg. *G.* 4.44 (bees are found) pumicibusque cavis exesaeque arboris antro. Note also the words which follow: Tu tamen et levi rimosa cubilia limo / ungue. On the explicative use of the conjunction, cf. n. 1.13.

2.465 velant: cf. Text. Comm. *ad loc.*

2.466–93: *Minos holds court at the confluence of Cocytus and Phlegethon. He separates the innocent from the guilty, passing condign sentences upon the latter.*

2.466 Est locus: on the cliché, cf. n. 1.123.

2.466 f. conciliantur in unum Cocytos Phlegethonque: cf. Hom. *Od.* 10.513 f. εἰς Ἀχέροντα Πυριφλεγέθων τε ῥέουσι / Κωκυτός θ'. Apparently Claudian is the only one to follow Homer as regards the confluence of the two streams: cf. Roscher (1937) s.v. *Phlegethon*, esp. 2377.10–13; s.v. *Kokytos*. Lucian (*Luct.* 3), like Statius (*Theb.* 8.30) and many others, mentions the two rivers together.

2.468 a hic volvit lacrimas, hic igne redundat: cf. the *Suda* s.v. Κήρ: ὁ μὲν ἀπὸ τοῦ φλέγειν . . . ὁ δὲ ἀπὸ τῶν θρήνων κωκυτῶν· κωκυτός δέ ἐστι φωνῆς μίμησις θρηνούντων.

2.468 b igne: on the form, cf. n. 1.9 d.

2.469 f. per geminos . . . amnes porrigitur: cf. Luc. 2.399 f. (the Apennines) mons inter geminas medius se porrigit undas / inferni superique maris.

2.469 a Turris: cf. Verg. *A.* 6.554 (at the gate of Tartarus) stat ferrea turris ad auras.

2.469 b flammis vicinior: Koenig (1808) *ad loc.* has great difficulty in understanding how, if the tower touches both Cocytus and Phlegethon, it can be said to be nearer the flames of the latter. It seems clear that Claudian means to locate the tower, not squarely athwart the median of the widened channel formed by the confluent streams, but rather with the larger part of it located to the left of mid-channel (cf. 2.470 f. sinistrum / . . . latus). The directions "left" and "right" are presumably from the standpoint of one making the *catabasis* from the world above.

2.470 rigens adamante: cf. Verg. *A.* 6.552 (Aeneas at the entrance to Tartarus) *porta adversa ingens solidoque adamante columnae*; BP 213 f.

2.472 *a* triste gemens: on the adverbial use of the neuter adjective, cf. n. 1.65 f.

2.472 *b* et: on the explicative use of the conjunction, cf. n. 1.13.

2.473 *a* emeritam . . . vitam: cf. Paul. *Fest.* 139 (= 123.4 Lindsay) *mortuus ab emerita vita dictus*. If this pseudo-etymology was known to Claudian, it may have influenced his choice of expression here (cf. Cameron [1968a] 389 on 1.154 *citavi*).

2.473 *b* mortalia saecula: cf. RP 2.311 (the shades crowd around to see Proserpina) *cuncta . . . praecipiti stipantur saecula cursu*. The expression *mortalia saecula* is of course Lucretian; cf. n. 2.208.

2.474–78 Ibi — sontes: cf. Lucian. *Nec.* 12 ὁ . . . Μίνως ἐπιμελῶς ἐξετάζων . . . ἕκαστον . . . ἐκείνων ἥπτετο τῶν ἐπὶ πλούτοις τε καὶ ἀρχαῖς τετυφωμένων. . . . οἳ δὲ ἀποδυσάμενοι τὰ λαμπρὰ ἐκεῖνα πάντα . . . γυμνοὶ . . . παρειστήκεσαν; 14 τοῖς μέντοι πένησι ἡμιτέλεια τῶν κακῶν ἐδίδοτο.

2.475 f. vano . . . exutum nomine regem proturbat plebeius egens: cf. RP 2.300–2 (Pluto to Proserpina) *purpurei venient . . . reges / deposito luxu turba cum pauperi mixti: / omnia mors aequat*.

2.476–78 Quaesitor . . . pertemptat crimina Minos et iustis dirimit sontes: cf. Verg. *A.* 6.432 f. *Quaesitor Minus urnam movet; . . . / . . . vitasque et crimina discit*. For *urnam*, cf. 2.459; on the Vergilian passage, cf. Norden (1916) 245 f. He cites [Asc.] *Ver.* (= Stangl [1912] 224) *Virgilius Minoem . . . tamquam si praetor sit rerum capitalium, quaesitorem appellat; dat illi sortitionem, ubi urnam nominat; . . . dat cognitionem facinorum, cum dicit vitasque et nomina discit*. The term *quaesitor* is used by Vergil and Claudian in its general sense of "examining judge," not as the equivalent of *quaestor* (cf. RE s.vv. *quaesitor*, *quaestor*).

2.478–80 Quos — agit: cf. Verg. *A.* 6.566 f. (Rhadamanthus forces the guilty to confess) *Gnosius . . . Rhadamanthus . . . / castigat*

... auditque dolos subigitque fateri; Page (1890) 466, on *castigat*: "The object for which Rhadamanthus uses the whip is to extract confession: 'he whips them and hears their deceits and forces them to confess.'" Cf. also Rushforth (1891) 232; Sidgwick (1891) 64; Platt (1891) 337. Rushforth is right in saying that, whatever Vergil meant by *castigat*, Page interprets Vergil the way Claudian did. Crépin (1933) wrongly translates *fateri* by "avancer," unless the French verb can convey a meaning not glossed in Robert (1960) s.v.

2.479 verbera: on the Roman use of torture to extort testimony (even from free men during the Empire) cf. DS s.v. *quaestio per tormenta*, s.v. *testimonium* 152 f.; RE s.v. *quaestio* 786.14–20, s.v. *Tormenta* 1777.34–1793.27.

2.480–93: on punitive metempsychosis as described in this passage, cf. Levy (1947a) 64–68, and the references there cited (in ftn. 8, in the final citation, for "p. 87" read "pp. 82–85"). To these should be added Fabbri (1916), Courcelle (1943) 121, and Long (1948).

It should be noted that, just as Seneca gives an elaborate description of a bottomless dice-box as a condign punishment for Claudius (*Apoc.* 14), only to have Aeacus, a brief while later, discard this punitive measure in favor of adjudicating Claudius to Caligula as a slave, so Claudian, after his learned disquisition on metempsychosis, has Minos abandon it in favor of eternal relegation beyond the bounds of Tartarus (2.522–27). In neither case is the artistic effect of the supplanted punishment reduced by its subsequent abandonment.

2.480 f. *a* Cum ... perspexerit: the perfect subjunctive here where the perfect indicative would be expected (cf. Hofmann-Szantyr [1965] 619) is typical of Claudian's free usage: cf. n. 1 Pr.3 f. *b*.

2.480 f. *b* gesta superni curriculi: cf. Verg. *A.* 6.568 f. (the earthly crimes of the shades) quae quis apud superos furto laetatus inani / distulit in seram commissa piacula mortem.

2.481 *a* curriculi: apparently not used in verse before Claudian in the sense "life career," though frequent in that sense in Cicero and other prose writers: cf. TLL s.v.

2.481 *b* actus: = *facta*: cf. n. 1.284.

2.482 damnum: for this word virtually equivalent to *poena*, cf. Gel. 20.1.32 (in a discussion of the XII Tables) iniurias atrociores ... impensiore damno vindicaverunt; TLL s.v. *damnum* 27.47–69. It is this word which defines the punitive nature of the metempsychosis: cf. n. 2.480–93.

2.482 f. muta ferarum ... vincla: Crépin (1933) here makes a nice distinction between the condition of being *muta*, "privés de la parole," which applies to all sub-human species, and "le silence absolu" in which the fish, 2.489 f., must live.

2.485–87: Bruère (1964) 238 sees here an echo of the description of Julius' winter of debauchery in Cleopatra's palace, Luc. 10.396. In Pl. *Phd.* 81E–82A it is the ass, not the hog, which typifies γαστριμαργία and φιλοποσία; cf. Levy (1947a) 65.

2.488–90: on the peculiarly allopathic nature of the punishment meted out to the *loquax*, cf. Levy (1947a) 65–68; cf. also n. 2.490. All the other offending shades become creatures who exemplify the very vices of which they were guilty as men; the *loquax* alone is transmuted into the opposite of his former self.

2.489 victurus: cf. Text. Comm. *ad loc.*; also 2.511 in tua mansurus migret praecordia vultur; Cameron (1968a) 399.

2.490 pensent: for this word in the sense "offset," "balance," cf. IE 1.73 (a woman's compensation for age) uxoris ... decus matris reverentia pensat; Stat. *Theb.* 5.710 f. (Hypsipyla is compensated for her sorrow) Quis superum tanto solatus funera voto / pensavit lacrimas?

2.491 *a* varias ... figuras: cf. Ov. *Met.* 15.171 f. (Pythagoras explains his doctrine of transmigration) animam sic semper eandem / esse sed in varias doceo migrare figuras.

2.491 *b* annis ter mille: for 3000 years as the period of the soul's various transmigrations before its return to a human body, cf. the Egyptian doctrine reported by Herodotus (2.123), esp. τὴν περιήλυσιν δὲ αὐτῇ γίνεσθαι ἐν τρισχιλίοισι ἔτεσι. Plato restricts the three-thousand-year limitation to philosophers, whose souls (*Phdr.* 249A) πτερωθεῖσαι τρισχιλιοστῷ ἔτει ἀνέρχονται. Elsewhere 3000 years is given as the measure of the *annus magnus*: Cic. *N.D.* 3, frag. 5 tria milia annorum ... magnum annum tenere (cf. Pease [1958] 668 f., 1230 [V]); a similar use of the period appears in Thphr. frag. 72 (= FHG 1.289), ascribed to the Magi: ἀνὰ μέρος τρισχιλία ἔτη τὸν μὲν κρατεῖν, τὸν δὲ κρατεῖσθαι τῶν θεῶν. Vergil uses 1000 (*A.* 6.748), Silius 5000 years (13.558 f.) as a period of purification before the soul's return.

2.492 Lethaeo purgatos flumine: the concept that Lethe has a purificatory function seems original with Claudian, and appears in his poems only here. Elsewhere Lethe is the conventional river of oblivion: cf. RP 1.282 f., BG 213 f.; Verg. *A.* 6.714 f., 750 f.; RE s.v. *Lethe* (1), Roscher (1937) s.v. *Lethe*, Rohde (1921) 1.316, 2.210, 382, 390. In Pl. *Phdr.* 249A, and in Lucian. *Cat.* 24, it is the practice of philosophy, and not the drinking of Lethe, that purifies; in Verg. *A.* 6.745-48 it is the lapse of time.

2.493 revocat: cf. Verg. *A.* 6.749 (a god summons the purified souls) Lethaeum ad fluvium deus evocat agmine magno.

2.494-527: *Noting Rufinus' approach, Minos interrupts the proceedings to hale him before the judgment-seat. He upbraids him sternly, and, after weighing various severe penalties, dooms him to imprisonment below the foundations of Night forever.*

2.494 Tum quoque: for these words serving as a resumptive transition from a general description to the particularities of the narrative, cf. Verg. *A.* 9.183 (after a general description of the friendship of Nisus and Euryalus) tum quoque communi portam statione tenebant.

2.495 *a* veteres ... reos ex ordine: the meaning of *veteres* is probably merely that these are the defendants whose cases have been on the docket for some time, and who are being examined in regular order with the well-known slowness of judicial deliberation. So Crépin (1933), who translates "d'après leur ordre d'ancienneté," apparently following Barth (1650) *ad loc.* Despite Sen. *Herc. F.* 579-81 (the infernal judges relent at Orpheus' plea) qui ... / ... veteres excutiunt reos / ... iuridici, our *rei* are probably not those "of old," as Platnauer (1922) renders *veteres*. Seneca's chorus was referring to a remembered past, Claudian's context is contemporary. For our *veteres rei* to be the "criminals of old" would give the court a static function like that of the villagers on Keat's Grecian urn, to judge and re-judge throughout eternity the same culprits.

2.495 *b* reos ... quaerit: probably means "seeks out," "cites," "summons before the bench," just as he summons Rufinus out of regular order in 2.498-501. Cf. Lucian. *Cat.* 23 f. (Rhadamanthus has the Fury and Hermes bring a group of 1004 defendants before him; at Cyniscus' request, he calls him up first, then speaks again to Hermes) Πρόσαγε αὐτούς, ὦ Ἐρινύ, σὺ δέ, ὦ Ἑρμῆ, κήρυττε καὶ προσ-

καλεῖ.... Δεῦρ' ἐλθὲ καὶ πρῶτος εἰς τὴν δίκην κατάστηθι....
ἄλλους προσκάλει. Platnauer (1922) and Crépin (1933) translate *quaero* here by "examine," "interroger." Despite Koenig (1808) *ad loc.* and Sandbach (1952) 7, it is unlikely that *reos quaerit = de reis (rem) quaerit*; at any rate, I have found no other example of this usage.

2.497 concussa sede: for the action of striking an inanimate object as a gesture of indignation, cf. Juv. 2.130 f. (Mars should be indignant at a homosexual marriage) *nec galeam quassas, nec terram cuspide pulsas, / nec quereris patri?*; Sittl (1890) 15 f. The triple use of *huc* (2.498–500) reflects the same emotional outburst. On Minos' indignation here, cf. Fargues (1933a) 231.

2.498–527: on direct quotation in IR, cf. n. 1.45–65, esp. sects. 4, 7.

2.498–500: Huc (*ter*): cf. n. 2.497.

2.498 *a* superum: here of the earth in relation to Tartarus (cf. 2.480 f. *superni / curriculi*; Sen. *Ag.* 4 [Thyestes, sent to earth from the realms of Dis] *fugio Thyestes inferos, superos fugo*); in 1.2 of the heavenly gods in relation to men; in 1.69 of the same gods in relation to those of the Lower World. Cf. Henry (1873) 3.326; he does not mention the third case.

2.498 *b* labes: in view (1) of the proximity of Verg. *A.* 6.745–47, *donec longa dies ... / concretam exemit labem purumque relinquit / aetherium sensum*, to other passages which have clearly influenced Claudian in this part of IR (cf. n. 2.469 *a*, n. 2.470, n. 2.478–80, n. 2.493), and (2) of *proluvies* in the next verse, it seems best to take *labes* here as meaning "corruption," "foul blot" (LS's *2. labes*), rather than "scourge" (Platnauer [1922]), "*fléau*" (Crépin [1933]), LS's *1. labes*. The phrase *superum labes* in Stat. *Theb.* 8.34 refers to an actual breakthrough from the Upper to the Lower World, and is thus, as Koenig (1808) *ad loc.* remarks, used *alio sensu*. The comment of Christiansen (1969) 87 is based, as far as *labes* is concerned, on the view that the word here means "destruction."

2.498 *c* insatiabilis: cf. Jerome *Ep.* 60.16.1 (Rufinus' right hand cut off) *ad dedecus insatiabilis avaritiae* (on Claudian's probable influence here, cf. Levy [1948a]); Zos. 5.7.6 τῷ ἀπλήστῳ (= Philostorg. 11.3); Eun. frag. 63 (= FHG 4.42) ἀμετροκάκου πλεονεξίας; Lyd. *Mag.* 2.10 'Ρουφῖνον τὸν ἐπίκλην ἀκόρεστον; Int. 15, ftn. 83.

2.498–501 auri proluvies pretioque nihil non ause parato ...

venditor: Bruère (1964) 238 compares Luc. 4.96 f. (Caesar's army is stricken by famine) pro lucri pallida tabes! / non deest prolato ieiunus venditor auro.

2.499 proluvies: Verg. A. 3.216 f. (the filth dropped by the Harpies) foedissima ventris / proluvies; Col. 12.38.1 (wine flavored with myrtle: a remedy for diarrhoea) ad tormina, et ad alvi proluviem, et ad imbecillum stomachum.

2.500 mihi: neither Platnauer (1922) nor Crépin (1933) takes account of this word, important as denoting the judge's personal sense of outrage at the venal perversion of the judicial process. On Rufinus' juridical functions, cf. Int. 12.

2.500 f. legum venditor: cf. Verg. A. 6.621 (among the miscreants being punished) vendidit hic auro patriam ... / ... fixit leges pretio atque refixit.

2.501 Arctoi stimulator ... Martis: cf. Text. Comm. *ad loc.*; 1.323–25 (of the Huns) genus ... / ... quo non famosius ullum / Arctos alit; Int. 23. Platnauer (1922) translates carelessly, "cause of that northern war," Crépin correctly, "qui as appelé à la guerre les peuples du Nord."

2.502 f.: Bruère (1964) 238 compares Luc. 6.704 f. (the Thessalian witch addresses Charon) o flagrantis portitor undae, / iam lassate senex ad me redeuntibus umbris. Cf. also Petr. 121.117–19 (Fortuna describes the results of the Civil War) vix navita Porthmeus / sufficiet simulacra virum traducere cumba; / classe opus est.

2.503 a plena lassatur portitor alno: cf. Stat. *Theb.* 4.479 (Manto evokes a multitude of shades) plena redeat Styga portitor alno.

2.503 b portitor: on the semantic development of this word from the meaning of "customs-collector" to that of "carrier," cf. Todd (1945), where (ftn. 16) our passage is cited.

2.504–6 Quid — tegunt: for the stains of guilt (στίγματα, σημεῖα, κηλῖδες) which make it possible for the infernal judge to identify malefactors, cf. Lucian. *Cat.* 24 f.; Ruhl (1903) 54–59.

2.504 f. inustae ... maculae: cf. Lucian *Cat.* 24 (Rhadamanthus discerns marks still visible, though faded, on Cyniscus' soul) ἴχνη ... καὶ σημεῖα πολλὰ τῶν ἐγκαυμάτων, and n. 2.504–6.

2.504 pectus: in Lucian. *Cat.* 24 the location of the stigmata is not given (though Harmon [1915] 74 translates "on your back"); merely ἐπὶ τῆς ψυχῆς περιφέρει and τῆς ψυχῆς ἀπελουσάμην. On the significance in Plato, Proclus, and Themistius of stigmata fore and aft, cf. Ruhl (1903) 38, 39, 44, 66. Claudian disregards the tenet that the wicked are marked on their backs.

2.505 vitii ... inolevit imago: cf. Text. Comm. *ad loc.* Of the reading *vitii*, Bieler (1957) 259 and Faider (1937) 680 approve warmly; Fargues (1936) 372 regards the change as unnecessary. Axelson (1944) 28–34 defends *vitiis* at great length, but begins by confessing (29) that, unless *vitiis inolevit imago* is inverted to *imagini inoleverunt vitia*, Claudian's words cannot be explained. He attempts to sustain the inversion with many formal, but, so far as I can see, no real semantic parallels. The crux of the matter is that Axelson takes *imago* to refer to Rufinus' shade (cf. his "sc. tua," p. 13); this, I now see, must be the interpretation reflected in the translations of Platnauer (1922) and Crépin (1933), and in the remark of Fargues cited above. But apart from the dramatic inappropriateness of having Minos refer to one of his defendants as an *imago* (the term Minos uses is *anima* or *umbra*, 2.520), Claudian nowhere else uses the word in the sense "shade"; in IE 1.122, which Axelson cites (29, ftn. 1), Eutropius is very much, if very loathsomely, alive. Axelson may have been deceived by the remark of Birt (1892) 521 s.v. *imago: de umbra quasi mortui.*

Imago is, in my view (cf. Koenig [1808] *ad loc.*), the σημεῖον (cf. n. 2.504–6) of Lucian: cf. LSJ s.v. σημεῖον 7. It is, then, the *vitii imago*, the "symbol of guilt," which has engrafted itself upon Rufinus' *pectus* as have the *multa diu concreta* upon the shades in Verg. *A.* 6.738. On *inolesco* of grafting, whether literal or symbolic, cf. Norden (1916) 311 on Verg. *A.* 6.738. Cf. also 6H 77 (the love of Rome is deeply implanted in Honorius' heart) Hinc tibi concreta radice tenacius haesit / et penitus totis inolevit Roma medullis, with the remarks of Müller (1938) *ad loc.*

2.506–20 Genus — umbris: for judicial hesitation on the appropriate punishment for an arch-criminal, and the final determination upon an unusual penalty, cf. Lucian. *Cat.* 28 τίνα ἂν οὖν κολασθείη τρόπον; ... ἐγώ σοι καινήν τινα καὶ πρέπουσαν αὐτῷ τιμωρίαν ὑποθήσομαι; Sen. *Apoc.* 14 De genere poenae diu disputatum est. ... Placuit novam poenam constitui debere; Lévy (1927) 120.

2.506 Genus omne dolorum: the punishment of metempsychosis is not mentioned, though it may be subsumed here; having served its artistic purposes (cf. n. 2.480-93 *fin*.), it is passed over in silence, and Claudian proceeds to enumerate several traditional Tartarean penalties.

2.507-11 dubio — vultur: for a similar enumeration, cf. RP 2.335-42, where Claudian mentions Ixion (cf. n. 2.508), Tantalus (cf. n. 2.509 f.), and Tityos (cf. n. 2.510), each with his traditional penalty. Here again we have three malefactors named, but four penalties: (a) the overhanging rock, (b) the wheel, (c) the elusive water, and (d) the vulture. Salmoneus' name appears here (without a specific penalty; cf. n. 2.512-19), but not in the RP passage; Tantalus and Tityos, each with penalty mentioned, are common to both; Ixion's name is omitted here, but his wheel is mentioned. The overhanging rock is omitted in the RP passage. No pattern of choice can be discerned; it may be, however, that the omission of a name for the victim of the overhanging rock reflects the confusion in the tradition (both mythical and textual) as set forth by Norden (1916) 285 f. on Verg. *A*. 6.601 f.

For a survey of such enumerations as those in our present passage, cf. Roscher (1937) s.v. *Tityos* 1039 f.

2.507 f. dubio tibi pendula rupes immineat lapsu: cf. Verg. *A*. 6.601-3 (the Sibyl enumerates some malefactors under torment) quid memorem Lapithas, Ixiona Pirithoumque, et / quos super atra silex iam iam lapsura ... / imminet?; n. 2.507-11.

2.507 dubio: for this word of that which is apprehensive of destruction, cf. 3H 64 (civil war imperils humanity) dubium ... quatit discordia mundi; Ov. *Tr*. 3.2.15 (on his journey into exile) terris dubius iactabar et undis; TLL s.v. *dubius* 2106.20-31.

2.508 volucer te torqueat axis: for Ixion, the prime sufferer from this penalty, cf. RP 2.335 (during a nuptial amnesty) non rota suspensum praeceps Ixiona torquet; Verg. *G*. 4.484 (Orpheus' music stops the wheel) Ixionii vento rota constitit orbis. For mention of the tormenting wheel without the name of a malefactor, as here, cf. Verg. *A*. 6.616 f. (among the culprits enumerated by the Sibyl) radiis ... rotarum districti pendent; Norden (1916) 290 *ad loc*.; Dieterich (1913) 203 on τροχίζειν.

2.509 f. te — sitis: for Tantalus' punishment, cf. RP 2.336 (during a nuptial amnesty) non aqua Tantaleis subducitur invida labris; Ov. *Met.* 4.458 f. Tantalus is not mentioned in Vergil's major works.

2.510 dapibus: for the vulture's traditional feasting-place, the liver and other vitals of Tityos, cf. Verg. *A.* 6.597–99 (among the torments enumerated by the Sibyl) vultur ... / immortale iecur tondens fecundaque poenis / viscera rimatur epulis; cf. also RP 2.338 (during a nuptial amnesty) Tityos tandem spatiosos erigit artus, 341 invitos trahitur lasso de pectore vultur; CM 53.25 f.

2.512–19: these verses are not in complete harmony with the rest of the poem. (1) Claudian sets up a group of malefactors, 2.512 omnes alii quos haec tormenta fatigant. Now the necessities of logic would seem to require that the names which follow belong to members of the group punished by *haec tormenta*: i.e. by one or more of the four enumerated in 2.507–11 (cf. n. 2.507–11). Salmoneus is an exception: his infernal penalty is not among those listed, nor is it described in any clear way by Vergil or any other ancient author, so far as I have been able to discover. The idea that Salmoneus was condemned in the Lower World to continue imitating Zeus' thunder and lightning throughout eternity (a penalty suspiciously mild, if one considers Verg. *A.* 6.585 crudelis ... poenas) rests upon a disputed interpretation of Verg. *A.* 6.585 f.; cf. Norden (1916) 282 f. *ad loc.*; Roscher (1937) s.v. *Salmoneus* 292 f. (2) The three specific evils mentioned in 2.514 f. are Salmoneus' *fulmen* (cf. n. 2.513 f.), Tantalus' *lingua* (cf. n. 2.514), and Tityos' *amor* (cf. n. 2.515 a). Only one of these, *lingua*, is really appropriate to Rufinus' guilty conduct as Claudian himself represents it: cf. 1.229 nusquam reverentia mensae; also 1.179 profert arcana; Levy (1947a) 67 f. But one is hard put to it to find any appropriateness to Rufinus in *fulmen*; even harder in the case of *amor*. Perhaps Rufinus' attempt to become Emperor is a case of *laesa divinitas* comparable to Salmoneus' imitation of Zeus. Or is Claudian thinking of the general destruction wrought by Rufinus (e.g. 2.61–70) as parallel to Salmoneus' assaults on his own people (cf. Hyg. *Fab.* 61)? As for *amor*, perhaps the *conubia ... aliena* (cf. n. 2.321 f.) are to be compared with Tityos' guilty passion for Latona, though the desire for such *conubia* seems to be attributed to Rufinus' followers rather than to the man himself. In fact, carnal lust is not among the vices with which Rufinus is taxed (cf. Int. 42, and ftn. 257). One must conclude that Claudian was elaborating a stock theme rather than working out a clearly conceived *schema*.

2.512 omnes alii, quos haec tormenta fatigant: cf. Ov. *Ib.* 189 f. (Aeacus will visit upon "Ibis" all the fabled punishments) In te transcribet veterum tormenta reorum: / omnibus antiquis causa quietis eris.

2.513 pars quota sunt, Rufine, tui?: cf. Ov. *Met.* 9.69 (Hercules taunts Achelous, who has assumed the shape of a snake) pars quota Lernaeae serpens eris unus echidnae?

2.513 f. audax fulmine Salmoneus: cf. Verg. *A.* 6.585 f. vidi et crudelis dantem Salmonea poenas, / dum flammas Iovis et sonitus imitatur Olympi (cf. n. 2.512–19); Lucian. *Tim.* 2 (Timon chides Zeus for being so lukewarm that Salmoneus was encouraged to rival him) ὁ Σαλμονεὺς ἀντιβροντᾶν ἐτόλμα; cf. also CM 51.13.

2.514 lingua Tantalus egit: cf. Hyg. *Fab.* 82 Iuppiter Tantalo concredere sua consilia solitus erat, et ad epulum deorum admittere; quae Tantalus ad homines renuntiavit; Ov. *Am.* 2.2.43 f. (Tantalus' fate a warning to slaves to be discreet) Quaerit aquas in aquis et poma fugacia captat / Tantalus: hoc illi garrula lingua dedit; *Ars* 2.605 f.

2.515 a inconsulto Tityos deliquit amore: cf. Hom. *Od.* 11.580 (the reason for Tityos' punishment) Λητὼ γὰρ ἕλκησε, Διὸς κυδρὴν παράκοιτιν; Men. Rh. p. 441 Spengel; Stat. *Theb.* 11.12 f. (Capaneus lies outstretched like Tityos) quantus Apollineae temerator matris Averno / tenditur; Fontenrose (1959) 22 f.

2.515 b Tityos: on the Greek nominative form, standard for Roman authors, cf. Roscher (1937) s.v. 1033.26–40.

2.516 f. si ... iungantur ... praecedes: on conditions of the *si sit ... erit* type, where the likelihood of the accomplishment of the condition is remote, but the author wishes to express a forceful conclusion, cf. Nutting (1925) 81 f., 205–9. For this pattern in legal language, cf. Cod. Theod. 9.14.1, quoted in n. 2.517 *b*.

2.517 a numero: for *numerus = ordo*, cf. Verg. *A.* 3.446 f. (the Sibyl puts the leaves in order) digerit in numerum (cf. 3.447 neque ab ordine cedunt). Presumably the single bearer of all the ancient crimes will come second, Rufinus will be first in order.

2.517 b piacula: for this word signifying crimes rather than atonement for them, cf. BG 390 (Mascezel has defected to the Romans) fugiens dira piacula fratris (cf. 392–98); Verg. A. 6.569 commissa piacula. The term had legal standing in Claudian's day: cf. Cod. Theod. 9.14.1 (A.D. 374) Si quis necandi infantis piaculum adgressus adgressave sit, erit capitale istud malum.

2.518 f. Quid — poenas: on a similar way of expressing the enormity of Rufinus' crimes, cf. n. 2.426 f.

2.520: Bruère (1964) 238 compares Luc. 6.313 (Rome's destiny might have been different) exire e mediis potuit Pharsalia fatis, 6.534 (Erichtho filches bones from pyres) e mediis rapit illa rogis.

2.520–23: on a similar series of brief utterances, cf. n. 2.217–19. Here the staccato is abandoned for the final adjuration. Bruère (1964) 238 compares Luc. 6.731 f. (Erichtho calls on Tisiphone and Megaera) non agitis saevis Erebi per inane flagellis / infelicem animam?

In our passage the imperatives *Tollite, parcite, purgate, agitate* are addressed to unnamed servitors. For Claudian to have introduced here the normal wielders of the *flagella*, the Furies, would have meant running the risk of arousing disturbing memories of the first infernal scene of IR. There the Furies Allecto and Megaera, the personifications of evil, set in motion the events whereby the latter's nursling, Rufinus, is let loose upon an unfortunate world. On this use of the Furies and its incompatibility with a view of them as the instruments of Justice (cf. 1.354–56), cf. Levy (1947a) 68–73.

2.522 Ditis ... domos: cf. Verg. A. 6.268 (Aeneas and the Sibyl commence their journey) Ibant obscuri sola sub nocte per umbram / perque domos Ditis vacuas et inania regna.

2.523–26 trans Styga, trans Erebum ... infra Titanum tenebras infraque recessus Tartareos nostrumque Chaos, qua noctis ... fundamenta latent: for the concept of a second underworld, below the realm of Dis, cf. Luc. 6.748 f. (Erichtho threatens the deities of the Lower World with a still more powerful divinity) cuius / vos estis superi. Cf. also the passages collected by Morawski (1917) 7.

2.523–25 Erebum ... Chaos: on these two words, cf. Pease (1935) on Verg. A. 4.26, 510.

2.524 Titanum tenebras: for the prison of the Titans as far below the infernal judgment-seat, cf. Verg. A. 6.577–81 Tum Tartarus ipse / bis patet in praeceps tantum tenditque sub umbras / quantus ad aetherium caeli suspectus Olympum. / Hic ... Titania pubes / ... fundo volvuntur in imo.

2.525 nostrumque: cf. Text. Comm. *ad loc.*

2.527 *a*: for eternal punishment, cf. Ov. *Ib.* 196 Hora ... erit tantis ultima nulla malis. Cf. also Norden (1916) 19. He cites, regarding the fate of the arch-criminals, Pl. *Grg.* 525C τὰ μέγιστα καὶ ὀδυνηρότατα καὶ φοβερώτατα πάθη πάσχοντας τὸν ἀεὶ χρόνον; *Phd.* 113E. τούτους ... ἡ προσήκουσα μοῖρα ῥίπτει εἰς τὸν Τάρταρον, ὅθεν οὔποτε ἐκβαίνουσιν.

2.527 *b* dum rotat astra polus: cf. Verg. *A.* 1.608 (Aeneas will remember Dido) polus dum sidera pascet, on which cf. Mjöberg (1944).

2.527 *c* feriunt dum litora venti: as does Vergil in *A.* 1.607 (Aeneas will remember Dido) in freta dum fluvii current, Claudian joins terrestrial with celestial phenomena as symbols of eternity (cf. n. 2.257 *b*), but Claudian reverses Vergil's order.

APPENDIX

INTRODUCTION

CHAPTER I

The Historical Background of Claudian's Invective, in Rufinum[1]

When Theodosius the Great died at Milan on January 17, 395, he left a troubled Empire to be divided between his two sons, the Augusti[2] Arcadius and Honorius. The former received the Eastern, the latter the Western portion of the Empire[3]. The strength of the dynastic principle[4] insured for them both a peaceful succession, but their youth[5] and their personal incapacity prevented them from playing more than a puppet's rôle in the realms of which they were the titular heads.

It is not, therefore, with them, but rather with the men who ruled in their names that we are chiefly concerned. In the period[6] immediately following the death of Theodosius, the real power in the West was concentrated in the hands of Stilicho, the Magister Utriusque Militiae; in the East, in those of Rufinus, the Praefectus Praetorio Orientis. Their conflicting interests soon resulted in a struggle; this struggle furnished the theme for Claudian's invective, In Rufinum.

---

[1]For the general history of the period, see Stein, 295-387 (especially 345-353); Seeck, 135-390, 484-593 (especially 263-279, 544-552); Bury, 1-173 (especially 106-115); Mommsen Stil., *passim;* Lot, 217-275. The sources are fully set forth by Dr. Stein and by Seeck. One who controls these sources, and the secondary works just mentioned will find little need to consult earlier discussions. The masterly works of Tillemont and Gibbon will, of course, always be read with interest.

The history of this period is also discussed, with special reference to Claudian, in Fargues, 57-127. M. Fargues's studies were not available to me until this chapter was completed in essentially its present form; any resemblances between my account of Rufinus and his (Fargues, 65-76) are therefore due to the use of identical sources. In my notes to this chapter I have added references to M. Fargues's opinions only where I differ from them.   [2]The title *Augustus* was granted to Arcadius in 383, to Honorius ten years later. See Seeck, 265.24-25, 267.16-18, 545.   [3]See Stein, Map of the Roman World in 390 (the maps in Dr. Stein's book are to be found in the pocket attached to the inside back cover). On the question of Eastern Illyricum (the dioceses of Dacia and Macedonia), see Appendix B, pages 32-34, below.   [4]See Seeck, 264.7-265.17.   [5]At the time of Theodosius's death, Arcadius was eighteen, Honorius eleven, years of age.

[6]January 17-November 27, 395.

[7]

Introduction

As is natural in an invective, the central figure of the poem is the person against whom the author inveighs; a careful examination of Rufinus's career and of the historical events surrounding it is therefore necessary for a complete understanding and appreciation of Claudian's vehement attack.

Flavius Rufinus[7] was a native of Gaul[8], from the town of Elusa, in Aquitania (the modern Eauze, in the Department of Gers, formerly part of the Province of Gascony[9]). Our ancient sources make no specific mention of his age at any point in his career, but it is probably safe to place the date of his birth between 350 and 365[10]. Of his early life we know nothing[11], nor is it possible to fix with certainty the date of his arrival at the Eastern Court[12]. The *terminus post quem* is of course the establishment of Theodosius's Court at Constantinople, November 24, 380[13]. A letter of Libanius, which Seeck[14] assigns with great probability to 388, shows Rufinus in a position of influence at the Court, and mentions details which make it seem that he was then

---

[7]My account of Rufinus's career is based, except where it is otherwise stated, on the sources indicated in Seeck Ruf., *passim*. I am, of course, indebted to Seeck for the interpretation of much of the source material.

[8]See IR 1.137–139. In Chron. 1.650 § 34 Rufinus is called *Bosporitanus*. This description is undoubtedly due to a hasty conclusion based on the locality of his later eminence. Zosimus 4.51.1, Κελτὸς τὸ γένος, supports Claudian, IR 1.123–141. Additional support is given by the fact that Rufinus understood Greek only imperfectly: Libanius, Epistles 784, addressing Rufinus, says τὴν <ἐμὴν> ἐπιστολὴν ἔφασκέ <τις>... γενέσθαι τοῖς διγλώσσοις ἆθλον..., σοῦ μὲν κελεύοντος ἑρμηνεύειν, τῶν δὲ ἐξελεγχομένων. Compare 1025 ἐγώ τέ σε θηράσω πάλιν κεκτημένον μὲν τὴν ἡμετέραν φωνήν, φάσκοντα δὲ οὐκ ἔχειν.

[9]See V. de Saint-Martin, Nouveau Dictionnaire de Géographie Universelle, 2.125 (Paris, Hachette, 1884).   [10]Claudian, IR 1.140–141, makes Megaera ask him *frustra... iuventae consumis florem?* This expression would seem most appropriate for a man in his twenties. The scene is supposed to take place a short while before Rufinus's arrival at the Eastern Court, and therefore within a few years, in either direction, of 385 (see pages 8–9, below). After his death, Symmachus (Epistles 6.14.1: see note 95, below) calls him *praedo annosus*, an expression which I take to mean 'a brigand of many years' standing' rather than 'an aged brigand'. The description of Philostorgius (quoted in note 113, below), which refers to the period just after Theodosius's death, best fits a man in his early prime.   [11]It is impossible to discover what germ of truth, if any, is concealed in Codinus, 74 (= Migne Gr. 157.548–549), Ῥουφίνου τοῦ σκυτοτόμου. The passage might, of course, refer to some mercantile enterprise or employment of Rufinus before he made a place for himself at Court. Tillemont, Histoire des Empereurs, 771, col. 1.29–48 (Paris, Robustel, 1701), calls it an error; no other modern scholar discusses the matter.   [12]See Appendix A, pages 27–31, below.   [13]Seeck Regesten, 255.   [14]Seeck Liban. 449.31–450.7, 451.1–2.

Magister Officiorum[15]. The letters of Symmachus which I have assigned to 389-390[16] lend support to this theory. For 390 we have definite proof: Rufinus is addressed as Magister Officiorum in a Constitution issued at Milan on March 8 of that year[17]. His position in 388 was certainly a lofty one. If we allow a few years for him to have reached that eminence, we are justified in placing Rufinus's entry into the Court at Constantinople scarcely later than 385, and perhaps a few years earlier[18].

From 389 on, his career becomes easier to trace. The letters of Symmachus[19] indicate that Rufinus was with Theodosius at Rome in 389, and that he returned with the Court to Milan in September of that year[20]. His presence at Milan in 390 is attested by the part which he played in the rift between Theodosius and Ambrose, Bishop of Milan.

Early in 390, a mob at Thessalonica had murdered one of Theodosius's officials. As a punishment, the Emperor ordered a promiscuous slaughter of the inhabitants, in which over 7000 were killed[21]. According to Theodoret[22], Rufinus had encouraged Theodosius in this brutal act. When the news reached Milan, Ambrose excluded Theodosius from the sacraments of the Church. Rufinus pleaded with the Bishop to forgive the Emperor. Though he was at first unsuccessful, he seems to have been instrumental in bringing about a reconciliation, thereby gaining the friendship of the Bishop[23] and the gratitude of Theodosius[24]. We may conclude from this episode that Rufinus,

---

[15]Libanius, Epistles 784 <ὁ ἀνὴρ> ἦν δὲ ἄρα τῶν σῶν, καί τι τῶν πολλῆς σπουδῆς ἀξίων ἀφῖκτο διοικήσων.... δέομαί σου τοῖς παρ' ἡμῶν πρέσβεσι πάντα ἀποφῆναι λεῖα. The man mentioned in the first sentence is probably one of the *agentes in rebus* (see Seeck Ruf., 1190.8-14), who were under the control of the Magister Officiorum. The latter also had charge of embassies and delegations. For a full discussion of the powers and the position of the Magister Officiorum, see Boak-Dunlap, 1-160, and compare Stein, 172.17-173.3.

[16]See Appendix A, pages 27-31, below.   [17]Cod. Theod. 10.22.3.

[18]Symmachus's expression *praedo annosus*, however interpreted (see note 10, above), would, in conjunction with Claudian, IR 1.140-141, lead us to assign an early date to this event.   [19]Especially Symmachus, Epistles 3.84. See page 31, below.   [20]Seeck Regesten, 277.   [21]Stein, 322.7-323.10.   [22]Theodoret, Historia Ecclesiastica, 5.18.10, makes Ambrose say to Rufinus, τοσαύτης... μιαιφονίας γενόμενος σύμβουλος...οὔτε ἐρυθριᾷς οὔτε δέδιας. Compare Palanque Ambr., 428-429.   [23]Ambrose, Epistles 52 (= Migne Lat. 16² [1866].1214-1215), Rufinus ... factus est ... praefectus praetorio. ... gaudeo ... illi, ut amico .... But see note 40, below. For Rufinus's part in the Thessalonica episode, see also Palanque Ambr., 227-250, 428-429.   [24]Seeck believes (Seeck Ruf., 1190.33-35) that Rufinus's consulship in 392 was a reward for this service. See also Seeck, 232.10-32.

though he was not baptized until some years later[25], was at this time a devout Christian. He had probably been so all his life[26].

Naturally, Rufinus did not lack rivals in the Emperor's favor. The letters of Symmachus give evidence of Rufinus's attempts to oust these rivals[27], and to replace them with men more to his liking[28]. He seems to have been on particularly bad terms with Theodosius's military leaders, a fact which, as we shall see, contributed largely to his final downfall. In 391[29], after the Court had returned to the East[30], Rufinus became engaged in a quarrel with the Generals Timasius and Promotus. Feeling reached such a pitch that Promotus actually laid violent hands on Rufinus[31]. As a consequence, the latter engineered the removal of Promotus from the Court, having him sent to Thrace, where he was killed by barbarians. According to Zosimus[32], Rufinus hired the barbarians to kill Promotus in ambush. Claudian makes no such charge, but he does state that, when Stilicho, a close friend of Promotus, attempted to avenge the latter's death, he was prevented by Rufinus from doing so[33]. The enmity between Stilicho and Rufinus which occasioned Claudian's In Rufinum was thus of long duration[34].

In 392 Rufinus received the high honor of a consulship, with Arcadius as his colleague[35]. When he became consul, the Praetorian Prefecture was held by the pagan Tatianus[36], whose son Proculus[37], likewise a pagan, was Prefect of the City of Constantinople[38]. Rufinus used his influence with Theodosius to bring about the removal from office of both Tatianus and Proculus, and was himself appointed Praefectus Praetorio Orientis[39] in the former's place[40]. Rufinus

---

[25]See page 15, below. [26]The Pilgrim Salvia was his sister (Seeck Ruf., 1189. 19–23). [27]Symmachus, Epistles 3.81.2, 3.85, 3.86.2. See Seeck Ruf., 1189. 68–1190.7. Seeck puts these activities much earlier (see Appendix A, pages 27–31, below). [28]Symmachus, Epistles 3.81, 87, 89, 90. See preceding note. [29]Shortly before Rufinus's consulship (Zosimus, 4.52.1; Seeck Ruf., 1190.30–32). [30]Seeck Regesten, 279. See Appendix C, pages 35–37, below, for a discussion of M. Palanque's theory that Rufinus spent part of 391 and of 392 as the Magister Officiorum of Valentinian II at Vienne.

[31]Zosimus 4.51 ὁ δὲ <Πρόμωτος> . . . ἐπήγαγε τῷ προσώπῳ τὴν χεῖρα καὶ ἔπληξεν. [32]Ibidem. [33]IR 1.316–320. Compare CS 1.94–115, and Bury, 107, note 3. [34]Claudian (CM 30.232–236) accuses Rufinus of having conspired to cause Stilicho's death. [35]Seeck Regesten, 279–281. [36]Seeck Liban., 285.10–288.29, especially 287.35–288.26; Pauly-Wissowa Zw. 4.2463.53–2467.26.

[37]Seeck Liban., 248.10–250.32, especially 250.11–29. [38]Seeck Regesten, 279–280. [39]The title appears also in the form *Praefectus Praetorio Per Orientem*. For the extent of his jurisdiction, see the map to which reference is made in note 3, above. On the question of the dioceses of Dacia and Macedonia, see Appendix

Chapter I [11] 229

entered upon his new office sometime between June 30 and September 10, 392[41], and held the position until his death. The frequent Constitutions[42] addressed to him as Praetorian Prefect are of great service to scholars in their efforts to reconstruct the history of the last three years of his life.

The power and the prestige of the office to which Rufinus thus attained were enormous: in the fourth, fifth, and sixth centuries the Praetorian Prefect[43] ranked as the highest official of the Empire[44]. The Praetorian Prefecture was in origin a military command[45]; it was instituted as such by Augustus. In the course of time, however, the Praetorian Prefect acquired so many and such extensive civil functions that, when Constantine[46] found it politic to deprive the office of its military powers, it remained as the foremost civil magistracy.

B, pages 32–34, below. [40]Seeck, 178; Stein, 327. The letter of Ambrose in which this event is mentioned (see note 23, above) is interesting as evidence of the extent to which Rufinus was feared and disliked: . . . Rufinus . . . ex magistro officiorum factus est in consulatu praefectus praetorio: ac per hoc plus posse coepit, sed tibi iam nihil obesse; est enim aliarum praefectus partium. Quam gaudeo vel illi, ut amico, quia honore auctus, invidia levatus est: vel tibi, ut filio, quia liberatus es ab eo, quem tibi graviorem iudicem arbitrabare . . . . See Appendix C, pages 35–37, below, for a discussion of M. Palanque's interpretation of this letter. [41]Seeck formerly (Seeck Ruf., 1190.46) held the limits to be June 30 (Cod. Theod. 12.1.127) and August 26 (Cod. Theod. 8.6.2). The dating of the latter, however, has been brought into doubt by a consideration of Cod. Just. 11.25.2, addressed to Tatianus. See Seeck Regesten, 97.18–42; for a Table of Indictions, see Willy Liebenam, Fasti Consulares, 125 (Bonn, Marcus and Weber, 1909). The date September 10 is obtained from Cod. Theod. 11.28.1.

[42]They are listed chronologically in Seeck Ruf. 1190.19, 48–50; 1191.15–22, 39–41; 1193.9–11. The dates should be checked with the Tables in Seeck Regesten, 427–446. In cases of discrepancy the reader should refer to the proper date in Seeck Regesten, 159–423, where much additional material will be found which is of great value for chronology. [43]On the suitability of this term as a translation of *praefectus praetorio*, see Stein, 53–54. [44]For the Praetorian Prefecture in general, see Stein, 178–182; Stein Verwalt., 364–380; Seeck Regesten, 141–149; Cosenza, 10–16; Bethmann, 46–58; Bury, 25–29. For a thorough study of the Praetorian Prefect's *officium* (administrative staff) see Stein Offic., *passim*. For the chronology of the Praetorian Prefects from 324 to 423, see Palanque, *passim;* see also Dr. Stein's extensive review of Palanque in Byzantion 9 (1934), 327–353, and M. Palanque's rejoinder to this review, *ibidem*, 703–713. Where it is possible, I have illustrated the various powers of the Praetorian Prefect by citing Constitutions addressed to Rufinus; for other citations, see the works just mentioned, particularly those of Dr. Stein and of Professor Cosenza. [45]Kromayer, 504–506; Stein, 53–56. [46]Probably in 317 or 318: Seeck, Rh. Mus. 49 (1894), 211–214; Stein, 178–179.

The Praetorian Prefect, alone of the officials of the Empire, was empowered to act on occasion in the Emperor's stead (*vice sacra*)[47]. His power was exercised in various fields.

(1) In his judicial capacity, he sat as a court of last resort[48]: from his decisions there was no appeal[49]. At most, a petition (*supplicatio*)[50] to the Emperor might result in his ordering a reconsideration (*retractatio*) by the Praetorian Prefect[51]. No more than one such *supplicatio* was permitted[52].

(2) His rulings had the force of law, provided that they did not conflict with Imperial legislation[53].

(3) He had control of the Post and the Post Roads[54]; here, however, his acts were subject to the scrutiny of the *agentes in rebus* (in the service of the Emperor) under the Magister Officiorum[55].

(4) He had charge of the erection and the maintenance of public buildings (except those in Rome and Constantinople)[56].

(5) He supervised the industrial corporations and guilds, and regulated the prices of commodities (in the latter function he was sometimes supplanted by the Emperor himself)[57].

---

[47]Stein Offic., 46; see note 49, below.
[48]Concurrently with the Emperor, of course. [49]Cod. Theod. 11.30.16 (331): A praefectis autem praetorio, qui soli vice sacra cognoscere vere dicendi sunt, provocari non sinimus, ne iam nostra contingi veneratio videatur. [50]Bethmann, 338–341. [51]The *supplicatio* was usually delayed until the Prefect who had given the original decision was succeeded by another, so that the *retractatio* might not fall under the jurisdiction of the former (Bethmann, 340). Viewed in the light of this practice, the provisions of Cod. Theod. 9.42.14 (recited in full, page 26, below) stand out in their full iniquity. [52]Cod. Just. 1.19.5 (365): Si quis adversus praefectorum praetorio sententias duxerit supplicandum victusque fuerit denuo, nullam habebit licentiam iterum super eadem causa supplicandi. [53]Cod. Just. 1.26.2 (235): Formam a praefecto praetorio datam, etsi generalis sit, minime legibus vel constitutionibus contrariam, si nihil postea ex auctoritate mea innovatum est, servari aequum est. [54]Stein Offic., 62, 64. Compare Cod. Theod. 8.5.52: IDEM AAA. <= Valentinianus, Theodosius et Arcadius> RUFINO P<RAEFECTO> P<RAETORI>O. Faciendarum evectionum licentiam in excidium publici cursus a comitibus Aegyptiaci limitis usurpatam sublimis magnitudo tua auctoritate huius legis inhibebit .... See also Cod. Theod. 8.5.40, 8.6.2. [55]Cod. Theod. 6.29.8. [56]Compare Cod. Theod. 15.1.31: IDEM AAA. <= Theodosius, Arcadius et Honorius> RUFINO P< RAEFECTO> P<RAETORI>O. Si qui iudices perfecto operi suum potius nomen quam nostrae perennitatis scribserint <sic>, maiestatis teneantur obnoxii .... Quod si quis in administratione positus sine iussu nostro aedificii alicuius iacere fundamenta temptaverit, is proprio sumptu et iam privatus perficere cogetur quod ei non licuerat inchoare.... [57]Compare Cod. Theod. 13.5.23: IDEM AAA. <= Valentinianus, Theodosius et Arcadius> RUFINO P<RAE-

Chapter 1 [13] 231

(6) He had administrative control over the institutions of higher education[58].

(7) He administered a considerable part of the public revenues, and had a treasury of his own[59].

(8) He acted as Paymaster General for all military and civil employees, and as Quartermaster General for the army; the accounts of the military leaders were sent to him twice yearly for his approval[60].

(9) He had charge of the conscription of recruits for the army[61].

(10) Through the *scrinium armorum* he controlled the magazines of arms (but not the manufactories of arms: see page 20, below)[62].

(11) He regulated the transportation of the grain-supply[63].

(12) He nominated the Provincial Governors, and supervised their actions. He acted as judge in matters which concerned them, and could remove them at his discretion[64]. He was also empowered to appoint their successors, pending the Emperor's approval. Even the Vicars, and officials of similar rank, whose power Diocletian[65] had meant to be concurrent with that of the Praetorian Prefect, were subordinated to the latter in the course of the fourth century[66].

(13) In addition to these specific duties and powers, the Praetorian Prefect was charged with the general maintenance of peace and order[67].

The outward magnificence of the Praetorian Prefect corresponded to his almost regal[68] position. Johannes Lydus[69] tells us that he wore

FECTO> P<RAETORI>O. Solos navicularios a vectigali praestatione immunes esse praecipimus. Omnes vero mercatores teneri ad supra dictam praestationem in solvendis vectigalibus absque aliqua exceptione decernimus . . . . See also Cod. Theod. 13.5.22; 15.7.11, 12; 10.19.13.   [58]Cod. Theod. 13.3.15; Libanius, Epistles 1025 'Ρουφῖνος . . . εἶπεν . . . πρὸς τοὺς ἐπὶ τῷ παιδεύειν καθημένους.

[59]Cod. Theod. 1.5.5 (compare 11.6.1); 11.1.23; 11.25.1 (see Pauly-Wissowa 3.832.26–32); 11.7.14 (see Pauly-Wissowa 4.370.13–376.44; Seeck Regesten, 281 [April 12]); Bury, 337, note 3.   [60]Cod. Theod. 7.4.20. See also Grosse, 158–160, 243; Stein, 61–62.   [61]Cod. Theod. 7.13.10, 13; Grosse, 158–160.

[62]Stein Offic., 71.   [63]Cod. Theod. 13.8.1; Cassiodorus, Variae, Praefatio 6 Ab hac <sede praefecti praetorio> victus quaeritur sine temporis consideratione populorum . . . .   [64]Cod. Theod. 1.7.2; Synesius, Epistles, 127 (= Migne Gr. 66.1508 B): see Seeck Liban., 150.3–16.   [65]Stein Verwalt., 377, § IV.

[66]Cod. Theod. 1.15.4 (362); 1.13.1 (394: see Seeck, Pauly-Wissowa 4.659–661); 1.5.12 (399).   [67]Cassiodorus, Variae 6.3.6 licet aliae dignitates habeant titulos praefinitos, ab ista paene totum geritur quicquid in imperio nostro aequabili moderatione tractatur.   [68]Lydus, De Mag. 2.5 τὸ μὲν περίβλεπτον τῆς ἀρχῆς . . . μόνῳ τῷ σκήπτρῳ παραχωροῦν . . . ἱκανοῖς ἄν τις καταλάβοι γνωρίσμασι: 'There are sufficient indications by means of which one may comprehend the glory of this office, which is subordinate only to the throne'. Compare *ibidem*, 2.9.

[69]*Ibidem*, 2.13–14.

a 'purple' tunic (παραγώδης), girdle, and cloak (μανδύης); the cloak reached to his knees (the Emperor's was full-length). A golden pen-case (θῆκαι or καλαμάριον)[70] weighing one hundred pounds, a large silver inkstand, and an imposing chariot[71] are also mentioned among his appurtenances. On his approach to the Palace, the highest military officials received him on bended knee[72]; the Emperor himself went on foot to greet him[73].

Our ancient authorities speak of the Praetorian Prefecture as an office of immense power and importance[74], and modern scholars are in substantial agreement with them[75]. Dr. Stein does not hesitate to apply the term Prefectorial Constitution ("Präfekturenverfassung"[76], "constitution préfectoriale"[77]) to the form of government which intervened between the Principate and the Byzantine system of Themes[78]. Dr. Stein also maintains that, in relation to the Empire as a whole, the great power of the Praetorian Prefect within a limited territory acted as a force of decentralization and later of disunion[79].

It must always be remembered that the power of the Emperor, who appointed and discharged Praetorian Prefects at his pleasure, could act as a mighty curb on their activities; but, even under a strong and vigilant ruler, the possibilities of extortion inherent in every one

---

[70]Professor Cosenza (15) errs in calling the case a *calamus;* compare Suetonius, Claudius 35 theca calamaria. [71]Compare Cassiodorus, Variae 6.3.2 ipse carpentum reverendus ascendit (*ipse* refers to the Biblical Joseph, whom Cassiodorus regards as the prototype of the Praetorian Prefect). Compare also Lydus, De Mag. 2.14. [72]Compare IR 2.443-444 supplex nobilitas. [73]Lydus, De Mag. 2.9. [74]*Ibidem,* 2.7 ... καθάπερ ὠκεανός τις τῶν πραγμάτων τῆς πολιτείας ἐστίν, "ἐξ ἧσπερ <read οὗπερ> πάντες ποταμοὶ καὶ πᾶσα θάλασσα <Iliad 21.196>". Further on in the same section Lydus refers to the Praetorian Prefecture as ἐκείνη ἡ ἀληθῶς ἀρχὴ τῶν ἀρχῶν (compare note 68, above). Compare Cassiodorus, Variae 8.20.3 nec immerito <praefectus praetorio> a legibus nostris pater provinciarum, pater etiam praedicatur imperii, *ibidem*, Praefatio 6 cui dignitati occupationes publicae velut pedisequae semper assistunt; Cod. Theod. 11.5.3 sedis excelsae; Ammianus 14.1.10 celsae potestates; Symmachus, Relationes 31.2 praetorianae sedis ... praecelsae potestatis; Sidonius, Epistles 2.3.1 amplissimae dignitatis; Synesius, De Providentia 1.2, 2.4 (= Migne Gr. 66.1213, 1272) τὴν μεγάλην ἀρχήν. I have not been able to locate a remark which Bury attributes to Eusebius, to the effect that the relation of God the Son to God the Father is like that of the Praetorian Prefect to the Emperor (see John Bagnell Bury, History of the Later Roman Empire[1], 1.43 [London, Macmillan, 1889]). [75]Bury, 27-28; Glover, 117-119; Seeck Regesten, 144.41-42; 147.40; 149.25-27; Stein Offic. 1. [76]Stein Verwalt., 379.3. [77]Stein, Byzantion 8 (1933), 312.34. [78]For a rather adverse discussion of this concept of Dr. Stein, see W. Ensslin, Gnomon 6 (1930), 498-500. [79]Stein, 179.20-180.7; Stein, Byzantion 8 (1933), 312.32-33.

of the Praetorian Prefect's functions afforded great opportunities for self-enrichment. Under Theodosius, who was given to trusting his favorites implicitly[80], and more particularly under a weakling like Arcadius[81], the opportunities of Rufinus in this direction must have been unlimited.

There is every indication that he used them abundantly. Rufinus's lust for wealth, a favorite theme of Claudian[82], is well attested by several independent sources[83]. When he began to accumulate his property it is of course impossible to determine, but in the last years of his life he was a very wealthy man. He possessed a magnificent estate in a suburb of Constantinople called Drys ('The Oak'). Here he erected a splendid mansion, and a shrine in which he placed relics of Saint Peter and Saint Paul. Nearby he built himself a magnificent mausoleum. Connected with the shrine was a monastery to which he invited monks from Egypt. It was at the dedication of the shrine that, already Praetorian Prefect, he received the sacrament of baptism, in the presence of numerous dignitaries of the Church[84]. The

---

[80]Seeck, 177.11–178.32; Stein, 296.8–10, 297.4–7.

[81]Seeck Regesten, 148.28–29. [82]IR 1.100-4, 186f., 220-2, 296, 299, 305; 2.99, 134–136, 410, 436–439, 498–501. [83]Symmachus, Epistles 6.14.1 praedonis annosi; Hieronymus, Epistles 60.16 abscissa manus dextera <Rufini> ad dedecus insatiabilis avaritiae; Zosimus, 5.7.6 τῷ ἀπλήστῳ (see also Philostorgius 11.3, where the same expression is found); Zosimus 5.1.1–4, 5.2.1; Eunapius, Fragment 63 (= FHG 4.42) ἀμετροκάκου πλεονεξίας; Lydus, De Mag. 2.10 'Ρουφῖνον τὸν ἐπίκλην ἀκόρεστον; Cod. Theod. 9.42.14 quae Rufinus ... quoquo pacto possedit. Even if the Greek writers draw from identical sources, we have evidence of at least four independent lines of tradition: Symmachus, Hieronymus, the Greek authors just mentioned, and the Theodosian Code. After all due allowance is made for hostile propaganda, Cod. Theod. 9.42.14 (quoted in full, page 26, below) is by its very existence an indication of Rufinus's wide-spread plundering (per omnes provincias). Whether Cod. Theod. 2.9.3 is another indication of the same activity is doubtful. Seeck (Ruf., 1189.51–52) seems to accept the interpretation of that Constitution advanced, but not wholly espoused, by Gothofred. 1.156 col. 1.42–col. 2.46. According to this view, the Constitution in question, which imposes harsh penalties upon those who would repudiate a sworn agreement, was a device on the part of Rufinus to prevent his victims from instituting proceedings to recover property which he had extorted. This is not impossible; it is also conceivable, however, that the enactment was another expression of Rufinus's religious fervor (compare Gothofred. 1.156 col. 2.46–end, and Cod. Theod. 9.7.8, 16.10.12). The interpretation of the motive behind such laws is often open to question; thus Cod. Theod. 7.3.1 may be regarded either as a laudable step toward a merit system, or as a device to justify Rufinus's promotion of his newly appointed favorites over the heads of men who had spent years in the service (see page 10, above). [84]For the practice of long-delayed baptism, see Augustine, Confessions 1.10.18. He censures the practice with vigor.

estate later became famous under the name of *Rufinianae;* it was occasionally used as a royal residence, and was at one time in the possession of the great Belisarius[85]. Whether Rufinus also founded a monastery in the City of Constantinople itself is a moot question[86]. He is known to have contributed on at least one occasion to a charitable religious enterprise[87].

In spite of the great devotion to orthodox Christianity which these activities indicate, Rufinus had found it politic to be on friendly terms with pagans who stood high in Theodosius's favor[88], particularly with Symmachus, Flavianus the Elder[89], and Libanius[90]. For the latter he may have had a sincere admiration[91].

The praises which are showered on Rufinus in the letters of Symmachus[92] and Libanius[93] are in strange contrast with what we hear of him from other sources[94]. But these letters were either addressed to Rufinus, or were intended to be brought to his notice. The hypocrisy of Symmachus is unmasked by his own words about Rufinus after the latter's death[95]. Libanius's encomiums of Rufinus also seem to have been dictated by self-interest[96]. A sentence in one of Libanius's letters betrays none too high a standard of honesty in regard to commendations which are spoken in the hearing of the person praised, or

---

[85]The sources pertaining to *Rufinianae* are collected in Seeck Ruf., 1189.25–42. Especially valuable is the article there cited of J. Pargoire, in Byzantinische Zeitschrift 8 (1899), 429–477. M. Pargoire absolutely identifies Drys with *Rufinianae* (429–430), and our Rufinus with the founder of the estate (431–435.26). His remarks on the various structures (435.27–458.7) and on Rufinus's mansion (458.8–460.24) are interesting and apparently well-founded. His identification (460.25–477) of the site of *Rufinianae* with the modern Djadi-Bostan (Jadi Bostan) is accepted by Bury (87.18).   [86]Pauly-Wissowa Zw. 1.1184.60–1185.2; Pargoire, in Byzantinische Zeitschrift 8 (1899), 430.   [87]Callinicus, Vita Sancti Hypatii 65.3. Seeck, in my opinion, generalizes too freely (Ruf., 1189.52–55) from this single instance. It should be noted that Rufinus was only one of several contributors ('Ρουφῖνος καὶ οἱ λοιποὶ τῶν μεγάλων . . . πλοῖα γεμίζοντες σίτου καὶ ὀσπρίων ἔπεμπον αὐτῷ).   [88]Seeck, 268.21–24.   [89]See Appendix A, pages 27–31, below.   [90]Libanius, Epistles 784, 1025, 1029. See also 900, 949, 972, 1028 b.   [91]Libanius, Epistles 1028 b.   [92]Symmachus, Epistles 3.81–91. See Appendix A, pages 27–31, below.   [93]See note 90, above.   [94]On the adjective μακάριος applied to Rufinus by Callinicus (Vita Sancti Hypatii 66.17), see Pargoire, Byzantinische Zeitschrift 8 (1899), 431.16–432.14.   [95]Symmachus, Epistles 6.14.1 Dubitare vos video, an Rufini poenam secuta sit etiam publicatio facultatum. Fides praesto est imperialibus signata praeceptis; et tamen praedonis annosi <see note 10, above> merita pendentibus non fuit ambigendum quod spolia orbis desideraret aerarium.   [96]In Epistle 949 Libanius is evidently trying by flattery to induce Rufinus to help him solve some difficulty (. . . σοῦ δέομαι λύσιν τινὰ τοῖς παροῦσιν εὑρεῖν).

Chapter 1

are likely to reach that person's ears[97]. It is a cause for regret that Libanius did not write his projected panegyric on Rufinus[98]; a comparison with the In Rufinum would have been most instructive.

It must be noted that no friendly relations between Rufinus and pagans need be dated later than 393[99], and it is probable that he broke off connections with them once his position was assured. Of Rufinus's orthodox zeal we shall have occasion to speak later in connection with his legislation directed against heretics and pagans.

Soon after his accession to the Praetorian Prefecture, Rufinus arranged to have his ousted predecessor Tatianus[100] brought before a court over which he himself presided. Proculus, the son of Tatianus, took to flight, and could not be found. Rufinus feared above all to have him at large. He therefore set about persuading Tatianus to have his son come back and stand trial, promising under oath that they would both receive pardons and be highly favored at Court. Deceived by these assurances, in which Theodosius seems to have joined[101], Tatianus persuaded Proculus to return, and they were both put on trial. In spite of all assurances, Proculus was sentenced to death, and beheaded, before his father's eyes[102], on December 6, 393[103]. According to Zosimus[104] an Imperial pardon arrived too late to save him. Tatianus was also sentenced to death, but at the last moment[105]

---

[97]Libanius, Epistles 1029 οὐ γὰρ ἴσον οὐκ ἴσον, ὁρώμενον φίλον ἐπαινεῖν, καὶ διὰ τοσούτου τοῦ μέσου, καὶ συνόντα κοσμεῖν ἢ πολὺ διεστηκότα. I translate this passage, which is difficult to understand apart from its context: 'It is one thing to praise a friend and adorn him with compliments to his face, when he is present; it is quite another thing to do so when he is separated from us by a great distance'. See also Pauly-Wissowa 12.2538.19–28; Seeck Liban., 250.3–11, 447.7–13. [98]See Libanius, Epistle 1029. Compare 1025 . . . τοῦτο καὶ νῦν δέομαι δοθῆναί μοι· τίνων τε ἐγένου γονέων, καὶ τὰ ἐν τοῖς διδασκαλείοις ἔργα δι' ὅσων πεπόρευσαι. . . . διδάσκειν οὐκ ὀλίγα δύναιτ' ἂν ὁ φίλος Θεόφιλος, ἀλλ' οὐδεὶς οἷος σὺ περὶ τῶν σῶν γένοιτ' ἂν ἡμῖν διδάσκαλος, and what follows, to the end of the letter. [99]Seeck, Liban., 446.35–447.6; Appendix A, pages 27–31, below. [100]See page 10, above. [101]Zosimus, 4.52 ὁ Ῥουφῖνος . . . ἀπάτῃ τὸν πατέρα καὶ ὅρκοις, καὶ τὸν βασιλέα πείσας ὑποφῆναι καὶ αὐτῷ καὶ τῷ παιδὶ μεγίστας ἐλπίδας. See also Eunapius, Fragment 59 (= FHG 4.40).

[102]Claudian (IR 1.246–247) is borne out by Asterius, Homily 4 (= Migne Gr. 40, 224 D) <ὁ ἐξ ὑπάρχων ἐκεῖνος (= Tatianus)> ἐπεῖδε τὸν ἑαυτοῦ παῖδα ἀποτμηθέντα τῆς κεφαλῆς. Zosimus makes no mention of this, and seems to imply that Tatianus was banished before his son's execution (4.52). [103]So the Chronicon Paschale, Chron. 1.245 (year 393), followed by Seeck (Ruf., 1190.51, 66). Dr. Stein (327.15–28) apparently places the trial and execution in 392. [104]4.52.

[105]Asterius, Homily 4 (= Migne Gr. 40.224 D–225 A) . . . εἶτα καὶ αὐτὸς τὴν ἐπὶ θανάτῳ ψῆφον ἐδέξατο, καὶ τῆς σχοίνου προσαχθείσης ἤδη τῷ στόματι, φιλανθρωπία βασιλικὴ ἐκώλυσεν ἐνεργῆσαι τὸν δήμιον.

Theodosius commuted his sentence to confiscation of his property, and banishment to his native province of Lycia. The Emperor, probably at the instigation of Rufinus, went so far as to deprive all Lycians of their dignities and of the right to hold office. This absurd and iniquitous law was not repealed until after Rufinus's death[106]. In the course of the year 393 laws were promulgated invalidating the official acts of Tatianus and Proculus[107].

In the Spring of 394[108], Theodosius set out for the West, at the head of all the troops he could muster, to crush the usurper Eugenius. With him as Generals went Rufinus's bitter enemies, Timasius and Stilicho[109]. The latter, a Vandal by birth, stood high in the favor of the Emperor, who had given him the hand of his favorite niece in marriage[110]. Theodosius left the seventeen-year-old Arcadius in Constantinople to rule the East in his absence[111], under the guidance of Rufinus. Actually, this was tantamount to placing Rufinus in full charge. Philostorgius, who knew them both by sight[112], depicts vividly the contrast between the tall, vigorous, and intelligent-looking Prefect, and the puny, dull, and somnolent Emperor[113].

[106]Compare Cod. Theod. 9.38.9 (August 31, 396): IMPP. ARCAD<IUS> ET HONOR<IUS> AA. AD CAESARIUM P<RAEFECTUM> P<RAETORI>O. Devotissimae nobis provinciae Lyciae priorem famam . . . renovari censemus . . . . Teneant honores suos . . . ; habeant praeteritas dignitates sperentque sui devotione venturas. Nec unius viri inlustris Tatiani tantum valuerit temporalis offensio teterrimi iudicis inimici ut adhuc macula in Lycios perseveret . . . . It is not easy to believe that the original edict depriving the Lycians of their rights and dignities had no other motive than that of manifesting the Emperor's displeasure against the Lycian Tatianus. I have been unable, however, to find a clue as to any other motive. [107]Cod. Theod. 9.42.12, 13; 11.1.23; 12.1.131; 14.17.12. The inscription CIL 3.737 (= Dessau 821) shows that the name of Proc<u>lus was effaced. It was later restored. [108]Stein, 333.34–35. Seeck's expression "gegen ende des Sommers" (Seeck Ruf., 1191.23) is apparently an error; see Gerard Rauschen, Jahrbücher der Christlichen Kirche, 409–410 (Freiburg, Herder, 1897); Seeck Regesten, 283–284, entries for April 29 and May 20. [109]Zosimus, 4.57.2. [110]For Stilicho's career, see Pauly-Wissowa Zw. 3.2523.4–2524.27. See also Mommsen Stil., *passim*; Bury, 106.9–107.7; Stein, 346.25–349.5. Seeck has a distinct bias against Stilicho (see note 145, below, and Seeck, 617, col. 1.1–3). [111]Stein, 333.35–334.1; Seeck Regesten, 285 (May 30, 394–January 9, 395). Arcadius had been Augustus since 383. See note 2, above. [112]Joseph Bidez, Philostorgius Kirchengeschichte, Preface 107.29–108.9 (Leipzig, Hinrichs, 1913); Bury, 107, note 1. [113]Philostorgius, 11.3 εὐμήκης δὲ . . . ὁ 'Ρουφῖνος ἦν καὶ ἀνδρώδης· καὶ τὴν σύνεσιν αἴ τε τῶν ὀφθαλμῶν κινήσεις ἐδήλουν καὶ τῶν λόγων ἡ ἑτοιμότης· ὁ δὲ 'Αρκάδιος βραχὺς τῷ μεγέθει καὶ λεπτὸς τὴν ἕξιν καὶ ἀδρανὴς τὴν ἰσχὺν καὶ τὸ χρῶμα μέλας· καὶ τὴν τῆς ψυχῆς νωθείαν οἵ τε λόγοι διήγγελλον καὶ τῶν ὀφθαλμῶν ἡ φύσις, ὑπηλῶς τε καὶ δυσαναφόρως αὐτοὺς δεικνῦσα καθελκομένους.

Just before Theodosius's death in January, 395, the boy Honorius, who had received the title of Augustus in 393, arrived at Milan, having been summoned post-haste from Constantinople[114]. It was Theodosius's intention that Honorius should rule in the West, but the boy stood in even greater need of a protector than did his older brother. In this strait Theodosius turned to Stilicho[115], whom he had raised to the rank of Magister Utriusque Militiae, the supreme military command[116]. The dying Emperor placed Honorius under Stilicho's direct protection, and it is not hard to believe that he bespoke[117] for both his sons the loyal services of a man who now controlled the combined armies of the East and the West[118]. The bond between Stilicho and the young Emperors was merely one of duty and sentiment: Mommsen has shown that there could be no question of a legal guardianship[119].

Theodosius has been severely criticized for leaving in control of the Empire two men, Stilicho and Rufinus, whom he knew to be bitter enemies[120]. It seems to me, however, that he had very little choice[121]. At any rate, he could count on the loyalty of Stilicho to the Imperial house, of which, as the Emperor's nephew by marriage, he was in a sense a part[122]. Theodosius may have intended his dying injunction as a plea to Stilicho not to allow his personal differences with Rufinus to endanger the safety of either son[123].

With the death of Theodosius, Rufinus reached the highest point in his career. Yet there is every reason to believe that he aimed even higher. The accusation of having attempted to become Emperor is one which is often unjustly brought against a fallen statesman; in the case of Rufinus, this charge[124] is supported not only by its inherent

---

[114]Stein, 336.3–11. In addition to the sources there cited, see Sozomen, 7.29.4.
[115]See note 110, above.
[116]Stein, 346.21–24; 368.15–18. I cannot agree with Seeck (Pauly-Wissowa Zw. 3.2523.37–41) that Cod. Theod. 7.4.18, 7.9.3 prove that Stilicho was Magister Utriusque Militiae in 393: the formula *Abundantio, Stilichoni et ceteris comitibus et magistris utriusque militiae* is ambiguous. But Cod. Theod. 1.7.3 proves that he held the office in 398, and there is no reason to believe that it was not conferred by Theodosius. Compare Zosimus 4.59, and see Birt Pr. 27.10–12, Bury, 106, note 3.   [117]Ambrosius, De Obitu Theodosii 5 nihil habebat novum . . . nisi ut eos praesenti commendaret parenti < = Stilichoni >.   [118]Seeck, 272.8–13.
[119]Mommsen Stil., 101.15–102.9. See also F. Martroye, Bulletin de la Société Nationale des Antiquaires de France, 1916, 202.26–206.   [120]Seeck, 267.24–31.
[121]The military leaders were all hostile to Rufinus (Seeck 269.5–25). Yet it was necessary to bind the army to the new régime. On the other hand, the peremptory removal of Rufinus would only have led to chaos.   [122]Zosimus, 4.57; Claudian CM 30, *passim*.   [123]Compare Birt Pr. 28.19–20.   [124]Seeck Ruf., 1191.59–63

probability, but also by several external indications. Through his own success in displacing Tatianus, Rufinus had shown the Court how a Praetorian Prefect might be dislodged; he must have feared that many were eager to follow the example which he had thus set. He had every cause for alarm in the ascendancy which Stilicho had gained in the West; whoever would be appointed by Stilicho to lead back the Eastern troops would be Rufinus's enemy. Moreover, because of his purely Latin name, and his birth in a thoroughly Romanized province, Rufinus did not suffer from the handicap of an Arbogastes, who had to be content with the rôle of king-maker[125], or from that of a Stilicho, who, a Vandal himself, could hope for a diadem only for his Roman-born son[126]. If his religion taught Rufinus any scruples, justification for his usurpation was not far to seek; accession to the throne would only be formal recognition of the position which he held in fact. Besides, no harm need come to Arcadius if all went well; even Claudian accuses Rufinus of no more than of wishing to be the young Emperor's colleague[127].

We have thus far been discussing the inherent probability of the view that Rufinus intended to become Emperor; several overt acts of Rufinus point in the same direction. The statement of Claudian[128] that Rufinus maintained an armed guard of barbarians is supported by an independent source[129]; a private army is the age-old weapon of the usurper. Rufinus's action in taking over the control of the manufactories of arms[130], which were usually in charge of the Magister Officiorum, and which he himself had supervised in that capacity[131], is also suspicious. He planned to have his daughter become the bride of Arcadius; the most obvious purpose of such an alliance is that of securing for his cause an appearance of legitimacy. Before

---

lists the passages in which this charge is made. Some of the passages, of course, go back to a common source. [125]Stein, 325.28–326.4. [126]Stein, 347.2–5; Seeck, 271.13–26. [127]IR 2.314–315 iubeatque coactus <Arcadius> in partem mihi regna dari; 383 participem sceptri, socium declaret honoris. [128]IR 2.76–77. See my note on IR 2.76. [129]Chron. 1.650, § 34 Chunorum, quo fulciebatur, praesidio. [130]This is the most natural interpretation of Lydus, De Mag. 2.10 (= 3.40). It is the interpretation given by Seeck (Ruf., 1192.1–5; compare Pauly-Wissowa 6.1926.14–30), accepted by Grosse (104.15–17), and supported with discussion by Professor Boak (Boak-Dunlap 87; compare Boak-Dunlap 36–37. It is not necessary to suppose, however, that Rufinus took over all the functions of the Magister Officiorum. The interpretation of Dr. Stein, which would assign the change described by Lydus to 341 or 346, is ingenious, but unconvincing (see Zeitschrift der Savigny-Stiftung für Rechtsgeschichte, Romanistische Abteilung 41 [1920], 220.10–223.25). [131]Cod. Theod. 10.22.3.

Chapter I

this plan matured, however, he seized a chance to play the rôle of defender of the Imperial dignity. Lucianus, the Comes Orientis, who had once been a protegé—for a consideration[132]—of Rufinus, had offended Eucherius, an uncle of the Emperor. Rufinus rushed with all speed to Antioch, and had Lucianus beaten to death. It may have been this absence of Rufinus, as Bury[133] suggests, which gave his enemies a chance to perfect a scheme which was to ruin his hopes of an Imperial alliance.

Eutropius, a wily old eunuch, Grand Chamberlain of the Palace[134], whose ambition matched that of Rufinus, had succeeded in interesting the young Emperor in the beautiful Eudoxia. She was the daughter of Bauto, a Frank, who had been Magister Militum under Gratian and Valentinian II, and had held the consulship in 385. After her father's death, she had been brought up in the house of the sons of Promotus, for whose death, as we have seen[135], Rufinus was held responsible. Eutropius showed Arcadius a portrait of Eudoxia, and contrived by glowing descriptions to raise his ardor to such a pitch that he determined to marry her. Elaborate preparations were made, but Eutropius's plans were so well concealed that everyone, including Rufinus, believed that the bride was to be the latter's

---

[132]Zosimus 5.2 οὗτος ἐχρῆτο προστάτῃ 'Ρουφίνῳ, τὰ τιμιώτατα τῶν ὄντων αὐτῷ κτημάτων εἰς ἐκεῖνον μετενεγκών. [133]Bury, 109, note 2. Zosimus (5.2) places this event after the death of Theodosius. Bury rightly maintains that Seeck (Ruf., 1190.51–56; compare Fargues 70.27–71.8) errs in assigning the journey in question to 393. A letter of Libanius (1025: see Seeck Liban., 465, § 492 b, 447.20–39) proves that Rufinus made a hasty journey to Antioch in 393, but there is no reason to believe that it was his only quick journey to that city. The language of Libanius does not in the least suggest a grim errand of vengeance; on the contrary, it shows Rufinus engaged in discussions with the city councils (βουλάς) and with the officers of the councils (τοὺς ὑπὲρ ταύτας), with the superintendents of education (τοὺς ἐπὶ τῷ παιδεύειν καθημένους), and even with ladies of the city (γυναῖκες . . . λόγων τυχοῦσαι πρᾴων). He did some hasty sight-seeing (τῷ πᾶσαν <τὴν πόλιν> ἐθέλειν εἰδέναι ἐν βραχεῖ, τὸ μὴ πᾶσαν ἰδεῖν κεκωλυμένος <'Ρουφῖνος>), and his doings and his speeches were the talk of the town (λόγος τε εἷς μόνος ἐν τῇ . . . πόλει 'Ρουφῖνος . . ., τί μὲν ἔπραξε, τί δ' εἶπεν). Contrast with the last quotation what Zosimus (5.2) says about the aftermath of Lucianus's death: ἡ μὲν πόλις ἐπὶ τῷ παραλόγῳ τοῦ δράματος ἐδυσχέραινεν ὁ δὲ τιθασσεύων τὸν δῆμον βασιλικὴν ᾠκοδόμει στοάν. It might be argued that Libanius is camouflaging the grim truth behind all his chatter, but on that principle anything might be proved. Furthermore, an act of such swift and despotic cruelty is much more likely after Theodosius's departure from Constantinople than before it; the Emperor had probably learned his lesson in the matter of the slaughter at Thessalonica (see page 9, above). [134]See Boak-Dunlap, 161–324. [135]See page 10, above.

daughter. It was only at the last moment that the truth became known. Arcadius married Eudoxia on April 27, 395.

This was Rufinus's first set-back. Even if he had not previously had a well-defined intention of becoming Emperor, this display of strength on the part of his enemies must have shown him the advisability of securing the protection which only the 'purple' could give.

However, he had not permitted these temporal concerns to interfere with his spiritual duties. The interval of ten months between the death of Theodosius and that of Rufinus is marked by no less than six Constitutions directed against pagans and heretics, particularly the latter[136]. On March 13, 395, Rufinus withdrew[137] from those who subscribed to the Eunomian heresy the testamentary rights which Theodosius had recently restored to them[138]. This measure was followed by others of equal or greater severity[139], the last of them preceding his death by just three days[140].

It is interesting to note in this connection that, in the spirit of the pagan literature of the period, Claudian nowhere alludes to these activities of Rufinus, or to the fact that he was a Christian. If Claudian's major poems were all that survived from the fourth century, we should have difficulty in believing that Theodosius and Honorius adhered to the Christian faith, or, indeed, that Christianity existed at the time.

As we have seen[141], the Eastern troops which Theodosius had led against Eugenius were still in Italy at the time of Theodosius's death. The Eastern provinces were thus left undefended, and soon became the prey of invading hordes. The Winter of 394-395 had been unusually severe. Barbarians poured over the frozen surface of the Danube[142], and down through the passes of the Caucasus. In addition, the Eastern part of the Empire was faced by a revolt of its Gothic allies. These had fought with Theodosius against Eugenius. Their losses had been very heavy, and they had every reason to believe that they had been deliberately placed where the fighting was hard-

---

[136]Seeck, 274.18-23, advances the interesting theory that Rufinus's severity toward heretics was the result of a belief that the barbarian invasions which we shall presently describe were the punishment meted out by God for the leniency of Theodosius.   [137]Cod. Theod. 16.5.25.   [138]Cod. Theod. 16.5.23 (June 20, 394). Compare 16.5.17. On 16.5.27 see Seeck Regesten, 101.31-33.   [139]Cod. Theod. 16.5.26; 2.8.22; 16.10.13; 16.5.28.   [140]See Cod. Theod. 16.5.29. This provides for the dismissal of all public officers of heretical leanings, and their banishment from Constantinople.   [141]See page 18, above. For the remainder of this discussion, in addition to Seeck Ruf., 1192.8-1193.35, see Stein, 349.28-352.26.   [142]Claudian, IR 2.26-28, is supported by Philostorgius 11.8, and Caesarius, Dialog. 1.68

est[143]. After the battle of the River Frigidus, they returned to the East before the rest of the army. There, further irritated by the omission of customary subsidies[144], they revolted. Under the leadership of Alaric they advanced, spreading devastation, to the very gates of Constantinople[145].

The rumor that Rufinus had invited the barbarians to attack the Empire out of sheer malice is, of course, absurd, but that it gained credence is a proof of Rufinus's unpopularity[146]. His private guard of barbarians lent color to the charge, and it may be that he made attempts to raise a mercenary army from among the invaders.

We have only Claudian's[147] word for it that Alaric spared Rufinus's estates during his raids, and that Rufinus, dressed in Gothic costume, made frequent visits to Alaric's camp. It seems very likely that Rufinus engaged in colloquies with Alaric in an attempt to recall him to his allegiance, or at any rate to induce him to withdraw from the city.

At this time a controversy was going on between Rufinus and Stilicho which concerned the territorial division of the Empire between Arcadius and Honorius. The bone of contention was Eastern Illyricum, comprizing the dioceses of Dacia and Macedonia[148]. Bury has pointed out the value of this territory as a recruiting-ground for the Roman armies[149]. Before 379, the dioceses in question had been subject to the ruler of the West. In that year, Gratian had ceded them to Theodosius, but this arrangement was not of long duration. Probably in 380, or soon thereafter, the territory was again made part of the Western division of the Empire, and so matters stood at the death of Theodosius. It was the contention of Rufinus, however, that Arcadius, as the older brother and the senior in point of accession to the throne, was entitled to Eastern Illyricum, since without it his share of the Empire would not represent a fair division. Stilicho,

---

(= Migne Gr. 38.936). [143]Claudian mentions this policy with approval (6H 221–222): et duplici lucro committens proelia vertit in se barbariem, nobis utrimque cadentem. See Schmidt, 425.10–14. [144]Schmidt, 426, note 5. On Alaric's position, see *ibidem*, 425.27–427.16. [145]Seeck, 272.17–274.15, maintains that Stilicho encouraged Alaric to lead his Goths against Constantinople. His purpose, according to Seeck, was to force Arcadius to summon him to defend the East. This theory is typical of Seeck's bias against Stilicho. [146]Seeck Ruf., 1192.10–16; Schmidt, 427.23–28. [147]IR 2.70–85. M. Fargues (73.12–19) rejects the reading *exceptis . . . suis* in IR 2.71. But *praeceptis . . . suis*, which he prefers, would certainly imply that Rufinus's estates were untouched: this seems to destroy the point of M. Fargues's argument. [148]See Appendix B, pages 32–34, below. [149]Bury, 111.10–26.

on the other hand, appealed to Theodosius's last wishes, in which he had sanctioned the perpetuation of the *status quo*[150].

Rufinus was without military resources to enforce his claim, but he seems to have persuaded Alaric to march into the debated territory. In this way he probably hoped to manoeuvre Stilicho into a position more favorable to his own interests; at any rate, this removed Alaric from territory which was Arcadius's undisputed possession.

When Stilicho became aware of Alaric's movements, he marched to meet him at the head of the combined forces of the East and the West. It was then Spring (395)[151]; we cannot determine how much time elapsed before Stilicho came face to face with Alaric in Thessaly. It may be, as Dr. Stein[152] suggests, that Stilicho was delayed in Western Illyricum by the necessity of crushing invaders. It is possible, however, that he arrived in Thessaly within a short time after his departure from Italy, but confined himself to Fabian tactics while he awaited the results of negotiations with Rufinus's enemies at the Eastern Court. We can judge from the sequel that he was in communication with a leader of the anti-Rufinian faction, most probably Eutropius[153]. But matters were brought to a head by the action of Rufinus himself. He persuaded Arcadius to send Stilicho a message commanding him to dispatch the Eastern troops to Constantinople, and to remove himself forthwith from a section of the Empire which Arcadius claimed for his own.

Though Stilicho probably had not foreseen any such move on Rufinus's part, he was not slow to see how it could be turned to his own advantage. By obeying the mandate of the senior Augustus, Stilicho could use the Eastern army to rid himself of Rufinus, and at the same time lay at the latter's door the responsibility for the devastation which Alaric was sure to spread upon Stilicho's departure[154].

On the other hand, to disobey would have placed Stilicho in the position of a rebel, and would have been most repugnant to his notions, doubtless sincere, of loyalty to the Imperial house[155]. With Rufinus out of the way, Stilicho must have felt, the matter of territorial division could easily be adjusted. He probably had not taken

---

[150]Ambrose, De Obitu Theodosii 5 Theodosius . . . de filiis . . . nihil habebat novum quod conderet quibus totum dederat . . . .; Olympiodorus, Fragment 3 (= FHG 4.58) . . . Στελίχων μετεκαλέσατο <'Αλάριχον> ἐπὶ τῷ φυλάξαι 'Ονορίῳ τὸ 'Ιλλυρικὸν (τῇ γὰρ αὐτοῦ ἦν παρὰ Θεοδοσίου τοῦ πατρὸς ἐκνενεμημένον βασιλείᾳ). [151]Claudian, IR 2.101–104. [152]Stein, 351.3–8.
[153]Zosimus, 5.8.1 Εὐτρόπιος δὲ πρὸς πάντα Στελίχωνι συνεργήσας . . . .
[154]Claudian, IR 2.186–196. [155]Compare Baynes, Journ. Rom. Stud. 12

into account the boundless ambition and guile of the eunuch Eutropius.

Later, when the Eastern Court refused to give up Dacia and Macedonia, Stilicho could claim, and actually did claim, that he had never really renounced a territory which belonged to Honorius by his father's will[156], but had merely acted to save Arcadius from an evil adviser who might have dragged him down in his own ruin[157].

Stilicho therefore obediently withdrew at the head of the Western troops, leaving Thessaly at the mercy of Alaric. The Eastern army marched to Constantinople under the command of the Goth Gainas, who seems to have received instructions from Stilicho. When the troops reached the vicinity of Constantinople, arrangements were made for Arcadius and Rufinus to meet and review them at the plain of the Hebdomon[158].

It is not difficult to believe Claudian's statement[159] that Rufinus expected this day to witness his elevation to the rank of Augustus. The place[160] and the spirit of the occasion must have seemed most favorable for a *coup*. Rufinus surely had nothing to gain by waiting until his enemies at Court should have a chance to win over the troops. Philostorgius[161] tells us that Rufinus expected his imposing appearance to influence the soldiers in his favor. But the day was fated to turn out otherwise.

On November 27, 395[162], when the troops had assembled on the plain, Arcadius and his Court went out to greet them. In the course of the review, Rufinus, who stood near the Emperor, was gradually surrounded by soldiers. At a signal from Gainas, they drew their swords and plunged them into his body[163]. The soldiers seem to have

---

(1922), 213.16–214.11. See, however, page 34, below. [156]Mommsen Stil., 102, note 4, 111.9–112.11; Stein Verwalt., 354.5–12; Stein, 380.20–28. [157]Claudian, CS 2.78–87, IR 2.165–168. [158]On the Hebdomon, see Van Millingen, 316–341; Glück, 3.38–4.4. See also my note on IR 2.350. [159]IR 2.297, 311–316, 340–347. M. Fargues (68, note 4), on the other hand, believes this accusation "particulièrement invraisemblable". He goes on, "en effet, s'il avait fait une pareille tentative, il aurait auparavant négocié quelque temps avec les principaux officiers, après leur retour, et il aurait fait des largesses aux troupes pour se les concilier". This reasoning does not seem to me cogent. Rufinus, already on bad terms with the military officers (see page 10, above), had little to hope for from negotiations with Stilicho's hand-picked subordinates; even Eutropius thought it best to pretend for a time to work in concert with Stilicho (see note 153, above, and Fargues, 65, note 2). Moreover, Rufinus's distribution of a donative to the soldiers *before* his elevation would have unmasked his plot prematurely. [160]The Hebdomon was often used for coronations. See Van Millingen, 328.3–334.6. [161]11.3.

[162]Socrates, 6.1.4. [163]The account given by Chron. 1.650 § 34 (interficitur

felt a violent animosity toward this civilian who had aspired to rule over them, for they proceeded to hack his body into pieces.

According to Claudian[164], the populace came streaming out of the city and gave vent to its hatred by trampling Rufinus's remains into the dust. His head was mounted on a pole, and was carried back to the city in mock solemnity. His severed right hand was carried from door to door with the words, 'Give to the insatiable!'[165] Such was the wretched end of His Sublime Highness, Flavius Rufinus, V. C., Praetorian Prefect of the East[166]. The contrast between the manner of his life and that of his death is striking, and Claudian knew how to bring it out in all its grim irony[167]. Rufinus's wife and daughter sought refuge in a Church; they were permitted to go to Jerusalem, where they lived in poverty. Rufinus's vast possessions were confiscated, but an Imperial law forbade their former owners to reclaim them. This Constitution[168] is worth reciting in full as a fitting conclusion to an account of Rufinus's career:

IMPP. ARCAD⟨IVS⟩ ET HONOR⟨IVS⟩ AA. CAESARIO P⟨RAEFECTO⟩ P⟨RAETORI⟩O. Serenitatis nostrae provisione solita commonemus, ut ea, quae Rufinus quondam, cum viveret, quoquo pacto possedit, in eodem statu interim maneant, nec quisquam sibi post eius obitum spontaneam vindicandi tribuat potestatem. Nam qui transacto tempore siluit ac Rufinum tenere concessit, fiscum quoque nostrum sine praeiudicio possideat patiatur. Hoc edictis propositis per omnes provincias praecipimus divulgari, quo cuncti sciant iacturam se perpessuros graviorem totiusque rei familiaris periculum, nisi ante praeceptum nostrum manus ab his, quae Rufinus vivus possederat, voluerint abstinere. DAT. ID. FEB. CONSTANTINOP⟨OLI⟩ ARCAD⟨IO⟩ IIII ET HONOR⟨IO⟩ III AA. CONSS.

Chunorum, quo fulciebatur, praesidio superato) is not supported by any other source. It may be that his body-guard of barbarians attempted to come to his rescue, but was overpowered.   [164]IR 2.427–432. The people of Constantinople must have hated him as an oppressor of foreign tongue. See Seeck, 267.33–268.2, and note 8, above. The belief that Rufinus was responsible for the barbarian invasions was probably another cause for the animosity of the people against him. See note 146, above.   [165]Philostorgius 11.3 τὴν ... κεφαλὴν ... τεμόντες ... ἐπὶ καμάκου δ' ἀναρτήσαντες πανταχοῦ περιέθεον. καὶ τὴν δεξιὰν ... τεμόντες ... περιῆγον, "Δότε τῷ ἀπλήστῳ" λέγοντες. Compare Hieronymus, Epistles 60. 16.11 Rufini caput pilo Constantinopolim gestatum est et abscissa manus dextra ad dedecus insatiabilis avaritiae ostiatim stipes mendicavit. The other sources agree with this account: see Seeck Ruf., 1193.1–5.   [166]Compare the following expressions in Constitutions addressed to Rufinus: Cod. Theod. 8.5.52 sublimis magnitudo tua, 12.1.139 sublimis auctoritas tua, 11.25.1 vestrae celsitudinis, 8.4.18 culminis vestri (on the use of *vester*, see Stein Verwalt., 372.34–373). Compare also CIL 9.6192 ARCADI ... E⟨T⟩ FLAVI RVFINI· VV· CC· ⟨= virorum clarissimorum⟩ ....   [167]IR 2.440–453.   [168]Cod. Theod. 9.42.14 (February 13, 396). See note 51, above.

APPENDIX A

Rufinus, Symmachus, and Flavianus

In his article in Pauly-Wissowa on Rufinus, Seeck[169] states that Rufinus was an influential official at the Eastern Court as early as 382. He bases this statement on the correspondence between Symmachus and Rufinus[170], in which the chronologically significant point is the mention of the elevation, first to the Quaestura Sacri Palatii, and then to the Praetorian Prefecture, of Virius Nicomachus Flavianus (Flavianus the Elder)[171]. The dating of these letters, and therefore the dating of Rufinus's entry into official life, depend entirely upon the date of Flavianus's first appointment as Praetorian Prefect. This date, in turn, must be determined in large part by the chronology and the attribution of various Constitutions of the Theodosian Code.

Cod. Theod. 7.18.8 and 9.29.2, ostensibly addressed to Flavianus the Elder as Praetorian Prefect, seem to fix his first tenure of this office in 383. On this basis alone, Seeck assigned the date 382-383 to Symmachus, Epistles 3.81, 90, and hence to Rufinus's appearance as a high official[172]. Dr. Stein[173], however, has pointed out that, on the basis of Seeck's own later studies, this entire chronology is subject to revision. It is evident that a new date for Flavianus's first Prefecture would change the chronology of Symmachus's letters to Rufinus, and would invalidate the statement with which this Appendix begins. It is therefore important for us to examine these matters closely.

To begin with, Seeck now[174] attributes Cod. Theod. 7.18.8 and 9.29.2 with great probability to the *Younger* Flavianus[175] as Proconsul of Asia[176]. On this basis, he removes the supposed Prefecture of 383 from the career of the Elder Flavianus, with whom we are concerned, and places his first Praetorian Prefecture in 390-391(392?)[177]. In this he is followed by Dr. Stein[178].

---

[169]Seeck Ruf., 1189.61–1190.5.   [170]Symmachus, Epistles 3.81–91.

[171]*Ibidem*, 3.81, 90. All references to 'Flavianus' are to be taken as denoting the Elder Flavianus, unless the Younger Flavianus is specifically named.   [172]Seeck Symm., Pr. 138–139. See note 169, above. For Symmachus, Epistles 2.22.2, see note 190, below.   [173]Stein, 323, note 1.5–6.

[174]Seeck Regesten, 116.28–31; 261 (February 27, 383). The Regesten (1919) represent this great scholar's last word on these problems. See note 182, below.

[175]Pauly-Wissowa 6.2511.24–2513.35.   [176]*Ibidem*, 2511.65–2512.12.   [177]Seeck Regesten, 453, col. 3.23–26; see also 260–261 (January–April 383).   [178]Stein, 310, note 1.3–5, 321.15–18; Stein Verwalt., 371. See also Palanque, 68.22–69.24, 76–78.

[27]

Two other bodies of evidence bear upon the correctness of the date 390 for the first Prefecture of Flavianus:

A. The inscriptions CIL 6.1782, 1783 (the pertinent portions are quoted below).

B. The chronology of the relations among Rufinus, Symmachus, and Flavianus.

In my opinion, the reasons for which I shall set forth below, the inscriptions rather favor, and certainly do not refute, the date 390. In a consideration of point B, I have found a confirmation of that date which, I believe, has not been noticed hitherto.

A. The Inscriptions

CIL 6.1782 (=Dessau 2947) Virio Nicomacho Flaviano V. C., Quaest⟨ori⟩, Praet⟨ori⟩, Pontif⟨ici⟩ Maiori, Consulari Siciliae, Vicario Africae, Quaestori intra Palatium, Praef⟨ecto⟩ Praet⟨orio⟩ Iterum, Co⟨n⟩s⟨uli⟩ Ord⟨inario⟩, Historico Disertissimo, Q. Fab⟨ius⟩ Memmius Symmachus V. C., Prosocero Optimo.

CIL 6.1783 (=Dessau 2948) Nicomacho Flaviano, Cons⟨ulari⟩ Sicil⟨iae⟩, Vicar⟨io⟩ Afric⟨ae⟩, Quaest⟨ori⟩ Aulae Divi Theodosii, Praef⟨ecto⟩ Praet⟨orio⟩ Ital⟨iae⟩ Illyr⟨ici⟩ et Afric⟨ae⟩ Iterum, virtutis auctoritatisq⟨ue⟩ senatoriae et iudiciariae ergo reddita in honorem filii Nicomachi Flaviani Cons⟨ularis⟩ Camp⟨aniae⟩, Procons⟨ulis⟩ Asiae, Praef⟨ecti⟩ Urbis Saepius, nunc Praef⟨ecti⟩ Praet⟨orio⟩ Italiae Illyrici et Africae . . . .

Certain points concerning the *cursus honorum* of the Elder Flavianus are undisputed: (1) he held the Quaestura Sacri Palatii under Theodosius[179], shortly before his *first* Prefecture (whenever the latter took place)[180]; (2) he was Praefectus Praetorio Italiae Illyrici et Africae in 390–391[181] (this is admitted by all; the question at issue is whether he had held this office *previously*); (3) at the time of his death in 394, he was Consul and Praetorian Prefect under the usurper Eugenius[182].

The problem is to bring into harmony with these facts the wording of the two inscriptions, both of which were erected after Flavianus's death. CIL 6.1783, a public inscription, in the recital of his *cursus*

---

[179]CIL 6.1783, quoted above.   [180]Symmachus, Epistles 3.90.   [181]See note 177, above.   [182]Pauly-Wissowa 6.2510.7-13. Seeck's words, "dritten Praefectur", correspond to his theory at the time (1909) when these words were written. In 1883 Seeck (Symm. Pr. 117.15-16) had held that Flavianus was Praetorian Prefect continuously from 389 to 394, but at the time that he wrote this article in Pauly-Wissowa 6 he had repudiated (Pauly-Wissowa 6.2509.59–2510.10) this theory, which is wholly untenable (see Seeck Regesten, 274–284, covering the period in question).

honorum entitles him Praefectus Praetorio Iterum. It must be noted that no mention is made of his consulship[183]. It is evident that the reason for the omission is the fact that he received it from a usurper. The question then arises, Was there in this inscription a similar suppression of Flavianus's last prefecture, and does the use of *iterum* therefore imply *two* prefectures under Theodosius[184]? Light is thrown on this question by the private inscription, CIL 6.1782, set up by a relative of Flavianus. Here the latter's consulship *is* mentioned, and yet he is again entitled Praefectus Praetorio Iterum. Now the relative who mentions Flavianus's discredited consulship could have no reason to ignore a third prefecture held under the same auspices, if there had been such a third prefecture. Therefore, so far as CIL 6.1782 is concerned we are justified in concluding that Flavianus had held the prefecture only twice, first under Theodosius in 390–391, and again under Eugenius in 394.

Returning now to the public inscription, we find that the Younger Flavianus is there entitled Praefectus Urbis Saepius. This strange formula[185] obviously contains a covert reference to the Younger Flavianus's Prefecture of the City under Eugenius[186], and shows that the author of the inscription was not altogether certain of how to treat the iteration of offices held under legitimate Emperors *as well as* under the usurper. The Elder Flavianus's consulship, held only under the usurper, could be ignored entirely; but, inasmuch as Flavianus had been raised to the Prefecture by Theodosius himself, it seems not unreasonable that the use of *iterum* was considered permissible in spite of the circumstances under which the second prefecture was held.

To sum up, I hold that the inscriptions CIL 6.1782, 1783 may support, and cannot be said to disprove, the theory that Flavianus the Elder held the Praetorian Prefecture only twice, first, under Theodosius in 390–391 (392?), perhaps with honorary iteration[187], secondly, under Eugenius in 394.

---

[183]M. Palanque (Byzantion 9 [1934], 707.23–24) is in error when he states that "Les mêmes inscriptions <CIL 6.1782, 1783> font état de son consulat, conféré par l'usurpateur en 394". The public inscription, CIL 6.1783, does *not* mention his consulship. This error invalidates M. Palanque's entire argument.   [184]Dr. Stein (Byzantion 9 [1934], 333.19–335.2) explains the use of *iterum* here by the theory of an honorary and purely formal iteration conferred on Flavianus by Theodosius subsequent to 390. This theory, if correct, only strengthens the main point, that Flavianus's first prefecture began in 390. M. Palanque's attempt at refutation of Dr. Stein's theory (Byzantion 9 [1934], 707.17–32), is invalid: see the preceding note.   [185]Compare Pauly-Wissowa 6.2512.25–27.   [186]*Ibidem*, 13–21.   [187]See note 184, above. If Dr. Stein's the-

B. The Chronology of the Relations among Rufinus, Symmachus, and Flavianus

We turn now to the correspondence between Symmachus and Rufinus. Two letters of Symmachus (Epistles 3.81, 90) addressed to Rufinus refer to the elevation of Flavianus the Elder to the Quaestura Sacri Palatii, and to his appointment as Praetorian Prefect, which soon followed. These letters give evidence of a certain degree of familiarity between Symmachus and Rufinus, even after all allowances are made for the former's epistolary exuberance. If the letters were written in 382–383, when, we may ask, did Rufinus and Symmachus become acquainted? If Rufinus had moved in high official circles at Rome *before* he went to the East, Claudian, in a poem intended for those very circles, could scarcely have represented him as being brought from an obscure Gallic town to the Court of Theodosius[188]. Nor is there any evidence that Symmachus ever visited Constantinople[189].

If, on the other hand, we accept the theory that Flavianus's first prefecture began in 390, and if we date Symmachus's letters accordingly, the manner in which the letters thus dated conform to what we know of Rufinus from other sources furnishes a striking confirmation of the theory.

There is nothing in Claudian or in the other sources[190] which stands in the way of our believing that Symmachus first became acquainted with Rufinus when the latter was in Rome with Theodosius, June 13–August 30, 389[191]. During his stay at Rome, Theodosius spent much of his time with the leading pagan officials and literary men of the old Capital[192]. Prominent among these were Symmachus and Flavianus. Rufinus thus had ample opportunity to make their acquaintance.

It may well be, moreover, that the brilliant Flavianus, during these festive months, made a lasting impression on the mind of the

---

ory is correct, we must believe (1) that the public inscription ignores the bestowal of the Praetorian Prefecture by Eugenius, and (2) that the private inscription ignores the Emperor's honorary iteration! I have purposely refrained from considering the possibility of a scribe's or stone-cutter's error. If account should be taken of that possibility, and an attempt be made to restore the inscriptions conjecturally, such restorations would, of course, be inadmissible as evidence.

[188]IR 1.170–172.   [189]See Pauly-Wissowa Zw. 4.1146.30–1158.24.   [190]There is no need to identify the *vir excellentissimus* of Symmachus, Epistles 2.22.2 with Rufinus; he may have been any prominent official who had furthered the appointment of the Younger Flavianus to the Proconsulship of Asia.   [191]Seeck Regesten, 275, 277.   [192]Stein, 321.

Appendix A

Emperor. A summons to Milan[193] late in 389 or early in 390 would be a natural outcome of such an impression, for men of literary ability were highly prized by the Emperors as Quaestores Sacri Palatii[194].

I therefore consider 3.84 to be the first letter of the correspondence between Symmachus and Rufinus, written shortly after Theodosius's departure from Rome in August, 389. If we accept this view, and regard this letter as the first, the other letters follow naturally. The acknowledgment (3.81) of Rufinus's letter announcing the appointment of Flavianus to the Quaestura belongs late in 389, or, more probably, early in 390. We may place 3.90 later in the same year, 390, or in the early part of 391. Epistle 3.82 probably belongs, as Seeck maintains[195], to the Autumn of 389, and therefore follows 3.84. Epistles 3.85 and 87 seem to have been written while Theodosius was at Milan[196]. To the same period belong 3.86 and 89. We know nothing of the circumstances surrounding the latter, but there is no reason to doubt that the Younger Flavianus joined his father at the Court of Theodosius at Milan, where the good offices of Rufinus might be of great advantage.

The remaining letters, 3.83, 88, and 91, contain no statements by which they can be dated, but I consider it more than likely that they were written during Rufinus's stay in Italy, 389-391[197].

For the reasons set forth in this Appendix I have rejected Seeck's statement[198] that Rufinus was an influential official at the Eastern Court as early as 382[199]. I am sure that Seeck himself would have rejected this view had he lived to revise his edition of Symmachus and his account of Rufinus in the light of his later researches.

---

[193]The language of Symmachus, Epistles 2.8 is more appropriate to a journey from Rome to Milan than to a voyage from Rome to Constantinople. Nowhere do the letters referring to Flavianus's Quaestura give the impression that he is at the other end of the Mediterranean. It must also be noted that placing Flavianus's Quaestura in 389-390 instead of in 382-383 disposes of several problems which troubled Seeck when he wrote the article on Flavianus in Pauly-Wissowa 6: (1) the presence of Flavianus at his Campanian villa in Autumn, 383 (Pauly-Wissowa 6.2509.8-17); (2) Flavianus's lack of influence in the Senate at that time (*ibidem*, 17-20); and (3) Flavianus's official position in 389-390 (*ibidem*, 24-42).   [194]Pauly-Wissowa 6.2508.43-46; compare Symmachus, Epistles 2.8.2.   [195]Seeck Symm. Pr. 138, last line.   [196]*Ibidem*, 139.   [197]See page 9, above.   [198]See note 169, above.   [199]M. Fargues (67, note 2) still adheres to this date.

APPENDIX B

The Partition of Illyricum

The question of the date or the dates of the partition of Illyricum between the Eastern and the Western division of the Empire has caused considerable discussion, and several theories about the matter have been advanced.

(1) Mommsen[200] and Bury[201] imply that, after Gratian ceded Dacia and Macedonia to Theodosius in 379[202], these dioceses remained permanently under Eastern control. This theory must be discarded, since it does not take account of Cod. Theod. 1.32.5[203], or of Cod. Theod. 16.1.3 and 11.13.1[204], which show that the territory in question was subject to the sovereign of the West at various times subsequent to 379.

(2) Seeck[205] agrees that Gratian ceded the dioceses to Theodosius in 379, but he further holds[206] (A) that they were handed back to Valentinian II, the Western Emperor, in 383, and (B) that Theodosius reassigned them to Arcadius during his last illness. The first of these theories (A) is refuted as to the date by Dr. Stein[207], who cites Cod. Theod. 16.1.3 and 11.13.1. For our purposes, however, the exact date of the recession of Dacia and Macedonia to the West is not of prime importance: it is certain that they were handed back before July 29, 386, the date of Cod. Theod. 1.32.5. Dr. Stein makes out a very good case for the year 380 as the date of the recession[208].

As for the second theory (B), I have found nothing in the sources, nor does Seeck cite anything, to indicate that Theodosius made any territorial changes during his last illness. On the contrary, Ambrose[209] gives the directly opposite impression[210].

(3) Dr. Alföldi[211] holds that there was only one partition of Illyri-

---

[200]Mommsen Stil., 102.13–103.12.   [201]Bury, 110.25–111.5.   [202]Sozomen, 7.4.1.   [203]Seeck, Rh. Mus. 69 (1914), 37, note 3; Seeck Regesten, 270–271.
[204]Stein Verwalt., 347, 364. I cannot, however, agree with Dr. Stein (Verwalt., 348.33–349.4) that CIL 6.1777–1779 are admissible in evidence: the word *Illyricum* in these inscriptions is too ambiguous, as Dr. Stein himself (Verwalt., 365) recognizes.   [205]Compare e. g. Seeck, 125.10–12.   [206]Rh. Mus. 69 (1914), 37–38.   [207]Stein Verwalt., 364–365.   [208]*Ibidem*, 347.26–348.10.   [209]See note 150, above.   [210]Professor Baynes (Journ. Rom. Stud. 12 [1922], 211, note 1) represents Seeck's view inexactly: compare Professor Baynes's words, "on the tyrant's defeat", with Seeck's, "während seiner < = Theodosius's> tödlichen Krankheit". See also Journ. Rom. Stud. 12 (1922), 216.41–44.   [211]Andreas Alföldi, Der Untergang der Römer-

Appendix B [33] 251

cum, and that it took place in 389. Dr. Stein[212] refutes this theory, which, on the one hand, does not take account of Sozomen 7.4.1 and Cod. Theod. 9.35.4, and, on the other, seeks to establish a date, 389, for which, so far as I can see, there is no foundation in the sources.

(4) The reconstruction of Dr. Stein[213], which I follow[214] in the main, seems to me to be entirely consistent with the sources, and to explain satisfactorily many otherwise confusing details in the events of 395–408. This view of Dr. Stein has been adopted by Dr. Kornemann[215], M. Palanque[216], and, apparently, by Dr. Schmidt[217].

(5) On the other hand, Dr. Stein's theory is rejected by Professor Baynes[218]. But, if I follow his remarks, the latter does not seem to have understood Dr. Stein's theory fully; besides, he assigns considerable weight to an *argumentum e silentio* which seems to me to lack cogency.

Professor Baynes[219] represents Dr. Stein as holding that Stilicho surrendered the territory in question to Eutropius in 396. Dr. Stein nowhere puts forth such a theory. He does say[220] that in *395* Stilicho acknowledged the senior Augustus as ruler of Eastern Illyricum. Professor Baynes seems to have misunderstood a preliminary statement of Dr. Stein's exposition[221].

Further, as I have said, the *argumentum e silentio* which Professor Baynes puts forth[222] is by no means conclusive. Briefly, it is that, had Stilicho renounced Eastern Illyricum, Claudian would have praised him for his generous sacrifice in the interest of domestic accord. On the contrary, I believe that Claudian's silence in respect to this cession of territory is quite understandable. As a matter of policy, Claudian upholds the essential unity of the Empire under Stilicho's protection[223]. From this point of view, the shifting of a strip of territory from one division of the Empire to the other is by no means as important as the damage done to Roman territory by barbarians

---

herrschaft in Pannonien I, 69–76 (Berlin, De Gruyter, 1924). [212]Stein Verwalt., 347–349. [213]Stein, 350–351, 380.20–23; Stein Verwalt., 347–354.12; Stein, Map cited in note 3, above. [214]See pages 23–25, above. [215]J. Vogt und E. Kornemann, Römische Geschichte³, 125.5–9, 34–38 (Leipzig, Teubner, 1933). [216]Palanque, 54, note 27. [217]Schmidt, 302.12–15, 427.28–428.7. [218]Journ. Rom. Stud. 18 (1928), 224.23–41. [219]See *ibidem*, 26–28. It may be of service to point out that, by inadvertence, Professor Baynes, in discussing the notes to Stein, 350–351, cites Claudian's "In Eutropium" instead of the In Rufinum. [220]Stein, 351.12–16; Stein Verwalt., 352.34–353.3. [221]Stein Verwalt., 351.22–27. Note especially lines 27–28: "*Von diesen Tatsachen aus* <the italics are mine> lässt sich der ursachlicher Zusammenhang der Begebenheiten von 395 besser erfassen". [222]Lines 34–38. [223]E. g. IR 2.4-6. See Professor Baynes's own remarks in

whom (so Claudian[224] claims) Stilicho could have checked had he been permitted to do so. In any case, Stilicho may have preferred that nothing be said about a renunciation which he may never have meant to be final[225]. The cession to Arcadius of soldiers who belonged to the East in the first place and were necessary for its defense was a far different matter.

Professor Baynes may have other and more valid objections, but those which he presents in the note which we have been discussing do not warrant the rejection of a theory which so adequately covers all aspects of the problem[226]. Professor Baynes's article on the policy of Stilicho, Journ. Rom. Stud. 12(1922), 211–217.13, in so far as it concerns Illyricum, is, of course, based on the theory that Dacia and Macedonia belonged to the East at the time of Theodosius's death.

Journ. Rom. Stud. 12 (1922), 212–213. [224]IR 2.186–194, 215–216. [225]Compare Stein Verwalt., 354.5–12, and see pages 24–25, above. [226]I am under the impression that I have read a rejoinder by Dr. Stein to Professor Baynes's criticism; if so, I have been unable to locate it again.

APPENDIX C

Rufinus and Valentinian II

M. Palanque[227] has proposed a new theory, that Rufinus served as Magister Officiorum under Valentinian II at Vienne after Theodosius's departure for the East in 391, and that he fled to Constantinople after Valentinian's death in May, 392. This theory, which is not supported by any direct evidence, is upheld by M. Palanque on the following grounds:

a) Ambroise, après avoir écrit à Titien (*Epist. LII*, 1⟨[228]⟩) que Rufin vient de quitter la maîtrise des offices pour la préfecture du prétoire, ajoute qu'il ne pourra plus lui nuire, car c'est pour d'autres régions qu'il est préfet (*est enim aliarum praefectus partium*): or, Rufin devient préfet d'Orient en septembre 392; c'est donc qu'il était maître des offices en Occident;

b) Il est consul en 392 avec Arcadius: or, Théodose choisit toujours un des deux consuls en Occident (sauf en 388 et en 393, où la rupture déjà ouverte avec un usurpateur occidental l'amène a nommer deux orientaux); comme Arcadius, qui doit régner à Constantinople, est évidemment désigné au titre de l'Orient, c'est donc que Rufin est encore au début de 392 un fonctionnaire d'Occident.

Several reasons have prevented my accepting this theory.

(1) The theory as a whole fails to take account of Zosimus's story[229] of Rufinus's quarrel with Promotus. This took place *after* Theodosius had returned to the East[230] and *before* Rufinus's designation as consul[231]. According to Zosimus, therefore, Rufinus returned to Constantinople with Theodosius in 391, and it was there that he received his consulship. M. Palanque makes no mention of the Promotus episode.

(2) In making his first point, M. Palanque has apparently overlooked a grave difficulty. A certain Titianus[232] was engaged, or expected to be engaged, in a legal action which came under the jurisdiction of the Magister Officiorum. It is agreed that this Titianus was an inhabitant of the Western part of the Empire (compare the words *aliarum . . . partium* in Ambrose's letter). Now if, as M. Palanque believes, Rufinus had fled to Constantinople after the death of

---

[227]Palanque Ambr., 273, note 42. Compare Palanque, 65.3-5. [228]See note 40, above, for the pertinent part of this letter. [229]4.51–52. [230]Zosimus, 4.50. [231]Zosimus, 4.52. See page 10, above. [232]Our complete ignorance concerning this Titianus is another reason why it is unwise to base so novel a theory on this letter. See Palanque Ambr., 479 § 13. Giovanni Mamone,

Valentinian on May 15, 392[233], this very act would have relieved Titianus of all his apprehension. Yet it is not this flight, but Rufinus's accession to the Praetorian Prefecture four months[234] later which seems to Ambrose to remove the cause for Titianus's worries, which had endured up to that moment.

I believe that a different interpretation of Ambrose's letter both removes this difficulty and is in complete accord with what we know from other sources of Rufinus's activities in 390-392. Upon the death of Valentinian II, it must have seemed very likely that Theodosius would return to Italy (as he did three years later). With him would come Rufinus as his Magister Officiorum (as he had done in 388-389), and he would take jurisdiction over Titianus's case. It is this likelihood which, according to my interpretation, caused Titianus's alarm. It may even be that the legal action had been commenced before Rufinus when he was in Italy, thus giving Titianus good reason to dread his resumption of the case. Now the news comes to Ambrose that Rufinus has been appointed Praefectus Praetorio Orientis. This means that, even if Theodosius returns to the West, Rufinus will remain in Constantinople (as he actually did in 394). Therefore Ambrose can say to Titianus, ". . . liberatus es ab eo, quem tibi graviorem iudicem arbitrabare".

(3) M. Palanque's second point is not without weight, but it is not sufficiently cogent to overcome the two objections which I have already mentioned. It must be remembered that the consular designations for 392 would of necessity be made in 391, a year which Theodosius spent partly in the West (January-June), partly in the East (July-September)[235]. It may well be that, before circumstances seemed to require his presence in the East[236], Theodosius had already decided to bestow the consulship on Rufinus, to whom he had reason

---

in Didaskaleion 2 (1924), 121-122, seems to believe that this Titianus is identical with the Tatianus <sic!> whom Rufinus succeeded as Praetorian Prefect (see page 10, above). This identification was most effectively disproved by Maximilianus Ihm, in (Fleckeisens) Jahrbücher für Classische Philologie, Supplementband 17 (1890), 52.   [233]Seeck Regesten, 280.   [234]For the purpose of this argument, I accept M. Palanque's date, September, 392 (see his section a], quoted above). M. Palanque has apparently chosen the latest possible date (see page 11, above) in order to lend verisimilitude to his theory: if Rufinus left Vienne immediately on May 15, 392, a full four months would be a short time indeed in which to reach Constantinople, reestablish himself at Court, oust Tatianus and Proculus, and have himself appointed in the former's place.
[235]Seeck Regesten, 278-279.   [236]Stein, 323.28-324.1.

to be grateful[237]. If, as is not improbable, he had mentioned this intention to Rufinus, it is not likely that a subsequent change in his own plans would cause Theodosius to alter this arrangement. Moreover, since Rufinus was of Western origin, and since Arcadius was theoretically Augustus in the entire Empire, it could not have seemed a serious infraction of Theodosius's rule (if rule it was) to name Arcadius and Rufinus as colleagues in the consulship.

---

[237]See page 9, above, and note 24.

CHAPTER 2

CLAUDIAN AND THE COMPOSITION OF THE INVECTIVE IN RUFINUM

Very little is known about the life of Claudius Claudianus[238]. He was almost certainly born in Egypt, probably in Alexandria[239]. The date of his birth is unknown, but may be placed with some assurance between 370 and 375[240]. We can judge from the works of Claudian that he received a thorough education in the literatures both of Greece and of Rome. In the latter he seems to have taken particular interest: the enthusiasm with which he writes of Rome's great history is surely the fruit of much early reading[241]. The correctness and the ease of his Latin verse even in his earliest productions testify to much assiduous practice on the part of one who was born and, apparently, educated in the Greek-speaking part of the Empire[242].

---

[238]Vollmer, in Pauly-Wissowa 3.2652.1–2660.37, sets forth and carefully analyzes our scanty sources of information. See also Fargues, 5–38. For general discussions of Claudian, besides the article of Vollmer just mentioned, and Fargues, *passim*, see Birt Pr., 1–75; Gaston Boissier, La Fin du Paganisme⁷, 2.237–253 (Paris, Hachette, 1913); Glover, 216–248; John C. Rolfe, Claudian, in Transactions and Proceedings of the American Philological Association 50 (1919), 135–149; Schanz, 3–32; Teuffel, 356–361; Weston, 101–120. For a list of editions and translations, see pages 53–54, below.

An attempt has recently been made to identify Claudian with a poet whose portrait appears on an ivory diptych now in the Treasury of the Cathedral at Monza, Italy: see Kurt Weitzmann und Stefan Schultz, Zur Bestimmung des Dichters auf dem Musen-Diptychon von Monza, in Jahrbuch des Deutschen Archäologischen Instituts 49 (1934), 128–138. The identification is supported by strong arguments on both artistic and historical grounds. [239]This is a conclusion drawn from all our sources (see Pauly-Wissowa 3.2652.19–30; Fargues, 6) but one. Lydus, De Mag. 1.47, calls him ὁ Παφλαγών. Birt's explanation (Birt Pr. 3–5) of this designation as a derogatory epithet has met with general acceptance. The question has been reopened by J. Turcevič, in Byzantinische Zeitschrift 34 (1934), 1–9. He would take Lydus's statement at its face value. According to this scholar, Claudian or his father really was a Paphlagonian, but the former, ashamed of his origin, pretended to be a native of Egypt. If this were true, it would be difficult to see how the tradition of Claudian's real birthplace survived over a century and a half to the time of Justinian, when Lydus wrote. There can be no doubt, at any rate, of Claudian's familiarity with and fondness for Egypt, which seem to point to long residence there (CM 19; 22.56–58; 27; 28). [240]Fargues, 7.

[241]See Clifford H. Moore, Rome's Heroic Past in the Poems of Claudian, in The Classical Journal 6 (1910–1911), 108–115. [242]Professor Rolfe, in the article cited in note 238, above, remarks (135–136) that the literary history of pagan Rome begins (in Plautus) and ends (in Claudian) with the miracle of a foreigner

Chapter 2

Claudian does not seem to have come to Rome until 394[243]. Upon his arrival in the capital city, he attached himself to the wealthy and illustrious senatorial family of the Anicii. When two young scions of this house, Olybrius and Probinus, were elevated to the consulship (now a purely honorary distinction), Claudian seized upon the occasion to make his début in Roman letters by writing a panegyric on the event. His skill in celebrating the accession of two insignificant youths to an obsolescent office presaged well for the future *vates* of Honorius and Stilicho.

In 395, the third consulship of the Emperor Honorius gave Claudian his first chance to gain the favor of the Court. His Panegyricus De Tertio Consulatu Honorii, composed late in that year, and read before the Emperor and his suite, celebrated the real achievements of Theodosius and the imagined virtues of his son. Significant are the verses in praise of Stilicho[244] which Claudian places in the mouth of Theodosius; with these, Claudian entered the service of a man whose praises he was to sing for the rest of his literary career.

The invective In Rufinum, the subject of the present study, was Claudian's first major effort as Stilicho's laureate. Outwardly an attack on Rufinus, the poem is of course intended as a eulogy of Stilicho[245] by contrast with the monster whom he had destroyed. It is for this reason that, as has been remarked, "... Claudian magnifies the personality, the evil personality, of Rufinus, to a point where he seems almost more than human, a being whose menacing shadow has darkened the world, whose 'bad eminence' entitles him to be named in connection with primal, cosmic forces"[246]. Claudian's hero is the new Apollo[247] who has slain this dread Python; the blacker Claudian paints Rufinus, the more dazzling appears the glory of the great Stilicho.

The two books In Rufinum, with the Preface to the first book, were written early in 396, and were read to an assemblage of Senators, in the absence of Stilicho and Honorius[248]. It was not until the middle of

---

who made the Latin idiom his very own and excelled in its use.   [243]Fargues, 10.

[244]3H 142–162. I see in 159–162 a clearer echo of Rufinus's recent death than in 185–189, which M. Fargues cites (Fargues, 13, note 1.14–17). Verses 159–162 read as follows:... rupta si mole Typhoeus prosiliat, vinclis Tityos si membra resolvat, si furor Enceladi proiecta mugiat Aetna, opposito Stilichone cadent.

[245]See my note on *servans ... regit*, IR I Pr. 17–18.   [246]Weston, 102.

[247]IR I Pr. 15.   [248]See Fargues, 15. The absence of Honorius and Stilicho, mentioned by M. Fargues as a possibility, seems to me a certainty. Had they been present, Claudian could not have failed to apostrophize them in his Preface.

397, after the return of Stilicho from his Arcadian expedition, that Claudian was able to recite the poem to his patron in person. For this occasion he wrote the Preface to the second book, which therefore mentions exploits of Stilicho which have no part in the second book itself[249].

The poem may be analyzed thus.

Book 1. Preface.—When Apollo killed Python, the world was rid of an oppressive monster. Now Stilicho, a new Apollo, has rid us of a new Python.

1–24: Exordium.—The death of Rufinus has justified the ways of gods to men. Tell me, o Muse, whence sprang this dread plague.

25–115.—The Furies, convoked by Allecto, rage at the triumph of Justice under Theodosius. Megaera offers to bring Rufinus, once her nursling, to the Court, where he will re-establish the reign of Evil.

116–175.—Megaera appears to Rufinus, and bids him travel to Constantinople. He obeys.

176–300.—The greed, cruelty, and violence of Rufinus crush and terrify the East. Only Stilicho can prevail against him.

301–331.—Rufinus incites the barbarians to invade the Empire.

332–353.—Stilicho girds himself to stem the barbarian tide; he prays to Mars, who comes to fight at his side.

354–387.—Megaera encounters Justice, and glories in the disorder which her pupil Rufinus has caused. Justice prophesies the return of the Golden Age under Honorius.

Book 2. Preface.—Helicon is freed from barbarian inroads. Rejoice, ye Muses. Stilicho, pause from your labors to hear my song.

1–6.—The dying Theodosius has left the twofold Empire in Stilicho's charge.

7–99.—Rufinus, feeling himself doomed, decides to involve the world in his own ruin. He summons barbarian hordes, and rejoices in the slaughter which they wreak. The oppressed people long for Stilicho.

100–129.—Stilicho marches East at the head of a mighty host, the combined armies of the East and the West. His very approach checks the barbarian raids.

130–170.—Rufinus, alarmed for his own safety, persuades Arcadius to bid Stilicho despatch the Eastern troops to Constantinople, and return to Italy with the Western forces.

---

[249]Fargues, 16, 103

Chapter 2

171-256.—The army is ready for battle with the barbarians when the Emperor's command arrives. Stilicho deliberates briefly, then decides to obey. The soldiers implore him not to separate the two forces, but he stands firm.

257-292.—The Eastern soldiers vow loyalty to Stilicho and vengeance upon his enemies. Their plan is kept secret as they march East.

293-347.—Rufinus rejoices with his friends at Stilicho's withdrawal. He prepares to ascend the throne as Arcadius's colleague. In sleep he beholds a vision which seems to promise him success. On the morrow he adorns himself for his coronation.

348-383.—The army is drawn up in splendid array at the Hebdomon. Rufinus and Arcadius review the troops. Rufinus is quietly surrounded. Not observing this, he urges Arcadius to declare him his colleague.

384-439.—A mighty voice denounces Rufinus. The soldiers draw their swords, and hack him to pieces. The citizenry stream forth to trample his remains in the dust.

440-453.—The fate of Rufinus teaches that pride goes before a fall.

454-527.—The spirit of Rufinus comes to the Lower World, where it is surrounded by his enraged victims. He is haled before the throne of Minos. That judge sternly upbraids him, and dooms him to imprisonment below the foundations of Night for ever and ever.

The In Rufinum deserves to rank among the most successful of Claudian's efforts. The simplicity and the coherence of the plan, the vigor of the execution, and the relative scarcity of elaboration and digression form a pleasing contrast to the tediousness and the repetition which mar many of the Panegyrics. It is no wonder that this poem took such a hold on the minds of medieval readers that Alain de Lille (1114-1203) felt obliged to write an Anticlaudianus De Antirufino[250].

It is not germane to our present purpose to discuss in detail Claudian's other works. They include Panegyrics on the Fourth and the Sixth Consulships of Honorius (398 and 404), Fescennines, and an Epithalamium, on the marriage of Honorius to Stilicho's daughter (398), a Panegyric addressed to the Consul Manlius Theodorus (399), poems on the Gildonic and on the Pollentine or Gothic War[251] (398 and 402), which are largely eulogies of Stilicho, three

---

[250]Alanus de Insulis, Anticlaudianus (= Migne Lat. 210.483-575).   [251]See Dr. Schroff's excellent edition (consult list of abbreviations, page 101, below,

books on Stilicho's Consulship (399), a group of minor poems on varied subjects, and an incomplete mythological epic, the De Raptu Proserpinae[252] (397), which has rightly been considered his masterpiece[253].

I have reserved for special mention the In Eutropium[254], which is a companion-piece to the In Rufinum. In this invective, written in 399, Claudian attacks another enemy[255] of Stilicho at the Eastern Court, the eunuch-consul Eutropius. There is an obvious similarity of theme between the two invectives, but the differences are no less marked: "The invective against Rufinus depends more on the epic element for effectiveness, and the style is more lofty and sustained. The satire is denunciation, never ridicule. There is no descent to burlesque or comedy.... With the satire against Eutropius, the case is somewhat different.... Eutropius is not represented as terrible, but as disgusting"[256]. The vile accusations and viler insinuations of lust and perversion which soil the pages of the In Eutropium[257] find no place in the earlier poem.

Claudian apparently enjoyed a great reputation among his contemporaries. In 400 or 401[258], the Emperor Honorius, at the request of the Senate, had a statue of the poet set up in the Forum, with an inscription which has been preserved[259]. The last two lines, which are in Greek, declare, with an exaggeration worthy of Claudian himself, that our poet combines in one person the mind of Vergil and the inspiration of Homer[260].

From this inscription we learn also that Claudian was recompensed for his services to Stilicho and Honorius by appointment to the post of Tribunus et Notarius[261], with the title of Vir Clarissimus.

under "Schroff"). [252]Recently published separately with an English translation: Claudian, The Rape of Proserpine, in English Verse, by R. Martin Pope (London, J. M. Dent and Sons, 1934. Pp. xiv, 97). [253]Glover, 217. [254]Two editions of this poem have appeared in recent years, the first mentioned with an English translation: Alfred Carleton Andrews, The *In Eutropium* of Claudius Claudianus, University of Pennsylvania Thesis (Philadelphia, Privately Printed, 1931. Pp. 135); Pierre Fargues, Claudien: Invectives contre Eutrope (Paris, Hachette, 1933. Pp. 137). [255]As we have seen (page 24, above, and note 153, above), Stilicho and Eutropius worked in concert for a while. The alliance, however, was short-lived, and was replaced by the most bitter hostility (Fargues, 76-77, § 3). [256]Weston, 117. Compare Theodor Birt, Zwei Politische Satiren des Alten Rom, 38 (Marburg, Elwert, 1888): "<Claudians In Eutropium> ist ein komisches Gegenbild zu dem tragischen Gedicht In Rufinum". [257]E. g. IE 1.66-68, 101-102, 280, 360-370. [258]Fargues, 27. [259]CIL 6.1710 (= Dessau 2949). [260]ΕΙΝ ΕΝΙ ΒΙΡΓΙΛΙΟΙΟ ΝΟΟΝ ΚΑΙ ΜΟΥΣΑΝ ΟΜΗΡΟΥ ΚΛΑΥΔΙΑΝΟΝ ΡΩΜΗ ΚΑΙ ΒΑΣΙΛΗΣ ΕΘΕΣΑΝ. [261]The *tribuni et notarii* were

Chapter 2

As we have seen, no poem of Claudian can be dated with certainty later than 404, the year in which he wrote the Panegyric on the Sixth Consulship of Honorius. One of his minor poems (CM 31), addressed to Serena, the niece of Theodosius and wife of Stilicho, informs us that that lady brought about the marriage of Claudian with a young protegée of hers who resided in Africa. It is a plausible suggestion[262] that this poem is Claudian's last work, and that he died in 404 during his honeymoon[263]. At any rate, his literary career, which began so abruptly in 395, ends in the same manner nine years later, and he vanishes henceforth from our sight.

Estimates of the literary value of Claudian's work are extremely varied[264]. My own reading has convinced me of the truth of Professor Glover's statement[265]: "There is about it ⟨the poetry of Claudian⟩ much to fascinate and charm the reader, who will take the trouble to learn the poet's mind".

---

attached to the Imperial Consistory. They acted as confidential agents of the Emperor in his relations with high officials, the Senate, and the Church. See Charles Lécrivain, Le Sénat Romain depuis Dioclétien, 31, § 7; 52–53, § 2 (Paris, Thorin, 1888). See also *idem*, article *Notarius*, in Daremberg-Saglio, Dictionnaire des Antiquités Grecques et Romaines, 4.105–106; Birt. Pr. 22; Fargues, 26.

[262] Pauly-Wissowa 3.2655.46–53. [263] Attempts have been made, with little justification, to link the Deprecatio ad Hadrianum (CM 22) with Claudian's death (see Fargues, 31–34). A new theory, which would eliminate CM 22 entirely from the sources of Claudian's biography, has been advanced by Emanuele Griset, in Il Mondo Classico 3 (1933), 329–335. [264] The extremes are the strictures of Walter C. Summers (J. Sandys, Companion to Latin Studies³, 644–646 [Cambridge: At the University Press, 1925]) on the one hand, and the praises of Teuffel and Schanz (cited in note 238, above) on the other. Fargues, 329–333, Glover, 216–248, and Rolfe (cited in note 238, above) seem to me to strike the correct note. [265] Glover, 217.

CHAPTER 3

THE TEXTUAL TRADITION OF THE IN RUFINUM

The following are the sources which the editors of the three critical editions of Claudian (Jeep, Birt, and Koch[266]) used in establishing the text of the In Rufinum.

A. NON-EXTANT MANUSCRIPTS

Certain readings of several manuscripts which are no longer extant have been preserved as interlinear or marginal notes in copies of early printed editions.

1. The Florentine[267] (or Lucensian) Excerpts[268]. These are found in a copy of the *editio princeps* (1482: see page 53, below), now in the Florentine National Library, numbered A 4.36. The readings of the printed text[269] of the *editio princeps* are designated by Birt as Λ. The variant readings were introduced during the fifteenth century by different hands. Birt distinguishes the following hands as having annotated the In Rufinum.

(a) Λ¹ denotes the first annotator, who made entries in the margin or between the lines of the text of the IR, mostly in IR 1. The source of these entries is not indicated.

(b) The entries of Λ² concern only IR 1. At IR 1.20 this annotator writes, "hinc coepi conferre cum vetustissimo codice amici cuiusdam Lucensis ⟨hence the designation 'Lucensian' for the Codex and for the Excerpts⟩, geminis punctis . . notaturus quae illinc emendabo". He also occasionally uses his two dots to show his approval of an entry of Λ¹. At IR 1.252 he announces his intention of denoting by a crux (†) readings in his old manuscript which are doubtful because the words were erased "ab improbis emendatoribus".

(c) A third annotator, whose entries Birt calls E when they are interlinear, Em when they are marginal, supplemented the work of Λ² by annotating IR 1 Pr. and IR 1.1–19 (seven entries in all), and con-

---

[266]See list of abbreviations, pages 99–102, below. See also note 306, below.
[267]Birt. Pr. 82–85, 109–112; Jeep 1 Pr. 31–32, 2 Pr. 27–57; Koch Pr. 15–16.
[268]In editions of Claudian the term 'Excerpts' (Excerpta) is used in two different senses: (1) as here, the term may denote variant readings copied from old manuscripts; (2) it is also used to denote quotations from Claudian extant in medieval florilegia (see page 47, § C, below). [269]Jeep 2 Pr. 29–57 gives a collation of the significant part of this edition with his own.

tinued from where Λ^2 left off (the end of IR 1). The writer of E and Em used at least two codices, for he occasionally denotes readings as coming from "antiquus a" or "antiquus b" (probably the Codex Lucensis). Where this annotation is found, Birt uses the symbols E^a or Em^a, E^b or Em^b respectively.

(d) The work of a fourth hand, Λ^3, is also found at some points in IR 1.

Jeep refers to Λ^2, Em, and E indifferently as G; compare Birt Pr. 86.30–32.

2. The Gyraldine Excerpts[270]. These are found in a copy of the Aldine edition (1523: see page 53, below), now at Leyden, numbered 757 G 2. The first page bears the notation "Gregorius Giraldus emendavit hunc codicem ex vetustiss(im)o exemplari, sumpto ab Aenea Gerardino". The Gyraldine Excerpts seem to be derived either from the Codex Lucensis, or, more probably, from a manuscript closely related to the Codex Lucensis. Birt denotes these readings by the symbol ϵ. Jeep refers to them by the symbol g; it must be noted, however, that, when he published the first volume of his edition, containing the IR, he knew these Gyraldine Excerpts only imperfectly, through reports of them in Heinsius's and Burmann's editions.

3. The Isengrinian Marginalia[271]. These readings, unlike the Florentine and the Gyraldine Excerpts, are printed in the margin of the Basel edition (1534: see page 53, below). They are derived in part from a non-extant manuscript which belonged to the religious reformer Wolfgang Fabricius Capito (he died in 1542); other variants were merely copied from the edition of Camers (see page 53, below). The Isengrinian readings are not referred to by Jeep; Birt cites them occasionally as "Isengr. mg.".

4. The Excerpta Cuiaciana[272]. These are found among the notes printed in the edition of Claverius (1602: see page 53, below). Claverius gives variants in great profusion. Koch has shown that some are derived from the extant Codex M (see Number 7 under B, below, and Koch Cuiac. 21–40), and thus have no independent value. Others are taken, sometimes with, sometimes without, acknowledgment, from previous editions (Koch apud Birt Pr. 196–198). Still other readings, however, are derived from a manuscript which, like M,

---

[270]Birt Pr. 85–91, 109.35–36; Jeep 1 Pr. 30–31, 2 Pr. 17–23; Koch Pr. 15–16.
[271]Birt Pr. 118, 187–193; Koch Pr. 6–15.   [272]Birt Pr. 194–199; Koch Cuiac. *passim*.

was once in the possession of Jacobus Cuiacius (he died in 1590), but is no longer extant. This manuscript Koch calls X; he arrives at its readings by a process of elimination (Koch Cuiac. 41-46, 53-62). The Cuiacian readings are not referred to by Jeep; Birt cites Koch's X occasionally as "vetus Cuiac.".

B. EXTANT MANUSCRIPTS CONTAINING THE WHOLE OF THE IR

1. Codex Vaticanus 2809 membr. (Birt's and Jeep's V)[273]. This belongs to the twelfth century[274]. Of the work of the original scribe[275] we have IR 1.215-387, and IR 2 entire. The first two leaves of the first quaternion, containing IR 1 Pr. 1-IR 1.214, were lost. The deficiency was supplied by five different hands of about the same period as V^1; these Birt designates indifferently by the symbol V. There are some corrections by V^1, and others by six different hands; the latter Birt divides into two groups, which he calls V^2 and V^3.

2. Codex Parisinus latin. 18,552 membr. (Birt's P)[276]. This belongs to the twelfth or to the beginning of the thirteenth century. There are corrections by P^1, and by two others, P^2 and P^3, not much later than P^1.

3. Codex Bruxellensis 5381[277] membr. (Birt's C, Jeep's B)[278]. This belongs to the eleventh century (possibly to the tenth). There are corrections by C^1; others by C^2, contemporary and perhaps identical with C^1; C^3 belongs to the fifteenth century.

4. Codex Parisinus 8082 membr. (Birt's Π)[279]. This belongs to the thirteenth century. It is beautifully written; it once belonged to Petrarch. There are corrections and variants added by $Π^2$, contemporary with $Π^1$.

5. Codex Neapolitanus Borbonicus (Farnesianus) IV E 47 membr. (Birt's B, Jeep's F)[280]. This belongs to the thirteenth century. There are corrections by various hands, slightly later than B^1; these are denoted collectively by the symbol B^2.

6. Codex Ambrosianus S 66 sup. membr. (Birt's A)[281]. This belongs to the fifteenth century.

---

[273]Birt Pr. 94-95, 106-109; Jeep 1 Pr. 33-34, 38; Koch Pr. 15. [274]Birt Pr. 94, note 2. [275]Birt calls him V^1. In Birt's notation, which I follow for convenience, the superior [1] always denotes the original scribe; Birt uses the superior [2] and [3] in various ways in dealing with different manuscripts: see the descriptions of the various manuscripts which follow in the text above. [276]Birt Pr. 95-96, 106-109; Jeep 1 Pr. 42. [277]So Birt 16, Jeep 1 Pr. 35; Birt Pr. 96 gives the numbers as 5380-5384. [278]Birt Pr. 96, 113-114; Jeep 1 Pr. 35, 38; Koch Pr. 15. [279]Birt Pr. 97, 114-118; Jeep 1 Pr. 42. [280]Birt Pr. 97, 114-118; Jeep 1 Pr. 39. [281]Birt Pr. 97, 114-118; Jeep 1 Pr. 51; Postgate, 164, col.

Chapter 3

7. Codex Ambrosianus M 9 sup. membr. (Birt's M, Jeep's A)[282]. This belongs to the thirteenth century.

8. Codex Laurentianus n. 250 membr. (Birt's and Jeep's L)[283]. This belongs to the thirteenth century (or possibly to the twelfth).

9. Codex Vossianus n. 294 membr. (Birt's Vo, Jeep's V1)[284]. This was written in the year 1218.

10. "Codices deteriores" (Birt's ς, Jeep's "deterr.")[285]. Readings from these manuscripts are occasionally cited by Birt and Jeep, who differ somewhat as to the exact constitution of this group.

C. MANUSCRIPTS OF MEDIEVAL FLORILEGIA CONTAINING SELECTIONS FROM THE IR

Certain manuscripts of medieval florilegia contain selections from the IR. These are enumerated and discussed in Birt Pr. 173–180. Birt employs none of them in establishing the text of the IR. Jeep uses one: Codex Monacensis (Frisingensis) lat. 6292 membr. (Jeep's M)[286], belonging to the eleventh century.

In establishing the text of the IR, the various editors follow different theories as to the interrelation and the value of the sources which they employ.

A. JEEP

For the IR, Jeep uses the Florentine Excerpts, the Gyraldine Excerpts as he knew them in 1876 (see page 45, above), Vaticanus 2809, Bruxellensis 5381, Laurentianus 250, Vossianus 294, and Monacensis 6292. These he distributes into four classes, in descending order of value[287]: (1) Gyraldine and Florentine Excerpts; (2) Vaticanus 2809; (3) Bruxellensis 5381, Monacensis 6292, Laurentianus 250; (4) Vossianus 294, and all other "deteriores".

B. BIRT

Birt[288] divides the manuscripts of Claudian into three groups, which, he believes, are descended from three non-extant manuscripts, x, z, and w. He derives z and w from a single manuscript y, and places the writing of x and y before the ninth century. In turn, he

---

1.4–24.   [282]Birt Pr. 118–119, Birt 16; Jeep 1 Pr. 35, 38, 48, 2 Pr. 160; Koch Cuiac. 21–40.   [283]Birt Pr. 120; Jeep 1 Pr. 36, 38.   [284]Birt Pr. 123; Jeep 1 Pr. 36–37, 38.   [285]Birt Pr. 118–128; Jeep 1 Pr. 38, 41–49.   [286]Birt Pr. 175–176, 178–179; Jeep 1 Pr. 35, 38; Jeep, Rh. Mus. 29 (1874), 74–80.   [287]Jeep 1 Pr. 37–38.   [288]Birt Pr. 97–98.

derives x and y from an "archetypus perantiquus", Ω, which he assigns[289] to the fifth or the sixth century. He presents the following stemma[290] (I omit manuscripts which do not contain the IR; designations of hypothetical manuscripts are in parentheses):

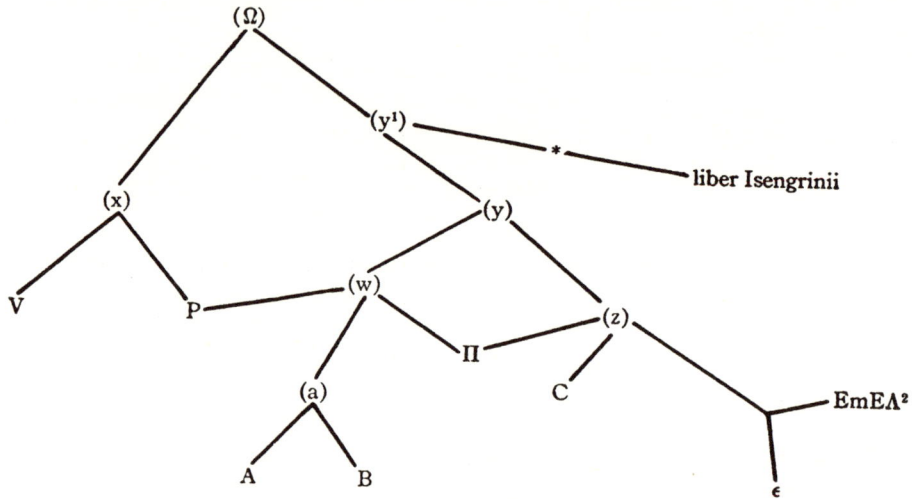

The words with which Birt describes his diagram are most significant[291]:

Hanc tamen cognationis magis umbratilem adumbrationem esse scias quam certissimam imaginem. Neque stemmata picta multum valent; nam manuscripta Claudiani sicut fit in poetis hisce non mera apographa esse solent, sed exemplis plus uno textus eorum fere componebatur([292]) confluxusque rivorum complurium in uno codice cernitur([293]).

Guided by his theory of the descent of our manuscripts, Birt discusses[294] the relative values of the families of manuscripts. He differs from Jeep chiefly in attributing less importance to the Florentine (and the Gyraldine) Excerpts, which he places[295] on a level with Vaticanus 2809. He seems to agree fairly well[296] with Jeep's judgment

---

[289]Birt Pr. 104.11–13.   [290]Birt Pr. 103.   [291]Birt Pr. 103.19–23. [292]Compare Birt Pr. 97.40–98.2, "Omnia haec apographa passa iam sunt manus interpolatorum, diversorum tamen et diversum in modum agentium .... singuli peculiares semper mutationes intulerunt". See also Postgate, 165, col. 1.55–60, col. 2.1–5.   [293]Lejay, in Revue Critique 1896 (part 1), 37, quotes these words of Birt, and remarks with truth, "Ces reflexions condamnent le *stemma*".   [294]Birt Pr. 104–118.   [295]Birt Pr. 109.35–40.   [296]Birt

of Bruxellensis 5381, but, as I noted above, he does not use the related Monacensis 6292, and relegates[297] Laurentianus 250 to the "deteriores". He sets a high value on the consensus of x and z (VP EC), but believes[298] that at some points their unanimous reading must be set aside in favor of the reading of the generally inferior w (ΠBA). Instead of Jeep's Vossianus 294, Birt uses M (Ambrosianus M 9 sup.) as a representative of the "deteriores", ς. Of the numerous manuscripts of this class, Birt says [299], "Intersunt qui codicem Π laude aequent, vincant B"[300].

In spite of the high antiquity which he assigns to the "liber Capitonis" (see stemma above, "liber Isengrinii"), Birt is diffident about accepting its readings as reported in the Isengrinian Marginalia[301]. He assigns no place in his stemma to the Cuiacian manuscript, but believes it closely related to the Isengrinian[302].

C. Koch

Koch follows Birt rather closely. He attaches great importance[303] to the consensus of V and C, or to that of V and E; in particular, he sets a higher value on V than either of his predecessors had done.

Of the various data set forth above, I consider one fact of salient importance. The extant manuscripts of Claudian, as we have seen[304], have all suffered greatly from contamination and interpolation. With a tradition of this sort, the establishment of a text by reference to the authority of a manuscript or a group of manuscripts seems to me a wholly unwarranted procedure. However excellent a given manuscript of Claudian may be as a whole, it is not homogeneous; the excellence of the majority of its readings is therefore no assurance of the correctness of any one reading[305]. The same considerations tend

---

Pr. 113–114.   [297]Birt Pr. 120.   [298]Birt Pr. 114.18–43.   [299]Birt Pr. 118.28–29.   [300]See also Birt Pr. 128.5–7.   [301]Birt Pr. 187–193, especially 192.23.   [302]Birt Pr. 195.25–26.   [303]Koch Pr. 15.   [304]See Birt's remarks, quoted on page 48, above, and note 292, above.   [305]Compare Maas, 4, § 10, ". . . wenn . . . einzelne Schreiber mehrere Vorlagen kontaminiert haben, so ist in dem Bereich dieser Kontaminationen die eliminatio stark behindert, wenn nicht unmöglich". See the rest of § 10. See also Collomp, 119, § B, "<S'il y a eu> contamination au Moyen Âge <,> aucune reconstitution scientifique n'est plus possible, quelle que soit l'origine et la filiation, même parfaitement établie, de nos manuscrits". See also A. Meillet, Bulletin de la Société de Linguistique de Paris 32 (1931), Comptes Rendus, 97. For the influence of papyrological discoveries on textual criticism, see John Garrett Winter, Life and Letters in the Papyri, 271–273 (Ann Arbor, University of Michigan Press, 1933), and the references there

to nullify the authority which might attach to the consensus of a group of manuscripts: such a consensus is always open to the suspicion that it is the result of contamination.

My procedure[306] in the attempt to establish the text of the IR has, therefore, been eclectic. I have tried to judge each case separately, and have based my choice of reading on the following criteria:

(1) The suitability of the reading, with reference both to the immediate context in which it appears, and to the purpose and the spirit of the In Rufinum as a whole.

(2) The language and the style of Claudian as shown in all his works, but particularly in the In Rufinum. Where Claudian's usage is not determinable, I have been guided by that of the poets whom he has evidently read and imitated (Vergil, Ovid, Lucan, Silius, Statius).

(3) The palaeographical probabilities. To this criterion I have assigned less weight than to the other two. Though I realize that much has been done toward the classification and the interpretation of errors in copying, I cannot have much faith in the rationalization of an essentially irrational process.

In the few instances where emendation seems necessary, I have, in examining the various conjectures, used the same criteria, assigning a little more weight to the third.

What has one the right to expect from a text constituted according to such principles[307]? I am not over-confident that, in doubtful places, I have printed the words which Claudian wrote. I am reasonably certain, however, that what I have printed approximates the sense which he intended to convey, and is in harmony with the language, the style, and the spirit of his works: more than this no editor of Claudian can hope to do with the manuscripts thus far discovered.

I have given an apparatus criticus[308] wherever Jeep, Birt, or Koch differ from one another or I differ from all of them. Where I thought it would be illuminating, I have added a discussion of my reasons for

---

cited.   [306]My knowledge of the manuscripts has been limited to the facts set forth in the Introductions and the critical notes of Birt's and Jeep's editions. So far as I know, no new manuscripts of the In Rufinum have been discovered or collated since the publication of Birt's edition. The preparation of a truly independent critical edition would, of course, require access to the manuscripts themselves.   [307]Both Birt (Pr. 107.38-39) and Koch (Pr. 15.5) state that they proceed *per electionem*. In their calculations, however, great weight is assigned to the authority of manuscripts and groups of manuscripts. Yet it is interesting to note how often they are obliged to disregard the readings of the sources which they severally consider the best.   [308]This is based on Birt's Introduction and

adopting one reading and rejecting others, that material may be at hand to support my views, or to correct my errors in judgment[309].

Tables showing the variations between this edition and those of Birt and of Koch appear below. These Tables take no account of purely orthographical differences; see note 309, below. Since the edition of Jeep has been almost completely superseded by those of Birt and Koch, I have not deemed it necessary to set forth separately a table of the variations between this edition and that of Jeep; a full list of such variations may, however, be obtained by consulting the apparatus criticus of this edition.

A. COMPARISON BETWEEN THIS EDITION AND THAT OF BIRT

Book and Verse	Reading of this Edition	Reading of Birt's Edition
1.47	corrupit	corrumpit
86	o sociae	sociae
91	refluis	fulvis
141	patriis	patriisque
151	gramine	germine
152	crimina	gramina
154	citavi	litavi
173	instabilesque	instabiles
238	parum est	parum
287	rebellis	rebellans
324	famosius	animosius
343	rapidos	trepidos
381	obunco	adunco
2.119	eximium	eximii
124	transgressus	egressus
141	faciem	rabiem
160	premet	premat
	Pontum	partem
163	fueris tantum	tantum fueris
239	qua	quo
274	solis	caeli
437	fraudes	poenas
505	vitii	vitiis

Apparatus Criticus; I have occasionally condensed his notes, less often expanded them by means of extracts from Jeep's apparatus. [309]In matters of orthography I follow Birt, except in IR 2.55 *Calchedonias;* 124 *nec iam* (Birt: *Chalcedonias, neciam*), and as noted in the textual commentary on IR 1.51, 253.

B. Comparison Between This Edition and That of Koch

(The symbol = marks readings which are common to the editions of Birt and of Koch.)

Book and Verse	Reading of this Edition	Reading of Koch's Edition
1.86	o sociae	sociae =
91	refluis	fulvis =
128	figuras	catervas
131	sensit	sentit
143	paret	parat
152	crimina	*gramina
154	citavi	litavi =
219	non ... non	nec ... nec
230	caesi	caesa
287	compressa	cum pressa
314	domari	domare
371	nec	non
381	obunco	adunco =
2 Pr. 2	permissis	promissis
2.49	causis	fatis
74	facultas	potestas
76	stipatus	stipatur
86	tunc vultus	tum vultus
87	nec	ne
106	complexus	amplexus
119	eximium	eximii =
124	transgressus	egressus =
159	fruetur	fruatur
160	premet Pontum	premat = Thracam
163	fueris tantum	tantum fueris =
167	umbras	undas
246	figet	figat
270	iam	clam
274	solis	caeli =
290	Hebrus	Haemus
323	quas *primum*	quae
350	tramite	limite
371	intendere	extendere
393	mucrone	rumore

Chapter 3

Book and Verse	Reading of this Edition	Reading of Koch's Edition
2.437	fraudes	poenas=
505	vitii	vitiis=
525	nostrum	ipsum

IMPORTANT EDITIONS AND TRANSLATIONS OF CLAUDIAN'S WORKS WHICH CONTAIN THE IN RUFINUM

A. Editions[310]

1. Barnabas Celsanus (Vicenza, Jacobus Dusensis, 1482). Editio Princeps[311].
2. Thaddeus Ugoletus (Venice, De Pensis, 1493–1500)[311].
3. Joannes Camers (Vienna, 1510)[311].
4. Antonius Francinus (Florence, Junta, 1519)[311].
5. Franciscus Asulanus (Venice, Aldus, 1523).
6. Michael Bentinus (Basel, Isengrinius, 1534)[311].
7. Theodor Pulmann (Antwerp, Plantin, 1571)[311].
8. Stephanus Claverius (Paris, Buon-Chaudière-Foüet, 1602)[311].
9. Joseph Scaliger (Leyden, Raphelengius, 1603)[311].
10. Caspar Barth (Hanover, 1612)[311].
11. *Idem*, Editio Altera (Frankfort, 1650)[311].
12. Nicolaus Heinsius (Leyden, Elzevir, 1650)[311].
13. *Idem*, Editio Altera (*Ibidem*, 1665).
14. Gesner, 1759[312].
15. Burmann, 1760[312].
16. Georg Ludwig Koenig (Göttingen, Dieterich, 1808)[311].
17. Jeep, 1876–1879[312].
18. Birt, 1892[313].
19. Koch, 1893[312].

---

[310]To my knowledge, the In Rufinum has never before been edited separately. In 1843–1845 Johann Caspar Orelli printed the texts of PO and IR for the use of his Seminar (Cl\<audii\> Claudiani In Probini et Olybrii . . . Consulatum Panegyris. In Rufinum Libri Duo . . . Recensuit Io\<annes\> Caspar Orellius. Turici . . . 1845. Pp. 49). On the worthlessness of this pamphlet (it has no introduction, no notes, and an antiquated apparatus) see Jeep 1 Pr. 59. [311]These books were not available to me. [312]See list of abbreviations, pages 99–102, below.

[313]See list of abbreviations, page 99, below. This is the standard edition of Claudian. The monumental Introduction (Birt Pr.) contains information about every phase of Claudian's life and works, and is the basis of all later studies on the subject.

B. Translations

1. V. Crépin, Claudien: Oeuvres Complètes. Traduction Nouvelle (Paris, Garnier, 1933. Two volumes. Pp. 328, 371).
2. Héguin de Guerle et Alphonse Trognon, Oeuvres Complètes de Claudien. Traduction Nouvelle (Paris, Panckouke, 1830–1833. Two volumes. Pp. xxxii, 393; 457).
3. Platnauer[314] (The Loeb Classical Library).
4. G. F. von Wedekind, Dichtungen des Claudius Claudianus Uebersetzt (Darmstadt, Jonghaus, 1868)[315].

[314]See list of abbreviations, page 101, below.
[315]This book was not available to me.

SIGLA

(Numbers in parentheses refer to pages above)

V   Vaticanus n. 2809 (46)
P   Parisinus latin. 18,522 (46)
C   Bruxellensis n. 5381 (46)
Π   Parisinus latin. 8082 (46)
B   Neapolitanus Borbonicus (Farnesianus) IV E 47 (46)
A   Ambrosianus S 66 sup. (46)
ω   consensus of VPC Π BA
φ   consensus of VPC Π BA except for those codices separately mentioned, on each particular occasion, in the note in which the symbol φ appears (e.g. suci CA, succi φ = suci CA, succi VP Π B)
ϛ   inferior codices
M   Ambrosianus M 9 sup. (47) [M is one of ϛ]
Λ   Editio Princeps, 1482 A.D. (44)
E, Em   Florentine Excerpts, interlinear (E) and marginal (Em) written in a copy of Λ (44–45)
$Λ^2$ Florentine Excerpts in the same copy of Λ, by a hand different from E,Em (44)
$Λ^1$ Annotations in the same book, by a hand earlier than E, Em, $Λ^2$ (44)
$Λ^3$ Annotations in the same book, by a hand later than E, Em, $Λ^2$ (45)
ε   Gyraldine Excerpts (45)
Isengr. mg.   Isengrinian Marginalia (45)
X   Cuiacian Excerpts (45–46)

[56]

CLAVDII CLAVDIANI
IN RVFINVM LIBER PRIMVS

INCIPIT PRAEFATIO

Phoebeo domitus Python cum decidit arcu
   membraque Cirrhaeo fudit anhela iugo,
qui spiris tegeret montes, hauriret hiatu
   flumina, sanguineis tangeret astra iubis:
iam liber Parnasus erat, nexuque soluto 5
   coeperat erecta surgere fronde nemus
concussaeque diu spatiosis tractibus orni
   securas ventis explicuere comas
et qui vipereo spumavit saepe veneno
   Cephisos nitidis purior ibat aquis. 10
Omnis "Io Paean" regio sonat; omnia Phoebum
   rura canunt; tripodas plenior aura rotat,
auditoque procul Musarum carmine dulci
   ad Themidis coëunt antra severa dei.

Nunc alio domini telis Pythone perempto 15
   convenit ad nostram sacra caterva lyram,
qui stabilem servans Augustis fratribus orbem
   iustitia pacem, viribus arma regit.

Pr. 17 servans *EB* (*sed* s *finalem in rasura B*) Birt Koch, servant φ Jeep
18 regit *EmB* (*sed* t *in rasura B; fuerat* regūt) Birt Koch, cadunt *A*, cadunt †
< = *vel*> regunt *P*¹, regunt φ (*omisit V*¹; *addidit V*²) Jeep

BOOK I

Pr. 17–18. servans ... regit: in spite of the separation of *qui* from its antecedent *domini* (15), Birt is justified in preferring this reading to *servant ... regunt*. The IR is primarily a glorification of Stilicho (1.259–267, 273–339, 369–371; 2.4–6, 94–129. See also pages 39–40, above). It is highly improbable, therefore, that Claudian would bestow on any other person or persons the high praise of sustaining the Empire (compare 2.4–6), while leaving Stilicho, the *dominus* of verse 15 (compare 2.402–404; CS 3.192), unadorned by a compliment. The reading *servans ... regit* is corroborated by another circumstance: Birt reports that Codex P has *dominus* as a gloss on *qui*. This gloss was undoubtedly copied mechanically from some point in the ancestry of P at which the manuscript reading was *servans ... regit*. For the separation of the relative from its antecedent, see Stolz-Schmalz, 795, Zusatz to § 2; see also 707, § 273 b, where Livy 21.26.2 is cited: <patres> C. Atilium praetorem cum una legione Romana et quinque milibus sociorum, dilectu novo a consule conscriptis, auxilium ferre Manlio iubent; qui < = Atilius!> sine ullo certamine ... Tannetum pervenit.

[57]

IN RVFINVM

LIBER I

Saepe mihi dubiam traxit sententia mentem,
curarent superi terras an nullus inesset
rector et incerto fluerent mortalia casu.
Nam cum dispositi quaesissem foedera mundi
praescriptosque mari fines annisque meatus 5
et lucis noctisque vices: tunc omnia rebar
consilio firmata dei, qui lege moveri
sidera, qui fruges diverso tempore nasci,
qui variam Phoeben alieno iusserit igni
compleri Solemque suo, porrexerit undis 10
litora, tellurem medio libraverit axe.
Sed cum res hominum tanta caligine volvi
aspicerem laetosque diu florere nocentes
vexarique pios, rursus labefacta cadebat
relligio causaeque viam non sponte sequebar 15
alterius, vacuo quae currere semina motu
affirmat magnumque novas per inane figuras

5 mari *C*Π *Birt Koch*, maris Λφ (*sed* ris *in rasura* B) *Jeep*   annisque] annique ω *Jeep*, amnisque ϵ, annisque *coniecit Heinsius, ediderunt Birt Koch*
16 vacuo ω *Birt Koch*, vano *anonymus in exemplari Cuiacii* (*Birt Pr. 195.13–16*), caeco *coniecit Paul edidit Jeep*

5. mari ... annis: Heinsius, who is responsible for the emendation *annis*, cites 4H 304 *praescriptos homini ... fines* as evidence that Claudian uses the verb *praescribo* with the accusative and the dative. The reading *amnis* of ϵ (see also Birt Pr. 178, note 1) probably arose from *annis* under the influence of *mari*.

The case of *lucis noctisque* (6) has no bearing on that of *mari ... annis*: *praescriptos* does not modify *vices*, which is a third object of *quaesissem*, parallel to *foedera* and *fines ... meatus <que>*.

16. vacuo ... motu: in retaining this reading, I interpret it, not as Gesner does, as meaning *motus vacuus rationis*, but rather as equal to *motus in vacuo*, 'movement in the void'. Compare Statius, Thebais 4.67 <funditores> assueti *vacuo ... diem praecingere gyro*, 'slingers wont to girdle the air with circles <which they describe> in empty space'. For Claudian's imitations of Statius, see Schamberger, 330, and L. Cerrato, Rivista di Filologia 9 (1880–1881), 356–393. For this free use of adjectives, compare CM 30.144–145 *naufraga ... otia*, 'the rest which follows the shipwreck <of Odysseus>'; IE 1.503 *inlustrat servilis laurea Crassum*, 'the laurels gained in a war against slaves ....'; IE 1.118 *brumalis hirundo*, 'a swallow in winter'. See also Kroll, 258–259, who quotes Culex 98–99, *apricas pastor agit curas*.

fortuna, non arte regi, quae numina sensu
ambiguo vel nulla putat vel nescia nostri.
Abstulit hunc tandem Rufini poena tumultum   20
absolvitque deos. Iam non ad culmina rerum
iniustos crevisse queror; tolluntur in altum,
ut lapsu graviore ruant. Vos pandite vati
Pierides, quo tanta lues eruperit ortu.
  Invidiae quondam stimulis incanduit atrox   25
Allecto, placidas late cum cerneret urbes.
Protinus infernas ad limina taetra sorores
concilium deforme vocat. Glomerantur in unum
innumerae pestes Erebi, quascumque sinistro
Nox genuit fetu: nutrix Discordia belli,   30
imperiosa Fames, leto vicina Senectus
impatiensque sui Morbus Livorque secundis
anxius et scisso maerens velamine Luctus
et Timor et caeco praeceps Audacia vultu
et Luxus populator opum, quem semper adhaerens   35
infelix humili gressu comitatur Egestas,
foedaque Avaritiae complexae pectora matris
insomnes longo veniunt examine Curae.
Complentur vario ferrata sedilia coetu
torvaque collectis stipatur curia monstris.   40
Allecto stetit in mediis vulgusque tacere
iussit et obstantes in tergum reppulit angues
perque umeros errare dedit. Tum corde sub imo
inclusam rabidis patefecit vocibus iram:
  "Sicine tranquillo produci saecula cursu,   45
sic fortunatas patiemur vivere gentes?
Quae nova corrupit nostros clementia mores?
Quo rabies innata perit? Quid inania prosunt

22 queror Λφ Birt Koch, querar Λ¹B Jeep   47 corrupit ΛVII (*sed rasura supra* u *in* II) Koch, corrūpit Λ²φ, corrumpit Jeep Birt

47–48. corrupit . . . perit: the finality of the perfect tense accords better with the context and with Claudian's manner. In defending the reading *corrupit*, Koch (Pr. 19) rightly takes *perit* as perfect; compare RP 3.273 quo leges cecidere poli? For the form *perit* as perfect, compare RP 2 Pr. 43 Caci flamma perit, rubuit Busiride Nilus. See also Neue 3.446–447; Birt Arch., 593–594; Sommer, 588. Brakman, 371–372, reads *corrupit*, but wrongly takes *perit* as present. For a similar problem (*diffundit* or *diffudit*, followed by *redit*), see BP 436–437, with Dr. Schroff's note.

verbera? Quid facibus nequiquam cingimur atris?
Heu nimis ignavae, quas Iuppiter arcet Olympo, 50
Theodosius terris. En aurea nascitur aetas,
en proles antiqua redit. Concordia, Virtus
cumque Fide Pietas alta cervice vagantur
insignemque canunt nostra de plebe triumphum.
Pro dolor! ipsa mihi liquidas delapsa per auras 55
Iustitia insultat vitiisque a stirpe recisis
elicit oppressas tenebroso carcere leges.
At nos indecores longo torpebimus aevo
omnibus eiectae regnis! Agnoscite tandem
quid Furias deceat; consuetas sumite vires 60
conventuque nefas tanto decernite dignum.
Iam cupio Stygiis invadere nubibus astra,
iam flatu violare diem, laxare profundo
frena mari, fluvios ruptis immittere ripis
et rerum vexare fidem". 65
            Sic fata cruentum
mugiit et totos serpentum erexit hiatus
noxiaque effudit concusso crine venena.
Anceps motus erat vulgi. Pars maxima bellum
indicit superis, pars Ditis iura veretur
dissensuque alitur rumor: ceu murmurat alti 70

51 Theodosius ω (n *supra* e V¹) *Koch*, Theudosius *Jeep Birt*   55 delapsa
Λφ *Birt Koch*, dilapsa ΠΛ¹Λ² *Jeep*

51. Theodosius: the exigencies of the dactylic hexameter require that violence be done either to the scansion or to the spelling of the name Thĕ-ŏ-dŏ-sĭ-us. Our manuscripts of Claudian all have *Theodosius* (Birt Pr. 211). The inscription CIL 3.737, which is bilingual, mentions Theodosius both in a Latin hexameter and in a Greek pentameter, in the former as *Theodosius*, in the latter as Θευδόσιος. Koch cites the former, Birt the latter, each to defend his own reading! Jeep refers to Lucian Mueller, De Re Metrica, 268 (edition of 1861 = second edition [1894], 316). Mueller supports *-eu-* by citations from Ovid, Claudian <!>, Venantius, Luxorius, and Sidonius. In verifying these citations, however, I found that in every case the manuscripts read *-eo-*, and that it is the editors who (in some cases only) have emended to *-eu-*. For the inscriptional evidence bearing on the treatment of the name Theodosius in the dactylic hexameter, see the hexameters in Anth. 285–289, 313, 314. *Theo-* is found there in 286, 288, 289, 313, 314, *Theu-* in 287 (doubtful), 285 (also doubtful: the actual letters of the inscription, which were of metal, are not extant. See Josef Strygowski, Römische Quartalschrift 7 [1893], 1–3). See Welzel, 31. On the danger of relying on inscriptions for matters of prosody, see A. E. Housman, Cl. Quart. 21 (1927), 3. I see no reason to depart from the unanimous reading of the manuscripts.

Liber Primus [61] 279

impacata quies pelagi, cum flamine fracto
durat adhuc saevitque tumor dubiumque per aestum
lassa recedentis fluitant vestigia venti.
   Improba mox surgit tristi de sede Megaera,
quam penes insani fremitus animique profanus   75
error et undantes spumis furialibus irae:
non nisi quaesitum cognata caede cruorem
illicitumve bibit, patrius quem fuderit ensis,
quem dederint fratres; haec terruit Herculis ora
et defensores terrarum polluit arcus,   80
haec Athamantheae direxit spicula dextrae,
haec Agamemnonios inter bacchata Penates
alternis lusit iugulis; hac auspice taedae
Oedipoden matri, natae iunxere Thyesten.
Quae tunc horrisonis effatur talia dictis: 85
   "Signa quidem, o sociae, divos attollere contra
nec fas est nec posse reor; sed laedere mundum
si libet et populis commune intendere letum,
est mihi prodigium cunctis immanius hydris,
tigride mobilius feta, violentius Austris   90
acribus, Euripi refluis incertius undis,
Rufinus, quem prima meo de matre cadentem
suscepi gremio. Parvus reptavit in isto

86 o sociae] socie *V* <*sic Birt; sed Jeep* o *litteram altera manu in V additam esse dicit*>, o socie φ, o sociae *Jeep*, sociae *Birt Koch*   91 acribus euripi •Λ² *Jeep* <*vide Jeep 2 Pr. 158*> *Birt Koch*, acrius hirpys Λ, acrius harpyis Λ¹, acrius arpiis ω.   91 refluis] fulvis *eB Birt Koch*, flavis Λφ *Jeep*, flavisque Λ¹ *quod probat* Λ² *sed addit vel fulvis*, refluis *Isengr. mg.*

86. o sociae: for the elision of the last syllable of *quidem*, compare 2.87 (also 2.216, *equidem et*). Birt, defending the reading *signa quidem, sociae*, cites IE 2.391 quid novus hic torpor, socii, as lacking *o*. Compare, however, BP 560 nunc, nunc, o socii; CS 3.262 O sociae. See Birt, 548, article *o*.

91. refluis: this reading is defended with cogent arguments by Muellner (182, note 1). He cites, among other examples, Statius, Thebais 7.333–334 refluumque meatu Euripum; Seneca, Hercules Furens 377–378 vicibus alternis fugax Euripus; Lucan 5.235 Euripus . . . cursum mutantibus undis. Claudian is using a comparison to illustrate Rufinus's inconstancy (*incertius*); it seems unlikely that he would qualify the Euripus by an almost otiose epithet, without referring specifically to its alternating current. In 2.113–114 Claudian goes out of his way to mention a similar characteristic of the Garonne. See also 6H 497–498; IE 2.259–269. For the word *refluus* in Claudian, we may cite BG 282–283 <Gildo> refluum . . . malignus commodat imperium; 3H 58 Tethyos alternae refluas calcavit harenas. Compare also Statius, Silvae 1.3.31–32 sic Chalcida fluctus expellunt reflui (there one manuscript reads *fluvii*, a clue to the corruption in our passage).

saepe sinu teneroque per ardua colla volutus
ubera quaesivit fletu linguisque trisulcis 95
mollia lambentes finxerunt membra cerastae.
Meque etiam tradente dolos artesque nocendi
edidicit: simulare fidem sensusque minaces
protegere et blando fraudem praetexere risu,
plenus saevitiae lucrique cupidine fervens. 100
Non Tartesiacis illum satiaret harenis
tempestas pretiosa Tagi, non stagna rubentis
aurea Pactoli; totumque exhauserit Hermum:
ardebit maiore siti. Quam fallere mentes
doctus et unanimos odiis turbare sodales! 105
Talem progenies hominum si prisca tulisset,
Perithoum fugeret Theseus, offensus Orestem
desereret Pylades, odisset Castora Pollux.
Ipsa quidem fateor vinci rapidoque magistram
praevenit ingenio; nec plus sermone morabor: 110
solus habet scelerum quidquid possedimus omnes.
Hunc ego, si vestrae res est accommoda turbae,
regalem ad summi producam principis aulam.
Sit licet ipse Numa gravior, sit denique Minos,
cedet et insidiis nostri flectetur alumni". 115
  Orantem sequitur clamor cunctaeque profanas
porrexere manus inventaque tristia laudant.
Illa ubi caeruleo vestes conexuit angue
nodavitque adamante comas, Phlegethonta sonorum
poscit et ambusto flagrantis ab aggere ripae 120
ingentem piceo succendit gurgite pinum
pigraque veloces per Tartara concutit alas.
  Est locus extremum pandit qua Gallia litus
Oceani praetentus aquis, ubi fertur Vlixes
sanguine libato populum movisse silentem. 125
Illic umbrarum tenui stridore volantum
flebilis auditur questus; simulacra coloni
pallida defunctasque vident migrare figuras.

96 membra φ *Birt Koch*, ora *VP Jeep*   99 fraudem φ *Birt Koch*, fraudes
V Jeep   119 nodavitque... comas φ *Birt Koch*, nodatamque... comam *V*,
nodavitque... comam *Jeep*   128 figuras φ *Birt*, catervas *V Jeep Koch*

128. figuras: Koch reads *catervas* on the ground that *figuras* is synonymous
with *simulacra*, and is therefore a gloss or interpolation; but compare 2.480–481
gesta ... actus. See also Parravicini, 75–113, Ripetizioni di Pensieri. Birt, 510,

Hinc dea prosiluit Phoebique egressa serenos
infecit radios ululatuque aethera rupit 130
terrifico: sensit ferale Britannia murmur
et Senonum quatit arva fragor revolutaque Tethys
substitit et Rhenus proiecta torpuit urna.
Tunc in canitiem mutatis sponte colubris
longaevum mentita senem rugisque severas 135
persulcata genas et ficto languida passu
invadit muros Elusae, notissima dudum
tecta petens, oculisque diu liventibus haesit
peiorem mirata virum; tum talia fatur:
"Otia te, Rufine, iuvant frustraque iuventae 140
consumis florem patriis inglorius arvis?
Heu nescis quid fata tibi, quid sidera donent,
quid fortuna paret: toto dominabere mundo
si parere velis! Artus ne sperne seniles!
Namque mihi magicae vires aevique futuri 145
praescius ardor inest; novi quo Thessala cantu
eripiat lunare iubar, quid signa sagacis
Aegypti valeant, qua gens Chaldaea vocatis
imperet arte deis, nec me latuere fluentes
arboribus suci funestarumque potestas 150

131 sensit φ *Jeep Birt*, sentit *A Koch* 141 patriis] patriisque *V Jeep Birt*,
patriis φ *Koch* 142 donent V^1 φ (*sed* d *ex* u *correxit* P^1) *Birt*, debent •CV^2
Koch, dedent $Λ^2$, dont *B*, dedant *coniecit ac edidit Jeep* 143 paret φ (*ex* patet
correxit P) *Jeep Birt*, parat *C Koch*   dominabere $Π^1 V^2 φ$ *Birt Koch*, donable
(*sic*) P^1, donabere $Π^2 V^1$ *Jeep*

col. 1, defends *figuras* by citing 2.491 and RP 3.124-125 somnia ... variis infausta figuris saepe monent.

131. sensit: in his apparatus, Birt writes "sentit *A, fort<asse> rectius*". Koch, influenced by this remark and by the tense of *quatit* (132), prints *sentit*. The change is an obvious one, and the reading of A is probably due to a conjecture of its fifteenth century scribe rather than to any manuscript reading in his exemplar. See Bednara, Arch. 14 (1905–1906), 574–577, for the adaptation of tenses to the exigencies of metre. Compare BP 476–480 aestuat ... piget ... visa <est> ... subeunt ... occultat ... iubet, with Dr. Schroff's note on verse 478.

142–143. donent ... paret: for *donare* in the sense of 'offer', compare RP 1.135 (Mars and Apollo, unsuccessful suitors of Proserpina, offer bride-gifts) Mars donat Rhodopen, Phoebus largitur Amyclas. This disposes of Koch's objection (Pr. 19): "*donent ... pro 'donatura sint' non facile acceperis*".

143. dominabere: if we read *donent* in 142, we cannot read *donabere* here. Moreover, the antithesis *dominabere ... parere* is quite in Claudian's manner; compare IE 1.142–144, and Parravicini, 59–62.

herbarum, quidquid letali gramine pollens
Caucasus et Scythicae vernant in crimina rupes,
quas legit Medea ferox et callida Circe.
Saepius horrendos Manes sacrisque citavi

151 gramine φ *Jeep Koch*, germine *A Birt*   152 vernant Λω *Birt Koch*, servant *coniecit ac edidit Jeep*   crimina] gramine Λω, gramina Λ² *Birt*, *gramina *Koch*, culmine *coniecit ac edidit Jeep*, crimina *coniecit Postgate*   154 citavi *X*, litavi ω *Birt Koch*, levavi Λ² *Jeep*

151. gramine: Postgate, Cl. Quart. 4 (1910), 258, supports this reading, and cites Propertius 2.1.53 seu mihi Circaeo pereundum est gramine. Compare also BG 173-174 adhuc ignota novercis gramina. The determination of the reading here depends largely on the solution of the problem raised by the penultimate word of the next verse.

152. vernant in crimina: conjectural attempts to remedy this "locus desperatus", as Koch calls it, have been many (Buecheler, quoted by Birt, would interpret the manuscript reading *in gramine* as equivalent to *inter alias herbas*, but this is too strained an interpretation to warrant the retention of *gramine*, especially after *gramine* [or even *germine*] in the preceding verse). Jeep's *servant in culmine* is pure invention. For Birt's *toxica*, compare Lucan 9.821 toxica fatilegi carpunt . . . Saitae, and Ovid, Ex Ponto 4.7.11; but the word *toxicus* does not occur elsewhere in Claudian. Heinsius's *carmina*, in the sense of 'magic arts', comes nearer the mark; but *in crimina*, the brilliant emendation of Postgate (Cl. Quart. 4 [1910], 258), is commendable on every ground. For *crimen* in the sense of 'evil deed', compare RP 3.386-387 . . . pestiferas animare ad crimina taxos . . . Megaera ruit. See also IE 1.27, 87; CS 1.7, 2.118; Birt, 491. The expression of purpose by the use of the accusative with the preposition *in* is frequent in Claudian: compare 1.311; CM 9.11-12 in proelia crescit . . . seges; PO 122-123 cornus in hastam porrigitur; CM 29.50, 6.3.

154. citavi: the difficulty with the reading *litavi* is the resultant construction of *litavi* with *manes* and *Hecaten*. For the meaning of *lito*, 'to sacrifice successfully', see Georg Wissowa, Religion und Kultus der Römer², 418 (Munich, Beck, 1912), and Cicero, De Divinatione, Edited by Arthur S. Pease, University of Illinois Studies in Language and Literature 8 (1920), 414, on De Divinatione 2.15.36 *litatur*. Because of this meaning, *lito*, when it is used with a case at all, is used with the *accusative* of the thing sacrificed, the *dative* of the recipient of the offering (see Harpers' Latin Dictionary, *lito* IB). In defense of *manes . . . litavi . . . Hecaten<que>* in the sense 'I worshipped the Manes and Hecate' Birt cites Cato, Disticha 4.38 and Claudius Marius Victor, Alethia 3.190-192. The first passage runs thus: Ture deum placa, vitulum sine crescat aratro; ne credas gaudere deum, cum caede litatur. But here *litatur* is certainly impersonal; the sense is 'when an offering is made by means of a slaughtered animal'. Compare IE 1.21-22 ipso . . . litandum prodigio, and the passage from Cicero to which reference is made above (. . . proxuma hostia litatur saepe pulcherrime). At any rate, nothing is proved by the citation from Cato. The second passage reads: . . . nam protinus omnes amplexae gentes scelus hoc sine fine litantes manibus inferias. Here we have the *accusative* of the sacrifice, the *dative* of the recipient: I am at a loss to understand what Birt meant this citation to prove. Koch (Cuiac. 59) quotes the theory of Servius

Liber Primus [65] 283

nocturnis Hecaten et condita funera traxi 155
carminibus victura meis, multosque canendo,
quamvis Parcarum restarent fila, peremi.
Ire vagas quercus et fulmen stare coëgi
versaque non prono curvavi flumina lapsu
in fontes reditura suos. Ne vana locutum 160
me fortasse putes, mutatos cerne Penates".
Dixerat, et niveae (mirum!) coepere columnae
ditari subitoque trabes lucere metallo.
 Illecebris capitur, nimiumque elatus avaro
pascitur aspectu. Sic rex ad prima tumebat 165
Maeonius, pulchro cum verteret omnia tactu;
sed postquam riguisse dapes fulvamque revinctos
in glaciem vidit latices, tum munus acerbum
sensit et inviso votum damnavit in auro.
Ergo animi victus: "Sequimur quocumque vocabis, 170
seu tu vir seu numen" ait, patriaque relicta
Eoas Furiae iussu tendebat ad arces,
instabilesque olim Symplegadas et freta remis
inclita Thessalicis, celsa qua Bosphorus urbe
splendet et Odrysiis Asiam discriminat oris. 175
 Ut longum permensus iter ductusque maligno
stamine fatorum claram subrepsit in aulam,

160 ne Λ² φ *Birt Koch*, neu ΛP *Jeep*, heu A   173 instabilesque] instabiles VII *Birt*, instabilisque Λ² *Jeep*, instabilesque φ *Koch*   175 discriminat φ *Birt Koch*, disterminat B *Jeep*

ad Vergilii Aeneidem 4.50: <sacris litatis:> "diis litatis" debuit dicere; non enim sacra sed deos litamus, id est placamus: ergo nove dixit. This remark of Servius is pedantic nonsense: compare Cicero, De Divinatione 2.38 Quid? cum pluribus deis immolatur, qui tandem evenit ut litetur aliis, aliis non litetur?; Pro Flacco 96 Litemus igitur Lentulo, parentemus Cethego. Compare also Koch's own citations! I have accepted *citavi*, the reading of the Cuiacianus (Koch Cuiac., 44, 59), which fits both the construction and the sense. Compare Seneca, Oedipus 568 manes voce ... citat; 4H 498 avida sector non voce citatur. See also Thesaurus *cito* (1) I B. *Levavi*, the reading of Λ², was apparently read by a scholiast in a French manuscript mentioned in Revue de Philologie 8 (1884), 81–99, especially 87, and note 2. I have been unable to find any parallel for the use of *levo* in the sense 'raise <from the lower world>', but I cannot agree with Koch (Cuiac. 59) that *levavi* here would be absurd: I consider it preferable by far to *litavi*.
 175. **discriminat:** compare 6H 290 <Appenninus> utraque perpetuo discriminat aequora tractu. See also PO 89–90 nodus, qui sublevat ensem, album puniceo pectus discriminat ostro, and Statius, Thebais 5.529–530 ... ab Arctois discriminat aethera plaustris anguis. *Distermino* is not found elsewhere in Claudian.

ilicet ambitio nasci, discedere rectum,
venum cuncta dari; profert arcana, clientes
fallit et ambitos a principe vendit honores. 180
Ingeminat crimen, commoti pectoris ignem
nutrit et exiguum stimulando vulnus acerbat.
Ac velut innumeros amnes accedere Nereus
nescit et undantem quamvis hinc hauriat Histrum,
hinc bibat aestivum septeno gurgite Nilum, 185
par semper similisque manet: sic fluctibus auri
expleri calor ille nequit. Cuicumque monile
contextum gemmis aut praedia culta fuissent,
Rufino populandus erat, dominoque parabat
exitium fecundus ager; metuenda colonis 190
fertilitas: Laribus pellit, detrudit avitis
finibus; aut aufert vivis aut occupat heres.
Congestae cumulantur opes orbisque ruinas
accipit una domus; populi servire coacti
plenaque privato succumbunt oppida regno. 195
   Quo, vesane, ruis? Teneas utrumque licebit
Oceanum, laxet rutilos tibi Lydia fontes,
iungatur solium Croesi Cyrique tiara:
numquam dives eris, numquam satiabere quaestu.
Semper inops quicumque cupit. Contentus honesto 200
Fabricius parvo spernebat munera regum
sudabatque gravi consul Serranus aratro
et casa pugnaces Curios angusta tegebat.
Haec mihi paupertas opulentior, haec mihi tecta
culminibus maiora tuis. Ibi quaerit inanes 205
luxuries nocitura cibos; hic donat inemptas

   186 manet Λφ *Birt Koch*, meat Λ¹ (Λ²?) *Jeep*   205 ibi *C Birt Koch*, tibi
φ *Jeep*   206 hic *C Birt Koch*, tibi *V*¹, mihi *V*³ φ *Jeep*

186. manet: according to Birt's apparatus, it is uncertain whether Λ² added his two dots of approval (see above, page 44) to *meat*, the reading of Λ¹. The verb *meo* occurs nowhere else in Claudian. Further, the verb is not Vergilian. Apparently it is not used by Martial, Juvenal, Statius, or Silius. It is rare in Ovid (twice) and in Lucan (twice). Moreover, the word *meat* is not particularly appropriate for Nereus. I believe that it may safely be discarded as a mistake or conjecture of Λ¹.

205-206. Ibi quaerit ... hic donat: Birt (Pr. 113.27-33) prefers this reading of Codex C to the reading *tibi quaerit ... mihi donat* of the other codices, rightly, on the ground that it is not in harmony with Claudian's usage in his longer poems to mention himself or his circumstances, or to compare himself with the characters

Liber Primus

terra dapes. Rapiunt Tyrios ibi vellera sucos
et picturatae saturantur murice vestes;
hic radiant flores et prati viva voluptas
ingenio variata suo. Fulgentibus illic   210
surgunt strata toris; hic mollis panditur herba
sollicitum curis non abruptura soporem.
Turba salutantum latas ibi perstrepit aedes;
hic avium cantus, labentis murmura rivi.
Vivitur exiguo melius; natura beatis   215
omnibus esse dedit, si quis cognoverit uti.
Haec si nota forent, frueremur simplice cultu,
classica non gemerent, non stridula fraxinus iret,
non ventus quateret puppes, non machina muros.

207 ibi φ *Birt Koch*, tibi *VΠBA Jeep*   208 saturantur φ *Birt Koch*, fucantur Λ²C *Jeep*   209 et prati] hic prati *Jeep ut ex V; sed Birt hanc lectionem in apparatu non praebet*   213 ibi Πφ *Birt Koch*, tibi VBII¹ *Jeep* <*qui dicit* (2 Pr. 20) *se* tibi *in libro* ϵ *vidisse, qua de re tacet Birt*>   218 gemerent Λ²V¹C *Birt Koch*, fremerent V²φ *Jeep*   219 non . . . non ω *Birt*, nec . . . nec Λ¹Λ² *Jeep Koch*

in his poems. In the Carmina Maiora, it is only in the Prefaces (e. g. 6H Pr., BP Pr.) that we find a reference to Claudian *in propria persona*. The reading *tibi . . . mihi* here (and *tibi*, 207, 213) may have resulted from an attempt to continue the *apparent* comparison of *mihi . . . tuis* (204–205).

It may not be too fanciful, however, to see in the variants here and in verses 207 and 213 a clue to the history of the passage. Verses 196–219 form a digression, complete in itself, on the inanity of wealth and the blessings of poverty. If we examine CM 2, CM 5, and particularly CM 6, we see that Claudian was accustomed to develop separate themes in the hexameter, perhaps with a view to later incorporation in longer poems (see Platnauer, 1.xviii, note 2). Our passage may have begun as a development of the commonplace *semper inops quicumque cupit*, in which *tibi . . . mihi* would not have been inappropriate. But, in incorporating the piece into the IR, Claudian may have changed *tibi . . . mihi . . . tibi . . . tibi* to *ibi . . . hic . . . ibi . . . ibi* in order to eliminate the personal note. The survival of the separate poem among Claudian's papers may then have caused the introduction of variants in our passage, with the resulting confusion which we find in the manuscripts.

208. saturantur: compare Ovid, Heroides 13.37 *saturatas murice vestes*.

218. gemerent: in defense of this reading, Birt cites Laus Pisonis 141–142 *nec . . . classicus horror . . . gemit*. See Birt, 516, and compare Thesaurus *gemo* II C, which cites Juvenal 7.71 *nihil gemeret . . . bucina*, and Corippus, Johannis 1.512 *gemit bucina*, 6.263–264 (for Corippus as an imitator of Claudian, see Pauly-Wissowa 4.1236.51–57, and Welzel, *passim*). See also Laus Pisonis, Edited by Gladys Martin, 73, note on Laus Pisonis 142 (Thesis, Cornell University, Privately Printed, 1917).

219. non . . . non: compare Ovid, Metamorphoses 1.98–99 *non tuba directi, non aeris cornua flexi, non galeae, non ensis erant*.

Crescebat scelerata sitis praedaeque recentis 220
incestus flagrabat amor, nullusque petendi
cogendive pudor: crebris periuria nectit
blanditiis; sociat perituro foedere dextras.
Si semel e tantis poscenti quisque negasset,
effera praetumido quatiebat corda furore. 225
Quae sic Gaetuli iaculo percussa leaena
aut Hyrcana premens raptorem belua partus
aut serpens calcata furit? Iurata deorum
maiestas teritur; nusquam reverentia mensae.
Non coniunx, non ipse simul, non pignora caesi 230
sufficiunt odiis; non extinxisse propinquos,
non notos egisse sat est; exscindere cives
funditus et nomen gentis delere laborat.
Nec celeri perimit leto; crudelibus ante
suppliciis fruitur; cruciatus, vincla, tenebras 235
dilato mucrone parat. Pro saevior ense
parcendi rabies concessaque vita dolori!
Mors adeone parum est? Causis fallacibus instat,
arguit attonitos se iudice. Cetera segnis,
ad facinus velox, penitus regione remotas 240
impiger ire vias: non illum Sirius ardens
brumave Riphaeo stridens Aquilone retardat.
Effera torquebant avidae praecordia curae,

222 cogendive ω *Birt Koch*, cogendique Λ² *Jeep*   227 partus Π¹ (*sed* rtus *in rasura*) *Birt Koch*, parthus V², parthum V¹Λ²ε *Jeep*   230 caesi *V Birt*, cęsti *C*, caesa φ *Koch*, caecis *coniecit Paul edidit Jeep*   238 parum est] parum est ω *Jeep Koch*, parum ϛ *Birt*

227. partus: Birt's contention that *partus* is necessary to define *raptorem* seems cogent; moreover, the word *Hyrcana* renders any other geographical adjective unnecessary. The manuscript change to *Parthus* and then (for agreement's sake) to *Parthum* looks like the result of pseudo-erudition on the part of an early scribe.

238. parum est: Birt omits *est* on the ground that Claudian avoids its use wherever such avoidance is possible (Birt Pr. 224, § 9.13–21; 225; 216.8–11. Compare Koch Pr. 20). Birt is correct in his observation of Claudian's usage, but he is not justified in formulating an iron-clad law ("lex", Birt Pr. 224, § 9.20–21). Compare PO 14 certum est de consule nasci, where *est* is not absolutely necessary either to metre or to sense, but is found in all the manuscripts. In CM 29.51, instead of quae tibi, saeve puer, non est permissa potestas, Claudian might have written, e. g. quae tibi, saeve puer, quae non permissa potestas (compare Vergil, Aeneid 9.97 cui tanta deo permissa potestas?, and see IR 2.385). The omission of *est* in our present passage would be very harsh, as Birt (Pr. 225.12–14) virtually admits.

Liber Primus

effugeret ne quis gladios neu perderet ullum
Augusto miserante nefas. Non flectitur annis, 245
non aetate labat: iuvenum rorantia colla
ante patrum vultus stricta cecidere securi;
ibat grandaevus nato moriente superstes
post trabeas exul. Quis prodere tanta relatu
funera, quis caedes possit deflere nefandas? 250
Quid tale immanes umquam gessisse feruntur
vel Sinis Isthmiaca pinu vel rupe profunda
Sciron vel Phalaris tauro vel carcere Sylla?
O mites Diomedis equi! Busiridis arae
clementes! Iam Cinna pius, iam, Spartace, segnis 255
Rufino collatus eris!
     Deiecerat omnes
occultis odiis terror taciticique sepultos
suspirant gemitus indignarique verentur.
At non magnanimi virtus Stilichonis eodem
fracta metu; solus medio sed turbine rerum 260
contra letiferos rictus contraque rapacem
movit tela feram, volucris non praepete cursu
vectus equi, non Pegaseis adiutus habenis.
Hic cunctis optata quies, hic sola pericli

 253 sylla *VCAΛ Koch*, silla φ, Sulla *Jeep Birt* 255 segnis *Birt Koch*, lenis *Jeep* <*de lectionibus codicum tacent Jeep Birt Koch*> 260 solus medio sed (*in eodem exemplari editionis Aldinae in quo sunt excerpta* ϵ, *scripsit haec Livineius ut ex Vaticano suo*) *Birt Koch*, medio solus sed *exemplar Aldinum*, ϵ *ante* medio *inseruit sese delevitque* solus sed, sese medio sed Λ, solus medio de Λ² *Jeep*, solus medio se *VC*, solus sed (*caret* medio) B, medio sese sed PΠA 264 hic *primum*] hic V²Λφ *Birt Koch*, hęc Λ¹ (*crucem, signum dubiae lectionis, addidit* Λ² *vel E*) C, hec V¹PΠ, haec *Jeep* hic *alterum*] hic Λφ *Birt Koch*, hęc Λ¹ (*crucem ut supra*) C, hec VPΠ, haec *Jeep*

 253. Sylla: Birt, 249 (on 6H 383), remarks: "Sylla etiam Ruf. 1.253 edendum fuit". See also Birt, 457; Pr. 40, note 1. For the spelling *Sylla* as an outgrowth of the legend that the name was a contraction of *Sibylla* see Pauly-Wissowa 4.1514. The legendary form of the name is appropriate to epic, and softens the harshness of a historical figure amid mythological characters. Compare Birt, 460 on *Thybris*, and see Dr. Schroff's note on BP 505 *Thybride*.

 260. solus medio sed turbine: Birt is undoubtedly right in following Livineius. In the reading of VC *solus medio se turbine*, I see the source of the confusion, the dropping of the final letter of *sed* (*set?*). The reflexive *se* or *sese* seems syntactically impossible, and Jeep's *de* is inappropriate.

 264. Hic . . . hic: uppermost in Claudian's mind is Stilicho, not the idea of *quies* or *turris;* moreover, verses 266–267, where *hic . . . sedes* and *hic castra* are both unanimously attested, favor our reading. The alterations in verse 264 which are found in the various manuscripts are undoubtedly due to emendatory zeal. See Kühner 1.36, Anmerkung 1.

turris erat clipeusque trucem porrectus in hostem, 265
hic profugis sedes adversaque signa furori,
servandis hic castra bonis.
                    Hucusque minatus
haerebat retroque fuga cedebat inerti:
haud secus hiberno tumidus cum vertice torrens
saxa rotat volvitque nemus pontesque revellit, 270
frangitur obiectu scopuli quaerensque meatum
spumat et illisa montem circumtonat unda.
  Qua dignum te laude feram, qui paene ruenti
lapsuroque tuos umeros obieceris orbi?
Te nobis trepidae sidus ceu dulce carinae 275
ostendere dei, geminis quae lassa procellis
tunditur et victo trahitur iam caeca magistro.
Inachius rubro perhibetur in aequore Perseus
Neptuni domuisse pecus, sed tutior alis:
te non penna vehit; rigida cum Gorgone Perseus: 280
tu non vipereo defensus crine Medusae;
illum vilis amor suspensae virginis egit:
te Romana salus. Taceat superata vetustas,
Herculeos conferre tuis iam desinat actus.
Vna Cleonaeum pascebat silva leonem; 285
Arcadiae saltum vastabat dentibus unum
saevus aper, tuque o compressa matre rebellis

272 illisa *C Birt Koch*, elisa *Vφ Jeep*   287 compressa *φ Jeep Birt*,
cumpressa *C*, cum pressa <*matre*> *Koch*   rebellis *V¹C¹φ Jeep Koch*, revel-
lis *C¹*, rebellas *V¹*, rebellans *coniecit ac edidit Birt*

272. illisa: *inlido* (*illido*) is well attested in Claudian (RP 1.257, IE 2.431), and is more appropriate to the sense of this passage than is *elido*. Contrast 2.222 *elisa tonitrua Coris*.

287. compressa matre rebellis: Claudian follows the later form of the Antaeus legend (see Roscher, 1.362–364), in which the giant receives new vigor from his mother Earth each time he is thrown by Hercules, until the latter defeats him by holding him aloft. Compare RP 2 Pr. 41 *non cadere Antaeo . . . profuit*; Ovid, Ibis 394 *qui <= Antaeus>, mirum, victor, cum cecidisset, erat*; Statius, Thebais 6.893–896; Juvenal 3.89; Lucan 4.590–655. To be sure, *compressa* in this sense is somewhat unusual, but compare Valerius Flaccus 3.106–107 <of a warrior 'biting the dust'> *compressa . . . mandens aequora*. The construction of an ablative absolute in a quasi-causal relation to an adjective is frequent in Claudian: CS 1.148–149 *turbida rupto ordine*; IR 2 Pr. 5 *securis pulsa formidine*; IR 1.277 *victo . . . caeca magistro*; 6H 137 *scissis . . . debilis alis*, 138 *antennis saucia fractis*. See also MT 247; CS 2.369; CM 32.19. Koch's *cum pressa matre* is not im-

Liber Primus

non ultra Libyae fines, Antaee, nocebas,
solaque fulmineo resonabat Creta iuvenco
Lernaeamque virens obsederat hydra paludem. 290
Hoc monstrum non una palus, non una tremebat
insula, sed Latia quidquid dicione subactum
vivit et a primis Ganges horrebat Hiberis.
Hoc neque Geryon triplex nec turbidus Orci
ianitor aequabit nec si concurrat in unum 295
vis hydrae Scyllaeque fames et flamma Chimaerae.
   Certamen sublime diu, sed moribus impar
virtutum scelerumque fuit. Iugulare minatur,
tu prohibes; ditem spoliat, tu reddis egenti.
Eruit: instauras; accendit proelia: vincis. 300
   Ac velut infecto morbus crudescere caelo
incipiens primos pecudum depascitur artus,
mox populos urbesque rapit ventisque perustis
corruptos Stygiam pestem desudat in amnes:
sic avidus praedo iam non per singula saevit. 305
Sed sceptris inferre minas omnique perempto
milite Romanas ardet prosternere vires
iamque Getas Histrumque movet Scythiamque receptat
auxilio traditque suas hostilibus armis
relliquias. Mixtis descendit Sarmata Dacis 310
et qui cornipedes in pocula vulnerat audax
Massagetes caesamque bibens Maeotin Alanus

294 geryon Λ² *Birt Koch,* geryones *V (sed* es *in rasura) Jeep,* gerion φ
295 aequabit] equabit *B,* aequabit *Birt Koch,* equabant *PΠ (duo puncti sub* n
in Π), aequabunt Λ²φ *Jeep* 302 primos ω *Birt Koch,* primo ς, primum
coniecit ac edidit Jeep 312 caesamque bibens maeotin alanus] *sic Birt Koch,*
patriumque bibens moeotis orontem *B*Λ *(sic fere P),* moeotin alanus Λ¹ *(sic fere*
*P*¹), cesamque bibens meotin alanus Λ² <*unde Birt Koch ego*>, patriamque
bibens maeotin alanus *A V (sic fere, sed* patriumque, *C*Π; alanus *in rasura V³*),
patriamque bibens maeotin alanus *Jeep*

possible, but, as Birt remarks, we should expect *pressa cum matre*, to conform
with Claudian's usage.

   312. caesamque bibens Maeotin Alanus: the confusion of readings at this
point, which I have only partially indicated in the textual notes (see Birt's apparatus), cannot be due to the ordinary mischances of manuscript copying. It
is my theory that some such alternate half-line as *patriumque bibens* ˘ ˘ - ˘ <e. g.
Apameus> *Orontem* was inserted at an early point in the manuscript tradition.
The readings *Maeotis* on the one hand, and *patriam* on the other would then
be the result of eclectic attempts to make a single harmonious verse. There can be
no connection between the Orontes and Lake Maeotis: the latter is over 500 miles
distant from any confluent of the former. Though the Orontes disappears under-
ground, it soon reappears (Strabo 16.750), and I have not been able to find any

membraque qui ferro gaudet pinxisse Gelonus,
Rufino collecta manus. Vetat ille domari
innectitque moras et congrua tempora differt.   315
Nam tua cum Geticas stravisset dextra catervas,
ulta ducis socii letum, parsque una maneret
debilior facilisque capi, tunc impius ille
proditor imperii coniuratusque Getarum
distulit instantes eluso principe pugnas   320
Hunorum laturus opem, quos affore bello
norat et invisis mox se coniungere castris.
　Est genus extremos Scythiae vergentis in ortus
trans gelidum Tanain, quo non famosius ullum
Arctos alit. Turpes habitus obscaenaque visu   325
corpora; mens duro numquam cessura labori;
praeda cibus, vitanda Ceres frontemque secari

314 domari ω *Jeep Birt*, domare *coniecit Birt edidit Koch*　　324 famosius Λ³V²CII *Jeep Koch*, deformius Λ, aniosius Λ², animosius V¹ *Birt*, formosius P　327 frontemque secari Λ²V¹ *Birt Koch*, frontemque secare εV³φ *Jeep*

trace of a legend such as that which connects the Alpheus with Arethusa (see IR 2 Pr. 9-12). Claudian can scarcely have mentioned the dwellers on the Orontes in this connection (compare IR 2.35 *imbellem . . . Orontem*). If my theory is correct, we must attribute the insertion of the alternate half-verse to some freak of reminiscence on the part of a scribe. The reading *patriam*, adopted by Jeep, is not impossible, but I have set forth my suspicions as to its origin; on the other hand, *caesam* is in complete harmony with Claudian's manner. He seems to have been deeply impressed by the freezing of bodies of water (perhaps because of his Egyptian origin): compare IE 2.414 duris haurire bipennibus Hebrum; IR 2.26-27; 3H 150 stantem . . . sulcavimus Histrum; also CS 1.125-126; RP 2.65-66; BP 338-339, with Dr. Schroff's note. Compare Encyclopaedia Britannica[14] 2.830: "It <the Sea of Azov> generally freezes from the end of November to the middle of April". For the Alani, see Pauly-Wissowa 1.1282. Josephus, Bellum Judaicum 7.7.4 τὸ δὲ τῶν 'Αλανῶν ἔθνος . . . Σκύθαι περὶ τὴν Μαιῶτιν λίμνην κατοικοῦντες, is there cited.

314. vetat ille domari: Birt remarks, "*Malim* domare; sc<ilicet> *Rufinus Stilichonem vetat barbaros domare*". Koch is not justified in adopting this suggestion into his text: compare Statius, Thebais 3.97 vetat igne rapi; Lucan 6.141-142 <locum> victoribus unus eripuit vetuitque capi.

324. famosius: Koch rejects Birt's *animosius*, rightly, on the ground that the word is too favorable to the Huns: compare IE 1.452-453 animosaque pauperis umbra Fabricii; MT 1-5 Virtus . . . divitiis animosa suis. For *famosus* as a word of reproach, compare IE 1.198 <Eutropius> caupo famosus honorum; MT 158 famosum luxum; Ovid, Heroides 9.134 Turpia famosus corpora iungit Hymen. The corruption in the manuscripts began probably with the omission of *f-*, and then proceeded *amosius > aniosius > animosius*.

Liber Primus

ludus et occisos pulchrum iurare parentes.
Nec plus nubigenas duplex natura biformes
cognatis aptavit equis; acerrima nullo 330
ordine mobilitas insperatique recursus.
    Quos tamen impavidus contra spumantis ad Hebri
tendis aquas, sic ante tubas aciemque precatus:
"Mavors, nubifero seu tu procumbis in Haemo
seu te cana gelu Rhodope seu remige Medo 335
sollicitatus Athos seu caligantia nigris
ilicibus Pangaea tenent, accingere mecum
et Thracas defende tuos. Si laetior adsit
gloria, vestita spoliis donabere quercu".
    Audiit illa pater scopulisque nivalibus Haemi 340
surgit et hortatur celeres clamore ministros:
"Fer galeam, Bellona, mihi nexusque rotarum
tende, Pavor. Frenet rapidos Formido iugales.
Festinas urgete manus. Meus ecce paratur
ad bellum Stilicho, qui me de more trophaeis 345
ditat et hostiles suspendit in arbore cristas.
Communes semper litui, communia nobis
signa canunt iunctoque sequor tentoria curru".
Sic fatus campo insiluit lateque fugatas
hinc Stilicho turmas, illinc Gradivus agebat 350
et clipeis et mole pares; stat cassis utrique
sidereis hirsuta iubis loricaque cursu
aestuat et largo saturatur vulnere cornus.
    Acrior interea voto multisque Megaera
luxuriata malis maestam deprendit in arce 355
Iustitiam diroque prior sic ore lacessit:
"En tibi prisca quies renovataque saecula rursus,
ut rebare, vigent? En nostra potentia cessit
nec locus est usquam Furiis? Huc lumina flecte.
Aspice barbaricis iaceant quot moenia flammis, 360
quas mihi Rufinus strages quantumque cruoris

    328 ludus $V^3\phi$ *Birt Koch*, lusus Λ^2 *Jeep*, luc||||us V^1, luctus *aut* ludus *C* (*incertum*), laudis *coniecit Birt*, luctus *Koenig*   343 rapidos $V^3\phi$ *Jeep Koch*, tepidos V^1, trepidos *Isengr. mg.; Birt*   358 en ϕ *Birt Koch*, et *V Jeep*

343. rapidos: I cannot agree with Koch (Pr. 20; he prints *rapidos*) that Birt's reading *trepidos* would be a suitable description of the horses of Mars, even under the ministrations of *Formido*. Compare CM 29.47 *feris . . . equis* <*Martis*>. See also CS 2.375–376; this passage shows that, according to Claudian's concept, *Formido* is a constant companion of the horses.

praebeat et quantis epulentur caedibus hydri.
Linque homines sortemque meam, pete sidera; notis
Autumni te redde plagis, qua vergit in Austrum
Signifer; aestivo sedes vicina Leoni   365
iam pridem gelidaeque vacant confinia Librae.
Atque utinam per magna sequi convexa liceret!"
    Diva refert: "Non ulterius bacchabere demens.
Iam poenas tuus iste dabit, iam debitus ultor
imminet et terras qui nunc ipsumque fatigat   370
aethera nec vili moriens condetur harena.
Iamque aderit laeto promissus Honorius aevo
nec forti genitore minor nec fratre corusco,
qui subiget Medos, qui cuspide proteret Indos.
Sub iuga venturi reges; calcabitur asper   375
Phasis equo pontemque pati cogetur Araxes,
tuque simul gravibus ferri religata catenis
expellere die debellatasque draconum
tonsa comas imo barathri claudere recessu.
Tum tellus communis erit, tum limite nullo   380
discernetur ager; nec vomere sulcus obunco
findetur: subitis messor gaudebit aristis.
Rorabunt querceta favis; stagnantia passim
vina fluent oleique lacus; nec murice tinctis
velleribus quaeretur honos, sed sponte rubebunt   385
attonito pastore greges pontumque per omnem
ridebunt virides gemmis nascentibus algae".

   366 gelidaeque] *sic Birt Koch,* gelidę *CA,* gelide *VPB,* gelidęque Λ², gelideque
Π, gemine ε, geminae Λ, geminaeque *Jeep*   371 nec vili Λφ *Jeep Birt,* nō ulla
Λ³, non ulli *B,* non vili *Koch*   374 subiget *V³φ Birt Koch,* subigat Λ² *Jeep,*
subigit *V¹*   proteret *V¹ (?)φ Birt Koch,* proterat Λ² *Jeep*   381 obunco Λφ
Jeep, adunco Λ¹Λ²*B Birt Koch,* ab unco Π   382 findetur Λω *Birt Koch,*
scindetur Λ¹Λ² *Jeep*

   371. nec vili: Koch is unnecessarily disturbed by *et . . . nec.* Compare 6H 482
et cui nec vigilem fas est componere Rhesum; Martial 12.31.3 *prataque nec bifero
cessura rosaria Paesto.* For *nec = ne . . . quidem,* see Kroll, Glotta 21 (1932),
106–107, and compare 6H 429, PO 147, CS 2.310–311. Postgate, 169, refers to
Koch's "superficial acquaintance with grammatical and lexical niceties" as his
"weak point".
   374. subiget . . . proteret: the future indicative is in much better accord with
the tone of the whole passage (372–387) than the present subjunctive would be.
   381. obunco: compare BG 470 <*aquila*> *morsu obunco.* On *obuncus* and *aduncus,* and the confusion in the manuscripts, see Mueller, Arch. 3 (1886), 249–250;
E. Norden, Aeneis Buch VI², 285, on Aeneid 6.597 (Leipzig, Teubner, 1916).
Aduncus is the Ovidian, *obuncus* the Vergilian form; I have been guided by the
well-attested reading *obunco* of BG 470.

IN RVFINVM LIBER SECVNDVS

INCIPIT PRAEFATIO

Pandite defensum reduces Helicona sorores,
   pandite. Permissis iam licet ire choris:
nulla per Aonios hostilis bucina campos
   carmina mugitu deteriore vetat.
Tu quoque securis pulsa formidine Delphis   5
   floribus ultorem, Delie, cinge tuum.
Nullus Castalios latices et praescia fati
   flumina polluto barbarus ore bibit.

Alpheus late rubuit Siculumque per aequor
   sanguineas belli rettulit unda notas   10
agnovitque novos absens Arethusa triumphos
   et Geticam sensit teste cruore necem.

Inmensis, Stilicho, succedant otia curis
   et nostrae patiens corda remitte lyrae,
nec pudeat longos interrupisse labores   15
   et tenuem Musis constituisse moram.
Fertur et indomitus tandem post proelia Mavors
   lassa per Odrysias fundere membra nives
oblitusque sui posita clementior hasta
   Pieriis aures pacificare modis.   20

   Pr. 2 permissis ω *Jeep Birt*, promissis *coniecit Birt edidit Koch*

BOOK 2

   Pr. 2. permissis: the conjecture *promissis* is neither necessary nor particularly apt. For the pleonasm *permissis . . . licet* compare 6H 265–266 laxata remisit frena; 261–262 relictis descivere favis; 498–499 nudata . . . litora . . . deserit <Nereus>; Catullus 64.179 discernens . . . dividit (see note *ad locum* in the edition of Wilhelm Kroll [Leipzig, Teubner, 1929]). Compare also Cicero, De Lege Agraria 2.34 ut complere liceat permittitur, . . . vagari ut liceat conceditur. See Brakman, 372; Stolz-Schmalz, 832, Zusatz; J. Vahlen, Opuscula 1.448–450 (Leipzig, Teubner, 1907); Enrica Malcovati, Bolletino di Filologia Classica 4 (1933), 8.3–11.

IN RVFINVM

LIBER II

Iam post edomitas Alpes defensaque regna
Hesperiae merita complexus sede parentem
auctior adiecto fulgebat sidere mundus,
iamque tuis, Stilicho, Romana potentia curis
et rerum commissus apex, tibi credita fratrum 5
utraque maiestas geminaeque exercitus aulae.
Rufinus (neque enim patiuntur saeva quietem
crimina pollutaeque negant arescere fauces)
infandis iterum terras accendere bellis
inchoat et solito pacem vexare tumultu. 10
Haec etiam secum: "Quanam ratione tuebor
spem vitae fragilem? Qua tot depellere fluctus
arte queam? Premor hinc odiis, hinc milite cingor.
Heu quid agam? Non arma mihi, non principis ullus
auxiliatur amor. Matura pericula surgunt 15
undique et impositi radiant cervicibus enses.
Quid restat, nisi cuncta novo confundere luctu
insontesque meae populos miscere ruinae?
Everso iuvat orbe mori: solacia leto
exitium commune dabit nec territus ante 20
discedam: cum luce simul linquenda potestas".
    Haec fatus, ventis veluti si frena resolvat
Aeolus, abrupto gentes sic obice fudit
laxavitque viam bellis et, ne qua maneret
immunis regio, cladem divisit in orbem 25
disposuitque nefas. Alii per terga ferocis
Danuvii solidata ruunt expertaque remos
frangunt stagna rotis; alii per Caspia claustra
Armeniasque nives inopino tramite ducti
invadunt Orientis opes. Iam pascua fumant 30

28 frangunt ω *Birt Koch,* stringunt *coniecit ac edidit Jeep*

28. frangunt: Jeep's emendation *stringunt* and Birt's suggestion *radunt* are unnecessary. The word *frangunt* well describes the grinding and crushing of the surface of the ice under the wheels of the heavy wagons. Compare Aeneid 1.178–179 fruges ... frangere saxo. See also note on IR 1.312, above.

[76]

Liber Secundus

Cappadocum volucrumque parens Argaeus equorum,
iam rubet altus Halys nec se defendit iniquo
monte Cilix. Syriae tractus vastantur amoeni
assuetumque choris et laeta plebe canorum
proterit imbellem sonipes hostilis Orontem. 35
Hinc planctus Asiae; Geticis Europa catervis
ludibrio praedaeque datur frondentis ad usque
Dalmatiae fines: omnis quae mobile Ponti
aequor et Adriacas tellus interiacet undas
squalet inops pecudum, nullis habitata colonis 40
instar anhelantis Libyae, quae torrida semper
solibus humano nescit mansuescere cultu.
Thessalus ardet ager; reticet pastore fugato
Pelion; Emathias ignis populatur aristas.
Nam plaga Pannoniae miserandaque moenia Thracum 45
arvaque Mysorum iam nulli flebile damnum,
sed cursus sollemnis erat campusque furori
expositus, sensumque malis detraxerat usus.
Eheu quam brevibus pereunt ingentia causis!
Imperium tanto quaesitum sanguine, tanto 50
servatum, quod mille ducum peperere labores,
quod tantis Romana manus contexuit annis,
proditor unus iners angusto tempore vertit.

Urbs etiam, magnae quae ducitur aemula Romae
et Calchedonias contra despectat harenas, 55
iam non finitimo Martis terrore movetur,
sed propius lucere faces et rauca sonare
cornua vibratisque peti fastigia telis
aspicit. Hi vigili muros statione tueri,
hi iunctis properant portus munire carinis. 60

45 nam *PCAΠ¹Em*ᵇ *Birt Koch*, iam P¹*VΠB Jeep*   46 mysorum Λ*VA Birt Koch*, moesorum "Excerpta Laeti" (vide Birt Pr. *127*) *Jeep, qui post hoc verbum signum* * *lacunae posuit*, misorum φ   49 causis φ *Birt*, fatis *Em*ᵇᵉ *Jeep Koch*   55 calchedonias *CP*¹ *Koch*, calcedonias Λ*VB*, chalcedonias *Jeep Birt*

46. **Mysorum**: the Moesi, who lived north of Mount Haemus, are meant. For the Greek form *Mysi* (Strabo 7.318 Μυσοί), see Pauly-Wissowa 15.2352.9–54. See also Birt Pr. 40, note 1, and my remarks on *Sylla*, 1.253.

49. **causis**: Koch's objection to *brevibus* . . . *causis* (Pr. 20, "*brevis causa* vix dici potest") is unfounded. Compare 4H 510–511 *quae sub te* . . . *causa brevis* . . . *neglegitur*, where the meaning of *causa* is different, but that of *brevis*, 'slight', 'insignificant', is the same. Compare also CS 1.42 *nil breve moliri*. See Paucker, 598; Thesaurus *brevis* III; Teuffel, 358; Brakman, 372.

Obsessa tamen ille ferus laetatur in urbe
exsultatque malis summaeque ex culmine turris
impia vicini cernit spectacula campi:
vinctas ire nurus, hunc in vada proxima mergi
seminecem, hunc subito percussum vulnere labi   65
dum fugit, hunc animam portis efflare sub ipsis;
nec canos prodesse seni puerique cruore
maternos undare sinus. Inmensa voluptas
et risus plerumque subit; dolor afficit unus,
quod feriat non ipse manu. Videt omnia late   70
exceptis incensa suis et crimine tanto
luxuriat carumque sibi non abnuit hostem;
iactabatque ultro, quod soli castra paterent
sermonumque foret vicibus permissa facultas,
egregii quotiens exisset foederis auctor   75
stipatus sociis, circumque armata clientum
agmina privatis ibant famulantia signis.
Ipse inter medios, ne qua de parte relinquat
barbariem, revocat fulvas in pectora pelles
frenaque et immanes pharetras arcusque sonoros   80
adsimulat mentemque palam proclamat amictu,
nec pudet Ausonios currus et iura regentem
sumere deformes ritus vestemque Getarum;
insignemque habitum Latii mutare coactae
maerent captivae pellito iudice leges.   85
    Quis populi tunc vultus erat! Quae murmura furtim!

67 nec φ *Birt Koch*, non *Em Jeep*   74 facultas *Emε V Jeep Birt*, potestas φ *Koch*   76 stipatus φ *Birt*, stipatur *V Jeep Koch*   81 proclamat amictu *Em*ᵇ *Birt Koch*, testatur amictus *E*ᵃω, testatur amictu *Jeep* <*ut ex* ε>   86 tunc vultus φ *Jeep Birt*, tumultus *C*, tum vultus *VII Koch*

76. stipatus sociis: Jeep and Koch read *stipatur*. Jeep places a comma at the end of verse 74, a full stop after 75; Koch places a full stop after verse 74, and a comma after verse 75. I follow Birt both in reading and in punctuation, since I believe, with him, that verses 73–78 are to be taken together, as part of a single sentence. The whole passage (73–85) is a description of the visits to the Gothic camp of Rufinus, surrounded by his barbarian retainers (*socii; armata clientum agmina*). These were his *bucellarii*, or private body-guard (the name is derived from *bucella*, the military biscuit; compare 'doughboy'!). Seeck *Gefolg.*, 109, believes that Rufinus was the first to introduce the custom of maintaining a corps of barbarian *bucellarii*, a practice which had become very frequent by the time of Justinian. See also Bury, 43, note 2; Stein, 365. The identity of these *socii* apparently escaped Koch, for he refuses to connect verses 75–77 with what precedes, on the ground that Rufinus alone had access to the camp of the barbarians. Yet

Liber Secundus

(nam miseris nec flere quidem aut lenire dolorem
colloquiis impune licet): "Quonam usque feremus
exitiale iugum? Durae quis terminus umquam
sortis erit? Quis nos funesto turbine rerum 90
aut tantis solvet lacrimis, quos barbarus illinc,
hinc Rufinus agit, quibus arva fretumque negatur?
Magna quidem per rura lues, sed maior oberrat
intra tecta timor. Tandem succurre ruenti
heu patriae, Stilicho! Dilecta hic pignora certe, 95
hic domus, hic thalamis primum genialibus omen,
hic tibi felices erexit regia taedas.
Vel solus, sperate, veni! Te proelia viso
languescent avidique cadet dementia monstri".
    Talibus urgetur discors Aurora procellis. 100
At Stilicho, Zephyris cum primum bruma remitti
et iuga diffusis nudari coepta pruinis,
partibus Italiae tuta sub pace relictis,
utraque castra movens Phoebi properabat ad ortus,
Gallica discretis Eoaque robora turmis 105
complexus. Numquam tantae dicione sub una
convenere manus nec tot discrimina vocum:
illinc Armeniae vibratis crinibus alae
herbida collectae facili velamina nodo;
inde truces flavo comitantur vertice Galli, 110
quos Rhodanus velox, Araris quos tardior ambit
et quos nascentes explorat gurgite Rhenus
quosque rigat retro pernicior unda Garumnae
Oceani pleno quotiens impellitur aestu.

87 nec φ *Jeep Birt*, nō B, ne C<?> *Koch*   106 complexus φ *Jeep Birt*,
amplexus E^bVC *Koch*

verses 78–83 plainly show that Rufinus's escort was composed of Goths, who would scarcely be excluded from their countrymen's camp.

87. nec . . . quidem: on this expression see Stolz-Schmalz, 641; Kühner, 2.45; and my note on *nec*, IR 1.371. The question is much confused by the tendency of editors to find reasons for emending rarities out of existence, a reprehensible practice (compare Maas, 7.5–6: "Das vereinzelte ist an und für sich ganz unverdächtig"). I take *nec . . . quidem* here as a superlative of negation, so to speak: 'verily, not even' (= οὐδὲ μήν).

106. complexus: Claudian uses this verb more frequently and with a wider sphere of meaning than he attaches to *amplector* (see Birt, 469, 486). Compare BG 519 partem <hominum> complectitur Olbia <urbs>; 6H 288 <Appenninus> populos complectitur omnes.

Mens eadem cunctis animique recentia ponunt 115
vulnera; non odit victus victorve superbit.
Et quamvis praesens tumor et civilia nuper
classica bellatrixque etiamnunc ira caleret,
in ducis eximium conspiravere favorem.
Haut aliter Xerxen toto simul orbe secutus 120
narratur rapuisse vagos exercitus amnes
et telis umbrasse diem, cum classibus iret
per scopulos tectumque pedes contemneret aequor.
 Vix Alpes transgressus erat nec iam amplius errat
barbarus adventumque timens se cogit in unam 125
planitiem tutoque includit pascua gyro:
tum duplici fossa non exsuperabile vallum
asperat alternis sudibus murique locata
in speciem caesis obtendit plaustra iuvencis.
 At procul exsanguis Rufinum perculit horror; 130
infectae pallore genae; stetit ore gelato
incertus peteretne fugam, veniamne subactus
posceret an fidos sese transferret in hostes.
Quid nunc divitiae, quid fulvi vasta metalli
congeries, quid purpureis effulta columnis 135
atria prolataeve iuvant ad sidera moles?
Audit iter numeratque dies spatioque viarum
metitur vitam. Torquetur pace futura
nec recipit somnos et saepe cubilibus amens

119 eximium *φ Jeep*, eximii||| Π *cum rasura unius fere litterae*, eximii *Birt Koch*, extremum *A* 124 transgressus *ω Jeep*, egressus *E*ᵇ *Birt Koch*
128 duplici fossa *φ Birt Koch*, duplicem fossam *V Jeep*

  124. transgressus erat <Stilicho>: Stilicho led his troops from Milan, where they were stationed at the death of Theodosius, overland toward the East (see pages 18–19, 24, above). The word *transgressus* is therefore physically accurate, and is much more in accord with Claudian's usual portrayal of Stilicho's swift movements than *egressus* would be; that word suggests emergence after a long and difficult march. Moreover, Claudian uses *egredior* in but one other place (IR 1.129), and there 'absolutely', of Megaera's emergence from the underworld. For *transgressus*, compare CS 1.53–54 Tigrim transgressus et altum Euphraten.
  Mommsen (Stil., 103, note 7) takes *barbarus* as the subject of this verb (he reads *egressus*). He is apparently followed by Dr. Schmidt (428, note 2). This is wrong. The point of *vix . . . nec iam amplius* is surely not how soon after their own crossing of the Alps the barbarians ceased their depredations, but rather how quickly the news of Stilicho's expedition drove them to cover (compare 125). For similar changes of subject (<Stilicho> transgressus erat . . . errat barbarus), compare IR 1.265–268; 2.336–340.

Liber Secundus [81] 299

excutitur poenamque luit formidine poenae. 140
Sed redit in faciem scelerumque immane resumit
ingenium sacrasque fores praedivitis aulae
intrat et Arcadium mixto terrore precatur:
"Per fratris regale iubar, per facta parentis
aetherii floremque tui te deprecor aevi, 145
eripe me gladiis; liceat Stilichonis iniquas
evitare minas. In nostram Gallia caedem
coniurata venit. Quidquid rigat ultima Tethys,
extremos ultra volitat gens si qua Britannos,
mota mihi. Tantis capiendi credimur armis? 150
Tot signis unum petitur caput? Vnde cruoris
ista sitis? Geminum caeli sibi vindicat axem
et nullum vult esse parem. Succumbere poscit
cuncta sibi: regit Italiam Libyamque coërcet;
Hispanis Gallisque iubet; non orbita solis, 155
non illum natura capit. Quascumque paravit
hic Augustus opes et quas post bella recepit,
solus habet, possessa semel nec reddere curat.
Scilicet ille quidem tranquilla pace fruetur,
nos premet obsidio? Quid Pontum invadere temptat? 160

141 faciem Λ$V^2\phi$ *Koch*, rabiem Λ$^1\epsilon V^1$ *Jeep Birt*   158 nec *V Birt Koch*, non ϕ *Jeep*   159 fruetur Π^{1}Λ$^1\phi$ *Birt*, fruatur Π^{2}M^{2}ΛEm^b *Jeep Koch*
160 premet V^{3}A, premit V^{1}P^1, premat P$^2\phi$ *Jeep Birt Koch*   *Jeep signum* * *lacunae post* obsidio *posuit*   pontum] partem ω *Jeep Birt*, spartem *Isengr. mg.*, aperta *coniecit Birt apud Koch (Pr. 21)*, partum *Brakman*, thracam *coniecit ac edidit Koch*, pontum *ego*

141. faciem: Koch supports this reading by referring to the parallels adduced by Birt: 4H 84 in vultus rediere suos; Ovid, Fasti 1.112 in faciem redii; Metamorphoses 4.231 in veram rediit faciem. Moreover, *faciem* is in better accord with *mixto terrore* (143) than *rabiem* would be.

159–160. fruetur ... premet: Birt reads and punctuates as follows: Scilicet ille quidem tranquilla pace fruetur; nos premat obsidio. The antithesis, however, seems to me to require the same mood and the same tense in both clauses. Koch, whose punctuation is that of Birt, reverts to Jeep's *fruatur ... premat*, apparently interpreting the sentence as an ironic jussive or volitive (his avowed reason for reading *fruatur* is very strange: "... v<ersus> 156–158 praesens ... poscunt, non futurum". In what way do they require the present? Even if they do, does *fruatur* really refer to present time? I fear that Koch was over-influenced by the term 'present' subjunctive!). I believe that Platnauer (who prints *scilicet ille ... pace fruatur; nos premat obsidio?*) is right in interpreting the sentence as an ironic question. The subjunctive in such a sentence is not unexampled: compare Silius 5.114–115 Scilicet has sera ad laudes Servilius arma adiungat ...? But for the indicative, which I prefer here, compare Ovid, Heroides 13.37–40 <Laodamia is

Deserat Illyricos fines; Eoa remittat
agmina; fraternas ex aequo dividat hastas,
nec sceptri fueris tantum, sed militis heres.
Quod si dissimulas nostrae succurrere morti
nec prohibere paras, Manes et sidera testor: 165
haec cervix non sola cadet; miscebitur alter
sanguis; nec Stygias ferar incomitatus ad umbras

 163 fueris tantum φ *Jeep,* tantum fueris II *Birt Koch*   167 umbras φ *Birt,* undas V *Jeep Koch*

speaking of herself and of Protesilaus> Scilicet ipsa geram saturatas murice vestes, bella sub Iliacis moenibus ille geret, ipsa comas pectar, galea caput ille premetur, ipsa novas vestes, dura vir arma feret? (the last verse, with its one verb, shows that *geram* and *pectar* are also future). Compare also Aeneid 2.577–578 Scilicet haec Spartam incolumis . . . aspiciet?; Lucan 1.314–315 Scilicet extremi Pompeium emptique clientes continuo per tot satiabunt tempora regno?

160. Pontum: the lack of an attribute for the manuscript reading *partem* led Jeep to indicate here a lacuna (his favorite remedy for textual difficulties, real or fanciful), and the other scholars to suggest various emendations, to which I have ventured to add a new one. It is conceivable, of course, that Claudian wrote Quid partem invadere temptat?, 'Why does he try to invade <your, our, the Eastern> part of the Empire?'; but the force of the question lies almost entirely in the modifier of *partem* which must be supplied. *Spartem,* a reading found in the Isengrinian edition, seems meaningless. Birt's *aperta* is, if anything, less satisfactory than *partem.* The reading *partum,* which Brakman, 372, suggests as equivalent to "*quod peperimus*", has nothing to recommend it save its resemblance to *partem.* Neither Rufinus nor Arcadius, nor even Theodosius, had 'won' the East. Compare 4H 69–71, where Claudian makes a distinction between Theodosius's peaceful accession in the East and his conquest of the West: sic traditus illi . . . Oriens.At non pars altera rerum tradita: bis . . . parta periclis. Moreover, to be really effective, *partum* would still require some sort of attribute. If recourse is to be had to emendation, the conjecture should be a proper name, which requires no qualification to make it definite. Koch apparently saw this, for he prints his conjecture *Thracam.* But *Thracam,* as has been pointed out by an anonymous reviewer (Lit. Cent. 45 [1894], 439), is hard to explain palaeographically. It is true, as Koch remarks, that Stilicho would have to pass through Thrace on his way to Constantinople. But it would be much more in keeping with the tone of the passage to have Rufinus accuse Stilicho of boldly aiming at the seat of the Eastern realm. I have therefore ventured to print *Pontum,* which is not dissimilar in appearance to *partem.* For Claudian's use of *Pontus* in connection with Constantinople, compare BG 225–226 At pater, intrantem Pontum qua Bosporus artat, Arcadii thalamis urbique inlapsus Eoae; see also IR 2.349–350. That Claudian uses the word *Pontus* as a proper noun is shown by IR 2.38–39. He is very fond, moreover, of denoting peoples and places by the names of neighboring bodies of water; compare 6H 414–415 timebant Tigris et Euphrates; 6H 220 debilitat . . . Histrum; CS 1.196 edomuit Rhenum. See Vollrath, 23–24.

167. ʰras: Claudian nowhere else refers to the waves of the Styx. On the other hand, he often uses the word *umbrae* to refer to the lower world or its in-

Liber Secundus

nec mea securus ridebit funera victor!"
   Haec ubi, dictatur facinus missusque repente
qui ferat extortas invito principe voces. 170
   Interea Stilicho iam laetior hoste propinquo
nec multo spatii distantibus aequore vallis
pugnandi cupidas accendit voce cohortes.
Armeniis frons laeva datur; per cornua Gallos
dexteriora locat. Spumis ignescere frena, 175
pulveris extolli nimbos lateque videres
surgere purpureis undantes anguibus hastas
serpentumque vago caelum saevire volatu.
Implet Thessaliam ferri nitor, antraque docti
cornipedis teneroque amnis reptatus Achilli 180
et nemus Oetaeum radiat. Clamore nivalis
Ossa tonat pulsoque fragor geminatur Olympo.
Intumuit virtus et lucis prodigus arsit
impetus; haut illos rupes, haut alta vetarent
flumina: praecipiti stravissent omnia cursu. 185
   Si tunc his animis acies collata fuisset,
prodita non tantas vidisset Graecia caedes,
oppida semoto Pelopeia Marte vigerent,
starent Arcadiae, starent Lacedaemonis arces;
non mare fumasset geminum flagrante Corintho 190

172 spatii φ *Birt Koch*, spacii Π, spatiis *C*, spatio *coniecit ac edidit Jeep*
189 arces Λ V²BΠ (rces *in rasura* Π) *Birt Koch*, agri V¹φ *Jeep*

habitants: IR 1.126–127; 2.328–329; see Birt, 604, *umbra* 5. Compare Ovid, Metamorphoses 1.139 Stygiis admoverat umbris; Statius, Achilleis 1.630 Stygiasque . . . raptus ad umbras; Thebais 11.85; Silius 5.617.
   168. nec—victor: to Birt and Koch this verse presents much difficulty. Birt thinks it spurious or corrupt; Koch affirms the latter view. I find justifiable neither their suspicions nor their attempts at a remedy (Birt: *ridebis;* Koch: *nec mea sola meus ridebit funera victor*). Koch brands as worthless ("inutilia") the suggestion of an anonymous critic in Lit. Cent. 44 (1893), 83.29–31. I, on the contrary, believe that this critic points to the correct interpretation: 'The victor <Stilicho> will not <be able to> laugh with unconcern at my death'. Stilicho was in a sense the protector of Arcadius (see page 19, above); his fidelity to the house of Theodosius was one of his prominent characteristics (see Stein, 346.30–32; see also pages 19, 24, above). A victory which would entail the death of one who was his protegé, his Emperor's brother, and his wife's kinsman (see page 18, above), would surely give him no cause for care-free laughter. To be sure, Rufinus does not expect Arcadius to be disturbed by Stilicho's prospective sadness, but by what would cause it, namely, Arcadius's own death. The indirectness of the warning is quite in keeping with the more or less veiled threat of 164–167.

nec fera Cecropiae traxissent vincula matres.
Illa dies potuit nostris imponere finem
cladibus et sceleris causas auferre futuri.
Invida pro quantum rapuit Fortuna triumphum!
Inter equos interque tubas mandata feruntur 195
regia et armati veniunt ductoris ad aures.
  Obstupuit; simul ira virum, simul obruit ingens
maeror et ignavo tantum licuisse nocenti
miratur. Dubios anceps sententia volvit
eventus: peragat pugnas an fortia coepta 200
deserat? Illyricis ardet succurrere damnis;
praeceptis obstare timet. Reverentia frangit
virtutis stimulos: hinc publica commoda suadent,
hinc metus invidiae. Tandem indignatus ad astra
extollit palmas et ab imo pectore fatur: 205
"Numina Romanis necdum satiata ruinis,
si iuvat imperium penitus de stirpe revelli,
uno si placuit deleri saecula lapsu,
si piget humani generis: prorumpat in arva
libertas effrena maris, vel limite iusto 210
devius errantes Phaëthon confundat habenas.
Cur per Rufinum geritur? Procumbere mundum
hoc auctore pudet. Mediis revocamur ab armis
(pro dolor!) et strictos deponere cogimur enses.
Vos, arsurae urbes perituraque moenia, testor: 215
cedo equidem et miserum permitto casibus orbem.
Flectite signa, duces. Redeat iam miles Eous.
Parendum est. Taceant litui. Prohibete sagittas.
Parcite contiguo—Rufinus praecipit!—hosti".
  His dictis omnes una fremuere manipli 220
quantum non Italo percussa Ceraunia fluctu,
quantum non madidis elisa tonitrua Coris,
secernique negant ereptaque proelia poscunt,
insignemque ducem populus defendit uterque
et sibi quisque trahit. Magno certatur amore, 225
alternamque fidem non inlaudata lacessit
seditio talique simul clamore queruntur:
  "Quis mihi nudatos enses, quis tela lacertis
excutit et solvi curvatos imperat arcus?

219 parcite *φ Birt Koch*, parcere <?> *E Jeep*

Liber Secundus

Quisnam audet stricto leges imponere ferro? 230
Inflammata semel nescit mitescere virtus.
Iam mihi barbaricos sitientia pila cruores
sponte volant ultroque manus mucrone furenti
ducitur et siccum gladium vagina recusat.
Non patiar. Semperne Getis discordia nostra 235
proderit? En iterum belli civilis imago!
Quid consanguineas acies, quid dividis olim
concordes aquilas? Non dissociabile corpus
coniunctumque sumus. Te qua libet ire sequemur.
Te vel Hyperboreo damnatam sidere Thylen, 240
te vel ad incensas Libyae comitabor harenas.
Indorum si stagna petas rubrique recessus
litoris, auriferum veniam poturus Hydaspen;
si calcare Notum secretaque noscere Nili
nascentis iubeas, mundum post terga relinquam; 245
et quocumque loco Stilicho tentoria figet,
haec patria est".
    Dux inde vetat: "Desistite, quaeso,
atque avidam differte manum. Cadat iste minacis
invidiae cumulus. Non est victoria tanti
ut videar vicisse mihi. Vos fida iuventus 250
ite, mei quondam socii". Nec plura locutus
flexit iter: vacuo qualis discedit hiatu
impatiens remeare leo, quem plurima cuspis
et pastorales pepulerunt igne catervae,
inclinatque iubas demissaque lumina velat 255
et trepidas maesto rimatur murmure silvas.
 Vt sese legio vidit disiuncta relinqui,
ingentem tollit gemitum galeasque solutis

---

230 stricto leges imponere ferro φ *Birt Koch*, leges vibrato imponere ferro *Em^b VC Jeep* 235 non φ *Birt Koch*, nun *V* (u *in rasura V*²), num *B Jeep*
239 qua libet] *sic Koch*, qualibet Λ¹φ († < = *vel* > quo Π²), quolibet Λ, quo libet *Jeep Birt* 246 figet ω *Jeep Birt*, figat *E Koch*

230. stricto leges imponere ferro: Birt (Pr. 114.31) prefers this to the reading of *Em^b VC*, on the ground that the former is without elision. In Claudian, elisions of long syllables between the fourteenth and fifteenth *morae* are rare: Birt Pr. 217. 12–14, 28–29, 218.16.

246–247. figet ... est: Koch, Pr. 21, prefers figat: "si enim *figet* legimus, sequi debet 'haec patria erit' ". With this I cannot agree (see my remarks on Koch's reading *fruatur*, 159, in my note on 159–160). The 'prophetic' present tense, *est*, is used for vividness, as if the expedition were an accomplished fact.

umectat lacrimis pressamque morantia vocem
thoracum validos pulsant suspiria nexus: 260
"Tradimur, heu, tantumque sequi prohibemur amorem!"
exclamant. "Spernisne tuas, dux optime, dextras,
quas tibi victrices totiens Bellona probavit?
Nos adeo viles? Adeo felicior axis
Hesperius, meruit qui te rectore teneri?   265
Quid nobis patriam, quid cara revisere tandem
pignora dilectosve iuvat coluisse Penates?
Te sine dulce nihil. Iam formidata tyranni
tempestas subeunda mihi, qui forte nefandas
iam parat insidias, qui nos aut turpibus Hunis   270
aut impacatis famulos praebebit Alanis;
quamquam non adeo robur defecerit omne
tantave gestandi fuerit penuria ferri.

270 iam ω *Jeep Birt,* clam *coniecit ac edidit Koch*   273 gestandi ω *Birt*
Koch, gestari *E,* gestati *coniecit Heinsius edidit Jeep*   penuria ω *Birt Koch,*
patientia *coniecit ac edidit Jeep*

270. iam: Koch's emendation *clam*, in spite of the approval of Postgate (169) and Gustafsson (Berliner Philologische Wochenschrift 14 [1894], 1359), seems to me neither necessary nor appropriate. Koch supports his conjecture by a citation from Marcellinus Comes (for the year 395 [= MGH 11.64.18–21]): Rufinus Patricius Archadio <sic> principi insidias tendens Alaricum Gothorum regem missis clam pecuniis infestum reipublicae fecit. . . . But in the expression *missis clam pecuniis, clam* is most significant: tribute in the form of 'gifts' was regularly sent to barbarian rulers (Jordanes, Getica 29; CS 1.204, 210–211); it is the secrecy of these particular subsidies which was unusual. When used with *insidias,* however, *clam* would be quite superfluous. *Iam,* on the other hand, emphasizes the soldiers' fear of immediate betrayal. I find the repetition *iam* (268) . . . *iam* (270) less offensive than the pleonasm *clam* . . . *insidias,* and certainly not disturbing enough to warrant emendation. Compare CS 2.320–321 annum redde tuum, quem *iam* secura sequatur posteritas, nec *iam* doleat defensa vetustas.

273. tantave gestandi fuerit penuria ferri: this passage has been suspected of corruption, perhaps justifiedly. The word *penuria* is not found elsewhere in Claudian; it is very rare in verse (it is found once in Vergil [Aeneid 7.113], once in Horace [Sermones 1.1.98]; apparently it was not used by Ovid, Lucan, Juvenal, Silius, or Statius). The meaning which it seems necessary to attach to *penuria* here, 'reluctance', 'niggardliness', and the construction used with it, are strained: I have not found even an approximate parallel. Compare, however, the opposite idea in MT 226–227 *nocendi prodigus.* The conjectures thus far proposed fall far short of adequacy. Paul, 12, suggests *tantave gestati fuerit periuria ferri;* he refers to Lucan 4.498–499 servataque ferro militiae pietas, and explains: "Gestatum Stilicone duce ferrum meminit miles, cuius se vel absentis imperio obtemperaturum esse declarat". This is at least as far-fetched as the manuscript reading. The same is true of Jeep's proposal, *tantave gestati fuerit patientia ferri.* Jeep refers

Tu, licet occiduo maneas sub cardine solis,
tu mihi dux semper, Stilicho, nostramque vel absens   275
experiere fidem. Dabitur tibi debita pridem
victima: promissis longe placabere sacris".
  Tristior Haemoniis miles digressus ab oris
tangebat Macetum fines murosque subibat,
Thessalonica, tuos. Sensu dolor haeret in alto   280
abditus et tacitas vindictae praestruit iras,
spectaturque favens odiis locus aptaque leto
tempora. Nec quisquam tanta de pube repertus
proderet incautis qui corda minantia verbis.
Quae non posteritas, quae non mirabitur aetas   285
tanti consilium vulgi potuisse taceri
aut facinus tam grande tegi mentisque calorem
non sermone viae, non inter pocula rumpi?
Aequalis tantam tenuit constantia turbam
et fuit arcanum populo. Percurritur Hebrus,   290

274 solis $V^1P^2\phi$ *Jeep*, caeli ϵV^3P^1B *Birt Koch*   277 longe *ω Birt Koch*, longum *unus ex* ς *Jeep*   290 *post* populo signum * *lacunae posuit Jeep* hebrus ϕ *Jeep Birt*, hẹmus *Em*, aemus ϵ, haemus *Koch*

to IE 2.542–543 exercitus ... fortis adhuc ferrique memor, which is pertinent to the passage as a whole, but lends no support to his conjecture. Perhaps the involved construction is purposely used to correspond with the veiled nature of the promise. Compare my note on 168.

  274. cardine solis: compare IE 1.397 *alio Phoebi de cardine*.

  290. Jeep marks a lacuna after *populo*, for two reasons: (1) *populo* lacks an attribute, and (2) no mention is made of the departure of the troops from Thessalonica. The first objection shows that Jeep did not appreciate the epigrammatic force of *fuit arcanum populo;* as for the second, Claudian is not obliged to mention every detail of the journey.

  290. Hebrus: Koch objects to this reading on two grounds: (1) "fluvius 'percurri' vix potest"; (2) "*Hebrus* ... in Thracia est et in Rhodopes latere orientali; itaque primum deseri Rhodopen memorandum fuisset, dein in Thraciam tendi, ultimo Hebrum percurri. Ergo *Haemum* restitui, nam Rhodopen quasi Haemi partem inductam *licentiae poetae* <the italics are mine> facile adtribuemus". Koch's first objection is very strange, coming as it does a few lines before he appeals to poetic license in support of another reading. For Claudian's extreme freedom of expression in regard to rivers, compare CS 2.199–200 *opacum vitibus Histrum conserit;* 6H 220 *debilitat ... Histrum;* see also my remarks on *Pontum*, 160. Compare also RP 2.68–69 *ripasque paternas percurrunt* <Nymphae>.

  Koch's second objection involves the determination of the army's route. The troops obviously marched East from Thessalonica by the Via Egnatia (see Pauly-Wissowa 5.1988.65–1993.33, especially 1992, col. 2; Konrad Miller, Itineraria Romana, 516–527 [Stuttgart, Strecker und Schroeder, 1916]). This road passes through the Rhodopean range between Brendice and Tempyra, and skirts it

deseritur Rhodope Thracumque per ardua tendunt
donec ad Herculei perventum nominis urbem.
　Vt cessisse ducem, propius venisse cohortes
cognita Rufino, magna cervice triumphat
omnia tuta ratus sceptrumque capessere fervet　　　　　　　　295
et coniuratos hortatur voce clientes:
"Vicimus, expulimus, facilis iam copia regni.
Nullus ab hoste timor. Quis enim, quem poscere solum
horruit, hunc tanto munitum milite vincat?
Quis ferat armatum, quem non superavit inermem?　　　　　　　300
I nunc, exitium nobis meditare remotus
incassum, Stilicho, dum nos longissima tellus
dividat et mediis Nereus interstrepat undis.
Alpinas transire tibi me sospite rupes
haut dabitur. Iaculis illinc me figere tempta.　　　　　　　　305
Quaere ferox ensem, qui nostra ad moenia tendi
possit ab Italia. Non te documenta priorum,
non exempla vetant? Quisnam conatus adire

303 interstrepat φ *Birt Koch*, interfluat *V Isengr. mg. Jeep*　　　308 nam φ
Birt Koch, pā *V*, par *Jeep, ut ex V*

again between Trajanopolis and Dyme. The Via Egnatia proper terminates at the Hebrus, between Dyme and Cypsela (Pauly-Wissowa 5.1991.51–53). The army, which was bound for Perinthus (Heraclea; the *Herculei . . . nominis urbem* of 292), would thus cross the Hebrus while it was still in sight of, or shortly after losing sight of, the Rhodopean range; a slight *hysteron proteron* will account for the order in which the places are mentioned. This is certainly less strained than to consider Rhodope a part of the Haemus range, which is far north of the Via Egnatia. For a similar manuscript confusion between *Hebrus* and *Haemus*, see Birt's apparatus on IE 1.504.

　303. interstrepat: compare RP 3.103 interstrepis urbes <the reference is to Cybele>. The word apparently does not occur before Claudian, but he may have read Vergil, Eclogues 9.36 as *argutos interstrepere anser olores*. Compare also *perstrepit*, IR 1.213; MT 285–286 sonipes . . . superbo perstrepit hinnitu Baetin.

　308. Quisnam: whether or not *pā* in Codex V is intended as an abbreviation of *par* (see Maurice Prou, Manuel de Paléographie, 147–148 [Paris, Picard, 1924]), the reading *par* is most inappropriate. The discussion in Koenig's edition, cited by Birt in his apparatus, was not accessible to me. However, it is clear (see Burmann's note) that *par* might be taken either as the substantive ('a gladiatorial pair') or as the adjective ('equal', 'on equal terms'). The first interpretation is too grotesque for consideration; the second introduces a *petitio principii*, or at least a serious limitation in a question which is intended to be as sweeping as possible. The *nam* of universal interrogation ('who in the world') is quite natural here: compare 230 Quisnam audet; 11 Quanam ratione. See Birt, 543; Stolz-Schmalz, 678–679.

Liber Secundus

has iactat vitasse manus? Detrusimus orbe
te medio tantisque simul spoliavimus armis. 310
Nunc epulis tempus, socii, nunc larga parare
munera donandumque novis legionibus aurum.
Opportuna meis oritur lux crastina votis.
Quod nolit rex ipse velit iubeatque coactus
in partem mihi regna dari. Contingat in uno 315
privati fugisse modum crimenque tyranni".
 Talibus acclamat dictis infame nocentum
concilium, qui perpetuis crevere rapinis
et quos una facit Rufino causa sodales:
inlicitum duxisse nihil; funesta tacere 320
nexus amicitiae. Iam iam conubia laeti
despondent aliena sibi frustraque vicissim
promittunt, quas quisque petat, quas devoret urbes.
 Coeperat humanos alto sopire labores
nox gremio, nigrasque sopor diffuderat alas. 325
Ille diu curis animum stimulantibus aegre

311 epulis *V Birt Koch*, epulas φ *Jeep Koch*, delicta fuere Λω *Jeep*, dilecta fuere *E Jeep Birt*, quae *Em Koch*   320 funesta tacere *Em*ᵇ *Birt*   323 quas *primum*] quas ω

320. funesta tacere: several factors combine to make this reading most attractive. The chiastic order of 319–321 (*causa* ... *duxisse* ... ⏑⏑–⏑ *nexus*) makes parallelism of construction very likely: compare IE 2.66–69 *contingere* dextram *ambitus, et votum* ... *oscula* ... *figere;* 6H 585–586 depositum *servasse, fides; constantia,* parvum *praefecisse* orbi. Secondly, *delicta fuere nexus amicitiae* is a mere repetition of *una facit Rufino causa sodales: inlicitum duxisse nihil* (319–320). Thirdly, the avoidance of a form of *sum* is characteristic of Claudian (even though it is not his invariable practice; see my note on *parum est,* 1.238). Had Claudian wished to use *delicta,* he is more likely to have written e. g. *delicta nefandae nexus amicitiae.* Finally, the expression *funesta tacere* is thoroughly in accordance with Claudian's usage: e. g. IR 2.90 *funesto turbine rerum;* CS 1.13 *partem tacuisse velim.*
 An anonymous reviewer in Lit. Cent. 44 (1893), 83.21–23 cites Corippus, Johannis 6.549–550 *delicta fuere tanti causa mali; fuerat non culpa regentis.* For Corippus as an imitator of Claudian, see my note on 1.218. But *delicta* is so frequent in Christian writers (see Thesaurus 5.460–461) that Corippus may well have been influenced by them in this decidedly religious passage. Moreover, the collocation *delicta fuere* is not so startling as to prove imitation at all.
 323. quas ... quas: Koch reads *quae quisque petat, quas devoret urbes,* in order to avoid what he calls the "pleonasmus molestus" of Birt's reading. In my opinion there is no pleonasm, but merely an instance of stylistic repetition (see Stolz-Schmalz, 834). *Quae* ... *petat* is too vague for this passage; the verse as I read it is equivalent to *quas urbes quisque petat devoretque.*

labitur in somnos. Toto vix corde quierat,
ecce videt diras alludere protinus umbras,
quas dedit ipse neci; quarum quae clarior una
visa loqui: "Pro! surge toro. Quid plurima volvis 330
anxius? Haec requiem rebus finemque labori
allatura dies: omni iam plebe redibis
altior et laeti manibus portabere vulgi".
Has canit ambages. Occulto fallitur ille
omine nec capitis sentit praesagia fixi. 335
   Iam summum radiis stringebat Lucifer Haemum
festinamque rotam solito properantior urget
tandem Rufini visurus funera Titan:
desiluit stratis densaeque capacia turbae
atria regifico iussit splendere paratu 340
exceptura dapes et, quod post vota daretur,
insculpi propriis aurum fatale figuris.
Ipse salutatum reduces post proelia turmas
iam regale tumens et principe celsior ibat
collaque femineo solvebat mollia gestu 345
imperii certus: tegeret ceu purpura dudum
corpus et ardentes ambirent tempora gemmae.
   Vrbis ab angusto tractu, qua vergit in Austrum,
planities vicina patet: nam cetera Pontus
circuit exiguo dirimi se tramite passus. 350

327 toto vix *V Birt Koch*, vix toto φ *Jeep* <*qui lectionem codicis V ignorare videtur*>   331 labori φ *Birt Koch*, timori *EmC Jeep*   345 solvebat *Em Birt Koch*, gestabat *P²B*, iactabat φ *Jeep*   350 tramite φ *Birt*, limite *Emϵ Jeep Koch*

345. solvebat: in support of this reading Birt cites Cicero, Brutus 225 *solutus et mollis in gestu*, and believes (Pr. 8–9, note 4) that Claudian was influenced by the uses of the Greek verb παραλύω. The reading *solvebat* seems to me particularly appropriate because of *femineo . . . mollia gestu*, with which *iactabat* is not in accord. The word *gestabat* would be more appropriate than *iactabat*, but less vivid than *solvebat*. This is the only opportunity Claudian has to twit Rufinus on effeminacy (compare IE *passim*), and he is likely to have made full use of it.
   The translation of Platnauer, ". . . he wore a woman's raiment about his neck . . ." seems to me incorrect; *gestus* refers to posture, not to raiment. See Thesaurus, *gestus* I A 1 a, where the present passage is cited (1970.2–3). The translation of Crépin (see page 54, above) is much nearer the mark, though Crépin reads *iactabat*: ". . . sa tête se balance doucement avec des gestes efféminés" (*gestum* in Crépin's text is obviously a misprint).
   350. tramite: Koch (Pr. 22) prefers the reading *limite*. He writes thus: ". . . magis placuit, quam *tramite*, quo haud ita apte terrae linguam in mare proiectam

Liber Secundus [91] 309

Hic ultrix acies ornatu lucida Martis
explicuit cuneos. Pedites in parte sinistra
consistunt. Equites illinc poscentia cursum
ora reluctantur pressis sedare lupatis;
hinc alii saevum cristato vertice nutant 355
et tremulos umeris gaudent vibrare colores,
quos operit formatque chalybs; coniuncta per artem
flexilis inductis animatur lamina membris.
Horribiles visu: credas simulacra moveri
ferrea cognatoque viros spirare metallo. 360
Par vestitus equis: ferrata fronte minantur
ferratosque levant securi vulneris armos.
  Diviso stat quisque loco. Metuenda voluptas
cernenti pulcherque timor, spirisque remissis
mansuescunt varii vento cessante dracones. 365
Augustus veneranda prior vexilla salutat.
Rufinus sequitur, quo fallere cuncta solebat
callidus affatu, devotaque brachia laudat;

353 illinc Λφ *Birt Koch*, illic PΛ¹ (*crucem, signum dubiae lectionis, addidit* Λ¹) *Jeep*   355 hinc φ *Birt Koch*, hic P *Jeep*   356 *ut supra* ω *Birt Koch*, et tremulo gaudent umeros vibrare colore *coniecit ac edidit Jeep*   357 format Π¹φ *Birt Koch*, firmat Π² *Jeep*   359 horribiles E *Birt Koch*, horribili C, horribilis φ *Jeep*   367–368 *ut supra* ω *Birt Koch*, rufinus sequitur devotaque bracchia laudat / callidus affatu quo fallere cuncta solebat *ordine verborum e coniectura mutato edidit Jeep*

significari credo". The distinction which he draws between *limes* and *trames* does not seem valid: indeed, neither word is particularly appropriate to a promontory (*terrae linguam*). However, by some word, whether *tramite* or *limite*, Claudian is describing, not the entire promontory, but the part of it which is not surrounded by water, that is to say, the portion which connects the out-jutting plain with the mainland. The present condition of the Hebdomon (see page 25, above) is thus described by Glück (2.19–21): "Die Küste zeigt hier ein stumpfwinkelige Ausbuchtung in das Meer hinaus, so das sie zwischen zwei flachen Buchten liegt ...". The promontory was probably much more like a peninsula in Claudian's day; Glück (2.25–26) refers to alluvial deposits. The word *tramite* would then refer appropriately to a narrow strip almost entirely occupied by a causeway. It may, however, be idle to go deeply into geographical questions here, since Claudian is often inaccurate in his topography (see Fargues, 41.1–4). Birt (Pr. 110.43) argues against *limite* because of the repetition of the letter *i*: *dirimi se limite.*

359. horribiles: Birt Pr. 109.43–46 supports this reading on the ground that *horribiles* with *equites* is much more forceful than *horribilis* with *lamina;* moreover, as he points out, *lamina* is modified by *flexilis*, and Claudian prefers to use only one adjective with a noun. Compare also Birt Pr. 221, § III.1, 2.

367–368. quo—affatu: for the word-order, compare EH Pr. 17–18 Tum Phoebus, quo saxa domat, quo pertrahit ornos pectine temptavit ... lyram.

nomine quemque vocat; natos patresque reversis
nuntiat incolumes. Illi dum plurima ficto 370
certatim sermone petunt, intendere longos
a tergo flexus insperatoque suprema
circuitu sociare parant; decrescere campus
incipit et clipeis in se redeuntia iunctis
curvo paulatim sinuantur cornua ductu 375
(sic ligat immensa virides indagine saltus
venator; sic attonitos ad litora pisces
aequoreus populator agit rarosque plagarum
contrahit anfractus et hiantes colligit oras).
Excludunt alios. Cingi se fervidus ille 380
nescit adhuc graviterque adprensa veste morantem
increpat Augustum: scandat sublime tribunal,
participem sceptri, socium declaret honoris—
cum subito stringunt gladios; vox desuper ingens
infremuit: "Nobis etiam, deterrime, nobis 385
sperasti famulas imponere posse catenas?
Vnde redi nescis? Patiarne audire satelles,
qui leges aliis libertatemque reduxi?
Bis domitum civile nefas, bis rupimus Alpes.
Tot nos bella docent nulli servire tyranno". 390
    Deriguit. Spes nulla fugae. Seges undique ferri
circumfusa micat; dextra laevaque revinctus
haesit et ensiferae stupuit mucrone coronae

369 natos *VEC Birt Koch*, natosque ΠΑε *Jeep*, notosque *PB*   371 intendere ω *Jeep Birt*, extendere Εε *Koch*   384 cum ω *Birt Koch*, tum *coniecit ac edidit Jeep*   393 mucrone ω *Birt*, rumore *coniecit ac edidit Jeep; edidit Koch*

369. natos patresque: in the oblique cases of the singular, and in the plural, Claudian prefers to treat the first syllable of *pater* as long: see Birt, 553. I have therefore preferred *natos patresque* to *natosque patresque*.

371. intendere: I cannot agree with Koch that *extendere* is more appropriate here. The figure is that of drawing together the ends of a bow (CM 9.38 intendunt taurino viscere nervos): compare the similes in 376-379. It is hypercritical to find cacophony, as Koch does, in the homoeoarchy of *incolumes* (370), *intendere* (371), and *insperato* (372).

393. mucrone: Koch objects to this reading on two grounds: (1) the "difficultas quae est in ipsa verborum compositione", and (2) the pleonasm of *mucrone* after the words *seges . . . ferri*. He supports Jeep's reading, *rumore*, because it corresponds to the *tertium comparationis* in 398-399: ille pavet strepitus . . . et tanti miratur sibila vulgi. His first objection I do not understand, unless he means the jingle of *mucrone coronae* (see my note on 371, last sentence): he cannot refer to the grammatical construction or to the arrangement of the words, both of

Liber Secundus [93] 311

ut fera, quae nuper montes amisit avitos
altorumque exul nemorum damnatur harenae   395
muneribus, commota ruit; vir murmure contra
hortatur nixusque genu venabula tendit;
illa pavet strepitus cuneosque erecta theatri
respicit et tanti miratur sibila vulgi.
    Vnus per medios audendi pronior ense   400
prosilit exerto dictisque et vulnere torvus
impetit: "Hac Stilicho, quem iactas pellere, dextra
te ferit; hoc absens invadit viscera ferro".
Sic fatur meritoque latus transverberat ictu.
    Felix illa manus, talem quae prima cruorem   405
hauserit et fessi poenam libaverit orbis!
Mox omnes laniant hastis artusque trementes
dilacerant; uno tot corpore tela tepescunt
et non infecto puduit mucrone reverti.
Hi vultus avidos et adhuc spirantia vellunt   410
lumina, truncatos alii rapuere lacertos.
Amputat ille pedes, umerum quatit ille solutis
nexibus; hic fracti reserat curvamina dorsi;
hic iecur, hic cordis fibras, hic pandit anhelas
pulmonis latebras. Spatium non invenit ira   415
nec locus est odiis. Consumpto funere vix tum

---

394 amisit $V^1C\Pi$ *Birt Koch*, dimisit $V^2\phi$ *Jeep*   404 meritoque $V^2\phi$ *Birt Koch*, meritumque EV^1P *Jeep*   410 vultus avidos ω *Birt Koch*, ravidos vultus E, rabidos vultus ϵ *Jeep* (*ut ex E*)   416 vix tum $A\Pi^1$ (ix tum *in rasura* Π^1) *Birt Koch*, vixtum P^2M^2, victor $Em\epsilon V^1$, vix tunc V^3, vix tam B, victum P^1C, vixdum *coniecit Heinsius edidit Jeep*

which Jeep's conjecture preserves. His second point is not without weight, but the pleonasm may be intentional. The argument based on the *tertium comparationis* is weakened by the practice of all Greek and Latin poets, from Homer down, of developing similes far beyond the logical necessities of the comparison. Compare IR 1.164–169; 2.460–465; RP 3.263–268. The word *mucro* is one of Claudian's favorite words: the list of occurrences which Birt, 542, gives is by no means exhaustive. If *mucrone* is corrupt, *rumore* is hardly the appropriate remedy; *rumor* would be a strange word for the bellow of that giant voice, *vox desuper ingens infremuit* (see 384–385, which Koch quotes!). The word *rumor* might perhaps be taken to refer to the murmur of the crowd, but a man who suddenly finds himself surrounded by a ring of steel is not likely to be stupefied by a murmur. Birt proposes *mutata coronae* (= *mutatam coronam*), which is farfetched, but not inappropriate in sense.

416. vix tum: Heinsius suggested *vixdum*, but the word, to judge from the lexica, does not occur outside of Terence and the prose authors. On the other hand,

deseritur sparsumque perit per tela cadaver.
Sic mons Aonius rubuit, cum Penthea ferrent
Maenades aut subito mutatum Actaeona cornu
traderet insanis Latonia visa Molossis. 420
Criminibusne tuis credis, Fortuna, mederi
et male donatum certas aequare favorem
suppliciis? Vna tot milia morte rependis.
Eversis agedum Rufinum divide terris.
Da caput Odrysiis, truncum mereantur Achivi. 425
Quid reliquis dabitur? Nec singula membra peremptis
sufficiunt populis.
    Vacuo plebs undique muro
iam secura fluit; senibus non obstitit aetas
virginibusve pudor; viduae, quibus ille maritos
abstulit, orbataeque ruunt ad gaudia matres 430
insultantque alacres. Laceros iuvat ire per artus
pressaque calcato vestigia sanguine tingui.
Nec minus adsiduis flagrant elidere saxis
prodigiale caput, quod iam de cuspide summa
nutabat digna rediens ad moenia pompa. 435
Dextera quin etiam ludo concessa vagatur
aera petens fraudesque animi persolvit avari
terribili lucro vivosque imitata retentus
cogitur adductis digitos inflectere nervis.
 Desinat elatis quisquam confidere rebus 440
instabilesque deos ac lubrica numina discat.
Illa manus, quae sceptra sibi gestanda parabat,
cuius se totiens summisit ad oscula supplex
nobilitas, inhumata diu miseroque revulsa

  421 credis φ (*in rasura* Π¹) *Birt Koch,* speras *EmC Jeep*   427 undique
φ *Birt Koch,* obvia *EmεVP Jeep*   437 fraudes *EmV¹C Jeep,* penas *V³φ,*
poenas *Birt Koch*   441 ac ω *Birt Koch,* et *E Jeep*

Claudian may have modelled *vix tum deseritur* on Aeneid 2.128-129 *vix tandem
. . . rumpit,* or Ovid, Epistulae 15.215 (217) *vix denique.* For two monosyllables
at the end of the verse, compare CS 2.201 . . . *fas est.*
 427. undique: since *obvius* (or *obviam*) *ire* is used only of going to meet someone or something which is coming toward one, I have preferred the reading *undique.* If *obvia* is the correct reading, the word is used in a tone of bitter irony: compare 435 digna rediens ad moenia pompa. See BP 461-462.
 437. fraudes . . . persolvit: I have ventured to adopt this reading on the theory that Claudian was influenced by uses of λύω (see my note on *solvebat,* 345; compare Statius, Thebais 10.586-587 fraudes . . . luam).

Liber Secundus [95] 313

corpore feralem quaestum post fata reposcit! 445
Aspiciat quisquis nimium sublata secundis
colla gerit: triviis calcandus spargitur ecce,
qui sibi pyramidas, qui non cedentia templis
ornatura suos exstruxit culmina Manes,
et qui Sidonio velari credidit ostro, 450
nudus pascit aves. Iacet en, qui possidet orbem,
exiguae telluris inops et pulvere raro
per partes tegitur nusquam totiensque sepultus.
 Senserunt convexa necem tellusque nefandum
amolitur onus iam respirantibus astris. 455
Infernos gravat umbra lacus. Pater Aeacus horret
intrantemque etiam latratu Cerberus urget.
Tunc animae, quas ille fero sub iure peremit,
circumstant nigrique trahunt ad iudicis urnam
infesto fremitu: veluti pastoris in ora 460
commotae glomerantur apes, qui dulcia raptu
mella vehit, pennasque cient et spicula tendunt
et tenuis saxi per propugnacula cinctae
rimosam patriam dilectaque pumicis antra
defendunt pronoque favos examine velant. 465
 Est locus infaustis quo concilientur in unum
Cocytos Phlegethonque vadis; inamoenus uterque
alveus; hic volvit lacrimas, hic igne redundat.
Turris per geminos, flammis vicinior, amnes
porrigitur solidoque rigens adamante sinistrum 470
proluit igne latus; dextro Cocytia findit
aequora triste gemens et fletu concita plangit.
Huc post emeritam mortalia saecula vitam

450 credidit Λ*CB V²P²Π² Birt Koch*, creditus *V¹P¹Π¹A Jeep*   459 iudicis ω *Birt Koch*, vindicis *coniecit ac edidit Jeep*   463 cinctae V (i *ex* u *correcta*) *Birt Koch*, ciñcte *P*, cinte *B*, cunctae *Jeep* <ut ex V>   465 velant ω *Birt Koch*, vallant *coniecit Heinsius edidit Jeep*   472 fletu ΠΒΑ *V²P² Birt Koch*, fluctu *Emε V¹P¹C Jeep*

450. credidit: the keynote of the passage (440–453) is the disappointment of the vainglorious person's hopes; the false expectations of others (qui creditus <est ab aliis>) are not in point.
 463. cinctae: as Birt saw, this reading is quite in accord with the mock-epic tone of the passage. Compare Aeneid 12.587–592; Statius, Thebais 10.574–579.
 465. velant: for *velo* in the sense 'cover protectingly', see CS 3.168 hanc <Romam> Tritonia Gorgone velat. Compare CM 2.1 urbs . . . montana cacumina velat; CS 2.188–189 amnem . . . domibus praevelat amoenis.

deveniunt. Ibi nulla manent discrimina fati,
nullus honos vanoque exutum nomine regem   475
proturbat plebeius egens. Quaesitor in alto
conspicuus solio pertemptat crimina Minos
et iustis dirimit sontes. Quos nolle fateri
viderit, ad rigidi transmittit verbera fratris:
nam iuxta Rhadamanthys agit. Cum gesta superni   480
curriculi totosque diu perspexerit actus,
exaequat damnum meritis et muta ferarum
cogit vincla pati. Truculentos ingerit ursis
praedonesque lupis; fallaces vulpibus addit.
At qui desidia semper vinoque gravatus,   485
indulgens Veneri, voluit torpescere luxu,
hunc suis inmundi pingues detrudit in artus.
Qui iusto plus esse loquax arcanaque suevit
prodere, piscosas fertur victurus in undas,
ut nimiam pensent aeterna silentia vocem.   490
Quos ubi per varias annis ter mille figuras
egit, Lethaeo purgatos flumine tandem
rursus ad humanae revocat primordia formae.
    Tum quoque, dum lites Stygiique negotia solvit
dura fori veteresque reos ex ordine quaerit,   495
Rufinum procul ecce notat visuque severo
lustrat et ex imo concussa sede profatur:
"Huc superum labes, huc insatiabilis auri
proluvies pretioque nihil non ause parato,
quodque mihi summum scelus est, huc improbe legum   500

491 quos φ *Birt Koch*, quos *editio Aldina*, *quod non delevit* ε, *supra scribens* hos, hos *E Jeep*

489. victurus: Postgate, in Cl. Quart. 4 (1910), 259, writes: "In the metamorphosis of the guilty in the world below the 'volgator arcani' becomes an ἔλλοψ ἰχθύς. But this transformation is neither expressed nor suggested by *victurus* which is worse than superfluous". He therefore suggests *naturus*, which, he admits, is not found in extant literature, or *taciturus*, which is, as he says, an improvement on Birt's suggestion *taciturnus*. But *victurus* appears to me to be perfectly sound. Compare 1.155–156 condita funera traxi carminibus victura meis. In our present passage, the chatterer has died; he is to live again in the silent depths of the sea: *how* is he to live there if not as some sort of fish? Postgate puts matters too strongly when he says that the transformation is not even "suggested by *victurus*". Emendation should be reserved for readings which present real difficulty, and not employed for those which merely admit of improvement.

venditor, Arctoi stimulator perfide Martis!
Cuius ob innumeras strages angustus Averni
iam sinus et plena lassatur portitor alno.
Quid demens manifesta negas? En pectus inustae
deformant maculae vitiique inolevit imago 505
nec sese commissa tegunt. Genus omne dolorum
in te ferre libet: dubio tibi pendula rupes
inmineat lapsu, volucer te torqueat axis,
te refugi fallant latices atque ore natanti
arescat decepta sitis dapibusque relictis 510
in tua mansurus migret praecordia vultur.
Quamquam omnes alii, quos haec tormenta fatigant,
pars quota sunt, Rufine, tui! Quid tale vel audax
fulmine Salmoneus vel lingua Tantalus egit
aut inconsulto Tityos deliquit amore? 515
Cunctorum si facta simul iungantur in unum,
praecedes numero. Cui tanta piacula quisquam
supplicio conferre valet? Quid denique dignum
omnibus inveniam, vincant cum singula poenas?
Tollite de mediis animarum dedecus umbris. 520
Aspexisse sat est. Oculis iam parcite nostris
et Ditis purgate domos. Agitate flagellis
trans Styga, trans Erebum, vacuo mandate barathro
infra Titanum tenebras infraque recessus
Tartareos nostrumque Chaos, qua noctis opacae 525

501 arctoi *CA Birt Koch*, arctori Λ, archthoi V³P², artoi *B*, arthoi Π, et sevi V¹P¹, et saevi *Jeep*   505 vitiique *coniecit Heinsius edidit Jeep*, vitiisque φ *Birt Koch*, viciisque Π¹ (*primum* viciique *scripserat; vide Birt Pr. 115.28–29*), que *omisit B*   510 arescat ω *Birt Koch*, ardescat *coniecit ac edidit Jeep*   516 iungantur φ *Birt Koch*, iungamus *E Jeep*   525 nostrumque φ (*in rasura* Π¹) *Jeep Birt*, ūrm *ex* ṅrmque *correxit* P, ipsumque *coniecit Birt edidit Koch*

501. Arctoi: Birt seems right in his ingenious conjecture that the reading *et saevi* came into the text of VP as a gloss on *ac torvi*, a blunder for *arctoi*. Compare 4H 50–51 gentes iam deserta suas in nos transfunderet Arctos.

505. vitii: *vitiisque inolevit imago* seems meaningless. I cannot see how Mr. Platnauer, who reads *vitiisque*, arrived at his translation: "... thy crimes have made their impress on thy spirit . . . ."

525. nostrumque: Koch (Pr. 23) later called into question his own acceptance of Birt's suggestion *ipsumque*. I do not believe that emendation is necessary. With Claudian, *chaos* is part of Pluto's realm (Koch cites RP 1.27–28 Proserpina . . . possedit dotale Chaos; compare also RP 2.13, 196); *nostrum* is therefore not unnatural in the mouth of Minos (compare IE 2.534–537 <Aurora is imploring

fundamenta latent; praeceps ibi mersus anhelet,
dum rotat astra polus, feriunt dum litora venti".

Stilicho to remain in the East>: Tantane te *nostri* ceperunt taedia mundi? . . . solamque tueris Hesperiam?). If emendation be deemed necessary, I should suggest *imum* rather than Burmann's *vastum*, or Birt's *ipsum:* compare IR 1.379.

LIST OF ABBREVIATIONS

For the abbreviations used in citing Claudian's poems, see below, page 102. In the Introduction with its notes, and in the Textual Commentary, where the number of a page, column, or note is followed by a period, any numbers following the period refer to lines of the text cited.

Anth. = Anthologia Latina, Volume 2, Part 1, Edited by F. Buecheler (Leipzig, Teubner, 1930. Pp. 398).

Arch. = Archiv für Lateinische Lexicographie und Grammatik.

Bethmann = Moritz August von Bethmann-Hollweg, Der Civilprozess des Gemeinen Rechts in Geschichtlicher Entwicklung, Dritter Band (Bonn, A. Marcus, 1866. Pp. VIII, 383).

Birt = Theodor Birt, Claudii Claudiani Carmina (= MGH 10. Berlin, Weidmann, 1892. Pp. CCXXX, 610).

Birt Arch. = Theodor Birt, Verbalformen vom Perfectstamme bei Claudian, in Arch. 4(1887), 589-594.

Boak-Dunlap = Arthur E. R. Boak and James E. Dunlap, Two Studies in Later Roman and Byzantine Administration (= University of Michigan Studies, Humanistic Series, Volume 14. New York, Macmillan, 1924. Pp. X, 324).

Brakman = C. Brakman, Observationes Criticae ad Claudianum, in Mnemosyne 58(1930), 371-384.

Burmann = Claudii Claudiani Opera ... cum ... Adnotationibus Petri Burmanni Secundi (Amsterdam, 1760. Pp. XXXII, 1112).

Bury = John Bagnell Bury, History of the Later Roman Empire from the Death of Theodosius I to the Death of Justinian, Volume 1^2 (London, Macmillan, 1923. Pp. xxv, 471).

Chron. = Chronica Minora, Edited by Theodor Mommsen (Two volumes, = MGH 9, 11. Berlin, Weidmann, 1892, 1894. Pp. XII, 756; 506).

CIL = Corpus Inscriptionum Latinarum.

Cl. Quart. = The Classical Quarterly.

Cl. Rev. = The Classical Review.

Cod. Just. = Codex Justinianus, Edited by Paul Krueger (Berlin, Weidmann, 1929. Pp. XXVI, 516).

Cod. Theod. = Codex Theodosianus, in Theodosiani Libri XVI, Volume 1, Part 2. Edited by Theodor Mommsen (Berlin, Weidmann, 1905. Pp. 931).

col. = column.

Collomp = Paul Collomp, La Critique des Textes (Paris, Les Belles Lettres, 1931. Pp. 128).

Cosenza = Mario Emilio Cosenza, Official Positions after the Time of Constantine (Dissertation, Columbia University. Lancaster, Pennsylvania, New Era Press, 1905. Pp. iii, 109).

Fargues = Pierre Fargues, Claudien: Études sur sa Poésie et son Temps (Paris, Hachette, 1933. Pp. 345).

FHG = Fragmenta Historicorum Graecorum, Edited by Karl Müller, Volume 4 (Paris, Didot, 1851. Pp. iii, 856).

Gesner = Joannes Matthias Gesner, Claudii Claudiani Quae Extant (Leipzig, Fritsch, 1759. Pp. XLVIII, 720).

[99]

Glover = Terrot Reaveley Glover, Life and Letters in the Fourth Century (Cambridge: At the University Press, 1901. Pp. xvi, 398).
Glück = Heinrich Glück, Das Hebdomon und Seine Reste in Makrikōi (Vienna, Österreichische Staatsdruckerei, 1920. Pp. VIII, 84, XI).
Gothofred. = Codex Theodosianus cum Perpetuis Commentariis Iacobi Gothofredi, Edited by Johannes Daniel Ritter (6 volumes. Leipzig, Weidmann, 1736–1745).
Grosse = Robert Grosse, Römische Militargeschichte (Berlin, Weidmann, 1920. Pp. XV, 346).
Heinsius = Notes of Nicolaus Heinsius on the IR, quoted by Burmann.
Jeep = Ludovicus Jeep, Claudii Claudiani Carmina (Leipzig, Teubner. Two volumes, 1876, 1879. Pp. LXXXI, 266; CLIX, 259).
Journ. Rom. Stud. = The Journal of Roman Studies.
Koch = Julius Koch, Claudii Claudiani Carmina (Leipzig, Teubner, 1893. Pp. LXI, 346).
Koch Cuiac. = Julius Koch, De Codicibus Cuiacianis Dissertatio (Marburg, Friedrich, 1889. Pp. 63).
Kroll = Wilhelm Kroll, Studien zum Verständnis der Römischen Literatur (Stuttgart, Metzler, 1924. Pp. 390).
Kromayer = Johannes Kromayer und Georg Veith, Heerwesen und Kriegführung der Griechen und Römer (Munich, Beck, 1928. Pp. IX, 649. 56 Plates).
Kühner = Raphael Kühner und Carl Stegmann, Ausführliche Grammatik der Lateinischen Sprache, Zweiter Band² (Hannover, Hahn. Two parts. 1912, 1914. Pp. XII, 828; VIII, 738).
Lit. Cent. = Literarisches Centralblatt (Zentralblatt) für Deutschland.
Lot = Ferdinand Lot, La Fin du Monde Antique et le Début du Moyen Âge (Paris, La Renaissance du Livre, 1927. Pp. XXVI, 515).
Lydus, De Mag. = Johannes Lydus, De Magistratibus.
Maas = Paul Maas, Textkritik, Section 2 of Gercke-Norden, Einleitung in die Altertumswissenschaft I³ (Leipzig, Teubner, 1927. Pp. 18).
MGH = Monumenta Germaniae Historica, Auctores Antiquissimi (Berlin, Weidmann).
Migne Gr. = Jacques Paul Migne, Patrologiae Cursus Completus, Series Graeca.
Migne Lat. = Jacques Paul Migne, Patrologiae Cursus Completus, Series Latina.
Mommsen Stil. = Theodor Mommsen, Stilicho und Alarich, in Hermes 38(1903), 101–115.
Muellner = C. Muellner, De Imaginibus Similitudinibusque Quae in Claudiani Carminibus Inveniuntur (= Dissertationes Vindobonenses 4[1893], 99–203. Vienna, Gerolds Sohn).
Neue = Friedrich Neue, Formenlehre der Lateinischen Sprache³, Revised by C. Wagener, Volume 3 (Leipzig, Reisland, 1897. Pp. II, 664).
Palanque = Jean-Rémy Palanque, Essai sur la Préfecture du Prétoire du Bas-Empire (Paris, De Boccard, 1933. Pp. XVI, 144).
Palanque Ambr. = Jean-Rémy Palanque, Saint Ambroise et L'Empire Romain (Paris, De Boccard, 1933. Pp. XVI, 599).
Parravicini = Achille Parravicini, Studio di Retorica sulle Opere di Claudio Claudiano (Milan, Scuola Tipografia Salesiana, 1905. Pp. X, 190).
Paucker = C. Paucker, De Latinitate Claudiani Poetae Observationes, in Rh. Mus. 35(1880), 586–606.

Paul = T. W. Paul, Quaestiónes Claudianeae (Berlin, Huelsen, 1866. Pp. 36).
Pauly-Wissowa = Paulys Real-Encyclopädie der Classischen Altertumswissenschaft. Revised by Georg Wissowa and (in recent volumes) Wilhelm Kroll. Pauly-Wissowa alone = First Series, commencing with the letter A; Pauly-Wissowa Zw. = Second Series, commencing with the letter R.
Platnauer = Claudian, With an English Translation by Maurice Platnauer. (The Loeb Classical Library. London, Heinemann, 1922. Two volumes. Pp. xxvi, 393; 413).
Postgate = J. P. Postgate, Review of Editions of Claudian by Birt and Koch, in Cl. Rev. 9(1895), 162–169.
Pr. = Preface. After this abbreviation, the Roman numerals of Prefaces so cited are changed to Arabic.
Rh. Mus. = Rheinisches Museum für Philologie.
Roscher = W. H. Roscher, Ausführliches Lexicon der Griechischen und Römischen Mythologie, Erster Band (Leipzig, Teubner, 1884–1890. Pp. VIII, 1440).
Schamberger = Maximilian Schamberger, De P. Papinio Statio Verborum Novatore (= Dissertationes Philologicae Halenses 17[1907], 231–336. Halle, Niemeyer).
Schanz = Martin Schanz, Geschichte der Römischen Literatur, Vierter Teil, Zweite Hälfte, von Martin Schanz, Carl Hosius und Gustav Krüger (Munich, Beck, 1920. Pp. XVII, 681).
Schmidt = Ludwig Schmidt, Geschichte der Deutschen Stämme bis zum Ausgang der Völkerwanderung. Die Ostgermanen² (Munich, Beck, 1934. Pp. 647).
Schroff = Helmut Schroff, Claudians Gedicht vom Gotenkrieg (= Klassisch-Philologische Studien Herausgegeben von F. Jacoby, Heft 8. Berlin, Ebering, 1927. Pp. 86).
Seeck = Otto Seeck, Geschichte des Untergangs der Antiken Welt, Volume 5, with Anhang (Berlin, F. Siemenroth, 1913. Pp. 619).
Seeck Gefolg. = Otto Seeck, Das Deutsche Gefolgwesen auf Römischen Boden, in Zeitschrift der Savigny-Stiftung für Rechtsgeschichte, Germanistische Abtheilung 17 (1896), 97–119.
Seeck Liban. = Otto Seeck, Die Briefe des Libanius Zeitlich Geordnet (Leipzig, Hinrich, 1906. Pp. 496).
Seeck Regesten = Otto Seeck, Regesten der Kaiser und Päpste für die Jahre 311 bis 476 n<ach> Chr<isto> (Stuttgart, Metzler, 1919. Pp. X, 487).
Seeck Ruf. = Otto Seeck, article Rufinus (23) in Pauly-Wissowa Zw. 1.1189.15–1193.35.
Seeck Symm. = Q. Aurelii Symmachi Quae Supersunt, Edidit Otto Seeck (= MGH 6.1. Berlin, Weidmann, 1883. Pp. CCXII, 376).
Sommer = Ferdinand Sommer, Handbuch der Lateinischen Laut- und Formenlehre³ (Heidelberg, Winter, 1914. Pp. XXVIII, 664).
Stein = Ernst Stein, Geschichte des Spätrömischen Reiches, Volume 1 (Vienna, Seidel, 1928. Pp. XXII, 590. Maps are in pocket attached to inside back cover).
Stein Offic. = Ernst Stein, Untersuchungen über das Officium der Praetorianer-Praefektur (Vienna, Rikola, 1922. Pp. 77).
Stein Verwalt. = Ernst Stein, Untersuchungen zur Spätrömischen Verwaltungsgeschichte, in Rh. Mus. 74 (1925), 347–394.
Stolz-Schmalz = Stolz-Schmalz, Lateinische Grammatik⁵, Revised by Manu Leumann and J. B. Hofmann (Munich, Beck, 1928. Pp. XXII, 924).

Teuffel = W. S. Teuffel, Geschichte der Römischen Literatur[6], Revised by E. Klostermann, R. Leonhard, P. Wessner, Wilhelm Kroll, and Franz Skutsch. Dritter Band (Leipzig, Teubner, 1913. Pp. VIII, 579).
Thesaurus = Thesaurus Linguae Latinae.
Van Millingen = Alexander Van Millingen, Byzantine Constantinople (London, John Murray, 1899. Pp. xi, 361).
Vollrath = Otto Vollrath, De Metonymiae in Cl<audii> Claudiani Carminibus Usu Dissertatio, Jena (Weide, Thomas und Hubert, 1910. Pp. 83).
Welzel = Alfred Welzel, De Claudiani et Corippi Sermone Epico Dissertatio (Breslau, Fleischmann, 1908. Pp. 100).
Weston = Arthur H. Weston, Latin Satirical Writing Subsequent to Juvenal (Thesis, Yale University. Lancaster, Pennsylvania, New Era Printing Company, 1915. Pp. vii, 165).

ABBREVIATIONS USED IN CITING CLAUDIAN'S POEMS

Abbreviation	*Poem*	*Gesner's Numbers*
BG	De Bello Gildonico	15
BP	De Bello Pollentino sive Gothico	25, 26
CM	Carmina Minora (cited as in Birt and in Koch)	
CS	De Consulatu Stilichonis	21–24
EH	Epithalamium De Nuptiis Honorii Augusti	9, 10
FH	Fescennina De Nuptiis Honorii Augusti	11–14
3H	Panegyricus De Tertio Consulatu Honorii Augusti	6, 7
4H	" " Quarto " " "	8
6H	" " Sexto " " "	27, 28
IE	In Eutropium	18–20
IR	In Rufinum	2–5
MT	Panegyricus Dictus Manlio Theodoro Consuli	16, 17
PO	" " Probino et Olybrio Consulibus	1
RP	De Raptu Proserpinae	32–36

Prefaces are cited thus: CS 3 Pr. 21 = the twenty-first verse of the *Praefatio* to the third book of De Consulatu Stilichonis.

INDEX

ab, 194
ablative, 124, 166; absolute, 83, 116, 118, 120
abstractions personified: *see* allegorical figures
acclamatio, acclamo, 190, 198
acer, 95, 97
Achilles, 88, 169
acies, 99
Acroceraunia, 177
Actaeon, 204 f.
actus, 82, 214
ad prima, 51
adjectives, adverbial use of neut., 29, 69, 193, 195, 213; contrasting, 38; extended use of, 15 f., 31, 50, 51, 70, 78
Adriatic, 177
adverb, 142
Aeacus, 210 f.
Aeneas, 88, 210
aestuo, 103 f.
aestus, 149
aetas, 71
aetherius, 156
Africa, 39
Agamemnon, 32
ago, 67
agriculture as sign of degeneration from Golden Age, 113
Alani, 90 f., 92, 183
Alaric, 68, 115 f., 117, 127, 133, 135, 138, 145, 150, 162, 171 f.
alchemy, 50
Alexander, 111, 130, 160, 180
alga, 114
Allecto, 18 f., 20, 21, 50, 105, 223
allegorical figures, 20, 21 f., 26, 102
allopathic punishment, 215
alludo, 191
aloft, carrying a conquering hero, 192

Alpheus, 117
Alps, 119, 151 f., 188, 200
alternus, 153, 178
ambages, 192
ambiguity, 192
Ambrose, 6
Ammianus, 94, 95, 195
amnesty, 149
amor, 178, 183, 221, 222
Andabilis, 131
Andromeda, 81
anfractus, 198
angustus, 194
anima, 211, 219
animals, first to be attacked in plague, 86 f.; images drawn from, 182
animi, 51
animosus, 95
annus, 71; *a. magnus*, 215
Antaeus, 82, 83
anti-Germanic sentiment, 88
Antioch, 131 f.
Aonius, 115 f.
apex, 120
appellations, various, applied to a god, 99
Apollo, 1 f., 4 f., 116, 118
apostrophe: *see* vocative; to Stilicho, 78, 86, 93, 98
Aquilo, 70
Aquitania, 39
Arabicus sinus, 81
Arar, 147 f.
Araxes, 109, 111 f.
Arbogastes, 119, 145
Arcadia, 115, 117
Arcadius, 6, 24, 110, 120, 123, 153 f., 155–57, 158, 163 f., 165 f., 172–74, 187, 190, 193, 197, 198
Arctous, 218
arcus, 140 f., 179

321

Ares: see Mars
aresco, 121 f.
Arethusa, 117
Argaeus, 131
Aristides, 150
Aristotle, 148
Armenia, 112, 128, 130, 146 f., 167
arrows, dense shower of, 150
Artemis, 204
arx, 104, 136
Asia, 131
asper, 111
aspero, 153
aspicio, 135 f.
ass, 215
Astraea: see Iustitia
astrology, 27, 43, 105
asylum, 154
at, 75, 144, 154
Athamas, 31 f.
Athena, 172
Athens, 172
Athos, 39, 99 f., 150 f.
Atilius: see Serranus
Atlas, 7, 79
Atreus, 31
atoms, 16
Audacia, 22
audio, 100, 200
Augustus, 112, 198
aurum, 189
Ausonius (poet), 1; (local adj.), 141
auspex, 32, 144
Auster, 33, 106
Autumnus, 106
Avaritia, 22
axis, 158, 220

Balkans, 133
barbarian attire, 139 f., 141 f.
barbarians, 87–89, 125 f., 127–29, 131, 139 f., 144, 152, 166, 171
barritus, 169 f.
basilikos logos, 110
Bastarnae, 88, 90
beast, tyrant as a, 76
bee-similes, 211 f.
Bellerophon, 76, 86
Bellona, 100 f., 183
bibo, 56, 92, 147, 181

biothanatoi, 48
Black Sea, 52
blood-offerings, 40
blood-pollution, 116 f., 121
bloodthirstiness, 31, 157, 179
boar, Arcadian, 82
bodyguards, barbarian, 139 f.
boni, 77
Bononia, 39
Bosphorus, 52
Boulogne-sur-Mer, 39
brevis, 134
Britain, 39, 157
Brittia, 39
bucellarii, 139
bull, Cretan, 82, 83
burial, lack of, 109; see also *inhumatus, inops, nudus*
Busiris, 74

cadaver, 204
caecus, 80
Caesar, 59, 108, 215
Caesarius, 128
Calchedonius, 135
calco, 181, 206 f.
caligo, 14 f.
Caligula, 214
calor, 57, 186; see also *flagro*
cano, 27, 49
cantus, 44
Cap de la Magnaure Jetée, 194
Cappadocia, 131
captatio, 57 f.
carcer, 73
carrago, 152
Caspian Gates, Sea, 129 f.
Caspius, 127–30
cassis, 103
Castalia, 116
castigo, 213 f.
Castor and Pollux, 79
castra, 77
catabasis, 209 f., 211 f., 213
cataphracti, 195 f.
caterva, 5 f.
Catiline, 123 f.
Cato, 79
Catullus, 1
Caucasus, 46, 128, 129 f.

INDEX

cavalry, Armenian, 146 f.; Hunnish, 140 f.
Cecropius, 172
Celts: *see* Gauls
Centaur, 97, 169
Cephisos, 4
Ceraunia, 177
Cerberus, 85, 210 f.
Ceres, 95 f.
certus, 193 f.
cetera, 69
Chaeronea, 116
chain of boats, 136
Chaldeans, 45
Chaos, 223
character, 45
chase, 198, 201
Chimaera, 76, 85 f.
Chiron, 169
Christianity, 99, 120, 121 f., 156, 185, 197, 203
chronology of IR 1 and 2, 63, 69 f., 87, 89, 119
Cicero, 9 f., 123 f.
Cilicia, 131
Cinna, 74
Circe, 47
Cirrhaeus, 2
Cithaeron, 205
civil wars, 200
clamor, 169 f.
classica, 63
Claudius, 214
claustrum, 127 f., 129 f.
Cleopatra, 61, 215
clipeus, 77
Cocytus, 212
coerceo, 159
cognatus, 97, 196
cognosco, 186 f.
coma, 112
comic poets, 1
commendatio, 198
community of property, 26, 113
comparison, second term of, disparaged, 76, 81
comparisons, series of, each w. abl., 33
complain, right to, suppressed, 142
complexity of Roman civilization, 62 f.
concilium deorum, 19
Concordia, 26

conditional expressions, 36, 64, 222
confero, 171
conflagration, extinction of, 124
confundo, 124
coniuratus, 93
conjunctions, explicative, 15, 36, 106, 212, 213
Constantinople, 38, 52, 135, 142, 143, 153 f., 158, 172, 185, 186, 193, 194, 206
consul, 141
contio, 187
convexa, 108, 210
coral, 114
Corinth, 171
corona, 200 f.
Corus, 177 f.
coruscus, 110
Crete, 82, 83
crimen, 55
crista, cristo, 102, 195
Croesus, 59
crudelitate, loci communes de, 66 f., 70, 136
crudesco, 87
cruentus, 29
culmen, 18
cum, 199
cuneus, 194 f.
Curae, 22
Curius, 59 f.
curriculum, 214
curro, 16
currus, 102 f.
cursus, 134

damnum, 214 f.
Damocles, 123
dangers, Rome's, 143, 174
Danube, 39, 127–29, 133 f.
Dariel, Pass of, 129 f.
darkness, 2, 21, 28, 41
dating of 3H and IR, 6
dative, 62, 159
daughter of Rufinus, 123, 154
dea, 41
death charms, 46, 48 f.; sentence: *see* execution
debitus, 109, 184
declamations: *see loci communes*
defendo, 178
defensive measures of Goths, 152 f.

defensor, 31
deification, 120
Delius, 116
Delphi, 4, 116
demonic personifications: *see* allegorical figures
Derbend, 129 f.
desuper, 199
deterior, 116
devastation, description of, 130, 132, 133, 171, 173
devius, 175
devotus, 197
Dido, 191
Diomedes, 74
Dionysus, 204
Dioscuri: *see* Castor
direct quotations, 23–25, 33, 42, 51, 99, 100, 105, 108, 156, 178, 181, 183, 187, 192, 199, 217; assigned to mythological characters, 24; beginning or ending within verse, 24; dialogue sequences, 24; exact words not given, 24; frequency, 23 f.; length, 24; rapid succession of brief sentences, 176, 223; resumption of narrative after, 29, 50, 52, 100, 103, 108, 127, 144, 165, 176, 181, 182, 184, 190, 192, 200, 202; *see also* speech, collective
Dis, 30
disasters, Rome's, 143, 174
Discordia, 21
discrimen, 146
dismemberment, 203, 204 f., 206
dispono, 127
dissimulo, 164
dito, 50
divido, 127
divitiis, loci communes de, 58 f.
Don, 94
donative, 189, 193
draco, 167 f., 197
dream, 191
dualism, 19, 28, 33, 41
dubius, 11, 220
dust-cloud, 167
dux, 176
dye-stuffs as sign of degeneration from Golden Age, 113 f.

East and West, 146, 159, 163

Eastern component of Stilicho's army, 145, 153 f., 158, 161 f., 172 f., 176, 181, 182, 184, 188
Eauze, 39 f.
Egestas, 22
egregius, 138
Egypt, 45, 141
Elatea, 116
Elis, 115
Elusa, 39 f., 42
embolodetes, 101
emeritus, 213
Empire, Roman, eastern boundary of, 111, 163; expansion of, 110 f.; unity of, 156
en, 105
ensis, 68, 123, 188
Eous, 145, 176
epic, Roman, speech in, 23–25
Epicureanism, 9, 15, 17
Epirus, 151
equator, 107
Erebus, 223
Ereğli, 186
est, 69; *est genus*, 94; *est locus*, 40, 212
et: *see* conjunctions
eternity, symbols of, 224
Eudoxia, 185
Eugenius, 119, 120, 145, 149, 179
Eunapius, 7, 54
Euripus, 33 f.
Europe, 132
Eutropius, 3, 208
exceptus, 137
execution, stay of, in death sentences, 53, 68; *see also* sword
exhortation of troops, 166 f.

Fabricius, 59
facinus, 185 f.
facultas, 138
Fames, 21
famosus, 95
famulus, 200
Fate and Fortune, 43; *see also* Fortune
fatum, 208
fera, 76
fero, 205; *fertur*, 40, 118
Fides, 26; *fides*, 28 f.
figura, 16 f., 41, 215

INDEX

fire and water, destruction of world by, 175
fishing, 198
Flaccus, Valerius, 23
flagro, 64; *see also calor*
flecto, 105, 176, 182
floods, 78
foedus, 11, 28 f., 138
foreshadowing, 17 f., 108, 125, 158, 164, 185, 189, 191, 192, 211
Formido, 102
formulae, repetition of, 32, 79, 81 f.
fortuna, loci communes de, 208
Fortune, 172; *see also* Fate
fragor, 169 f.
frango, 30, 78, 129
fraternus, 163
fratricide, 31
friends, inseparable, 36
frons, 96
funus, 204
Furies, 18 f., 20, 24, 25, 28, 29, 32, 38–42, 50, 52, 105, 107 f., 112, 209, 223
Furor, 108

Gainas, 173, 185, 199
Ganges, 84
Garonne, 147, 148 f.
Gaul, Gauls, 38 f., 145, 146, 147 f., 157, 159, 167
Geloni, 90 f., 92
gemino, 170
geminus, 120, 158, 171
gemma, 194
genialis, 143 f.
geocentric theory, 14
geographical allusions, 34, 41, 147, 168, 180
Germanic components in Stilicho's Western army, 145
Germans, 148; *see also* anti-Germanic sentiment; Germanic components; Goths
geronticide, 96
gerundive, 157
Geryon, 82, 84 f.
Gesoriacum, 39
Getae: see Goths
Gildo, 5, 68, 117, 125, 145, 159
gleam of arms, 168
gods on trial, 18, 205

gold, transformation of baser substances into, 50, 51
Golden Age, 26, 104, 105, 109 f., 112 f.
Gorgon, 80 f.
Goths, 20, 87–90, 92, 94 f., 98, 115, 117, 128 f., 132, 133 f., 135, 139, 145, 152 f., 166, 179
Gradivus, 103
Gratian, 139
Greece, 115, 133, 162, 171
Greek origin, possible influence of on Claudian's Latin, 61, 200
grief-stricken army, 182 f.

Hades, 209 f.
Haemonius, 185
Haemus, 39, 99, 186
Haik, 147
hair, 112, 147
Halys, 131
hand, kissing the Emperor's, 208
hasta, 163, 168
heart as seat of anger, 23
heat: *see calor, flagro*
heavenly vs. chthonic powers, 2; *see also* light, darkness
Hebdomon, 194
Hebrus, 98, 186
Hecate, 47
Helicon, 115
Hellespont, 150 f.
Heracle, 186
herbidus, 147
Hercules, 31, 79, 82, 83, 86, 186
hereditary transmission of imperial power, quasi-, 162 f., 164
heres, 163 f.
Hermus, 35
heroic past, Rome's, 72, 200
hesitation, judicial, 219
Hesperia, 119, 183
Hiberi, 84
Hister, 90
hog, 215
Homer, 182, 195, 209, 212
honestum, 59
honey, 113
Honorius, 6, 108–10, 120, 139, 143, 156, 159, 163 f., 173, 190
honos, 114

horses, winds and waters compared to, 28, 175
hortor, 187, 201 f.
hucusque, 77
humankind as recipients of plagues, 87
humanum genus, 175
hundreds, verses numbered in even, 86, 144
Huns, 90 f., 93 f., 95–98, 128 f., 130, 139, 140 f., 183
hunting, 198, 201
Hydaspes, 181
hydra, Lernaean, 82, 84, 85
Hyperboreus, 180

iacto, 138
iam, 87, 89; *iam non*, 87, 135
Iazyges, 96
ice crushed by wagon-wheels, 129
ictus, 199
ignesco, 167
ignis, 13, 56, 212
ilicet, 52 f.
illinc, 142, 146
Illyricum, 159, 163, 173
images, 20, 27, 30, 33, 36, 41, 56, 65, 75, 77, 78, 79, 86, 103, 121, 122, 123, 126 f., 132, 133, 142, 143, 144, 177, 182, 184, 191, 193, 198, 201, 211
imago, 219
impatiens, 21, 182
imperfect tense, 11, 12, 15, 18
Imperial court, 5 f., 174; legislation in West, 7
impono, 123
imprisonment of evil forces, 28, 108, 112
in, 51
Inachus, 80 f.
inanis, 16 f., 61
inde, 146
India, 111; Indian Ocean, 81, 180 f.
indicative mood, 203
iners, 58, 77, 134 f.
infinitive w. *do*, 23; historical, 54; pres., of fut. action, 94, 209
ingemino, 55
inhumatus, 208; *see also* burial, *inops*, *nudus*
innecto, 92
inolesco, 219
inopinus, 130

inops, 59, 209; *see also* burial, *inhumatus*, *nudus*
insanity, 31
insilio, 103
interiaceo, 132
interstrepo, 188
intervention, divine, 209
intransitives, development of into transitives, 46
intumesco, 170
inundation, 28
invado, 162, 202
invidia, 173 f., 181
Iolcos, 52
ipse, 37, 67
irony, 154, 158, 192
iste, 34
Isthmiacus, 72 f.
Italus, 177
Italy, 115, 143, 144, 148, 152, 153, 158, 159
iubar, 44, 156
iubeo, 159 f.
iungo, 102 f.
iuro, 66, 96
ius, 141, 211
Iustitia, 18, 27, 104, 223; as constellation (= Virgo), 27, 106 f.
iuvat ire, 206
Ixion, 220

Jason, 52
Jerome, 128, 130, 131, 132, 143
John of Antioch, 120 f., 154
Julian, 148, 168
Jupiter, 99; earthly rulers compared to, 26
Justice: *see* Iustitia
justification of the ways of supernatural powers, 18, 205
Justinian, 139
Juvenal, 9, 150

kissing the Emperor's hand, 208
knee, bending of before the Emperor, 208

labarum, 168, 197
labes, 217
Lactantius, 121
Ladon, 117
Latinity of Claudian, 61, 122
Latium, 84, 142

INDEX

laus Stilichonis, 75, 97, 119, 144, 166, 199
laws, 27 f., 141 f., 218
Leo, 107
leonine rhyme, 184
Lethaeus, Lethe, 216
libertas, 200
libo, 203
Libra, 106, 107
Libya, 132 f., 159, 180
licet, 184
"licking into shape," 34
light, 2, 41, 112, 210
limes, 113, 175
lion, Nemean (or Cleonaean), 82
lion-similes, 65, 182, 196, 201
lito, 47
lituus, 102, 176
Livor, 22
localities, various, connected with a god, 99
loci communes, 58, 66 f., 110 f., 136, 150, 169, 183, 208, 210
longe, 184
Lower World, 209 f.; entrance to, 40
Lucan, 1, 19, 23, 25, 40, 41, 69, 71, 72, 90, 91 f., 121, 124, 133, 141, 181 f., 191, 197 f., 203, 204, 208 f.
Lucian, 72, 150, 210–12
Lucianus, 53, 55, 69 f.
Lucretius, 9, 16, 82
Luctus, 22
ludus, 96, 207
lunar myth, 2
Luxus, 22
Lycians, 53, 67
Lydia, 50, 59

Macedonia, 163
Macetes, 185
Maenads, 204
Maeonia, 50
Maeotis, 92
magic, 43–50; Claudian's relative avoidance of, 44
maiestas, 66
malefactors, historical and mythical, 72
Manes, 47, 164
Manichaean controversy, 19
Manlius, 144
mansuesco, 133

Mar Apas Catina, 147
Marcomanni, 133
Mars, 39, 97 f., 99 f., 102–4, 118, 194, 218
Martial, 1
martial fury, 170
martyrology, 203
masculine allegorical figures included among feminines, 20
Massagetae, 90–92, 96
maturus, 123
Maximus, 63, 119, 200
meatus, 12
Medea, 46 f.
Medes: *see* Persians
medius, 188
Medusa, 81
Megaera, 19, 31, 38, 39 f., 50, 104, 105 f., 108, 112, 223
mensa, 66
mentior, 42
metempsychosis, 214, 215, 219 f.
Midas, 50 f.
milk, 113 f.
Minos, 37, 211, 213, 214, 217
Minucius Felix, 10
mixtus, 91
mobilitas, 95, 97
modus, 190
Moesia, 134
moles, 103
Molossian hounds, 205
monologue, 122
monosyllables, 35
mood-variation, 3, 122, 203
moon, 13, 44
morning, 193
Moses of Chorene, 147
mugitus, 29, 116
multi-ethnic troops, 145 f.
mundus, 7, 26, 33, 43, 175, 181
Muses, 4, 9, 18, 115
mutus, 215
Mysians, 134
mythological themes, 2, 19, 24, 52, 72

narrative, resumption of after speech, 29
natura, 160, 161
navigation, 63, 79 f., 143
nec, 205; *nec . . . quidem*, 142
necdum, 174

necromancy, 47–49
necto, 64
nego, 178
nefas, 28, 33, 71, 200
Nekyia, 38–40, 209 f.
Neptune, 81
Nereus, 56
nescio, 133
nexus, 101 f.
niger, 100
Nile, 56, 81, 181
nimbus, 110, 156
non, 35, 63, 67, 81
North and South, 146
Notus, 181
novus, 16, 124, 189
Nox, 21; *nox*, 191
nudus, 209; *see also* burial, *inhumatus*, *inops*
Numa, 37
numerus, 222
nuncupatio, 198

obex, 127
Oceanus, 58 f.
Odrysius, 52, 118, 205
Oedipus, 32
Oeta, 39
oleum, 113 f.
olim, 180
Olympiodorus, 6 f.
opes, 161 f.
Oratio Obliqua, 24, 198; *Recta: see* direct quotations
orbis, 7, 26, 43, 58, 127, 150, 175, 203, 209
orbita, 160 f.
Orcus, 85
Oriens, 130
Orkney Islands, 180
Orontes, 131 f.
Ovid, 40, 204 f.
oxymoron, 69, 178, 196

Pactolus, 35 f.
Paean, 4
pando, 115
panegyrists, 56, 71, 82, 122, 143, 144
Pangaea, 100
Pannonia, 133 f.
papyri, magical, 43
parade, 194 f.

paradox, 155
paraxonion, 101 f.
Parcae, 49
parens, 119
parenthesis, exclamatory, 176
parliamentary atmosphere, 22 f., 31, 36, 37
Parnassus, 205
pars, 162 f., 190
parsimony of traditional Roman heroes, 59
partition of world among major deities, 30, 105 f.
paternity, test of, 148
Pavor, 102
pax Theodosiana, 20, 25, 107, 145, 162
pearls, 114
pecus, 81
pedes, 151
Pegasus, 76
Pelion, 39
Pelopeius, 171
penalties, enumeration of, 220 f.; eternal, 224
Peneus, 152
penso, 215
Pentheus, 204 f.
penuria, 184
pereo, 25
perfect indicative, 4
Perfekt, constatierendes, 22
Perinthus, 186
Perithous, 36
periuria, 184
permissio, 188, 205
Perseus, 80 f.
Persians, 111
personification, 179; *see also* allegorical figures
Phaëthon, 175
Phalaris, 73
Pharsalus, 39, 192 f.
Phasis, 111
Philostorgius, 128, 130
Phlegethon, 38, 212
Pholoe, 115
phronêsis, 58
piaculum, 222 f.
picturatus, 61
Pietas, 26
Pindus, 39
plagues, 86 f.

pleonasm, 115, 138
Pliny, 146
plural, 60, 180
poena, 155; Rufinus' murder as, 18, 109, 203
pollution: *see* blood-pollution
polyglot character of Stilicho's troops, 145 f.
Pompey, 141, 175, 186, 191, 209
Pontus, 162
portitor, 218
posco, 187
possum, 33
posterity, wonderment of, 185
poverty: *see* wealth
prae- (prefix), 65, 155
praeceptum, 137
praedo, 87
Praetorian Prefect, 58, 86, 141
prayer, gesture in, 174
prefaces, 1, 5, 115
present, 30, 209
primus, 34, 84; *see also ad prima*
Probinus and Olybrius, 33
Procopius, 38 f.
Proculus, 53, 70 f.
prodigus, 170
proditor, 93, 134
prolepsis: *see* resultative-predicate
proluvies, 217 f.
Promotus, 88, 93
prooemium, 17 f.
prophecy: *see* foreshadowing
Propontis, 186
providentia, 9, 10–12, 14
Prudentius, 1
psogos-pattern, 11, 33, 34, 35, 52, 56, 58, 59, 63, 65, 66, 72, 75, 80, 84, 86, 104, 121, 134, 154, 186
Ptolemies, 209
pudor, 64
punishments: *see* penalties
purpur, purpureus, 155, 168, 194, 209
Pyrenees, 39
Pyrrhus, 59 f.
Pythia, 4
Python, 1–5

Quadi, 133
quaero, 216 f.

quaesitor, 213
quantum non, 177
quatio, 65
-que: *see* conjunctions
quisque, 65
*quod-*clause, 138
quondam, 19, 182
quotiens, 138

radio, 61, 123, 168 f.
rapio, 61, 150
rarus, 198
re- compounds, 51, 105
recepto, 91
recipio, 155
recursus, 95, 97
Red Sea, 81
refluus, 34
regalis, 156
rego, 159
relative, separated from antecedent, 7; clauses with subjunctive, 57
rending of garments, 22
resultative-predicate use of adjective, 11, 49, 61, 87, 102, 114, 115, 193, 204, 206
retentus, 208
revisions, poet's own: *see* variants
revoco, 140
revolt of powers of darkness, 28, 30, 107 f.
revolvo, 41 f.
rex and its derivatives, of Roman Emperor, 36 f., 156, 172
Rhadamanthus, 213 f.
rhetoric, 41, 54, 58, 100, 155, 160, 169, 179 f., 181 f.; *see also loci communes*, oxymoron, *permissio*, *psogos*-pattern, tyrants
Rhine, 39, 42, 147, 148
Rhodope, 99
Rhone, 147
Riphaean Mts., 70
rising to address a gathering, 31
river-names used to designate adjacent peoples, 84
river-similes, 77 f.
rivers, as plague-carriers, 87; bearing signs of carnage, 117; drunk by armies, 150, 181; enumeration of, 111
Rome, 33, 84, 135
Rubrum Mare, 81, 180 f.

Rufinianae (Rufinus' estate), 155, 193, 208 f.
Rufinus, 1, 2, 3, 5, 6, 7, 9, 18, 19, 21, 22, 24, 30, 34, 35, 38, 39, 42, 52, 53, 54, 67, 93, 104, 109, 112, 121, 125, 153 f., 155, 158, 159, 162, 165, 172, 185, 186 f., 188, 189, 191, 192, 197, 199, 203, 210; ambition, 54; and Arcadius, 164, 165 f., 187, 189, 198; and Honorius, 156; and Theodosius, 37, 53, 55, 71, 92; anxiety, 191, 192; aspirations toward Imperial crown, 155, 187, 189, 192, 199; avarice: *see* greed; barbarian dress, 139–41; barbarians, dealings with, 87–89, 136, 137 f., 139, 154, 179; incitement of, 86, 122, 125–27, 137, 218; bodyguard, 139 f., 141; *catabasis*, 210–24; crimes, 205, 223; cruelty, 35, 52, 67, 70, 136, 155; daughter, 123, 154; deceptiveness, 36, 55, 64; depredations, extent of, 58, 86, 209; dismemberment of, 203–8; estate: *see Rufinianae*; evil-doing, 53 f., 221 f.; frightfulness, 75, 143; greed, 22, 35 f., 46, 52, 56 f., 59, 64, 85, 87, 137, 144, 154, 190, 203, 207; hatred inspired by, 122, 135, 185, 206 f.; hypocrisy, 35, 56; inconstancy, 34; ineptitude, military, 58, 69, 77, 135, 187; insatiability: *see* greed; intelligence, 58; juridical functions, 141 f., 211, 218; maltreatment of corpse of: *see* dismemberment; mansion, mausoleum: *see Rufinianae*; murder of, 203–5; murders committed by, 191 f., 211; oppression of universe by, 109, 210; perjury, 64, 66; pride, 208; provocation of dissension among others, 36; speech, skill in, 197; supporters, 190; swiftness, 33, 54; treachery, 93, 134; two-fold demand, 158, 175; unburied state, 109, 208 f.; untrustworthiness, 55, 66; venality, 54 f., 57; victims, 191 f., 210, 211; violence, 52; wife, 154
rumpo, 186
rural life, idealization and reality, 60, 62
rursus, 105

sacer, 5, 155
sacramentum, 184, 189
sacrifice, human, 165

saecula, 174 f., 213
saeculo, loci communes de, 58
Sallust, 123 f.
Salmoneus, 220–22
Salona, 132
Sarmatae, 90 f.
saturo, 104
sceptrum, 89, 163 f., 187
Sciron, 73
Scylla, 85
Scythia, Scythians, 46, 94, 96
sea, insatiability of, 56
securis, 72
semel, 64
senatorial party, 8
Seneca, 76, 210, 214
Senectus, 21
Senones, 39
sepelio, 75
Septimus, 141
Serena, 143
serpent-similes, 66
Serranus, 59 f.
Servius, 47
Shetland Islands, 180
shield, defender as, 77
Sicily, 117
sidereus, 103
Signifer, 106 f.
signum, 45, 139
silence, enforced, as an element of tyranny, 75
Silius Italicus, 23, 25, 40, 91
Silvanus, 168
similes, 198, 204 f.
singular in collective speech, 178–81
Sinis, 72 f.
Sinon, 183
sinuo, 197
skins, costume of, 139 f.
sky as first locus of plague, 86 f.
slaying, vengeful, viewed as providing with escort the soul of the revenged person, 164 f.
snaky locks, 23, 105, 112
Socrates, 128, 130, 133, 144, 152
solito, 193
sors, 105 f.
South, North and, 146
Sozomen, 128 f., 130

Spain, 39
Spartacus, 74
spectaculum, 136 f.
speech, collective, 142, 179–81, 199
Sperchius, 169
spiro, 203 f.
spondees, 72, 191
stars, as navigational guides, 79; metamorphosis of deified rulers into, 119
Statius, 23, 34, 40, 91, 211
statue to Claudian, 8
stigmata, 218 f.
Stilicho, 1, 2, 4, 5, 6, 7, 8, 24, 35, 52, 54, 55, 75, 88, 89, 92, 93, 97 f., 103, 109, 115, 116, 118, 119, 123, 126, 133, 140, 142, 143, 144, 145, 149, 150, 151, 152, 153 f., 157, 158, 159, 161, 165, 166 f., 170 f., 172 f., 174, 176, 181, 182 f., 184, 186, 188, 191, 197, 199, 202, 206, 210; achievements, 7 f., 79; alleged guardianship of young Emperors, 6 f., 119; and Christianity, 98 f.; and legendary figures, 76, 80, 118; clemency, 154; generosity, 86; in war and peace, 7 f.; love of army for, 178; of people for, 122; two-fold army, 120 f., 123, 144; *see also laus Stilichonis*
Stoicism, 9–11
striking an inanimate object, 217
Styx, 210, 223
subject, grammatical, change of, 34, 77, 151, 193; in Indirect Discourse, omission of, 36
subjunctive, 2 f., 62, 138, 170, 183, 187, 189, 203, 214
sublimis, 86
subrepo, 53
succurro, 164, 173
suffragium, 55, 57
Sulla, 72–74
sunrise, 193
superus, 217
supremus, 197
sword as instrument of execution, 68, 72
sympatheia, 11 f.
Symplegades, 52
Syria, 128, 131

taedae, 32
Tagus, 35 f.

Tanais, 94
Tantalus, 220–22
tantus, 65, 134, 146, 157
Tartareus, Tartarus, 214, 223
Tartesiacus, 35
Tatianus, 53, 67, 69, 70 f.
Taurus, 131
Tchaouch bachi déré, 194
Tchirpédji déré, 194
teichoskopia, 136, 206
tempestas, 35
tendo, 97 f., 101 f., 188
tense-usage, relation to chronology of, 63, 75
tense-variation, 3, 37, 41
tenuis, 117 f.
terra, 7, 26, 43, 122
terror, 155 f., 164
Tethys, 39, 41 f.
thaumaturgy, 43
theatrum, 202
Thebes, 116
Themis, 2, 5
Theodosius, 6 f., 20, 25 f., 37, 53, 55, 68, 71, 88, 92, 99, 107, 111, 119, 120, 143, 145, 149, 156, 159, 173, 174, 179, 183, 184, 185, 189, 190
Thermopylae, 116
Theseus, 36
Thessalonica, 53 f., 55, 185
Thessaly, 24, 44, 52, 133, 144, 151 f., 163, 166, 168, 185
third person, ironical, 165
Thrace, 98, 100, 118, 134, 186
thunder and lightning, 177 f.
Thyestes, 2, 31, 32
Thyle, 180
tiger-similes, 33, 65 f.
tis, 165
Tisiphone, 19
Titan, 193, 223 f.
Tityos, 220–22
torture, 214
totus, 29
tower of strength, 77
tractus, 3
traho, 211
trames, 194
transmigration: *see* metempsychosis
tribunal, 199

tripod at Delphi, 4
Trogus, 94
troops, multi-ethnic, 89; mustering of, 167
trophy, 100
tum quoque, 216
tumeo, 51, 193
tumultus, 18
tuque o, 83
turba, 36
turma, 103, 145, 193
Turnus, 50
turris, 77, 136, 212
two-fold: army, Stilicho's, 120 f., 123, 144 f., 161, 179 f.; t.-f. demand of Rufinus, 158, 175; t.-f. invasion of Empire by barbarians, 128
tyrants, 66 f., 74, 76, 136 f.

vacuus, 15, 203, 206
vallum, 153, 166
variants traceable to author, 58, 61, 179
Vatican Library, 32
venatio, 201
Vergil, 21, 23 f., 25, 40, 72, 90, 91, 108, 148, 158, 201, 210, 211
verse, speeches beginning or ending within, 24
vetus, 216
Via Egnatia, 194
Virgo (constellation): *see Iustitia*
Virtus, 26
Visigoths, 89 f., 94, 133
vocative, 75, 83, 185
voice, shift in, 96
volito, 157

voting by show of hands, 37
votum, 98, 104, 193
Vulgate, 121 f.
vulture, 221

wagon-barricade, 152 f., 166
war-cry, 169 f.
warrior-gods, 100
water, bodies of, affected by noise, 41; by metonymy for the banks thereof, 169
water, fire and: *see* fire
waves, violence of, 177
wealth and poverty, *sententiae* on, 59, 62
weapons, hostility attributed to, 179
West, East and, 146, 159, 163
Western components of Stilicho's forces, 145, 153 f., 157, 161, 181
wife of Rufinus, 154
wind similes, 127
winds as plague-carriers, 87; as reined horses, 127; by metonymy for region of origin, 181
wine, 113
witchcraft: *see* magic
word-order, 21, 51, 84
word-patterns, 21, 51

Xerxes, 99 f.

years, three thousand, 215

Zephyrus, 144
Zeus, 221; *see also* Jupiter
Zodiac, 106 f., 161
Zosimus, 54, 133, 144, 154